MW01640988

GOOD FOOD GUIDE 2004

EDITED BY SALLY LEWIS

with COUNTRY EDITOR
DANI VALENT

Principal sponsor

24th edition, September 2003
Fully revised and reset for this edition

Published by The Age Company Limited
250 Spencer Street, Melbourne, 3000
ABN 85 004 262 702

ISBN 1 876132 14 0

Every effort has been made to ensure that the information contained in this book was correct at the time of going to press.

Production editor Robyn Carter
Copy editor Roslyn Grundy
Production team Carolyn Bain, Michelle Griffin, Thomas Hunter, Felicity Lewis, Felicity Robinson, Dani Valent
Art director Anita Belia
Design Susan Charalambidis
Cover photograph Brett Brogan
Additional photography Jo Gamvros; *The Age* Photo Library
Features photography Brett Brogan; *The Age* Photo Library; thanks to the Adelphi Hotel, Flower Drum and Small Block
Styling Lisa Chivers

Books manager Steve Berry

Colour reproduction and digital imaging Richard Wilson, *The Age* Imaging Department
Printer BPA Print Group
Distributor Penguin Books Australia Ltd

Advertising manager Christine Bell
Advertising production coordinator Esther Ellero

Contents

Introduction

Maybe it's the post-war climate, the rise and rise of naked celebrity chefs, or the booming Melbourne bar scene. Whatever it is, we've noticed, while on the food trail this year, that eating out is more fun than ever. It's as if the restaurant scene no longer needs to take itself quite so seriously. And we love it.

By 'fun', we don't mean theatre restaurants, places with zany names or wisecracking waitstaff, and we certainly don't mean revolving restaurants. We mean places where the service is assured without being intimidating, the ambience allows diners to relax and even share dishes, and where the wines are interesting and well priced. And of course, we mean places that serve food prepared with creativity and pride, and maybe with a sprinkling of humour, too.

This year, how could you not have fun with Botanical's wall of wine or Reserve's rococo-au-go-go couches and boundary-breaking menu? You can't help but smile at Donovans' dangerously decadent bombe Alaska, the cheeky 'year of the goat' curry at Blakes Cafeteria and Pearl's gold-spangled taro dumplings. Upstairs at Stokehouse is party time, all the time, and downstairs at Stefano's is as love-drenched as ever. And remember, each of these restaurants is serving some of the best food this state has ever seen.

We can't get enough of all this because dining out *should* be fun. It should be about relaxing with friends and counting Victoria's blessings – great produce and talented cooks.

This year many of the restaurants we salute have managed that tricky double-act – fabulous food plus a fun atmosphere – without going soft on important things like service or tableware. They're places we really enjoy and know the dining public of Victoria love, too.

The Age Good Food Guide 2004 will probably be considered a more contentious guide. But we're certain it's also a more conscientious guide.

Never in the *Guide's* history have more restaurants been visited more often by such a professional group of critics. Each of the three-hat restaurants, and most of the two- and one-hat restaurants, have been visited at least three times by different reviewers. This year, the editorial panel met more often and discussed more openly its opinions of restaurants and the overriding industry trends.

As a result, we can say more confidently than ever that we are able to provide you with the nation's most authoritative restaurant guide.

This year, for instance, there are more one-hat restaurants than ever but fewer three-hat restaurants. Why? Because we think it is a more honest appraisal of Victoria's dining scene right now. And we have decided that the Restaurant of the Year and the Country Restaurant of the Year should be just that – the places that best sum up the past 12 months, rather than the ones that garnered the most hats.

This year may have proved a turning point in our dining history. Brilliant food no longer has to be served with starchy solemnity, meaning diners can unwind, and maybe even undo a belt notch or two.

Don't get us wrong, we still adore our institutions and our culinary temples. But this year it seems the grand old dame that is the Victorian restaurant scene might just have snuck off and gotten her belly button pierced.

What on earth can we look forward to next year?

Enjoy the *Guide* and please send any feedback to: goodfoodguide@theage.com.au or *The Age Good Food Guide*, 250 Spencer Street, Melbourne, 3000.

Sally Lewis – Editor

About this guide

Reviewing policy

The Age Good Food Guide is an independent publication, produced by *The Age*.

Each restaurant is visited anonymously by one of our experienced reviewers (see page 12). They pay for each meal in full and do not accept inducements of any kind.

The *Guide* carries advertising, but this does not influence editorial content in any way.

Each three-hat restaurant has been visited at least three times by different reviewers; likewise many one- and two-hat restaurants.

How to use this book

Restaurants in the metropolitan area are listed alphabetically in the front section of the book. The country section is divided into widely recognised regions. Interstate restaurants are in the final section.

If you are looking for a restaurant in a particular area, use the maps (pages 260 to 269) or the 'Index by suburb or town'. If you are after a particular style of food, check the 'Cuisine index'.

The symbols, which are explained on page 12, are also indexed. For example, all restaurants that carry a bar symbol will be in the 'Good bars index'. We have also indexed restaurants with private rooms, those that serve yum cha and that allow BYO.

Accuracy

While we make every attempt to ensure that the information in this *Guide* is correct, chefs move, restaurants close and menus change. This is, unfortunately, beyond our control.

Maps

In addition to the maps printed at the back of the *Guide*, every city review carries a map reference from the *Melway Greater Melbourne Street Directory* (30th edition).

In the country section, each review carries a map reference from the fifth edition of the *VicRoads Country Street Directory of Victoria*, other than those in Geelong and Bellarine Peninsula, and the Mornington Peninsula, which take Melway references. In addition, we have included the review page number after each restaurant's name on the country maps on pages 267 to 269 of the *Guide*.

Opening hours

In most cases, we have given the time the kitchen accepts last orders, rather than the restaurant closing time.

Prices

We have listed prices for each course, from lowest to highest. Prices change frequently, so these are intended as a guide only. Where space permits, we have also included details of the restaurant's best-known menu.

Rating the restaurants

Restaurants are awarded marks out of 20. We also award chefs' hats, from one to three. These ratings and hats are determined by the reviewer and a seven-member editorial panel, made up of some of the most experienced food writers in Victoria (see page 12).

The restaurants in the *Guide* are very diverse and those with similar ratings may be quite different. A score of 13 for a casual cafe is excellent but disappointing for a restaurant with loftier ambitions.

The scoring system

The score comprises 10 for food, five for service (including wine list/service, if applicable), three for ambience and two for the overall experience. Places that score 11 out of 20 or less are not included in the *Guide*.

12 Fair: don't expect too much

13 Good: a place we can recommend

14 A good all-round package: a place we can confidently recommend

15 (one hat) Very good: especially recommended or notable in its class

16 (two hats) Great: worth seeking out

17 (two hats) Truly excellent: up there with the best

18 (three hats) An outstanding experience on all fronts

19-20 (three hats) Approaching perfection: the restaurant pinnacle

AWARDS 2004

Restaurant of the Year
Botanical
The name on everyone's lips, Botanical draws together seriously good food, lavishly renovated surrounds, superior service and an innovative approach to wine.

Country Restaurant of the Year
Lake House, Daylesford
Two decades of passion and experience are spun into magnificent meals in Lake House's welcoming dining room. Few Victorian restaurants match it for fine flavours and a sense of occasion.

The Vittoria Coffee Best New Restaurant
Reserve
Dressed in swirly turquoise and gold brocade, Reserve sashays past the competition with some of the most daring food Melbourne has seen in years.

Chef of the Year
Donovan Cooke & Philippa Sibley-Cooke (joint winners), Ondine
Donovan Cooke's highly evolved Eurocentric dishes are crowned by stunning desserts from partner Philippa Sibley-Cooke at their suave basement restaurant.

Young Chef of the Year
George Calombaris, Reserve
Calombaris' food is whimsical and wonderful in equal measure. This driven young bloke is one to watch.

***The Age* Award for Service Excellence**
Michael Sapountsis, Melbourne Wine Room
MWR's Michael Sapountsis is conductor of a sometimes chaotic orchestra. That Melbourne Wine Room is so good, so much of the time, is down to Sapountsis' rare talent with the baton.

***The Age* Award for Professional Excellence**
Alla Wolf-Tasker
The driving force behind the 2004 Country Restaurant of the Year, Alla Wolf-Tasker has mentored an army of aspiring chefs while fostering and promoting excellent Victorian produce.

Best Wine List
Circa, the Prince
Circa's mammoth wine list is a savvy summation of the world's best wines, serviced by some of the most passionate sommeliers in the country.

Special categories

Best Chinese
Flower Drum

Best French
Ondine

Best Greek
Pireaus Blues

Best Indian
Bhoj Docklands

Best Italian
Cafe Di Stasio

Best Japanese
Hanabishi

Best Malaysian
Ah Mu

Best Middle Eastern
Mo Mo

Best Steakhouse
A & V Lazar Charcoal Grill & Seafood Restaurant

Best Vietnamese
Oanh's Kitchen

City hats

ezard at adelphi
Flower Drum
Ondine

Becco
Botanical
Cafe Di Stasio
Cecconi's
Circa, the Prince
Diningroom 211
Donovans
Grossi Florentino
Hanabishi
Jacques Reymond
Mask of China
Matteo's
Pearl
Red Emperor
Reserve
Scusami
Stokehouse
Vue de Monde

Abla's
Ah Mu
Akita
Araliya
Bamboo House
Blakes Cafeteria
Bok Choy Chinese Cuisine
Chine on Paramount
Choi's
Cicciolina
Da Noi
David's
Fenix
France-Soir
The Graham
Harveys
Il Bacaro Cucina e Bar
Kenzan
Koots
Langton's Restaurant & Wine Bar
Le Restaurant
Luxe
mecca
Melbourne Wine Room
Mercer's Restaurant
Middle Brighton Baths
Mo Mo
Nihonbashi Zen
No. 3 Station Pier
Number 8 restaurant & wine bar
Ocha
O'Connell's
The Point Albert Park
radii
Saucier Restaurant
Sud
Tea House on Burke
Toofey's
Treasure Restaurant
Verge
Yu-u
Zio's Ristorante

Country hats

Stefano's, Mildura

Lake House, Daylesford

Gigi's of Beechworth, Beechworth
Healesville Hotel, Healesville
Joseph's at the Mansion Hotel, Werribee
Montalto Vineyard & Olive Grove, Red Hill South
Oscar W's Wharfside, Echuca
Pettavel Winery & Restaurant, Waurn Ponds
Pippies by the Bay, Warrnambool
Royal Mail Hotel, Dunkeld
Salix at Willow Creek, Merricks North
Simone's of Bright, Bright
Stonelea Country Estate, Acheron
The Victoria Hotel, Port Fairy

Symbols

given to a restaurant that has an exceptional wine list, including depth and breadth of selection, relevance to the food served, and value for money.

$ given to a restaurant where it is possible to eat at least two courses for $25 or less a head.

V for restaurants that offer a wide selection of vegetarian dishes, or which have special vegetarian menus.

for restaurants or cafes that serve excellent breakfasts most days of the week.

given to restaurants with excellent bars that could stand alone.

for country restaurants that also offer accommodation.

for a restaurant connected with a winery.

AE American Express BC Bankcard DC Diners Club MC Mastercard V Visa

The contributors

Editorial panel
Roslyn Grundy, Foong Ling Kong, Ralph Kyte-Powell (wine), John Lethlean, Sally Lewis, Matt Preston, Dani Valent, Necia Wilden

Country editor
Dani Valent

Contributing reviewers
Gayle Austen, Janet Austin, Ben Canaider, Michael Cave, Richard Cornish, Larissa Dubecki, Matt Eckhaus, Jane Faulkner, Megan Fletcher, Claude Forell, Siew-Ching Goh, Robert Haldane, Michael Harden, Angus Holland, Siu Ling Hui, Thomas Hunter, Foong Ling Kong, John Lethlean, Sally Lewis, David McClymont, Matt Pirrie, Liz Porter, Matt Preston, John Schauble, David Sutherland, Leanne Tolra, Dani Valent, John Weldon, Tricia Welsh, Necia Wilden, Patrick Witton

Interstate contributors
Matthew Evans: Adelaide, Brisbane, Canberra, Perth, Sydney, Tasmania
Sally Lewis: Darwin, Queensland resorts

Features
Michael Harden (city), Dani Valent (country): at a glance
Carolyn Holbrook: breakfasts, cellar doors, coffee, country markets, gourmet getaways, rooms with a view, signature dishes, vegetarian
Melinda Houston: bars
Ralph Kyte-Powell: wine lists
David Sutherland: directory

THE CITY

Abla's

LEBANESE

109 Elgin Street,
Carlton **9347 0006**

BYO
Corkage none
Open Thurs-Fri noon-3pm; Mon-Sat 6-11pm
Seats 90
Owner & chef Abla Amad
Cards AE BC DC MC V
Prices entrees $8-$12; mains $15-$18; desserts $1.50-$2; set menus $38-$43 (13 courses, compulsory for 2 or more Fri-Sat nights)
Map page 262 **Melway** 2B H6

WHILE some Melbourne restaurants suffer more facelifts than Joan Rivers, this homely Carlton terrace is ageing gracefully. Design snobs might cringe at the candelabra and sage paint, but these details matter little once the traditional Lebanese dishes stream from the kitchen, where chef, proprietor and national living treasure Abla Amad presides like a beneficent grandmother. The 13-course banquet, compulsory on Friday and Saturday nights, is enchanting. There's smoky baba ghanoush; thick house-made labna; cumin-spiked lamb and beef sausages; and silverbeet rolls crammed with rice and chickpeas, perfumed with allspice. Regulars know to leave space for the ladies' fingers – filo parcels stuffed with mince and pine nuts – and the kibbe, egg-shaped bombs of burghul and lamb. The hero dish is fluffy rice pilaf, strewn with shredded chicken, but vegetarians will feel only slightly short-changed by majadra, a concoction of lentils and rice with yoghurt. Few diners have room for baklava and Turkish delight, but an aromatic coffee rarely goes amiss. A reminder: Abla's is BYO. That there's no corkage adds to the pleasant aftertaste.

15/20 $ V

Ah Mu

MALAYSIAN/MODERN ASIAN
Best Malaysian

51 Bourke Street,
City **9654 6800**

Licensed
Open Mon-Fri noon-2.30pm; daily 6-10.30pm
Seats 72
Owners Julian Pang & Allen Woo
Chef Allen Woo
Cards AE BC DC MC V
Prices entrees $7.50-$17.50; noodles & rice $15-$17; mains $18-$29; desserts $9-$9.50
Map page 260 **Melway** 1B U5

AH MU'S interior is at once classic and contemporary: a very now colour scheme of jade and raspberry combines with timber screens that hint at a Nonya and British colonial past. Co-owner and chef Allen Woo takes a similar approach to the food, refining and redefining the northern Malaysian hawker and home-style dishes of his childhood with modern twists. To start, succulent grilled Thai sausage, savoury rice and pork wrapped in corn husk is a must, as are the pan-fried wontons filled with crunchy yam bean shards and garlic chives, all drizzled with Indonesian sweet soy. Wadaan noodles are everything they should be – silky egg sauce over wok-charred rice noodles with fresh prawns and chicken. Thai laksa (rice noodles in a spicy, fishy coconut soup) comes with the surprising addition of pickled mustard cabbage, and 'Dad's fish curry' is an unusual Malaysian-Indian curry based on a tamarind stock with hints of fenugreek. Dessert might be sticky rice pudding with coconut milk or creamy cheesecake scented with pandan leaves. The wine list is short and savvy, but a tad pricey.

15/20

Akita

JAPANESE

Corner Courtney & Blackwood Streets,
North Melbourne **9326 5766**

Licensed & BYO
Corkage $2 a head
Open Mon-Fri noon-2pm, 6-10pm
Seats 60
Owner & chef Toshio Furuhashi
Cards AE BC DC MC V
Prices entrees $6-$14; mains $11-$24; desserts $3-$7
Map page 262 **Melway** 2B A9

AKITA'S fans, of whom there are many, pay no mind to the rabbit-warren interior, unadorned tables and restrained decor. They come here for the exquisite food prepared by chef Toshio Furuhashi. His à la carte menu is brief – it's the daily-changing specials that are the real focus. Worth crossing town for, in fact. There is much rubbernecking among tables as diners check out each other's pickings before deciding that they'll have what you're having. On offer may be kara age (John Dory rolled with spring onions and shiso leaves, then deep-fried) or kani ten (sweet crabmeat and shiso leaf tempura) – both showing off impeccable produce. There may also be grilled quail, ocean trout, lamb salad or squid legs, all cooked simply to coax the best out of each ingredient. Like any self-respecting Japanese restaurant, the sashimi and sushi are very fine, and the dengaku (halved eggplant with chicken mince and sweet miso) is a buttery delight. The wine list is small, but Japanese beer and sake bump up the options. All this, and at such humble prices, too. Make sure you book.

15/20 **$**

Antipodes

MODERN GREEK

195 Lonsdale Street,
City **9663 4760**

Licensed & BYO wine
Corkage $3 a bottle
Open Tues-Fri 11.30am-2.30pm; Mon-Sat 5-10pm
Seats 60; outdoor seating
Owners Stephen Kirk & Sam Veskoukis
Chef Con Derlis
Cards AE BC DC MC V Eftpos
Prices entrees $6.50-$15; mains $12.50-$37; desserts $6-$7.50
Map page 260 **Melway** 1B Q3

NO holiday snaps of the Parthenon, or Nana-heavy muzak: at first glance, Antipodes seems Greek in name only. But that's co-owner Stephen Kirk's family in the black-and-white photographs of Greek villagers lining the glossy bluestone walls, and the menu is crammed with traditional Greek dishes, albeit with a mod-Oz twist. So the juicy moussaka might come with a peppery tomato salsa, the charred lamb cutlets with mash and jus, and the lightly floured, deep-fried calamari is propped on a bed of rocket and served with house-made mayonnaise. Seafood is usually sweet and tender – lucky diners can sometimes catch plump, char-grilled prawns on the specials board, perfect with a chunky Greek salad or wedges of waxy spuds. Sparrows might like to pick at a mix of simple mezze (olives, dolmades, crisp-then-tender saganaki), or try the piatella (platter) of crunchy whitebait, moist dolmades, taramasalata and tzatziki, olives, feta and, often, a lamb meatball or two. All these salty, garlic-laden dishes demand a bold Greek wine, of which there are several on the brief list, including the Contiki favourite, retsina. Reality check: this *is* Lonsdale Street.

13/20 **$**

the apartment

MODERN AUSTRALIAN

401-405 Little Bourke Street,
City **9670 4020**

Licensed
Open Mon-Fri noon-3pm, 3pm-late (bar menu only);
Sat 8pm-late (bar menu only)
Seats 90; bar
Owners Tally Konstas & Daniel Verheyen
Chef Marshall Richards
Cards AE BC DC MC V Eftpos
Prices entrees $9-$14; mains $18-$25.50; desserts $9-$12;
bar menu $1.50-$12
Map page 260 **Melway** 1A J4

THINGS have changed a lot since the apartment moved into the first of the empty Marchetti's properties. The former Marchetti's Tuscan Grill is now a neutral, mushroom-toned space that looks like a hotel lobby but operates as a restaurant by day and a bar by night (with impressive cocktail and tapas menus). Lunch is the main event and chef Marshall Richards keeps things adventurous without being wacky. Sukiyaki scallops are teamed, perhaps, with a tangy seaweed salad. Smoky squid might be plated with buds of braised fennel. Agnolotti could come stuffed with wild rabbit and served with baby beets, radicchio and caramelised apple. And linguine might arrive with clams and snapper, pepped up with vinegary onions. Richards earnt his stripes at Blakes, and his cooking shows real spark and an enthusiasm for interesting pairings. Service is not always as smooth as the food, but the attitude is similarly enthusiastic. Come after 3pm and you'll find the apartment reconfigured as a lounge bar complete with plush couches, slinky sounds, and interesting small bites such as green olive biscotti with hummus.

14/20

Araliya

SRI LANKAN

611 Glenferrie Road,
Hawthorn **9818 5120**

Licensed & BYO wine
Corkage $3 a head
Open Fri noon-2.30pm; daily 6-11pm
Seats 50
Owners Sriyan & Dee Wedande
Chefs Sriyan Wedande & Ajith Fernando
Cards AE BC DC MC V Eftpos
Prices entrees $9-$15; mains $17-$25; desserts $6-$12
Map page 265 **Melway** 45 D11

ARALIYA'S co-owner and chef, Sriyan 'Sam' Wedande, has been cooking exquisitely crafted examples of Sri Lanka's distinctive cuisine for more than 17 years in this relaxed sand- and sea-toned space. A favourite Hawthorn hangout, drawcards include knowledgeable service, a short, well-chosen list of modestly priced wines and beers, and of course, the food. All the dishes display harmonious, complex spicing of quality ingredients. Among the standouts are blackened fish in a coriander and lemongrass sauce, and Araliya's superior rendition of beef smore (they call it fried beef sour), the sliced fillets served with an intricate sauce spiked with lime pickle. And eating your vegies is pure pleasure with the likes of creamy red lentils with spinach or tiny cauliflower florets and pumpkin nuggets with onions, mustard seeds and grated coconut. Phone ahead to ensure there are plenty of hoppers (soft bowl-shaped pancakes) to mop up sauces, or order string hoppers (lacy pancakes) and pittu (crumbles of rice flour and coconut). But save room for 'love cake' (almond meal and semolina flavoured with honey) and vattalappam (baked coconut custard).

15/20

Arc Cafe

MODERN AUSTRALIAN

160 Rathdowne Street,
Carlton **9349 3933**

Licensed & BYO wine
Corkage none
Open Wed-Fri noon-2.30pm; Tues-Sat 6-10pm
Seats 34; private rooms
Owners Catherine Cooke & Alex Roser
Chef Alex Roser
Cards AE BC DC MC V Eftpos
Prices entrees $14.50-$16.50; mains $26-$28; desserts $11.50
Map page 262 **Melway** 2B H5

OVER nine years, this corner-shop restaurant has built up a fiercely loyal following. Wine-lovers are chief among Arc's acolytes, lured by its commitment to BYO and a no-corkage policy (a concise, reasonably priced wine list is on hand for those arriving without a special bottle). The simplicity of the interior – all delicate cream and butternut tones, blondwood chairs and tubs of bone-handled cutlery – is reflected in the food. Clean, robust flavours are paramount in chef and co-owner Alex Roser's imaginative Italian and Asian-influenced offerings. The shortish menu might include fine-skinned ginger and chicken dumplings lolling in a sweet soy broth, plump pumpkin and pine nut raviolo with burnt butter, lemon and sage, and tender roast duck slices on watercress salad. Larger plates range from braised beef shin with three veg and gremolata, to Sri Lankan-style chicken curry with coconut rice. Desserts are intricate and artful: pineapple and passionfruit icecream is served as a triangular terrine with a mini football of mango sorbet, while creamy honeycomb semifreddo arrives sandwiched between florentines.

13/20

Asiana

MODERN ASIAN

181 Victoria Avenue,
Albert Park **9696 6688**

Licensed & BYO wine
Corkage $8 a bottle
Open Sun-Fri noon-3pm; Sun-Thurs 6-11pm; Fri-Sat 6-11.30pm
Seats 40; outdoor seating
Owners Bee Yap, Chuen Low & Randolph Cheung
Chef Chuen Low
Cards BC DC MC V
Prices entrees $6-$15; mains $19-$28; desserts $8-$10.50; degustation menus $45-$55 (7-8 courses)
Map page 264 **Melway** 2J J9

THE minimalist dark-wood and off-white interior, chocolate banquettes and crisp linen don't advertise the restaurant's oriental pedigree but relax, you're in expert hands. Having earned their stripes at Choi's in Hawthorn, front-of-house (and resident wine nut) Randolph Cheung and chef Chuen Low now pair smart mod-Asian cuisine with a superlative wine selection (more than 700 labels) at the bayside end of Vic Ave. Many dishes list wine suggestions, so a Mesh riesling may match a tangy calamari salad while cult Torbreck Juveniles is teamed with sticky pork ribs. While Asiana's popularity has the partners looking to expand to St Kilda, it may also account for some less-than-impressive dishes on recent visits. Nonetheless, the Peking duck (they roast their own daily) is sublime with a fragrant pinot, and the degustation menus give a sweep of seasonal or more popular dishes like oyster shooters, crunchy coconut scallops or Black Angus steak with kung bo sauce. Don't come expecting ultra-refined Asian cooking. Instead, delight in a restaurant willing to indulge in the shock of the new.

14/20

Attica

MODERN MEDITERRANEAN

74 Glen Eira Road,
Ripponlea **9530 0111**

Licensed
Open Mon-Fri 6pm-late; Sat-Sun 9am-late
Seats 40; outdoor seating; private room; bar
Owners David & Helen Maccora
Chef Perry Peters
Cards AE BC DC MC V Eftpos
Prices breakfasts $4-$8.50; entrees $9.50-$14; mains $18.50-$24.50; desserts $11.50
Map page 266 **Melway** 67 E1

AFTER a long stretch on the market (as Owensville), followed by a renovation, this elegant old bank on a kosher shopping strip has reopened. Chef Perry Peters cooks from a mod-Med menu. As he proved at Syracuse, he knows his harissa from his chermoula, and Middle Eastern inflections pep up many dishes. Entrees are particularly sound. A rough-hewn chickpea soup with saffron labna is satisfyingly balanced; bastilla-style chicken pie is amped up with wild mushrooms. Desserts are teasingly good, from the mandarin and cardamom crème brûlée to the moist fig pudding with butterscotch icecream. Main courses can be hit and miss. Wiener schnitzel on caraway sauerkraut might feature flabby meat in a soggy crust, while pappardelle with leeks and melted feta is a one-dimensional dish that loses its charm. Better is a nicely grilled slab of swordfish with pear and rocket salad. Slick, if slightly nervy, service suits the revamped dining room, with its small phalanx of tables behind the handsome bar. The compact wine list offers plenty of interest at reasonable prices. With its weekend breakfasts and snack menu, Attica is a boon to the neighbourhood.

14/20

@ A GLANCE

For those who read the last page first

DESSERTS

ezard at adelphi
187 Flinders Lane,
City, 9639 6811
Teage Ezard's pace does not slacken as he nears dessert – his sweet stuff is as interesting as everything else on the menu. Citrus, spice and palm sugar are all involved.

Harveys
10 Murphy Street,
South Yarra, 9867 3605
Rosewater, pistachios and honey get cosy with meringue and icecream in Kurt Sampson's Middle East-accented desserts.

Mercer's Restaurant
732 Main Road,
Eltham, 9431 1015
Can't decide which of Stephen Mercer's intricate desserts to devour? Opt for Le Grand Dessert, a platter containing up to eight scaled-down dishes from the carte.

No. 3 Station Pier
3 Station Pier, Beacon Cove,
Port Melbourne, 9646 6299
A dessert is not a dessert here unless it includes fruit. Dianne Kerry puts cherries in the chocolate soufflé and pear, quince and rhubarb in the fritters.

Ondine
299 Queen Street,
City, 9602 3477
For many, Philippa Sibley-Cooke's artful and highly crafted desserts are the highlight of the meal. She is a chef who understands the true beauty of chocolate.

Pearl
631-633 Church Street,
Richmond, 9421 4599
Doughnuts, panna cotta and chocolate pudding get a Geoff Lindsay makeover and exit the kitchen looking and tasting revitalised. If you're lucky, fried hibiscus flowers might feature.

Aya

JAPANESE

1193 High Street,
Armadale **9822 9571**

Licensed
Open Tues-Sun 6-10.30pm
Seats 100; private rooms
Owner Leony Siauw
Chef Kenichi Okumura
Cards AE BC DC MC V
Prices entrees $3.80-$29.80; sushi & sashimi $2.20-$48.90; mains $14.20-$48.90; desserts $2.70-$8.80; set menus $30-$45 (5-8 courses)
Map page 265 **Melway** 59 B7

IN a city that offers many standard Japanese restaurants, it's a joy to report that this eastern suburbs pleaser seeks to rise above the pack. The menu features everything from sashimi to shabu shabu (a mix that doesn't happen in Japan), so rest assured that your favourite dish will be there. But wait, there's more. Modern touches abound and there are enough specials to keep things interesting. Seaweed rolls may combine salmon with basil and tomato, and a salad of King Island crabmeat could come with a thousand island-style dressing on mesclun. Traditional dishes arrive on soulful ceramics, served with customary generosity – tempura is a well-cooked mound of seafood and vegetables, and the sukiyaki is recommended enthusiastically by regulars. The sushi bar, which runs along one side of the long, cheery dining room, turns out impeccable creations, including spicy salmon hosomaki (seaweed layered rolls) and a seared salmon sushi. The wine list has been chosen to complement the food, there's a generous selection of sakes, and tatami rooms are available for large parties.

14/20

Aziz Middle Eastern Restaurant

MIDDLE EASTERN

270-272 Park Street,
South Melbourne **9645 9996**

Licensed & BYO wine
Corkage $2.50 a head
Open Wed-Fri noon-3pm; Tues-Sun 6-10pm
Seats 70; outdoor seating
Owner & chef Amal Malouf
Cards AE BC MC V
Prices lunches $7.50-$13.50; entrees $8.50-$12; mains $14.50-$18.50; desserts $1.20-$5.50
Map page 264 **Melway** 2K C3

MELBURNIANS' enthusiasm for modern Middle Eastern labna-and-latte outfits is undiminished. Last September, in the cavernous space left by Curry Bizarre, Amal Malouf (yes, she's Greg Malouf's sister-in-law), unveiled Aziz. Amal, who previously managed the kitchen at sister restaurant Cafe Zum Zum (see page 43), works a predominantly traditional and moderately priced menu drawing on flavours from Lebanon to Morocco to Syria, in a spacious, rug-covered dining room. With Arabic music as a backdrop, entrees focus on authentic dips circled with olives; crisp falafel with tahini and labna; tightly wound filo fingers of lamb and pine nuts, drizzled with pomegranate essence; and a coriander-rich pot of sauteed mushrooms and Hungarian peppers. All are good rather than great, and mains follow this trend. The pressed mince beef kebab (kofta) is recommended, while the ris'a dejaj (chicken slivers on stock-cooked rice, dotted with fried almonds) doesn't reach anticipated heights. Desserts include commendable Turkish delight and mahalabia (chilled, milky custard topped with crushed pistachio), and exceptional pastries.

12/20 $

Bacash

MODERN AUSTRALIAN/SEAFOOD

175 Domain Road,
South Yarra **9866 3566**

Licensed
Open Mon-Fri noon-3pm; Mon-Sat 6pm-late
Seats 80; outdoor seating; private room
Owners Michael Bacash & Fiona Perkins
Chefs Michael Bacash & Kate Dalziel
Cards AE BC DC MC V
Prices entrees $14-$18.50; mains $24-$30; desserts $14-$15
Map page 264 **Melway** 2L C2

AFTER a year and a half as Bac's, owner-chef Michael Bacash has taken the plunge and splashed his whole surname across the front of his restaurant. Along with the demise of the nickname, breakfasts are no more and there's less of a drop-in feel. Bacash is now a semi-formal restaurant with an emphasis on seafood. It makes sense, really. Bacash helmed the kitchen at seafood restaurant Toofey's for 12 years and his passion for a great piece of fish is still fierce. Entrees might include tuna tartare garnished with slivers of anchovy or a substantial steaming bouillabaisse. Grilled fish – perhaps whole garfish or sweet-flavoured flounder – comes with generous bowls of fries and salad. Terrific terra firma dishes might include goats' cheese tart in a tourniquet of pear slivers or fettuccine with a juicy rabbit ragout. Desserts are consistently good: the nougat parfait is a harmony of pistachio, hazelnut and almond. While some may find the Vic-centric wine list a little pricey, the service has much improved since Bacash's reincarnation, a wise move since this slice of Domain Road is more competitive than ever.

14/20

Bala Da Dhaba

INDIAN

56-58 Glen Eira Road,
Ripponlea **9523 8683**

Licensed & BYO wine
Corkage $1 a head
Open Tues-Sun 5.30-11pm
Seats 70
Owner Inder Prasad
Chef Khushel Singh
Cards AE BC DC MC V
Prices entrees $2.50-$12.70; mains $8.70-$16.90; desserts $4.40-$5.40; set menu $24.50 (3 courses)
Map page 266 **Melway** 67 E1

AS the sole curry house in Ripponlea, Bala Da Dhaba plays to a captive audience, belting out the medleys like a trouper and only occasionally singing off key. Staff do their best but can be tardy, forgetful and sometimes cheeky: 'Sorry for the delay, the microwave exploded.' Business is obviously very good; why not hire more waiters? Groups are commonplace in Bala's noisy confines, where shiny butcher's paper over cloth and fresh carnations on the tables spruce up surrounds that bear signs of the restaurant's longevity. The menu is an extensive, cheap and familiar repertoire of tandoori treats and well-balanced curries. You can't go wrong with chunky vegetable samosas and stews like gosht sada bahar that surprises with its velvety, cumin-flavoured gravy and tender lamb chunks. A handful of Nepalese dishes, like creamy potato salad vibrant with turmeric, make a worthy diversion from the regular fare. Accompaniments vary in quality from sugary, flaccid keema bread to huge serves of aromatic pilau rice with peas. Although licensed, BYO is the best way to go. *Also 1455 Malvern Road, Glen Iris, 9822 5069.*

12/20 $ V

Bamboo House

CHINESE

47 Little Bourke Street,
City **9662 1565**

Licensed
Open Mon-Fri noon-3pm; Mon-Sat 5.30-11pm; Sun 6-10pm
Seats 110; private rooms
Owners Alex Tseng, Robert Wong & Simon Chan
Chef Simon Chan
Cards AE BC DC MC V
Prices entrees $6.60-$21.50; mains $18-$29.50; desserts $14-$18.50; banquet menus $44-$66 (9 courses)
Map page 260 Melway 1B U4

IF walls could talk, those at Bamboo House would have some tales to tell: the round tables at this Chinatown veteran are favoured by food-lovers from the worlds of politics, industry and the arts. They come for hallmark Chinese dishes from the north and south, so duck may be enjoyed in the Sichuan or Peking styles – the former tea-smoked and served with steamed buns, the latter roasted and served in Mandarin pancakes. Both are as polished as an MP on polling day. The provincial dishes are magnificent: the unctuous Sichuan eggplant is one of the best in town; the cold platter selection offers divine textural treats like saltwater pork hock and drunken chicken; and the kitchen is justly famous for its hand-pulled noodle dishes, perhaps stir-fried with shredded pork and Shanghai pickled vegetables. While these dishes continue to shine, others disappoint (lifeless seafood, tired pastry) and the '80s interior is far from glossy. You get the feeling that Bamboo House is happy cruising rather than powering ahead. The service continues to ooze professionalism and the wine list is a genuine notch above for Little Bourke Street.

15/20 V

Bamboo Terrace

CHINESE

201 Bulleen Road,
Bulleen **9852 0541**

Licensed & BYO wine
Corkage $2 a head
Open Mon-Sat noon-3pm; Sun 11am-3pm; Sun-Thurs 6-10pm; Fri-Sat 6-11pm
Seats 160; private room
Owners Alex Tseng & Robert Wong
Chef Wai Keong Leong
Cards AE BC DC MC V
Prices yum cha dishes $3.50-$8; entrees $6-$11; mains $20-$28, desserts $7-$7.50; banquet menu $36 (8 courses)
Map page 266 **Melway** 32 D7

BAMBOO TERRACE has a lot to live up to and it meets that challenge well. It might not be as suave as big brother Bamboo House (see above), but it's just as savvy and smoothly run. The capacious dining room is large enough for clan celebrations and its leafy carpark is big enough to get lost in. No wonder it's hugely popular with families. Just watch them trooping in – dot-commers, baby boomers and sun-setters, making time for each other over some jolly good chow. And what are they eating? Peking duck (a bestseller), Mongolian lamb, Cantonese beef, and Sichuan eggplant smothered in spices and garlic. Dishes come from all over a familiar road map. The Terrace is specially good for its yum cha, which lists many northern delicacies, such as spring onion pastries and pot-stickers, which are a welcome change from the steamed dumplings at southern-style 'yum' times. The dinner menu changes with the seasons, but some things are perennials, like velvety green pea omelette made with eggwhites, and sweet-sour pork in a judicious mix of vinegar and sugar. Finish off with red-bean pancakes; it's a satisfying round of happy families.

13/20

B.coz

MODERN AUSTRALIAN

403 Riversdale Road,
Hawthorn East **9882 7889**

Licensed
Open Wed-Fri noon-2.30pm; Tues-Sat 6-10pm
Seats 50
Owners Rodney & Neville Barbey
Chef Rodney Barbey
Cards AE BC DC MC V
Prices entrees $14.30-$17.60; mains $24.20-$33; desserts $11.55-$16.50; sampling menu $55 (8 courses)
Map page 265 **Melway** 59 H1

FOOD gets a real workover at B.coz. There's the usual roasting, grilling and braising, but when you settle down with a menu in the stark white dining room, be prepared for 'coriander toss', 'pumpkin and lentil splash' and 'cashew drizzle'. Chef-owner Rodney Barbey is obviously having fun with his Asian-Cajun fusion, making for fascinating – if unpredictable – ultra-modern meals. You'll want to order the smoked salmon with wok-tossed lime-marinated salmon and wonton crisp just to see if it really comes with a single snowpea tendril as promised. And the 'frozen licorice allsorts semifreddo with colour toffee drops' is mind-blowing before you even see it. Perhaps inevitably, execution can be less exciting than the menu's rhapsodies. Oriental flavours are good (barbecued, marinated quail is enlivened with an Asian pesto) but some dishes, like wokked Cajun lamb with prawns and tamarind chilli jelly, turn into a flavour brawl. The choc-cherry soufflé has been known to fail occasionally: it must be the pressure of living up to the menu description. The wine list is excellent, though matching a bottle to the melange of flavours can be tricky.

13/20 V

Beate's

MODERN EUROPEAN

Studley Park Boathouse, 1 Boathouse Road,
Kew **9853 1828**

Licensed
Open Wed-Fri & Sun noon-3pm; Wed-Sat 6.30pm-late;
Studley Park Boathouse Cafe Mon-Fri noon-3pm; Sat-Sun 9-11am, noon-4pm
Seats 74; outdoor seating; private room; cafe
Owner Beate Tierney
Chef Oliver Fulljames
Cards AE BC DC MC V
Prices breakfasts $8-$14.50; entrees $10.50-$19.50; mains $26-$33; desserts $13.50-$14.50; less in cafe
Map page 265 **Melway** 2D E8

THIS handsome Federation-era boathouse shines by day. Diners are seated comfortably in high-backed chairs on the glassed veranda while, down below, the river sparkles and kids, boats and ducks go about their business. Chef Oliver Fulljames' clean, bright – if conservative – food is just right for a leisurely, sun-dappled breakfast or lunch. You might choose tiger prawns flamed in Pernod and garlic butter, or a tian of smoked salmon with avocado and cucumber salsa. Service is smooth and assured. By night, things can run a little awry. Lacklustre interior lighting does not compensate for the absence of river views – best to avoid the veranda and ask for a fireside table inside. And dishes that are pleasantly non-threatening at lunch seem somehow less satisfying at dinner. Aged fillet of beef on creamed potatoes is tender and perfectly cooked but the cabernet jus fails to lend distinction; crisp-skinned salmon on baked roma tomatoes is simply that. A rich chocolate and raspberry cake and a glass-rich wine list make some amends, though Beate's needs to recapture some of the sparkle if it's to keep luring diners down to the river.

13/20

Beaumaris Pavilion

MODERN AUSTRALIAN

472 Beach Road,
Beaumaris **9589 3251**

Licensed
Open Mon-Fri 11am-late; Sat-Sun 9am-late
Seats 98; outdoor seating; bar
Owner Leawarra Hospitality Group
Chef Gracion Dassanayake
Cards AE BC DC MC V Eftpos
Prices entrees $8.50-$18; mains $16-$28.50; desserts $6.50-$7.50
Map page 266 **Melway** 86 E9

FORMERLY known as a fine dining establishment with cafe attached, this bayside eatery has relaunched itself as a more casual bistro. The water views remain a highlight, especially at sunset. Another is the cool Chris Connell-designed interior, featuring an intimate central bar, with a gleaming white marble counter and low-slung leather ottomans. But a first glance at the dinner menu would give few hints of the changes in direction. The prices don't scream 'casual' and, although the glossary of French foodie terms is gone, the new menu still features a couple of items such as 'velouté' (served with barramundi) and 'assiette' (as in a plate of oysters done six ways). So what's new? Asian tastes now take main billing on the once Eurocentric menu. So for starters, squid may come wearing a coat of chilli-salt and Asian coleslaw could accompany Peking duck spring rolls. For mains, gastro-pub standards like laksa and beer-battered whiting sit alongside chicken with a slick of tandoori paste. The only desserts on offer at the time of review were a disappointing selection of cakes, served chilled, straight from the fridge. Tsk, tsk.

12/20 

Becco

MODERN ITALIAN

11-25 Crossley Street,
City **9663 3000**

Licensed
Open Mon-Sat noon-3pm, 6-11pm; bar Mon-Wed noon-1am; Thurs-Sat noon-3am
Seats 75; bar
Owners Elizabeth Egan, Simon Hartley & Richard Lodge
Chefs Elizabeth Egan & Domenic Pipicelli
Cards AE BC DC MC V
Prices entrees $9-$17.50; mains $21.50-$34.50; desserts $13.50-$14.50
Map page 260 **Melway** 1B T5

CONSISTENCY is prized in a restaurant, as is a well-made Campari. You can get both at Becco, a sexy, clubby city laneway establishment that, after seven years, still attracts Melbourne's smart set and a smattering of starry-eyed out-of-towners. The split-level interior is studded with leather banquettes and linen-clad tables. The service, overseen by the ever-present Becco boys, Simon Hartley and Richard Lodge (last year's winners of *The Age* Award for Service Excellence), is exemplary. Regular diners settle into a satisfying ritual of drinks at the bar with a bowl of the signature meaty stuffed olives. Next up? Wonderful big-flavoured modern Italian dishes. Perhaps superb boned quail, wrapped in pancetta on a semolina pudding with a sweet grape dressing. Or faultless baked snapper, with one of the best-dressed salads in town. Coveted desserts include a lush vanilla bavarois with poached plums, ideal with something sticky from the impressive wine list, chased by a chunk of chewy torrone. This is one of Melbourne's most consistent performers, as much a part of the city as the trams and the Arts Centre spire.

17/20 

Bellas

MODERN SEAFOOD/VEGETARIAN

273 Glen Huntly Road,
Elsternwick **9530 0849**

Licensed & BYO wine
Corkage none
Open Wed-Fri noon-2pm; Tues-Sat 6pm-late
Seats 90; outdoor seating; private room
Owners David & Rose Patterson
Chef Avraam Avramidis
Cards AE BC DC MC V Eftpos
Prices entrees $9.50-$16; mains $19-$26; desserts $10.90
Map page 266 **Melway** 67 F3

THE beauty of the whimsical nudes that grace the walls at Bellas is more likely to win favour with the patrons of the nearby Classic Cinema than the clientele of another well-known neighbour, the Daily Planet. The ladies gaze down from the soft green and grey walls over a simple timber-floored dining room. Leave any staunch carnivores at home or try to lure them over to the 'other side' with the serious yet safe seafood and vegetarian menu. Start with Atlantic salmon and asparagus spring rolls or a crunchy salad of rocket, pear, parmesan and pecan. Service is relaxed and unpretentious; easy-going staff will help you choose between main courses like an eggplant tower with an avocado and cream sauce or a Moroccan-style vegetable stew. Seafood choices are as simple as flathead in a crisp jacket or as gutsy as blue-eye fillets in a lemongrass and coriander curry sauce, or a laksa chock-full of fish, shellfish and calamari. Dessert decisions are the hardest part of the evening. Will it be a lemon delicious pudding with memorable vanilla bean icecream, or poached pear atop a delighfully warm and sticky gingerbread cake?

13/20 V

---

bellezain

MODERN MEDITERRANEAN

HMAS Apartment Building, 1 Beach Street,
Port Melbourne **9646 6706**

Licensed
Open daily 11am-11pm
Seats 75; outdoor seating; bar
Owner Fab Hamka
Chef Leah Crathern
Cards AE BC MC V Eftpos
Prices tapas $4.50-$15; pizzas $11-$18; mains $16-$25; desserts $9-$12
Map page 264 **Melway** 2J E8

WHEN you're on a good thing, stick to it. That seems to be the thinking at bellezain, the new Port Melbourne home of some former key players from the popular Ragazzi in Middle Park. There are certainly similarities. Terrific pizza. That family-friendly ambience that characterises good neighbourhood cafe-restaurants. A few relatively ambitious mains, such as roasted duck breast on baharat-spiced lentils with harissa; and crisp-skinned salmon on lemon and tomato cous cous with sauce vierge. And a nice little wine list (though it would be more neighbourly to also offer BYO). Where Ragazzi-al-mare differs most obviously from the original is in its smarter fitout, bayside views – ideally enjoyed from the deck – and the welcome Middle Eastern influence on the Mediterranean menu. If the spicing seems rather tame, perhaps that's because bellezain is trying to please all comers. Criticisms? The absence of free bread sends out all the wrong signals, and desserts can disappoint, as in a half-baked apple. But you've got to love those pizzas: crisp-bottomed, great value, with bright, fresh flavours.

13/20

Benito's

ITALIAN

Temple Court Building, 445 Little Collins Street,
City **9670 5347**

Licensed
Open Mon-Wed 7.15am-8pm; Thurs 7.15am-9pm; Fri 7.15am-late
Seats 45; bar
Owners Joshua Brisbane, Con Christopoulos, Chris Kerr & Teresa Reginato
Chef Chris Kerr
Cards AE BC DC MC V
Prices breakfasts $6.50-$14.50; lunches $14-$25; antipasti $15-$25; desserts $6.50-$8
Map page 260 **Melway** 1A G6

BENITO'S is the newest shoot on the family tree that sprouted the European (see page 63) and Pelican (see page 127), so it's no surprise that this Italian cafe already feels so established. It's helped along by the faux antique decor – a beautiful green and cream stone-paved floor, cosy booth seating, marble-topped bar and 1930s light fittings. But it's the degree of confidence in the food and service that really makes Benito's seem wise beyond its years. Chef Chris Kerr is up early every morning baking pastries, breads and croissants to round out a breakfast menu of frittatas, bruschetta and good versions of eggs benedict and florentine. He also makes most of the pasta on the ever-changing lunch menu, layering lasagne sheets with duck bolognese and gorgonzola bechamel, or tossing squid-ink tagliatelle with sardines, tomatoes and salsa verde. There's always a roast – usually chicken or pork – and if you are lucky, Kerr might have made his chocolate and Stregà-laden cassata. Lunch is the main food event at Benito's. At nightfall it becomes a flatteringly lit wine bar serving antipasti and a brief but interesting range of wines by the glass.

13/20 

Bhoj Docklands

INDIAN
Best Indian

54 New Quay Promenade,
Docklands **9600 0884**

Licensed
Open daily noon-3pm, 5.30-11pm
Seats 115; outdoor seating
Owner Bhoj on Docklands Pty Ltd
Chef Rajesh Mehta
Cards AE BC DC MC V Eftpos
Prices entrees $4.90-$13.90; mains $7.90-$20.90; desserts $4.50-$6.50; set menus $30-$50 (3 courses)
Map page 264 **Melway** 2E E4

THIS is Bhoj's second venture – the more modest original in Templestowe has held the *Guide's* Best Indian restaurant award since 2000. Enter Bhoj Docklands. Here, the interior boasts stylish timber and tiled floors, rendered walls and persimmon lightshades, and the wine list is easily the best going around the Indian traps. The menu is similar to that at Templestowe, albeit with higher prices. Chef Rajesh Mehta, who has shifted his attention to this kitchen, continues to use only choice produce. Tandoori meats are succulent, be it marinated Rajasthani lamb, whole barramundi or minced chicken kebabs with a minty spinach puree. Most curries are distinctive: saffron and orange rind brighten a murgh dilruba (mild chicken curry) and vegetable dishes continue to impress. Since it opened in late 2002, the confusing array of menus has been streamlined and the owners are addressing early service issues, no doubt in response to high expectations of the clientele at this waterside precinct. But Docklands has become the jewel in Bhoj's crown. *Also Bhoj, shops 13-14, level 2, rear 114-116 James Street, Templestowe, 9846 7799.*

14/20 

Birdcage

MODERN JAPANESE

129 Fitzroy Street,
St Kilda **9534 0277**

Licensed
Open Tues-Fri noon-11pm; Sat-Sun 5pm-1am;
bar Tues-Fri noon-1am; Sat-Sun 5pm-1am
Seats 40; bar
Owners Widwath & Sharmaine Subasinghe
Chefs Anura Delpa Chitra & Anuruddha Subasinghe
Cards BC MC V Eftpos
Prices sushi & sashimi $4-$42; cold 'tapas' $11-$19; hot 'tapas' $9-$19;
noodles & rice $17-$19; Wagyu beef $12-$25; desserts $9-$12
Map page 261 **Melway** 2P A4

SECTIONED from the deliberately faded grandeur of the George Hotel foyer by a metal grille, this bar (under new management since late last year) serving tapas-style Japanese is equal parts birdcage and goldfish bowl, and ever so popular with the St Kilda designer crowd. Arrive early and claim a prized position at one of the closely corralled tables overlooking Fitzroy Street, or prepare to elbow a space at the bar, where flirting with staff over an Asahi or two is the main game. Nibble alluringly at bar snacks including wasabi peas, the Asian equivalent of beer nuts, or display your sophistication with the niku-dango – pork meatballs with tomato sauce, spring onion and sesame. Tiny deep-fried crab dim sims, and chicken pieces marinated in sake and herbs are well done 'Japanesque' dishes, but the cold beef salad has been known to suffer from unpleasantly chewy slices of grilled porterhouse – quite a lapse considering that dishes are both small and expensive. But sushi and sashimi lovers will be kept happy by the traditional moriawase, a selection of fish arranged on a plate with the cute addition of a hollowed cucumber candle.

12/20 

Bistro 1

MODERN EUROPEAN

126 Little Collins Street,
City **9654 3343**

Licensed
Open Mon-Fri noon-3pm; Mon-Wed 6-10pm; Thurs-Fri 6-10.30pm; Sat 6-10pm;
bar Mon-Fri 8.30am-10.30pm
Seats 70; bar
Owner Lee family
Chef Nick Ward
Cards AE BC DC MC V
Prices entrees $14.50-$22; mains $26-$34; desserts $12; less in bar
Map page 260 **Melway** 1B R6

FOR a place that bills itself as a Parisian-style bistro, there's not much 'messieursdames' here. But with its rich timber surfaces, black leather banquettes, moody lighting, pinafored waiters and adjoining bar, Bistro 1 gets top marks for atmosphere. Suits file in at lunch to talk business, or come at night to flirt by the evocative glow of red table lamps. The menu is a feast of modern bistro hits, each matched with wine from a predominantly Australian, occasionally French list. Entree favourites include home-made gnocchi with duck ragout, mushroom-filled ravioli with asparagus and leeks, and an elaborate calamari dish stuffed with basil and parsley. Mains play it straight: expect King George whiting in beer batter, roast pork with pear and basil relish and a stand-out dish of lightly smoked Wannon River lamb loin on a potato galette. It's not glitch-free: the kitchen can play fast and loose with the salt, and vegetables can sometimes be undercooked. Desserts are reliably good, though: favourites like panna cotta, luxurious crème brûlée, rich raspberry soufflé and soft-centred chocolate pudding are all there for the scoffing.

13/20 

Bistrot d'Orsay

EUROPEAN

184 Collins Street,
City **9654 6498**

Licensed
Open Mon-Fri 7.30am-11pm; Sat 9am-11pm
Seats 60; outdoor seating
Owners John Tully & Kenneth Meere
Chef Matthew Palmer
Cards AE BC DC MC V
Prices entrees $12-$17.50; mains $18.50-$31.50; desserts $9.50-$10.50
Map page 260 **Melway** 1B P7

THE name screams 'Paris' but the menu suggests that 'Bistrot Uffizi' might be more apt. There are a few nods to the west side of the Mount Blanc tunnel – perhaps a clean-tasting bouillabaisse crowded with garlicky seafood or a classic crème brûlée – but you're just as likely to enjoy a perfectly al dente duck and artichoke risotto. There's usually a garlicky 'white' marinara or soft pillows of gnocchi, perhaps under a creamy mushroom sauce. The thrill is that Matthew Palmer (ex-bluestone) is a chef who can cook this honest food with great finesse. He runs up a great coffee panna cotta and makes a simple dish like lightly battered zucchini flowers with Yarra Valley feta and a balsamic reduction a thing of angelic beauty. (If you look up to see if those are seraphim and cherubim you can hear singing, you'll discover the ceiling is covered in the little rascals.) The mural ceilings add quirk to the decor of this cosy cubby of a restaurant that is all dark wood and comfy red leather banquettes. The wine list has a few unusual selections, including half bottles for the pre- or post-theatre crowd.

14/20

Bistro Thierry

FRENCH

511 Malvern Road,
Toorak **9824 0888**

Licensed
Open daily noon-10pm
Seats 60; outdoor seating
Owner Thierry Cornevin
Chef Paul Dunlop
Cards AE BC DC MC V
Prices entrees $10-$16.50; mains $19.50-$29.50; desserts $11-$15.50; lunch set menu $25 (2 courses)
Map page 265 **Melway** 2M C10

BISTRO THIERRY shamelessly evokes a slew of French clichés, with its striped awnings, Parisian menu typography and waiters with natty waistcoats and long white aprons. Resist, if you will, but the moment one of these waiters unleashes a twinkling 'bonsoir', you're bound to be seduced. It helps that the lighting is kind, the service solicitous and the ambience warm, jollied along by a chatty Trak pack every evening. But it's not just froth and frou-frou: the French food might be familiar, but it's none the worse for that. There's beefy onion soup capped with a searing cheesy crouton, and steak tartare with the classic accompaniments: finely chopped gherkins, shallots, capers, parsley and a quivering egg yolk. Grilled steaks are good, too, especially with a great bearnaise – sharp, herby and creamy all at once. The shoestring fries are always hot and crisp, and salads come with a nicely balanced vinaigrette. Some meat servings can feel a little meagre: one chop does not a rack make. Desserts skip down the same classic path: maybe a crème brûlée, chocolate soufflé or a tarte du jour made with lemon or figs and mascarpone.

13/20

BREAKFASTS

Set the alarm to sample these morning glories

Babka
358 Brunswick Street, Fitzroy, 9416 0091
Babka has elevated to cult status dishes like spicy Georgian baked beans with crumbled feta, and cottage cheese blintzes with citrus caramel sauce and cinnamon sugar. Breads, pastries and jams are made out the back, and there's freshly squeezed OJ and excellent coffee.

baker D. Chirico
Shop 3-4, 149 Fitzroy Street, St Kilda, 9534 3777
The D. stands for Daniel, Daniel Chirico. Remember it, because he's one of the most talented bakers in town. Breakfast here could be as simple as toasted natural sourdough with Jam Lady conserves or as satisfying as oven-baked granola with warm poached fruit and yoghurt. But the ultimate experience is a custard bomboloni (doughnut) with a strong coffee chaser.

Benito's
Temple Court Building, 445 Little Collins Street, City, 9670 5347
This Italian-inspired newcomer is shaping up as one of the CBD's best breakfast options. Each morning, chef Chris Kerr bakes his own friands, spicy fruit scrolls and fruit-and-nut bread. Bigger appetites will be sated by panino stuffed with fried egg, bacon and chutney, or frittata flavoured with house-made duck sausage and sage. See page 25.

Cafe Fidama
34 Ballarat Street, Yarraville, 9687 0133
Fidama's regulars customise their breakfast, choosing from a list that includes house-baked bread and croissants, endless bacon and egg combos and fab cheese kranskies from the nearby butcher. Newcomers might prefer to stick to the written menu, where you'll find the likes of stewed tomatoes with pancetta, spinach and a poached egg. Coffee is Grinders and juices are squeezed to order. See page 38.

Harveys
10 Murphy Street, South Yarra, 9867 3605
This South Yarra restaurant combines sterling breakfast fare with professional service. Squeeze in a bowl of porridge with zingy green raisins and poached pears, or fluffy pancakes with caramelised apples and dates, between appointments with your personal trainer and hairdresser. There are tables on the streetside terrace when the sun shines. See page 73.

Pearl
631-633 Church Street, Richmond, 9421 4599
Perhaps Melbourne's most glamorous weekend breakfast destination, early-morning Pearl appears to be populated by people who buy most of their clothes and accessories up the road in Chapel Street. Geoff Lindsay's food is a match. There are delicate smoked salmon and crème fraîche omelettes, exquisite French-toasted peach sandwiches and more robust sweetcorn cakes with bacon and grilled tomato. See page 126.

Rathdowne Street Food Store
617 Rathdowne Street, Carlton North, 9347 4064
Success has not bred complacency at this smart cafe-foodstore, where owner Ricky Holt is constantly dreaming up new dishes to add to favourites like ricotta hotcakes and the petit déjeuner (a bowl of milky coffee and a house-baked croissant). Depending on the season, look out for raspberry pancakes with raspberry swirl icecream and maple syrup, or grilled figs with Greek yoghurt and mint. See page 133.

Spoonful
543 High Street, Prahran, 9521 5212
Shabby-chic Spoonful does simple things superbly, using the best available ingredients, like organic free-range eggs and Pure Bread organic sourdough. Try sunset-hued smoked salmon omelette, Red Hill muesli topped with grated pear, poached rhubarb and Meredith sheep's milk yoghurt, or crisp baguette smothered with creamy French butter and Cunliffe & Waters jam. See page 144.

Blakes Cafeteria

MODERN AUSTRALIAN

132a Greville Street,
Prahran **9510 3900**

Licensed
Open Mon-Fri 7.30am-late; Sat 8am-late; Sun 8am-5pm
Seats 72; private room; bar
Owner Andrew Blake
Chef Richard van Deursen
Cards AE BC DC MC V Eftpos
Prices breakfasts $5-$15; entrees $12-$18; mains $21-$25; desserts $6-$10
Map page 265 **Melway** 2L G11

PRICES have edged up at Blakes since last year, but its quality still puts most cafes of the same price-bracket to shame. Now that Emma Mackay and Daniel Wilson, joint winners of the *Guide's* 2003 Young Chef of the Year Award, have moved on, Andrew Blake has rejoined the kitchen crew and the Caf is as good as ever. Greville Street's trendiness helps explain the pared-back fitout: bare light globes draped over stainless steel ceiling rails, neat wicker chairs, nude timber tables. And the small list of wines is as fashionable as the clientele. There's a cheeky menu that might include kfq (Kentucky fried quail), 'year of the goat' curry and world's best practice chicken schnitzel. Beyond the catchy names are wonderful dishes: pan-fried squid showered with tiny dots of luscious pawpaw; plump gnocchi smothered in a hot and sour veal ragu; even brisket gets charismatic when it's Wagyu beef cooked in red peanut curry with eggplant. Desserts are still special – a brioche waffle may come with roast peach and mocha sauce – and service is casual but efficient. You can't book, so use the bar next door as a holding pen until a table becomes available.

15/20

Blue Chillies

MALAYSIAN

182 Brunswick Street,
Fitzroy **9417 0071**

Licensed & BYO wine
Corkage $2.80 a head
Open daily noon-2.30pm; Mon-Thurs 6-10.30pm; Fri-Sat 6-11pm; Sun 6-10pm
Seats 70; outdoor seating
Owners Hilda Frith & Linh Cao
Chef David Sum
Cards AE BC MC V
Prices entrees $3.30-$7.90; noodles $9.30-$12.50; mains $10.20-$20.80; desserts $5.90-$7.50; banquet menus $25-$30 (5-6 courses)
Map page 263 **Melway** 2C A8

THE younger sister restaurant to Chinta Blues (see page 50), Blue Chillies proves that a decent seafood laksa tastes great in a handsome wood-panelled room cooled by the soft breeze of rattan ceiling fans. The menu has changed little since opening day more than three years ago. No matter. It offers confident Malaysian fare with top-quality ingredients; aromatic curries, seafood sambal, and wok-tossed everything. Entrees are always good – taro-stuffed prawn spring rolls or snacky sambal ikan bilis. Standards like mee goreng and Singapore noodles are cooked with practised precision, but stand-out dishes include BB's beef, tender strips of beef tossed in a textured peanut sauce with lemongrass, ginger and cumin, and Assam prawns, plump king prawns served in a tamarind-based sauce with okra, tomatoes and pineapple. Soak up the sauces with the excellent roti. Blue Chillies lends itself equally to the casual night out (locals sing praises for its BYO status) and a special occasion at a table upstairs. The super-friendly staff are super-efficient. Those who like breathing space between courses should ask the kitchen to back off.

13/20 $ V

Bluecorn

MODERN MEXICAN

205 Barkly Street,
St Kilda **9534 5996**

Licensed & BYO wine (groups of 10 or fewer)
Corkage $3 a head
Open Mon-Fri 5.30pm-late; Sat-Sun 10am-late
Seats 35; outdoor seating
Owner & chef Justin Pola
Cards BC MC V Eftpos
Prices entrees & salads $10.50-$15; mains $15-$19.50; desserts $3.50-$8
Map page 261 **Melway** 2P C10

ALTHOUGH still a tot, this Barkly Street baby is doing business like it's been around for a decade. It's the balance between fresh ideas and familiarity, struck by both the decor and the menu, that confirms Bluecorn's monopoly on creative, modern Mexican food in Melbourne. The unpretentious dining space and cerveza-friendly courtyard are filled with functional steel furniture and curious touches of Mexican folk art, including eerily cheery skulls and skeletons. The menu, designed by chef Justin Pola (formerly of Stokehouse), kicks off with sugar-muddled caipirinha cocktails (drinks specials change fortnightly), then launches into entrees such as hearty baked jalapeno and mozzarella bread, seared tuna and asparagus tortilla, or a special's board tuna salad drenched in a bracing peach jalapeno vinaigrette. A mod-Mex influence continues with adventurous mains like baby octopus and chilli prawn tostada or barbecued lamb tacos, while for those enamoured of traditional options, the tightly bundled chilli beef enchilada will more than satisfy. All that, and it's a great spot for groups regardless of age or funkiness.

13/20 V

bluestone restaurant bar

MODERN AUSTRALIAN

349 Flinders Lane,
City **9620 4060**

Licensed
Open Mon-Fri noon-3pm; Tues-Fri 6-9.30pm; bar Mon-Fri 10am-late
Seats 120; bar
Owners Jason & Valerie McLean
Chef Mickael Gaultier
Cards AE BC DC MC V Eftpos
Prices entrees $14-$16; mains $23-$29; desserts $10-$14; bar menu $6-$13
Map page 260 **Melway** 1A H9

THE upstairs restaurant in this former woolshed evokes a past era of grand dining: there are gilt-edged mirrors, crimson curtains and a giant painting featuring uniformed officers and ladies in tiaras at an elaborate table. The room's contemporary diners look much happier. Seated at well-spaced linen-dressed tables, they choose from an upmarket menu of modern Australian dishes prepared with finesse then served with friendly aplomb. French chef Mickael Gaultier ensures bluestone is a class act, from the house-baked rye bread and an amuse-gueule of salted blue-eye bruschetta, through to an accomplished dessert list that includes the perfect chocolate pudding. Take advantage of Gaultier's winning ways with seafood. You might come upon calamari marinated in Moroccan spices, scallops baked with parmesan and dill, and lemongrass-infused prawns with wilted watercress. The kitchen has fun with meatier dishes, too. A decadent duck dish comprises pan-fried breast, succulent confit leg, roasted figs and a Drambuie-spiked jus. The downstairs bar is a different world, all lounges, low tables, wood-fired pizzas and after-work buzz.

14/20 

Blue Tongue

MODERN AUSTRALIAN

62 Ormond Road,
Elwood **9531 3011**

Licensed
Open daily noon-late; Sat-Sun 9am-late
Seats 35; outdoor seating; bar
Owners Matthew Little & Nick Savage
Chef Matthew Hutchison
Cards AE BC MC V Eftpos
Prices entrees $8.50-$15; mains $16-$23; desserts $6.50-$9.50
Map page 261 **Melway** 67 C3

IT'S odd that a restaurant with such a cheeky name doesn't make more of it. There's no blue tongue lizard sprawled across the window, nor on the door. In fact, the only place it makes an appearance is on the front of the global-roaming menu, where risotto might come piled with jerked chicken, Caribbean-style; beef could be chilli-spiked and ready to roll in a fluffy fajita; and duck could be confit-cooked and peppered with a ginger and anise dressing. Vegetables also get glammed-up, as in a terrine of pickled eggplant and sheep's milk feta with pomegranate molasses. Chef Matthew Hutchison's food isn't gasp-worthy but it's inventive and well cooked, easily the stand-out on Ormond Road. Elwood locals love the place, and when they're not feasting or doing double espressos, they're lounging like lizards on the pavement with a coldie, or raising glasses of Clare riesling in the simple honey-coloured dining room/bar. The wine list is razor-sharp, with a mix of fashionable and cult labels, and touches like cold unsalted butter and mini grinders on the table make up for small service glitches. It's also a good spot for weekend breakfast.

13/20

@ A GLANCE

Spots to sup before or after curtain call

PRE- & POST-THEATRE

EQ
Melbourne Concert Hall, 100 St Kilda Road, Southbank, 9645 0644
Be careful. The dramatic city views, combined with Bernard McCarthy's clever food, could have you forgetting you have a show to go to.

The European
161 Spring Street, City, 9654 0811
The theatrical decor provides an ideal backdrop to a pre- or post-show bite. There are great snacks and wines by the glass for those racing for the first act.

Hairy Canary
212 Little Collins Street, City, 9654 2471
Good pizzas, chilled sherry and a constant parade of groovers shaking their tailfeathers turn this long catwalk of a place into pre- or post-theatre theatre.

mecca
Mid-level Southgate, Southbank, 9682 2999
As you order, the waiter is likely to ask whether you're heading for the theatre. Supper afterwards is an elegant and fragrant treat, with desserts hitting all the right notes.

Phoenix
82 Flinders Street, City, 9650 4976
Plonk yourself on a couch after the show, order a snack and a drink and workshop what you have just seen. The loud, fun vibe prevents arguments.

Supper Inn
15 Celestial Avenue, City, 9663 4759
Feeling drained after the theatre? Revive yourself with congee, suckling pig or hot and sour soup at this Chinatown icon, which bustles until 2.30 every morning.

Blush Foodroom

MODERN AUSTRALIAN

43 Epsom Road,
Kensington **9376 1222**

BYO wine
Corkage $4 a bottle
Open daily 8am-11pm
Seats 60; outdoor seating
Owners Jeff Booth & Robin Neaves
Chef Ashley Ord
Cards AE BC MC V Eftpos
Prices breakfasts $4-$12.50; entrees $8-$15; mains $19.90; desserts $10.90
Map page 264 **Melway** 2T H4

AS gentrification sweeps aside the industrial past of many inner suburbs, cool cafe-restaurants like Blush Foodroom are bobbing up like Pilates classes. Despite Blush's busy roadside location, plenty of punters sit at the tables out front. Inside, a fireplace keeps things cosy, charcoal and burgundy walls carry arty photos, and tables sparkle with linen and fine glassware. Open all day, the space is tended by experienced staff and the menu features flashy mod-Oz selections. For breakfast, there's Bircher muesli with rosewater-poached dried fruit and honey yoghurt. The lengthy lunch list starts with focaccia, passes through salad and pasta, and ends with seafood. Dinner is more formal, with the duck breast special likely to arrive atop a dukkah-spiced fig tart, the eye fillet wearing a tangy citrus marinade and plump ravioli parcels containing truffle-scented quail. Prices are generally reasonable, and like any culinary player in an increasingly hip suburb, the coffee is reliable. This place has matured since it opened in 2002 and its reputation is growing. Be sure to book later in the week.

13/20

Bok Choy Chinese Cuisine

CHINESE

300a New Street,
Brighton **9592 0253**

Licensed
Open Mon-Fri noon-3pm; daily 5pm-late
Seats 80
Owner New Street Pty Ltd
Chef David Yap
Cards AE BC DC MC V
Prices entrees $3.30-$11; mains $11-$23; desserts $6.50-$8; banquet menu $55 (8 courses)
Map page 266 **Melway** 67 D9

THIS newly arrived restaurant shares family traits with its Hawthorn cousin, Choi's (see page 51): a smart but relaxed environment, professional service dominated by Flower Drum and Red Emperor alumni, outstanding food (with chef David Yap doing laps between Brighton and Hawthorn), and a wonderful wine list. The extensive collection draws on Yap's private cellar, running from quality quaffers to Grange and grand cru burgundies. Conservative dishes of the sweet-and-sour/black-bean/almonds-or-cashews variety are all present. Of greater interest, however, are the chef's suggestions and daily specials. Shanghainese pan-fried dumplings are filled with delicious fish paste instead of traditional pork. Poultry is excellent, be it roasted squab, kung bo chicken or various styles of duck. Don't miss the tender soybean-braised duck in a salty sauce nesting on greens and ovals of crispy-outside, creamy-inside tofu. Vegetable dishes, like stir-fried fungi, are also superior. Forget the predictable listed desserts; instead, ask for off-menu specials like the delicately fruity pumpkin-paste pancake, a brilliant take on the red-bean classic.

15/20

Bollywood on the Park

INDIAN

Corner Elgar & Riversdale Roads,
Box Hill South **9888 7575**

BYO
Corkage none
Open Tues-Fri noon-2.30pm; Mon-Sat 5.30-10.30pm
Seats 49
Owners & chefs Rakesh & Ranjana Goel
Cards AE BC DC MC V
Prices entrees $3.50-$11; mains $15-$21; desserts $6-$6.50; set menus $28-$45 (3 courses)
Map page 266 **Melway** 61 A3

BOLLYWOOD ON THE PARK'S wall-to-wall celebration of Hindi filmmaking always raises a smile (particularly the Errol Flynn look-alike on the bulkhead above the shop windows), and the noisy surrounds are well suited to groups and families. Although many of the posters are fading, two wall-mounted TVs bring the latest Indian stars to your attention. The menu is formulaic when compared with the decor, but there are still enough culinary sub-plots to make for a highly enjoyable meal. The Bollywood entree platter (featuring six tandoori kebabs) is the most popular item on the card, but vegetarians fare equally well with the vegie platter: a sizzler loaded with pumpkin, red onion, tofu and capsicum, all daubed with a sweetish marinade. Mains are unlikely to amaze, but the old faves are executed with assurance: saagwala chicken is inundated with ginger in a creamy spinach sauce; mughlai korma is studded with crushed cashew nuts and the odd sultana for texture. BYO six-packs are de rigueur, and after a vindaloo, a glass of badam milk, spiked with crushed almonds, almond meal and sugar, is the perfect salve.

13/20 $ V

The Bombay Beat

INDIAN

93 Burwood Road,
Hawthorn **9819 0262**

Licensed & BYO wine
Corkage $2 a head
Open Thurs-Fri noon-2pm; Mon-Sat 5.30-10.30pm
Seats 60; outdoor seating
Owners Harry & Shubi Oberoi
Chef Chander Singh Bungla
Cards AE BC DC MC V Eftpos
Prices entrees $5.50-$14.20; mains $9.90-$22; desserts $4.50-$5.50; set menus $24-$29.50 (3 courses)
Map page 265 **Melway** 45 B10

BOMBAY BEAT applies the keep-it-simple principle to its operations, with great success. Energetic staff and wholesome cooking compensate for a small space and rudimentary decor. It's good to see a genuine specials board, as opposed to the permanent 'chef specialities' on many Indian menus. The kitchen might offer mango chicken as well as mango kulfi (icecream) when the fruit is in season; or lamb dhansak, a tender, mild mix of meat, red lentils and vegetables from India's Parsi community. Marinated tandoori mushrooms stuffed with cheese and herbs complement the dozen or so main vegetarian dishes. The mains are always well prepared: bhuna ghosht combines astringent fenugreek leaves with warm ginger in the gravy for its chunky lamb pieces; chicken makhani has the velvety tones of a Las Vegas crooner, its sauce smoothed with cream and yoghurt. Accompaniments are top-notch, from the smoky flavours of minty pudina paratha bread to nutty lemon rice. There are a handful of imported beers and the wine list is handy, offering more than a dozen drops by the glass.

13/20 $ V

Bombay by Night

INDIAN

355 North Road,
Caulfield South **9578 6150**

Licensed & BYO wine
Corkage $2.50 a head
Open Tues-Sun 6-10pm
Seats 90; private rooms
Owners Jaspal & Arvind Gandhi
Chef Jaspal Gandhi
Cards AE BC DC MC V
Prices entrees $4.80-$9.50; mains $9-$22; desserts $5.50-$7; set menu $28.50 (3 courses)
Map page 266 **Melway** 68 B8

FEW commuters would suspect that Bombay by Night, a 14-year-old family business housed in an innocuous strip of shops on busy North Road, is one of Melbourne's most innovative Indian restaurants. The interior is more Italian cafe than curry house: moody black-and-white photographs, candlelit tables, linen tablecloths. Among the curries are a few creative specials that change every four to six weeks. More exotic offerings include barramundi and mussels dressed in tamarind, ginger and coriander. Of the regular fare, don't miss the much-lauded batatawada: two delicate, lightly fried pastries filled with curried potatoes. Old faithfuls will also please: tandoori lamb in a lurid orange marinade; creamy aloo gobi (cauliflower and potato curry); ultra-mild chicken makhani. Chef Jaspal Gandhi is particularly proud of his desserts, like the fluffy gulab jamun (milk dumplings in a cardamom syrup) and three types of kulfi (icecream). The traditional pistachio and mango flavours are less cloying than inferior recipes elsewhere that overdose on condensed milk, while the praline adds a distinctly French twist.

14/20 $ V

Botanical

MODERN AUSTRALIAN
Restaurant of the Year

169 Domain Road,
South Yarra **9820 7888**

Licensed
Corkage $15 a bottle (in-house bottle shop purchases only)
Open daily 8-11.00am; noon-4pm; 6-11pm
Seats 170; outdoor seating; private room; bar
Owner Chris Lucas
Chef Paul Wilson
Cards AE BC DC MC V Eftpos
Prices breakfasts $7-$14; entrees $14-$19.50; mains $22.50-$32.50; desserts $10.50-$16.50
Map page 264 **Melway** 2L C2

BOTANICAL'S rebirth came with the burden of implied promise. A great chef (Paul Wilson), an iconic site (historic watering hole the Bot), and the fiscal resources of Chris Lucas, who gutted and rebuilt the joint: what couldn't they do? Botanical's chic, sparkling dining hall hit the ground running – breakfast, noon and especially at night. The wine protocol (you can buy from the on-site shop and pay a service charge to drink in) is only one example of this restaurant's innovative approach. As ever with a Wilson restaurant, the chef's rustic food is more than a little ingenious. Flavour comes first, in classic dishes from his radii days (egg and truffled polenta; wood-fired chorizo and calamari; tuna sashimi with wasabi custard), or new favourites (scallop cassoulet with brandade and black pudding; Asian broth with steamed dhufish and lobster rice-noodle roll; taleggio, truffle and mushroom omelette with wood-roasted banana prawn). The same bold approach applies to the desserts. This is exceptional food at fair prices and, despite some predictable early chaos, Botanical looks like an institution in the making.

16/20

Bottega

ITALIAN

72-74 Bourke Street,
City **9654 2252**

Licensed
Open Mon-Sat noon-10.30pm
Seats 80; outdoor seating; private rooms
Owners Denis Lucey, Kenneth Meere & John Tully
Chef Daniel Schelbert
Cards AE BC DC MC V
Prices entrees $9.50-$15.50; mains $17.50-$26.50; desserts $10.50-$13.50
Map page 260 **Melway** 1B T5

BOTTEGA belongs to a new breed of eateries cropping up around Melbourne: informal, impeccably run by people with great experience (Bistrot d'Orsay, see page 27), wine-centric but essentially culinarily unambitious. The brief here is to provide uncomplicated, Italian-inspired food, prepared from quality ingredients, at a competitive price. Bottega fills that brief. Chef Daniel Schelbert has done time with the Bortolotto clan (Cecconi's), and his grasp of the genre is firm. Grilled calamari on charred kipfler potato with black olive is the sort of starter that works year round, as is the retro dish of spaghetti with meatballs. Mains offer a fine piece of protein, simply cooked with suitable sides: spatchcock with prosciutto, served with braised chicory, or very fine Flinders Island lamb rack roasted and served with broccoli puree. Wines reflect the culinary style, contemporary and well chosen. The spirit's Italian, the execution very much Australian and the extensive use of recycled-look timber gives this approachable Bourke Hill restaurant a sense of history. Informality is the key here. Bottega knows its target and is hitting it.

14/20

Burmese House

BURMESE

303 Bridge Road,
Richmond **9421 2861**

Licensed & BYO wine
Corkage $2 a head
Open Mon-Sat 5.30-10.30pm
Seats 50; private rooms
Owner Mimi Elton-Bott
Chefs Richard & Mimi Elton-Bott
Cards AE BC DC MC V Eftpos
Prices entrees $7.50-$19.80; sides $2.80-$4.80; mains $9.80-$21
Map page 265 **Melway** 2H A6

COCONUT, chilli or curry cravings don't have to mean Malaysian, Thai or Indian feasts. Burmese cuisine relies on chilli, lime, shrimp paste, tamarind and coconut milk, then uses these ingredients in slow-cooked curries, flash-cooked meats over rice, and zesty salads. At Burmese House, these are served in a casual but bustling dining room that contrasts exposed brickwork, Buddhist artwork and dashes of saffron yellow. Marrow fritters are typical of the kitchen's light touch: fleshy vegetable strips fried in a delicate batter and served with a rich tamarind dipping sauce. The fishcakes are also worth a look – deep-fried but still fragrantly herby, they're accompanied by a sour cucumber and chilli sauce. Mains are generous and powerfully flavoured. Mohinga, the classic Burmese fish soup, comes with a tangle of rice noodles; Mandalay mout-te features egg noodles, tossed with chicken, crushed peanuts and the obligatory chilli paste and citrus. A decent range of vegetarian dishes includes yellow split-pea curry and a sour vegetable curry with tamarind. Filling up on savouries makes sense – they're cheap and there's no dessert menu.

13/20 $ V

cafe a taglio

ITALIAN/PIZZERIA

157a Fitzroy Street,
St Kilda **9534 1344**

Licensed
Open daily noon-late
Seats 60; outdoor seating
Owners Kathy & Jean-Paul Cellier, Marcus Wilson
Chef Maurice Santucci
Cards AE BC MC V Eftpos
Prices pizza slices $3.50-$5.50; pastas $8.50-$15.50; salads $6; desserts $5.50
Map page 261 **Melway** 2P B4

NO cardboard boxes and soggy garlic bread at cafe a taglio. Instead, this Fitzroy Street fixture offers pizza by the slice at a large communal table (or snazzily wrapped to go) in an ochre-painted dining room. Ordering takes place at a glass-fronted counter, guests wandering its length pointing out their selections – with up to 20 original combos on offer, picking an interesting jumble of colours and flavours is easy. Options range from simple (spinach, ricotta), to creative (broccoli, chilli, anchovy, sultanas, pine nuts), to new age (carrot, zucchini, mozzarella, fresh tomato) and back to familiar (beef sausage, mozzarella and onion). Good-sized serves of pasta, risotto and salad are executed with less finesse than the pizzas (and pricey in comparison), but a portobello and porcini mushroom risotto will fill any rumbling belly, as will the seafood selections, maybe a linguine with local snapper and slivers of garlic. The brief wine list covers all bases, the service is fast and friendly, so if it's quick, casual and cost-effective you're after, a taglio is hard to beat. *Also basso, 195 Little Collins Street, City, 9650 0077.*

12/20 $ V

Cafe Di Stasio

ITALIAN
Best Italian

31 Fitzroy Street,
St Kilda **9525 3999**

Licensed
Open daily noon-3pm, 6-11pm
Seats 60; outdoor seating
Owner Rinaldo Di Stasio
Chefs John Snelling & Michael Darmanin
Cards AE BC DC MC V
Prices entrees $16-$33; mains $27-$39; desserts $14-$15; lunch set menu $25 (2 courses)
Map page 261 **Melway** 2N K5

FIFTEEN years on, we're still aflutter about Cafe Di Stasio. It might be controversial, even capricious, but it's never dull. For this we must thank the ebullient Ronnie Di Stasio, mastermind of this idealised slice of Italian life, whose vision and energy have made his restaurant one of the city's most enduringly successful. The devil is in the details: the line-up of white-jacketed waiters to fete you at the door, the cool jazz soundtrack, the soft, glowing light that flatters everyone, whether they're in jeans or Versace. But the main act is the food, imbued with Italian brio and respect for the primacy of ingredients. From the long menu or recited specials list, you might choose melting gnocchi pomodoro, superb gratin of scallops served on the shell, or densely flavourful herb-stuffed rabbit loin with an envelope of char-grilled polenta. Salad greens and vegetables are superior here, too, as are desserts (the white chocolate, mascarpone and pistachio torte is dream fuel). Cafe Di Stasio can be fickle, on occasions delivering less than it promises. And it is expensive, including the Di Stasio-studded wine list. But at its best, it's sublime.

17/20

Cafe Fidama

MODERN AUSTRALIAN

34 Ballarat Street,
Yarraville **9687 0133**

Licensed
Open daily 9am-11pm
Seats 42; outdoor seating
Owners Mark & Louise Cohen
Chefs Mark Cohen & Darren Morgan
Cards AE BC DC MC V Eftpos
Prices breakfasts $4.50-$12.50; entrees $7-$13; mains $15-$22; desserts $7-$12
Map page 264 **Melway** 42 A9

CAFE FIDAMA embodies the post-industrial chic of the new Yarraville. Inside its huge front windows is a neat space lined with dark-timber furniture, black leather banquettes and whitewashed walls hung with local art, the bar lit by orange pendant lights. The kitchen, visible through a narrow void behind the bar, spices up its mod-Oz menu by borrowing ideas from near and far. Shucked-to-order oysters, for instance, may come tempura-fried and wearing dainty dollops of wasabi mayo. As well as offering homely dishes like sausages and mash, the menu makes a strong commitment to seafood, with grilled ocean trout accompanied, perhaps, by a green pawpaw salad glistening in a lime and chilli glaze, while the baked salmon may arrive draped on moghrabieh (giant semolina balls) and a minty cucumber relish. Some meals can arrive slightly oily, but this is fast forgiven when the strawberry shortcake touches down – layers of golden biscuit separated by tangy strawberry sorbet, studded with unsweetened berries. The small wine list offers a modest range by the glass. A Yarraville highlight at breakfast-time too.

14/20 

Cafe Four Seasons

MODERN VIETNAMESE

377 Malvern Road,
South Yarra **9826 5353**

Licensed & BYO wine
Corkage $2 a head
Open daily 6.30-11pm
Seats 32
Owners Bornia Choy, Trang Phan & Betty Choy
Chef Trang Phan
Cards AE BC DC MC V
Prices entrees $3.80-$12.50; salads $8.80-$10.50; mains $8.50-$17; desserts $6-$7.50
Map page 265 **Melway** 2M A10

THIS intimate little restaurant celebrates the versatility of Vietnamese cuisine. Some dishes show the influence of Chinese and French colonisers, others borrow elements from neighbours as distant as India and Japan, and all are brought together with more than a smidge of mod-Oz know-how. The menu lists standard Viet-in-Melb dishes like chilli beef and spring rolls, then kicks along briskly with lesser known summer, autumn and winter rolls, the latter featuring peppery minced pork and wood-ear mushrooms. Regional Vietnamese dishes are another feature: there's a sizzling fish dish from Hanoi, cooked with turmeric, lime juice and fish sauce, and a southern-style pancake with pork and prawns that has a touch of the Indian dosa about it. Grill, claypot and wok are all kept busy: you might eat tender charred pork ribs with the oomph of lemongrass and chilli; gently gingered claypot chicken; and seasonal vegetables stir-fried with a fragrant hot and sour paste. Japan gets a look-in with an udon noodle stir-fry, and there are obvious Gallic influences in dishes such as green beans cooked in garlic butter, and crème caramel.

13/20 $ V

Cafe Jus

MODERN EUROPEAN

287 High Street,
Kew **9852 7788**

Licensed
Open Tues-Sat 6pm-late
Seats 42
Owners Justin & Kate Dooley
Chef Justin Dooley
Cards AE BC DC MC V Eftpos
Prices entrees $7-$15.50; mains $19.50-$24.50; desserts $7.50-$9.50
Map page 265 **Melway** 45 D6

THIS unassuming restaurant became an instant neighbourhood favourite when it opened in April 2002. It seems that Kew was hanging out for a low-key bistro with sweet service and creative food at modest prices. Owner-chef Justin 'Jus' Dooley has crafted an immensely appealing, Euro-flavoured menu that includes a long list of snacks, pastas, and wood-fired pizzas. They're good, but the larger plates, augmented by the specials, really hum with freshness and flavour. There might be juicy roasted quail with lentils and shavings of parmesan and truffle, house-made ravioli filled with fluffy prawn mousse in a delicate beurre blanc, or exemplary duck confit – moist, tender and falling from the bone – resting on a wonderfully buttery parsnip puree. The Moreton Bay bug linguine is a signature dish in the making, full of generous shellfish chunks and tossed with plenty of herbs. Desserts are skewed to the Italian: tiramisu and panna cotta feature, alongside puddings (perhaps with date and macadamia) and cakes. A petite wine list completes the package, ensuring Jus is a very welcome arrival indeed.

13/20

Cafe Latte

MODERN ITALIAN

521 Malvern Road,
Toorak **9826 5846**

Licensed
Open Mon 8am-5pm; Tues-Sat 8am-late; Sun 9am-5pm
Seats 45; outdoor seating
Owners Luca & Carol Lorusso
Chef Riccardo Momesso
Cards AE BC DC MC V
Prices breakfasts $3-$9.50; entrees $6.50-$18.50; mains $24-$28.50; desserts $11.50
Map page 265 **Melway** 2M C10

LIKE a smooth latte on a hectic Saturday morning, this restaurant makes you feel good. The staff laugh with the locals and shamelessly lay on the Italian flourishes as they run through the specials. Naturally, there's a beautiful coffee machine, surrounded by biscotti, wine and liqueurs, in the centre of the white-walled room. The Pugliese (south-east Italian) menu hits some high notes with dishes like an entree of calamari lolling in a rich tomato, pistachio and garlic sauce and a main veal scaloppine, tangy with white wine, lemon and caperberries. Panzerotti, pockets of pasta in a lamb broth, contain the distilled essence of roast lamb with all the trimmings. Occasionally, there is a flat moment, as in an unremarkable pasta dish of ricotta and tomato with orecchiette. But find a regular who cares – they're too busy lapping up this place's *gioia di vivere*. Not to mention the lemon crepes and fresh muffins for breakfast, or the three kinds of bruschetta that lunching ladies dally over on the footpath tables. The wine list, half Italian and half Australian, is another incentive to stay and enjoy.

13/20 

BARS

Raise your glasses and be upstanding

Carlton Yacht Club
298 Lygon Street, Carlton, 9347 7080
Don't boast about your sea legs until after you've sampled the first-rate cocktails at the land-locked Carlton Yacht Club. Prices are reasonable and the simple snack menu runs from pide and dips to salmon-and-prawn skewers and mini pizzas. The fact that CYC is smoke-free will also win friends – and influence others to seek the outdoor seating.

The Deanery
13 Bligh Place, City, 9629 5599
The ambience (chic), the wine list (extensive) and the service (knowledgeable) all make the Deanery work superbly as a bar. But it's so much more. Aside from the restaurant and a great snack menu (try the taleggio toasties), this discreet and stylish venue offers you the chance to cellar your own collection, drink it (or sell it) in the bar, or just pop down from your funky CBD apartment to buy some bottles for your dinner party.

Cookie
Level 1, 252 Swanston Street, City, 9663 7660
This vast, friendly mixed business manages to segue seamlessly from student lunches to apres-work drinks to late-night digestifs – and all points in between. Whether you're after cocktails, Italian wines, Belgian beers or fab fishcakes, look for the signage shouting 'Cookie! Bar! Food! Come on in!'

Melbourne Supper Club Bar
Upstairs, 161 Spring Street, City, 9654 6300
You haven't earned your night owl stripes in this town until you've found Melbourne's best-known secret doorway and hauled yourself upstairs to the Supper Club to escape the dawn. The wine list is impressive, the staff smooth and assured, and the snacks a smart blend of the sophisticated (dainty bruschettas) and the restorative (party pies).

Melbourne Wine Room
125 Fitzroy Street, St Kilda, 9525 5599
People migrate to Melbourne to be closer to this sprawling corner pub, which makes drinking fine wine as convivial, relaxing and just plain fun as downing a few pots. Whether you do it in the rackety front bar or the more civilised dining room, you have access to the same fine selection of Australian and European vino, and the friendly, well-informed service. See page 107.

Public House
433-435 Church Street, Richmond, 9421 0187
A Six Degrees refit has turned a sad old blues bar into a hip, modern pub. Grandma's carpet, antique wood panelling (sourced from a Toorak mansion) and vintage beer taps are dragged up to date with clean angles, raw finishes, and robust modern tapas. Drinking perches include streetside porches, a big communal table and a jutting concrete bar. A rooftop beer garden is in the works. See page 130.

Vin Cellar Cafe
212 High Street, Prahran, 9510 2820
It may be above ground, but concrete floors, burnt umber walls and wine bottles by the thousands make this bar-cafe-restaurant perfectly cellar-ish. Indulge your vin obsession by working your way through a short but interesting list of wines by the glass, or flight, or choose from the racks at retail, plus five bucks. Service is expert but not overbearing, and in winter the huge open fire is a bonus.

Wine Bar
Victorian Wine Precinct, Federation Square, 2 Swanston Street, City, 9654 6499
With more than 40 choices by the glass, and plenty more in the cellar, this is wine buff heaven. There are rustic wooden tables outside, perfect for hanging with the gang. Inside, it's sleek and modern. The service is friendly and prompt, there's a long list of snacks (from deep-fried bocconcini to grilled lamb cutlets) and, of course, there's wine, much of it rare, much of it affordable, and all of it Victorian.

Cafe Noir

MODERN AUSTRALIAN

1094 High Street,
Armadale **9509 0182**

Licensed & BYO wine
Corkage $3 a head
Open Thurs-Fri noon-2pm; Tues-Sat 6.30pm-late
Seats 65; private room
Owners Sarah & Eric Ettridge
Chefs Eric Ettridge & Nicole Cavigan
Cards AE BC DC MC V Eftpos
Prices entrees $14-$17; mains $23-$28; desserts $13-$16; lunch set menu $25 (2 courses)
Map page 265 **Melway** 59 A7

CAFE NOIR fits in well on one of Melbourne's glossiest shopping strips. Slide on to a cream banquette in a lemon-toned room hung with mirrors and gilt-framed art, and enjoy dishes like twice-cooked blue swimmer crab soufflé with a creamy bisque that looks good enough to star on a magazine cover. There are two other dining spaces as well: a cosy wine-stocked area and an airy atrium. The menu mixes bright and fashionable notions – like a fillet of Atlantic salmon crusted with black sesame – with some of Cafe Noir's own signature dishes, like crisp mature-cheddar fritters and liquid-centred chocolate and jaffa pudding. A simple stack of roast vegetables layered with Persian feta is just plain good. And the desserts can be striking. A semifreddo may ooze honeycomb and come encased in biscotti, while a white chocolate and rosewater crème brûlée could arrive with a melon citrus salad. Sensitive to the clientele's whims, the menu's carb-minimalising and gluten-free dishes are indexed. The service, however, can be slow and vague, and wines by the glass can seem jaded from the bottles having been left open.

13/20

Cafe Saffron

INDIAN

238-240 Upper Heidelberg Road,
Ivanhoe **9497 1084**

Licensed & BYO
Corkage $2 a head
Open Tues-Fri noon-3pm; daily 5pm-late
Seats 65; outdoor seating
Owner & chef Vijay Negi
Cards AE BC DC MC V
Prices entrees $5-$12.90; mains $8.90-$19.90; desserts $3.50-$3.90
Map page 266 **Melway** 31 F7

CAFE SAFFRON is the pick of the eateries along Upper Heidelberg Road, offering a broad range of specialities to spice up its uniformly excellent curries. Overlook the ho-hum facade, maroon carpets and piddling fountain in the middle of the dining room – first impressions don't do justice to owner-chef Vijay Negi's splendid cookery. The mainly north Indian menu includes three salads and two soups, notably tamatar ka shorba (an earthy tomato puree seasoned with curry leaves) and kale moti ka (chickpeas with red cabbage). The menu is replete with popular Indian dishes, but there are more flamboyant numbers vying for your attention, among them, perhaps, tandoori chicken stuffed with a dry, fruity mince or tender meatballs studded with sunflower seeds. The kormas (braised meats) are invariably velvety and well balanced; perhaps cubed lamb teamed with turnips or the auspicious murgh chabahar, chicken cooked and served in a coconut shell that imparts its own sweetness to the dish. The savoury lassi drinks are super and the service is cheery, on song with the chirpy sitar music that plays ceaselessly in the background.

13/20 $ V

Cafe Zum Zum

MIDDLE EASTERN

645 Rathdowne Street,
Carlton North **9348 0455**

Licensed & BYO wine
Corkage $2 a head
Open Wed-Sun noon-10pm; Tues 6-10pm
Seats 40; outdoor seating
Owners Geoff Malouf & Dahouk White
Chef Dahouk White
Cards BC MC V
Prices entrees $7.50-$9.50; mains $14.50-$17.50; desserts $5-$7
Map page 262 **Melway** 2B J2

ZUM ZUM has it all: great food, good staff, and a growing reputation among fans of Middle Eastern food. Mo Mo's Greg Malouf is not in the kitchen, but has had a hand in the menu. His brother Geoff and partner-chef Dahouk White (from the Dunyazad/Kanzaman restaurant family) are running the show, and what a show it is. The small, simple space is dotted with Middle Eastern curios, painted the colours of sunset and decorated with ornate Mediterranean tilework. The menu offers expertly rendered variations on Middle Eastern standards. Grilled ma'anek sausages may appear under harissa-spiced potato salad, and lightly fried haloumi arrives, perhaps, over zaatar-sprinkled baby spinach. Mains look familiar, but the kitchen exceeds expectation on almost every front. There could be harissa-spiced chicken with almond-speckled rice and yoghurt, and grilled snapper fillet showered with walnuts, coriander, chilli and tahini. Dessert is a small range of pastries, and there's a Persian tea alternative to the syrupy, stove-cooked coffee. All that and two could eat here for a very reasonable sum.

13/20 $

Caffe e Cucina

MODERN ITALIAN

581 Chapel Street,
South Yarra **9827 4139**

Licensed
Open Mon-Sat 7am-midnight; Sun 8am-4pm
Seats 72; outdoor seating
Owner Arthur Georgiou
Chef Franco Italia
Cards AE BC DC MC V Eftpos
Prices breakfasts $4.50-$10.50; entrees $9.80-$18.80; pastas & risottos $15.80-$21.80; mains $21.80-$27.80; desserts $6.80-$12.80
Map page 265 **Melway** 2L J6

CAFFE E CUCINA is a bit like that old black polo neck jumper at the back of the cupboard. It's not the sassy item it used to be, but hey, it's comfy and in the right light it's still chic. This iconic Melbourne restaurant, the place that made antipasto on silver stands and crusty bread with olive oil and balsamic essentials for any restaurant with Italian credentials (or pretensions), is still looking just fine to its many devotees. But a certain heaviness comes from the kitchen these days, with oiliness weighing down entrees like deep-fried zucchini flowers stuffed with ricotta, mushroom and truffle pesto, and the once delicate pan-fried crumbed veal now tastes thick and dumpy under its rocket mantle. The pesto and goats' cheese spaghetti is stock-standard, too. But designer sunglasses still glint in the darkness as the delicate calamari St Andrea gets a squeeze of lemon, and the waiters love to banter in Italian as they offer a glass of espresso to splash over your vanilla semifreddo with pistachios. Who needs cutting edge when you can sneak a bit of comfort and still look cool?

12/20

Caffe Per Te

ITALIAN

66 Church Street,
Brighton **9592 0169**

Licensed & BYO wine
Corkage $3 a bottle
Open Sun 9am-3pm; Mon 8am-5pm; Tues-Fri 8am-late; Sat 9am-late
Seats 40; outdoor seating
Owners Tony Kropach & Michael Gleeson
Chef Grant Waters
Cards AE BC MC V
Prices breakfasts $3.60-$14.50; entrees $4.80-$16.50; pastas & risottos $16.50-$19.80; mains $24.50-$29; desserts $8-$10.50
Map page 266 **Melway** 67 E11

CAFFE PER TE'S creamy walls, dark timber and low lights offer more intimacy and Euro refinement than many of the bayside area's big, boldly coloured cafes. The waitstaff also know how to turn on the continental charm. By day, breakfast offerings include frittata and buttermilk hotcakes, then from lunchtime, there are Italian standards – pasta plus focaccia and panini filled with top-shelf ingredients (pancetta, semi-dried tomato and mascarpone, for example). At night, the cafe morphs into a *ristorante* with a classically Italian menu and tables dressed in linen. Food is lovingly prepared, from a delicate entree of thinly sliced roast beef with a parmigiano and pistachio crust, reclining on slivers of crisp vegetables, to char-grilled calamari heaped on rocket. Penne smothered in fresh tomato, rocket and olives is delicious, and a special of risotto with duck meatballs and spinach is interesting in both flavour and texture. Don't skip desserts – the chef could be whipping up a gossamer-light zabaglione or have baked a cheesecake with sour cherries, which he serves in a slab. There's also a decent list of Italian and Australian wines.

13/20

Carlisle Wine Bar

ITALIAN

137 Carlisle Street,
Balaclava **9531 3222**

Licensed
Open Mon-Thurs 5pm-1am; Fri noon-1am; Sat-Sun 8am-1am
Seats 65; outdoor seating; bar
Owners Marco Santucci & Steven Milic
Chef Marco Santucci
Cards AE BC DC MC V
Prices entrees $7.50-$15.50; mains $14.50-$24; desserts $6.50-$8
Map page 261 **Melway** 2P G9

CARLISLE bills itself as a wine bar, and you could easily amuse yourself among the Australasian and European wines and well-constructed cocktails organised by sommelier Lazlo Everhuis (ex-Melbourne Supper Club), while a record spins behind the glowing underlit onyx bar. But why stop there? In the kitchen at the rear of this dark and handsome space, crafted from an old butcher's shop, chef Marco Santucci is working his charm. Santucci has cooked everywhere from the Latin to Termini, and his take on Italian food is big-flavoured and big-portioned. Oven-baked figs are filled with mascarpone and wrapped in prosciutto, and a huge skein of house-made spaghetti is flavoured with fennel and tomato and bristles with sand-crab legs. The cacciucco, a Tuscan stew with fish, prawns, calamari, clams and spicy juices, is a regular on the daily-changing menu. There's veal Milanese, crumbed with herbs and pine nuts, and tender grilled aged eye fillet topped with provolone and served with stuffed eggplant rolls. Desserts can include an addictive dark chocolate zabaglione. Good weekend brekkies fill a Carlisle Street void.

13/20 $

The Carringbush Dining Room

MODERN EUROPEAN

228 Langridge Street,
Abbotsford **9417 2918**

Licensed
Open Mon-Fri noon-2pm; Mon-Sat 6pm-late
Seats 50; outdoor seating; private room; bar
Owners Pat Harris & Helen Loyall
Chef Troy Anthony
Cards AE BC DC MC V Eftpos
Prices entrees $12-$15; mains $22.50-$27.50; desserts $10-$12.50; bar menu $6-$17
Map page 263 **Melway** 2C H12

THERE is a strange time warp operating at the Carringbush Hotel. The charmingly dim public bar is a throwback to the '40s, the dining room's exposed brick and rattan ceiling fans are city chic circa '72, and the menu makes retro gestures to the '80s. Chef Troy Anthony once cooked with Philippe Mouchel, and the menu bears evidence of the Frenchman's influence in its fondants and fricassees. The food, while generally well executed, often seems unnecessarily fiddly for a neighbourhood pub: haricot beans become a frothy cappuccino garnished with a prawn; rack of lamb comes with an over-the-top retinue of peperonata, powerful salsa verde and crumbed sweetbreads; roast chicken with lentils and cotechino sausage is crowned with a puny leek tart. The chunky pork and hazelnut terrine works well, and the warm rice pudding with passionfruit icecream puts an interesting spin on an old favourite. Service wobbles as waiters struggle with the menu's upmarket aspirations, and the wine list is patchy at best. Simple, well-cooked lamb chops in the front bar are likely to make for a more satisfying meal.

12/20

Caterina's Cucina e Bar

ITALIAN

Basement, 221 Queen Street,
City **9670 8488**

Licensed
Open Mon-Fri noon-3pm; bar Mon-Fri noon-late
Seats 90; bar
Owner Caterina Borsato
Chef Michele Usci
Cards AE BC DC MC V
Prices entrees $12-$17.50; mains $22-$28; desserts $12.50
Map page 260 **Melway** 1A H3

A TRUE lunching legend, clubby Caterina's powers on with a gobsmacking wine list and an inspired northern Italian menu (some rustic dishes from new chef Michele Usci's central Italy are also promised). Corporate and legal types fill the dim cellar space, talking shop and relishing the rich, reliable food over a glass – 'oh, might as well get a bottle' – of great wine. The formally-clad waitstaff pitch it just right: they're welcoming and efficient, and unobtrusive once they've recited the preposterously long specials list. The written menu is a hefty tome, too. The huge antipasto plate is always a good start, perhaps featuring crisp whitebait, air-cured beef and slabs of polenta and herb cake. Otherwise, try paper-thin tuna carpaccio with radicchio, orange segments, capers and a drizzling of olive oil. Meaty business-bloke fare rules among the mains: wonderfully tender lamb is stewed in a carefully composed agrodolce (sweet and sour) tomato sauce; a risotto of pork sausage, mushrooms and spinach groans with creamy goodness. Keep an eye out for the charming Caterina herself – she makes a lap of the room most lunchtimes.

13/20

Cecconi's

MODERN ITALIAN

Ground level, Crown Entertainment Complex, Southbank **9686 8648**

Licensed
Open Sun-Fri noon-3pm; daily 6pm-late
Seats 170; outdoor seating; private rooms; bar
Owner Bortolotto family
Chefs Olimpia Bortolotto & Harry Lilai
Cards BC DC MC V
Prices entrees \$15-\$25; mains \$34-\$35; desserts \$15.50
Map page 264 **Melway** 1D M3

CECCONI'S is a class act. Who wouldn't want to be a tourist, discovering the place by happy chance after a visit to the casino or a stroll by the river? First impressions would be positive: there's the smart terrace, the vast, bustling interior, the courteous staff and the well-spaced, linen-clothed tables topped with quality hardware. It's a biggie, too – those 170 seats make it one of Melbourne's largest upmarket restaurants. But the real surprise for the first-time visitor would be the food: unusually fine for a place this size. Whether it's two fillets of superb chickpea flour-battered King George whiting with kipfler salad; rust-coloured, tender quail with chorizo and grapes; or a flourless chocolate pudding, molten in the middle and correctly bittersweet, it's all about top ingredients, accomplished cooking and flash presentation. And the steep prices? Stick to a plate of good pasta (perhaps angel hair with pan-fried tuna, olives and lemon), a generous side of excellent fried potatoes or green bean salad, a glass of wine from the extensive list and you can see why Cecconi's has no trouble filling all those tables seven nights a week.

16/20

@ A GLANCE

Love is an intimate table for two

ROMANTIC

Circa, the Prince
2 Acland Street, St Kilda, 9536 1122
After five years, Circa can still put you in the mood for love. Wafting drapes, leather couches and chef Michael Lambie's deft touch may have you considering a room in the Prince hotel.

ezard at adelphi
187 Flinders Lane, City, 9639 6811
There's a frisson of excitement about this room, the combination of flattering lighting, plush furnishings, sparkling food and discreet service.

Ici
359 Napier Street, Fitzroy, 9417 2274
Friday and Saturday night dinners turn this tiny, backstreet cafe into a candlelit love shack. Small tables are perfect for hand-holding and the whispering of sweet nothings.

Mo Mo
Basement, 115 Collins Street, City, 9650 0660
The basement location, shadowy spaces, mysterious screens and enticing aromas from Greg Malouf's kitchen give your night an exotic and clandestine edge.

Syracuse
23 Bank Place, City, 9670 1777
Old-world good looks provide the perfect setting for pretending you are honeymooning in Europe: some wine, some tapas, then back to the pensione.

Tides
Pier 35 Marina, 263-329 Lorimer Street, Port Melbourne, 9645 6433
With the docks as an industrial backdrop, this secluded seafood restaurant is made for the discreet affair, or at least the one you're pretending to have.

Centonove

MODERN ITALIAN

109 Cotham Road,
Kew **9817 6468**

Licensed
Open Tues-Fri 10am-10pm; Sat 9am-10pm
Seats 40; private room
Owners Gale Davidson & Brent Baigent
Chef Brent Baigent
Cards AE BC DC MC V Eftpos
Prices entrees $13-$18; pizzas & pastas $14-$22; mains $25-$32; desserts $7-$13
Map page 265 **Melway** 45 E6

THIS small, slick restaurant performs two roles. On the one hand, it's a modern Italian cafe playing contemporary music and serving smart pizza and pasta to customers in jeans. On the other, it's a restaurant serving classic Italian-inspired meat dishes to patrons old enough to expect silver service. And they get it. That's the key to Centonove: what they do, they do very well, for a broad spectrum of diners. Service is impeccable and personal; tactile fittings are of a high standard. And, while the Italian menu is hardly groundbreaking, it is executed with style and finesse, employing raw materials of a quality beyond similar operations. Pasta dishes – perhaps spaghettini with seafood and roasted cherry tomatoes – are close to perfect. Simplicity is difficult to pull off, but here a simple caprese pizza comes with a thin crust, lovely tomato, bocconcini and fresh torn basil. And a carpaccio of salt-cured ocean trout may arrive with a confetti of radicchio and baby capers. Within the parameters of its menu, Centonove is a rather sophisticated place indeed, an impression reinforced by an extensive wine list and knowledgeable wine service.

14/20

Centro Ristorante Italiano

ITALIAN

225 Clarendon Street,
South Melbourne **9699 5904**

Licensed & BYO wine
Corkage $5 a bottle
Open Mon-Fri noon-3pm, 6-10.30pm; Sat 6-10.30pm
Seats 90; outdoor seating; private rooms
Owners Pietro & Ruth Caluzzi
Chef Luke Smith
Cards AE BC DC MC V
Prices entrees $9-$17; mains $20.50-$27; desserts $9-$12.50
Map page 264 **Melway** 1C H12

ONE of Melbourne's bedrock lunch haunts, this colourful cucina has been operating in the same location since 1977. Count on a warm welcome from longtime host Pietro Caluzzi, Italian pop on the stereo, and a bit of blokey belt-loosening after another long high-carb lunch and a dabble in the more-than-decent wine list. Luke Smith (Centro's chef for eight years until 1999) is back after a few years' sabbatical at Centonove, Caffe e Cucina and r.bar. He's returned with a renewed focus on the lighter dishes from his northern Italian repertoire: calamari strips tossed with chilli, garlic and parsley; seared ocean trout salad with potatoes, beans and egg; and house-made gnocchi with mushrooms, roasted red peppers and pancetta. The regulars are just as likely to start with garlicky spaghettini with prawns, calamari and mussels, followed by man-sized veal scaloppine, char-grilled aged Western District eye fillet or the restaurant's signature dish of braised rabbit in white wine, juniper berries and mushrooms served with rabbit sausage. True gourmands make it through to dessert, finishing with strawberry semifreddo or a towering chocolate soufflé.

13/20

Chamber Food & Wine Room

MODERN AUSTRALIAN

189 Nelson Place,
Williamstown **9397 6666**

Licensed & BYO wine
Corkage $7 a bottle
Open Wed-Fri 11am-3pm, 6pm-late; Sat 11am-late; Sun 10.30am-late
Seats 110; outdoor seating; private rooms
Owners Brook & Benbow families
Chef Paul Brook
Cards AE BC DC MC V
Prices entrees $12-$15; mains $20-$26; desserts $9
Map page 264 **Melway** 56 D9

EVERY year this restaurant, in a stately old bank, shrugs off a few more fine dining orthodoxies. The tablecloths and upholstered chairs were turfed last year in favour of a comfortable clutter of shabby-chic antiques. Chef Paul Brook has lightened up the menu, offering antipasto with house-made beer bread, fat chips and muffins, along with unpretentious restaurant meals. Brightly flavoured dishes include sang choy bao with barbecued pork and capsicum, calamari with chilli-lime mayonnaise, and parmesan-crumbed schnitzel. Some of the more complex dishes work well: slow-roasted duck with glazed peaches, and ocean trout with a teriyaki glaze. Others, such as Moroccan-spiced chicken, are disappointingly bland. The specials board has better pickings – perhaps beautifully presented red mullet with asparagus or 'Dad's snags', the sausages made by Brook's butcher father. Desserts are a delicious remnant of Chamber's fancy past: chocolate and raspberry pudding or caramelised lemon tart with citrus and lychee salad. The wine collection, featuring a few older-vintage Australian classics, is stored in the bank vault. You can also BYO.

12/20

Charcoal Grill on the Hill

STEAKHOUSE

289 High Street,
Kew **9853 7535**

Licensed
Open Fri noon-3pm; Mon-Sat 6-11pm
Seats 80
Owners Peter & Dejan Derbogosian
Chef Fabian Caminiti
Cards AE BC DC MC V
Prices entrees $9-$11; mains $29-$35; desserts $9
Map page 265 **Melway** 45 D6

THIS suburban steakhouse has two things that make it very special: a wonderful wine list and stunning steak. In that order. The wine list runs to nine pages (in the tiniest print imaginable) and there are pages devoted to Australian cult reds (including older vintages), excellent burgundies and a great selection of Italian wines, some of them imported solely by father and son Peter and Dejan Derbogosian. Quality glassware is a given, but unlike other wine-obsessed restaurants, prices are not in the outer ionosphere. The setting is homely, with RSL-style carpets, fittings and bright lighting. The staff are attentive and seem happy as they ferry great fries and some of the best steak in Melbourne to the pub-style tables. Get your juices flowing with soup or startlingly simple grilled vegetables, before moving on to the real business: exemplary scotch fillet, rump or porterhouse – all perfectly cooked. On the side, there's steakhouse coleslaw, cos lettuce salad and plenty of good-quality condiments. There are standard icecreams and crepes for dessert; better to order cheese and ask Dejan to help you settle in with another brilliant red.

14/20

---

chez phat

MODERN AUSTRALIAN

Level 1, 7 Waratah Place,
City **9663 0988**

Licensed
Open Tues-Sat 6pm-midnight; Sun 4-11pm
Seats 57; bar
Owners Sol & Rufino Ramos
Chef Catriona Freeman
Cards AE BC DC MC V Eftpos
Prices entrees $8-$13; tapas $3-$12; mains $18-$25; desserts $6-$10
Map page 260 **Melway** 1B Q4

CHEZ PHAT'S kitsch reworkings of classic '70s dishes and offbeat location seemed to capture the zeitgeist back in 2000. But since founding chef Elena Bonnici left, the phat has struggled to regain its initial self-assurance. City types still weave past the dumpsters of Waratah Place to perch on retro chairs and revel in the spartan interior. But the moody downlighting and beige walls are starting to look turn-of-the-century. Dishes are smart and playful – open lasagne with parmesan soufflé, for example – but sometimes display more style than substance. A shredded salad of sand crab, avocado, cos, radish and tomato may arrive a tad watery, and a plump leg of free-range chicken begs for more than a handful of ricotta gnocchi and peas as an accompaniment. Better are a generous fillet of barramundi rubbed in red miso and swimming in a soybean broth, and salty jamon wrapped around balls of baked mozzarella. At press time there were plans to introduce more Spanish-style dishes, an upshot, no doubt, of the popular 'tapas Sundays', and second chef, Catriona Freeman, was also stepping up to take the reins.

13/20

China Max

CHINESE

6 Keilor Road,
Essendon North **9374 1988**

Licensed & BYO wine
Corkage $5 a bottle
Open Mon-Sat 11.30am-2.30pm; Sun 11am-3pm; daily 5pm-late
Seats 80
Owners William Lee & Paul Chan
Chef Paul Chan
Cards AE BC DC MC V
Prices yum cha dishes $4-$7; entrees $5-$8; mains $15-$25; desserts $5; banquet menus $26-$38 (5-7 courses)
Map page 264 **Melway** 28 E1

EVERYONE knows that real Chinese restaurants are crammed with painted screens, lanterns, gaudy red and gold carpet, and bad wine lists, right? Someone must have forgotten to tell China Max. Its pleasing good looks, a broad list of keenly priced wines, and the scarcity of 'name' restaurants in the immediate vicinity have proved a winning combination. But, as they say in the trade, how does it taste? The whitebait – teeny-weeny fish in extra-crisp batter coats – are delicious. Bigger things like jumbo prawns in an XO-butter-garlic sauce, spicy plump quail and grilled giant green mussels are as good as they get. Pastries, as in deep-fried yam with a moist filling of duck, are also good. While the menu is pretty standard, the specials list changes seasonally, so quiz the waiters about what's good. Prices have started to creep up lately, and like everyone else, the Max does have its moments ('deboned duck' that arrives with bones), but with perks like a BYO policy and daily yum cha, this big western suburbs restaurant makes most people happy most of the time.

13/20

Chine on Paramount

CHINESE

Shops 9 & 10, Paramount Centre, 101 Little Bourke Street, City **9663 6556**

Licensed
Open Mon-Sat noon-3pm; Sun-Thurs 6-11pm; Fri-Sat 6-11.30pm
Seats 70; private room
Owner Banksia Rose Pty Ltd
Chef On Kwan
Cards AE BC DC MC V
Prices entrees $5.80-$15.80; mains $17.80-$69; desserts $6.80-$9.80; banquet menus $69 or $88 (6 courses)
Map page 260 **Melway** 1B S4

THE well-dressed tables and elegantly draped windows of Chine reflect the unhurried pace here. An upmarket wine list features a selection of iconic wines, including a pair of Grange vintages, and service is swift and knowledgeable. The menu matches the mood with a thoughtful blend of current trends from Hong Kong and Taiwan, where, our spies tell us, nutrition has regained the ascendancy over flash flavours. Medicinal herbs such as huai san (a rhizome) and qi zi (wolfberry or boxthorn fruit) are returning to restaurants. You'll find them in Chine's new 'herb-enriched duck', skinned, deboned, steamed and tasting too good to be medicinal. A clear soup infused with the slight sweetness of boxthorn accompanies the duck. Also new is ox tongue, marinated in a reduced stock with rice wine and star-anise, and served cold with sesame seed and seaweed. Old faithfuls like Peking duck and steamed whole fish are all prepared with meticulous care. Even the fried rice (fluffy, specked with dried scallop and eggwhite) rates highly. And when a kitchen elevates such a staple to a taste sensation, it's well worth repeat visits.

15/20 V

Chinta Blues

MALAYSIAN

6 Acland Street, St Kilda **9534 9233**

Licensed & BYO wine
Corkage $5 a bottle
Open Mon-Sat noon-2.30pm; Mon 6-10.15pm; Tues-Thurs 6-10.30pm; Fri-Sat 6-11pm; Sun noon-10pm
Seats 80; outdoor seating
Owner Hilda Frith
Chef Michael Cho
Cards AE BC MC V
Prices entrees $4.40-$7.50; mains $10.80-$20.50; desserts $6-$7.50
Map page 261 **Melway** 2N K6

CHINTA BLUES is part of the St Kilda landscape – the saxophonist statue on the terrace is almost as familiar as Luna Park's gaping mouth. The open kitchen and produce-stocked shelves are stylishly informal, but on busy nights, it feels like a student cafeteria, with understandably stressed waitstaff. Grab a seat on the terrace, heated during the colder months, if only to escape the din of boisterous conversations and spatulas scraping on woks in the bustling kitchen. Regulars can recite the menu like relatives' birthdays – spring rolls, curry puffs and satay chicken skewers. Prices are still low, but watch those creeping credit card charges (to compensate, they've installed an ATM in-house). Piquant soups like the coconut-based vegetarian laksa tong are a treat on cold nights. Slurp the soup noodles with impunity, including the hearty Chinta soup – egg noodles with chicken, prawns and bean shoots in a chicken broth. Decent curries include a correctly crumbly beef rendang. The house speciality of a spicy and slightly bitter tamarind-based Assam sauce lends silkiness to fish or prawns.

12/20 $ V

Chocolate Buddha

MODERN JAPANESE

Federation Square, 2 Swanston Street (corner Flinders Street), City **9654 5688**

Licensed
Open daily noon-11pm
Seats 100; outdoor seating; bar
Owners Paul & Jo-Anne Mathis
Chef Yoshi Fujiu
Cards AE BC MC V
Prices entrees $3.90-$12; mains $12.90-$16.90; desserts $9
Map page 260 **Melway** 1B P10

PAUL MATHIS puts his money where his food ideology is. At his St Kilda canteen Soulmama (see page 137), that means all-vegetarian eating; at this bubbly Fed Square ramen and donburi bar, it means the meat, eggs and noodles are organic and free-range. For customers, it adds up to a few extra dollars on the bill and the satisfaction of knowing that the animals you're eating have enjoyed a 'more abundant and a more natural life', as the menuspeak puts it. Your own life may certainly feel more abundant while you sit in this spunky, Buddha-lined, inevitably crowded room, slurping up noodles and char-grilled salmon from a fishy broth, or chopsticking juicy grilled teriyaki eel from a deep bowl of white rice. The sake cocktails are terrific – try the apple crunch with vodka, apple schnapps, fruit juice and a cinnamon stick – but desserts tend to be unimpressive and overpriced. It's possible to quibble with the no bookings policy, the backless stools, and the staggered arrival of each party's meals (they arrive as they're ready). But if you can get into the spirit of the place, Chocolate Buddha is a top spot for fresh, feisty food.

13/20 $ V

Choi's

CHINESE

186 Riversdale Road, Hawthorn **9818 2299**

Licensed & BYO wine
Corkage $2.50 a head
Open Mon-Fri noon-2.30pm; Sun-Thurs 5-10pm; Fri-Sat 5-11pm
Seats 70; bar
Owner & chef David Yap
Cards AE BC DC MC V
Prices entrees $7-$12; mains $16-$23; desserts $6-$7; banquet menu $39 (6 courses)
Map page 265 **Melway** 45 E12

BLUE-BLOODED Riversdale Road doesn't seem like the place for a dazzling Hong Kong-style restaurant. But Choi's brings glitz to Hawthorn with its triple-domed ceiling, splashy downlights and gaudy play of marble, tiles, glass and brass. Smartly attired waiting staff go about their tasks with the fluidity that comes with constant practice. Choi's isn't just glitter and action: the impressive and often innovative Cantonese menu (with diversions into Shanghainese and Sichuan cuisine) offers seriously good food. The marvellous spinach turnover is crisp to the tooth before melting away, and the ha ha roll (a reinvented spring roll) is filled with a balanced blend of minced chicken, shiitake mushrooms and dried shrimps. Even the humble eggplant looks more noble when it's stewed in spiced, coconut-flavoured tomato puree in the house version of Sichuan eggplant. And then there is the duck – a fine Peking for the conservative punter, and East Village for the adventurous, with sparky apple sauce and deep-fried bird. The choice of 4000 bottles from owner-chef David Yap's cellar only enhances the experience. *Also Bok Choy, Brighton, page 33.*

15/20 V

SURROUND YOURSELF WITH FLAVOUR
ROSEMOUNT ESTATE
SHIRAZ
ESTATE BOTTLED
OSEMOUNT
ROSEMOUNT
FULL FLAVOURED • EASY DRINKING

Ciccia Bomba

MODERN ITALIAN

37 Toorak Road,
South Yarra **9866 3237**

Licensed
Open Tues-Sat noon-3pm; Mon-Sat 6pm-late
Seats 90; private room
Owners Rita Wessels & Nina Ripani
Chef Richenda Pritchard
Cards AE BC DC MC V Eftpos
Prices entrees $13.50-$16.50; pastas & risottos $12.50-$26.50; mains $23.50-$28.50; desserts $10-$13.50
Map page 265 **Melway** 2L F5

THE inspiration for the baroque interior of this two-storey terrace could have come from Peter Greenaway's film *The Cook, The Thief, His Wife and Her Lover*. But for all the opulence (tapestries, chandeliers, gilded mirrors), the mood is relaxed and the service attentive. The short wine list offers choices for every budget, but speak to the man with the exquisitely coiffured moustache, head waiter Vincenzo Tomaino – he may have something interesting out the back. Crusty bread may come with a too-delicious cannellini bean paste as you study the modern Italian menu. Entrees and pastas are built around good ingredients simply prepared, such as shallow-fried calamari with chilli, garlic and parsley, and twisted casarecce pasta with asparagus, zucchini, peas and oregano topped with shaved ricotta. Mains balance protein and greens well enough to dispense with side dishes, as in twice-roasted duck with sauteed chicory and Campari sauce. From the Italian dessert selection, the tartufo affogato (chocolate-coated icecream with nuts and candied fruit, drowned with espresso) is good, but bombolini, custard-filled dumplings, are great.

13/20

Cicciolina

130 Acland Street,
St Kilda **9525 3333**

Licensed
Open Mon-Sat noon-11pm; Sun noon-10pm; bar Mon-Sat 4.30pm-1am; Sun 3.30-11pm
Seats 45; bar
Owners Barbara Dight, Lisa Carrodus & Virginia Redmond
Chef Virginia Redmond
Cards AE BC DC MC V
Prices entrees $7.50-$14.50; mains $17.50-$28; desserts $3.50-$12.50; bar menu $4.50-$14.50
Map page 261 **Melway** 2P B9

THERE are two bores about Cicciolina: that you'll need a map (and a key on a huge chunk of wood) to visit the lavs and that you can't book. To snare a table you'll need to turn up early or put your name down and wait in the cosy (read: crowded) bar out the back. And yet there is no shortage of groovers willing to queue to eat hugga mugga in this glowing, down-to-earth dining room. The reasons are myriad. The buzzy atmosphere encourages laughter and intense conversation. Despite the casual attitude, service seldom misses a beat. There's a petite but intriguing wine list with some brave selections by the glass – be it a Gembrook Hill chardonnay or Charlie Melton's Nine Popes. Oh, and there is also the food. Intelligent, spirited food that will have you mopping the plate – perhaps a hunk of veal cutlet on Jerusalem artichoke puree with a sticky jus, or prosciutto-wrapped brains served with roast garlic mayo. The same finesse is displayed in dishes like red snapper fillet with a champagne and saffron velouté, or a salad niçoise blessed with scallops rather than tuna. Return to the bar for a cleanser or full-throttle espresso. A Melbourne gem.

15/20

Circa, the Prince

2 Acland Street,
St Kilda **9536 1122**

MODERN EUROPEAN
Best Wine List

Licensed
Open daily 7am-11am, noon-3pm, 6.30pm-late
Seats 90; private rooms; bar
Owners Michael Lambie, John & Frank Van Haandel
Chef Michael Lambie
Cards AE BC DC MC V
Prices entrees $19.50-$24; mains $35-$38.50; desserts $17.50-$19.50; set menu $85 (6 courses); vegetarian set menu $70 (6 courses)
Map page 261 **Melway** 2N K6

SECURE in its status as one of Melbourne's best restaurants, Circa dishes up excellent food and a sense of occasion. The romantic dining room has worn well – the drapes shimmer, the cream banquettes are still sexy and comfortable, and there's just enough light to read the menu. Creative seafood dishes are still a long suit, as in a quenelle-shaped barramundi soufflé, or roasted scallops with chorizo oil. Refined pastas (say, delicate pigeon ravioli with showy white bean foam) and game also feature. Occasionally, Michael Lambie and crew seem to be seduced by the wizardry of their sauces at the expense of the protein components of the mains. An unexceptional snapper fillet comes in a transcendent star-anise and caramel broth; and eye fillet is not as tender as might be hoped, though it sits in a gloriously sticky jus. Desserts are on track: the soufflés range from blood orange to pear and chocolate, and many sweets come with house-made ices like playful gingerbread. Circa's wide-roaming wine list (winner of the *Guide's* Best Wine List award) is rendered even more tantalising by the enthusiasm of sommelier Chris Crawford.

17/20

V

Citrus

8-10 North Concourse,
Beaumaris **9589 2199**

MODERN AUSTRALIAN

Licensed
Open Mon-Fri noon-3pm; daily 6pm-late
Seats 90; private room
Owners & chefs Todd Roydhouse & Armin Pfister
Cards AE BC DC MC V Eftpos
Prices entrees $10-$16; mains $21-$29; desserts $10.50-$14.50
Map page 266 **Melway** 86 D7

WITH sand-coloured walls and lots of shiny wood, Citrus bears more than a passing resemblance to a Brighton display home. Perhaps it's a ruse to lure those conservative diners who might otherwise be deterred by the more ambitious dishes emerging from the kitchen. To begin, classics like French onion soup seem pedestrian next to jasmine tea-smoked ocean trout on a pared-back Waldorf salad, and positively pale beside the intricate five-tastes starter that may comprise of an oyster shooter, tender chilli squid, salt-and-sugar-cured porterhouse, pumpkin ravioli and good-quality smoked salmon. A main course of, say, dory fillets on a creamy cauliflower korma is equally sparky. The roast duck is more conservative, although the mandarin glaze adds an intense, semi-sweet flavour. Desserts are less reliable; a bland coconut bavarois appears to lack depth next to a spirited steamed apple and calvados pudding, accompanied by a rich melt of apple crumble icecream. A wine list, offering plenty of drops by the glass, is competently chosen; less impressive is the service, which can be amateurish or aloof at times.

12/20

Claypots

CLAYPOT/SEAFOOD

213 Barkly Street,
St Kilda **9534 1282**

BYO
Corkage none
Open daily noon-3pm, 6-10.30pm
Seats 40; outdoor seating
Owner Renan Goksin
Chefs Christian Byrne & Thanh Vu
Cards none
Prices entrees $4.50-$6.50; claypots $10-$15; fish to share $15-$120
Map page 261 **Melway** 2P C10

WHEN chef Adam Dalton left last year, regulars at this lively seafood restaurant waited with bated breath to see whether newcomers Christian Byrne and Thanh Vu would upset their claypots. They can relax: the baked, steaming fish stews are still on the menu, perhaps with a Moroccan-flavoured mix of cous cous, eggplant, harissa and chickpeas. Or maybe combined with coconut milk to create a laksa-style feast full of mussels and clams. Today's catch could be steamed, grilled, or baked – perhaps trevally with harissa and chermoula, swordfish oozing tapenade butter or a prized whole coral trout. Serves are generous and garlicky fingers almost unavoidable. A caveat: Claypots is purely BYO, doesn't do desserts or credit cards, and staff don't take bookings (but ask nicely and they'll call your mobile phone when a table becomes free). On balmy summer nights, the best tables are out the back – go through the cramped, cosy front dining room, past the kitchen billowing steam and into the pebbled courtyard, with its perspex roof, strings of coloured lights and the occasional possum parading the back fence.

13/20 $

courthouse dining room

MODERN AUSTRALIAN

86-90 Errol Street,
North Melbourne **9329 5394**

Licensed
Open Mon-Fri noon-3pm; Mon-Sat 6-10.30pm
Seats 36; bar
Owner The Courthouse Pty Ltd
Chef Scott Thomas
Cards AE BC DC MC V Eftpos
Prices entrees $10-$14; mains $22-$26; desserts $10-$12; lunch set menu $19.50 (2 courses)
Map page 262 **Melway** 2A J9

THIS cream-brick Art Deco corner pub was once a notoriously rough watering hole, but new owners have exorcised the ghouls and given the hotel a conventional dark-wood renovation. The old bistro is now the courthouse dining room, a simple wainscotted space that is sunny by day and illuminated by a cherub chandelier at night. Chef Scott Thomas is a recently repatriated Melbourne bloke who cut his teeth at A-list London restaurants such as Pied à Terre. His entree menu straddles different cuisines easily, running from Thai-style hot and sour soup to silky sashimi tuna salad, and braised pig cheek with fennel and hazelnut oil. The mains are more Euro-elegant: lamb may be stuffed with a fondant of potato and scented with rosemary, and salmon could arrive with prosciutto and white bean tortellini, perfumed with truffle oil. Velvety Japanese ices, flavoured with plum wine and green tea, finish the meal. The wine list is compact yet diverse and there's unsalted French butter to slather on the house-baked bread. Too-leisurely service doesn't prevent courthouse from being a welcome addition to the up-and-coming North Melbourne scene.

14/20 

Da Noi

ITALIAN

95 Toorak Road,
South Yarra **9866 5975**

Licensed & BYO wine (Mon only)
Corkage $8 a bottle
Open Fri-Sun noon-3pm; daily 6pm-late
Seats 60; outdoor seating; private room
Owner Pietro Porcu
Chef Steven Salce
Cards AE BC DC MC V
Prices entrees $14-$18; mains $27-$34; desserts $9-$13; chef's set menu $69 (5 courses)
Map page 265 **Melway** 2L G5

A MEAL at this delightful restaurant throws up a few curly questions. Like, how come *that* table's antipasti is different to ours? And, when everyone in this arms-width two-storey nook has ordered the chef's menu, why do *we* have spaghettini with bottarga (mullet roe) and pipis, while over there *they* have terrine of rabbit, pigeon and confit fennel? Just go with it – a large part of Da Noi's charm is the spontaneity of the kitchen, which might reinterpret the set menu a dozen times a night. A structure certainly exists: a little focaccia, some antipasti, a broth of sorts, followed by pasta and a Sardinian braise or fish dish, topped off with a dessert plate. A small à la carte menu – if you insist – is there for committed independents. Usually, the format succeeds, but at times, the meal's balance does not appear clearly thought through. Individual dishes can be very special, but a succession of bready things or a repetition of meats tarnish the lustre of some meals. Da Noi remains, however, a charming and unique restaurant, its identity reinforced by an all-Italian wine list. There's a courtyard in summer and a fire when winter takes hold.

15/20

David's

CHINESE

4 Cecil Place,
Prahran **9529 5199**

Licensed
Open Mon-Fri noon-3pm; Sat-Sun 11.30am-3pm; Fri-Sat 6-11.30pm
Seats 100
Owner David Zhou
Chef Fan Wingming
Cards AE BC DC MC V
Prices yum cha dishes $4-$6; entrees $4.80-$15; noodles & rice $13.80; mains $17-$26; banquet menus $29-$49 (6-8 courses)
Map page 265 **Melway** 2L J11

IN the beginning, tea leaves were not just brewed, they were chewed. At David's, you can have them either way. Brewed teas include Iron Buddha and Silver Tip, tea infusions (jasmine, lychee) and even a frothy chai latte. From the menu, shrimp with Dragon Well leaf tips is delicately delicious, while the chicken is sweetly smoked in Pu Er tea. David's mostly Shanghainese menu, including a top yum cha, promises good health and fine dining – try juicy pan-sticker dumplings and silken bean curd with mushrooms. The eponymous owner is a Chinese herbalist (and tea-shop owner) who adds ingredients like ginseng or wolfberries (for vigour) to his dishes. The decor is designer teahouse, mixing antiques with polished wood and white drapery. There's an excellent wine list, including a Chinese wine (Hua Tiao Chiew) served warm in a ceramic pot with a water jacket. Recent scientific studies suggest that tea really does prime the immune system. Don't wait until they study David's double-boiled soups, such as crocodile with red dates or quail with gingko nuts. If these soups are half as good for you as they taste, ancient wisdom wins again.

15/20

De Lacy

MODERN AUSTRALIAN

29 Niagara Lane,
City **9670 9099**

Licensed
Open Mon-Fri noon-3pm
Seats 45; private room; bistro
Owner Jan Willingham
Chef Andrew Irwin
Cards AE BC DC MC V
Prices entrees $12.50-$14; mains $22.50-$26.50; desserts $9.50-$12; less in bistro
Map page 260 **Melway** 1A K4

THIS business meal trouper opened its doors just as Paul Keating closed the books on the tax-deductible lunch. It's a credit to De Lacy's reliably good food and semi-formal atmosphere that it's thrived in the challenging post-FBT years. Tucked down a laneway in a 19th-century warehouse, De Lacy's interior is '80s-style salmon and green. The food is more up-to-date. To cater to the regulars, the menu is reworked every six weeks, so pasta one month might be delicate pumpkin and emmenthal tortellini; the next it could be scallop and chive ravioli; and the next, pillows of house-made gnocchi with mushroom ragout. Mains cater to those who have had a hard morning on the squash courts. There might be a slab of roasted blue-eye with green curry, superb pink-cored lamb rack with a cumin crust and char-grilled Angus porterhouse with sweet roasted shallots. Desserts are classic, ranging from a fruity bavarois to homey bread and butter pudding. Swift, discreet service suits the besuited crowd, as does the reasonably priced list of mainly big-company Australian wines. Quicker and cheaper bites are available in the downstairs bistro.

14/20

Diningroom 211

MODERN EUROPEAN

211 Brunswick Street,
Fitzroy **9419 7211**

Licensed
Open Sun & Wed noon-3pm; Tues-Sun 6.30pm-late
Seats 40
Owners Andrew McConnell & Pascale Gomes-McNabb
Chef Andrew McConnell
Cards AE BC DC MC V
Prices entrees $15-$17; mains $26-$31; desserts $13-$16; lunch set menu $26 or $31 (2 or 3 courses); dinner set menu $75 (5 courses)
Map page 263 **Melway** 2C A8

CO-OWNER and chef Andrew McConnell must have graduated from Hogwarts School of Witchcraft and Wizardry. His knack of transforming the most unsexy ingredients into elegant Euro-style dishes has cast a spell over modish Melbourne and conjured up another restaurant, Mrs Jones (see page 114). Take nettles for example. They might be transfigured into a silky soup, topped with sweet scallops and drizzled with yoghurt. Or salsify, a deeply unfashionable root vegetable that he might braise with artichokes and serve with a zucchini flower. It won't appeal to everyone – some would prefer not to have to think so intensely about the menu – but mostly it works. Duck may arrive as a crisply fried leg and roasted breast with a wicked prune tart; tender pork belly might partner a poached, then fried, pigeon with mustard fruits, and to finish, rhubarb could come with a gingery yoghurt custard. Whatever your take on the food, you'll be bewitched by the swish dining space with its uber-arty sculptures, twinkling lights and granny-ish butter dishes. Beware the wine list, however. Like the menu, it favours the obscure and unusual over the user-friendly.

16/20

---

dish

MODERN AUSTRALIAN

Royce Hotel, 379 St Kilda Road, City **9677 9933**

Licensed
Open Mon-Fri 6.30-10.30am, noon-2.30pm; Sat 6.30am-noon, 6-10.30pm; Sun 6.30am-noon
Seats 100; outdoor seating; bar
Owner Bursztyn family
Chef James Vardis
Cards AE BC DC MC V Eftpos
Prices breakfasts $7-$18; entrees $13-$17; mains $21-$27.50; desserts $10-$16; lunch set menu $25 (2 courses)
Map page 264 **Melway** 2K K3

WITH its determinedly lower-case name and low-key interior, this stylish hotel restaurant is trying to do everything right. Chef James Vardis' unfussy and inventive approach gives dish the jump on its competitors on culinarily-starved St Kilda Road, and huge bronze-framed windows (from its Rolls Royce showroom days) provide a great view of this bustling boulevard. New citizens of postcode 3000 come here with business travellers and tourists to sample the decisively mod-Oz carte. Entrees emphasise seafood and are mostly good – like pan-fried tiger prawns crusted with coconut flakes and served with slices of nectarine, or a well-executed salmon sushi terrine, let down by a timid wasabi dressing. Main courses, such as crisp-skinned baby barra fillets served with pumpkin and feta-rolled lasagne, sauteed spinach and pine nuts, are a carnival of textures and flavours. For dessert, a delightfully evanescent 'soufflé of the moment', perhaps wicked hot raspberry, proves something good is worth waiting for, while providing an excuse for another glass of wine and more surreptitious glances at neighbouring business identities.

14/20

Donovans

MODERN MEDITERRANEAN

40 Jacka Boulevard, St Kilda **9534 8221**

Licensed
Open daily noon-late
Seats 120; private room; bar
Owners Gail & Kevin Donovan, Richard Fisher & Jeanne Donovan Fisher
Chef Robert Castellani
Cards AE BC DC MC V
Prices entrees $15-$28; pastas $17.50-$36; mains $24-$38; desserts $10-$16.50
Map page 261 **Melway** 2N K9

EVER-PRESENT hosts Gail and Kevin Donovan might occasionally tweak the interior of their Californian-style, bayside restaurant, but they've resisted the urge to make more wide-reaching changes. Good call. Dining at Donovans follows a particular and satisfying course. Guests click across the wooden floors to the plump, fireside sofas for an aperitif, before moving to white-clad tables with million-dollar views. Robert Castellani's cooking is sunny and polished. Over the past 12 months, great produce and redoubled effort have lifted standards higher than ever. Starters might include just-shucked oysters, or an antipasto of honey-glazed ham, gravlax and char-grilled vegetables with feta. A country-style chicken and tarragon pie with a buttery crust, or line-caught, barbecued fish, are uncomplicated but refined. The dessert list is skewed towards the traditional, as in an irresistible apricot upside-down tart with pouring cream or dazzling bombe Alaska. Service is warm and accomplished, never rushed. After a long and hearty meal, the bill might cause a minor flutter, but it's worth it. And a Californian lifestyle rarely comes cheap.

17/20

Dumpling King

CHINESE

570-572 Station Street,
Box Hill **9890 3719**

Licensed & BYO
Corkage $1.50 a head
Open daily 11am-3.30pm, 5-10.30pm
Seats 130; private room
Owner & chef Kwok Keung Sze
Cards AE BC MC V
Prices yum cha dishes $4.80-$10; entrees $4.80-$8.80; mains $13.80-$38.80; desserts $4.80-$8.80
Map page 266 **Melway** 47 D10

DUMPLING KING'S Armadale branch served its last dumpling in mid-2002, but the original Box Hill business is going great guns. They have expanded into the shop next door, and installed seafood tanks, a new oven for roasting ducks and dotted the rooms with Asian-style art and gloating buddhas. The energy and effort shows: the King is a lively, family-friendly, East-meets-eastern-suburbs hot spot for good-value Chinese food. Exploring the extensive menu will involve an occasional miss, as in battered barra that comes with a rather perfunctory sweet and sour sauce. But the handmade northern Chinese dumplings are a highlight, particularly the beautiful four seasons dumplings, open-topped treasures filled with a colourful quadrella of pureed vegetables. Chicken dumplings are more robustly flavoured, with a little cooking liquor inside the tender steamed pastry. Sichuan tea-smoked duck comes with spicy salt, or, if you're an organised eater, call a day ahead to order braised eight treasure duck, a rich assemblage of whole boned bird stuffed with sticky rice, pork and prawns. Dumpling-heavy yum cha is served at weekends.

13/20 $ V

Dunyazad

LEBANESE

329 Doncaster Road,
Balwyn North **9857 8778**

BYO
Corkage $1 a head
Open daily 6pm-1am
Seats 186; private room
Owners Walid & Najwa Talj
Chef Nouhad Talj
Cards AE BC DC MC V
Prices entrees $7.50; mains $17-$27.50; desserts $5.50; banquet menus $35-$45 (9-10 courses)
Map page 266 **Melway** 46 H2

HALF-HIDDEN in a shopping strip, this family-run restaurant is an Aladdin's cave. The dimly lit dining room, covered in intricate, hand-painted murals, evokes a decadent Middle Eastern mood, so an exotic banquet seems entirely appropriate. Bowls of lemon-enriched hummus and smoky baba ghanoush come with rough-chopped tabbouleh. Sambousik (filo parcels filled with feta, mint and spices), crunchy falafels and pudgy, lamb-stuffed ladies' fingers follow, chased by succulent scallops and prawns in a peppered tomato, lemon and coriander broth. Baked snapper is doused in nutty tahini, a delightful counterpoint to the white, bright fish flesh. Old faithfuls, such as shish kebabs, with tender hunks of lamb, and grilled, marinated chicken fillets, served with tomatoes and green beans, are satisfying enough, but more unusual dishes might include kraidis meshwee, barbecued prawns swimming in a sharp, balsamic dressing. Among the desserts, only the delicate orange-scented mahalabia custard tempts, though the belly dancers on Friday and Saturday nights might also prove a little seductive.

13/20

Dutton Enoteca

MODERN ITALIAN

527 Church Street,
Richmond **9428 7898**

Licensed
Open Mon-Sat 11.30am-3pm; 6pm-late
Seats 100; private rooms; bar
Owner Cat Club Pty Ltd
Chef Roger Serjent
Cards AE BC DC MC V
Prices entrees $11-$18; mains $24-$30; desserts $7-$15
Map page 265 **Melway** 2G K12

THE elegant Enoteca has changed gear in the past year. The bistro and restaurant have been combined, creating a formal, but by no means stuffy dining room with linen-dressed tables, fine Riedel glassware, a comfortable lounge, and an underlying automotive theme. There have also been changes in the kitchen: well-credentialled British chef Roger Serjent took the steering wheel in early 2003 and has continued with the modern Italian approach, spinning top-quality produce into beautifully balanced meals. Ingredients do most of the talking as in a pizzetta of gorgonzola, fig and walnuts, and crumbed veal cutlets with vegetable ragu. Sometimes, Serjent lets loose with mostly happy results, as with the butternut pumpkin pasta 'bonbonieri' in a butter sauce flavoured with sage and almond macaroons. Desserts are good without grandstanding: the luscious vanilla icecream 'chimney sweep' is sprinkled with ground coffee and a sniff of bourbon. Service is polished, with the staff more than capable of talking diners through an excellent wine list that showcases a number of small wineries. Dutton continues to purr along nicely.

14/20

Empress of China

CHINESE

120-122 Little Bourke Street,
City **9663 1883**

Licensed & BYO wine
Corkage $2.50 a head
Open Sun-Fri noon-3pm; Mon-Wed 6-11pm; Thurs-Sat 6-11.30pm; Sun 6-10.30pm
Seats 110; private rooms
Owners Ken & Eugene Louey
Chef Chuen Butt
Cards AE BC DC MC V
Prices entrees $4-$12.80; mains $17-$31; desserts $5.50-$6; banquet menu $45 (6 courses)
Map page 260 **Melway** 1B S4

IN her 33 years, the Empress has seen dynasties come and go. But despite a new chef occupying the kitchens, this Chinatown dowager continues on her steady course as if nothing has changed; not the '70s decor, not the courtly manner, and, amazingly, not the owners. Father and son Ken and Eugene Louey balance menu favourites, garnered over a third of a century, with culinary Canto pop, and it pays to try something old and something new. Among the veterans are the elegant drunken prawns, halved to display streaks of orange-coloured coral against the plump white flesh, and steamed with ginger slivers in an aromatic rice wine. Scallops wokked with spring onions and ginger are also simple but delicious. Among the newbies are calamari filled with prawn mince and mandolin crabs (crabmeat and tofu moulded on a mandolin-shaped spoon) steamed in a silken white sauce. Tests of craftsmanship, both of these must be ordered ahead. But if you don't pre-plan, there is a fine list of 'all ords' to fall back on – sang choy bao (lettuce cups), beef rolls filled with enoki mushrooms, barbecued meats and noodles.

14/20

Enzo

MODERN ITALIAN

435-437 Blackburn Road,
Mount Waverley **9887 9477**

Licensed
Open Mon-Fri noon-3pm; Mon-Sat 6pm-late
Seats 100; bar
Owners James & Joanne Mavros
Chef James Mavros
Cards AE BC DC MC V Eftpos
Prices entrees $10.20-$17.90; mains $17.20-$24.90; desserts $8.90-$13.90
Map page 266 **Melway** 70 J5

SMART thinking to open a contemporary Italian with a pinch of pizazz in Melbourne's comfortable eastern suburbs. There's a surfeit of similar places within cooee of the CBD but out here, the safe and pleasant hallmarks of an international lounge bar (display wine racks, flattering lighting, linen tablecloths and quality table settings) make Enzo a special occasion favourite. The food is cleverly conceived without being too startling. There's squid-ink risotto with roasted Moreton Bay bugs, chicken mousse tortellini tossed with blue cheese and purple basil, and the creamy house speciality of gnocchi with prawns, mascarpone and pesto. Secondi are substantial enough to make side dishes unnecessary. You might eat roasted lamb rump with broad beans and sweet potato mash, or ham-stuffed saddle of rabbit in a tomato and olive reduction. Seafood specials are worth a look: whole calamari stuffed with a knock-out mince of chicken, pork and pistachio indicate the kitchen's flexibility and flair. Desserts stick mostly to well-executed traditionals like baked lemon tart and rich dark-and-white chocolate panna cotta.

13/20

EQ

MODERN MEDITERRANEAN

Melbourne Concert Hall, 100 St Kilda Road,
Southbank **9645 0644**

Licensed
Open Tues-Sun 11am-1am
Seats 240; outdoor seating; bar
Owner Dur-é Dara
Chef Bernard McCarthy
Cards AE BC DC MC V
Prices entrees $8-$16; mains $19-$27; desserts $9.50-$12.50
Map page 264 **Melway** 1D V3

EQ does an efficient job catering to pre-performance Arts Centre crowds looking for a quick bite. But the food is good enough to bring many one-course fly-bys back through the door on other occasions – without tickets to a show – for a proper, no-rush meal. The menu is sensibly flexible, running from shareable bites of mostly Mediterranean inspiration, to entree and main-sized pastas, all the way to big slap-'em-down meaty plates. Organic produce is used whenever possible. So you might share saganaki, pumpkin dip and a Greek-style barbecue platter of ocean trout and feta-stuffed calamari, then scoot to the theatre, just as the next table settles in with moussaka and stuffed free-range chicken. And you might come back after the show for wine and cheese (with house-made quince paste), or luscious rhubarb pavlova. Best to perch at the bar, or snare a terrace table with views of the Yarra, as parts of the interior are a little gloomy. Service ranges from efficient to downright brisk, probably because so many diners are trying to get fed before the curtain goes up. The wine list offers an interesting range by the glass.

14/20 

The European

EUROPEAN

161 Spring Street,
City **9654 0811**

Licensed
Open Sun-Thurs 7.30am-11pm; Fri-Sat 7.30am-midnight
Seats 55; outdoor seating; bar
Owners Joshua Brisbane & Con Christopoulos
Chef Paul Jones
Cards AE BC DC MC V
Prices breakfasts $6-$15.50; tapas $5.50-$8.50; entrees $10.50-$17.50; mains $16-$34; desserts $3.50-$11.50
Map page 260 **Melway** 1B V5

TALK about a package: the black-and-white tiled floor, dark-wood furniture and fittings, and parchment-coloured Parisian-style bistro menu all come together to make this five-year-old spot feel, well, European. On Spring Street, that means somewhere between suave and comfy. In the morning, read the paper over panettone with poached fruit, then return in the afternoon for char-grilled octopus and baked polenta with a glass of wine drawn from the passionately compiled list of more than 700 all-Euro bottles. Dinner is the best time to appreciate the European's charms: the one-page carte trips through light offerings like smoked tuna niçoise salad and plump roasted pumpkin ravioli, before ploughing on with corned beef or tender char-grilled rib-eye with a spritzy salad of coriander, mint and parsley. Not all dishes sing – duck confit, for example, might come a little dry – and the service can be aloof. Desserts offer comfort: try the excellent chocolate soufflé and house-made cinnamon icecream. The European's owners have recently expanded the family to include Benito's (see page 25).

13/20

ezard at adelphi

MODERN AUSTRALIAN

187 Flinders Lane,
City **9639 6811**

Licensed
Open Mon-Fri noon-2.30pm; Mon-Sat 6-10.30pm
Seats 70
Owner & chef Teage Ezard
Cards AE BC DC MC V
Prices entrees $16.50-$19.50; mains $33-$36; desserts $16.50-$17.50; degustation menu $95 (8 courses)
Map page 260 **Melway** 1B P9

TEAGE EZARD'S food will enter your dreams. It's stimulating and provocative with the right mix of mystery and mischief to keep you buzzing long after your visit. All his Asian-inspired dishes look beautiful: lime-cured cuttlefish puddled in bonito mayonnaise sits in a Chinese spoon; crisp shredded leek and seaweed hover above. The pleasure always continues from palette to palate. The oxtail wontons are a tantalising collision of melting meat and sweet and sour tamarind broth. Sumac-spiced rack of lamb comes with punchy pomegranate syrup, luxurious baba ghanoush, eggplant fritters and a lemony herb and feta salad. Some regulars grumble that Ezard's signature dishes at this much-loved special occasion restaurant keep a lid on innovation. But complaints seem churlish when faced with spectacular perennials like oyster shooters, served in a shot glass with mirin, tamari, sake and a dab of wasabi. The classy basement dining room is appropriately self-contained, with comfortable seats and well-spaced tables suitable for sweet nothings or dotted lines. The dapper waitstaff are passionate and knowledgeable about both food and wine.

18/20

COFFEE

Things go better with a dose of caffeine

The European
161 Spring Street, City, 9654 0811
Dressed in bentwood chairs, timber tables, wood-panelled walls and chequerboard floors, this city restaurant looks the goods. The coffee, made by staff who have been put through their training paces, tastes the goods. Ease into the day with a silky latte and free-range eggs benedict, or unwind after a hard day's night with a smooth espresso and a slice of creamy rhubarb cheesecake. See page 63.

Gravy Train
83 Gamon Street, Yarraville, 9687 9866
At Gravy Train, they do things a little differently. The coffee is ceremoniously served on an oval platter with an espresso glass of cold water to refresh the palate. And where else would you get eggs baked in papa pomodoro (a rustic Italian bread soup) alongside cheese on toast for brekkie? Breakfasts go all day, but at some point you might like to try a pasta or grill from the lunch menu.

Kanteen
150 Alexandra Avenue, South Yarra, 9827 0488
Kanteen has shrugged off its ignominious origins as a toilet block on the banks of the Yarra and these days it's thoroughly flushed with success. Take your morning java with black sticky rice porridge, dressed with coconut milk and banana. Lunch might be house-made gnocchi, pide stuffed with tuna niçoise or massaman curry. The atmosphere is cool and slightly kooky.

Postal Hall Cafe
Corner Russell & Little Collins Streets, City, 9663 0998
With Cafe Racer owner and barista-extraordinaire Danny Colls calling the shots, little wonder the coffee here is so good. Breakfast can be as simple as an organic pastry from baker D. Chirico, or as satisfying as smoked ham, cheese, tomato and poached egg atop Phillippa's pane toscano. For lunch, choose from salads, soups and generously packed panini.

The Pound
Shop 5, 566 Chapel Street, South Yarra, 9826 1114
If the Pound were a person, it would be a slim and funky black-clad fashionista. But just to prove that beauty is more than skin deep, the coffee here is first-rate. Match it with the berry bomba breakfast of stewed berries stacked in a glass with honey, yoghurt and flaked almonds. Lunch and supper are also available.

Ray
332 Victoria Street, Brunswick, 9380 8593
Ray is one of a batch of unlicensed, oh-so-cool cafes spawned by the success of Wall Two 80 (see right). The formula is familiar: kerbside box-stools, communal table, great coffee and simple, good food. The latter gets a Middle Eastern twist, with the likes of egg, bastourma (air-dried beef) and chutney jaffles, and open pides topped with mint, haloumi and carrot marinated in spicy pomegranate dressing.

Small Block
130 Lygon Street, Brunswick East, 9381 2244
Small Block owner and barista Sarah Croston says the key to making good coffee lies almost entirely in the preparation. Her ultra-hip cafe collects raves for its smooth, creamy lattes and espressos made without a trace of ugly bitterness. Take your dose of caffeine with a full-on fry-up, Phillippa's crunchy corn toast, or a hefty stack of fluffy pancakes and maple syrup, with or without bacon. Fabulous burgers and BLTs are very fairly priced.

Wall Two 80
Rear, 280 Carlisle Street, Balaclava, 9593 8280
'Wall' still dispenses some of the finest coffees in town, with lots of crema and plenty of depth and richness. Every cafe proprietor and his or her bank manager have jumped on the filled pide bandwagon these days, but it's worth remembering that these guys were among the first. Look for the crowd of bystanders outside, and don't miss the divine Portuguese tarts.

Fedele's

ITALIAN

460 Springvale Road,
Glen Waverley **9561 7327**

Licensed & BYO wine
Corkage none
Open Sun-Fri noon-3pm; daily 6pm-late
Seats 110; private room
Owner Fedele's Restaurant Pty Ltd
Chefs Maria Di Scala & David Poskus
Cards AE BC DC MC V
Prices entrees $11.50-$17.90; pastas $16.50-$23.90; mains $25.90-$28.90; desserts $10.90-$13.50
Map page 266 **Melway** 71 C6

IT can be hard for first-timers to believe that this is the restaurant their friends recommended so warmly. This faded barn with the traffic thundering by outside? Even inside, the exposed brick and gingham doesn't inspire much excitement. The crowds are a good sign, though, and the menu means business. As soon as your first mountainous plate hits the table, it's obvious that there's so much love and generosity in the kitchen, very little TLC is left for the building. The pasta list includes staples such as gnocchi napoli, alongside odd house specialities like penne alla salsa Indiana (with thinly sliced porterhouse). Sound classical cooking technique is evident in the sticky veal shanks, braised in barolo, and served with saffron-tinged risotto Milanese. No less impressive is the humbly titled grigliata mista (mixed grill). This feast for one comprises confit duck leg, boned quail and ox cheek pie. Fresh, modern dishes, such as grilled Atlantic salmon with cumin-scented mussels, get a look-in too. The banana crepe stars on the dessert list and there's a good list of Italian reds for those who've forgotten to bring their own special bottle.

13/20

Fenix

MODERN AUSTRALIAN

680 Victoria Street,
Richmond **9427 8500**

Licensed
Open Mon-Fri noon-3pm, 6-10pm; Sat-Sun 8.30am-3pm, 6-10pm
Seats 140; outdoor seating; private room
Owners & chefs Raymond Capaldi & Gary Mehigan
Cards AE BC DC MC V Eftpos
Prices breakfasts $6.50-$13.50; entrees $15-$17; mains $26-$33; desserts $14-$15; cafe menu $8-$26
Map page 265 **Melway** 2H H2

TIME and hard work have finessed Fenix, docked alongside the slow-moving Yarra and surrounded by trees. On balmy nights, the balcony tables are some of Melbourne's best. A harder choice is where to sit indoors. One side of the room is plush banquettes and broad, classically clothed tables; the other is blondwood casual. The menus make similar distinctions. The restaurant's food is intricate, marrying classical techniques from Asia and Europe in dishes like caramelised barra with fried snake beans, sang choy bao and egg drop broth, or roast loin of rabbit with garlic butter raviolo and rosemary juice. The cafe's style is simpler – things like risotto Milanese with chorizo and lemon mascarpone; Chinese red braised beef with turnip cake; and Bermagui swordfish with sweet peanut butter – and perhaps more in step with Melbourne's dining habits. Either way, the kitchen team, led by hotel-trained owners Raymond Capaldi and Gary Mehigan, is adept at wringing fine flavours from simple combos, such as the restaurant's roma tomato sorbet with heirloom tomato tartare, candied olives and basil oil. The wine list is pricey, with little under $40.

15/20 

Flower Drum

17 Market Lane,
City **9662 3655**

CHINESE
Best Chinese

Licensed
Open Mon-Sat noon-3pm; daily 6-10pm
Seats 120; private rooms
Owners Anthony Lui, Patricia Fung & William Shek
Chef Anthony Lui
Cards AE BC DC MC V
Prices entrees $6-$23; mains $34-$48; desserts $12; set menu $128 (6 courses)
Map page 260 **Melway** 1B S5

GILBERT LAU has apparently left the building. The celebrated restaurateur has sold Flower Drum to his staff, but he just can't seem to stay away. When Mr Lau is in the house, he greets regulars and clears plates, just as he has always done. Consistency is a Flower Drum watchword. Diners adore the restaurant's eternally intuitive service. Nothing is overblown; not the spacious dining room, nor the deceptively simple food from chefs skilled in showcasing first-rate produce. Sweet live scallops steamed in their shell may come dressed with chicken stock and soy. Shanghai dumplings filled with King Island crab are soft as clouds. Beautifully lacquered Peking duck comes with juicy flesh and parchment-thin skin, sitting on the filmiest pancakes. Grain-fed fillet, partnered with a vibrant and peppery Sichuan sauce, eats like veal. Coral trout, steamed or stir-fried straight from the tank, sparkles with freshness. The wine list is extravagant in depth, breadth and price. When can you get a table? Some time next month, perhaps. The prices? Don't ask. Abandon yourself to hedonistic luxury, and for a few hours, pretend that money is no object.

18/20

Fortuna Village

CHINESE

235 Little Bourke Street,
City **9663 3044**

Licensed & BYO wine
Corkage $5 a bottle
Open Sun-Fri noon-3pm; Mon-Wed 6-11pm; Thurs-Sat 6-11.30pm; Sun 6-10pm
Seats 150; private rooms; bar
Owner Jim Khong
Chef Yuin Sung
Cards AE BC DC MC V
Prices entrees $4-$13.20; mains $18.90-$52; desserts $7.50-$12
Map page 260 **Melway** 1B P4

INTRICATE lattice windows, bamboo eaves and a ceiling hung with ruby lanterns make the dining room of this Melbourne institution seem magical. The menu is enchanting, too. This is one of the few Chinese restaurants in the city offering both home-style and more elaborate dishes from north of the Yangtze river, plus spicy favourites from Sichuan. Many unusual dishes are concealed behind romantic names. To begin, you might try 'Thousand Layered Wind', a simmered sow's ear, finely shredded and served unadorned. Dumplings range from pot-stickers to delicate vegetarian parcels. Jasmine tea-smoked duck makes a rich, aromatic alternative to the ubiquitous Peking, and comes with baby bok choy; beans are dry-fried with preserved vegetables and minced pork. Fish-infused eggplant and ma po bean curd, with ground pork, are old favourites. Mop up with northern-style steamed breads, washed down by a drop from the extensive wine list. And leave room for intriguing desserts that include fried icecream and Chinese date pudding. Service, under the watchful eye of owner Jimmy Khong, is attentive; the atmosphere, relaxed.

14/20 V

France-Soir

FRENCH

11 Toorak Road,
South Yarra **9866 8569**

Licensed & BYO wine (except Sat night & public holidays)
Corkage $9.50 a bottle
Open daily noon-3pm, 6pm-midnight
Seats 68
Owner Jean-Paul Prunetti
Chef Geraud Fabre
Cards AE BC DC MC V
Prices entrees $10.50-$17.50; mains $25.50-$29.50; desserts $10.50
Map page 265 **Melway** 2L F5

THIS venerable bistro has been a touchstone for a certain 'quartier' of Melbourne society for two decades. It's favoured by those who love French things or just keen to reminisce about French kisses on the Riviera during their gap year. Love it, as many regulars do, and you'll swear by the moules, the goats' cheese crouton salad, the steak with bearnaise sauce and the chocolate mousse. But for the novice, squeezing through the crowds to a pocket-sized table, it might be hard to see what all the fuss is about. You might even find the famously theatrical waiters (with EU-approved accents) aren't nearly as sniffy as they are cracked up to be. The food is standard bistro fare – brains with caper sauce, caesar and niçoise salads, boeuf bourguignon – and they're usually fine, but seldom soar. Chinks in the armour are causing grumbles among some devotees, however. They're not happy about underdone or chewy steaks and tepid frites, nor about îles flottantes that might as well sink. The prices on the admittedly spectacular wine list have also crept upwards of late. Yet they still return for double-helpings of bonhomie – priceless.

15/20

@ A GLANCE

The pick of Melbourne's catch

SEAFOOD

Claypots
213 Barkly Street,
St Kilda, 9534 1282
In this tiny place, the menu features stingray, mussels, fish, crab and whatever else looked good when the boat came in – all served in huge slow-cooked portions.

Halikarnas
820 Sydney Road,
Brunswick, 9384 1096
There are other things available at this cheap, bustling taverna, but you're best off hooking beautifully fresh seafood, cooked simply to let the flavours shine.

Livebait
55b New Quay Promenade,
Docklands, 9642 1500
Brilliant views over Victoria Harbour, a Greek Island atmosphere and a menu full of sea-salty Med-inspired dishes make this the spot for a fishy feeding frenzy.

Pacific Seafood BBQ House
Shop 8, 240 Victoria Street,
Richmond, 9427 8225
Look your wriggling fish dinner in the eye before it is hauled off to the kitchen to be dispatched, steamed with ginger and shallots and dropped back on your table.

Toofey's
162 Elgin Street,
Carlton, 9347 9838
A change of owners has caused scarcely a ripple on the surface of Toofey's much-loved style – top-quality seafood, simply cooked and served in soothing surrounds.

Watergrill
300 Toorak Road,
South Yarra, 9827 6248
Based on a New England chowder house, this seafood restaurant offers everything from sashimi and chilli crab to clam chowder.

Fu Long

942 Whitehorse Road,
Box Hill **9890 7388**

Licensed & BYO wine
Corkage $3 a bottle
Open Mon-Fri 11.30am-3pm; Sat-Sun & public hols 11am-3pm; daily 5.30-11pm
Seats 200
Owner Fu Long Pty Ltd
Chef Lurk Law
Cards AE BC DC MC V
Prices yum cha dishes $3.20-$6.50; entrees $4-$7; mains $14.80-$23.80; desserts $5-$12
Map page 266 **Melway** 47 C9

THIS capacious pink China diner did duty as a G.J. Coles discount store in the 1930s, when no-one in Box Hill had ever picked up a chopstick, and nothing was over two shillings and sixpence. Fu Long has held its own in this competitive eating neighbourhood for a few years now and is particularly popular with big banqueting groups. The dim sum are fair rather than spectacular: top dishes include stuffed eggplant, and eel in a mild XO sauce. The à la carte menu sticks mostly to fail-safe Cantonese fare. Check the scrolling LED ticker suspended at the restaurant's rear for surprises like steamed abalone and sweet mud crab. There are good pickings among the side dishes – unadorned pea shoots, for example, provide welcome crunch alongside a succulent (if slightly oily) chicken hotpot. Desserts traverse standard lychees, fritters and toffee apple territory – the best way to finish your meal is by calling for the inevitably modest cheque. In the best traditions of Chinese family restaurants, Fu Long is child-friendly – if you've got a problem with zooming grommets, this isn't the place for you.

12/20 $

Ginger Garlic

Shop 9, 9 Dudley Street,
Eltham **9439 4423**

BYO
Corkage none
Open Tues-Fri noon-2.30pm; Tues-Sun 5pm-late
Seats 40; outdoor seating
Owners Ashok & Ritu Sikand
Chef Kirpal Singh
Cards AE BC MC V
Prices entrees $4.50-$14; mains $10.50-$20; desserts $4.50; Thurs night set menu $30 (2 courses)
Map page 267 **Melway** 21 K5

GINGER GARLIC is an original take on traditional Indian cookery. The cramped interior is worn at the edges and the views from the concrete patio aren't exactly scenic, but most visit for the sights and sizzle coming from the kitchen. It's worth trying aloo ki tikki first up, as these smooth, crisp balls of mashed potatoes and peas won't dampen your enthusiasm for hefty mains. Interesting seafood options include grilled prawn mirchiwalla, or tandoori fish cubes transformed to meen mollee by a korma sauce. Wednesday nights mean balti, including two molten-hot 'earthquake' curries of either prawns or beef. Thursday nights are for nakhas ki boti, a set-price meal of five snacks (stuffed mushrooms, chicken drumsticks or spicy shrimps served on deep-fried puri bread) and two mains, say, tandoori machhi snapper, marinated, grilled, then served sizzling with onion, capsicum and a yoghurt dip. Sundays bring the set-price 'India on a banana leaf' platters, when a range of dishes are plated about the banana leaf (when in season). All of which gives chef Kirpal Singh further opportunity to extend his impressive repertoire.

13/20 $ V

Gourlays Restaurant

MODERN FRENCH

529 High Street,
Prahran **9521 5566**

Licensed & BYO (Tues only)
Corkage $10 a bottle
Open Tues-Sat 6.30-11pm
Seats 28
Owner Rosetta Le Compte
Chef Anthony Siketa
Cards BC MC V Eftpos
Prices entrees $13-$17; mains $28-$30; desserts $13- $16; degustation menu $95 (5 courses; minimum 8 people)
Map page 265 **Melway** 58 G7

FEW restaurants rival the ambience of Gourlays on a wintery night, when a fire crackles in the grate and the snug little room seems to glow. The room, part medieval French inn (exposed beams, panelled walls, heraldic motifs), part bohemia (pith helmets, mirror ball), has hosted a string of chefs. The latest to grace the tiny kitchen is Anthony Siketa, whose food, like the decor, draws influences from France. He may offer gratinated onion soup or a duxelles and foie gras pithiviers with your roast poussin. While Siketa can undoubtedly cook, there's a big difference between flying solo in this tiny kitchen and his last role as executive chef for Eleonore's at Chateau Yering. To survive, you need a switched-on floor crew to remind you on those rare occasions when you forget the chanterelle mushrooms on a plate of John Dory fillet with black truffle butter, or to mollify diners disappointed when the almond and rhubarb crumble materialises as a cold tart. Sadly, this support was not evident in Siketa's early days and service generally needed work. There is, however, a nice boutique wine list and that crackling fire to console you.

14/20

The Graham

MODERN AUSTRALIAN

97 Graham Street (corner Esplanade West),
Port Melbourne **9676 2566**

Licensed
Open daily noon-3pm, 6-10pm
Seats 50; outdoor seating; private room
Owners Tony & Peter Giannakis, Peta Curran
Chef Rodney Nevin
Cards AE BC DC MC V
Prices entrees $10.50-$15.50; mains $22.50-$26.50; desserts $9.50
Map page 264 **Melway** 2J F6

THIS accomplished restaurant in a restored corner pub was already a top option for memorable meals at neighbourly prices. With new chef Rodney Nevin on board, the Graham has become irresistible. Nevin's CV includes stints at Jacques Reymond and O'Connell's, and given his background, it's no surprise that the Euro-based menu features splashes of Asia and the Middle East. Happily, you haven't seen it all before. The pork salad is a revelation: snowpea tendrils tangle with succulent belly meat, dates and Vietnamese mint, all drizzled with a citrus soy vinaigrette. Perfectly seared lamb loin comes with a piquant mustard glaze and a creamy radicchio and red wine risotto. The twice-baked pear soufflé is a minefield of green peppercorns. Dishes are innovative, occasionally overly busy, but taste is never sacrificed for novelty. Seamless service is headed up by identical twins (and part-owners) Tony and Peter Giannakis. The simple white dining room works well for casual catch-ups and intimate evenings propped by a champagne bucket. There are wine recommendations for each dish on the well-wrought wine list.

15/20

The Great Provider

MODERN AUSTRALIAN

St Kilda Marina, Marine Parade,
Elwood **9525 5855**

Licensed
Open Mon-Fri 11am-late; Sat-Sun 8am-late
Seats 90; outdoor seating; bar
Owners Andrew Rolleston & Simon Schofield
Chefs Ashley Richey, Tim McWilliam & Fiona Verwoerd
Cards AE BC DC MC V
Prices breakfasts $4.50-$15; entrees $8.50-$15; mains $21-$29; desserts $8-$9
Map page 261 **Melway** 2P A12

THE GREAT PROVIDER'S bayside terrace is a great place to chill, soaking up the cruisy ambience, and contemplating those big yachts and cruisers at the St Kilda Marina. It's a popular spot for snacks, lunch and big breakfasts, such as a pikelet stack with pecan and maple butter, or porridge with banana and coconut. The service is enthusiastic and casual but the food, like the Provider's driftwood balustrades, sometimes seems bleached out. Sure, the menu has taken on board the latest provisions and flavours (salsa verde, sumac yoghurt, quince paste) but dishes don't always float the boat when assembled. Char-grilled tiger prawns sound like the business, but the accompanying harissa yoghurt and tomato and coriander salad lack the necessary zing. More straightforward dishes – perhaps char-grilled rib-eye with mash and roasted beetroot, or roast chicken with pumpkin, feta and bean salad – are good and satisfying. The wine list is compact but well chosen, with many options by the glass (there's a reserve wine list if you want to dig deeper). The adjoining gazebo bar is a great spot to break a beachy Sunday afternoon stroll.

13/20

Grossi Florentino

ITALIAN

80 Bourke Street,
City **9662 1811**

Licensed
Open Mon-Fri noon-3pm; Mon-Sat 6-11pm; Cellar Bar Mon-Sat 7.30am-1am; Grill Mon-Sat noon-3pm, 6-11pm
Seats 140; private rooms; bar
Owner Grossi family
Chefs Guy Grossi & Chris Rodriguez
Cards AE BC DC MC V
Prices entrees $28-$32; mains $42-$47; desserts $20; degustation menu $110 (8 courses); less in Cellar Bar & the Grill
Map page 260 **Melway** 1B T5

SURELY this is the best-dressed table in Melbourne. Let's count the ways: silver salt and pepper shakers. One dish of salted butter, another with unsalted. A cruet of olive oil. A dish of marinated olives. Home-made grissini in a silver vase. Riedel glassware. Christofle cutlery. All of it on double damask linen. Visit Grossi Florentino's historic Mural Room and it's clear that rumours of the death of special occasion dining have been exaggerated. The wine list is impressive and the menu is distinguished and respectful of Italian regional traditions. The kitchen may prime the palate with a spoonful of chicken and walnut salad, before a primi of crayfish on Russian salad with quail egg and bottarga; then rabbit with veal and porcini stuffing and gruyère-filled leg. Servings are heroic, but lately the food has seemed heavy (chewy pasta, overcooked meat, too-rich saucing) and service lacking the personal touch. Flash surrounds are all very dandy, but to maintain Florentino's first-class reputation, the owners must refocus on the main issues: food and service. We're certain they can. After all, no-one else does this grand European style quite so well.

17/20

Haggers

MODERN AUSTRALIAN

268 Toorak Road,
South Yarra **9827 7733**

Licensed
Open Tues-Fri noon-3pm; Tues-Sun 6pm-late
Seats 60
Owner Craig Fennell
Chef Matthew Thurley
Cards AE BC DC MC V
Prices entrees $12-$18; mains $22-$30; desserts $9-$14; set lunch $25 (2 courses)
Map page 265 **Melway** 2L K5

HAGGERS is the kind of local bistro that makes you want to take out a hefty mortgage and move to South Yarra. Deco lamps, dark wood, linen napery and a split-level with balustrades give Haggers a classic look rare in this flashy part of town. It's a hangout for diners of a certain stripe – those attracted to its clubbish charm, thoughtful service and knockout mod-Oz food. The entrees feature something for everyone: chef Matthew Thurley's longstanding 'Haggers' snaggers' (skinless veal and pork sausages) for the traditionalists, and, for the fashion forward, a Japanese-influenced salmon gravlax with wasabi-avocado cream. Three plump tortellini filled with a feather-light mixture of ricotta, pine nuts and currants, smothered in a creamed spinach sauce, approach the status of culinary velvet. Seafood is a standout: maybe a barbecued swordfish steak with black olive tapenade, or roasted salmon on panzanella (the rustic Italian bread salad). Desserts also hit the mother lode – a chocolate tart ultra-rich in Belgian chocolate, or a Frangelico and almond soufflé served with the creamiest praline icecream.

14/20

Hanabishi

JAPANESE
Best Japanese

187 King Street,
City **9670 1167**

Licensed
Open Mon-Fri noon-2.30pm, 6-10.30pm
Seats 65; private rooms
Owner & chef Akio Soga
Cards AE BC DC MC V
Prices entrees $12-$16; mains $19-$30; desserts $6-$18
Map page 260 **Melway** 1A C5

GIVEN the far-from-glamorous location (among a clutch of gentlemen's clubs, backpacker hostels and takeaway joints), you wouldn't expect this to be the venue for some of the best Japanese in town. But that's the contradiction of Hanabishi. It has always attracted a good lunch trade – its bento boxes have sustained many a QC through afternoon proceedings – but it's at dinner that owner-chef Akio Soga comes out to play. The specials showcase his skills in balancing textures and flavours, perhaps thin lobes of ponzu-marinated salmon with salmon roe, seaweed and radish, or a small earthernware pot (complete with coal-burner) of ocean trout simmered in miso with shiitake mushrooms and leek. Just as impressive are the fish parcels smoked in cedar shavings – the smokiness from the cedar and accompanying candied walnuts add ineffably woody notes, soothed by the side of earthy spinach. Sushi and sashimi lovers will be enchanted, and there are perennials such as tempura and sukiyaki for the fish-phobic. The modest peacock-blue rooms have a few tasteful props; the lack of ostentation allows you to focus on the plates.

16/20

Harveys

MODERN MEDITERRANEAN

10 Murphy Street,
South Yarra **9867 3605**

Licensed
Open Mon-Fri 7am-2.30pm; Sat-Sun 8am-3pm; Mon-Sat 6-10pm
Seats 60; outdoor seating
Owners Sarah Harvey & Bob Kuna
Chef Kurt Sampson
Cards AE BC DC MC V
Prices breakfasts $5.50-$16; entrees $13.50-$16; mains $24.50-$30; desserts $14-$16.50; lunch set menu $27.50 (2 courses)
Map page 265 **Melway** 2L G5

MELBOURNE'S love affair with all tastes Mediterranean blooms at Harveys. Chef Kurt Sampson is dexterous at combining a bit of Morocco with a dash of Spain and a sprinkling of Greece and Portugal to craft a satisfying, well-balanced, intriguing menu, even at breakfast. The food purrs with confidence. Delicate, plump ravioli might be stuffed with haloumi and mint, then finished with a burnt butter sauce. Pickled ox tongue may be tossed with chickpeas and spiced tomatoes in a tangy, boisterous salad. Old favourites are rejuvenated: a venison schnitze is cloaked in olive-green zaatar crumbs, and served on feta-studded mash. Goat often appears on the specials list, perhaps as a fabulously flaky wild goat and feta pie. The sweet stuff is excellent: hazelnut pavlova with rosewater peaches and cream is a delicately perfumed argument for mixed marriages. The dining room is comfortable and soothing, featuring warm wooden floors, burnt yellow walls, fireplaces, linen-draped tables and wrinkle-friendly lighting. The service is not always as honed as in the past, but efficient, friendly, detail-oriented waiters are still the rule.

15/20

Hibari

JAPANESE

479 Malvern Road,
South Yarra **9827 0155**

BYO
Corkage $1 a head
Open Tues-Sat 6-10pm
Seats 30
Owner & chef Takeshi Kojima
Cards AE BC DC MC V
Prices entrees $3-$7; noodles $10-$12; mains $13.50-$22; desserts $3.50
Map page 265 **Melway** 2M C10

THE user-friendly menu at Hibari reads like it's built from a popular vote of Japanese Dishes Most People Like. Sushi and sashimi? Check. Gyoza, miso and agedashidofu? Check. Noodles and rice dishes, maybe some Japanese curry? Yes, yes, and yes. Teriyaki? As if you had to ask. The indefatigable Hibari is a restaurant for the people, who flock to this modest dining room, with its sushi bar down one side, dark-wood tables and chairs, and bustling staff, to eat Japanese comfort food at skinny prices. Among entrees, the brittle batter of the kaki fry (deep-fried oysters) shatters pleasingly, offering a briny hit of the oyster within. Also recommended are the crisp salmon and coriander spring rolls (harumaki). The inside-out spicy tuna rolls, tumbled in pepper, are deservedly popular, and the sashimi is reliably fresh. Mains are conservative but competent. Their nabeyaki udon, which arrives in a special 'UFO' pot, is the real deal, the broth scaldingly hot and seriously good. Hibari's takeaway trade speeds up after seven, so you may need to be a little patient while the kitchen sorts out its timing.

13/20 $

Hibiscus Restaurant & Bar

MODERN AUSTRALIAN

167 St Georges Road,
Fitzroy North **9497 8101**

Licensed
Open Tues-Sat 9am-late; Sun 9am-4pm
Seats 60; outdoor seating; bar
Owners Steve & Caroline Rogers
Chef Steve Rogers
Cards BC MC V Eftpos
Prices breakfasts $5-$11; entrees $10-$15; mains $19-$24; desserts $9.50
Map page 263 **Melway** 30 B12

ENGLISH chef Steve Rogers – seen most recently at Peach, the Rainbow Hotel's dining room – has moved away from the hooplah of Fitzroy proper to the burgeoning foodie enclave in Fitzroy North. His sleek new place is in the spot that once housed hippie hangout Sub Terrain, but it's been given a good sprucing. There's a bar and casual seating up front and a smart dining room at the rear, with stark white walls offset by giant feature lampshades and Middle Eastern-inspired lightboxes. Indulgent brunches are a feature and go way beyond the standard fry-up. Bacon and egg jaffles come with a lively kasoundi; potato roesti is served with buffalo bocconcini and loads of fresh basil. The dinner menu gives Rogers a chance to show off his charcuterie specialities, often partnered with a fruity side. Duck terrine might come with pickled pear, and boudin blanc with a salad of chickpeas, spiced apple and watercress. Other mains are less adventurous: there might be pumpkin and almond ravioli or a pub-grubbish barbecued scotch fillet. Reasonable prices make up for the occasional flat spot.

12/20 

Hotel Spencer

MODERN EUROPEAN

475 Spencer Street,
West Melbourne **9329 5111**

Licensed
Open Mon-Fri noon-3pm; Mon-Sat 6.30-9.30pm;
Sun noon-3pm (Apr-Dec)
Seats 36; bar
Owners Garry & Michele Edgley
Chef Blair Mathieson
Cards AE BC MC V Eftpos
Prices entrees $10.50-$13.50; mains $23-$32; desserts $10-$14.50
Map page 262 **Melway** 2E J1

DINING at the Hotel Spencer is like getting a big hug from a friend – it's warm, it's comforting, and you feel good for a long time afterwards. The meat-centred chalkboard menu travels the 'rich and hearty' route. An entree of roast tomato, smoked bacon and lentil soup is virtually a meal in itself, but there have been some concessions to lighter dining. A salad of slow-roasted figs is a textural treat, the soft fruit offset by layers of crisp sliced apple, prosciutto and a light gorgonzola and honey dressing, while a main dish of salmon fillet arrives on a bed of mashed peas, topped with crunchy pancetta and a soft poached egg, and drizzled with a tart sauce bois boudran of balsamic vinegar cut with tomatoes and herbs. Since the departure of co-owners and long-time Melbourne gastropub legends Peter and Janelle McLeod in late 2002, the service has seemed less polished, and the food doesn't have quite its previous flair – evidenced, perhaps, by an overcooked fish fillet, or a grainy sorbet. But don't get us wrong – the proven formula of meat, mateship and fine wine can still draw you into its embrace.

14/20 

idibidi

MODERN AUSTRALIAN

356 Brunswick Street,
Fitzroy **9419 2482**

Licensed & BYO
Corkage $5 a bottle
Open Mon-Sat 7am-late; Sun 8am-late
Seats 70; outdoor seating; bar
Owners Alex, Jim & John Mihailidis
Chef Raoul Symmons
Cards AE BC DC MC V
Prices breakfasts $4-$13; entrees $7.50-$11; pizzas $10-$12; mains $14.50-$22; desserts $7
Map page 263 **Melway** 2C B6

THERE are lots of cookie-cutter cafes on Brunswick Street; idibidi is one of the few with the culinary smarts to back it up. The brothers behind the city's popular Cafe Segovia set their hearts on a Fitzroy outpost a while back, then jumped at the chance to secure this prime people-watching spot, with shady pavement seating and a huge upstairs function space – idibidi in size it is not. A swift reno has left regulation dark timber, dim lamps and faux-1970s touches in its wake, but better-than-average food and service help idibidi pull ahead of the bunch. The menu is cutely segmented into 'littles', 'bigs' and 'idibits' and, though the dishes listed are far from revolutionary, the food is fresh, well presented and great value for money. Perfectly grilled snapper might come with a summery tomato, basil and red onion salad; chicken breast might be miso-poached and served with buckwheat noodles and refreshing ginger broth. Even better, idibidi is one of those round-the-clock joints you can drop into for a slap-up breakfast, a Tuscan sausage pizza, or a glass of wine from the blackboard list.

13/20 $

Il Bacaro Cucina e Bar

MODERN ITALIAN

168-170 Little Collins Street,
City **9654 6778**

Licensed
Open Mon-Sat noon-midnight
Seats 50; bar
Owners Graeme Ballentine & Joseph Mammone
Chef Jason Jujnovich
Cards AE BC DC MC V
Prices entrees $12-$22; mains $24-$35; desserts $14
Map page 260 **Melway** 1B Q6

IT would take more than an economic slowdown and ownership changes to dent the popularity of this dimly lit Italian restaurant, with its chocolate-and-cream interior and racks of wine bottles. City types and well-heeled shoppers relish the clubby atmosphere, bolstered by prices just this side of acceptable. For starters, goats' cheese and summer leaves ravioli with seedless grapes, shallots and verjuice is as sophisticated as it is subtle; beef carpaccio, almost obscured by a thicket of rocket spiked with parmesan shards, is everything it should be. Regulars can't go past the roasted half duck, with wet polenta and an orange and Campari sauce the colour of a Queensland sunset. Other mains are more prosaic – rib-eye with caramelised onion and roma tomatoes, or baked baby snapper – but equally satisfying. You might order panzanella (bread and tomato salad) or a side of sauteed spinach if the boss is paying, and mop up with Daniel Chirico's sourdough bread. Desserts are stylishly traditional (tiramisu, grilled peaches with amaretto) and service is brisk, with waiters eager to offer advice on the broad wine list, on which Italians feature strongly.

15/20

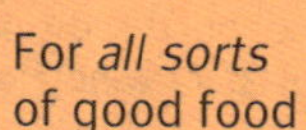

For *all sorts*
of good food

Bridge Road **Brunswick Street** St Georges Road **Swan Street** **Nicholson Street** Gertrude Street **Victoria Street** Queens Parade Rathdowne Street **Church Street** Johnston Street **Smith Street**

SANPSPIN1747
SPARKLING NATURAL MINERAL WATER
S.PELLEGRINO
SAN PELLEGRINO TERME
Attenzione: può far sorgere amicizie prolungate.
PELLEGRINO
S.PELLEGRINO
Whatever language you speak, *live in Italian.*

Il Fornaio

ITALIAN/BAKERY

2 Acland Street,
St Kilda **9534 2922**

Licensed
Open daily 7am-10pm
Seats 40; outdoor seating
Owners John & Frank Van Haandel, Warren Guest & Glenn Tobias
Chefs Joe Grbac, Daniella Turinski & Murray Whale
Cards AE BC DC MC V Eftpos
Prices breakfasts $3.80-$7; filled baguettes $6.90; pastries $2.50-$4.50; entrees $9-$15; mains $10.50-$20
Map page 261 **Melway** 2N K6

IT'S chockers with urban hipsters most nights, serves a mean breakfast and it's been name-dropped on *The Secret Life of Us*. Il Fornaio has cemented a well-deserved reputation as a St Kilda standard. During the day, it's a snack stop par excellence, with fabulous Grinders coffee, pastries, biscotti, breads and crusty filled rolls. Come 6pm, the kitchen starts dishing out satisfying house-made pasta dripping with buttery sauces, like a heart-stopping linguine with Balmain bugs, or veal and sage tortellini alla panna. Carbo-phobes and Atkins diet acolytes can choose from a small, straightforward selection that might include garfish stuffed with lemon roasted fennel and wrapped in cabbage. The daily specials board proffers dishes for smaller appetites, like an entree of beetroot-and-vodka cured salmon gravlax. The prices won't hurt too much, either. Digestion time before dessert could be spent people-watching on the terrace, or in trying to catch the staff's attention in the heavily polished industrial interior. It's worth persisting for the glorious lemon and passionfruit tart.

13/20 $

Il Solito Posto

ITALIAN

Basement, 113 Collins Street (enter from George Parade),
City **9654 4466**

Licensed
Open Mon-Fri 7.30am-late; Sat 9am-late
Seats 47; bistro; bar
Owners Michael Tenace & Theo Poulakis
Chef Grant Phelan
Cards AE BC DC MC V
Prices entrees $16.50-$18.50; mains $28.90-$35; desserts $7.50-$11; bistro menu $15.90-$18.50
Map page 260 **Melway** 1B R8

ON weekday mornings this stylish cafe-cum-trattoria hums with the city's hollow men filling up on fresh pastries and strong espresso before work. Later, they join the shoppers sipping bloody marys in the front bar, or slip into the relative calm of the basement restaurant. Down here, the decor is a mix of granny-chic and city-slick, with bare tables cosying up to plump banquettes, but the food is resolutely Italian. The charge for the crusty bread and olives waiting on each table is equally authentic, if unwelcome. Antipasti might include roasted sweet red onion, artichokes, prosciutto-wrapped sardines and peppers, or a plate of prosciutto and three-year-old parmigiano to share. Pasta is freshly made; spaghettini with anchovies, parsley, garlic and chilli is agreeably light, while gnocchi cushioned by a rich gorgonzola sauce is a more satisfying main. The cotechino, slow-cooked with Puy lentils, is pure comfort food. The fluid dining set-up ensures a lively atmosphere, but service can be patchy during busy periods. There's a reasonable wine list, with plenty by the glass, and an interesting choice of vintage drops.

13/20 

Indian Harvest

INDIAN

111 Waverley Road,
Malvern East **9571 0472**

Licensed & BYO wine
Corkage $1.50 a head
Open Tues-Sun 5-10.30pm
Seats 45
Owners Amarjit & Raman Wahi
Chefs Amarjit Wahi & Ram Jaiswar
Cards AE BC DC MC V Eftpos
Prices entrees $6-$12; mains $10.25-$17; desserts $4-$5.50; set menu $30 (3 courses)
Map page 266 **Melway** 68 G1

INDIAN HARVEST fashions itself as 'Malvern's own' Indian restaurant, but there is enough subtlety in Amarjit Wahi and Ram Jaiswar's cooking to attract customers from further afield. With its brick archways, large timber candelabra, exposed ceiling joists and rendered walls, the dining room is reminiscent of a taverna, but a troupe of cheery wall-mounted Rajasthani puppets make pretty distractions. The kitchen dishes up fine northern Indian staples like paneer tikka, generous cheese patties in a piquant tandoori marinade, and creamy dhal makhani with black lentils and red kidney beans. Seafood takes well to curry and here, the kitchen flavours both the house speciality, scallops (unusual on Indian menus), and perch with nutty Bengali five spice (no relation to Chinese five spice). Some sides are less successful, as in a bland lemon rice and staid coconut chutney, but there's a commendable level of authenticity overall. Service is efficient but homely, so don't be surprised if your waiter reads a paper at a spare table or one of the chefs sits down for a bite himself towards the end of the night.

12/20 $ V

Indochine

VIETNAMESE

51 Carrington Road,
Box Hill **9890 2966**

Licensed & BYO wine
Corkage $3 a bottle
Open daily 11am-3pm, 5.30-10pm
Seats 120
Owners Chu Thi Yen & Loc Chu
Chefs Chu Thi Yen, Lang Bau, & Nguyen Toan
Cards AE BC MC V Eftpos
Prices entrees $3.50-$11.50; mains $8.50-$24.50; desserts $7.50
Map page 266 **Melway** 47 C10

INDOCHINE is an island in a sea of suburban shops on bustling Carrington Road. Its clever layout (two dining areas separated by a wall), muted lighting, cheery Asian artefacts and noise-muffling strawboard ceiling give it an intimacy that belies its size. Service is welcoming and efficient, without being in-your-face, and prices are wallet-friendly. The food won't rock your world, but Viet staples like rice-paper rolls are as fresh and plump as you'll find, and soups like chicken and corn, with shredded bird and corn kernels in a clear broth, are both comforting and fortifying. Vietnamese specialities include a sweet-sour prawn broth, studded with pineapple, tomatoes, bean shoots, celery and fresh basil; and gargantuan banh xeo, a crisp, golden-hued pancake wedged with minced pork, prawns, bean shoots and mung beans. Sweet, juicy chilli prawns, stir-fried with onions, capsicum, crisp green beans and lemongrass, pack a fiery punch. And the delicious bo luc lac is rich with sauteed beef and mushroom-flavoured soy. The drinks list has a decent line-up of Asian beers and wines, even if the vintages aren't addressed.

13/20 $ V

Isthmus of Kra

MODERN ASIAN

50 Park Street,
South Melbourne **9690 3688**

Licensed
Open Mon-Fri noon-3pm; daily 6pm-midnight
Seats 90; outdoor seating
Owners Beh Kim Un, John Dunham & Ma Kim Poay
Chefs Beh Kim Un & Sanguan Phuakrai
Cards AE BC DC MC V
Prices entrees $9.50-$18.50; mains $15-$24.50; desserts $7.50-$10.50; banquet menus $45-$60 (minimum 4 people)
Map page 264 **Melway** 2K H2

ON the map, the Isthmus of Kra is the skinny strip of Thailand linking Myanmar and Malaysia. On the plate, this South Melbourne stayer blends flavours from all over Asia to create strikingly modern meals. A magnificent antique statue of Hanuman, the monkey god, presides over the rust and eggplant-toned restaurant, but the interior can't outshine the small miracles on the plate. Dishes harmoniously meld sweet, salty, sour and spicy in multi-textural compositions. Exquisitely crafted morsels include celadon-blue dumplings filled with peppery minced chicken, and pan-fried king prawns wrapped in coconut crepes with caramelised shrimps. Stellar main dishes include stir-fried venison with Thai basil, the signature roast duck red curry, and ocean trout steamed with spicy coconut custard and cinnamon. Meat-free offerings include a sour tamarind curry of organic tempeh and greens but a full vegetarian menu is available with a day's notice. For dessert, order the challenging platter of coconut fudge, sticky rice and mung bean paste pastries. Service shows the same TLC as the food and for bonus points, there's a food-friendly wine list.

14/20 V

Italy 1

MODERN ITALIAN

823 Burke Road,
Camberwell **9804 0944**

Licensed
Open Mon-Sat 10am-10pm; Sun 5.30-10pm
Seats 60; outdoor seating
Owner Lee family
Chef Henry Honner
Cards AE BC DC MC V
Prices entrees $12-$17.50; mains $18.50-$29; desserts $11.50
Map page 265 **Melway** 45 J12

THERE'S something rather magical about Italy 1 and its unflagging consistency. Even the locals, often too busy checking out chi-chi new venues in other neighbourhoods, marvel at how this Burke Road bistro continues to impress time and time again. Is it the dark-wood interior with its oh-so-flattering lighting? The attentive service from smart, apron-clad waitstaff? Or the wine list featuring plenty of friendly labels at prices that please? Whatever the reasons, the contingent of women dining in twos is a sure sign of a high comfort factor. They flock for familar dishes like creamy risotto with duck, pancetta, porcini and baby spinach, or simple fusilli primavera, with roasted tomatoes, asparagus, zucchini and peppered goats' cheese. A silky tortellini of sweet baby peas with seared scallops and caper raisin butter is as good as a Pavarotti solo. Gutsier options like ossobuco cushioned on mash or prime porterhouse with mushrooms and red wine sauce almost evoke standing ovations. And desserts like bread and butter pudding with roasted peaches or zuppa inglese with tarty rhubarb ensure an encore.

14/20

Jacques Reymond

MODERN AUSTRALIAN

78 Williams Road,
Windsor **9525 2178**

Licensed
Open Thurs-Fri noon-2pm; Tues-Sat 6.30-10pm
Seats 60; outdoor seating; private rooms
Owners Jacques & Kathy Reymond
Chef Jacques Reymond
Cards AE BC DC MC V
Prices fixed price menus $68, $90 or $115 (2, 3 or 4 courses); vegetarian menu $80 (6 courses); degustation menu $115 (6 courses)
Map page 265 **Melway** 58 G7

JACQUES REYMOND is a master of reinvention. His venerable Windsor restaurant is a different place since a makeover in 2002, yet it remains at the top of the city's food chain. Now glamorous and striking, rather than grand and stuffy, the reborn JR attracts a livelier – at times even bubbly – crowd, though elements such as double linen, Christofle and giddy prices still mark this as a serious dining experience. What hasn't changed is the classically trained Frenchman's border-busting cuisine that, with its multiple ingredients and complex techniques, stands in stark contrast to the prevailing mood of simplicity in Melbourne. Where else will you find ingredients like kohlrabi and bantam chicken rubbing up against shark's fin and dashi jelly? Such inventiveness has its risks, and the combinations can be dazzling, or sometimes just contrived, as in cured oysters and foie gras with cucumber pickle, circling garlic and parsley-flecked spaghettini with brains. Desserts are a highlight and the wine list has all the heavy-hitters, though mark-ups may deter. Arintji, JR's casual Fed Square diner, was to open August 2003.

17/20 V

Jamon Sushi

JAPANESE

472 Church Street,
Richmond **9427 1233**

Licensed
Open Tues-Fri noon-3pm; Tues-Sat 6.30pm-late
Seats 60
Owner & chef Charles Greenfield
Cards AE BC DC MC V Eftpos
Prices entrees $3.50-$15; sashimi & sushi platters $25-$150
Map page 265 **Melway** 2G 10K

SUSHI is now so commonplace, every other hole-in-the-wall eatery seems to offer it. But aficionados know that there's sushi, and then there's sushi. Jamon Sushi, now in the Richmond restaurant that was Anak Ku (kitted out with long low benches and coloured feature walls), offers the real stuff, thanks to fanatical owner-chef Charles Greenfield. He turns people away when the restaurant is half full, telling wanna-eats they have to wait an hour or to come another time. Pleading doesn't work, so book ahead. To get the best out of the menu, order a platter (several sizes available) of the daily changing specials. Depending on which boat comes in, you might look forward to garfish, salmon belly, bream, kingfish or tuna. Freshly landed kingfish may be sushi-ed; oysters could be served in their shells with a smear of dill wasabi, chilli mayo and salmon roe caviar; and squid could arrive shredded into a salad. There are some hot food options, such as the ramen noodle dishes offered at lunch, but most go, when they can, to share Greenfield's pursuit of perfect sushi. He also has plans to open a sake bar.

13/20

jarrah

MODERN AUSTRALIAN

26 Southgate Avenue (enter from podium level),
Southbank **9693 6060**

Licensed
Open Mon-Sat 6.30-11am; Sun 7.30am-noon; Tues-Thurs 6-10pm; Fri-Sat 6-10.30pm; bar daily noon-late
Seats 51; outdoor seating; bar
Owner Mirvac Hotels Pty Ltd
Chef Michael Bagnato
Cards AE BC DC MC V
Prices breakfasts $6-$25.50; entrees $10-$16; mains $21-$28; desserts $10-$13.50; pre-theatre set menus $23-$32 (1-2 courses)
Map page 264 **Melway** 1D T3

THIS wraparound restaurant on the Southbank thoroughfare, attached to the Quay West apartments, is a lively place without the usual blandness of hotel restaurants. Locals traipse in for after-work drinks on the terrace while pre-theatre diners choose from a dedicated eat-and-run menu. For those who can linger longer in the comfortable dining room, the kitchen comes up with some refreshingly different spins on mod-Oz standards. Seared scallops arrive with a terrific prosciutto-wrapped terrine of shiitake mushrooms and pink-eye potatoes; marinated tuna carpaccio is served with pickled ginger and snowpea salad; and a simple salad of baby spinach and peas comes with warm brie crostini. Well-considered mains include baby veal medallions with aniseed-inflected jus, and a robust seafood masala with shellfish, salmon chunks and house-made roti. Creative sugar hits might include a trio of sorbets arranged like paints on a shortbread palette, or a layered blood orange and raspberry jelly in tuile casing. Service is attentive and the wine list well priced. A casual $12 blackboard lunch menu operates for the bar and terrace.

14/20

Jimmy's the Original Greek Tavern

GREEK

130 Lygon Street,
Carlton **9663 5138**

Licensed & BYO
Corkage $3 a bottle
Open Tues-Sun 6-11pm
Seats 60; outdoor seating
Owners Paul & Helen Triandos
Chef John Vogiatzis
Cards AE BC DC MC V Eftpos
Prices entrees $5-$15; mains $18-$29.50; desserts $3-$5; set menus $35-$40 (7 courses; minimum 4 people)
Map page 262 **Melway** 2B F10

THE relaxed atmosphere in this family-run taverna offers a welcome respite from the Lygon Street touts. Perhaps it's the room-length mural with its idyllic islands, boats and Aegean-blue sky (enough to bring out the Shirley Valentine in us all). Or the fresh, clean flavours of traditional Greek food. Diners are advised to squeeze plenty of lemon over the sizeable triangle of hot, chewy saganaki, while deep-fried zucchini wafers should be piled with sloppy skordalia, a potato and garlic mash that's a smart alternative to the ubiquitous dips and bread. As you'd expect, the kitchen has got the traditional mix of lamb souvlaki, juicy cutlets and spit-roasted meats down pat, but seafood is the scene-stealer. Fresh from the grill come, perhaps, a slab of moist, delicate blue-eye, served with a scattering of chewy, deep-fried calamari strips, sweet mussels steamed in a rich tomato sauce, and plump prawns. The wine list is brief (it's wise to BYO), but this is no-frills dining – generous portions in a genial environment. Waitstaff are friendly but have little time for pleasantries when the going gets tough.

12/20

Jimmy Watson's

MODERN AUSTRALIAN

333 Lygon Street,
Carlton **9347 3985**

Licensed
Open Mon 10.30am-6pm; Tues-Sat 10.30am-late
Seats 70; outdoor seating; private rooms; bar
Owner Watson family
Chef Michael Bannerman
Cards AE BC DC MC V
Prices entrees $12.90-$15; mains $17.90-$28; desserts $7.50-$11.50
Map page 262 **Melway** 2B G6

JIMMY WATSON'S has always been an egalitarian chophouse, attracting students by day, couples by night and Carlton bohemians as the fancy takes them. The white-faced exterior of the Robin Boyd-designed building opens into a bar and dining room with a terracotta-tiled floor and classic bistro furniture – not flash, but its conviviality gives the place panache. The dusty Watson cellar of a thousand bottles means the wine list has serious and sprightly offerings, many available by the glass. The menu is full of bistro favourites, mostly Mediterranean by birth but brought up with Middle Eastern and Asian influences. Chef Michael Bannerman sates the appetite with entrees such as a well-cured gravlax flecked with dill; duck terrine; or saganaki with preserved lemon tart. For mains, you can always count on steak, perhaps a giant T-bone with an earthy jus, and duck, with Chinese flavourings or baked in a mustard crust. Vegetarian dishes are also available. Desserts, such as the poached quince with cinnamon mascarpone and pistachios, are satisfyingly indulgent, as is the service from the everpresent Watson boys – son and grandsons.

14/20

Jim's Greek Tavern

GREEK

32 Johnston Street,
Collingwood **9419 3827**

BYO
Corkage none
Open daily 6pm-midnight
Seats 200
Owners Kostas Tziotzis & Leo Panagopoulos
Chef Chris Katopodis
Cards AE BC DC MC V Eftpos
Prices entrees $6.50-$15.50; mains $17.50-$29; desserts $3.50-$4.50; set menus $38 (6-8 courses)
Map page 263 **Melway** 2C E7

JIM'S has a reputation for being raucous and ready to party, with a history as chequered as the blue-and-white cloths draped over every table. It's utterly deserved. In the cavernous back room, replete with burbling water features and kitsch Greek paraphernalia, boisterous diners compete with waiters shouting orders over the counter. There are no menus – you eat whatever is good that day, starting, perhaps, with golden saganaki drizzled with lemon juice; thick calamari rings sprinkled with oregano; or plump scallops, seared and served in an ancient, battered pan. On the grill, sweet prawns and octopus in red wine vinegar might vie for space with tender, juicy lamb and onions. King George whiting, butterflied and sizzled over charcoal, has dazzling white flesh that sings out for a squeeze of lemon and sprinkle of salt. It's something of a blessing that waiters operate on Mediterranean time, leaving plenty of space between courses, though desserts of sweet kataifi (angel-hair) pastries, dripping with sugar syrup, are too tempting to resist. For those drunk on the atmosphere (or BYO stubbies), a jolt of Jim's coffee brings instant sobriety.

14/20

Kabana Bros

MODERN GREEK

623 Glenferrie Road,
Hawthorn **9819 1377**

Licensed & BYO wine
Corkage $4 a bottle
Open daily noon-3pm, 5pm-late
Seats 160; outdoor seating
Owners James & Joanne Mavros
Chef James Mavros
Cards AE BC DC MC V Eftpos
Prices entrees $5-$12; mains $16-$24; desserts $2.80-$8; set menus $23-$45 (3 courses)
Map page 265 **Melway** 45 D10

WHILE most local Greek restaurants try to replicate that Aegean island holiday experience, Kabana delivers modern, mezze-style dishes in a contemporary space of polished wood floors and muted colour schemes that's definitely more Conran than Con. If it's too hard to choose from the array of mezedes, the Kabana Bros Tray is a neat summary: standard dips, olives, feta, barbecued red peppers and a stout pork and beef loukaniko sausage. Mains veer from traditional (moussaka, souvlaki, a seafood platter with prawns, scallops and calamari) to the slightly unusual, like roast kid served with pasta and feta. The Hunter's Catch is intriguing: slow-cooked and char-grilled game that varies according to what looked tasty at the market. Today it might be braised duck, or quail marinated in lemon, garlic and oregano, or slow-baked ox cheek so satiated with red wine it almost falls apart on the plate. Salads are pleasant, if uninspired, and the wine list is concise and reasonably priced. To finish, the sweet, rich and custardy galatoboureko could anchor a small boat. At press time, co-owner James Mavros was about to take charge of the kitchen.

14/20

Kanzaman

LEBANESE

458 Bridge Road,
Richmond **9429 3402**

Licensed & BYO wine
Corkage $2 a bottle
Open daily noon-3pm, 6pm-midnight
Seats 150
Owners Bilal & Mona Talj
Chef Bilal Talj
Cards AE BC DC MC V
Prices entrees $7.50-$10; mains $18.50-$28; desserts $7-$9; banquet menus $35-$46 (12-15 courses)
Map page 265 **Melway** 2H D6

WITH its bold spicy colours, heavy drapes, Persian carpets, cool blue lights and exotic murals, Kanzaman seems more exotic bazaar than restaurant. Unload the family wagon and opt for one of the crowd-pleasing banquet menus (seafood optional), or order several of the snacky mezze choices: oniony sambousik, triangles of filo filled with feta and spiced with cumin; chicken wings in a lemony zaatar dressing; lamb and pine nut filo fingers, or fat cabbage-leaf cigars stuffed with lamb and jasmine rice and served in a rich lemon, mint and garlic sauce. The hummus and baba ghanoush dips are excellent served with warm pide, but why fill up on bread when you can nibble crisp, moist barbecued quail, slathered in a coriander and labna marinade? Garlicky falafels come with tahini and slivers of baby-pink pickled turnip that add acidity and crunch. Lamb comes with spicy tomato and coriander; fish of the day with tahini, walnuts and paprika. Just wait until the koosa arrives – white zucchini plump with rice and tomatoey lamb mince spiked with mint. But save space for mahalabia, a blancmange-like dessert drizzled with orange blossom syrup.

13/20

Kazen

MODERN JAPANESE

201 Brunswick Street,
Fitzroy **9417 3270**

Licensed & BYO wine
Corkage $2 a bottle
Open Tues-Fri noon-3pm; Tues-Sun 6-10.30pm
Seats 60; private room
Owners Kazu Ueda
Chefs Kazu Ueda & Masa Harada
Cards AE BC MC V Eftpos
Prices entrees $3.50-$15; mains $15-$22; desserts $7-$9
Map page 263 **Melway** 2C A8

ONLY in Fitzroy can you find antipasto misto, carpaccio and linguine sharing menu space in a cheerfully minimalist Japanese cafe. These Japanese-Italian mixed marriages are Kazen's signature – happily, there's no fusion confusion under the chef's steady hand. The antipasto plate is a lovely precis of the kitchen's ability – dishes like marinated octopus, grilled eggplant with shaved bonito, sardines in tomato sauce, chicken terrine, and cream cheese rolled in nori and deep-fried bean curd. Check the daily specials, written on butcher's paper, for excellent grilled quail. Seared beef carpaccio with garlic and ginger is reliably good and the sashimi and sushi are well regarded, especially the spicy tuna rolls. Similarly dependable are Japanese classics such as char-grilled eel, and gyoza, with its chewy top, crisp bottom and lively pork and spring onion filling. Big-bowl noodle dishes would sate any salaryman's hunger, and the aforementioned linguine, with mountain vegetables and shiitakes, has an earthiness that soothes the soul. Mains span the tempura-tonkatsu-teriyaki options, and some come with mashed potato, rice and salad.

14/20 $ V

The Kent Hotel

MODERN AUSTRALIAN

370 Rathdowne Street,
Carlton North **9347 5672**

Licensed
Open daily noon-midnight
Seats 140; outdoor seating; private room; bar
Owner Michael Cappelleri
Chefs Jason Aitken & Anthony Caruso
Cards AE BC DC MC V Eftpos
Prices snacks $4.90-$13.50; entrees $8.50-$14.50; mains $17.50-$24.50; desserts $6.50-$8.90
Map page 262 **Melway** 2B J2

THE Kent's leafy Curtain Square vista, wooden floors, and banks of concertina windows that open out on to outdoor tables are all quintessentially Carlton North, as is the rowdy crowd. On busy nights, the noise can be deafening as drinkers and diners pack the place out. Luckily, the service is brisk and competent. The mainly mod-Oz menu caters for those who want a full-on pub feed or those who prefer beer to be the main calorific intake of the day. Smaller bites include wood-fired pizzas (one comes topped with tandoori chicken, Spanish onion, peanuts, chutney and yoghurt), and pub standards like fries and wedges. More refined and modish dishes might include an excellent house-cured gravlax of ocean trout, teamed with shallots, fried capers and mascarpone crostini, or plump Sydney Rock oysters if the season is right. Mains are big and mostly meaty. Lamb cutlets may come with a tomato and black olive salsa, and pan-seared veal on wild mushroom risotto. Red wine jus is 'drizzled' a little too frequently, but mostly the flavours are bright and interesting. If only all pub food were this good.

13/20

Kenzan

JAPANESE

Lower ground floor, Collins Place, 45 Collins Street, City **9654 8933**

Licensed
Open Mon-Fri noon-2.30pm; daily 6-10pm
Seats 100; private rooms
Owner Takanao Murayama
Chefs Kaname Komatsu & Koichi Minamishima
Cards AE BC DC MC V
Prices entrees $7.50-$16.50; sushi & sashimi $15.40-$75; mains $23.50-$28.50; desserts $5-$8.80
Map page 260 **Melway** 1B U8

KENZAN has a reputation as the place to go for sashimi, and rightly so. Not only is the fish well stored and well cut, it's served at just the right temperature, not over-chilled. Equally impressive is the huge range of sushi available: uni (sea urchin), toro (tuna belly), aji (mackerel), sake (salmon), and more. Daily specials offer astute pairings such as roasted eggplant with sea urchin in dashi – the sensation of cooled ingredients with hot stock is wonderful. Or perhaps half-boiled organic eggs, served in their shell with sea urchin – an earthy, creamy hit. The chawan mushi shows off the Kenzan's dashi stock to full advantage; the trembling custard full of seafood and mushrooms barely holds together. Favourites such as teriyaki, tempura and hotpots are handled competently, as is a simple dish of grilled fish with miso, its caramel crust cut by a citrusy ponzu. Those who like Japanese desserts will enjoy the black sesame mousse with red azuki beans; otherwise there's green tea or vanilla icecream. Staff are attentive, the wine list is very good, and the room, though simple and modest, is comfortable and inviting.

15/20

Kimchi Grandma Restaurant

KOREAN

125 Koornang Road, Carnegie **9569 2399**

Licensed & BYO wine
Corkage $1.50 a head
Open daily 5-10.30pm
Seats 80
Owner Jim Lee
Chefs Jim Lee & Min Lee
Cards BC MC V Eftpos
Prices entrees $2.50-$8.50; stir-fries $12.90-$18.50; noodles $12.90-$14.90; mains $12.90-$26
Map page 266 **Melway** 68 J4

SLICKER than most of Melbourne's Korean restaurants, Kimchi Grandma is an enduringly popular and unflappable place. Sandblasted red-brick walls, dark timber tables and tasteful spotlighting lend warmth to a functional space. When it's busy (and that's most nights), the volume in the room ramps up from buzzy to frankly cacophonic. Luckily, the staff run a tight ship and you'll rarely have to shout above the din to ask what's happened to your sizzling Korean barbecue. Grandma – who runs the kitchen out back – has crafted a menu that honours her heritage while making a few concessions to Korean cuisine newbies. Goon-man du (crunchy pan-fried spiced meat dumplings) are an easy entry point, while ttokbokki, stir-fried rice-flour 'gnocchi', makes for a fiery start. Korean classics among the mains include bulgogi, barbecued soy-marinated beef slivers, and whole 'small chicken' stuffed with ginseng, rice and garlic and served in a chive and water chestnut broth. Half a dozen kimchi side dishes arrive as a matter of course: chilli pickled cabbage is a given, but there might also be sweet and sour white radish and slivers of steamed zucchini.

13/20 $

Koko

JAPANESE

Level 3, Crown Entertainment Complex,
Southbank **9292 6886**

Licensed
Open daily noon-3pm, 6-11pm
Seats 130; private rooms
Owner Crown Ltd
Chef Allan Koh
Cards AE BC DC MC V
Prices entrees $13.50-$20; sushi & sashimi $20-$34; mains $23-$40; desserts $12-$20
Map page 264 **Melway** 1D M3

KOKO'S dining room screams 'high roller', with its umber-toned fitout, stone steps that dance away to tatami rooms and a reflection pool that bisects two teppanyaki zones. The menu is a compilation of Japanese favourites and slightly more modern dishes; there's also a separate bespoke sushi list. Daily specials are dutifully recited by staff, though they can't always be relied upon for further explication. Koko's most memorable and lavish dishes are the seafood ones, made from impeccable fish and shellfish. The soft-shell crab tempura with mirin wasabi is consistently good; salmon belly tataki is livened with wasabi soy sauce, and works well with a sprightly three-seaweed salad tossed with mirin and sesame oil. Freshly cut sashimi is a study in texture and variety, but it's crammed on to a platter without the expected care for presentation. Meat alternatives can be a little listless, as in sizzling beef shogayaki in a pallid ginger sauce. The comprehensive wine and sake list offers plenty of interest, but Koko will need to improve its service and attention to culinary detail if it's to return to the ranks of Melbourne's best Japanese.

14/20

Koots

MODERN FRENCH

479 Glenferrie Road,
Kooyong **9822 3809**

Licensed
Open Tues-Fri noon-3pm; Tues-Sat 6.30-10.30pm
Seats 45
Owners Patrice & Catherine Repellin
Chef Patrice Repellin
Cards AE BC DC MC V
Prices entrees $14-$15.50; mains $24-$27.50; desserts $10-$15; lunch set menu $25 (2 courses)
Map page 265 **Melway** 59 C3

FOR three years, without much fuss, Patrice and Catherine Repellin have been crafting the perfect restaurant for the polite suburb of 'almost Toorak'. Coups like hiring Olivier Ferretjans – sommelier from the Roux brothers' Waterside Inn – have largely gone unheralded. But the Repellins run one of Melbourne's better local restaurants and word is getting out. The room has changed little over the years. Polished concrete floors make the room feel a little austere although the baronial fireplace, ochre walls and view of crab-apples and wisteria out of the back window add character. Patrice Repellin delivers light French-accented food, which veers from something as simple as tomato tarte tatin with pissaladière-like hints of olive and sweet onion to more intricate offerings such as chicken leg stuffed with chestnuts, sage and prosciutto or sliced porterhouse lifted by the tang of tarragon and confit onions. Desserts are a high spot, with excellent sorbets (maybe grapefruit, green apple, chocolate) or a simply elegant and excellent crème brûlée. The wine list is petite and predominantly Australian, with a smattering of French charm.

15/20

ROOMS WITH A VIEW

See the sights without leaving your table

Beate's
Studley Park Boathouse, 1 Boathouse Road, Kew, 9853 1828
At lunch, ensconced in a comfortably upholstered chair on the historic boathouse's sheltered veranda, you can take in a treetops view of the meandering Yarra, accompanied by bird calls and the sounds of dipping oars as canoeists glide by. At night, hole up by the fire inside. See page 22.

Donovans
40 Jacka Boulevard, St Kilda, 9534 8221
At Donovans, the golden sands and lapping waters of St Kilda Beach are but a Ligurian olive pip's throw from your linen-clad table, and cyclists, strollers and the sunset provide a spectacular nightly floorshow. Call well ahead to reserve a window table. The best views are reserved for guests in the private dining room, which comes with its own beach-front terrace. See page 59.

Le Restaurant
Level 35, Hotel Sofitel, 25 Collins Street, City, 9653 0000
When you're not marvelling at the careful artistry of Le Restaurant's French-inspired food, the sparkling crystal glasses, and Christofle cutlery, you can gaze down on the city from 35 floors up. The best views are to be had when night falls, and the darkened cityscape lights up like a jawful of fluorescent teeth. See page 95.

Livebait
55b New Quay Promenade, Docklands, 9642 1500
Walk up the stairs and past the oyster-shell wall before settling into this glass-enclosed eyrie for Med-inspired seafood dishes. By day you can watch the pleasure craft come and go, and at night there's a mesmerising wide-angled view that takes in neon-lit skyscrapers, the Docklands stadium and the imposing pillars of the Bolte Bridge, all reflected in the waters of Victoria Harbour. See page 97.

Middle Brighton Baths
251 The Esplanade, Brighton, 9539 7000
This place is a giant window on Port Phillip, with an all-day cafe downstairs and an up-market restaurant above. In summer, you can observe beautiful bodies baking on the U-shaped pier as you tuck into beer-battered King George whiting with tartare sauce and ponder how you will ever fit into your bathers. See page 108.

No. 3 Station Pier
3 Station Pier, Beacon Cove, Port Melbourne, 9646 6299
You might not be able to afford to live the new Port Melbourne lifestyle, but you can survey it at leisure from your perch at No. 3 Station Pier. The three-sided view takes in the flashy Beacon Cove apartments and the comings and goings of the Tasmanian ferry. Casual dining is below, or head upstairs for formal dining and more expansive views. See page 118.

Sarti
6 Russell Place, City, 9639 7822
While Sarti's new owners have ditched the tailoring business and changed chefs, they haven't tinkered with one of the restaurant's most precious assets: its standout rooftop terrace. Lined with cumquat and olive trees in terracotta pots, and shaded by stylish market umbrellas, the two-tier space feels like a Mediterranean courtyard in the heart of the CBD. See page 140.

Tides Seafood Grill & Oyster Bar
Pier 35 Marina, 263-329 Lorimer Street, Port Melbourne, 9645 6433
From the outdoor decks at Tides, you can almost reach out and stroke the massive concrete pillars of the Westgate Bridge, and boat-spotters will be able to tick off anything from luxury cruisers to lumbering container ships as they pass by. Not surprisingly, in this waterside setting, the menu is dominated by the fruits of the sea.

Kri Kri Mezethopoleion

MODERN GREEK

39-41 Little Bourke Street,
City **9639 3444**

Licensed
Open Tues-Fri noon-3pm; Mon-Sat 5-11pm
Seats 210
Owners Ren Bastone & Melete Roussis
Chef Sattar Abdus
Cards AE BC DC MC V Eftpos
Prices appetisers $6.60-$12.50; mains $10.80-$17.90; desserts $6-$9; banquet menus $21.50-$39 (7-14 courses)
Map page 260 **Melway** 1B U4

THIS is the place to go if you love to order a little of this and a bit of that. Kri Kri Mezethopoleion (surely Greek for 'I want it all'?), specialises in mezze. But be warned – the food comes out in the order in which it is prepared, not ordered. Still, this is a menu to really have fun with, so skip the taramasalata, tzatziki and melitzanosalata dips (why fill up on bread?) and launch into strips of deep-fried calamari, skewered swordfish chunks or char-grilled lamb cutlets that arrive pink at the bone. Vegetable lovers will be happy with the list of options, which might include giant beans stewed in tomato or zucchini fritters ready to be plunged into skordalia. Keep an eye on the specials board for dishes such as chicken livers, or boned sardines, both cooked in oil and lemon, the sardines finished with sweet red wine vinegar. A classic Greek salad is served at the end of the meal just in case you haven't had your fill. Desserts are restricted to sticky Greek pastries like baklava or loukoumades, cinnamon-laced honey doughnuts. Be brave and order a bold, fruity Greek white wine, which is more than able to compete with flavour-packed food.

13/20 $ V

@ A GLANCE

Dim sum guaranteed to get the lazy Susans spinning

YUM CHA

Bamboo Terrace
201 Bulleen Road, Bulleen, 9852 0541
The building looks like the Brady Bunch house but the food would be a treat no matter what the setting. If you don't like crowds, weekday yum cha will suit.

David's
4 Cecil Place, Prahran, 9529 5199
A soothing, airy room, excellent service and a treasure-laden selection that never stops provide all the right ingredients for recovering from the night before.

Pepper Chilli
85 Little Bourke Street, City, 9662 9662
Well-spaced tables and a low-lit atmosphere make this one of Melbourne's less frenetic yum cha pitstops. Trays of dishes keep coming so relax and make it a leisurely one.

Plume Restaurant
546 Doncaster Road, Doncaster, 9840 1122
Those pining for a bit of bustling Hong Kong style come to Plume for yum cha. Cruising trolleys provide a parade of old favourites.

Red Emperor
Upper level, 3 Southgate Avenue, Southbank, 9699 4170
This is big city yum cha, complete with big city views. Squads of waiters make sure you're well fed before the next sitting arrives.

Taipan
237-239 Blackburn Road, Doncaster East, 9841 9977
The long queue out the door and the full carpark attest to the popularity of the food here. Weekday yum cha provides an alternative to the weekend maelstrom.

Kuni's

JAPANESE

56 Little Bourke Street,
City **9663 7243**

Licensed & BYO wine
Corkage $2 a head
Open Mon-Fri noon-2.30pm; Mon-Wed 6-10pm; Thurs-Sat 6-10.30pm
Seats 80
Owners Kunihiro Ichikawa & Ron Harrison
Chefs Terry Hirata & Masa Kuriki
Cards AE BC DC MC V
Prices sushi & sashimi $3-$27; entrees $5-$12; noodles $12-$14; mains $17-$23; desserts $6-$10
Map page 260 **Melway** 1B T4

SLIPPING into reliable Kuni's is like coming home after a time away. Kuni's renditions of Japanese classics have long served as a benchmark, and combined with its roster of daily specials, there is more than enough to keep diners' interest piqued. There's a sushi bar and a dining room proper, simply dressed in pine furniture and cheery yellow walls. Vividly fresh red and white fish make up the well-cut sashimi, and sushi is available à la carte, featuring occasional delicacies such as toro (tuna belly), uni (sea urchin) or scallop. Shumai (steamed prawn and scallop dumplings wrapped in dough), served with hot mustard and soy, are meaty yet delicate, and the noodle dishes, such as kamo nanban (buckwheat noodles with sliced duck and leek in a dashi-shoyu base) offer endless comfort in a bowl. A main dish such as gyu yanagawa – beef cooked with onion, gobo (burdock root) and egg – is one of those one-pot meals served in a cast iron pot that the Japanese do so well. Limited dessert offerings include green tea icecream, but as with everything else, it's done well.

14/20

La Luna Bistro

MODERN MEDITERRANEAN

320 Rathdowne Street,
Carlton North **9349 4888**

Licensed & BYO wine
Corkage $4.50 a bottle
Open Tues-Fri noon-10pm; Sat-Sun 9am-10pm
Seats 75; outdoor seating; private rooms
Owner & chef Adrian Richardson
Cards AE BC DC MC V Eftpos
Prices breakfasts $3.50-$16.50; entrees $11.50-$16.50; mains $19.50-$27.50; desserts $12.50
Map page 262 **Melway** 2B J3

PERHAPS it's the notice about the chef-owner Adrian Richardson's monthly master classes on the door. But from the moment you walk into La Luna's vanilla-walled, terracotta-floored dining room, you know you're in expert hands. Nibbling on an appetiser of, say, garlicky olives, you contemplate the brief menu. You expect entrees of char-grilled octopus and calamari, sauteed with spinach, chilli, garlic and olive oil, to be tender and snapping with flavour. They will be. You consider the main course of Moroccan-spiced chickpeas, served with spinach and saffron-spiked yoghurt. Or the famous trio of grilled pork sausages, one flavoured with red capsicum, another with olives, and the last with parsley, sage, rosemary and thyme. But really, you want to hear the specials. Perhaps there'll be a main course 'barrel of pork' – different cuts of pork rolled together, then infused with garlic, and served enveloped in crisp, salty crackling – the ultimate roast pork fantasy come true. Or a less calorific dish of seared rare tuna with a salsa of parsley, olives and capers. Desserts like warm crepes filled with hazelnuts and almonds make up for lost kilos.

14/20

La Madrague

FRENCH

171 Buckhurst Street,
South Melbourne **9699 9627**

Licensed
Open Tues-Fri noon-3pm; Mon-Sat 7-11pm
Seats 45
Owners & chefs Alain Blanc & Leisa Campbell
Cards AE BC DC MC V Eftpos
Prices entrees $16-$18; mains $27-$32; desserts $12; degustation menu $70 (6 courses; minimum 2 people)
Map page 264 **Melway** 2J H1

IF the departure of Annie and Jacques Heraudeau after 21 years at La Madrague caused regulars no little heartache, at least the takeover by new arrivals Alain Blanc and Leisa Campbell has been reasonably seamless. There's been no slick renovation, Edith Piaf still sings from the speakers, and the menu is still the kind you might find in regional France. It's robust, honest and a little old-fashioned, but above all tasty. Bar occasional dishes employing offal – lamb sweetbreads and kidneys with a lamb noisette; snails on pig trotter ragout – the menu is unlikely to offend those squeamish about the French eat-everything approach. Faithfuls such as onion soup, duck confit on mash, and eye fillet with green peppercorn and cognac sauce make up the bulk of the carte, leavened by slightly more modern dishes such as seared scallops with tomato beurre blanc, and venison with a prune and cabernet reduction. The food is not unreservedly excellent (fatty duck confit; crepes with gluey Grand Marnier custard), but easy parking, genteel service and low noise levels allow diners to relax. A few French wines add character to the steady-as-she-goes list.

13/20

Langton's Restaurant & Wine Bar

MODERN EUROPEAN

61 Flinders Lane,
City **9663 0222**

Licensed & BYO (Tues only)
Corkage $15 a bottle
Open Mon-Fri noon-2.30pm; Mon-Sat 6-10.30pm; wine bar Mon-Sat 7.30am-11pm
Seats 100; outdoor seating; private room; bar
Owners Stewart Langton & partners
Chef Walter Trupp
Cards AE BC DC MC V
Prices breakfasts $3.50-$15.50; entrees $15-$22.50; mains $29-$36; desserts $14.50-$17; degustation menu $95 (6 courses)
Map page 260 **Melway** 1B T9

WHEN visitors come to Melbourne, Langton's is almost certainly on their itinerary. They love the Euro elegance of this back-street basement restaurant. There's a suave brown fitout; one of Australia's best wine lists; and a lengthy cheese carte. The European influence permeates the open kitchen. Frenchman Philippe Mouchel was the founding chef, succeeded by Brit Jeremy Strode. Now Austrian-born Walter Trupp is in charge. While his pedigree (Marco Pierre White's Criterion and Titanic) suggests he has what it takes to continue the Langton's legacy, the food can be hit and miss. Entrees shine, as in a ballottine of salmon – a triangle of silky pink flesh with a pea and mint cream. And a dessert of cranberry soufflé with apple gelati is a model of its kind. But some mains seem messy and confused: a pool of 'pecorino foam' alongside delicate king dory jars with a tomato-based razor clam stew on the plate. Service can lapse (jackets not hung, delays with drinks) and the lighting is too low. But given time to adapt to local conditions, Trupp, with owner Stewart Langton, should return the restaurant to its position of strength.

15/20

A & V Lazar Charcoal Grill & Seafood Restaurant

STEAK/SEAFOOD
Best Steakhouse

87-89 Johnston Street,
Fitzroy **9419 2073**

Licensed & BYO wine
Corkage none
Open Mon-Fri noon-3pm; Mon-Sat 6-10pm
Seats 200
Owners Alojz & Vera Lazar
Chefs Alojz Lazar (meat) & Raymond Oei (fish)
Cards AE BC DC MC V
Prices entrees \$7-\$15; mains \$21-\$29; desserts \$7-\$12; set menu \$59 (4 courses)
Map page 263 **Melway** 2C A7

WHEN it comes to refined ambience or sophisticated dining, Melbourne's established steakhouses are not really in the frame. Lazar's is a barn-sized chocolate brick chalet still living in the '70s. Inside, mounted heads of Herefords stare mournfully from the wall, surrounded by photos of other beasts fated for the plate. But when you consider Lazar's steak, who cares about decor? Without doubt, it's the best scotch fillet and porterhouse in Melbourne, big rustic grass-fed slabs rippling with fat, perfectly cooked and incredibly juicy. It's served with the standard coleslaw and iceberg lettuce but the condiments are terrific – a sharp Dijon mustard and a respectably fresh horseradish. Sure, there's fish on the menu, too, but let's face it – you come here for the beef. The set menu is \$59 and includes beef broth, ordinary sausages, sublime steak and dated desserts like strawberry crepes. The staff are charming older European men who really know their beef. The wine list is a little predictable, but it's BYO and there's no corkage, so take a bottle of your best red to match the best steak in Melbourne.

14/20

Le Gourmet

EUROPEAN

366 Albert Street,
East Melbourne **9416 3744**

Licensed
Open Tues-Fri noon-3pm; Tues-Sat 6-10.30pm
Seats 100; private rooms
Owners Erich & Barbara Mohr
Chef Erich Mohr
Cards AE BC DC MC V
Prices entrees \$10.50-\$17.90; mains \$23.90-\$32.90; desserts \$10.50-\$13.90
Map page 263 **Melway** 2G B1

SITTING surrounded by burgundy walls, floral tablecloths, candles and Christofle, you can catch glimpses of the Fitzroy Gardens through Le Gourmet's flounced drapes and Victorian picture windows. Your hostess, discreet but welcoming, slips a pot of entenschmalz (Austrian pork rillettes) on the table as you mull over the choice of leberknodel suppe (liver dumpling soup) or gratin of snails with cognac and paprika butter. Then there's the saddle of venison with braised cabbage, spaetzle and porcini or the wiener schnitzel with mashed potatoes and cranberries – all prepared by Austrian chef Erich Mohr. The wine list could see you weighing up the finest (and oldest) of Australia against France's best. The atmosphere is as time-warpish as the menu, but the European manner is beguiling and the traditional flavours excellent. The duck (served with pumpkin tart and spinach) is richly flavored with a perfectly crisp skin. Try extravagant Viennese desserts like sacher torte, or Salzburger nockerln (meringue-soufflé), but remember that Erich Mohr also excels with fruit. His crumbles, grilled fruit and icecreams are very, very good.

13/20

Lemongrass

THAI

176 Lygon Street,
Carlton **9662 2244**

Licensed
Open Mon-Fri noon-3pm; Mon-Sat 5.30-11pm; Sun 5.30-11pm
Seats 140; outdoor seating
Owner Michael Mah
Chefs Namoi Meesa-ard & Tassanee Kerdpikul
Cards AE BC DC MC V
Prices entrees $11.50-$18.50; mains $19.50-$34.50; desserts $8.80-$11.50
Map page 262 **Melway** 2B F9

LEMONGRASS is a sanctuary of style and tranquillity in hectic Lygon Street. The stark, washed-charcoal interior, in a Victorian building overlooking leafy Argyle Square, is warmed by pools of downlighting, polished timber tables and an ambient soundtrack. With such a setting (and lofty menu prices), it's a shame this once shining example of royal Thai cuisine has lost a little of its lustre. Mieng plates remain an interesting DIY starter – lettuce and rice paper are topped with fillings such as chicken, pork, pomelo, lime, green mango, garlic and chilli, then rolled into bite-sized parcels. Tom kha gai, the classic coconut-rich chicken soup, smacks of excellent sweet and sour flavours. But tauhu thod (fried tofu pockets), seem bland and joyless by comparison, and a roast duck red curry lacks the subtlety of flavour usually associated with this refined cuisine. Better to order wok-fried noodle dishes, such as pad moo goong gai (with pork, chicken and prawn), which have a satisfying, smoky zing. Desserts include sang-kaya, an intensely flavoured coconut crème caramel. The wine list includes plenty of food-friendly varieties and a few by the glass.

13/20 V

Le Petit Bourgeois

FRENCH

330 Waverley Road,
Malvern East **9571 0909**

Licensed & BYO wine
Corkage $3 a head
Open Tues-Sat 7pm-midnight
Seats 30
Owners Wendy & John Salisbury
Chef John Salisbury
Cards AE BC MC V
Prices entrees $13.50-$16; mains $24; desserts $10-$11
Map page 266 **Melway** 68 J1

REMEMBER those great neighbourhood BYO restaurants of the '80s? Just one neat room in a suburban shopping strip, and a kitchen that paid homage to well-cut pieces of meat with great sauces, and potatoes that came 'pureed', 'sauteed' or 'gratineed'? The snug room at Le Petite Bourgeois is full of grinning diners who still delight in these traditions, practised with aplomb by chef-owner John Salisbury. He balances classics like smoked salmon with sauce gribiche, confit of duck, and liqueured soufflés with more contemporary creations. There could be a feather-weight blue goats' cheese tart, or delicate King George whiting, perhaps paddling in an oyster-studded vermouth and chive sauce. There may be a chicken, cucumber and walnut oil salad, mustard-smeared kangaroo or braised beef with Vietnamese peppercorns – all evidence that time hasn't stood still in the kitchen (although some diners complain that time drags at the table). If you last the distance, finish with a soufflé that might just clear the ceiling or the 'floating island' of caramelised meringue, adrift in a sea of crème anglaise.

13/20

Le Restaurant

MODERN EUROPEAN

Level 35, Hotel Sofitel, 25 Collins Street,
City **9653 0000**

Licensed
Open Tues-Sat 6.30pm-late
Seats 100
Owner Accor Asia Pacific
Chef to be announced
Cards AE BC DC MC V
Prices entrees $26-$32; mains $37-$43; desserts $16-$18; menu gourmand $110 (8 courses)
Map page 260 **Melway** 1B U8

THIS ultra-luxe restaurant transcends its hotel setting to stake a claim as one of Melbourne's most refined (and expensive) dining experiences. It's not just the extraordinary views from the 35th floor, or the flattering light, comfortable club chairs and tables dressed with linen, crystal and silver. You may also be served admirably by the same impeccable staff who looked after you on your previous visits. Start, perhaps, with roasted scallops, celeriac and truffle, then move on to flavourful venison with, say, an intense porcini and juniper jus. Pan-fried John Dory could be teamed with fennel, lobster and duck giblet sausage, which balances strong flavours in a twinkle-toed composition. Desserts – such as the caramelised fig soufflé with balsamic icecream – are luscious. Intelligent wine service, from award-winning sommelier Christian Maier, completes the experience. As the *Guide* went to press, Le Restaurant's head chef, Steve Smith was leaving after three years of serving up his finely wrought food, and the hotel was searching for a new chef to replace him.

15/20 V

Lever & Kowalyk

MODERN AUSTRALIAN

42 Ferguson Street,
Williamstown **9397 6798**

Licensed & BYO wine
Corkage $4 a bottle
Open Mon 8am-5pm; Tues-Fri 8am-10pm; Sat 9am-10pm; Sun 9am-5pm
Seats 45; outdoor seating; private room
Owners Rohan Lever, Helen & Mark Kowalyk
Chef Rohan Lever
Cards AE BC MC V Eftpos
Prices breakfasts $4-$12; lunches $9-$16; entrees $9-$12; mains $18-$23; desserts $9
Map page 264 **Melway** 56 C8

L&K is one of a growing number of mixed businesses on Melbourne's cafe scene. It was one of the first to combine a cafe with a foodstore supplying high-quality ingredients, such as infused oils and boutique muesli. The neat dining space is decked out with ultra-mod white chairs, banquettes and polished buttercup-coloured tabletops. L&K rethinks brunch staples like the ham and cheese toastie – here it's crammed with ham, gruyère and egg, and at lunch, baguettes could burst with prawns, Vietnamese salad and poached chicken. But at dinner, when the menu and prices go upscale, L&K seems less comfortable with the flourishes of fine dining. While the ideas are there, they're not always matched by the execution. An entree of salmon gravlax with celeriac remoulade is a perfect balance of fish and creamy vegetable, but a lukewarm kangaroo fillet, perched on an ungainly fig and prosciutto risotto, is not as successful a combination as it sounds. Choosing wine is a doddle – they are all either $6 a glass or $30 a bottle. For dessert, the chocolate tart with orange icecream is the stuff of local legend.

13/20 

Li Li's

CHINESE

71-73 Stanley Street,
West Melbourne **9326 5790**

Licensed & BYO wine
Corkage $3 a bottle
Open daily 6-11pm
Seats 55; private rooms
Owner & chef Li Li
Cards AE BC DC MC V
Prices set menus $55-$138 (16-18 small courses)
Map page 262 **Melway** 2A J12

THERE'S nothing outside to suggest that you'd come to this unprepossessing backblocks restaurant for exquisite Imperial Court cuisine. Inside, the modest dining room is peaceful but far from regal. However, the family of owner-chef Li Li has a history of creating greatness behind the scenes: her great-grandfather oversaw the royal kitchens of Dowager Empress Ci Xi, grandmother of Pu Yi, the last emperor of China. You better believe it when Li Li says her repertoire comprises 300 authentic court dishes handed down by her forebears, served here in traditional banquet style. Every set menu starts with seven or eight entrees (perhaps deep-fried lotus root, smoked pork balls and glazed walnuts), before branching off into three price schedules, depending on whether you choose stir-fried chicken fillet in fragrant rice wine, fried crabmeat with bamboo shoot, or stewed shark's fin or fried breaded lobster. The budget menu chicken can be bland, but the tenderness and flavour of the other set dishes (deep-fried scallops, Mandarin fish, whole green prawns and exquisite Peking duck) more than make up for it. You'll also be treated like royalty.

14/20

Lim's Nyonya Hut

MALAYSIAN

240 Blackburn Road,
Glen Waverley **9802 3763**

BYO
Corkage $1 a head
Open Tues-Fri 11.30am-3pm; Sat-Sun noon-3pm; Tues-Sun 5.30-10pm
Seats 60
Owners & chefs Beng Lai & Bee Lee Lim
Cards BC MC V
Prices entrees $4-$6.50; mains $8.50-$18.80; desserts 60 cents-$3.80
Map page 266 **Melway** 61 J12

YOU don't have to travel all the way to the rickety food stalls in Gurney Drive, Penang, for fabulous hawker and Nonya dishes. In downtown Glen Waverley, you'll find the true flavours of Penang cuisine in this simple laminate-table cafe, set up by the Lim family in 1999 following stints in Singapore and London. Their loss is Melbourne's gain. There are no substitutions or shortcuts in the Lim kitchen. Sour, fishy Assam laksa, redolent of bunga kantan (ginger flower), uses the proper plump white noodles and arrives with a healthy drizzle of prawn paste. The fabulous nasi lemak comes with achar (pickled vegetables), crunchy fried whitebait and peanuts, and a choice of curry chicken or beef rendang. Lunch is mostly noodles and rice but dinner could be inche kabin (spice-marinated and crisply fried chicken), otak-otak (spiced steamed custards) of either prawns or fish, and specials like hong bak (spiced braised pork). At weekends, they make poh piah, pliant crepes stuffed with braised shredded yam bean, pork, prawns and shredded fried bean curd, all bundled into a roll. There is a range of kueh (Nonya sweets) available, too.

14/20 $ V

The Lincoln Hotel

MODERN AUSTRALIAN

91 Cardigan Street (corner Queensberry Street),
Carlton **9347 4666**

Licensed
Open Mon-Fri noon-3pm; Mon-Sat 6-9.30pm
Seats 38; bar
Owners Glenn Fletcher & Donelle Coates
Chefs Michael DeJong & Graham Sutherland
Cards AE BC DC MC V Eftpos
Prices entrees $12.50; mains $18.50-$32; desserts $10
Map page 262 **Melway** 2B E10

THIS is a little cracker of a backstreet pub. No great surprise, as Lincoln's kitchen was kick-started in 2002 by Peter and Janelle McLeod, who built the food legend of those meat-and-wine temples, West Melbourne's Hotel Spencer (see page 74) and Richmond's All Nations. The McLeods have moved on, but chef Michael DeJong remains, and the blackboard menu in the simple, yellow-walled dining room still offers great value with its hearty flavours. A charcuterie platter is packed with meaty goodies like unctuous rabbit rillettes and a huge slab of intense wild pork terrine, while a more delicate seafood assiette includes tender char-grilled scallops, and silky sashimi on spicy avocado. Tuck into one of the sizeable mains, like a super-rich beef and mushroom pie, and you'll be full for days. More modest is the chicken and duck bastilla, buttery pastry enclosing a sweet, spicy mound of slow-cooked poultry, served with a dollop of yoghurt and roasted tomato. The new owners have upgraded the wine list, adding many iconic Australian drops, including some hard-to-get and aged bottles straight from their private cellar.

14/20 

Livebait

SEAFOOD/MODERN MEDITERRANEAN

55b New Quay Promenade,
Docklands **9642 1500**

Licensed
Open daily noon-3pm, 6-11pm
Seats 110; outdoor seating
Owners Damian Trytell, Julian Lee & Cath Claringbold
Chef Darron Paul
Cards AE BC DC MC V
Prices entrees $12-$19; mains $20-$40; desserts $10.50
Map page 264 **Melway** 2E E4

LIVEBAIT is an unpretentious, modern seafood restaurant where dishes bask in the southern Mediterranean flavours of Portugal, Spain, Greece, Italy, Provence. These are big, sunny, fishy flavours mixed with salt and spice. The kinds of flavours that partner and executive chef Cath Claringbold, who also has a hand in Mecca Bah downstairs, and Southbank's mecca (see page 106), understands well. Here, fish fiends come to feast at bare tables standing on seagrass matting, with a wall of windows offering panoramic views of the city, Docklands and Bolte Bridge. Salt cod fritters might be served with a robust aioli, fried calamari nuzzles a cheeky skordalia, and six chilli-spiked king prawns (heads off, tails on) bake in a terracotta dish. There are fish stews brimful of peppers and saffron and generous pans of paella, though the simple 'fish with a choice of salads' – say, char-grilled swordfish with a salad of chickpeas, chorizo, tomato and parsley – is popular. Simple desserts such as panna cotta are enlivened with smart touches like poached peaches with a smashed praline crust. All this, and a perky wine list? One visit and you'll be hooked.

14/20

The London

MODERN EUROPEAN

92 Beach Street,
Port Melbourne **9646 4644**

Licensed
Open Mon-Fri noon-3pm; Mon-Sat 6pm-late; bistro daily 9am-late
Seats 90; bistro; bar
Owner Lion Nathan
Chef Darryl Hand
Cards AE BC DC MC V Eftpos
Prices entrees $14-$18; mains $22-$29; desserts $11.50-$13.50; less in bistro
Map page 264 **Melway** 2J B6

THE London's upstairs restaurant is an intimate room with a scattering of nicely spaced tables and a terrific view across the bay. It's spectacular at night when the Tasmanian ferry is docked, lights ablaze. While the bistro downstairs caters to the pub-lunchers and cappuccino-rollerbladers, upstairs is far more ambitious. A menu weighted towards seafood bristles with challenging offerings: 'Veal chaud-froid, celeriac remoulade, black truffle and Gippsland blue cheese emulsion' or 'Confit of salmon with ventrèche ham, softened garlic, crumbed oysters, sauteed spinach and a pinot noir jus'. Crabmeat rillettes, swathed in salmon, are moulded into a sphere; risotto sits in a moat of green velouté like a creamy island; a witty reinvention of the mixed grill sees vertical cylinders of duck sausage teamed with delicate slices of lamb, a chunk of poached ham and a tiny quail egg. The disparate elements don't always work so well together in the mouth. Still, it's an entertaining way to eat. The service staff are diligent and there's an expansive wine list, though you won't find much for under $50.

13/20

Luxe

MODERN EUROPEAN

15 Inkerman Street,
St Kilda **9534 0255**

Licensed
Open Fri & Sun noon-3pm; daily 6-10.30pm
Seats 85; outdoor seating; private room; bar
Owner Zeth Romanis
Chef Leigh Dundas
Cards AE BC DC MC V Eftpos
Prices entrees $8-$16.50; mains $16.50-$29.50; desserts $9-$13
Map page 261 **Melway** 2P D7

SUBTLE refinements to Luxe's moody interior – paintings, stylish fabric light shades, interesting paint finishes – have softened its hard edges. It's evolution, not revolution, but the result is a space that once again captures the zeitgeist, the way the original incarnation did back in 1997. Former Langton's sous chef Leigh Dundas now runs the kitchen. His pared-back menu displays predominantly European inspiration and classical training, with an emphasis on good ingredients. Dishes such as raviolo of confit ocean trout on a cauliflower puree, with a red wine and anchovy sauce; sublime potato gnocchi pan-fried with prosciutto and parmesan; or a signature dish of pot-roasted pork chop with potato puree, braised lettuce and a sauce diable demonstrate Dundas' enthusiasm and maturity. Dessert might be a perfectly roasted peach, halved and served one cheek up, the other down, with sticky vanillin roasting syrup and pistachio and amaretto icecream. Luxe takes its wine seriously, without being too precious. There's a dynamic global-roaming list chosen with Dundas' food in mind.

15/20

Lynch's

INTERNATIONAL

133 Domain Road,
South Yarra **9866 5627**

Licensed
Open Mon-Fri noon-2.30pm; Mon-Sat 6.30-10.30pm
Seats 90; private rooms; bar
Owner Paul Lynch
Chef Frederic Naud
Cards AE BC DC MC V
Prices entrees $14-$28; mains $31-$39; desserts $14-$17.50; lunch set menu $27.75 (2 courses)
Map page 264 **Melway** 2L C2

FEW places carry the imprimatur of the owner as strongly as this velvet and brocade salon in South Yarra. Pictures of the irrepressible Paul Lynch share wall space with naughty artwork, and the baby-banning mobile phone-phobe often cruises the floor sharing a tipple with his regulars or talking loudly on his own phone. Hypocrite? Moi? All this creates the atmosphere of a Belle Epoch bordello with Lynch presiding as the madam – and we mean that in the nicest possible way. Dining here does not come cheap. Especially if you choose the ferociously expensive steaks, well-executed duckling with caramelised red cabbage, or really retro prawns in a creamy Pernod and cheese sauce. Go for lunch, or choose judiciously – maybe the chilli-salt calamari and the house favourite, corned beef – and you won't need to mortgage the Portsea weekender. Lynch's feels like it's frozen in a time when dinner at a restaurant was a Big Night Out, but Melbourne would be a poorer place without characters like Paul Lynch. While you may never be asked to join the Melbourne Club, getting a table here is as easy as a phone call.

14/20

Madam Fang

MODERN ASIAN

27-29 Crossley Street,
City **9663 3199**

Licensed
Open Mon-Fri noon-3.30pm; Mon-Sat 6-10.30pm
Seats 50
Owners Beh Kim Un & Kin Chen
Chef Beh Kim Un
Cards AE BC DC MC V
Prices entrees $11.50-$19.50; mains $21.50-$31.50; desserts $10.50-$12.50; set menu $69 (7 courses)
Map page 260 **Melway** 1B T5

A VISIT to Madam Fang is like a short trip to French-colonial Asia. The chop-socky name mirrors the decadent set-up: a salon-like interior with dusky pink walls, soft spot lighting, Asian artefacts and incense (although the looped New Age soundtrack can be distracting). Many dishes, such as tender noisettes of beef wrapped in pandan leaves and pan-seared with sweet teriyaki, are available as both entrees and mains. Can't decide? Try the entree sampler, featuring an oyster, beef noisette, rice-battered tempura avocado roll with sesame coriander sauce, and mushroom agnolotti warmed with Thai basil garlic oil. But it would be a shame to miss the zesty grilled oysters served in individual spoons with chilli, lime and lemongrass. The delightful East-West frisson continues with mains such as charred king prawns and wild rocket with a tapenade of black bean, ginger and peppercorns, and a laksa-style seafood bouillabaisse. The wine list is long and well chosen, with selections that won't break the bank. Desserts are deluxe and European, like the tian of Callebaut chocolate cake with mandarin mascarpone.

14/20 V

THE LONDON

Embrace Melbourne's affinity with the water. No matter what the season, The London offers breathtaking panoramic views all year round. Overlooking the bay and the bustling activity on the foreshore, this fashionable Port Melbourne restaurant provides a spectacular backdrop for everything from a romantic dinner for two, to the largest of social events. The decor of crisp white linen, polished jarrah floors, luxurious leather lounges and open fire, are simply a prelude of what's to come.

Chefs Darryl Hand and Matthew Jefferies have created a seasonally inspired, innovative Modern Australian. Attention to detail is evident in all dishes. The extensive wine list focuses on Victoria's premier regions and you will always find a few little gems hidden on the rack from some of the lesser known local and overseas wineries. Particular attention has been paid to establishing a cellar of great "food &wines" and the knowledgeable waiting staff are delighted to offer their expertise in finding the perfect complement to your meal.

The London
92-94 Beach Street
Port Melbourne 3207
p: 9646 4644 f: 9646 4631
e: london@hmc.net.au
w: www.thelondon.com.au

The PROVINCIAL

The Provincial
299 Brunswick Street Fitzroy 3065
P: 9417 2228 F: 9486 9205 www.provincialhotel.com.au

Overlooking the corner of Brunswick and Johnston Streets you'll find The Provincial. Winner of the AHA best casual dining award (state & national). Our cafe cuisine combines both classic and modern French and Italian dishes. Gorgeous wood fired pizzas, over baked Atlantic salmon with pink peppercorns, or confit duck legs with roasted kiplfler potatoes are just the beginning. Dine under our vine covered courtyard, or snuggle up on a chesterfield in front of the fireplace and take in the delights of bohemian Brunswick Street. Offering ambience and character found in the streets of Europe, The Provincial is one of those places that has something for everyone.

Yarra Burn
PINOT NOIR

Manju

MODERN JAPANESE

135 Maling Road,
Canterbury **9836 3236**

BYO
Corkage $2 a head
Open Mon-Fri noon-2.30pm; Mon-Sat 6-10pm
Seats 45
Owner & chef Ikuei Arakane
Cards AE BC MC V
Prices entrees $12.50-$18.50; mains $25.50-$35.50; desserts $10-$12; lunch set menu $21.50 or $26.50 (2 or 3 courses)
Map page 266 **Melway** 46 D11

A BUTTERFLY flapping its wings in Japan is making waves in suburban Canterbury. Chef Ikuei Arakane plays oh-so-gently with chaos theory, tweaking traditional Japanese dishes with European influences, and the effect can be little short of spectacular. The surroundings, by contrast, are blandly beige – a cunning ploy to focus attention on the food? You might start with prawn gyoza, four plump dumplings filled with minced and whole prawns, steamed with greens and Japanese pickles. A nori-style salmon and green tea roll in light-as-a-feather tempura batter looks as good as it tastes in its earthenware bowl, while a noisette of the tenderest grilled eye fillet with a viscous fruit-soy sauce, served with a potato croquette and sukiyaki beef, is weirdly reminiscent of the traditional English roast. Other dishes draw together ingredients such as red miso and blueberries, or smoked salmon and mango, but there's traditional sushi and first-rate sashimi. The dessert experiments are less successful: a delicate green tea soufflé cake is overwhelmed by crunchy wasabi icecream. Quaffers remember to take a bottle – this part of Canterbury is still dry.

14/20

Man Mo

CHINESE/MALAYSIAN

42 New Quay Promenade,
Docklands **9642 1997**

Licensed
Open Mon-Sat noon-3.30pm; Sun noon-late; Mon-Sat 5.30pm-late
Seats 120; outdoor seating
Owners Eric Duong & Louis Yap
Chef Louis Yap
Cards AE BC DC MC V Eftpos
Prices yum cha dishes $4.50; entrees $6-$24.50; mains $13-$28; desserts $7-$12
Map page 264 **Melway** 2E E4

MAN MO is named after a celebrated Hong Kong temple dedicated to the worship of two divinities: Man Cheung, the god of literature, and Kwan Yu, the god of war. But never fear: the menu isn't a literary challenge and the only battles you'll face are with the stiff sea breeze buffeting the promenade tables. Stereotypical Chinese and Malaysian dishes take up a fair proportion of the menu, but if you're prepared to forgo garlic prawns and lemon chicken, there are some more interesting offerings among the four pages of chef's suggestions. Try excellent deep-fried king prawns cocooned in crisp shreds of taro, or delicate stuffed garfish rolls smothered with silky mushrooms. The Singapore-style chilli sauce that dresses the barramundi and the mud crab is exceptionally fragrant. Shandong fried duck is also good, the juicy crisp-skinned fillets poached, then deep-fried and blanketed in sweet Chinese vinegar and garlic sauce with a lick of chilli. Service staff are still finding their feet – diners sometimes get the sense that they have become invisible. This sleek space also hosts yum cha at weekends.

13/20

Mao's

263 Brunswick Street,
Fitzroy **9419 1919**

Licensed & BYO wine
Corkage $3 a bottle
Open Tues-Sun 6-10.30pm
Seats 45
Owner Cindy Wu
Chef Jimmy Chiu
Cards AE BC DC MC V
Prices entrees $4.20-$7.50; mains $15.50-$24; desserts $5.50; duck banquet $40 (6 courses)
Map page 263 **Melway** 2C B7

CHINA'S Hunan province has at least two claims to fame: it's where Chairman Mao took his first steps, and it boasts some wonderful regional specialities. There are no gelatinous sauces at this funky little place on Brunswick Street, popular enough most nights that drop-ins might have to wait in line like good little communists. Hunan cuisine is generally hot and spicy, loaded with garlic, chilli, spring onions and honey. Meats are often smoked and quick-fried: wok-centric mains include the decadently rich double-smoked pork with vegetables, and a gratifying number of juicy prawns are tossed with blackened chilli and cashew nuts. Mao's chicken and sweetcorn soup will cure whatever ails you. Vegetarian offerings, such as a garlicky steamed eggplant with Chinese aged vinegar, are excellent, and dishes are large enough to share, as is only correct and proper. The six-course Luv a Duck banquet is a bargain. The comfortable interior, created by architects Six Degrees, looks like a designer take on the Mao family home. Add some Communist Party iconography, including a portrait of a smiling Mao, and it's the last word in great local Chinese.

13/20 $ V

Masani

313 Drummond Street,
Carlton **9347 5610**

Licensed & BYO wine
Corkage $7.50 a bottle
Open Mon-Sat noon-2.30pm, 6-11.30pm
Seats 80; private room; bar
Owners Richard & Luciana Maisano
Chefs Richard Maisano & Lennox Bull
Cards AE BC DC MC V
Prices entrees $12.50-$28.50; mains $22.50-$38; desserts $10.50-$16.90
Map page 262 **Melway** 2B G7

AROUND the corner from the spruiker-filled footpaths of Lygon Street, the Maisano family has been quietly building the Masani legend over the past 20 years. The big boomtown terrace was once the clubrooms of the original Carlton Club, but now houses a big, airy space, with all the expected trappings of a slightly upscale Italian restaurant – white napery, dark timber accents, rustic decorative touches. The imposing bar is a good spot for an aperitif or a chance to preview an elegant but expensive wine list featuring Grange and Hill of Grace antiquities. At the table you'll find comfort food in true northern Italian style, miles ahead of some of the hastily prepared offerings in nearby places. Try the huge serve of tender ossobuco with zingy gremolata, or, if you are lucky, a special of goat casserole served with sweet-sour savoy cabbage. Recent visits have been let down by inexperienced service and less-than-refined dishes – home-made duck ravioli with heavy pasta, or timid mushroom risotto. But the tiramisu, made from a generations-old recipe, will make you weak at the knees.

13/20

Mask of China

115-117 Little Bourke Street,
City **9662 2116**

CHINESE

Licensed
Open Sun-Fri noon-3pm; daily 6-11pm
Seats 90; private rooms
Owner Alfred Chan
Chef Yeung Pui Ming
Cards AE BC DC MC V
Prices entrees $7.80-$13.80; mains $16.80-$49.80; desserts $5.90-$8.80
Map page 260 **Melway** 1B S4

THE emblem of this restaurant, a black-and-white Chinese opera mask, has been watching over Little Bourke Street for about 16 years, but age has not wearied owner Alfred Chan and his kitchen team, headed by Yeung Pui Ming. A bank of aquariums lines the entry, telegraphing the house speciality. Three dining zones allow for discreetly spaced tables and the knowledgeable staff will help you get the most from the menu. The impressive wine list is well matched to the food, mainly Chiu Chow dishes from Guangdong province, in China's south. The food is deceptively simple: minced seafood dumplings in egg-white wrappers have clean, subtle flavours; minced pork with green beans in black olive paste is joyfully pungent, perfect with traditional soupy congee or rice. The soy duck in master stock with bean-curd puffs is herbal and aromatic. The steamed fish is so fresh, you only nudge it with your chopsticks and the flesh falls from the bone. Also recommended are the Chinjew-sauced venison or squab, and other Chiu Chow favourites. Whether ruggedly simple or impressively grandiose, there's something to please everyone here.

16/20 V

@ A GLANCE

Eating places that are fun for all the family

KID-FRIENDLY

Cecconi's
Ground level, Crown Entertainment Complex, Southbank, 9686 8648
Cecconi's twice-yearly family days are wildly popular but the Bortolottos welcome kids any time. Helpful waiters will find something hearty for junior to eat.

Donovans
40 Jacka Boulevard, St Kilda, 9534 8221
Gail and Kevin Donovan's super-welcoming attitude extends to the kids, who are treated to their own 'cubby house menu'.

Livebait
55b New Quay Promenade, Docklands, 9642 1500
A casual, light-filled space with great views and a relaxed approach. This attitude extends to the kids' menu, which includes excellent home-made fish fingers.

Mezuna Pantry
36 Bluff Road, Black Rock, 9589 2200
With breakfast and lunch menus for both children and adults, a cheerful attitude and reasonable prices, why wouldn't you bring your offspring?

Num Fong
271 Swanston Street, City, 9663 1477
Behind the venetian blinds, you'll find youngsters tucking into Cantonese classics, and finishing with banana fritters, just as they have for the past 20 years.

Retro Cafe
413 Brunswick Street, Fitzroy, 9419 9103
The kids' menu runs from Coco Pops to noodles, but when that's not enough they can get busy with the toy box and crayons.

Matsuya

JAPANESE

146 Station Street,
Fairfield **9482 6088**

Licensed & BYO wine
Corkage $1.50 a head
Open Mon-Sat 11.30am-3pm; Mon-Thurs 5-10.30pm; Fri-Sat 5-11pm; Sun 5-10.30pm
Seats 64
Owner & chef Peter Chan
Cards AE BC DC MC V
Prices entrees $6.50-$9; sushi & sashimi $5-$13; mains $10.50-$19.50; noodles & rice $9-$13.50; desserts $3.50-$5
Map page 266 **Melway** 30 K10

ENTER Matsuya and your eye will inevitably be drawn to the row of Japanese beckoning cats (believed to bring wealth and success) sitting above the sushi bar. The cats' magic must work – the pale-yellow room is cheery and warm, and by 7.30pm, most of the pine tables are filled with families and too-tired-to-cooks poring over the eager-to-please menu. It's hard to imagine anyone being disappointed with the rollcall of Japanese favourites, from sushi to hotpots, and bento boxes to noodle dishes. 'House special sushi and sashimi' comes in wooden boats for two to share. Unusual sushi offerings include bitey seaweed rolls of chillied squid or mussels. Sashimi is glisteningly fresh and eggplant with miso is sweetish, salty and silky. Wafu steak offers good chewy flavour; tempura and katsudon get the thumbs-up from the kids. Heads turn and follow the vapour trails from cook-at-your-table shabu-shabu and sukiyaki beef dishes and bubbling yosenabe (chicken and seafood soup). The food is satisfying, servings are generous, and service is efficient. For sheer value and honesty, Matsuya is hard to beat in these parts.

13/20 $

Matteo's

MODERN EUROPEAN

533 Brunswick Street,
Fitzroy North **9481 1177**

Licensed & BYO wine
Corkage $12 a bottle
Open Sun-Fri noon-3pm; daily 6-10pm
Seats 150; outdoor seating; private rooms
Owners Matteo & Franca Pignatelli
Chef Frederic Quemin
Cards AE BC DC MC V
Prices entrees $16; mains $28; desserts $13; degustation menu $70 (5 courses)
Map page 263 **Melway** 2C B3

SOME restaurateurs know how to craft an enjoyable experience, one that begins with 'can I take your coat?' and ends with 'thank you and goodnight'. Matteo Pignatelli is one of them. Spry and engaging, he's a regular presence in the dining room and works hard behind the scenes to fine-tune his staff. But a good restaurant needs to serve more than bonhomie. Matteo's new chef, Frederic Quemin, cooks food that continues the modern European trajectory. Quemin's menus bring bold flavours together in intelligent dishes like boned saddle of lamb stuffed with braised kid on creamy polenta. Game usually features, perhaps an entree of venison carpaccio with fromage blanc and pomegranate syrup, or a rousing meat plate with grilled venison, squab breast and hare pithiviers. Pastry chef John Comiskey makes a bellissimo panna cotta, served, perhaps, with honeyed pears and chocolate sauce. The terracotta and timber dining room shows its age, but is still warm and welcoming. Excellent degustation menus (including a vegetarian feast) and shared platters are also on hand at this accommodating and entirely agreeable restaurant.

16/20 V

mecca

Mid-level Southgate,
Southbank **9682 2999**

Licensed
Open daily noon-3pm, 6pm-late
Seats 70; outdoor seating; private room; bar
Owners Damian Trytell, Julian Lee & Cath Claringbold
Chef Cath Claringbold
Cards AE BC DC MC V
Prices entrees $15-$20; mains $25.50-$30; desserts $12-$14
Map page 264 **Melway** 1D T3

IT'S very Melbourne, the trend to modern Middle Eastern cuisine, and mecca is one of its leading exponents. In spacious, upmarket surrounds, high-profile chef and co-owner Cath Claringbold keeps the emphasis firmly on the modern, with refined, handsome food. Her enticing menu – ideally perused at a table on the wraparound balcony – promises Moroccan, Tunisian, Egyptian and Lebanese flavours. Must-haves are the chicken bastilla, a traditional filo pie rich with sweet spices; and the mezze platter, distinguished by the quality and variety of its components – hummus, tabbouleh, falafel, ladies' fingers. Other dishes are more subdued, falling into the 'Middle Eastern lite' category: a harissa-spiced barramundi with preserved lemon and okra salad had no discernible taste of the hot-blooded paste. Service is friendly but can be unfocused. There's a sense that the team's attention has strayed since baby sister, Mecca Bah (see below), opened in late 2002. Desserts, however, continue to display the Claringbold Midas touch, with things like Middle Eastern nougat parfait striking a good balance between the familiar and the exotic.

15/20

Mecca Bah

MODERN MIDDLE EASTERN

55a New Quay Promenade,
Docklands **9642 1300**

Licensed
Open daily 11am-11pm
Seats 96; outdoor seating; bar
Owners Damian Trytell, Julian Lee & Cath Claringbold
Chef Nicky Riemer
Cards AE BC DC MC V Eftpos
Prices mezze $6-$10; mains $15-$19; desserts $6.50-$9.50
Map page 264 **Melway** 2E E4

CHERMOULA. Mujaddarah. Bastourma. The language and tastes of the Middle East, encountered at upmarket establishments like O'Connell's and Mo Mo, are now beamed to a wider audience at the easygoing, no-bookings sibling to Southgate's mecca (see above). Lounge on Mecca Bah's cushion-strewn banquettes (better than the bum-numbing chairs) for homely, well-priced food ideal for sharing. There's no way two people can do justice to the mouthwatering mezze list: you might wolf down juicy olive-studded Tunisian carrot salad; cheese-filled kataifi pastries; and sweet potato falafels with a creamy tahini sauce – but there are still 15 to try. And that doesn't take into account the spicy Moroccan tagines, the grills – perhaps vine-leaf-wrapped flathead fillets on a terrific parsley and artichoke salad, or boat-shaped Turkish pizzas. Desserts make good shareable fodder, too: the halva icecream and walnut maamoul (crumbly, floral-scented biscuits) are worth your attention. On still days, head for the deck with its harbour views, iron and timber tables and overhead heaters for chilly evenings.

14/20 $ V

Melbourne Wine Room

MODERN ITALIAN

125 Fitzroy Street,
St Kilda **9525 5599**

Licensed
Open Wed-Sat 6-11pm; bar Mon-Thurs 3-11pm; Fri-Sun noon-11pm
Seats 60; outdoor seating; bar
Owners Maurice Terzini, Marino Angelini, Michael Sapountsis & Karen Martini
Chef Andrew Kubale
Cards AE BC DC MC V
Prices entrees $10.50-$14.50; mains $16.50-$34; desserts $8.50-$12.50
Map page 261 **Melway** 2P A4

THE Wine Room is part of the fabric of modern St Kilda. In years past this studied, spartan dining room has been the home of clever modern Italian cooking, a fascinating wine list and excellent service led by co-owner Michael Sapountsis (winner of *The Age* Award for Service Excellence). But, with the move to Sydney of partner-chef Karen Martini, changes have been made. Sights have been lowered and ambitions reined in, meaning the style is now more 'clever rustic' than innovative and less refined than it once was. Among the better dishes are squid in a rich tomato ragu served with a crunchy risotto cake, veal with tomatoey cannellini beans and an excellent balsamic strawberry salad with sheep's yoghurt parfait. And there is still the famous (and pricey) rib-eye. But some dishes – like dull fish croquettes – are a little too cafe-style for the Wine Room's heritage, proving once again that Martini's move is Melbourne's loss. In the main, prices are in line with industry medians, making the Wine Room something of a bargain, given that service remains a long suit and the wine list a joy.

15/20

Meli Melo

MODERN ITALIAN

107 Acland Street,
St Kilda **9593 8855**

Licensed
Open daily noon-late
Seats 48; private room
Owners George Redwan & Chris Goulding
Chef Chris Goulding
Cards AE BC DC MC V
Prices entrees $9-$14; mains $14.50-$26; desserts $8-$9.50
Map page 261 **Melway** 2P B9

HERE'S a story so familiar, yet so appealing. Two guys with loads of experience – one a chef, the other a manager in the same company (Italy 1) – pool their resources to do it for themselves. This time it's Meli Melo, in the heart of Acland Street. With its generic timber and bancuette interior, it could be just another passion-free crowd-pleaser. Think again. Chris Goulding's cooking, Italian with French flourishes, has real integrity. He takes the presentation of his dishes beyond mere assembly, but never close to fussiness. The prosciutto-wrapped eye fillet, served with a mushroom panna cotta, and the quail saltimbocca with a balsamic-apple puree, are destined for signature status. The desserts show considerable flair. The creamy 'passionfruit-scented agnolotti' float in a passionfruit and mint consommé with a scoop of tart limoncello gelati. Meli Melo is well run, with a good selection of wines that come in at fair – rather than bargain – prices. There's no doubt the fundamentals are in place to make Meli Melo a long-term St Kilda proposition. Two talented owners – on the ground and trying – should ensure that.

14/20

Mercer's Restaurant

732 Main Road,
Eltham **9431 1015**

Licensed
Open Thurs-Fri & Sun noon-3pm; Wed-Sun 6.30-9.30pm
Seats 60
Owners Stephen & Ute Mercer
Chef Stephen Mercer
Cards AE BC DC MC V
Prices entrees $13.50-$17; mains $23-$29.50; desserts $13-$16; set menu $68 (7 courses)
Map page 267 **Melway** 21 J7

YOU'RE in caring hands when hosts Stephen and Ute Mercer welcome you to their flower-rimmed Federation-style cottage on the urban fringe. In this part of the world you might expect country comfort. But challenging modern dishes are Mercer's mainstay, with a few non-threatening dishes added for good measure. An amuse-gueule, maybe a tiny tomato cappuccino, flags the restaurant's haute ambitions. There's no let-up with dishes like honey-soy spiced quail on an Asian eggplant salad with shiitake mushrooms and a zesty yoghurt sauce; smoked salmon rolled with rice noodles and crabmeat; and sumac-spiced free-range chicken with orange risotto cake. The dishes are not all equally successful. The scotch fillet with sugar-cured beef tortellini is not as 'country tender' as the menu promises, and the confit duck leg's apricot and prune stuffing seems cloying. But most experiments come off: the Salzburger nockerln coconut soufflé with curried peaches still manages to shock and please in equal measure. The wide-reaching wine list is great value, studded with fine vintages from Victoria and further afield. Worth the detour.

15/20

Middle Brighton Baths

251 The Esplanade,
Brighton **9539 7000**

Licensed
Open Mon-Sat noon-3pm, 6pm-late; Sun 8am-3pm; cafe daily 7am-1am
Seats 120; outdoor seating; bar
Owner Jonathan Dixon
Chef Paul Raynor
Cards AE BC DC MC V Eftpos
Prices entrees $13.50-$18.50; mains $28-$34; desserts $11.50-$14.50
Map page 266 **Melway** 67 C10

BRIGHTON has been crying out for a restaurant to measure up to its bayside location. Now it has one. This smart dining room looked the goods when it opened in early 2002, but patchy food and service let the setting down. Now the restaurant's cool grey, green and buff tones, and its views over the old sea baths and across the bay, are matched by crisp, efficient work from the staff and consistently good food from chef Paul Raynor. His Euro-inspired creations are both innovative and uncompromising: the soufflé 'épices' taste like a fleeting memory of spiced bread while the white chocolate crème brûlée veined with macerated cherries is so rich, it's almost brutal. Delicate and punchy flavours are deftly matched, as in spice-rubbed calamari with a vermilion harissa spark, and a dish of fat little scallops sandwiched with chorizo. Main courses are complex without being too fussy: you might find veal accompanied by gently wilted leeks, onion jam dolloped in a pie crust and morel gravy. This isn't a particularly blokey restaurant, but there is one special treat for men. You'll need to visit the loos to discover just what it is.

15/20

Milan Tandoori Indian Restaurant

INDIAN

44 Cotham Road,
Kew **9853 5379**

BYO
Corkage none
Open Wed-Mon 6-11pm
Seats 45
Owners & chefs Sadhana & Satya Prakash
Cards AE BC DC MC V Eftpos
Prices entrees $3.50-$9.50; mains $9.50-$22.50; desserts $3.50-$6; set menu $35 (3 courses)
Map page 265 **Melway** 45 C6

MILAN nonchalantly dishes up classy mainstream Indian fare to a loyal contingent of wine-wielding locals. The floor-to-ceiling glass shopfront frames a small, sparsely decorated dining-room. The interior is not without charm, although the electric-blue paint job and lurid fan-shaped uplights might be best admired wearing sunglasses. Complimentary cumin-seed pappadams get all meals off to a great start. But if you can desist until mains arrive, you can enjoy these delicious wafers as Indians do, sprinkled over curries for texture. The obligatory entree is raan-e-alishaan, five tender lamb roundels marinated in a delicate, rum-infused masala and presented on a large, white plate garnished with lettuce and tomato. After this, some of the mains can appear a little pedestrian – butter chicken, kormas, vindaloos – but are all above-average renditions of the classics. The well-balanced saagwala curries (chicken or lamb pieces in a deep green spinach sauce) go especially well with a dry dish such as crunchy string beans tossed in a tart, grainy mustard. The usual dessert roster of kulfi and golden gulab jamun winds up the feast.

14/20 V

Misuzu's

MODERN JAPANESE

3-7 Victoria Avenue,
Albert Park **9699 9022**

Licensed
Open daily noon-3pm, 5.30-10pm; sushi bar daily noon-10.30pm; sake bar daily 5.30-10.30pm
Seats 75; outdoor seating; private room; bar
Owners Warwick Lobb & Misuzu Kawano
Chef Misuzu Kawano
Cards AE BC MC V Eftpos
Prices entrees $6.80-$11.80; mains $10.80-$17.20; desserts $5.80-$7.50
Map page 264 **Melway** 2J K7

OVER eight years, this little corner of Japan has mushroomed into a buzzy little complex, comprising two floors, three shopfronts and a pavement space lit at night with traditional red lanterns. Most devotees dine on the simple village-style fare of the original restaurant – good gyoza, tempura, noodles and hearty chicken, pork and tuna 'sets' – while the more adventurous head next door to the newer Umami (sake bar), where there's a choice of 32 rice wines and a selection of refined, delicate tastes. Pull up a hand-crafted stool at the free-form wooden bar to nibble fabulous pre-prepared entrees like sashimi, slow-cooked salmon or seared tuna with a sake or two. Also good are the tender-crisp octopus balls, paper-thin slices of scotch fillet in teppanyaki sauce and tender slivers of teriyaki duck breast, all beautifully presented on handmade crockery. There's a dedicated vegetarian menu, and the helpful waiters are happy to offer guidance. There's no problem hopping from room to room: you might have sake and sushi in the bar, then move next door for wok-fried calamari and sukiyaki beef.

13/20 $ V

Mizu

JAPANESE

133 Commercial Road,
South Yarra **9827 1144**

Licensed & BYO wine (Sun only)
Open Tues-Sun 6.30pm-late
Seats 50; outdoor seating
Owners Kiyoko Fukumura, Koji Takahashi & Michael Mills
Chef Koji Takahashi
Cards AE BC DC MC V Eftpos
Prices entrees $3-$13.50; mains $13-$26; desserts $6-$8
Map page 265 **Melway** 2L G9

THIS South Yarra spot is where black-clad young things zoom in for takeaway, couples stop to slurp bowls of udon, and early in the evening, kids munch excellent tempura seafood and vegetables with their parents. The split-level contemporary dining room has something to please most, with intimate, moodily lit tables or an elegant rear courtyard complete with zen-inducing pool. The menu ranges from the drinks-friendly edamame (steamed soybeans) and deep-fried golden octopus balls, ready to be plunged into tonkastu sauce and mayo, to modern Japanese creations such as the satisfyingly salty mentaiko spaghetti, salted and chilli-spiked cod roe tossed in butter with al dente spaghetti. The satiny sashimi is fresh and well cut, and sushi rolls have generous fillings. Indecisive diners opt for an entree bento box, featuring morsels such as deep-fried calamari, crab croquettes and steamed plump dumplings. Teriyaki comes as beef, chicken and seafood options and donburi and noodle dishes round off the menu. The friendly staff make this a welcoming drop-in place.

13/20 $

Mo Mo

MODERN MIDDLE EASTERN
Best Middle Eastern

Basement, 115 Collins Street (enter from George Parade),
City **9650 0660**

Licensed
Open Mon-Fri noon-3pm; Mon-Sat 6-10.30pm
Seats 90; bar
Owners Geremy & Dean Lucas
Chef Greg Malouf
Cards AE BC DC MC V
Prices entrees $17.50-$21.50; mains $29.50-$35; desserts $16.50-$18.50; degustation menu $80 (5-6 courses)
Map page 260 **Melway** 1B R8

ONE taste of chef Greg Malouf's poached then fried duck, perched on a bed of the evocatively named 'jewelled Iranian rice', saffron-scented and studded with dried fruit, and you'll realise why he's the master. It's a triumph – the skin crisp, the meat succulent and the accompanying flavours and textures in perfect balance. You might come back to Mo Mo for this dish alone, but the master's talent also shines through the rest of the repertoire at this city basement restaurant. Roasted scampi with ras-el-hanout spices, silverbeet risotto and caramelised onions is similarly excellent. Even the names of dishes take you on a magic carpet ride: bastilla (Moroccan pigeon pie); mishmishiya (Syrian stuffed lamb kibbe); passionfruit mahalabia (milk custard). Unfortunately, the rest of the experience doesn't quite equal the food. Value sometimes seems questionable – an entree of three seared scallops with shavings of Turkish air-dried beef for $21.50? Gloomy lighting makes it difficult to see your food. Professional staff and a good by-the-glass wine list make up lost ground but Malouf's brilliance deserves a more dazzling stage.

15/20

Mongusto Mamma

ITALIAN

200 Camberwell Road,
Hawthorn East **9813 1099**

Licensed
Open Mon-Fri 8am-10.30pm; Sat-Sun 10.30am-10.30pm
Seats 60; outdoor seating
Owners Helen Higgins, Geremy & Dean Lucas
Chef Michael Hall
Cards AE BC DC MC V
Prices entrees $6.50-$16.50; pastas & risottos $14.50-$19.50; mains $21-$25.50; desserts $9.50; lunch set menu $20 (2 courses)
Map page 265 **Melway** 59 J1

MONGUSTO MAMMA is happily engaged in a symbiotic relationship with its co-tenant, the Rivoli cinema, and does a fine line in coffee and cake at all times of the day and night. Within well-defined parameters, it also provides reassuring Italian fare in faux-Roman surroundings to revive cineastes reeling from the latest excursion into social realism. Entrees are enticing. Try nutmeg and tea-smoked chicken tossed with a salad of rocket, asparagus, pine nuts and a honey-herb dressing, or comforting suppli (rice balls), crumbed and fried, oozing melted cheese and topped with a rich tomato sauce. Pastas and risottos take centre stage, with a to-die-for veal and pork bolognese, and pappardelle with pan-fried chicken livers, sage and pancetta among the main players. Big meaty mains include roasted lamb rump lifted with a zesty lemon and oregano marinade. The specials board – three listings including soup of the day – bumps out the options with things like ocean trout on spiced kipflers, with green olive, lemon and basil tapenade. Staff are attuned to moviegoers' timelines and won't dawdle with the lattes and the tiramisu.

13/20

Moretons Brasserie

MODERN FRENCH

166 Rathdowne Street,
Carlton **9349 4422**

Licensed & BYO wine
Corkage $4.50 a bottle
Open daily 6pm-late
Seats 35; private rooms
Owners & chefs Jenny Walsh & Chris Rees
Cards AE BC MC V Eftpos
Prices entrees $9-$12; mains $19-$23; desserts $9-$10
Map page 262 **Melway** 2B H5

ONCE you've squeezed into one of the chairs in this tiny shopfront, prepare yourself for a ride. This is a well-priced Australian take on the classic French family bistro. As both owners Jenny Walsh and Chris Rees are in the kitchen and aren't above critiquing each other's cooking, this can add a sitcom angle to a meal. The honest food deserves a starring role in its own right. Scrawled across the blackboard you'll find the usual French favourites like moules marinière, snails in garlic butter and thin porterhouse or fat eye fillet served with chips and a three-dimensional bearnaise or spirited green peppercorn sauce. Specials might include lamb rump on cauliflower puree or duck breast with poached pear. To start, there's usually pâté or a goats' cheese salad, but it's hard to go past the intensely flavoured warm salads topped with scallops or soy-marinated chicken livers. Desserts are the true triumph. They make a sensational summer pudding, the bread casing sodden with berry juices, and an excellent individual tarte tatin – caramelly apples under a puff pastry blanket. The apple and quince crumble and the apricot bread and butter pudding are also charming.

13/20

GRANDE ANNÉE
1990
BOLLINGER
CHAMPAGNE
VINTAGE ROSE
LOUIS ROEDERER
CHAMPAGNE
BRUT
REIMS
750 ml e
GRAND CRU
2000
1994
ROBERT MONDAVI
CABERNET
BLANC DE BLANCS

WINE LISTS

Label-conscious diners are spoilt for choice

Asiana
181 Victoria Avenue, Albert Park, 9696 6688
Asiana's list is the work of a true lover of fine wines, with an extraordinary selection of mouth-watering vintages. Alongside hard-to-find Australian wines are excellent representatives from Germany, Austria, Spain and the United States. 'Special pours of the week' challenge you to try something interesting by the glass. See page 17.

Charcoal Grill on the Hill
289 High Street, Kew, 9853 7535
This list is testament to Dejan Derbogosian's vinous love affair. On the densely packed pages you'll find a range of French burgundies the like of which you'd rarely see in France, along with plenty of iconic Italians and Australians. There's an esoteric selection by the glass, and prices aren't too scary, considering the quality. As they say in the *Guide Michelin*, worth a detour. See page 48.

Circa, the Prince
2 Acland Street, St Kilda, 9536 1122
An amazingly comprehensive round-up of the great wines of Australia and the world awaits diners at Circa. Obscure examples of the winemaker's art share space with great classics, and expert staff are on hand if it's all too hard. There are plenty of older vintages, a carefully chosen range by the glass and high-quality glassware – little wonder Circa has won the *Guide's* Best Wine List award for the second time. See page 55.

France-Soir
11 Toorak Road, South Yarra, 9866 8569
France-Soir is like a Paris bistro transplanted to South Yarra, with one notable exception: you'd never find a wine list like this on the Champs Elysee. France-Soir's list takes diners on a tour of France's vignobles. But just to show that the proprietor isn't completely one-eyed, there's a spectacular list of Australian wines, too. Prices are fair, but it's easy to be led astray by rare and impressive vintages. See page 68.

Langton's Restaurant & Wine Bar
61 Flinders Lane, City, 9663 0222
Winemakers make a point of calling into Langton's when they visit the big smoke, and a glance at the wine list reveals why. It's a truly expert selection, with wonderful wines from around the globe. A feature is their 'flight' of three different but complementary wines served together in 60ml tastes. See page 92.

Number 8 restaurant & wine bar
Crown Entertainment Complex, 8 Whiteman Street, Southbank, 9292 7899
If you want to sip 1928 Chateau Mouton-Rothschild and happen to have picked up $9020 on the roulette wheels, drop in. Among the encyclopedic selection of wines (they claim to have 888 examples) are flagship wines from home and abroad. Off-beat producers are thin on the ground, and mark-ups vary from reasonable to hefty, but there is a fair choice by the glass. See page 119.

Verge
1 Flinders Lane, City, 9639 9500
Verge's eclectic list defies convention. There's a wide range of pinot noirs, plenty of good Italians, a smattering of wines with some bottle age, obscure dessert wines, an interesting selection by the glass, and an overriding sense that the whole thing has grown out of personal enthusiasm. Prices are fair, too. See page 163.

Walter's Wine Bar
Upper level, Southgate, Southbank, 9690 9211
Walter's continues to boast one of Melbourne's best wine lists. There's something for even the most world-weary winelover, with fascinating wines by the glass, a degustation selection that lets you compare flights of three wines, and some of the rarest drops around. Informed service and good glassware complete the package. See page 166.

Mrs Jones

MODERN EUROPEAN

312 Drummond Street,
Carlton **9347 3312**

Licensed & BYO
Corkage $10 a bottle
Open Fri noon-3pm; Tues-Sat 6pm-late
Seats 50; private room; bar
Owners Pascale Gomes-McNabb & Andrew McConnell
Chefs Andrew McConnell & Brent Savage
Cards AE BC DC MC V
Prices fixed price menu $35 (2 courses)
Map page 262 **Melway** 2B G7

MRS JONES is an interesting response to the times: how to satisfy demand for more informal dining from an increasingly food-literate audience. The solution here is a tiny fixed-price menu aimed at adventurous eaters, in a simple space with excellent service and fairly priced wines or BYO. Andrew McConnell, chef and co-owner of Diningroom 211 (see page 58), conceived Mrs Jones as a more streetwise second label. He steers a menu that is different every day. The menu (two entrees, two mains, two desserts) is posted on the restaurant's web site each week. You can bank on a 'special' in each category plus vegetarian options. On Tuesday night, you might eat red mullet, braised pheasant dumplings in brodo, or a saffron-rich Spanish fish stew. The next night, it could be grilled mackerel with salsa verde, or a pot-au-feu with various delicious meaty offcuts and superb baguette. Or Jerusalem artichoke soup with crabmeat. The cooking is simple but professional, although desserts lack punch. With co-owner Pascale Gomes-McNabb's flair for interiors, the room is surprising, if a little stark. The quintessential quirky local bistro.

14/20 

Murasaki

JAPANESE

24 Russell Street,
City **9654 5437**

Licensed
Open Mon-Fri noon-2.30pm; Mon-Sat 6-10pm
Seats 80; private room
Owner Hisao Sato
Chef Hiro Hayashi
Cards AE BC DC MC V Eftpos
Prices entrees $4-$16.50; noodles $10-$15.50; mains $17.50-$31; desserts $3-$8
Map page 260 **Melway** 1B R9

THERE are many Japanese faces (tourists and locals) in the cavernous dining room of this city eatery, a sign that the food must scrub up OK. While parts of the menu seem designed for the tourists (there's crocodile at least two ways), the daily specials offer a few dishes seldom seen in Melbourne's Japanese restaurants, such as maguro yamakake, a wonderful combination of garnet-red tuna, shredded nori and pureed yam in a bowl. To eat, slosh in some soy sauce and stir (although the gluey consistency of the yam may be an acquired taste). The vast menu has something to please most people: impressive sushi and sashimi, a range of hot and cold entrees, teppanyaki, teriyaki and noodle dishes and table-cooked sukiyaki, yosenabe and shabu shabu. A seafood hotpot comes brimful with sea creatures in a simple sauce of sake, butter and soy. For sweets, try matcha shiratana – warm rice-flour dumplings flavoured with green tea and filled with red bean paste. There's a good selection of Japanese plum wines, sake and beer. The room is appealling with butter-coloured walls and diffused lighting; service is warm and helpful.

13/20

Mylyn

VIETNAMESE/CHINESE

1135 Burke Road,
Kew **9817 4488**

BYO
Corkage $1.50 a head
Open Thurs-Fri noon-2.30pm; Tues-Sat 5.30-10.30pm; Sun 5.30-10pm
Seats 55
Owners Joe & Mary Nguyen
Chef Mary Nguyen
Cards BC MC V Eftpos
Prices entrees $3.50-$8.50; mains $7.50-$17; desserts $4-$6
Map page 265 **Melway** 45 J9

THIS neighbourhood eatery on a heavily trafficked stretch of Burke Road is virtually hidden behind its glass-bricked frontage. It's pleasant enough and entirely unpretentious – fake flower beds, pink and purple hues, and an FM rock soundtrack (mercifully low in volume) are as far as the owners go to create an atmosphere. But the food – fine, uncomplicated fare – is what matters here. The menu is separated into Vietnamese and Chinese: you'll find lovely, fresh rice-paper rolls, pork with lemongrass and chilli, and salt-and-pepper chicken on the Vietnamese list; crab claws, ginger beef, and barbecued pork spare ribs feature on the Chinese carte. The daily specials tend to blur the national boundaries. Beef rolls in 'lalop' are the spicy, star-anise-infused house version of beef wrapped in betel leaves. Another signature dish is the simply named beef with potatoes, featuring thinly sliced potatoes fried into crisp chips, then added in the last seconds to a peppery beef casserole to soak up the wonderful meaty juices. Vietnamese greens stir-fried with garlic are the perfect crunchy accompaniment. Service is smiling and efficient.

13/20 $ V

The Near East

MODERN ASIAN

254 Park Street,
South Melbourne **9699 1900**

Licensed & BYO wine
Corkage $5 a bottle
Open Mon-Fri noon-3pm; daily 6-10.30pm
Seats 120
Owners John & Joanne Che
Chef Ken Wong
Cards AE BC DC MC V Eftpos
Prices entrees $9-$13.50; mains $18.50-$35; desserts $11
Map page 264 **Melway** 2K D3

THE NEAR EAST was one of Melbourne's first Asian restaurants hip to the value of stylish contemporary presentation. Its pan-Asian menu also broke the mould, covering Indonesian, Thai, and Malay classics as well as some hybrid dishes that exploit Australia's abiding love affair with ginger and lemongrass. Many have since adopted the formula – and that's probably one of the reasons the Near East seems less special these days – and some flavours are less intense than you'd expect. An attractive dish of trumpet mushrooms comes in a pockmarked clay pan dotted with a pork and prawn mince and coconut dressing, while the stuffed squid arrives as four golden puffs of battered squid tubes dressed in a super-sweet chilli sauce. The duck curry, which can be slightly fatty, comes with a brew of pineapple, pumpkin and kaffir lime in thick coconut gravy, while the Nonya seafood in a galangal and ginger flower ragout is not the quality you expect for the price. If the attention to detail shown to this South Melbourne shopfront's interior and presentation were echoed in the food, the Near East's star would be on the rise again.

13/20

Neill's on Central Park

MODERN AUSTRALIAN

134 Burke Road,
Malvern East **9886 0458**

Licensed
Open daily 8am-4pm, 6.30-10pm
Seats 70; outdoor seating; private room
Owners Melissa Neill & Tim Reardon
Chef Dinesh Peethamparam
Cards AE BC DC MC V Eftpos
Prices breakfasts $3.80-$15.50; entrees $10.50-$16.50; mains $22.50-$28.50; desserts $11.50-$14.50
Map page 265 **Melway** 59 G10

'A NICE restaurant for a nice suburb' is how some locals describe this impressive and popular bistro that delivers exactly what the well-to-do locals want. That's crisp, friendly service with good numbers on the floor and an equally crisp orange-splashed interior featuring bonsai trees, inspired by co-owner Melissa Neill's time in Japan. The food shows the same popular and populist edge, although some may find the flavours a little sanitised. Still, dishes like beef served with horseradish butter and beetroot mash or juicy quail on a white bean salad sparked with feta offer a decent feed. Other choices might include favourites like corned beef; char-grilled veal fillets marinated with oregano and garlic with roast Med veg and rocket pesto; Thai sweet potato soup with coriander pesto; or five-vegetable tagine. Prices suggest that locals are willing to pay for the suburban proximity. Seek out the good crème brûlée with white choc icecream or chocolate soufflé, rather than the stolid panna cotta. Breakfast is served daily, boosted at weekends by the full gamut of egg dishes, including the indulgent egg salmon, with sugar-cured fish and scrambled eggs.

13/20 

New Royal Garden

CHINESE

562-570 High Street Road (corner Blackburn Road),
Syndal **9886 1388**

Licensed & BYO wine
Corkage $1.50 a head
Open Mon-Fri 11.30am-3pm; Sat-Sun & public hols 11am-3pm; Sun-Thurs 5.30-10.30pm; Fri-Sat 5.30-11.30pm
Seats 220; private room
Owners Bang C. Hua & Johnny Cheung
Chef David Hung
Cards AE BC DC MC V
Prices yum cha dishes $3-$4.50; entrees $4-$12; mains $12.50-$22.50
Map page 266 **Melway** 61 J12

RESTAURANTS that offer 'one menu for the Chinese, another for others' are heading down a slippery slope these days. New Royal Garden is comfortable enough with its clientele not to try this tack. The egalitarian menu is clear, but it still pays to ask for recommendations. They've made their name catering to big crowds with good yum cha and fresh seafood, and the roasts from the front window, such as the mixed platter of juicy duck and suckling pork, are something of a house speciality. Many dishes are delicate and detailed. Fresh scallops are steamed in the shell with ginger, mushrooms and shallots. Golden rolls of light egg pancake are stuffed with roast duck slivers, finely chopped carrot, celery, cabbage and mushrooms, then refried. Another duck dish that tastes as good as it looks comprises pieces of bird stuffed with prawn meat and enclosed in the duck's crisp skin. Some sauteed een choy (Chinese spinach) helps ease the guilt and the digestion. For dessert, there are banana fritters and lychees, but fresh fruit is always a pleasant way to cleanse the palate at the end of a rich Chinese meal.

14/20 $

Nihonbashi Zen

87 Little Bourke Street,
City **9639 7050**

Licensed
Open Tues-Fri noon-2pm; Tues-Sun 6-11pm
Seats 38; private room
Owner & chef Hiro Yano
Cards AE BC MC V Eftpos
Prices kushiyaki $5.50-$12; kushiyaki sets $19.50-$24.50; sashimi platters $40-$52; noodles & rice $3.50-$10.50; hot & cold dishes $5-$28; desserts $3.50
Map page 260 **Melway** 1B S4

THIS small, subterranean bento box doesn't seem especially zen-like, but its authenticity and intelligent restraint make dining here such a pleasure. The restaurant specialises in kushiyaki, a cooking style from south-west Japan – basically yakitori for grown-ups, where food is skewered and grilled. Small dishes arrive in stately procession and are ideal for those who like lots of small tastes. Four kushiyaki sets are offered (chicken, meat, seafood or vegetarian), or you can mix and match from the à la carte list. Recommended are the skewered pinwheels of squid rolled in basil; the beef sirloin; sweet, meaty scallops; and okra rolled in salty bacon. A side salad of daikon, cucumber, tomato and nori in a wafu (soy-based) dressing adds a yin antidote to the yang food, and may well represent true zen when chased down with an Asahi beer. They do sashimi very well, often featuring unusual suspects such as velvety school prawns and sea urchin alongside the usual mackerel, perch, salmon and tuna. Onigiri (filled rice balls), noodle dishes, hotpots and daily specials round off the compact menu. A little jewel.

15/20

North Fitzroy Star

32 St Georges Road South,
Fitzroy North **9482 6484**

Licensed
Open daily noon-2.30pm, 6.30-9.30pm; Sat-Sun 10am-12.30pm
Seats Blue Room 30; outdoor seating; private room; bar
Owners Patricia O'Donnell & James Richards
Chef Adrian Watson
Cards AE BC DC MC V
Prices snacks $4-$9; meals $9-$21.50; desserts $9; Blue Room set menu $35 (2 courses, Tues-Sat); Sun lunch set menu $40 (4 courses)
Map page 263 **Melway** 2C A3

THE STAR dances a dangerous multi-purpose line: it's simultaneously a bar, a casual pub dining room and a more formal restaurant. Luckily, it comes up trumps on all fronts. Patricia O'Donnell (sister of Mietta) and James Richards gave the place a gypsy Six Degrees makeover about three years ago, creating rooms with individual character and appeal. There's a snacky all-day menu, and a menu for the cosy Orange and chintzy Garden rooms, mixing pub classics (spag bol, beef and mushroom pie, beer-battered flathead) with fancier dishes like superb beef sirloin on white truffle mash. The formal Blue Room has table service and set-price menus, and is the only area for which bookings are taken. Rice-studded chicken brodo might be the set entree, followed by a choice of sirloin with red wine sauce, gnocchi with mushrooms, peas and mascarpone, or roast salmon with red onion salsa. Italo-Melbourne cooking legend Silvana Palmira is in charge of the four-course Sunday lunch, market-driven meals that might include vitello tonnato and chicken breast stuffed with prosciutto, ricotta and olives.

14/20 

No. 3 Station Pier Mezzanine Restaurant

MODERN AUSTRALIAN

3 Station Pier, Beacon Cove,
Port Melbourne **9646 6299**

Licensed
Open Sun-Fri noon-3pm; daily 6-10.30pm; brasserie daily 8am-late
Seats 110; outdoor seating; bar
Owners Sam & Shadi Zenedin
Chef Dianne Kerry
Cards AE BC DC MC V Eftpos
Prices entrees $16-$22; mains $28-$33; desserts $14.50-$16; degustation menu $75 (6 courses)
Map page 264 **Melway** 57 A4

DOCKED at the foot of Station Pier, with Beacon Cove's apartment towers filed behind, this deluxe restaurant serves very fine food and wine. Chef Dianne Kerry cooked up a storm at Blakes, Lip and Red Orange; now her very Melbourne, very contemporary food has a showstopping setting to match. The dining room has well-spaced tables, long banquettes, chocolate and cream furnishings and serious tableware. You don't get a faceful of bay (the windows face the beach, not the sea), but views are more than decent. Service could improve – not all waiters are equally knowledgeable or adept. But the food waves away most quibbles. An intense spinach soup, heady with bay leaves and thyme, is garnished with labna and green harissa. Game dishes feature on the mains list, perhaps pheasant with ratatouille, grilled venison with pomegranate dressing or rabbit in a Basque-style stew of chorizo and peppers. There's always something clever for vegetarians, say, delicate fennel tart with elaborate stuffed vegetables, or polenta and white truffle cake with pine mushrooms. Downstairs, the airy, easygoing brasserie serves food and drink all day.

15/20

Nudel Bar

MODERN ASIAN/NOODLES

76 Bourke Street,
City **9662 9100**

Licensed
Open Mon 11am-10pm; Tues-Thurs 11am-10.30pm; Fri 11am-11.30pm; Sat noon-11pm; Sun 4-10pm
Seats 100; outdoor seating
Owners John Mackay, Dur-é Dara, Yorgos Tserexidis, Helen Saniga & Marijan Klym
Chef John Mackay
Cards AE BC DC MC V Eftpos
Prices entrees $7.80-$11.80; mains $14.90-$18.50; desserts $7.50
Map page 260 **Melway** 1B T5

THE eponymous Nudel Bar hardly overstates the case. Noodles in their four humours – cold, wokked, wet and in broth – are the cornerstone of the menu. Occupying a 1960s slot between the grand Victorian facades of Florentino's and Bottega, the Nudel Bar attracts salarymen, families (children welcome) and the supper crowd. Service is confident and friendly, and the mains are large and filling. Noodle dishes traverse Asia, reflecting Indian, Chinese and Japanese influences. Cold buckwheat noodles tossed with orange chilli oil, spinach, sesame paste and prawns hits the spot in summer, while the chicken broth noodles with pork, Chinese mushrooms and chives is truly restorative. Italian noodles include spaghetti aglio e olio and good old macaroni cheese. There's zesty Malaysian ikan bilis (spicy fish sambal on toast with pickled cucumber), peanutty gado gado or a selection of garden-variety salads. The ever-evolving wine list displays well-chosen drops by the glass. Desserts continue the Asian theme, with things like house-made icecream in vanilla, ginger and pandan, or 'silken threads', chilled soybean curd with ginger syrup.

12/20 $ V

Number 8 restaurant & wine bar

MODERN ITALIAN

Crown Entertainment Complex, 8 Whiteman Street, Southbank **9292 7899**

Licensed
Open daily noon-3pm, 6-11pm
Seats 140; outdoor seating; private room; bar
Owner Crown Ltd
Chef Joseph Vargetto
Cards AE BC DC MC V
Prices entrees $11.50-$17.50; mains $24.50-$31; desserts $9.50-$11.50
Map page 264 **Melway** 1D M3

WHO says restaurants run by major corporations have to be bland? Number 8 – part of the PBL/Crown behemoth – defies the cynics with a personal – and personable – approach, sealed with a pleasurable professionalism. But what about the food? Chef Joseph Vargetto, latterly at the Venetian, brings an Italian-Australian's heritage and classical training to the table, producing elegant, contemporary food that's a synthesis of those influences. Vargetto is flexible without being faddish. A wonderful quail and foie gras terrine sits beside a brilliant risotto of fresh shiitake mushrooms. A pea soup with a ricotta and mint tian shares the stage with a classic beef carpaccio crumbled with truffled parmigiano. A clever fish dish, like barramundi stuffed with mussels and finished with a vanilla dressing, can be matched by a golden-grilled spatchcock with apricot and rosemary juice. For the elegance offered, Number 8 is a steal. But the extremely impressive wine list is priced to discourage excessive consumption. A warm night on the terrace, with this food and service, justifies a few more dollars on your wine tab.

15/20

Oanh's Kitchen

VIETNAMESE
Best Vietnamese

916 Glenferrie Road,
Kew **9818 4366**

Licensed & BYO wine
Corkage $2.50 a head
Open Tues-Sun 6pm-late
Seats 30
Owners Oanh & Si Pham
Chef Oanh Pham
Cards AE BC DC MC V Eftpos
Prices entrees $7-$10; mains $11-$20; desserts $3-$5
Map page 265 **Melway** 45 E6

LOOKING for a contemporary take on Vietnamese dining? Then you'll love Oanh's. A narrow shop has been tricked up with polished floorboards, white paint and a long, low waiter's station. Chef Oanh Pham, who ran French restaurants in Ho Chi Minh City, offers food to match the mood. Dishes like her Peking duck-inspired tortillas – divine wraps of roasted duck, cucumber and spring onion daubed with hoisin sauce – step outside the usual Viet square. But for the most part, she presents stylish interpretations of the traditional dishes of her homeland. Most diners opt for the classy mixed entree, a platter bearing glass teacups of pho soup, spring rolls with a shot glass of nuoc cham (dipping sauce), chicken skewers served vertically, and duck wraps. Other favourites include tom ram, the prawns stir-fried with lemongrass in a caramelised sauce, then arranged on a raft of steamed green beans, and bo xao la lot, the sweetly tender pieces of beef stir-fried with fragrant betel leaves (la lot) and fermented soybeans. Front-of-house staff can be run off their feet and the wine list won't win any awards, but as the locals know, it's wise to book.

14/20 $

Ocha

MODERN JAPANESE

156 Pakington Street,
Kew **9853 6002**

Licensed & BYO wine
Corkage $2 a head
Open Mon-Fri noon-2.30pm; Mon-Sat 6-10.30pm
Seats 35
Owners & chefs Yasu Yoshida & Michelle Fong
Cards AE BC DC MC V
Prices entrees $8-$19; mains $11-$26; desserts $3.50-$9.50
Map page 266 **Melway** 45 D3

FIRST, catch your table – and that means booking many weeks in advance. This jewel box of a restaurant seats only 35, and chef Yasu Yoshida's food is very many people's cup of Ocha, so be organised. The dining room is small, and the cloth-covered tables close, but the combination of mood lighting, whimsical artwork and attentive staff ensures happy lingering. A printed menu, boosted by blackboard and daily specials, offers a decent selection of mainly seafood dishes, all served with careful precision. Mussel salad wears a silky miso dressing; tuna is braised in sweet soy and ginger; oysters are sauced in ponzu. Sushi and sashimi are finely wrought; the eel options terrific. Many dishes come in two sizes, so diners can sample many dishes, or go with entrees and mains. Don't pass up the teriyaki duck, with its balanced deep flavours and glossy sauce. Noodle-lovers will enjoy the nabeyaki udon, a flavoursome broth with tempura prawn, shiitake mushrooms and egg (break the yolk so that it runs and thickens the hot broth). And if by chance you have room after all that, there's plum wine and sake jelly for afters.

15/20 V

O'Connell's

MODERN AUSTRALIAN

407 Coventry Street,
South Melbourne **9699 9600**

Licensed
Open daily noon-3pm; Sun-Thurs 6-9.30pm; Fri-Sat 6-10pm
Seats 100; outdoor seating; private rooms; bar
Owner Lockhurst Pty Ltd
Chef Cath Kalka
Cards AE BC DC MC V
Prices entrees $9-$16.50; mains $14.50-$28; desserts $8.50-$9.50; set menus $38-$65 (2-3 courses)
Map page 264 **Melway** 1C A12

THE stream of cabs dropping off and picking up at this South Melbourne watering hole would make you think it's the Spencer Street taxi rank. It's not, of course, but the awesomely busy O'Connell's. Seven days a week, punters gather elbow-to-elbow in the front bar for dark murky Guinness and ice-cold Coopers, and one of Melbourne's best pub dining room meals. Out back, it's high-backed dining chairs, Jeffrey Smart look-alike urban paintings and a menu that's at once so now (pork belly and scallops) and yet so then (beef and Guinness pie). Chef Cath Kalka manages to combine first-rate ingredients and flavours in special ways. There may be Clarence River octopus with borlotti beans and feta, or mussels with a crust of garlic, parsley and chorizo. Rockling could morph into moussey dumplings soused in a red curry sauce, and crème fraîche icecream may accompany a rich chocolate cake. O'Connell's continues to delight with its exciting and superbly executed food and soothe with its familiarity and charm. The wine list is also worth a guernsey and remember, you won't need to book a cab.

15/20

Okra

SOUTH-EAST ASIAN

159 Camberwell Road,
Hawthorn East **9813 1623**

Licensed & BYO wine
Corkage $1.70 a head
Open Wed-Fri & Sun noon-3pm; Tues-Sun 6-10.30pm
Seats 75
Owners Irene & Joao Lay, Joe Wu
Chef Joao Lay
Cards AE BC DC MC V
Prices entrees $5.90-$9.90; noodles & rice $11.90-$14.30; mains $16.50-$29.90; desserts $3.80-$7.80; Sunday hawker-style lunch $6.80-$9.80
Map page 265 **Melway** 45 H12

TOUR South-East Asia in two hours by visiting Okra – you can eat Thai, Malaysian Indonesian, plus a bonus selection of Chinese. This double-storey restaurant, with polished floorboards and white tablecloths, is more Camberwell than Bangkok, but that's in keeping with Okra's mildly upmarket pitch. The menu incorporates Asian restaurant staples like satays and Thai soups, as well as more unusual dishes like fried chicken wrapped in pandan leaf, murtabak (grilled roti stuffed with minced meat and fried egg) and Nonya-style chicken curry with lime leaves. Balance a coconut-rich curry with a salad such as yum nuer (Thai beef salad) or grilled sweet potatoes in a mint, fresh coriander and lemon dressing. Service can sometimes be a little unpolished, but interesting desserts, such as coconut icecream with sticky black rice and custard help make amends. On Sundays, the hawker-style lunch features traditional dishes like poh piah (soft spring rolls stuffed with pork, prawns and yam bean root) and yong tow foo laksa, an assortment of bean curd morsels and vegetables stuffed with fish paste.

13/20 V

Old Kingdom

CHINESE

197 Smith Street,
Fitzroy **9417 2438**

BYO
Corkage $1 a head
Open Tues-Fri noon-2.30pm; Tues-Thurs & Sun 5-10.30pm; Fri-Sat 5-11.30pm
Seats 90
Owner Simon Lay
Chef Ly Ron Gy
Cards none
Prices entrees $1.50-$5.50; mains $8-$20; whole duck $43; desserts $3-$5.50
Map page 263 **Melway** 2C D9

WHOLE flocks of ducks have passed through this unprepossessing double-storey restaurant since its doors opened 19 years ago. This is a popular Peking duck haunt and everyone knows about the 24 hours' notice – there's Peking duck everywhere you look. The bird arrives whole at your table, where its head is unceremoniously wrenched off and the body expertly sliced before you. After you demolish the meat and skin wrapped in warm pancakes with spring onion and cucumber, the rest of the carcass returns as stir-fry shredded duck with vegetables, followed by duck soup. But Peking duck isn't the only drawcard. Affable owner Simon Lay's East Timorese background comes through in the specialities. (The rest of the menu is a throwback to '70s Australian-Chinese.) Crisp-skin boned chicken comes with a spicy chilli, vinegar, onion, garlic sauce; Timorese roast chicken is marinated in tamarind, garlic, and black pepper, finished with fresh lemon, sesame seeds, spring onion and sweet soy sauce. There's also Portuguese fried rice, laced with clove-spiced Portuguese sausage, finely chopped capsicum, tomato paste and shrimp.

12/20 $

Ondine

299 Queen Street,
City **9602 3477**

MODERN FRENCH
Best French

Licensed
Open Tues-Fri noon-2.30pm; Tues-Sat 6.30-10pm
Seats 100; outdoor seating; private room
Owner Nonda Katsalidis
Chefs Donovan Cooke & Philippa Sibley-Cooke
Cards AE BC DC MC V Eftpos
Prices entrees $18-$25; mains $34-$40; desserts $15-$18; degustation menu $110 (5 courses)
Map page 260 **Melway** 1A H1

IF any Melbourne restaurant offers a dynamic model of 21st-century fine dining, Ondine is it. It's at once ambitious and approachable, serving some of the city's most exciting food in a suave, split-level basement space. Tables are set formally and waiters are black-suited, but the affluent urban crowd dresses up or down at will. In the same way, Donovan Cooke and Philippa Sibley-Cooke's (joint winners of the *Guide's* Chef of the Year award) food fuses classic and contemporary notions. A terrine of chicken, shiitake mushroom and leek typifies the style – intricate but unfussy, with vibrant flavours. Vegetables are integral, as in silky wild mushroom tortellini in champagne foam surrounded by plump poached oysters, or a blanquette of veal on polenta galette with baby root vegetables and onion puree. The wine list offers a broad selection of high-end local and imported offerings, and desserts like Ondine's signature Valrhona chocolate soufflé with its molten truffle centre or spiced quince, apple and chestnut crumble will give you sweet dreams. It all comes together to make Ondine a thoroughly professional, ever-evolving package.

18/20

one fitzroy street

MODERN AUSTRALIAN

1 Fitzroy Street,
St Kilda **9593 8800**

Licensed
Open Mon-Fri noon-3pm, 6pm-midnight; bar & cafe Mon-Fri noon-midnight; Sat-Sun 10am-midnight
Seats 120; outdoor seating; bar
Owners Chris Lucas, John Psanis & Nicholas Harvey
Chef John Psanis
Cards AE BC DC MC V
Prices entrees $12-$17.50; mains $24.50-$33.50; desserts $13.50-$14.50; cafe menu $7.50-$20
Map page 261 **Melway** 2N J6

THE scallop-shaped dining room and elliptical balcony with fabulous views has always held promise. Now, after a good deal of tweaking, one fitzroy street has gone a long way towards realising its potential. Paul Wilson, now at the Botanical, consults on the menu and his influence can be seen in the bold, rustic cooking, with an emphasis on fish and seafood. Spain and the Middle East make their mark, as do Thai and Indian flourishes, although the kitchen does best with the flavours of the Mediterranean. Ocean trout with spiced eggplant, fattoush and tahini dressing is a robust dish while char-grilled pork chop, served with a rich stew of tomato, beans, peppers, chorizo and morcilla, the Spanish black pudding, is positively ballsy. The roasted fish platter with oregano and white beans is generous in every sense, and one of the owners puts his own Black Angus beef on the menu: it's excellent meat, served char-grilled with a salt crust. A good wine list and fair prices boost the appeal further, and as the new team settles in, this restaurant should slice itself a bigger piece of the Melbourne dining pie.

14/20

Orita's

MODERN JAPANESE

34 Jackson Street,
Toorak **9826 2111**

Licensed & BYO
Corkage $10 a bottle
Open Tues-Sat noon-3pm; Tues-Sun 6-11pm
Seats 40
Owner & chef Hikaru Orita
Cards AE BC DC MC V Eftpos
Prices entrees $12-$46; mains $25-$46; desserts $12-$15; degustation menu $65 (6-7 courses)
Map page 265 **Melway** 2M F6

ORITA'S has a tendency to divide or conquer fans of Japanese food. But even purists who disapprove of owner-chef Hikaru Orita's fusion approach will agree that he is uncompromising in his dedication to quality produce and to every element of the experience in this dramatic timber and black granite space. Orita-san likes to suggest diners try his omakase (degustation) menu, the better to showcase his technique and impeccable ingredients. Whether you bow to his wishes or choose à la carte, the array of sushi and sashimi is certainly striking; Orita's crafts in rice and fish are of the highest quality. To follow, an entree of grilled duckling breast 'saikyouyaki' may be served with a dark miso paste, and there may also be some Italian touches, such as a memorable carpaccio of salmon with a carrot and onion sauce. Mains, perhaps barramundi in soy butter, grilled veal loin and sea perch teriyaki are generous, but all might come with the same garnish and may even involve juggling cutlery and chopsticks. Service is well meaning and prices are rather steep, but no-one could accuse Orita of sticking blindly with tradition.

13/20

Pacific Seafood BBQ House

CHINESE/SEAFOOD

Shop 1, 210 Toorak Road,
South Yarra **9826 3838**

Licensed & BYO wine
Corkage $6 a bottle
Open Sun-Thurs 11am-11pm; Fri-Sat 11am-11.30pm
Seats 110
Owners Gabriel Chan & Nam Lau
Chef Raymond Tang
Cards AE BC MC V
Prices entrees $4-$4.50; mains $10.50-$19.80; roast dishes $12.80-$43
Map page 265 **Melway** 2L J5

THE South Yarra sibling to Pacific House's Victoria Street original has been bursting at the seams since it opened in early 2003. The new kid has a little more elbow room – you can even walk between the tables without dipping a sleeve in your neighbour's claypot. Coloured paper flags list numerous specials; the hanging roasted meats and fish and crustacean tanks are self-explanatory. Complimentary bowls of 'lei tong' (home-style soup) are served while you contemplate the menus. Perennial favourites include a mixed platter of roasts, steamed fish, crab in XO or ginger sauce with noodles, and the myriad claypot dishes, perhaps oxtail simmered with garlic and Chinese barbecue sauce. Venison is excellent either stir-fried with spring onions and ginger, or dry-fried with rice noodles. Good tofu dishes range from pi-pa bean curd (in which the star ingredient is minced, then mixed with Chinese sausage, and deep-fried) to preserved bean curd with water spinach and chilli. A special munch-and-go lunch menu focuses on rice dishes, noodles and congee. *Also Pacific Seafood BBQ House, shop 8, 240 Victoria Street, Richmond, 9427 8225.*

14/20 **$ V**

Paradise Indian Restaurant

INDIAN

Shop 34, Wheelers Hill Shopping Centre, 190-200 Jells Road, Wheelers Hill **9561 6661**

Licensed & BYO wine
Corkage $1.50 a head
Open Thurs-Fri noon-2.30pm; Sun 11am-3pm; Tues-Sun 5.30-10.30pm
Seats 100
Owners Robert Rabel & Shiva Kolambe
Chef Shiva Kolambe
Cards AE BC DC MC V Eftpos
Prices entrees $5-$17.50; mains $9.50-$26.50; desserts $5-$6; set menu $32.50 (4 courses)
Map page 266 **Melway** 71 J10

PARADISE might be overstating it, but after trying some of the more ambitious food at this unlikely Indian oasis, a qualified dose of bliss is guaranteed. You'd be forgiven for noting that the restaurant's Wheelers Hill outlook does not live up to the tropical sunset illustrated on the laminated menus. But the complimentary pappadams and pickles will allay any reservations – closely followed by entrees like a hearty mulligatawny soup; or ulundu vada, a mouth-watering street snack of chickpeas and coriander seeds mixed to form a wrinkly-skinned doughnut. The mains list includes some engaging options. Whole snapper gets the tandoori treatment to great effect; dhal maharani combines heady, simmered brown lentils and haricot beans. Keema naan should come with a warning that consumption is addictive – it's like a mini calzone filled with minced lamb, cheese and tomato. The Sunday brunch buffet, with its assorted dosas (crepes of fermented rice-flour and dhal that can be filled with any number of ingredients), offers a fine sampling of southern Indian fare.

13/20 V

Pearl

MODERN AUSTRALIAN

631-633 Church Street, Richmond **9421 4599**

Licensed
Open Mon-Fri noon-3pm; Sat-Sun 9am-3pm; daily 6-10.30pm; bar Mon-Fri 11am-midnight; Sat-Sun 9am-midnight
Seats 66; outdoor seating; bar
Owners Andrew Gunn & Geoff Lindsay
Chef Geoff Lindsay
Cards AE BC DC MC V
Prices breakfasts $4-$14; entrees $16-$32; mains $29-$33; desserts $14-$18; bar menu $5-$16
Map page 265 **Melway** 2L K1

THE danger in running a spectacular restaurant is that return diners expect to be wowed every time. Once you've had Geoff Lindsay's amazing watermelon salad with tomato jelly and feta, or his coconut duck with sweet fish sauce, the bar is set very high. Impressively, Lindsay is still finding new ways to express his signature Aussie-boy-within-a-drop-punt-of-Victoria-Street style. You might get scallops with dashi custard, or a teasingly subtle entree of wok-fried pearl meat dressed with shiitake mushrooms, ginger and soy. Dinner envy can be a problem. Sure, the moo shoo pork comes with a springy omelette and hand-rolled rice noodles, but it doesn't have Jerusalem artichoke crumble (like the beef) or pomelo and snake beans (like the chicken). And the passionfruit custard, good as it is, doesn't have the quivering gold leaf of the unmissable taro dumplings. Pearl's loud, young crowd deals with these highs and almost-highs just fine, helped by a very good wine list (with helpful headings like 'pinot noir, young and fresh'), down-to-earth waiters, and the knowledge that the next culinary marvel is just around the corner.

17/20 V

Pelican

MEDITERRANEAN/TAPAS

16 Fitzroy Street,
St Kilda **9525 5847**

Licensed
Open daily 7.30am-late
Seats 55; outdoor seating; bar
Owners Paul Olynyk & Con Christopoulos
Chef Roger Van Der Bogaert
Cards AE BC DC MC V
Prices breakfasts $3.50-$13.50; tapas $5.50-$9.50; mains $18-$21; desserts $7.50
Map page 261 **Melway** 2N K6

PELICAN is the Melbourne definition of 'hangout'. It's an attractive, flexible restaurant and bar where young St Kilda types come to sit comfortably at the bar with a magazine and coffee, dawdle with workmates over a jar or three at the communal table, or catch up with the gossipy gang at a heated outdoor terrace table with rather good wine and cocktails. The food is just as easygoing. Breakfast can be as simple as the house muesli or crumpets, or as decadent as fried egg and feta bruschetta. The page-long tapas list includes dishes ripe for sharing, like beetroot dip, molten feta fritters with garlicky aioli, or a chickpea and chipolata stew with tomatoey juices begging to be sopped up with thick-cut pide. Other small bites – say, sardines on sourdough and salmon bruschetta with red onion – work better for one. The short list of main dishes runs from pies to pastas to decent grills, such as lamb cutlets with a yoghurt dressing. It's all good tucker rather than brilliant cuisine, and the service is cheery and casual rather than expert. But the Pelican style washes down very well, so long as you're just hanging out, too.

13/20 $

Penang Coffee House

MALAYSIAN

395 Burwood Road,
Hawthorn **9819 2092**

BYO
Corkage 70 cents a head
Open Tues-Fri & Sun 11.30am-2.30pm; Tues-Sun 5-9.30pm
Seats 36
Owners Jimmy Hong, Sharon Tang & Jeffrey Sing
Chefs Karen Hong, Sharon Tang & Jeffrey Sing
Cards none
Prices entrees $2.20-$5.40; mains $9.20-$17.50; desserts $3-$5
Map page 265 **Melway** 45 D10

IF it ain't broke, don't fix it. Happily, nothing has been tinkered with at this veritable embassy of Penang hawker food, with its open kitchen, crowded chatter and laminate tables. The stars here are the noodle dishes, whether fried or in soup. The Penang-style char kwai teow, which you can have in any degree of chilli heat, emits the essential wok-charred flavor and is about the best in town. They would have few rivals for their Penang har mee (yellow noodles and rice vermicelli in a prawn-pork stock, with prawns, sliced pork, hard-boiled egg and greens), Assam laksa (rice noodles in belachan-loaded fishy broth sans coconut milk, over which true Penang-ites can drizzle black shrimp paste sauce called 'hay koh') and mee goreng. Rojak, a salad of fruit and vegetables dressed in hay koh, is also excellent. There are curries to accompany rice or roti. Try the nasi padang, a platter of four curry dishes with rice. Hainanese chicken rice often pops up as a special. Desserts like sago pudding, pulot hitam (sticky black rice 'porridge' with coconut milk) or ice kachang are the best ways to wrap up a Penang feast.

14/20 $

Pireaus Blues

GREEK
Best Greek

310 Brunswick Street,
Fitzroy **9417 0222**

Licensed & BYO wine
Corkage $5 a bottle
Open Wed-Fri noon-3pm; Sun noon-late; Mon-Sat 5pm-1am
Seats 85; private room
Owners John & Athanasia Rerakis, Tony Tracas
Chefs George Stournaras, Niki Loukopoulos & Katina Rerakis
Cards AE BC DC MC V Eftpos
Prices entrees $5-$12; mains $16.50-$27.50; desserts $6.50-$8.50; banquet menu $33 (3 courses)
Map page 263 **Melway** 2C B7

THERE'S a welcoming bustle about Pireaus Blues, a family business with snaps of the kinfolk on the sunny yellow walls and a mother in the kitchen – owner John Rerakis' mother Katina, the queen of Cretan cuisine. The staff are always friendly and the Mythos is always cold, but it's the specials board that makes Pireaus Blues such a pleasure. Baked kid is a dark, luscious affair, with meat that's held on to the bone by circumstantial evidence alone. When zucchini flowers are blooming, the kitchen crew stuffs them to bursting with grains of mint-flecked rice. Then there's tasty baked okra with tomatoes and onions, which teams up wonderfully with soutzoukakia; taut lamb rissoles redolent of rosemary. And no self-respecting Greek restaurant could fail to offer dishes from the char-grill: here, the lamb cutlets and octopus both come smoky and tender. Desserts are often overlooked by the banquet brigade but there is one more special that should be tried and that is icecream with halva. Try imagining creamy vanilla with intense sesame paste rippled through it and then try saying no – it simply can't be done.

14/20

Plume Restaurant

CHINESE

546 Doncaster Road,
Doncaster **9840 1122**

Licensed
Open Mon-Fri noon-3pm; Sat-Sun 11am-3pm; daily 5.30pm-late
Seats 330
Owner Plume Chinese Restaurant Pty Ltd
Chef Chi-Keung Cheung
Cards AE BC DC MC V
Prices yum cha dishes $4-$8.30; entrees $6.50-$11; mains $18-$55; desserts $6-$11
Map page 266 **Melway** 47 C1

THIS upmarket suburban Chinese is huge. So huge that there might be a wedding reception in full swing behind you, and a multigenerational birthday gathering on the floor below, and you'll still be able to have a low-key family meal without feeling that you're in the way. The food here is good – sound interpretations of mostly Cantonese standards with a sprinkling of surprises. If the idea of Peking duck or garlic prawns has you snoring, order instead house specials like the succulent wine-cooked pigeon flavoured with osmanthus blossoms, and served cold. Or emu fillet in a spicy sauce, garfish stuffed with prawn mousse or pork intestines on silky bean curd. It's not all excitement: some dishes (the law hon jai vegetarian stew among them) are too bland and many sauces have a mass-produced feel about them – perhaps inevitable in a 330-seat restaurant. The selection of desserts is fairly predictable, though there is a nice line in fruity flambés. Daily yum cha features tripe cooked in rice wine and tasty eel. Ask about esoteric delicacies like duck tongues – the staff have a tendency to forget to mention them.

13/20 V

The Point Albert Park

MODERN EUROPEAN

Aquatic Drive,
Albert Park **9682 5566**

Licensed
Open daily noon-3pm, 6-10pm; cafe 8am-10pm
Seats 90; private rooms; bar
Owner Leawarra Fall Pty Ltd
Chef Stephen Wright
Cards AE BC DC MC V
Prices entrees $17.50-$21.50; mains $29-$34.50; desserts $16-$18; lunch set menu $29.50 (2 courses); less in cafe
Map page 264 **Melway** 2K G7

THERE are few better appointed Melbourne restaurants than this modern glass-sided dining room, with its epic panorama over Albert Park Lake. It's the perfect spot for a languid corporate lunch or for lingering over a romantic dinner. You'll get a clue about the sort of food that will arrive from the kitchen by reading the menu, which is scattered with tricky French cooking terms, necessitating a glossary. It's intricate stuff employing several elements on the plate. So Milawa chook breast might come with crushed kipflers, *étuvée* of asparagus and roasted foie gras sauce; pumpkin and pine nut *velouté* with mushroom filo and truffled pumpkin *ecrasse*; or rack of lamb *farced* with sweetbreads, *pastiade* of confit lamb shoulder, baby peas and lettuce. Service ranges from starched efficiency to ennui; it's a slick package but sometimes lacks a little soul, perhaps hinting that this doubles as a function centre. Some welcome humour is creeping in with new chef Stephen Wright's recent dessert menus: look out for things like parsnip icecream with a chocolate silk tart or 'three things from a banana'.

15/20

V

Precious Morocco

MOROCCAN

173 Victoria Avenue,
Albert Park **9686 8681**

Licensed & BYO wine
Corkage $4 a bottle
Open daily 5-10pm
Seats 48; outdoor seating
Owner & chef Mustafa Yacine
Cards AE BC DC MC V Eftpos
Prices entrees $7-$14; mains $15-$25; desserts $9-$11.50; banquet menus $45-$55 (6 courses)
Map page 264 **Melway** 2J J9

THIS clever, casual diner offers Melburnians a rare chance to experience traditional Moroccan food. Owner and chef Mustafa Yacine has tricked up this single shopfront with bright colours, gold-brocade banquettes and copper vases. The fez-wearing staff are knowledgeable enough to help diners pick something light or piece together a feast. The wine list is short but it's BYO as well. The house-made merguez sausages, accompanied by an earthy grilled eggplant-tomato combo, are an excellent starter, as are prawns sauteed in a ras-el-hanout spice mix and served on tomato and cucumber cous cous. Tagines range from a subdued traditional seven-vegetable stew to a tender lamb dish reinforced with preserved lemon, potato and olives. The bastilla is excellent. A delicate pie formed from warqa (a filo-like pastry), it is filled with chicken meat spiced with cumin, cinnamon and turmeric, sweetened with sugar, thickened with egg and dusted with icing sugar. Superb. Finish off with Morrocan sweets such as knafa, layers of warqa and coarsely ground almonds, scented with orange-flower water and enriched with rice cream.

13/20

Prodigy

MODERN AUSTRALIAN

166 Wellington Parade,
East Melbourne **9419 5700**

Licensed
Open Mon-Sat noon-3pm, 6-10.30pm
Seats 60; private room; bar
Owners Howard Lam & Paul Dickson
Chef Jason Burrows
Cards AE BC DC MC V Eftpos
Prices entrees $14.50-$16.50; mains $24.50-$32.50; desserts $9.50-$13.50
Map page 263 **Melway** 2G E5

THIS cool mint-green space beneath a city-edge apartment block is full of surprises, not least of which is the innovative menu designed by former Marchetti's Tuscan Grill chef Jason Burrows. His food has strong Asian flavours and the odd Mediterranean note. Plump Tasmanian scallops sit on sesame seaweed salad with ponzu butter in the half shell, while deliciously light goats' cheese and orange dumplings are sensational on a roasted butternut pumpkin mash with basil and nut-brown butter. Judicious use of seasonal fruit lifts tender baked lamb rump served on home-made 'fregolone' pasta (like plus-size cous cous) with apricot and basil chutney, and revamps char-grilled swordfish on soba noodles with red grapes and wilted rocket. Desserts are also fruity: things like poached blood plums on a soft cardamom and orange meringue, hot chocolate pudding served with roasted banana sauce, or the subtle ginger lime brûlée with lime zest wafers and a red berry salad. The wine list is well priced and there is also a cellar list. Service has sharpened over the past few months, and so far, this Prodigy promises not to burn out.

14/20 

Public House

MEDITERRANEAN/TAPAS

433-435 Church Street,
Richmond **9421 0187**

Licensed
Open Mon-Thurs 4pm-midnight; Fri-Sun noon-1am
Seats 100; outdoor seating; bar
Owners Julian Gerner & Paul Olynyk
Chef David Danks
Cards AE BC DC MC V Eftpos
Prices small plates $4.50-$9.50; mains $17-$23; desserts $5-$10
Map page 265 **Melway** 2G K12

THE people behind Public House fantasised about what a modern pub could be and – with help from architects Six Degrees – transformed a bland former rock venue into a place like no other in Melbourne. It's a great place to meet and drink, with all sorts of pub references (swirly carpet, recycled timber panelling and a vintage CUB clock). But it's also a very social place to eat. The menu is built around sharing, with tapas and flatbreads making up the bulk of the list, and a few main courses thrown in for traditionalists. Chef David Danks has an easy, generous way with big Spanish, Middle Eastern and Mediterranean flavours. His long, fun list of gutsy finger food might include grilled fish fillets with green olive relish, or polenta-crusted quail with hummus. And no visit here is complete until you've paired a glass of wine with char-grilled flatbread topped, perhaps, with goats' cheese, prosciutto and figs or tomato, chorizo and rocket. There's something irresistibly youthful and intoxicating about Public House. But is it a pub, a bar, a cafe or a restaurant? Who knows? But if you're fixated on an answer, you're probably not its type.

14/20 $

Punch Lane

MODERN AUSTRALIAN

43 Little Bourke Street,
City **9639 4944**

Licensed
Open Mon-Fri noon-11pm; Sat-Sun 5-11pm
Seats 65; private room; outdoor seating; bar
Owner Martin Pirc
Chef Mark Johnstone
Cards AE BC DC MC V
Prices entrees $4.50-$16.50; mains $22-$32.50; desserts $6.50-$12.50
Map page 260 **Melway** 1B U4

THE atmosphere at Punch Lane is so welcoming that you feel free to wander in by yourself, grab a magazine from the bar rack, and relax in a red leather armchair. Timber-panelled and dimly lit, the wine bar-cum-restaurant's back wall is lined with wine bottles, while side wall chalkboards display some of the Punch Lane cellar's best drops by the glass and an ever-changing list of French, English and local cheeses. The look is a bit gentleman's clubby, but there's nothing blokey about the eclectic Asian-meets-Mediterranean menu, which is divided into 'tastes', 'smaller courses' and 'larger courses'. Star 'tastes' include skewers of eye fillet marinated in red Thai curry, and coconut-battered prawns, while small courses range from an almost transparent shellfish ravioli to seared Spring Bay scallops and vegetarian moussaka. The main course highlight is a crisp-skinned rack of pork: tender cutlets served with crossed swords of crackling on a sweet, nutty bed of sauteed cabbage with walnut and apple compote. Desserts excel, especially the home-made pineapple and passionfruit sorbet and apple and calvados icecream. But don't forget the cheeses.

14/20

Purple Sands

CHINESE

862-866 Doncaster Road,
Doncaster **9848 8022**

Licensed & BYO wine
Corkage $1.80 a head
Open Mon-Fri noon-3pm; Sat 11.30am-3pm; Sun 11am-3pm; daily 6-10pm
Seats 120
Owner John Wong
Chef Cheung Yu
Cards AE BC DC MC V Eftpos
Prices yum cha dishes $3.20-$7.80; entrees $5.50-$7.50; mains $17.80-$25; desserts $6-$6.50
Map page 266 **Melway** 47 J1

PURPLE SANDS' owner John Wong is a graduate of the Flower Drum school and it shows. The dining room is unprepossessing, but his Flower Drum training is evident in the linen cloths, exemplary service, and the unwavering consistency of the stylish Cantonese food, despite recent changes of chef. Seafood is the speciality and it begins with the entrees. Crisp deep-fried whitebait sprinkled with a spicy salt are like little puffs of sea breeze. Fleshy prawns swim in thick seafood stock with slippery vermicelli. A whole barramundi is poached in soy sauce and spring onions. Subtly flavoured to reveal its delicate flavor, the fish is deboned by the waiter. The beef and pepper hotpot is less distinguished, although the meat is tender. Banquet menus are available for those who like their decisions made for them. There's a modest but well-chosen selection of domestic wines starting at $16 a bottle. The daily yum cha is notably good, and often intriguing – strips of tripe bedded on bean curd, or sweet duck tongues paired with chillied seaweed. Desserts are both sweet (buttery custard tarts) and fun (lotus penguins and pastry swans).

13/20

Qizine

MODERN EUROPEAN

230 Dorcas Street,
South Melbourne **9690 3261**

Licensed
Open Mon-Fri noon-4pm; Mon-Sat 6pm-late
Seats 60; outdoor seating; private rooms
Owners Val & Helena Szedow
Chef Helena Szedow
Cards AE BC DC MC V
Prices entrees $14.50-$15.50; mains $25.50-$28.50; desserts $10.50
Map page 264 **Melway** 2K C2

RESTAURANTS in converted terrace houses feel like blasts from the past in a city pulsing with temples of timber and stainless steel. The framed Toulouse-Lautrec and Moulin Rouge posters on the scarlet walls in Qizine's front room only add to the retro-perspective. But the regulars all seem very comfortable, because Qizine feels like their own neighborhood dinner party. And the food, influenced by chef and co-owner Helena Szedow's French upbringing, with a small nod to her Polish heritage, is strictly contemporary. The entrees range from excellent seared scallops to her signature dish of smoked salmon slices wrapped around a traditional Russian potato salad. The mains are heavy on meat, running from fillet of beef, through pork fillet wrapped in bacon and on to a memorable moist roast duckling with ginger and plum sauce, served with braised cabbage and potato gratin. Lighter options might include the daily grilled fish on bok choy or a lime-marinated roast chicken fillet. Desserts are always good, and might include butterscotch pud or a selection of home-made icecreams – cinnamon, blood orange and Grand Marnier.

13/20

---

radii

MODERN EUROPEAN

Park Hyatt Hotel, 1 Parliament Square (off Parliament Place),
East Melbourne **9224 1211**

Licensed
Open daily noon-2.30pm; Sun-Thurs 6-10.30pm; Fri-Sat 6-11pm
Seats 138; private rooms; bar
Owner Hyatt International
Chef Sean Donovan
Cards AE BC DC MC V Eftpos
Prices entrees $22-$27; mains $34-$42; desserts $16-$22;
express lunch menu $35 (2 courses); degustation menu $110 (7 courses)
Map page 263 **Melway** 2G A2

FILLING the shoes of former executive chef Paul Wilson was always going to be tough. The 2002 Chef of the Year upped the ante for hotel dining in Melbourne and his earthy style of cooking attracted much acclaim to this glitzy space in the luxuriously over-the-top Park Hyatt. Wilson's former sous chef, Sean Donovan, now heads the kitchen and is continuing radii's big-hearted approach. To start, you might have shellfish roasted in the wood-fired oven and served with summer minestrone, or hickory-smoked oysters with prosciutto, pears and sage. Dishes for two or more are a feature, and might include juicy lamb loin with lamb's offal, and rotisserie-cooked wild duck with peaches. Other mains could be a saffron-infused fish stew with shellfish and smoky chorizo. The food is skilfully prepared but not as dazzling as it once was, and the habit of using multiple side plates, pans, dishes, boards and gravy boats clutter the table to little purpose. To finish, desserts such as house-churned icecreams are simply delicious. Service remains top-notch, keeping pace with the prices, which have climbed since last year.

15/20

Rathdowne Street Food Store

MODERN AUSTRALIAN

617 Rathdowne Street,
Carlton North **9347 4064**

Licensed & BYO wine
Corkage $6 a bottle
Open Mon-Sat 8am-late; Sun 8am-5pm
Seats 50; outdoor seating
Owners Ricky Holt & Janine Ballantyne
Chef Ricky Holt
Cards AE BC MC V
Prices breakfasts $6-$13.50; entrees $7.50-$16.50; mains $16.50-$29.50; desserts $6-$9.50
Map page 262 **Melway** 2B J3

STREETSIDE or inside, the Rathdowne Street Food Store is Carlton personified: cool, urban, busy, but thankfully also down-to-earth. By day, chic Carltonians crowd the counter, buying pastries and inventive salads, such as warm beef, dates and rocket tossed in a sweet pomegranate molasses to go. Others grab tables in the small, crisp-clothed restaurant for coffee, brunch or lunch. Specials are tempting, with owner-chef Ricky Holt chalking up seasonal dishes such as baked quinces or grilled figs with honey, basil and goats' milk curd. At night, the lights dim and the mood becomes warm and intimate. Queues still form for takeaway meals, but diners are just as likely to linger, persuaded by a rich asparagus risotto fragranced with truffle oil or a piquant Mexican red bean and chipotle (smoked jalapeno) ragout. Or perhaps its signature lamb curry, richly spiced with a mean ginger kick, devised more than 20 years ago by well-known British chef Gary Sweetman and perfected by Holt. Desserts are gloriously indulgent; praline-stuffed, chocolate-covered dates are naughty nuggets of sweetness.

14/20

r.bar

ITALIAN

67 Beach Street,
Port Melbourne **9646 0707**

Licensed
Open Mon-Fri 11am-late; Sat-Sun 9am-late
Seats 80; outdoor seating; bar
Owner Roberto Scheriani
Chef Josh Doherty
Cards AE BC DC MC V
Prices entrees $7.50-$17; mains $16-$25; desserts $11
Map page 264 **Melway** 2J C7

WITH so few Melbourne restaurants taking advantage of the city's waterfront location, r.bar is in a prime position, with views across the fashionable Port Melbourne shorefront and out to the bustling Station Pier. Its downstairs bar is often rollicking, but the upstairs restaurant doesn't quite kick the goals it should, given its location and ambitions. An airy warehouse space, r.bar's minimalist look is tempered by some plush finishes and flickering candles. With its burger and fries and battered fish 'n' chips, the menu makes obvious concessions to casual dining, but stick with the classic Italian dishes to get the best from the kitchen. A risotto of shredded duck and mushrooms is meaty and comforting, while a huge serving of bruschetta topped with tomato and basil is simple but good. A generous slab of tuna might be a little overdone, but it's saved by a fresh lemon and olive oil dressing and a decent side of roasted vegetables. Better yet are the simple meat dishes like corned beef with baby vegetables, or twice-cooked duckling with white bean puree. For a casual seaside meal in a room with a view, you could do far worse.

13/20

Red Emperor

CHINESE

Upper level, 3 Southgate Avenue,
Southbank **9699 4170**

Licensed
Open Mon-Sat noon-3pm; Sun 11am-4pm; daily 6pm-late
Seats 250; private room
Owners Charles Ng, Simon Lo, Ngau Lee, Raymond Cheung & Christine Hua
Chef Hon Kau Hui
Cards AE BC DC MC V
Prices yum cha dishes $4-$9; entrees $5.30-$28.60; mains $17.60-$66; desserts $7-$14
Map page 264 **Melway** 1D T3

YOU can tell a lot about Red Emperor from its crisply dressed tables, Yarra views, rapier-sharp service and handsome wine list. But if you need further proof that it aims high, look to the menu, where you'll find shark's fin in loose or comb forms, rarities such as bird's nest soup and what many believe is Melbourne's best yum cha. This is a classy place, staffed by Flower Drum graduates (the chef, two co-owners, several floor staff) striving for greatness. Not that the Emperor plays only with top-shelf ingredients – braised pork knuckle, and pork with taro, are Hakka provincial dishes rarely seen in Chinese restaurants. Both transcend their humble origins. When you have good ingredients, you don't need to muck around – perfection is fish simply steamed in soy and sesame oil and finished with spring onions, ginger and coriander. Technique is flaunted in the Sichuan tea-smoked duck with crisp, lacquered skin served in a steamed flower bun. Desserts are highly unusual – on offer are steamed bird's nest soup ($128), made from the saliva of the sea swallow, and double-boiled hasima (snow frogs' glands, no less) with red dates and lotus seeds.

16/20 V

Red Rice

MODERN ASIAN

193 Brunswick Street,
Fitzroy **9415 7513**

Licensed
Open Tues-Sun noon-3pm; Tues-Thurs & Sun 6-10.30pm; Fri-Sat 6-11pm
Seats 65; outdoor seating
Owner & chef Danni Dinh
Cards AE BC MC V Eftpos
Prices entrees $4.50-$8; noodles $9.50-$13.50; mains $9.90-$20.50; desserts $5.90-$7
Map page 263 **Melway** 2C A9

ALTHOUGH Brunswick Street appears to have reached restaurant saturation point, Red Rice is a welcome addition. It's ready proof that friendly but informative service, smart surrounds (muted lighting, timber fittings, wicker chairs), decent wines and imaginative food don't have to lift prices into the stratosphere. The kitchen takes Vietnamese as a springboard, before diving off into other cuisines. Entrees might include chewy Thai-style fishcakes, aromatic with coriander, lime, lemongrass and chilli; or crisp spring rolls crammed with salmon, wood-ear mushrooms, bean shoots, asparagus and squiggles of rice vermicelli. Mains range from a simple stir-fry of chicken and lemongrass, to more complex dishes such as grilled fish with a cross-cultural pesto of Asian basil and coriander, or rice noodles with chicken, prawns and eggs with a lime-lifted peanut sauce. And what to eat with all that? Rice, of course, coloured red with annato seed extract. For dessert, check out the icecream smothered in a tangy lemon and berry compote and served in a glass. It's rich, sweet and smooth as velvet.

13/20 $

Reserve

Federation Square, 2 Swanston Street (corner Flinders Street), City **9654 6002**

MODERN EUROPEAN
Best New Restaurant

Licensed
Open Mon-Fri noon-3pm, 6-10pm; Sat 6-10pm
Seats 90; bar
Owner Andrew O'Brien
Chef George Calombaris
Cards AE BC DC MC V Eftpos
Prices entrees $15.90-$21; mains $22-$33.90; desserts $15; 'journey fare' menu $65 (4 courses)
Map page 260 **Melway** 1B N10

WITH its over-the-top interiors and focus on fine dining, Reserve, at the Victorian Wine Precinct, thumbs its nose to the prevailing culture of safe design and 'every occasion' accessibility. But it's Reserve's food, orchestrated by George Calombaris (the *Guide's* Young Chef of the Year), that puts the B in Bold. Calombaris' cuisine synthesises French haute cuisine with the intellectual fringe of modern European food, particularly that of Spain's Ferran Adria. Foams, savoury icecreams and frozen oils add unpredictable twists to the often-stunning food here. Conservatives will try beef tenderloin with horseradish foam, and be thrilled. The adventurous will take on spiced venison carpaccio with raspberry icecream, or a beef and bone marrow croquette with onion icecream and passionfruit-chive syrup, and be equally happy. Not everything works, but this is not style over substance. A strawberry consommé served with preserved strawberries, watermelon cubes and a lime and basil sorbet is a triumph. A serious wine list and good, experienced management both help make this the year's most exciting restaurant debut.

16/20

Richmond Hill Cafe & Larder

48-50 Bridge Road, Richmond **9421 2808**

MEDITERRANEAN

Licensed
Open Mon 9am-5pm; Tues-Fri 9am-late; Sat-Sun 8.30am-late; larder Mon 9am-5pm; Tues-Fri 9am-5.30pm; Sat 8.30am-7pm; Sun 8.30am-5pm
Seats 65
Owners Stephanie Alexander, Angela Clemens, Lisa Montague, Karl Walder & Michael Lee Richards
Chef Lance Rosen
Cards AE BC DC MC V Eftpos
Prices breakfasts $6-$16.50; entrees $18; mains $28; desserts $15
Map page 265 **Melway** 2G H5

WHEN it opened six years ago, Richmond Hill Cafe and Larder was a revelation. Stephanie Alexander had seen the future: no-fuss food celebrating terrific produce, particularly cheese (via her association with cheese guru Will Studd), in casual surroundings. Today the Larder is more brand than place: wine and cheese shop, gift and bookshop, cafe. The popular (no bookings) breakfast is a sprawling affair – muesli *and* granola, kippers, and 'Baghdad eggs' (in demand during Gulf War 2). Lunch is inventive pastas, salad niçoise and cheeseboards. Come dinner, creeping prices and starchy service means it's fine dining time. The frequently changing evening menu has been whittled to a handful of choices for each course and it works well. The flavours are Mediterranean, focusing on quality ingredients, such as superb baby artichokes garnishing ricotta-stuffed tortellini with sage and burnt butter, or super-tender sirloin in a roast dinner that mocks grandma's grey Sunday lunches. Happily, they haven't pruned the extensive wine list, with plenty by the glass, many bottles under $30 and a cellar collection for special occasions.

13/20

VEGETARIAN

No animals were harmed in the production of these meals

Bhoj Docklands
54 New Quay Promenade, Docklands, 9600 0884
Rajesh Mehta's creative and carefully executed cooking has raised the bar for Indian cuisine in Melbourne. Dishes like crisp fried potato and cheese dumplings, unctuous okra curry, and spinach and paneer (with fenugreek-flavoured cheese) prove there is more to the subcontinental vegetarian repertoire than vegetable samosas and mixed veg curry. See page 25.

Jacques Reymond
78 Williams Road, Windsor, 9525 2178
Jacques Reymond may have renovated his Windsor restaurant and reworked the menu format, but his outstanding vegetarian degustation stands firm. The six-course card is true to Reymond's French-rooted fusion style and offers imaginative dishes such as vichyssoise wasabi with baby beans and fresh sultanas, and potato and corn crepe with Vietnamese salad and enoki tempura. See page 81.

Lake House
King Street, Daylesford, 5348 3329
Carnivores are as likely as vegetarians to order Lake House's inventive six-course veg deg menu, according to owner Alla Wolf-Tasker. It's a seasonally moving feast, and might include herb tortellini with zucchini custard and fried zucchini flowers, or beetroot carpaccio with a salad of rocket, pear, walnut, baked Meredith feta and sheep's milk labna. See page 216.

Matteo's
533 Brunswick Street, Fitzroy North, 9481 1177
Intricacy and finesse are the key characteristics of Frederic Quemin's cooking. No hastily rustled-up omelette for vegetarians here. Rather, they're treated to carefully crafted dishes based on the day's fresh produce, along the lines of butternut pumpkin, spinach, oyster mushroom and chevre pithiviers with roasted bell pepper piperade, shallot and herb cream. See page 105.

Mecca Bah
55a New Quay Promenade, Docklands, 9642 1300
Vegetarian dishes get equal billing on the Mecca Bah menu. Crunchy sweet potato falafels are served with tahini, dolmades-style silverbeet parcels are plump with rice, herbs and chickpeas, and there are dips, salads and tagines to fill any gaps. But ultimate accolades go to the Turkish pizzas, topped with things like zucchini, cheese, lemon and mint. See page 106.

Pearl
631-633 Church Street, Richmond, 9421 4599
Geoff Lindsay's regular menu invariably includes a couple of desirable meat-free dishes, but if nothing takes your fancy ask to see his special vegetable-based list. All the hallmarks of his passionate, inventive style are evident in dishes like chickpea soup with zaatar, feta fritters, parsley and shaved radish, and buffalo mozzarella salad with stewed red and gold peppers, torn basil and grilled olive bread. See page 126.

Shakahari
201-203 Faraday Street, Carlton, 9347 3848
While the food at Shakahari has moved with the times, regulars won't let some dishes budge from the list. Still rocking after all these years are the tempura-coated avocado, eggplant and red capsicum rolls (sound odd, taste great) and wholemeal flour-based seitan skewers with a rich satay sauce. See page 142.

Soulmama Global Vegetarian Cafe
St Kilda Seabaths, 10-18 Jacka Boulevard, St Kilda, 9525 3338
Soulmama combines a brilliant waterside location with a daring food concept – the all-vegetarian buffet. Steve Cumper cooks a daily changing range of dhals, curries, stir-fries, salads and noodle dishes. Depending on his whim, the constantly replenished glass cabinet might house chickpea tagine, potato and leek curry, or tomato, zucchini and mushroom pasta.

Riva

MODERN AUSTRALIAN

St Kilda Marina,
Elwood **9537 2224**

Licensed
Open daily noon-late (Wed-Sun in winter)
Seats 140; outdoor seating; private room; bar
Owners Drewe Bellmaine & Jeff Glover
Chef to be announced
Cards AE BC DC MC V Eftpos
Prices entrees $10.90-$14.90; mains $18.90-$27.90; desserts $12.90; winter lunch set menu $25 (2 courses)
Map page 261 **Melway** 2N K12

WHO can resist an outside seat at Riva? By day, diners on this boatshed restaurant's deck look over palm trees and across the blue stretch of the bay. By night, they gaze across to the lights of Williamstown. And listen to the thumping music from the adjacent bar heaving with text-messaging twentysomethings. If it's raining, they can gaze out the floor-to-ceiling windows from the burgundy-walled dining room. Riva's tables are bare (although the napkins are cloth), the service is attentive, and the cooking is accomplished, dispelling any prejudices about restaurants with views. A fried calamari entree is crisp and tender in the right places, while grilled scallops come served on the shell with a pea puree and truffle cream just begging to be mopped up with the crusty bread served when you are seated. Mains might include a well-executed seared rare tuna, baby barramundi fillets with dill risotto, or a beef tenderloin on soft chilli polenta. However, the raspberry panna cotta is so bland it might as well be junket. Perhaps all this seaside kitchen's passion goes into the fish. A new chef was to be appointed as the *Guide* went to press.

13/20

Saigon Rose

VIETNAMESE

206 Chapel Street,
Prahran **9510 9651**

Licensed & BYO wine
Corkage $3 a bottle
Open Mon-Thurs 11am-10pm; Fri 11am-11pm; Sat 5-11pm; Sun 5-10pm
Seats 60
Owners Van Nguyen & Quy Le
Chef Cuong Nguyen
Cards AE BC DC MC V
Prices entrees $5.50-$10; soups $4-$8; mains $7-$19.50; desserts $3-$4
Map page 265 **Melway** 2L J12

SAIGON ROSE on Chapel is one of those places that is so consistent, you know what you're going to get before you even set foot inside. It's going to be madly busy (but the brisk waitstaff will get you to the movies on time); there'll be the same list of blackboard specials as last time around (the scallops with XO sauce are tickety-boo) and the lengthy menu will continue to list the roll-call of South-East Asian favourites available at most Viet diners around town. Why worry? It's cheery and you're thinking more dash than cash. Choose from light-as-a-feather spring rolls, ready to be stuffed into crispy iceberg and dipped in nuoc cham, or go the see-through version plump with lettuce, vermicelli, rose-pink prawns and pork. Move on to juicy chicken tumbled with chilli, lemongrass, tamarind and crunchy capsicum, or the crisp salted flounder that laps the plate. Nursery-style Asian restaurant desserts like fritters, fried icecream and lychees are uninspiring, but the small selection of Australian wines, with ever-changing specials by the glass, is quite grown-up. Now that's a surprise. *Also 86 Victoria Street, Richmond, 9429 8328.*

12/20 $ V

Sails on the Bay

MODERN AUSTRALIAN/SEAFOOD

15 Elwood Foreshore,
Elwood **9525 6933**

Licensed
Open daily noon-3pm, 6pm-late (closed Sun nights & Mon-Tues in Jun-Aug)
Seats 100; bar
Owners Derek & Monica Fuller, Peter & Gisa Gillon
Chef Richard Wood
Cards AE BC DC MC V
Prices entrees $13-$22; mains $23-$31; desserts $11.50-$14.50; set lunch $25 or $30 (2 or 3 courses; not Dec-Jan)
Map page 266 **Melway** 67 B5

A CHAMPAGNE cork's pop from the sands of Elwood Beach, Sails is a licence to print money. In they troop, generations of families seeking weekend lunches and twilight dinners. It's like Mother's Day seven days a week. They start, perhaps, with a glass of Aussie bubbly at the pebble-encrusted bar, then adjourn to the nautically inspired dining room, filled with red banquettes and sailcloths for a menu bristling with the day's catch and every other form of protein. While Sails could cruise along with the likes of beer-battered fish and a good salad niçoise, it takes another tack, serving food that might seem too adventurous for the safe-as-houses clientele. Seared bugs might come with snails and a verdant parsley sauce, tuna carpaccio could arrive wearing a Cajun crust and dribbled with pomegrante syrup, and salmon might be bundled into bean curd and set adrift in a coconut and paprika broth. Some dishes work, some don't, but who's to care? The tables hum and good glassware is filled constantly with wines from a smart wine list. Beware the charge on your bill if you've chosen to park outside.

13/20

Saragossa

MODERN AUSTRALIAN

369 Bridge Road,
Richmond **9429 7880**

Licensed
Open Mon-Fri & Sun 7am-10pm; Sat 7am-4pm, 6-10pm
Seats 75; outdoor seating
Owner Bryan Barendregt
Chef Darren Daley
Cards AE BC DC MC V Eftpos
Prices breakfasts $3.50-$12; meals $7.50-$22; desserts $6.50
Map page 265 **Melway** 2H C6

THIS spacious corner store starts the day as a breakfast nook, dishing out porridge with orange syrup or steamed rice with fried egg and Thai condiments. It buzzes through the day as a shoppers' retreat and pram-pushers' hangout, before shifting into a neat little local dinner spot and wine bar. Whatever the hour, the pavement tables are the most congenial choice in fine weather. The grey-walled, concrete-floored interior with stainless steel bar, forgettable wine glass-themed paintings, bare tables and suspended lighting, is far less appealing. Still, the napkins are linen, meals start with good bread and olive oil, and there are interesting European drops on the wine list. Moreover, the waiters are friendly, the prices reasonable and the menu interesting, with some hits, the occasional miss and the odd puzzlingly creative combination. Successful dishes include healthy chunks of seared salmon served with a thicket of rocket on a pile of warm potatoes, and a generous bowl of pappardelle with cavolo nero. Less enjoyable is the dull antipasto plate and a too-subtle cold curry soup. To finish, replace desserts with a selection of French cheeses.

12/20 

Sarti

MODERN MEDITERRANEAN

6 Russell Place,
City **9639 7822**

Licensed
Open Mon-Fri 10am-1am; Sat 4pm-1am
Seats 55; outdoor seating; bar
Owners Fiona Sheeran & O'Connell's Hotel
Chef Mark Wilby
Cards AE BC DC MC V
Prices entrees $10-$16; mains $12-$26; desserts $3-$12
Map page 260 **Melway** 1B P6

A LITTLE CBD gem that was just waiting to be polished, Sarti finally sparkles under new ownership from the people behind O'Connell's. The tailors that used to share the timber-panelled space are gone, allowing diners to focus on the food. Linen-covered tables fill the stained plywood floor, and arched windows and a rooftop terrace add charm. Part-owner Fiona Sheeran runs the floor with aplomb, the wine list is affordable and appealing, and new chef Mark Wilby (formerly of Owensville) cooks satisfying, strongly flavoured dishes showing both French and Italian influences. Entrees might include a sturdy ham hock, artichoke and gruyère terrine, handsome eggplant fritters with frisée and beetroot, and simple pasta dishes like penne with tomato, creamy blobs of bocconcini and prosciutto. For mains you might choose from confit of belly pork on spiced lentils, with brittle salty crackling, or a steaming bowl of mussels and octopus cooked in tomato and red wine, and dotted with white bean and preserved lemon salsa. Stylish desserts might include a mellow lime and coconut tart with caramelised pineapple.

14/20 

@ A GLANCE

Away from prying eyes, you're free to party, smooch or broker a deal

PRIVATE ROOMS

Circa, the Prince
2 Acland Street,
St Kilda, 9536 1122
There are plenty of options to be by yourself here but the private room, opening on to the courtyard, is the primo experience. Gather up to 20 friends and bask in the warm glow of good design.

Dutton Enoteca
527 Church Street,
Richmond, 9428 7898
A room with a real sense of occasion, separated from, but with enough glass to gaze out upon, the hoi polloi. Big enough for 12 of your closest friends.

Lynch's
133 Domain Road,
South Yarra, 9866 5627
Of course Lynch's has private rooms – the quaint libertine atmosphere demands it. You can do it in private here with between eight and 32 guests.

Mrs Jones
312 Drummond Street,
Carlton, 9347 3312
A circular table seating between 12 and 24 would dominate this upstairs room, but for the ornate chandelier overhead. It's a smart flourish in a coolly minimal room.

Silks
Crown Entertainment Complex,
8 Whiteman Street,
Southbank, 9292 6888
Soaring ceilings and walls of glass framing the city add to the glamour of dining privately here. Impress between 10 and 60 people.

Yu-u
137 Flinders Lane,
City, 9639 7073
Call well ahead to book one of the two tatami rooms – an enigmatic attitude makes this Melbourne's hottest Japanese restaurant. The rooms seat up to 12.

Saucier Restaurant

MODERN EUROPEAN

1007 High Street,
Armadale **9822 8515**

Licensed & BYO wine (except Sat)
Corkage $10 a bottle
Open Tues-Fri noon-3pm; Tues-Sat 6.30-10pm
Seats 40; private rooms
Owner & chef Eric Frahamer
Cards AE BC DC MC V
Prices entrees $17; mains $32; desserts $16; degustation menu $75 (6 courses)
Map page 265 **Melway** 59 A7

CIVILISED Saucier, in the heart of conservative and affluent Armadale, is very much a product of its environment. With its brass and gilt decor and mannered ambience, it remains the quintessential smart dining room for the local demographic. Chef-owner Eric Frahamer's regulars come for professional service, a wine list rich in rare back vintages (particularly iconic Australian labels such as Henschke), and modern European cooking, which is neither cutting-edge nor bogged down in tradition. Honey-glazed Peking duck breast, expertly cooked and served with a pinot noir and duck sauce, is typical of the chef's contemporary touch. Teamed with Austrian fig dumplings and a cabbage and caraway salad, it offers a glimpse of all of Frahamer's main influences – France, Asia and his native Austria. A crayfish consommé with oloroso sherry and seafood works well, as does the combination of wonton-fried prawns with a Thai-inspired tatsoi salad. Desserts, like the coconut bavarois with passionfruit centre, gingersnap tuile and tropical fruit salad, can be excessively arty, but always maintain the restaurant's high standards.

15/20

Scusami

MODERN ITALIAN

Mid-level, Southgate,
Southbank **9699 4111**

Licensed
Open daily noon-3pm, 6pm-late
Seats 80; bar
Owner Theo D'Souza
Chef Simon Humble
Cards AE BC DC MC V
Prices entrees $9.50-$21; mains $22-$48.50; desserts $7-$17.50; set menus $65 or $82 (2 or 3 courses)
Map page 264 **Melway** 1D T3

YOU know when globetrotting friends return saying they didn't eat as well overseas as they can in Melbourne? They are talking about restaurants like the 11-year-old, Italian-fuelled Scusami. The dream team, led by longtime chef Simon Humble, hasn't skipped a beat since a change of owners in 2002. The service guarantees an anxiety-free experience, starting with a deftly managed greeting, seating and wine-pouring within the first five minutes. Take time to peruse the wine list's strong by-the-glass selection, and the long, satisfying menu, which balances contemporary offerings with a shorter list of 'Cucina Tradizionale' classics. Luxury ingredients abound and dishes are priced accordingly. A roasted free-range baby chicken stuffed with black truffle might be one of the best dishes you'll eat all year. Dizzyingly good, too, is a roasted and boned duckling with amarena cherries and balsamic vinegar sauce. Desserts like zuccotto Toscano, a lavish mix of sponge, custard and nuts maintain the standard. Only Scusami's bland decor detracts from the splendour. Go in fine weather and snare a balcony table, with Melbourne skyline views.

16/20 

Shakahari

VEGETARIAN

201-203 Faraday Street,
Carlton **9347 3848**

Licensed
Open Mon-Sat noon-3pm; Sun-Thurs 6-9.30pm; Fri-Sat 6-10pm
Seats 65; outdoor seating
Owners John Dunham, Beh Kim Un & Ma Kim Poay
Chefs Beh Kim Un & Beh Hang Noe
Cards AE BC DC MC V
Prices entrees $8-$10.50; mains $14.50-$15.50; desserts $8-$9.50
Map page 262 **Melway** 2B G7

THIRTY years ago, a strictly vegetarian restaurant must have seemed a risky proposition. But Shakahari's brightly hued interior and clever, complex fusion of Asian and European flavours has proved a winning formula. The menu is amusingly earnest (a rice salad is described as 'immortal', while the herbal hotpot is 'ethereal'), but the wine list is sound and food is presented with wit and flair. A stylish garnish of Vietnamese mint and radicchio brightens a simple dish of pan-seared nori parcels, packed tightly with julienned sweet turnip, carrot and bean-thread noodles, which rest in a miso mayonnaise. A salad of seasonal greens, bean curd and chewy tempeh slices tossed in lemon sambal might make an invigorating contrast, followed by a deceptively mild laksa, rich in galangal, chilli and coconut, and riddled with organic linguine. Or perhaps croquettes of mashed yam, polenta and red beans, with a tangy peppercorn sauce. Service is friendly, professional and persuasive; you might not feel like dessert, but the black rice congee with coconut cream and chunks of honeydew is a delight. On a balmy evening, try for the palm-fringed courtyard.

14/20 $ V

Shark Fin House

CHINESE

131 Little Bourke Street,
City **9663 1555**

Licensed
Open Mon-Sat 11.30am-3pm; Sun 11am-3pm; daily 5.30-11pm
Seats 350
Owner Shark Fin Group Pty Ltd
Chefs John To & Fung Chau
Cards AE BC DC MC V
Prices yum cha dishes $3.30-$12; entrees $5-$6; mains $14-$45; desserts $5-$6; banquet menu $30 (6 courses)
Map page 260 **Melway** 1B R4

THE success of the Shark Fin network has largely been due to its devotion to live-catch cuisine. Add to this the daily ritual of yum cha and it's a combo that has kept Shark Fin restaurants bobbing along happily for many years. The flagship, Shark Fin House, draws regulars for dim sum supremo John To's dumplings, yam puffs and savoury pastries – they are seldom below par. Adventure-seekers will scurry after fish head with black beans, braised beef tendons and spongy tripe. But the best things are fished from the state-of-the-art tanks – six double-decker aquariums brimming with promise. Giant crab, accompanied by noodles stewed with soft roe, is a standout for POA occasions and mud crabs are always a treat. If seafood's not your catch, look for dishes like taro duck, honey-glazed beef, double-boiled soups and meaty lamb hotpots. The hospitality in this three-storey building is not their strong point and service can be slow. *Also Shark Fin Inn, 50-52 Little Bourke Street, 9662 2681; 155 Burwood Highway, Burwood East, 9866 5777; and 328 Cheltenham Road, Keysborough, 9798 8788.*

13/20

Shavan's Tandoori Indian Restaurant

INDIAN

Shop 15, Harbour Plaza, Thompson Road,
Patterson Lakes **9773 0639**

Licensed & BYO wine
Corkage $1 a head
Open Thurs-Fri noon-2.30pm; daily 5.30pm-late
Seats 80; outdoor seating
Owner Marcus Peiris
Chefs Narebhar Khatri & Charlise Krishna
Cards AE BC DC MC V
Prices entrees $5-$11; mains $9-$19; desserts $4.50-$5; set menu $32 (3 courses)
Map page 267 **Melway** 97 H5

TUCKED away in a nondescript shopping centre, Shavan's brings a good selection of classic curries to the waterways of Patterson Lakes. The decor is basic but neat: a peachy paint job, imitation palms and wall-mounted ornamental platters make little impression, and service is reliable but impassive. Pleasingly, most dishes highlight one or two key ingredients rather than being swamped by overly complicated masalas. Lamb boti kebabs, for example feature lamb cubes the size of children's play blocks, lightly marinated and served on a bed of fried onions, while Hyderabadi chicken uses only tender breast fillets stewed in a smooth tomato gravy. Vegetarian offerings also benefit from the kitchen's light touch, as with the sizzling platter of diced pumpkin with whole curry leaves and almonds. For dessert, it's perhaps safest to stick to time-honoured kulfi, rather than the more ambitious vattalappam, a Sri Lankan coconut milk and palm sugar dessert like a treacly crème caramel. Drinks are not Shavan's strong suit – bring your own chilled white instead.

12/20 **$ V**

Shira Nui

JAPANESE

247 Springvale Road,
Glen Waverley **9886 7755**

Licensed
Open Tues-Fri noon-2pm; Tues-Sun 6-10.30pm
Seats 35
Owner Hiro Nishikura
Chefs Yuki Ueno & Hiro Nishikura
Cards AE BC DC MC V Eftpos
Prices entrees $5-$9; sushi & sashimi $6-$26; mains $12-$18; desserts $8-$9
Map page 266 **Melway** 71 C2

IT doesn't take long for sushi fans to nose out a place that's doing justice to their beloved delicacies. Within months of opening in mid-2002, Shira Nui was packed with diners, mostly Japanese, for most meals. Why? Because Hiro Nishikura's sushi is among the best in town. The classic prawn, salmon and tuna offerings are stellar. But there's also sweet, buttery sashimi squid; nori-wrapped sea urchin roe; and tempura maki (prawn and cucumber roll), which delivers a double whammy with wasabi and hot mustard. The best way to enjoy Nishikura's talents is to dine omakase at the sushi bar, allowing the maestro to feed you. Cooked dishes are good, too, prepared by French-trained chef Yuki Ueno. Options include tender dengaku daikon (radish grilled with miso) and silky eggplant in a delicate fishy stock. Zousi – traditionally a poor man's dish designed to make rice go further – is another gem. Here, the staple grain is cooked in chicken stock, studded with seafood and nori and finished with beaten egg – it's soupy happiness in a bowl. Food is definitely the focus here: the primrose dining room is modest; staff are cheerful and relaxed.

14/20 **$ V**

Silks

CHINESE

Crown Entertainment Complex, 8 Whiteman Street,
Southbank **9292 6888**

Licensed
Open daily noon-3pm; Sun-Thurs 6pm-midnight; Fri-Sat 6pm-1am
Seats 120; private rooms
Owner Crown Ltd
Chef Ki Wah Lau
Cards AE BC DC MC V
Prices entrees $8-$24.50; noodles & congee $18.50-$36; mains $26-$44; lunch banquets $50-$85 (5 courses); dinner banquets $60-$110 (5 courses)
Map page 264 **Melway** 1D M3

NOTHING beats Silks for oriental splendour. Antique and reproduction vases, ornate artwork, and even a Mongolian tent decorate a room dominated by seven-metre glass windows looking out across the Yarra to the Melbourne skyline. The accoutrements of the table are no less lavish: diners use gold-plated cutlery and eat from fine china edged with gold leaf, seated in chairs with backs of burnished mahogany. The food plays second fiddle, but that's to be expected when the kitchen turns out both high-end oddities such as combs of shark's fin ($198 a serve), steamed abalone and lobster sashimi, and more homely dishes like fish congee and noodles. The staples are competently handled and the service is, naturally, courteous. Delicate whitebait could come coated in a crisp, seasoned batter; beef fillet is gorgeously tender, and teamed, perhaps, with spring onions and ginger, and vegetables such as crunchy Chinese broccoli come trimmed to their core. The wine list is accordingly flashy, with prices to match. Which brings us to the bottom line on this restaurant: come for the view, enjoy the sumptuous setting, and eat and drink lightly.

13/20

Spoonful

MODERN AUSTRALIAN

543 High Street,
Prahran **9521 5212**

BYO
Corkage $1.50 a head
Open Mon-Sat 8am-5pm; Tues-Thurs 6.30-9.30pm
Seats 28
Owner & chef Melly Beilby
Cards BC MC V Eftpos
Prices breakfasts $5-$14.50; lunches $9.50-$18.50; entrees $9.50-$14.50; mains $16.50-$22.50; desserts $7.50-$9.50
Map page 265 **Melway** 58 G7

THIS purple one-roomer is a friendly place, with a long banquet table and a scattering of smaller perches. An open kitchen and shelves of produce add to the communal feel. The cafe works a double shift, the first as a meeting spot for local mums and business types, then, three nights a week, upping gear to offer casual but classy dinners. Break your fast with farm eggs and crisp smoky bacon and vibrant smoked salmon omelettes.The daily-changing lunch menu moves easily from Vietnamese coleslaw or haloumi-stuffed capsicum to spaghetti marinara. Dinner is a first-class act at second-class prices. Perhaps delicately tangy tuna carpaccio dressed in citrus-infused soy, or zucchini flowers stuffed with lemon and ricotta. Flathead may come baked Lebanese-style with walnuts, coriander and tahini, and imam bayildi, the Turkish baked eggplant classic, could be served with chickpea salad and yoghurt dressing. There's usually beef, perhaps minute rump steak with tarragon crème fraîche, or fillet steak with smashed spuds. Desserts are triumphant, as in mango pavlova roulade or poached figs with vanilla, cardamom and saffron.

14/20

Stavros Tavern

GREEK

183 Victoria Avenue,
Albert Park **9699 5618**

BYO wine
Corkage $2 a bottle
Open Tues-Sun 6pm-late
Seats 85; outdoor seating
Owners Stavros Abougelis, Andrew & Theo Panayi
Chef Theo Panayi
Cards AE BC DC MC V
Prices entrees $7-$10.50; mains $9-$15.50; desserts $5-$6
Map page 264 **Melway** 2J H10

THIS restaurant is proudly Greek, from the big bristling moustache on the welcoming face of Stavros himself, to the walls hung with images of Greek fishing villages, through to the brazenly Greek menu. The colour scheme is eggplant and yoghurt, the stone floor primed for plate smashing. Of course, there is great lamb: casseroled, wrapped in filo with herbs and feta, or best of all, sliced straight from the gyros – crunchy and sweet on the outside and succulent and tender inside. Many dishes come with pide, including grilled calamari rings bathed in a vinegary tomato and kalamata olive salsa, so beware of filling up early when ordering starters. That said, the entree of green mussels baked in a tomato sauce flavoured with ouzo and crumbled feta shouldn't be missed – the saltiness of the cheese and the fennel flavours of the ouzo add depth to an already intense sauce. The recent addition of a fresh seafood cabinet and an increase in the number of vegetarian options, including a warming taro casserole, complement old favourites such as interested friendly service and a convivial atmosphere.

13/20 V

Stokehouse

MODERN MEDITERRANEAN

30 Jacka Boulevard,
St Kilda **9525 5555**

Licensed
Open daily noon-2.30pm, 6-10pm
Seats 140; outdoor seating; private room; bar
Owners John & Frank Van Haandel
Chef Maurice Esposito
Cards AE BC DC MC V
Prices entrees $12-$20; mains $28-$38; desserts $15-$19
Map page 261 **Melway** 2N K9

IS it any wonder that a seaside window table here is one of the most keenly sought, and most romantic in Melbourne? It helps that this airy, relaxed first-floor dining room, suspended above a still-life of swaying palms and St Kilda sands, also has Maurice Esposito's Mediterranean-inspired food to put on the tables. Esposito's fish dishes show the usual Stokehouse flair – perhaps crisp-skinned barramundi, battered-whiting fish and chips, or prawn-filled calamari on cous cous – but they're now backed by more meaty options. That's good news when they're as fine as the fat drumstick of a veal chop with spinach and a slab of cheesy potato or the impeccably juicy quail wrapped in pancetta and sage, perching on a cakey pear tarte tatin. And the mouth-watering wine list balances trendy, obscure and cultish labels from home and abroad. There's just one niggling concern: lately the service, while mostly efficient, is occasionally perfunctory, with a subtle undertow of upselling that can, on a busy night, make you feel like just another 'cover'. Find yourself at table 19 or 38, however, and you'll be really stoked.

16/20

Strega

ITALIAN

Crown Entertainment Complex, 8 Whiteman Street,
Southbank **9645 5400**

Licensed
Open daily noon-3pm; Sun-Thurs 6-10pm; Fri-Sat 6-11pm
Seats 140; outdoor seating; private room
Owner Fab Nicolao
Chef Pasquale Villella
Cards AE BC DC MC V
Prices entrees $12.50-$16.50; pastas & risottos $15-$26; mains $26.50-$32; desserts $12.50
Map page 264 **Melway** 1D L3

THERE'S something a little American about Strega. Martha Stewart's been doing that country-house thing with the decor – subdued prints, tobacco suede, polished dark timber – and Vegas is happening all around, compliments of Crown's riverside pyrotechnics and the swarms of punters on the promenade at Strega's door. You settle into your big chair with your big view and your big menu and wait for big flavours to burst off your plate. And they do. Delicacy is not much seen on the menu here. A dish of 'chitarra' (guitar string) spaghetti with prawns and asparagus is a simple and thoughtful pairing, but more typical, perhaps, is tortelloni filled with duck and porcini, swimming for its life in a heavy grappa and pear jus. The gutsy jus may also appear with both crisp-skinned duck, on a porcini and potato mash, and with roasted pork cutlets on soft polenta. For dessert, zuppa inglese (trifle) is all casino chic – lolly-pink layers, a fair slap of booze and a long way from home. The service is amiable, the wine list commendable and the room buzzing. Roma it's not, but it's glossy good fun.

12/20

Strictly Thai

THAI

170 High Street,
Kew **9853 0723**

Licensed & BYO wine
Corkage $1.50 a head
Open Sun-Thurs 5.30-10pm; Fri-Sat 5.30-10.30pm
Seats 80
Owner & chef Alice Tchen
Cards AE BC DC MC V
Prices entrees $7.50-$9.90; mains $11-$20.50; desserts $5.50
Map page 265 **Melway** 45 C6

THIS cheerful, two-storey High Street shop fills nightly with Kew families, who adore their local Thai's generous serves, reasonable prices and subtle style. The tables may be paper over linen and the chairs are the type you'd find at a convention centre, but the carved wood Thai friezes make an exotic counterpoint to the clickety-clack of passing trams. The well-priced wine list is small, and the traditionally costumed staff are attentive, but not overly interactive. The food is, indeed, strictly Thai, although the sweet-sour balance of many dishes dips heavily towards the sweet. Best to start with, say, succulent marinated chicken thighs wrapped in pandan leaves or goong maplao, a rewarding mouthful of deep-fried prawn coated in crunchy shards of shredded coconut. A main like rich red curry with roast duck is fragrant with kaffir lime leaves, while the steamed curry fish, served on a clay dish with seven little tagine-like lids, is a melting spoonful of juicy meat and coconut, infused with sweet basil. The kitchen is less strict with desserts, serving an OK sticky date pudding alongside a sweet Thai sago dish with coconut milk.

13/20 $ V

Strozzi Restaurant

ITALIAN

333 Collins Street,
City **9629 4844**

Licensed
Open Mon-Fri 7.30am-5pm
Seats 75; outdoor seating; bar
Owner Michael Tenace
Chef Rupert Smith
Cards AE BC DC MC V
Prices entrees $12.50-$16.50; mains $26.50-$34; desserts $11; bistro-bar menu $8.60-$16.90
Map page 260 **Melway** 1A J8

SITTING at the base of a palace of commerce, Strozzi murmurs 'business class' all the way from its port bottles and leather-bound books to the thick individual handtowels in the loo. Open early to caffeinate and fuel bankers and stockbrokers, this sister restaurant to Il Solito Posto (see page 78) now clocks off at 5pm – lunch is where it's at in this part of town. A long central bar separates a casual bistro-bar from the ochre and grey dining area, with its high-backed upholstered chairs and gentle lighting. Waiters in black Mao suits explain the daily specials: there might be spicy capsicum risotto with buttery zucchinis, pappardelle with duck ragout, or stand-out salmon sashimi flavoured with preserved lemon and served with basil, baby tomatoes and hummus. The regular menu is much less adventurous, sticking tight to well-rendered Italian classics like paper-thin, herbed beef carpaccio, house-made oxtail ravioli, slowly braised sticky pork with creamed cabbage, and seared tuna. Desserts merely cover the bases: count on tiramisu, sorbets and crumbles. Service is efficient, the wine list means business, and the coffee is first class.

13/20

Sud

ITALIAN

219 King Street,
City **9670 8451**

Licensed
Open Mon-Fri noon-3pm, 6pm-late
Seats 40
Owner Phillip Tran
Chef Rick Mikus
Cards AE BC DC MC V
Prices entrees $10.90-$17.90; mains $19.90-$30.90; desserts $10
Map page 260 **Melway** 1A C3

OFTEN, the ingredient critical to a restaurant's success cannot be found in any larder. At Sud, a smart, vanilla-hued dining space in the heart of lap-dancing land, the essential element is, appropriately, passion. Founding proprietors-waiters Umberto Lallo and Giovanni Patane tapped into the source, and new owner, Singaporean Phillip Tran, vows to maintain both their menu and their methods. It helps that Sud is a snug, one-room space, made cosier with chocolate banquettes and low lighting. Chef Rick Mikus is still in the kitchen, which operates on a simple premise: quality. Only fine, seasonal ingredients are used, and the menu changes every day. The neat Italo-centric wine list is also constantly evolving. Both cartes are written on huge metal sheets hung from the walls, and they'll be explained at great length. You might order calves' liver with peppers and tomato, or handmade fusilli with artichokes and wilted rocket. To follow, there could be lamb with chicory and mustard fruits. Settle back on your chocolate banquette and await dessert, perhaps pear and fig tart with a luxurious pear sorbet and pear bavarois.

15/20

LAVAZZA
Improve your performance.

Sukhumvit

THAI

1258 Malvern Road,
Malvern **9824 7099**

BYO
Corkage $1.10 a head
Open daily 6-10pm
Seats 50; private room
Owner & chef Boonaek Aoumbowtount
Cards AE BC MC V
Prices entrees $7.70-$9.90; mains $14.20-$17.50; desserts $5.50-$6.60
Map page 265 **Melway** 59 D6

SUKHUMVIT has waxed and waned over its 14 years. Now under new ownership, its star is rising. Huddled between homes on busy Malvern Road, the inconspicuous two-storey building is cheerful inside, with Thai statuettes and wall-hangings adding spark to the somewhat dreary green and yellow colour scheme. The new owner-chef's background in Bangkok hotels is apparent in the efficient service, '80s muzak and often Westernised versions of this royal cuisine. The food can sometimes be too sweet, but it's fresh and well prepared all the same. Entrees are particularly good, as in steamed pork dumplings with crisp roasted peanuts, and a bland sweet-sour soup proves a refreshing foil for intense, salty dishes like the roast duck salad, which arrives with a naff grape and strawberry garnish. The wok-hot, fishy pad Thai is more authentic. Some more inventive dishes include deep-fried calamari stuffed with minced chicken and prawn, and crisp-fried rainbow trout doused in a punchy ginger-inflected sauce. In another retro flourish, Sukhumvit is BYO only. Thankfully, the bottle shop is only a quick sprint across the road.

12/20 $ V

Supper Inn

CHINESE

15 Celestial Avenue,
City **9663 4759**

Licensed & BYO
Corkage $2 a head
Open daily 5.30pm-2.30am
Seats 80
Owners John Lau & Steve Lau
Chef Tony Lu
Cards AE BC DC MC V
Prices entrees $3.50-$6; noodles & rice $11-$30; mains $11.50-$55; desserts $3.50-$4.50
Map page 260 **Melway** 1B P4

LITTLE has changed at Supper Inn in 25 years of quick-smart Chinese food and late-night clatter. Sure, its reputation for hearty Chinese cooking has spread beyond Asian students and families. These days, you'll queue on the grotty carpeted stairs alongside clubbers, chefs and city-dwellers. But the fabulous congees (perfect with crullers – deep-fried doughnuts – for dunking) or fried hor fun (fat rice noodles) with beef are as reliably tasty as ever. Other favourites are found among the claypot dishes: it's hard to choose between chicken and salted fish, seafood with bean curd or homely eggplant with minced pork. The pig is celebrated from snout to tail, whether it's the feather-light, deep-fried intestine, 'venerable pork' (sweet and sour) that really lives up to its name, or roast suckling pig. Vegetable dishes are good for crunch and colour: spinach with dried scallops makes eating greens pure pleasure, and the fungus dishes are meaty and spooky in equal measure. Service can be brusque, but value is excellent, and the rather respectable wine list incorporates helpful food-matching hints.

14/20 $ V

The Swallows

MODERN AUSTRALIAN

192 Station Street,
Port Melbourne **9646 2746**

Licensed
Open Sun-Fri noon-2.30pm; daily 6-9.30pm
Seats 60; bar
Owners Gillian Weinberger & John Fitzpatrick
Chef Cath Budd
Cards AE BC DC MC V Eftpos
Prices entrees $8.50-$15; mains $15.50-$30; desserts $9
Map page 264 **Melway** 2J G2

SWALLOWS is the ultimate comfortable pub night out. Prop at the bar for clean, frothy tap beer or drink from the exceptional wine list dotted with rare back vintages while you enjoy the clubby motor-racing decor and the crackle of the double-sided fire. Then carry your glass through to the dining room and sit down at a linen-clothed table for top-flight pub food that, usually, has gourmet appeal to spare. The mammoth rib-eye steak is a signature; cooked precisely to order, it comes with a mountain of mash and quality condiments. There's always a pot pie on the menu, too, perhaps rabbit and hot English mustard, or chicken and tarragon. The repertoire could also include corned beef with sauteed cabbage, tempura flathead tails with fat chips, the odd Asian excursion like sang choy bao, and a pasta of the day, such as chicken and pancetta agnolotti in a butter sauce. Just about everything has a home-cooked feel to it, the only niggle being a rather too pubby salad with dull production-line dressing. It's a minor issue when the staff are so convivial, there's a friendly resident border collie and live jazz on Sunday nights.

13/20

Sweet Basil

THAI

209 Commercial Road,
South Yarra **9827 3390**

Licensed & BYO wine
Corkage $2 a head
Open Tues-Sun 6pm-late
Seats 90; outdoor seating
Owners Sangvorn Meemulthong & Fran Horace
Chefs Sangvorn & Nathakarn Meemulthong
Cards AE BC DC MC V
Prices entrees $7.90-$9.50; mains $12-$19.90; desserts $5.50-$6.50
Map page 265 **Melway** 2L H9

THE addition of an upstairs eating area may have eased the dinner-time rush, but it hasn't hushed the hubbub at this vibrant, modern Thai cafe. The crowds are no mystery. Bangkok-trained chef Sangvorn Meemulthong and his daughter Nathakarn play fearlessly with flavours, pushing the balance between sweet and sour to craft dishes that are beautifully complex and satisfying. The tom som is indicative: a dynamic bowl of sweet fish stock with plump fish fillets is soured with tamarind and lifted with ginger. Pra hoy is just as sophisticated, featuring warm oysters melting into a rich fish sauce, and the gaeng ped pet (roast duck in a sweet red curry) is unusually good, thanks to the addition of fragrant lychees. Most tempting among the salads is the yum gai, steamed chicken strips in lime and lemongrass-infused coconut cream, crunchy with cashews and red onion. Reasonably priced seafood includes pla lui san, crisp-fried trevally fillets in a sauce sweetened with palm sugar and sharpened with lime. The waiters are engaging, and have a good understanding of the affordable menu. The compact wine list is sufficient but BYO is an option.

13/20 $ V

Syracuse

MODERN MEDITERRANEAN/TAPAS

23 Bank Place,
City **9670 1777**

Licensed
Open Mon-Fri 7.30am-11pm; Sat 6pm-late
Seats 70; bar
Owners Paul Lumicisi & Charlie Sirianos
Chef Hal Riches
Cards AE BC DC MC V
Prices breakfasts $4-$10.50; tapas $3.20-$10.50; entrees $11.50-$16; mains $19.50-$24; desserts $6.50-$10.50
Map page 260 **Melway** 1A G7

SYRACUSE'S velvet curtains reveal a voluptuous room, part of what was once a 19th century bank or hotel, depending on who you talk to. There are statues, columns and marble-topped tables, but there's also a genteel shabbiness that ensures the room is comfortable rather than imposing. What's more impressive – the room, the sterling wine list or the food? You'll need a few hours to sample all and decide. New chef Hal Riches (ex-Dutton Enoteca) has replaced Perry Peters, now at Attica. Riches has dropped Peters' Moroccan touches, but retained the Italian keynotes and high standards. A simple and satisfying breakfast menu is followed by a more elaborate lunch carte. There's pasta (perhaps semolina gnocchi with roast tomato and ricotta) or platters of capocollo (cured pork neck) with green olive tapenade and fennel. Whiting might be polenta-crusted; lamb could come with beans and saffron aioli. The evening menu focuses on tapas such as grilled quail and octopus, though six main plates are thrown in, too. The sparky waiters can steer you towards a choice bottle from the list, or a glass from the always-interesting blackboard.

14/20

Taipan

CHINESE

237-239 Blackburn Road,
Doncaster East **9841 9977**

Licensed & BYO wine
Corkage $1.50 a head
Open Mon-Fri noon-3pm; Sat-Sun & public hols 11am-3pm; daily 6-11pm
Seats 200
Owners Charles Ng, Simon Lo & Ngau Lee
Chefs Li Man Kit & Simon Lo
Cards AE BC DC MC V
Prices yum cha dishes $3.20-$6; entrees $4.50-$12; mains $17.50-$28.50; desserts $3-$7.50
Map page 266 **Melway** 34 C11

BEFORE you even get to Taipan's front door, you'll notice a steady stream of takeaway containers heading out. Upstairs on the mezzanine floor is the 200-seater dining room, which does yum cha during the day and mainly Cantonese at night. It's decorated with imposing stone lions, mirrored panels and Chinese kitsch, and crammed most nights with large groups chattering around the lazy Susans. Service is swift, but can be erratic, and there's a small but sound wine list, featuring some well-matched whites. The dim sum, such as the crisp spring rolls and satay sticks, are adequate. Chinese speakers may have better access to delicacies such as braised abalone or the cold platter of jellyfish and pig's ear. At night, try the succulent spicy-fried quail, or the perfectly cooked pan-fried Tassie salmon in a light soy and spring onion sauce, or excellent Buddha-style fried noodles, piled high with mushrooms, broccoli and snowpeas. Less could be said for the Sichuan-style pork – a handful of chilli does not convert a stir-fry into a Sichuan treasure. It's often best to finish with fresh fruit, but many swear by the gooey red-bean pancake with banana.

13/20

Tandoori Den Camberwell

INDIAN

261-263 Camberwell Road,
Camberwell **9882 5353**

BYO
Corkage $2 a head
Open Tues-Fri noon-2.30pm; Tues-Sun 6-10pm
Seats 66; private rooms
Owners Prakash Mirchandani & Gaurav Khanna
Chefs Paul Anthony, Sansar Chand & Balwant Singh
Cards AE BC DC MC V Eftpos
Prices entrees $6.50-$12; mains $11-$18; desserts $4.50-$5.50; set menu $31 or $34 (4 courses)
Map page 266 **Melway** 59 J1

YOUNG and old alike love suburban stalwart Tandoori Den, not least because of its marvellously homely ambience. The carpet, paint job and pleated two-tone drapery are looking a bit tatty, but you have to admire the Den's consistency over two decades. Any BYO bottles are swept away on arrival, one to return uncorked in moments, a foretaste of the switched-on service throughout the meal. Begin with southern-style coconut crab, spiked with chilli and ginger, and served in potato skins. Meat dishes are generous and wonderfully cooked, be it mustard-pickle lamb stewed to a rosy hue in an earthy gravy dotted with caraway seeds, or succulent chicken jalfrezi, boneless pieces casseroled with capsicum and tomatoes. Tandoori dishes like gobi (cauliflower) are baked to perfection and, like most entrees, served with peppery mint and tamarind sauces. Only the greediest should try the filling semolina pudding, unusual among the kulfi- and dumpling-loaded dessert menus at most local Indian restaurants. Despite the proximity to Camberwell junction, parking is generally OK.

14/20 V

Tea House on Burke

CHINESE

911-913 Burke Road,
Camberwell **9882 9088**

Licensed & BYO wine
Corkage $4.50 a bottle
Open Sun-Fri noon-3pm; Sun-Thurs 6-10.30pm; Fri-Sat 6-11pm
Seats 100; private room
Owners Lawrence Tse, Shannon Chan, Sum Cheung & Kam You Chen
Chefs Sum Cheung & Kam You Chen
Cards AE BC DC MC V
Prices entrees $4-$12; mains $13.50-$30; desserts $5-$6
Map page 265 **Melway** 45 J11

TEA HOUSE has been set up by graduates of Flower Drum college, demonstrated by the excellent Chinese cuisine, well-spaced tables, gentle lighting and impeccable service, which doesn't miss a beat, even at peak times. The menu is conservative, but even dishes like roast lacquered duck, sweet and sour pork or fried rice are raised to an artform. The supplementary list of chef's suggestions reveals the kitchen's potential, but for a truly extraordinary meal, ask about what's in the kitchen that day. The staff might tell you about steamed baby abalone, or cold platter of drunken squab, jellyfish and vegetarian goose. Prawns might be steamed and served with a soy dipping sauce, caramelised with soy to enhance their natural sweetness or coated with duck-egg yolk, then deep-fried. Chinese marrow might be teamed with dried scallops. Shanghainese pancakes with sweetened taro or red-bean paste bring the meal to a fine conclusion. On the beverage side, choose a tea such as 'Monkey-picked oolong', or a wine from the pinot noir-heavy wine list. *Also Tea House at Chinatown, 11 Cohen Place, City, 9639 2526.*

15/20 V

Termini

ITALIAN

60a Fitzroy Street,
St Kilda **9537 3465**

Licensed
Open daily noon-11pm
Seats 50; outdoor seating
Owners Michele Francavilla, Mauro Marcucci, Cordell Khoury & Donato Toce
Chefs Cordell Khoury & Donato Toce
Cards AE BC DC MC V
Prices entrees $6-$16.50; mains $16-$22.80; desserts $6.50-$7.50; lunch set menu $18 (2 courses)
Map page 261 **Melway** 2P A4

ALL good restaurants have one or two shining attributes. At Termini, it's the refreshingly rustic menu. The enormous chalkboard offers a dizzying array of choices, some familiar (ossobuco, fish soup), others less so (vine leaves filled with ricotta and breadcrumbs, risotto with prawns, fennel and saffron). Termini's signature grilled baby calamari on lemony radicchio displays finesse, but some of the rather plain mains, like char-grilled rock ling, simply anointed with olive oil, are not such good value once you add the requisite side dishes. It's the sort of food you'd rave about were it served in a little trattoria just outside Siena. In the old St Kilda railway station, it loses something in the translation – straightforward rather than inspirational. The small, airy room, with outdoor annexe, is decorated in the usual style of Caffe e Cucina's offspring (wine bottles stacked to the ceiling, spartan tables, banquettes). It can get loud but it's more of an energetic buzz than a nuisance. The service is warm and confident, and regular patrons are greeted with a kiss, Roman-style. There is a short but considered wine list with plenty by the glass.

13/20

@ A GLANCE

Pack up your bottles in your own kitbag

BYO

Abla's
109 Elgin Street, Carlton, 9347 0006
Like the BYO concept, Abla's is a Melbourne classic. Figure some beer into the equation here – it suits the homespun Lebanese flavours and the low-key setting.

Da Noi
95 Toorak Road, South Yarra, 9866 5975
Monday night is the time to grab that vermentino you've been saving and see how well the Sardinian wine partners Da Noi's Sardinian-inspired food.

Gourlays Restaurant
529 High Street, Prahran, 9521 5566
If you come on Tuesday nights you can ignore Gourlays' well-chosen list and test your skills matching your wine with the modern French food.

La Luna Bistro
320 Rathdowne Street, Carlton North, 9349 4888
La Luna has a decent wine list of its own but, as Carlton is the spiritual home of BYO, you can tote your own to marry with the gutsy mod-Med dishes.

Langton's Restaurant & Wine bar
61 Flinders Lane, City, 9663 0222
Tuesday night is Cellar Night, where you get to raid your collection and drink that special wine. They'll even arrange a degustation menu to match, if you phone ahead.

Manju
135 Maling Road, Canterbury, 9836 3236
Canterbury is a dry area so bring sake for the Japanese classics and pinot noir for the fusion dishes and really enjoy this surprising addition to Maling Road's sea of lace.

Thai Saffron

THAI

135 Church Street,
Brighton **9592 9097**

Licensed & BYO wine
Corkage $3 a bottle
Open daily 5.30-10pm
Seats 65; private room
Owner Thai Saffron Pty Ltd
Chef Supis Voranopakul
Cards AE BC DC MC V
Prices entrees $3.50-$10.50; mains $12.50-$21.50; desserts $6.50
Map page 266 **Melway** 67 E12

EXQUISITE black ceramic tableware, resort-style staff uniforms and contemporary South-East Asian art help this breezy bayside Thai stand out from the pack. There's attention to culinary detail, too. Chef Supis Voranopakul uses plenty of fresh herbs and chillies to make her curry pastes, achieving a pleasing balance between sweet, sour and fiery. Deep-fried entrees such as curry puffs are better than most – crisp-crusted and light-centred – but they're no match for the excellent Thai Saffron soup. This house special consists of a sweet-sour broth, tinged with saffron and brimful of fleshy barra fillets. Grilled offerings such as king prawns with lemongrass also hit the mark. Chilli lovers should try the lingeringly hot jungle chicken curry, a wet, aromatic red curry made without coconut. Vegetable fans get their own version, plus a few more options to choose from. Unfortunately, the enthusiasm displayed in the main menu does not extend to the desserts, with only four unimaginative choices available. There's also a modest wine list. Beware the minimum charge at weekends.

13/20 $ V

Thien An

VIETNAMESE

59 Irving Street,
Footscray **9687 0398**

BYO
Corkage none
Open daily 9am-9pm
Seats 50
Owner & chef Hong Chuc
Cards none
Prices entrees $2.50-$8; mains $6-$8.50; juices $2-$2.50
Map page 264 **Melway** 2S F9

BRIGHTLY coloured walls, a cabinet full of tropical fruit for juicing, and a front door in perpetual motion combine to give Thien An a feeling of bustling good cheer. Customers tuck happily into fare that's good and cheap (even for Footscray) and, while service is brisk, smiling waiters take the time to ask how you're enjoying your meal. The brief menu is a round-up of Vietnamese standards, plus an acceptable Aussie steak and chips. The rice-paper rolls, stuffed with either vegetables or pork, are freshly wrapped and beautifully minty. The broken rice with marinated grilled pork chop, crowned with a fried egg, would make a great recovery brunch, and the crisp chicken is a finger-licking highlight: tender and tasty meat under a crunchy skin. Soups step outside the usual beef-or-chicken pho double-act to include an unwieldy but worthy duck version, sunk in an intense stock with bamboo shoots and vermicelli, accessorised with purple cabbage, mint leaves and lemon. Choose from fruits like avocado, durian and custard apple for a slushy-like 'fruit tingle', or for some hardcore protein-enhancement, there's a soda drink with beaten egg and milk.

12/20 $

Tides Seafood Grill & Oyster Bar

SEAFOOD

Pier 35 Marina, 263-329 Lorimer Street,
Port Melbourne **9645 6433**

Licensed
Open Mon-Sat noon-3pm; daily 6-10pm
Seats 85; outdoor seating
Owner Lou Jovanovski
Chef Geoff Lamb
Cards AE BC DC MC V
Prices entrees $13; pastas & risottos $20; mains $24; lobster platters $120-$230; desserts $12
Map page 264 **Melway** 42 E11

THE panoramic view of the old (industrialised) Port Melbourne from Tides' panoramic windows is quite a counterpoint to the restaurant's lean, stylish interior. There are linen-clothed tables, good glassware and a deck to take full advantage of the sights up and down the river. An enormous cargo ship could glide by as you swallow an oyster dolloped with vivid green wasabi and tobikko (flying-fish roe). Chef Geoff Lamb has a fine way with seafood. There may be crabmeat and pork salad, spiked with sweet chilli sauce and tossed with shards of fresh coconut and Vietnamese mint, or more robust dishes like roasted fillets of blue-eye with a sparky harissa vinaigrette. But the hero dish (with price tag to match) is the rock lobster platter, a whole crustacean plattered with whatever's fresh off the boats, perhaps calamari, mussels and fish. Meatier options include a succulent tenderloin teamed with semolina gnocchi in a good cabernet jus. The smallish wine list offers several fish-friendly whites by the glass. Desserts are mainly fruity and creative: maybe roasted pineapple with gingerbread icecream, or strawberry soup with mascarpone mousse.

14/20

Toey's

MODERN AUSTRALIAN

62 Wellington Parade,
East Melbourne **9415 8639**

Licensed
Open Tues-Fri 11am-late; Sat-Sun 6pm-late
Seats 50; private room; bar
Owners Trent & Georgina Bromley, Kevin Clodumar
Chef Pierre Barelier
Cards AE BC DC MC V Eftpos
Prices entrees $16-$23; mains $15-$29; desserts $14-$16; lunch set menu $26 (2 courses)
Map page 263 **Melway** 2G F5

A GLITTERING renovation has transformed the space that was once the old Balzac into an ultra-mod, 'welcome to the noughties' restaurant. Gone are the boho Mirka Mora murals and ivy facade, replaced by modish furnishings, stainless-steel fittings and gleaming mirrors. French chef Pierre Barelier, formerly of Jacques Reymond and his own Soupiere, has taken charge of the kitchen, where he combines ingredients in unlikely, and mostly delicious, ways. The downstairs bar serves simpler dishes like fishcakes and stir-fries around a communal table, but it's a different story in the upstairs restaurant, with its chandeliers and mammoth window overlooking Wellington Parade. Sauteed scallops may be served with a parcel of cabbage and zucchini flower filled with Peking duck; radish gazpacho might come with tuna sashimi; and pillows of goats' curd ravioli could accompany slow-cooked ocean trout. Execution doesn't always live up to expectations, as in an overdone eye fillet. Desserts, however, are the business: you'll be wowed by pineapple pudding with sesame nougatine and wasabi icecream. A good wine list adds further cred.

14/20

Tolarno Bar & Bistro

MODERN AUSTRALIAN

42 Fitzroy Street,
St Kilda **9525 5477**

Licensed
Open Tues-Fri & Sun noon-1am; Sat 6pm-1am
Seats 90; bar
Owners Iain Hewitson & Ruth Allen
Chef Iain Hewitson
Cards AE BC DC MC V
Prices entrees $8.50-$14; mains $11.50-$25; desserts $9.50-$11.50
Map page 261 **Melway** 2P A5

IN the constant race to be the coolest new kid on the St Kilda block, Tolarno is so far out of the running, it just doesn't matter. It's barely changed in 20 years, bar a lick of paint on the Mirka Mora murals and the occasional experiment on the menu. What Tolarno does offer is something many of the newcomers don't: effortless reliability. It's a comforting blend of French bistro and Aussie pub – there aren't many places where you can order a gruyère cheese soufflé with a fine pinot noir and eat it perched on a stool in front of the cricket. Huey's food is more *Two Fat Ladies* than Jamie Oliver but few would deny the simple appeal of deep-fried crumbed mushrooms with tartare sauce (never oily, always piping hot) or minute steak topped with a knob of garlicky Paris butter. Not to mention the 'famous bar burger', an imposing stack of beef, bacon, caramelised onion, mustard aioli, beetroot chutney and salad, which can only be eaten (gracefully, at least) with knife and fork. It's not all pub grub, either, with forays into duck confit tagine, an Asiany noodle soup, and crumbed polenta fingers with aioli.

13/20

Tomoshibi

JAPANESE

5 Armstrong Street,
Middle Park **9699 1810**

Licensed & BYO wine
Corkage $2 a bottle
Open Tues-Sun 6-10.30pm
Seats 30
Owner & chef Motonori Hayashita
Cards AE BC DC MC V
Prices entrees $2.50-$12; mains $13-$27; desserts $5-$10
Map page 264 **Melway** 2K E11

THIS quaint corner shop has its fans. It's the place to meet friends or colleagues for simple, unpretentious Japanese food, or for a quick in-and-out dinner before a session (beer-fuelled or flicks) at the George. The dim room, full of chunky pine furniture and bold flower arrangements, is peopled with happy diners fighting over the last gyoza or murmuring quietly in appreciation over spanking fresh sashimi and sushi. As befitting a kitchen run by Kenzan alumni, the fish is well chosen: the tuna glowing red, the ocean trout's flavor complex, their mouthfeel and texture enhanced by the chef's cutting techniques. Get a combination sushi-sashimi mix to enjoy the full range. Deep-fried morsels such as kaki furai (bread-crumbed oysters) are oil-free, the crumb flyaway light; and the kani mushi, steamed dumplings of crab, are delicate and flavoursome. On offer for mains are the various yaki (teri, suki, shoga) with fish, chicken or steak; or slippery udon or ramen noodles in steaming soup. The sakana no shioyaki (grilled fresh fish) is swiftly plucked clean by appreciative Japanese diners – no further comment needed, surely?

12/20 $ V

Toofey's

162 Elgin Street,
Carlton **9347 9838**

SEAFOOD

Licensed
Open Tues-Fri noon-3pm; Tues-Sat 6-10.30pm
Seats 75; private room
Owners Michael Conrad & Mary Kass
Chef Michael Conrad
Cards AE BC DC MC V
Prices entrees $14.50-$21.50; mains $25-$32; desserts $12.50-$15
Map page 262 **Melway** 2B G6

ON the surface, little has changed at Toofey's since longtime owner-chef Michael Bacash sold in late 2002. The white walls and dark furniture, the fishy artwork and the heavy linen have kept their casual sophistication, the service remains switched on and, of course, the menu is still fish-focused. But new owner-chef Michael Conrad is making welcome changes, offering more complex dishes alongside Toofey's traditional simple fare. A trio of prawns could include a powerful tom yum soup, crisp spring rolls and a mini prawn cocktail. Salmon gravlax may be diced and served with pickled cucumber and teamed with lavosh bread and anchoiade. There's plenty of excellent fish – maybe barramundi, flathead and John Dory – simply served grilled or meunière but hapuku may now come with kipflers and topped with a green olive salad, and tuna could be teamed with green-tea noodles and bok choy. Desserts are an unfussy selection that might include home-made icecream and panna cotta. Toofey's may not be setting the pace, but in a city where good fish restaurants are hard to find, it's a leader.

15/20

Treasure Restaurant

482 Springvale Road,
Forest Hill **9803 2388**

Licensed & BYO
Corkage $2 a head
Open Mon-Fri noon-3pm; Sat-Sun 11am-3pm; Mon-Thurs 5.30-11pm; Fri-Sat 5.30-11.30pm; Sun 5.30-10.30pm
Seats 140
Owner Good-View Pty Ltd
Chef Alex Fung
Cards AE BC DC MC V Eftpos
Prices yum cha dishes $3-$6.50; entrees $4.50-$9.50; mains $15-$29
Map page 266 **Melway** 62 D5

OTHER than an expanded car park, it's steady as she goes at this bland but brightly lit dining room on a rise overlooking Springvale Road: same owners, same chef, same front-of-house faces. But that consistency is the Treasure's greatest virtue – those long-stayers know what they are doing, and do it so well. The service is courteous and the food (Hong Kong-Cantonese style) is always seasonal and of the highest quality. Year-round there is silky emerald green spinach-seafood soup, with diced scallops; fried squab with rich, moist meat enhanced with spicy salt; and lamb straps in a ginger-mustard sauce, which put paid to the notion that the Chinese can't cook lamb. In winter they do goat, too, in a homely, warming hotpot with bean curd flakes, water chestnut and dried orange peel. But the most memorable dishes come from the tanks. Drunken prawns – live, doused in brandy and flamed on a trolley – make a spectacular entree for diners and a stunning exit for the prawns. This verges on drama in a restaurant that is otherwise simple, understated, but always quite perfect.

15/20

Treasury

MODERN AUSTRALIAN

394 Collins Street,
City **9211 6699**

Licensed
Open Tues-Sat 6.30am-late; bistro daily noon-late
Seats 120; private rooms; bar
Owner The Sebel Melbourne
Chef Simon Duff
Cards AE BC DC MC V
Prices breakfasts $7.50-$25.50; entrees $9.50-$18; mains $22-$29; desserts $11-$17; bistro menu $7.50-$17.50
Map page 260 **Melway** 1A H7

AFTER a couple of bumpy years, Treasury has settled on a less ambitious, more realistic path. Gone are the gastro-temple pretensions, and in their place is a solidly cooked menu of mod-Oz favourites, well-pitched for weary hotel guests and lunching office workers. The room – an old banking chamber – is surprisingly comfortable for somewhere so cavernous but the quality of the linen and the finesse of the service have been scaled back along with the menu. Entrees are mostly familiar – smoked salmon with sourdough toast – but there is the occasional flourish, such as scallops mixed with sweet confit pork and a tiny pawpaw salad. Simply cooked mains tick all the chicken-beef-fish boxes but tend towards superfluous garnishing. A crisp-skinned breast of Barossa chicken disappears under a mountain of sweet potato chips. A skilfully cooked beef fillet shares the plate with a scalped tomato. Desserts continue the greatest hits approach – a flourless chocolate cake with chocolate and Kahlua sauce or a classic crème brûlée. Treasury is not the place it once was but seems all the happier – and busier – for it.

13/20

Tribeca Restaurant Bar

MODERN AUSTRALIAN

436 Toorak Road,
Toorak **9827 4484**

Licensed
Open Mon-Fri 11am-1am; Sat-Sun 8am-late
Seats 100; private room; bar
Owners Billy Sakkas & Nick Agnew
Chef Steve Rasmussen
Cards AE BC DC MC V
Prices entrees $9-$18; mains $16-$28; desserts $10; set menus $40-$60 (1-3 courses)
Map page 265 **Melway** 2M F6

YOU can learn a lot about a restaurant from its on-hold telephone message. Tribeca's perky advertorial insists the chef is 'a master of style'; that its function room can make your 'do' the event of the year; and that Tribeca is open late, every night 'as any good bar should be'. Is it a bar? A restaurant? Or a nightclub? Tribeca is a bit of everything. Let's start with lunch. On warm days, the floor-to-ceiling windows slide back to reveal a chocolate and cream dining scene. It's the spot to be seen sipping a sauv blanc or sampling a light crab and avocado terrine, sexed up with a coriander dressing. At night, the menu is pricier and weightier – porterhouse steak, veal medallions, or well-cooked seafood such as crisp-skinned barramundi in an orange 'saffron' mussel broth with sauteed potatoes. It's mostly good and non-confronting for the blue-chip clientele. For dessert, the house-made icecreams and sorbets are excellent. Don't expect the service to be as polished as your neighbour's sling-backs, although the waiters are pleasant and well meaning. The wine list is short and predictable, and there's a bar upstairs.

13/20

SIGNATURE DISHES

From simple and rustic to complex and luxe, some of Melbourne's finest

Chicken and rice, $7
Abla's, 109 Elgin Street, Carlton, 9347 0006
Abla Amad prepares a long-grain rice pilaf with lamb mince, a dash of pepper, cardamom and chicken stock. Then she lines a cake mould with shredded chicken breast and flaked almonds, and piles in the pilaf. To serve, she inverts the mould, crowns the rice with more chicken and almonds, and dusts it with cinnamon. It's amazing that something so simple can taste so good. See page 14.

Fiorina's stuffed olives, $9
Becco, 11-25 Crossley Street, City, 9663 3000
Marco Lori has long since departed the stoves at Becco, but his mother, Fiorina, still prepares the restaurant's snack of renown. Fleshy green olives are pitted and filled with a subtly spiced pork and veal mixture. They're then crumbed and fried in olive oil, resulting in a rustic appetite whetter. See page 23.

Baghare baigan, $12.90
Bhoj Docklands, 54 New Quay Promenade, Docklands, 9600 0884
Always a winner at Bhoj in Templestowe, this dish seems to taste even better in the glam surrounds of harbourside Docklands. Baby eggplants are simmered with ground cashews, sesame seeds, peanuts and coconut. Tamarind lends tang, providing a perfect foil to the richness of the eggplant and nuts. See page 25.

Warm poached egg with soft polenta, parmesan and truffle, $19.50
Botanical, 169 Domain Road, South Yarra, 9820 7888
This dish was conceived at Georges, and grew up to fame and glory at radii. Now, proud dad Paul Wilson has taken it with him to the Bot. Wilson stores his free-range eggs with fresh truffles, before poaching and serving them on a bed of truffle-infused polenta, enriched with parmigiano reggiano, then finished with shavings of parmesan and truffle for good measure. See page 35.

Crespelle al limone, $15.50
Cafe Di Stasio, 31 Fitzroy Street, St Kilda, 9525 3999
It's one of the most memorable desserts you'll eat and a tricky one to get right. Thin crepes are poached in a piquant lemon syrup, brûléed until crisp, then served with vanilla bean icecream. If the crepes are too hot, they fall apart when poached. If they're too cold, they taste stodgy. It's a fine balancing act but one the Di Stasio team has perfected. See page 37.

Crispy fried pork hock with chilli caramel, Thai basil, marinated bean shoots and jasmine rice, $32.50
ezard at adelphi, 187 Flinders Lane, City, 9639 6811
The amazing Mr Ezard has taken a hunk of pork and worked his fusion magic on it. He bones out the hock, poaches it in master stock and hangs it to dry for a couple of days. He then coats it with palm sugar caramel, lime juice and chilli and deep-fries it until the skin is crisp and the flesh is moist. See page 63.

Peking duck, $35 (for 2)
Flower Drum, 17 Market Lane, City, 9662 3655
Perhaps the most celebrated dish in all of Melbourne, the Drum has been 'doing duck' for 28 years. Blanched and seasoned birds are roasted vertically until their skins are crisp and the flesh moistened by the rendered fat. Service is pure theatre: chopstick-wielding waiters deftly position duck, spring onions and cucumber on to delicate steamed pancakes, which are daubed with sweet plum sauce. See page 67.

Truffle-centred chocolate soufflé, $19
Ondine, 299 Queen Street, City, 9602 3477
The only dish that never leaves Ondine's menu. Dessert queen Philippa Sibley-Cooke tucks a disk of ganache inside her Valrhona chocolate soufflé before it is baked to order, so when you break through you're greeted with a luscious, melting centre. The soufflé comes with an equally decadent icecream, perhaps mint and caramel or orange and cardamom. See page 122.

The Trust

MODERN ITALIAN

405-411 Flinders Lane,
City **9629 9300**

Licensed
Open Mon-Fri noon-3pm; Mon-Sat 6pm-late
Seats 130; bar
Owners Lou & Lora Baccini
Chef Leandro Panza
Cards AE BC DC MC V
Prices entrees $14.50-$18; pastas & risottos $14.50-$27; mains $27.50-$32; desserts $11.50-$14
Map page 260 **Melway** 1A F9

WANT a quiet meal? Avoid the Trust on Friday nights, when workers pack the cavernous front bar of this heritage-listed building. The rest of the week, however, diners rule. The dining room is a magnificent expanse of high ceilings, original wood panelling, crisp linen and white-painted wooden chairs, upholstered in raspberry. There's a wine list with plenty of familar, well-priced labels, so you might team Shadowfax pinot noir with a main course of tender twice-cooked duck on a muscatel and barley risotto. Upmarket pastas, like ribbons of al dente tagliolini in an inky ragu of tender cuttlefish, come in entree and main sizes. Other dishes are less successful in execution – a heavy hand with seasoning in a prawn farce weighs down a dish of fried, stuffed zucchini flowers, and calling tomato slices 'fillets' is just silly. The Trust is an expensive restaurant, more so as side dishes ($10.50 for sauteed spinach and garlic) are needed to balance the mains. Desserts set things back on track: the white peach semifreddo with prosecco jelly and raspberry coulis is a well-worked and stylish ending.

12/20

Union Food and Wine

MODERN AUSTRALIAN

10-12 Armstrong Street,
Middle Park **9699 4244**

Licensed & BYO wine (groups of 6 or fewer)
Corkage $10 a bottle
Open Tues-Fri noon-2.30pm; Tues-Sat 6pm-late; Sat-Sun 9am-3pm
Seats 50; outdoor seating; private room; bar
Owner Julian Nelson
Chef Bob Millynn
Cards AE BC DC MC V Eftpos
Prices entrees $8-$18.50; mains $16.50-$28.50; desserts $12; less in bistro
Map page 264 **Melway** 2K E11

UNION FOOD AND WINE covers several bases: it's a wine bar; it's a drop-in bistro; and it's a formal restaurant with an elaborate menu. It's all spread across two neutrally renovated Victorian shopfronts, with contemporary art on the walls, chalkboard menus, a crackling fire in winter, and a leafy courtyard that packs out in warmer months. New chef Bob Millynn, previously at Middle Park's Gunn Island Brew Bar, has a deft touch, and he crafts a menu with wide appeal, covering everything from veal loin saltimbocca with a shallot tarte tatin to the signature corned beef with mash. His tasting plate replaces the usual antipasto suspects with, say, chicken spring rolls, risotto balls, and cotechino sausage. The fillet steak may come with pan-fried spaetzle noodles to soak up the rich jus. There's a good range of wines by the glass and many attractively priced bottles. There's the occasional hiccup, such as scatty service, or scorched macadamias in the otherwise superb white chocolate and banana steamed pudding, but this is a polished performance from a neighbourhood restaurant.

13/20

Vao Doi

VIETNAMESE/CHINESE

300 High Street,
Kew **9852 8366**

Licensed & BYO wine
Corkage $1.50 a head
Open Mon-Fri 11am-11pm; Sat-Sun 6-11pm
Seats 110
Owner Vo family
Chef Tom Vo
Cards AE BC MC V
Prices entrees $3-$9; soups $4.50-$6.50; mains $9-$55; desserts $4-$5
Map page 265 **Melway** 45 D6

THERE'S little on Vao Doi's menu that you wouldn't find on Victoria Street. But with its linen tablecloths, colourful lightshades, formally clad staff and well-appointed bar, Vao Dao is a notch above most Viet stalwarts, without inflicting fiscal GBH. All the family's Sino-Viet favourites are there: charry beef wrapped in mint; huge sang choy bao, the lettuce leaves enfolding minced pork, vegetables and Chinese sausage; succulent chilli-salted quails; and rice-paper rolls with various stuffings. You'll even find dishes from further afield, such as Thai-style tom yum soup spiked with chilli and sour with citrus, and ever-popular Singapore noodles. Lemongrass sauteed prawns are worth ordering: fragrant and garlicky, with a lick of chilli. Skip the Oz-Chinese classic of sweet and sour pork: light on pork, heavy on batter. But leave room for the deliciously coconutty rice pudding, sprinkled with roasted sesame seeds. Overall, the dishes are cooked competently and delivered swiftly, service is courteous, if sometimes inexperienced, and the wine list is quite respectable: two dozen well-chosen Antipodean labels, some by the glass.

13/20 $

Verge

MODERN AUSTRALIAN

1 Flinders Lane,
City **9639 9500**

Licensed
Open Mon-Sat noon-3pm, 6-11pm; bar Mon-Sat 10am-1am
Seats 70; outdoor seating; bar
Owners Michelle Bowen, Simon Denton & Karen White
Chef Karen White
Cards AE BC DC MC V
Prices entrees $12.50-$16.50; mains $18.50-$29.50; desserts $12.50; cheeses $8.50-$19.50
Map page 260 **Melway** 1B V9

VERGE is all that's good about the boom in CBD apartment living in the past five years, being the offspring of one such project. It's easygoing yet smart, seamlessly combining a vibey bar with a minimalist restaurant upstairs. Karen White maintains the menu's basic size and structure through the seasons, leaning more towards epicurean European cooking than Asian standards, and flavours are as restrained and subtle as the decor. That said, the gyoza have been a fixture since day one, their pleated fringes and ivory-coloured casings filled with particularly sweet and juicy pork. Fish dishes might include snapper with crème fraîche or a thick steak of ocean trout that arrives with a rare orange core. While red meats are choice, be it roast lamb cutlets or rondels of finely minced veal girdled by delicate pasta, you may need a snappy side dish like baby spinach bound in chilli oil to balance the meal. Verge attracts a loyal following of style-mongers won over by its consistency and chic surrounds. Service is hyper-alert, unobtrusive and a little impersonal – courses are delivered with the timing of a great actor, belying all the hard work backstage.

15/20

Viet's Quan

VIETNAMESE

Shop 6, 300 Toorak Road (enter from Cunningham Street),
South Yarra **9827 4765**

BYO
Corkage none
Open Mon-Sat noon-3.30pm, 6-11.30pm
Seats 60
Owner & chef Huynh Viet
Cards AE BC DC MC V Eftpos
Prices entrees $7-$12; mains $14-$20; desserts $5-$6
Map page 265 **Melway** 2L K5

IT'S hidden metres from Toorak Road, up a little side street, but cluey locals are happy to keep quiet about Viet's Quan. It's a nifty, colourful (lots of reds and oranges) little place doing a line in imaginative, contemporary Vietnamese food at very reasonable prices and a BYO permit keeping the bill down still further. Order the calamari if it's on the specials board, as it's some of the best salt-and-pepper squid in town, with hints of chilli and ginger and flesh that's rarely chewy. The grilled cho lon beef rolls are an interesting contrast, heavier and more filling, with marinated beef fillet wrapped around crunchy onion and served with a hoisin-based dipping sauce. Tender meat also features in the sizzling diced beef dish, a rich, sweet stir-fry with sesame and oyster sauce. And the fizzling platter theme continues with a braised prawns and vegetable combination, redolent of those Vietnamese staples, lemongrass, chilli and garlic. It's less successful than the beef, but still good. Among desserts is a rare and popular find – a French-style chocolate mousse. As Quan says: 'Nothing is bad. Everything good. OK.'

13/20 $ V

Vista Bar & Bistro

INTERNATIONAL

123-125 Bridport Street,
Albert Park **9699 7757**

Licensed
Open Tues-Fri & Sun noon-3pm; Tues-Sun 6pm-late
Seats 65; outdoor seating; bar
Owners Josef & Eileen Fiederling
Chef Josef Fiederling
Cards AE BC DC MC V
Prices entrees $11.25-$17.50; mains $19-$29.50; desserts $11.50-$15
Map page 264 **Melway** 2K A6

IF you were having an affair, Vista is the last place you'd want to rendezvous. It may be the perfect vantage point for the comings and goings of Albert Park village, but that means everybody else can see what you're up to, too. Pity, as it's an evocative spot, with splashes of deep red on the walls, honey-stained floors and glowing candle-lamps. It's certainly the pick of the big-night-out venues around these parts, with confident service, a good wine list (including a 'premium selection') and a menu of contemporary favourites served with a mild twist: mix and match Tasmanian sugar-cured salmon with brioche, 'Indian spiced' quail with lentil salsa, and duck with Chinese flavours. Moroccan, classic French and Italian dishes make an appearance, too. The signature dessert is the 'Coupe Vista', a melee of icecreams and fresh fruit in an enormous goblet. The food is of a decent standard, although you could expect a little more polish at this price level – there's not much 'wow' factor. Still, dining at Vista is reliably enjoyable. It plans to introduce a bar menu, too, which might offer the ambience without the price tag.

13/20

Vlado's

STEAKHOUSE

61 Bridge Road,
Richmond **9428 5833**

Licensed
Open Mon-Fri noon-3.30pm; Mon-Sat 6-11pm
Seats 80
Owner & chef Vlado Gregurek
Cards AE BC DC MC V
Prices set menu $62 (4 courses)
Map page 265 **Melway** 2G H5

THE front inside wall of Vlado's says it all: it's one big photograph of a herd of cattle staring down the barrel of a camera. The 40-year-old formula at this Bridge Road chophouse remains unchanged: beef cevapcici appetiser, mixed grill entree (liver, bacon, eye fillet), beefsteak main, strawberries and icecream or pancakes for dessert, accompanied by a few local beers or something from a short but affordable wine list (plus Grange). Vlado himself still cooks the man-size cuts of porterhouse, rump or scotch fillet exactly to order. He's happy to debrief you after the meal on the beef's breed and dietary habits, but you won't learn whether it's grain- or grass-fed by reading the menu. The waiters still wear ill-fitting polycotton shirts and slacks; the restaurant's interior is still dark baronial homestead; and the walls are still covered in awards, celebrity photographs, and objets d'art celebrating beef – its execution, cooking and eating. The coleslaw is fresh, the chips plentiful, and the beef is at the more densely textured end of the spectrum. Which all make this de facto businessmen's club an enjoyable anachronism.

13/20

Vue de Monde

MODERN FRENCH

295 Drummond Street,
Carlton **9347 0199**

Licensed
Open Tues-Fri noon-2.30pm; Tues-Sat 6.30-10pm
Seats 50; private room
Owner & chef Shannon Bennett
Cards AE BC DC MC V
Prices entrees $18.50; mains $35.50; desserts $15.50; dinner set menu $49 or $65 (2 or 3 courses); menu gourmand $80-$130 (5-9 courses)
Map page 262 **Melway** 2B G7

EVERY city should have a Shannon Bennett – a chef fanatical about doing things the right way. Grapes that accompany foie gras have been peeled, and gravies have been wrung from bones over many hours. This uncompromising foodiness is not to everyone's taste, but the formality has softened slightly over the years, making Vue de Monde an increasingly enjoyable experience. A memorable but simple (for Bennett) pastry tart of confit tomato is paired with an almond gazpacho sorbet, crisped sage and anchovy fritter. But if you're longing for elaborate, classical technique, you'll find it in dishes like trotters stuffed with caramelised sweetbreads, bound in a chicken and wild mushroom mousse, or oysters topped with scrambled duck egg, crayfish bits and a champagne velouté. The set-price menu with supplementary charges for high-end ingredients means the 'menu gourmand' offers the best value. If the monstrous, marvellous wine list scares you, let the sommelier be your guide. Vue de Monde delivers a memorable experience because of Bennett's obsessive focus on quality – and in spite of the current trend away from fine dining.

16/20

Walter's Wine Bar

MODERN AUSTRALIAN

Upper level, Southgate,
Southbank **9690 9211**

Licensed
Open daily noon-late
Seats 90; outdoor seating; bar
Owners Walter & Maria Bourke
Chef Justin Cortellino
Cards AE BC DC MC V
Prices entrees $16-$17.50; mains $24-$33.50; desserts $14-$17.50
Map page 264 **Melway** 1D T3

A BAR, a wine destination, a big night out, a post-theatre supper or a quick lunch, Walter's versatility is all in its favour. But creeping prices and expensive ingredients (Wagyu beef, truffle oil) suggest that it's aiming beyond fancy bistro, a label that's served it so well for more than a decade. The geranium-trimmed balconies with views to the CBD, the tinkling piano, and the awesome 22-page reserve wine list – indexed by varietals and/or regions – still impress, but the food is not as good as it once was. A sage gnocchi entree, perhaps, may be weighed down with butter and oil. In contrast, a tomato and zucchini lasagne is light and deft enough, happily keeping company with a deep-fried zucchini flower stuffed with goats' cheese. Mains are all generously portioned and might include a tender and juicy quail saltimbocca, a retro dish of garlic prawns, or a well-cooked chicken breast atop a truffle-infused risotto. Service seems more distracted than in the past, and the place a little run down – bent fork tines, chipped paint, frayed aprons. Ambience can be everything, but the little things still count.

14/20

Warung Agus

BALINESE

305 Victoria Street,
West Melbourne **9329 1737**

Licensed & BYO wine
Corkage $3 a bottle
Open Thurs-Sun 6-10.30pm
Seats 60
Owners Mary & Agus Ida Bagus
Chef Agus Ida Bagus
Cards BC MC V
Prices entrees $1-$12; mains $11-$28; desserts $6; juices $5.50
Map page 262 **Melway** 2A J11

IN Bali, a warung is a place to get together, eat and chill out. And so it is here, where smiling staff guide you from the potted green jungle at the entrance to tables clothed in batik, under a sky of mirrored quilts. Agus himself produces innovative flavours alongside more simple dishes. The requests of vegetarians and vegans will not faze him – try soybean dishes like nasi campur, which proves that tofu and tempeh can be tasty when dressed up in soy, ginger, garlic and coconut sambal. Interesting sauces abound; more delicate in the king prawn coconut curry with kaffir lime leaves and chilli oil; darker, with hints of tamarind, for the braised calamari. Both are excellent. Likewise flathead fillets, with a sauce of, say, palm sugar, chilli and tamarind, flecked with spring onions. The traditional Balinese roast pork is baked with lemongrass, galangal, prawn paste and palm sugar and served with a candlenut sauce. It's large enough to work easily as a plate for two to share. Same goes for the desserts – generous treats like the dadar crepes filled with coconut and palm sugar will send you off on a Bali high.

13/20 $ V

Wharf 8 Grill

MODERN AUSTRALIAN

8a South Wharf Road,
Southbank **9686 2468**

Licensed
Open Tues-Sun 5.30-10pm
Seats 65; outdoor seating; bar
Owner Lou Jovanovski
Chef Bas Van Uyen
Cards AE BC DC MC V
Prices entrees $12; sides $5; pastas $18; mains $20; desserts $10
Map page 264 **Melway** 2E J9

NESTLED next door to the Polly Woodside on the edge of the Yarra, this ambitious diner has transformed a difficult space into a comfortable and stylish restaurant. The colour scheme is dark chocolate and cream, trimmed with glass and steel. Chef Bas Van Uyen, whose CV reads like a Melbourne international hotel directory, offers a casual 'grill-style' menu: plenty of meat plus some creative seafood and pasta dishes. Entrees are seafood-rich, such as oysters done six ways, the steamed chilli and lemongrass version a standout. Other entrees might include cured salmon with a dill crème fraîche, or grilled calamari over rocket and preserved lemon. Mostly meaty mains include chicken cooked two ways, Cajun- and Thai-style. Both arrive lightly spiced and crisp-skinned, the flesh wonderfully moist. The New York T-bone combines flame-grilled meat with a potent red wine and capsicum jus. Sides include chunky fries and marinated olives, while the desserts trend toward comfort. A bread and butter brioche, served with a jammy sauce, is luscious but heavy. Best to stick to a plate of house-churned icecream or sorbet.

13/20

Wildflower

MODERN AUSTRALIAN

1 Theatre Place,
Canterbury **9888 6662**

BYO
Corkage $2.75 a head
Open Mon-Sat noon-2.30pm, 6.30-9.30pm; Sun 9am-3pm
Seats 40; outdoor seating; private room
Owners Natalie Canavan & Anthony Phelan
Chef Anthony Phelan
Cards AE BC DC MC V Eftpos
Prices breakfasts $5-$18; entrees $14.50-$16; mains $24.50-$30; desserts $11-$12.50; lunch set menus $25 or $30 (2 or 3 courses)
Map page 266 **Melway** 46 D11

SIX-PACKS and even the occasional cask make their way to this delightful but strictly BYO restaurant – one of the best of the few left in town. The downside is that you'll drink your favourite wine from cheap, chunky glassware. The dining room of this two-storey terrace is uncluttered, as are the tables, and the chairs are comfortable. Co-owner and chef Anthony Phelan is a dab hand at modern Australian flavours, presenting dishes with the minimum of fuss and without frivolous garnishes. The oft-changing menu is small but well-rounded: five choices for each course, plus a handful of good-looking sides, such as roast pumpkin and pesto. Thus, tender seared scallops might be served today with a lemon-scented mash, and next time with char siu pork, lime-vanilla mash and chilli jam. The beef fillet – perfectly cooked, served with potatoes, baby spinach, mushrooms and a rich jus – will match your best shiraz. Desserts breathe life into restaurant favourites – panna cotta might be flavoured with cinnamon, and chocolate brownies sparked up with nectarine and plum-pudding icecream.

14/20

Windows on the Bay

MODERN AUSTRALIAN

Peter Scullin Reserve, 333 Beach Road,
Mordialloc **9580 5854**

Licensed
Open Mon-Fri noon-3pm, 6pm-late; Sat-Sun 9am-late
Seats 180; private rooms
Owner & chef Alex Almatrah
Cards AE BC DC MC V Eftpos
Prices breakfasts $5-$15.50; entrees $10-$19; mains $14-$42; desserts $10-$14
Map page 267 **Melway** 92 E1

WINDOWS, a nicely revamped former bathing pavilion by the water's edge, has a subtle marine-themed decor that reels in the hopefuls. There's not much fine-dining competition in Mordialloc, and the food here mostly sustains local expectations. The wine list is wide-ranging, with a large by-the-glass selection, and service is pleasant, but not particularly thoughtful. Extra offerings like a basket of bread would help, considering the prices. Entrees include an antipasto platter featuring good house-made delicacies (beef carpaccio, semolina-crumbed calamari, marinated vegetables), and boned quail that's been steeped in chilli, garlic, ginger and soy then char-grilled. Mains lift the standard. A simple dish of pan-seared king tiger prawns in a buttery, garlicky sauce is hard to fault. A Moroccan-spiced rack of lamb is just as good, its minted peas, mash and pomegranate molasses striking a delicate balance between sweetness and tang. A side dish of garlic mushrooms enhances both meals. Desserts are predictable but reliable and may include gelati, tiramisu, sticky date pudding or lemon tart.

12/20 

The Windsor, One Eleven Spring Street

INTERNATIONAL

103 Spring Street,
City **9633 6004**

Licensed
Open (afternoon tea) daily 3.30-5.30pm; Mon-Fri 6.30am-11.30pm; Sat-Sun 7am-11.30pm
Seats 100, private room
Owner Oberoi International
Chef Tom Milligan
Cards AE BC DC MC V
Prices breakfasts $8-$27; entrees $17-$30; mains $22-$32; desserts $12.50-$16; afternoon tea $30 (Mon-Fri), $45 (Sat-Sun); lunch set menu $32 (2 courses)
Map page 260 **Melway** 1B V6

YOU'VE got to love the Windsor. The soothing brown and cream colour scheme, the swags and flounces at the windows, the Persian rugs on polished floors – it's all very atmospheric. Which is just as well, because the food at One Eleven Spring Street just adds to the sense of a bygone era. Many of the offerings are homely in style and flavour – one pudgy Thai fishcake on cucumber salad might not be authentic but it's delicious, while the Windsor roast at lunchtime, perhaps roast pork loin with crackling, is like your mother's Sunday best. Lamb chops and mash, however, transport you straight back to the 'burbs, circa 1968. On the more exotic dinner menu, a brochette of king prawns on a turmeric and green pea risotto or an almond-crumbed veal cutlet sound stylish, but it's the sort of 'international' hotel food found across the globe. Desserts can be lavishly creamy, or painfully plain, but it all seems acceptable when your wrists rest on crisp damask and a solicitous waiter is hovering nearby. And then, of course, there's the famous high tea: tiered trays of point sandwiches, scones and cakes. Take your mum.

12/20 

Ying Thai 2

THAI

110 Lygon Street,
Carlton **9639 1697**

Licensed & BYO
Corkage $2 a head
Open Tues-Sun noon-10pm
Seats 40; outdoor seating
Owners Boston & Pornlapat Phrutthiarphakul
Chefs Santaya Panghom & Pornlapat Phrutthiarphakul
Cards BC MC V Eftpos
Prices entrees $6.70-$11.90; mains $10.90-$16.90; desserts $4.20-$6.90
Map page 262 **Melway** 2B F10

SPAWNED from its busy mother restaurant in Abbotsford, Ying Thai 2 serves Thai market food in a funky two-level dining room at the city end of Lygon Street. The decor is a riot of colour, with airbrushed cartoons of traditional Thai village life. The mainly Asian crowd is young, boisterous and not too fussed with the lax service. The food can be blisteringly hot, but once you've passed through the chilli pain barrier, authentic flavours creep through. (The owner's mother had a cafe in the Bangkok market and still makes all the curry pastes, sauces and condiments.) For entree, try the northern Thai sausage, a fat fiery pork snorker laced with kaffir lime leaves. Salads can be intense , but like the roast duck salad with lemon and fish sauce, refreshingly sour. Six curries range from the relatively mild Panang curry – beef, pork, chicken or seafood in a luxurious coconut sauce – to a sweet and sour curry topped with fat strips of omelette. Sweet, salty, hot and sticky – the taro or sago desserts are confronting but delicious. Some will find Ying Thai 2 too much, others will keep flocking back. *Also Ying Thai, 235 Victoria Street, Abbotsford, 9419 1225.*

12/20 **$**

Yu-u

JAPANESE

137 Flinders Lane,
City **9639 7073**

Licensed
Open Mon-Fri noon-2.15pm (or until sold out);
Mon-Fri 6-9.30pm
Seats 28; private rooms
Owners Daisuke & Noriko Miyamoto
Chef Daisuke Miyamoto
Cards AE BC DC MC V
Prices all dishes $5-$10 (minimum $30 a head after 7.30pm);
lunch set menu $15 (6 dishes)
Map page 260 **Melway** 1B R9

THE wispy smoke rising from the yakitori grill, the cool grey and purple room, the hushed tones of the clientele, food that arrives artfully presented on Japanese ceramics – Yu-u is ultra-smart in a minimal, understated way. Lunch is teishoku (chef decides) bento boxes – a curry, perhaps, or minced chicken, with soup, soba noodles, rice and pickles. Dinner is served izakaya-style: snacks designed to be eaten with sake or beer. Yu-u's menu separates the dishes according to temperature, not size. Assured staff orchestrate the meal's progression, ensuring a series of contrasts between soft-crisp, spicy-cleansing, hot-cold. Cold dishes include dashimaki (rolled omelette with vegetables and seaweed); dominos of thickly sliced salmon or kingfish sashimi; and braised octopus in soy – each plate honed in flavour and texture. The hot shishamo (grilled sun-dried sardines) are to be eaten whole, and nizakana (sea perch simmered in soy and sake) is homely and warming. Yu-u offers the traditional Japanese dish of green tea poured over steamed rice with either pickled plums or cooked salmon. For dash without much cash, Yu-u is it. Remember to book.

15/20

Zen's

CHINESE

23-25 Anderson Creek Road,
Doncaster East **9841 7566**

Licensed & BYO wine
Corkage $2 a head
Open Mon-Fri noon-3pm; Sat-Sun 11am-3pm; Sun-Thurs 5.30-10pm; Fri-Sat 5.30-11pm
Seats 120
Owner Amy Yu
Chef On Kwan
Cards AE BC DC MC V
Prices yum cha dishes $3.20-$6; entrees $4-$24; mains $15-$50; desserts $5-$6.50
Map page 266 **Melway** 34 D10

THIS nondescript eating barn on the edge of town, dressed with requisite calligraphy banners and Chinese screens, draws on a substantial local Chinese population. It seems slightly less buzzy since a recent change of ownership but the chef, the food and the service remain accomplished. At first sight, the menu offers the standard Cantonese fixtures, but there are some hidden treasures, so it pays to seek out recommendations. To begin, you might order crunchy fried lotus cake or deliciously light whitebait fritters. Shredded pork may come wrapped in pancakes à la Peking duck – a variation on a similar dish popular in northern China. Zen's is noted for its hotpot dishes, and a highlight is a bubbling casserole of chicken and black beans, succulent and satisfying on a wintry evening. Those looking for something with a kick should order the shelled prawns in spicy chilli salt. Pro forma desserts include red-bean pancakes, sweet soup or a cheesecake with coconut icecream. Live seafood is available, along with daily yum cha service. The wine list is modest, but you may bring your own.

12/20

Zio's Ristorante

MODERN ITALIAN

14 Lansdowne Street,
East Melbourne **9419 0252**

Licensed & BYO wine
Corkage $7.50 a bottle
Open Tues-Fri noon-3pm; Tues-Sat 6pm-late
Seats 85; private room
Owners Paul & Myrto Recinella
Chef Paul Recinella
Cards AE BC DC MC V
Prices entrees $14.90-$23.90; mains $21-$32.90; desserts $12.90
Map page 263 **Melway** 2G B1

FOR 14 years, loyal diners have visited the elegant green dining room of this two-storey terrace for heartfelt hospitality and some of the most consistently good modern Italian food in town. Chef Paul Recinella uses choice ingredients (the herbs, free-range eggs, and vegetables often come from his father's garden) in a menu that plays with Italian traditions, but takes a more-than-occasional soy or wasabi side-trip. Zio's signature is the 'six tastes of the sea' – an entree sampling platter of six (and sometimes even eight) seafood bites. Expect morsels such as salt-and-pepper cuttlefish, creamy ocean trout gravlax with coriander, steamed prawn dumplings and wasabi-seared tuna. Pasta, perhaps a hand-rolled duck tortellini or linguine with creamy bocconcini and chilli, is always well cooked. And it's worth checking the specials list for things like a spinach salad, tossed with fresh figs, prosciutto, walnuts and gorgonzola and dressed with apple balsamic. Desserts range from fruity (poached pears) to rich (chocolate parfait with coffee biscotti and vanilla fairy floss). There's a short list of reasonably priced wines, but you can also BYO.

15/20

THE COUNTRY

EDITED BY DANI VALENT

Black Paddock Restaurant & Receptions

MODERN AUSTRALIAN

Evelyn County Estate, 55 Eltham-Yarra Glen Road,
Kangaroo Ground **9437 2155**

SO striking is Black Paddock that it stops many daytrippers from venturing any further than Kangaroo Ground. But the streamlined restaurant doesn't just trade on its metallic good looks – innovative food is part of the package, too. Pâtés and terrines make regular appearances: you might happen upon a chunky chicken and apricot terrine with a plummy sauce. Middle Eastern and Asian flavours are employed in many dishes. Roast lamb comes in preserved lemon jus; saganaki is sparked up with pomegranate molasses; braised chicken is served with iceberg lettuce and Asian herbs. This fusion food sometimes falls short, as in flathead tails bundled with noodles and an oversupply of pickled ginger. Desserts are always good, though, whether it's the zingy sorbets drizzled with fruit coulis or orange cake with rosewater syrup.

Licensed
Open Sun 9-11am; Wed-Sun noon-5pm; Thurs-Sat 6pm-late
Seats 44; outdoor seating; bar
Owners Robyn & Roger Male
Chef Gordon Brown
Cards AE BC DC MC V Eftpos
Prices breakfasts $5-$11.50; entrees $8.50-$12.50; mains $19-$23; desserts $7.50-$14
Map page 267 **Melway** 23 B1

13/20

De Bortoli Winery & Restaurant

ITALIAN

58 Pinnacle Lane,
Dixons Creek **5965 2271**

THE approach – up a pretty lane, bordered by pear trees and backed by vines – is marred somewhat by the squat brick restaurant and cellar door complex. Never mind – it's better from the inside, where the cottagey decor sits well with the unfussy regional Italian food. Dishes range from delicate (baby beet salad with piquant vinaigrette) to rich and well-rounded (melting rabbit ravioli) to rustic (pork sausages with braised lentils, or eggplant and fontina 'lasagne' with a dollop of white bean puree). Desserts are pure pleasure, especially when savoured with De Bortoli's botrytis semillon. Try hazelnut semifreddo with zabaglione or baked fig with fluffy rice pudding. The little things are done well: water is regularly refreshed, the waiters always have a moment to banter and moist macaroons are presented with the coffee. Sundays lunches are by set menu only.

Licensed
Open daily noon-3pm; Sat 7pm-late
Seats 130; outdoor seating
Owner De Bortoli family
Chef Robert Monteau
Cards AE BC DC MC V Eftpos
Prices entrees $12.50-$19; mains $16.50-$31; desserts $12; Sun lunch set menu $55 (5 courses)
Map page 267 **Melway** 267 K1

13/20

Eleonore's at Chateau Yering

MODERN EUROPEAN

42 Melba Highway,
Yering **9237 3333**

AMONG Victoria's most stately restaurants, Eleonore's grand dining room boasts lofty ceilings, starchy napkins and double-glazed windows with exceptional views of perambulating house guests, cow paddocks and distant forested hills. The food is highly worked, consisting of multiple elements in elaborate arrangements. The kitchen's trickery is patently worthwhile in dishes like the baked tomato, stuffed with herbed cous cous and anchored by pea puree in a refined tomato tea. Other dishes do not coalesce: poached rabbit loin is rolled with a delicate basil mousse and plated with cheesy crayfish. And it's frankly mystifying to find a very good fillet of seared local salmon draped over an oyster and pancetta tart. Desserts are deliciously decadent, as in the baked apple filled with joyously obvious white chocolate fudge.

14/20 

Licensed
Open Sat-Sun noon-5pm; daily 6 30pm-late
Seats 10
Owners Len & Elly Milner
Chef Shane Delia
Cards AE BC DC MC V Eftpos
Prices entrees $18-$22; mains $30-$39; desserts $14-$22; lunch set menus $49.50 or $59.50 (2 or 3 courses)
Map page 267 **Melway** 275 B5

Healesville Hotel

MODERN REGIONAL

256 Maroondah Highway,
Healesville **5962 4002**

THE Healesville has the lofty pressed-metal ceilings, open fires and beer garden of a small town hotel, but it's far from your normal country pub. Chef Richard Hauptmann (ex-Sweetwater Cafe) cooks smart dishes with plenty of spirit. Yarra Valley farmyards, pastures and waterways supply much of what ends up on the plate: free-range pork and pheasant are used for his rillettes; chermoula-rubbed local salmon turns up on a moghrabieh and preserved lemon salad; a millefeuille of Silvan raspberries is sandwiched with mascarpone and Campari jelly. Hauptmann makes his own prosciutto and sausages (scoff these in the front bar with potato salad) and the owners grow hydroponic herbs, lettuce and cress for the restaurant. The wine list is excellent, chosen with style and written with humour.

15/20 

Licensed
Open Sat-Sun 9-11.30am; daily noon-3pm, 6-9pm; bar daily noon-9pm
Seats 50; outdoor seating; private room; bar
Owners Michael Kennedy & Kylie Balharrie
Chef Richard Hauptmann
Cards AE BC DC MC V Eftpos
Prices entrees $12.50-$15; mains $22.50-$29.50; desserts $11; bar meals $12-$17
Map page 267 **Melway** 278 C1

Rochford's Eyton

MODERN AUSTRALIAN

Rochford Wines, Corner Maroondah Highway & Hill Road,
Coldstream **5962 2119**

WITH its concert series, loft gallery, busy cellar door and functions trade, Eyton obviously has the big picture in mind. So much so that everyday restaurant operations can get a little lost. The expansive, sun-drenched venue – and the high prices – suggest that eating here will be a special experience indeed. But, while some dishes are winningly theatrical, others just flounce about the plate. Successful dishes include an elaborate nori-wrapped seafood terrine with firm scallops and sashimi tuna, and a spritely tomato salsa topped with coiled snake beans. Less impressive is the overwrought chicken mignon, stuffed with cheesy scrambled eggs, trussed with bacon and plonked indelicately on an avocado and corn salad. But stay tuned. A new chef and set-price menu regime were instituted as the *Guide* went to press.

13/20 

Licensed
Open daily noon-3pm; Fri-Sat 6pm-late
Seats 200; outdoor seating; private room; bar
Owner Helmut Konecsny
Chef Leonard Kysnezow
Cards AE BC DC MC V Eftpos
Prices lunch set menu $45 (2 courses); dinner set menu $55 (3 courses)
Map page 267 **Melway** 277 D9

Rustic Charm Restaurant

MODERN REGIONAL

Corner Warburton Highway & Beenak Road,
Wandin North **5964 3694**

IT started in 1899 as Wandin North's general store, and tripped through the decades as real estate office, stove shop and antique emporium. Now this modest building is firmly established as the proud yet personable Rustic Charm. The decor is a confused mix of barn door and boudoir, but the food is a victorious mix of country comfort, international ideas and home-grown twists featuring native produce. Start with homely flowerpot bread served with dukkah made from indigenous herbs. Move on to gamey rabbit and prune terrine with bush tomato chutney or kangaroo sirloin in a riberry and pepperberry glaze. The mocha soufflé comes with local berries and icecream from Yarra Valley chocoholics Kennedy and Wilson. A handy menu glossary talks newbies through native ingredients.

13/20

Licensed
Open Wed-Sun 12.15-5pm; Mon & Wed-Sun 6.15pm-late
Seats 40; outdoor seating
Owners Scott & Jeynelle Forrest
Chef Scott Forrest
Cards AE BC DC MC V Eftpos
Prices entrees $8-$15.50; mains $18.50-$26; desserts $9-$10.50
Map page 267 **Melway** 119 D11

Sacrebleu!

FRENCH

Shop 5, 1526 Mount Dandenong Tourist Road,
Olinda **9751 2520**

IN a region better known for its mock Tudor teahouses, it's a surprise to come upon a classic French bistro, complete with the mirrors and bentwood chairs of a Parisian cafe. But over half a dozen years, Sacrebleu! has established itself as a reliable destination for French food. Chef and co-owner Thierry Mauran leads a Francophilic team that obviously enjoys doing what it does, so service is professional and the atmosphere is warm. The best eating is the least complicated: grilled fish, steaks (including steak tartare) and ragouts all come with lashings of excellent frites. More adventurous dishes have a lower success rate. Stick to familiar suspects on the dessert list, too: Mauran makes a mean crème caramel and very good crepes suzette. A nice selection of local and French wines tops things off.

14/20

Licensed & BYO wine
Corkage $5 a bottle
Open daily noon-3pm, 6-11pm
Seats 45; outdoor seating
Owners Thierry Mauran & Michel Le Page
Chef Thierry Mauran
Cards AE BC DC MC V Eftpos
Prices entrees $9-$15.50; mains $23.50-$25.50; desserts $8.50
Map page 267 **Melway** 66 H7

Sweetwater Cafe at Chateau Yering

MODERN AUSTRALIAN

42 Melba Highway,
Yering **9237 3333**

SWEETWATER, the informal foil to the grandeur of Eleonore's (see page 173), is in the restored and extended home of Victoria's first vineyard. The cafe spills from the rear veranda of the old house – it's somewhat cavernous and can be noisy, but there are fine views of the gardens and glimpses of the valley beyond. The food is mildly innovative and nicely prepared. Portions are always generous. The antipasto platter is a guaranteed pleaser, served with house-made sausage and sourdough. Succulent crumbed flathead fillets come with chilli mayo and fat chips; crisp-skinned salmon sits on fennel and pea risotto; roast lamb loin comes with lentils, leeks and sage jus. The afternoon tea spread includes traditional tortes and a daily fruit tart. Slapdash service can let the food down, especially at busy times.

14/20 

Licensed & BYO wine
Corkage $20 a bottle
Open daily 7.30am-5pm; Sat 6.30pm-late
Seats 90; bar
Owners Len & Elly Milner
Chef Selina Timms-Basich
Cards AE BC DC MC V Eftpos
Prices entrees $12-$18; mains $22-$28; desserts $3-$8; cheese platters $16.50
Map page 267 **Melway** 275 B5

Woods Sherbrooke

MODERN AUSTRALIAN

21 Sherbrooke Road,
Sherbrooke **9755 2131**

FIRST a poky post office and store, then a tearoom, new proprietors have taken Woods further, crafting a light-splashed dining area, with loads of polished wood and bold artwork. It opens on to a delightful cottage garden for alfresco dining. The 'dimensions' menu departs from the traditional configuration of entree and main, preferring to distinguish between lighter and more substantial dishes. Lunch includes warm pumpkin salad, porterhouse on house focaccia, and summer barbecues. At dinner, the mezze platter of char-grilled vegetables and garlicky white bean dip makes an especially good shared starter. Heavier dishes don't have such a good strike rate, as in an overly fatty duck breast served with roasted stone fruits. Much better are the house-made cakes, including a light-as-air vanilla slice. Service can be a little haphazard.

13/20

Licensed & BYO wine
Corkage $5 a bottle
Open Thurs-Sat 9am-11pm; Sun 9am-5pm
Seats 40; outdoor seating; bar
Owners Philip Staer, Gillian & William Spurrier
Chef Jason Dousset
Cards BC MC V Eftpos
Prices breakfasts $3.50-$14; lunches $13.50-$18; dinners $14-$20 desserts $10.50
Map page 267 **Melway** 75 H2

Yarra Restaurant

MODERN AUSTRALIAN

The Heritage Golf & Country Club, Heritage Avenue,
Chirnside Park **9760 3300**

THE challenge at this two-year-old country club restaurant is to tear your eyes from the stellar views of verdant St John golf course and the rolling hills beyond. At least between bites. The food is easily good enough to warrant this small discipline. Chef Iain Lawless runs a clever menu of essentially upmarket pub dishes. You may start with oysters partnered with caramelised pork pieces, or al dente asparagus with prosciutto, then move on to a fairway-sized scotch fillet. Char-grilled and tender, the steak is plated unfussily with mash and mustard aioli. Desserts include a refined apple and berry crumble and excellent local cheeses. The fairly priced wine list is about as broad as an exclusively Yarra Valley list could be. Bella, the brasserie-style little sister to Yarra, is but a putt away at the adjoining Sebel Lodge.

14/20

Licensed
Open Sun 8.30-11.30am, 1-4pm; Fri-Sat 6-10pm
Seats 100; bar
Owner Sebel Lodge Yarra Valley – MIRVAC
Chef Iain Lawless
Cards AE BC DC MC V Eftpos
Prices entrees $16-$19; mains $26-$28; desserts $9-$11; Sun breakfast buffet $34.50; Sun lunch set menu $49.50 (3 courses)
Map page 267 **Melway** 279 D6

Yering Station

MODERN AUSTRALIAN

38 Melba Highway,
Yering **9730 1107**

YERING STATION'S imposing, modern restaurant dominates this historic property and offers sweeping views of the Yarra Ranges, pastures and neighbouring vineyards. Chef Colin Swalwell boasts experience in the kitchens of Langton's, Paul Bocuse and Stephanie's. Here, he masterminds an ever-changing menu crafted to complement estate-grown wines. A penchant for seafood shines through in dishes like plump crayfish medallions with champagne and lemon risotto, and beautifully executed tournedos of ocean trout, served with tangy rhubarb, asparagus and a drizzling of smoked salmon butter. Heartier dishes might include cardamom-marinated pork rack with caramelised apples and lemon sauce, or lamb loin with cashew curry crust. The botrytis cake with sticky apples is a good idea, but works better on the menu than on the plate.

14/20

Licensed
Open Mon-Fri noon-3pm; Sat-Sun noon-4pm; wine bar daily 10am-6pm
Seats 120; outdoor seating; private room; bar
Owner Rathbone family
Chef Colin Swalwell
Cards AE BC DC MC V Eftpos
Prices entrees $14.50-$16.50; mains $22.50-$27.50; desserts $11
Map page 267 **Melway** 275 C6

Bob's Gate @ Bianchet

ITALIAN

187 Victoria Road,
Lilydale **9739 0378**

A DETOUR to bluestone-and-glass Bianchet is rewarded with Italian-style meals and a backdrop of tumbling vines. Seafood is a good option, perhaps flathead tails on saffron mash or pipi-laden spaghetti marinara. There's a cellar of plonk to choose from, or count on assiduous staff to give the guff on a complementary drop.

Licensed
Open Thurs-Sun noon-3pm; Thurs-Sat 6pm-late
Prices entrees $9-$14; mains $16.50-$29.50; desserts $9
Map page 267 **Melway** 280 C6

Cunningham's Inn

MODERN REGIONAL

24 Warburton Highway,
Yarra Junction **5967 1080**

CUNNINGHAM'S takes local produce and creates standard pub fare with some enticing tweaks. There might be harissa with your lamb cutlets, tapenade with your ravioli, and lemon-dressed rocket with your prawn salad. Munch atop a bar stool within elbow's reach of a beer-drinking local, in the mellow dining room or on the veranda.

Licensed
Open Tues-Sun noon-2.30pm, 6-8.30pm
Prices entrees $7-$12; mains $13-$23; desserts $7.50
Map page 267 **Melway** 288 D8

Kenloch

MODERN AUSTRALIAN

Mount Dandenong Tourist Road,
Olinda **9751 1008**

WITH its sweeping lawns, antiques, fresh-cut flowers and open fireplaces, the atmosphere at Kenloch is steadfastly olde-worlde. Things are on the up, however: chef Alan Harding (ex-Healesville Hotel) came on board as the *Guide* went to press, a development sure to add some spark to the grand old dame's food.

Licensed
Open Wed-Sun noon-4pm; Fri-Sat 6.30pm-midnight
Prices entrees $12-$14.50; mains $22-$30; desserts $10-$12
Map page 267 **Melway** 66 J9

Oakridge Winery Cafe

MODERN AUSTRALIAN

864 Maroondah Highway,
Coldstream **9739 1920**

CHEF Ross McAuliffe (formerly of Sydney's Buon Ricordo) is running a pleasing minimalist menu at this winery cafe. Simple flavours shine in Italian dishes like ossobuco and rigatoni with bacon, tomato and mustard. Otherwise, there are curried lamb pasties and chicken pies. Desserts include an upside-down raspberry soufflé.

Licensed
Open daily 11am-3pm
Prices entrees $8.50-$24.50; mains $15.50-$22.50; desserts $9-$14
Map page 267 **Melway** 276 H10

Potters Restaurant

MODERN AUSTRALIAN

321 Jumping Creek Road,
Warrandyte **9844 2270**

NEW owners have spruced up Potters' grounds – the water features and bush vistas are looking lovely. Kitchen creations remain straightforward and hearty. Take a seat in the vast yet welcoming dining area and choose from a menu of wild mushroom terrine, grilled Tasmanian scallops, stuffed zucchini flowers and local venison.

Licensed & BYO wine
Open Tues-Sun noon-4pm; Wed-Sat 7pm-late
Prices entrees $9.50-$15.50; mains $22-$25; desserts $8.50
Map page 267 **Melway** 35 J2

Roundstone Winery

MEDITERRANEAN

54 Willowbend Drive,
Yarra Glen **9730 1181**

A DIRT road, a lake, requisite vines and an unpretentiously rustic dining area are just the introduction to Roundstone's appeal. The food takes matters further, employing wood-fired ovens to create Med-inspired meals such as crusty pizzetta with melting taleggio, duck roasted in pinot and golden chook with garlic juices.

Licensed
Open daily 10am-5pm
Prices entrees $6.50; mains $15-$19; desserts $7.50
Map page 267 **Melway** 266 K1

Shantell Vineyard & Winery

MODERN AUSTRALIAN

1974 Melba Highway,
Dixons Creek **5965 2155**

SHANTELL'S light, vibrant lunches are designed to be consumed with the pleasing house wines. You might drink semillon with Tarago River cheeses and capsicum dip on the antipasto platter, then move to wild yeast chardonnay for the chicken braised in lemon yoghurt, or cabernet sauvignon for Indian-spiced lamb.

Licensed
Open Thurs-Mon noon-4.30pm
Prices entrees $10-$14; mains $16-$18; desserts $8; platters $14-$22
Map page 267 **Melway** 267 K1

Watson's in Yarra Valley

MODERN AUSTRALIAN

25 Bell Street,
Yarra Glen **9730 2122**

WATSON'S is a well-run family business. John and Ronietta Watson own the place, their son Jay (apprenticed at Chateau Yering) is chef, and daughter Sheridan manages the floor. Herb-laden zucchini soup and creamy smoked trout fettuccine are the order of the day; at night the linen is unfolded and more formal meals take centre stage.

Licensed & BYO wine
Open Wed-Sun noon-3pm, 6.30-9pm
Prices entrees $8-$15.50; mains $23-$25; desserts $8-$15.50
Map page 267 **Melway** 275 A2

Wild Oak Cafe

MODERN AUSTRALIAN

232 Ridge Road,
Olinda **9751 2033**

A FEW years back, this cafe led the Hills away from the twee and stodgy restaurants of yore. It's a lovely room, looking out over a wrap-around nursery. In summer, you'll sit down to light Asian-inspired dishes; in winter, richer comfort food might include buffalo sausages. Year-round, there's good coffee and fabulous florentines.

Licensed & BYO wine
Open Wed-Fri 10am-10pm; Sat-Sun 9am-10pm
Prices entrees $8-$15.50; mains $18.50-$27.50; desserts $6.60
Map page 267 **Melway** 66 H5

Yarra Valley Dairy

MODERN REGIONAL

McMeikans Road,
Yering **9739 0023**

THE farm's 200 cows are responsible for much of the cheese for sale, both in the mouth-watering display cabinet and on the popular platters served in this rustic old dairy. Sample the signature Persian feta and the tangy ash-covered goats' cheese before noshing on slow-cooked rabbit, or salmon and feta ravioli.

Licensed
Open Mon-Fri 10.30am-4pm; Sat-Sun 10.30am-5pm
Prices mains $19-$25; desserts $12; platters $22.50-$70
Map page 267 **Melway** 275 C10

MORNINGTON PENINSULA

Acqua

MODERN ITALIAN

20 Ocean Beach Road,
Sorrento **5984 0484**

WITH its likeable Ikea-look interior and impressive rear courtyard, Acqua has a touch of Noosa about it. But the kitchen is driven by an Italian spirit, moving from primi piatti through pasta and on to secondi. The menu embraces mostly familiar bistro favourites – the carpaccio, rocket and parmesan routine gets a good work-out – with solid rather than breathtaking results. That carpaccio might be of tuna with capers and a citrus and passionfruit dressing; there might be squid-ink spaghettini with a classic combo of scallops, garlic, chilli and oil. Fish features prominently. Naturally, there's a pesce del giorno, perhaps decent saffron tempura-battered fillets of local snapper, served with aioli and shoestring fries. A useful little wine list and fine service add to Acqua's appeal.

12/20

Licensed
Open daily 10am-10pm (limited hours Apr-Nov)
Seats 80; outdoor seating
Owner Bruce Dowding
Chef Marnie Bretherton
Cards AE BC DC MC V Eftpos
Prices entrees $8-$17; mains $21-$30; desserts $12-$14
Map page 267 **Melway** 157 A8

Albert Street Restaurant

FRENCH/MEDITERRANEAN

1c Albert Street,
Mornington **5976 1444**

PREVIOUSLY known as Provence, Algerian-French chef Pierre Khodja has renamed his restaurant and pared back the North African influences in favour of more traditional French-Mediterranean fare. As before, it's a pleasant place, with a buttery colour scheme and full-length sliding windows that open in balmy weather. Good ingredients come to the fore in dishes like juicy roasted prawns with well-spiced boudin noir, and rack of lamb with lamb sausage. The occasional splash of North Africa shows in dishes like the bouillabaisse with Moroccan spices. Not everything comes off: caramelised onion and goats' cheese tarte tatin is merely a chewy pastry disc topped with onions and blobs of cheese. There's always something tempting to finish, though: perhaps rhubarb crème brûlée with home-made strawberry icecream. The small but considered wine list is a paean to the peninsula.

13/20

Licensed & BYO wine
Corkage $5 a bottle
Open Tues-Sat noon-3pm, 6.30-10pm
Seats 65
Owner & chef Pierre Khodja
Cards AE BC DC MC V
Prices entrees $14; mains $26.50; desserts $8-$9.50
Map page 267 **Melway** 104 D10

Bittern Cottage

FRENCH/MEDITERRANEAN

2385 Frankston-Flinders Road,
Bittern **5983 9506**

A NIGHT here is like visiting old friends – if you happen to have pals who specialise in French provincial cooking. Jenny and Noel Burrows love travelling within cooee of the Mediterranean, and their passion for the region is evident in the rustic dining room with its open kitchen, and of course, in their lovingly prepared food delivered at a leisurely pace. A typical feast could start with a herb-strewn roma tomato tart, served with a pot of home-made pesto. Next, there might be baked ham with a maple syrup and mustard sauce. Then, moist chocolate and sour cherry cake made with Red Hill morellos or the night's cheese – perhaps an unfeasibly creamy brie – and coffee from the old-fashioned percolator. Just like a mate's place, the Cottage is BYO – do the right thing and arrive with a bottle.

14/20

BYO
Corkage none
Open Sun noon-6pm; Fri-Sat & middle two Mons of each month 7pm-late
Seats 30
Owners & chefs Jenny & Noel Burrows
Cards BC MC V
Prices entrees $8-$14; mains $24-$28; desserts $10-$12 (à la carte Fri only); set menu $52 (3 or 4 courses)
Map page 267 **Melway** 164 F6

Castle at Delgany

MODERN AUSTRALIAN

3809 Point Nepean Road,
Portsea **5984 4000**

A MEAL at this fairytale 1920s castle is no everyday occasion. The dining room – part of a Peppers Group conference centre and retreat – is sophisticated and intimate with bonny views of rolling lawns and established trees. The Saturday evening degustation (obligatory) offers a good overview of the regular carte's depth and variety. You might begin with a creamy celeriac soup, served with a truffled oyster, followed by zucchini flowers stuffed with goats' cheese and accompanied by seared scallops. The flavour-packed parade might continue with prosciutto-wrapped salmon on blue cheese aioli, then a big slab of peninsula beef with pureed potato, hearty vegetables and anchovy butter. Valrhona chocolate pudding with pistachio icecream makes a luscious finale. Prices are up there with Melbourne's finest but the sense of occasion is priceless.

14/20

Licensed
Open daily 7am-late
Seats 120
Owner Peppers Group
Chef Craig Gorton
Cards AE BC DC MC V Eftpos
Prices entrees $12-$22; mains $20-$35; desserts $10-$15; Sat night degustation menu $65 (5 courses)
Map page 267 **Melway** 156 E2

Kook

MODERN AUSTRALIAN

Shop 2, 3760 Point Nepean Road,
Portsea **5984 3434**

KOOK – it's a play on the way a Scottish chef tells you what he does – is overseen by Raymond Capaldi of Richmond's Fenix. This country cousin, in the old Browns Bakery premises, serves up simple seaside versions of Capaldi's complex city dishes. Excellent bistro food (at very realistic prices) includes winners like pan-fried scallops wrapped in smoked salmon and served on cauliflower risotto, and a very fine salad of peeled asparagus, tomato jelly, candied and fresh black olives, boiled egg and kipfler potato. These summery dishes are as fine as any you'd care to name. Brunch choices range from white peach crumble pancakes with King Island yoghurt to poached free-range eggs with ham jaffles. Staff are generally on the boil and efficient, though a long winter lay-off is sure to test management as they regroup each summer.

14/20

Unlicensed
Open Tues-Sun 9am-2pm, 6.30-10pm (closed Jun-Sep)
Seats 86; outdoor seating
Owner Portsea Cafe Group Pty Ltd
Chef to be announced
Cards BC DC MC V Eftpos
Prices breakfasts $7-$14; dinners $15-$36
Map page 267 **Melway** 156 E2

La Baracca Trattoria

ITALIAN

T'Gallant Winemakers, 1385 Mornington-Flinders Road,
Main Ridge **5989 6565**

THIS appealing stalwart of the peninsula's vineyard restaurant scene chewed through a slew of kitchen staff not long after wine giant Beringer Blass bought the property in the autumn of 2003. The current crew is aiming for a provincial Italianate feel with dishes like handmade spinach and ricotta gnocchi, mussels poached in the winery's own pinot gris, cotechino sausage on lentils, and grilled salmon with brown butter and broad beans. Desserts may include panettone pudding with cashews and muscatels or ricotta cakes on vine leaves with verjuice dressing. La Baracca's tone is easygoing and fun, but informality has come at a cost: front-of-house rigour and charm is not all it was and prices have crept beyond many city counterparts. Cheaper pizzas and steak sangers are available in the adjoining Spuntino Bar.

13/20

Licensed
Open daily noon-5pm; Fri-Sat 7pm-midnight (closed Fri night in winter); Spuntino Bar Sat-Sun noon-5pm
Seats 60; outdoor seating; bar
Owner Beringer Blass
Chefs Marcos Amando & Louise Lechte
Cards AE BC DC MC V Eftpos
Prices entrees $12-$16; pizzas $14-$26; pastas $17; mains $20-$26; desserts $12
Map page 267 **Melway** 190 E12

Lime Restaurant & Lounge

MODERN AUSTRALIAN

3183 Point Nepean Road (corner Terry Street),
Sorrento **5984 4444**

TUCKED away in semi-obscurity by the roadside, Lime has survived several incarnations. The latest, as a hip bar-restaurant aimed at a younger crowd, may be the best yet. Certainly, the food, service and wine list now match the arty interior. What's surprising about Lime, however, is how well the somewhat unfashionable fusion food works on the plate. Asian and Mediterranean ideas collide incongruously on paper but rather pleasingly in the flesh: scampi and asparagus risotto, for example, also embraces Persian feta, Thai peanut crumble and mint coriander pesto. Sounds weird; is, in fact, excellent. Or confit ocean trout in a mushroom consommé with roasted chilli salsa. This is ambitious stuff but it's carried off well. The flip side is that Lime is relatively expensive, but with so little serious cooking in the area, it's a case of grin and wear it.

14/20

Licensed
Open Thurs-Mon 6.30-11pm (daily in summer; closed Aug)
Seats 45; outdoor seating; private room; bar
Owners Danny Petrone, Al Pitman & Shpresa Beca
Chef Evan Seaward
Cards AE BC DC MC V Eftpos
Prices entrees $12-$18; mains $23.50-$29.50; desserts $9.50-$14
Map page 267 **Melway** 157 D9

The Linden Tree Restaurant

MODERN AUSTRALIAN

Lindenderry at Red Hill, 142 Arthurs Seat Road,
Red Hill **5989 2933**

THIS attractive modern conference centre has engaged renowned chef Andrew Blake to guide the restaurant. Blake designs the menus and makes periodic swoops into the kitchen – no doubt dishes like roast scallops with yellow curry and green mango are spectacular when he's rattling the pans. But things can falter without the maestro on the piano: your Jerusalem artichoke soup might be bland; you might find ice chips in the pistachio icecream. On most occasions, though, execution lives up to the ideas. Roast duck is served with deliciously bitter orange sauce and mascarpone-stuffed fig; crisp-skinned salmon is plated with tiny yellow beets and pink grapefruit. Linden Tree also does lavish buffet-style breakfasts, and afternoon teas. Things may settle under a new chef, due to start as the *Guide* went to press.

12/20

Licensed
Open daily 7.30-10am, 12.30-2.30pm, 6.30-9pm
Seats 90; outdoor seating; private rooms
Owner Lancemore Group
Chef to be announced
Cards AE BC DC MC V Eftpos
Prices breakfast buffet $27.50; entrees $15-$18; mains $24-$28; desserts $11-$13
Map page 267 **Melway** 190 K3

Montalto Vineyard & Olive Grove

MODERN AUSTRALIAN

33 Shoreham Road,
Red Hill South **5989 8412**

SINCE opening two years ago, Montalto has rocketed to wine-dine hero status on the peninsula. The location is delightful, next to an established vineyard with views of rolling hills and billabongs, and the airy dining room feels like it floats above the fields. James Redfern cooks French-inspired rustic food boosted by rigorously sourced local produce. An excellent chicken and duck terrine might be served with local slippery jack mushrooms. Aged Red Hill goats' cheese turns up in the soufflé, peninsula fisherman Tim Mirabella provides the catch of the day. Redfern knows his way around a piece of meat: his eye fillet is a rhapsody to beef; his roasted duck breast is succulent and pink. Wonderful desserts include an authentic tarte tatin with caramelised apples. The wine list continues to improve, as does the quality of the estate wines.

15/20

Licensed
Open daily noon-3pm; Fri-Sat 6.30-11pm (extended hours in summer)
Seats 70; outdoor seating; private room
Owners John & Wendy Mitchell
Chef James Redfern
Cards AE BC DC MC V Eftpos
Prices entrees $12-$18; mains $23-$32; desserts $12-$15
Map page 267 **Melway** 256 B2

Paringa on a Plate

MODERN EUROPEAN

44 Paringa Road,
Red Hill South **5931 0136**

PARINGA ESTATE'S famed pinot noir is responsible for most pilgrimages to this one-room cellar door and restaurant. There's a reason for that: the wine is reliably fabulous but the restaurant is prone to stumbles. Musical chairs in the kitchen have resulted in the demise of à la carte dining. The food, much of it tasty and creative, is now served on shared platters. Charred rare salmon nuggets dressed with pomegranate molasses may appear as one of three salads on an entree platter; cotechino could roll up alongside barbecued maple-marinated chicken on the main course platter. But such culinary assemblages can result in awkward mixes, and the inflexibility of this style of dining is not compensated for by lower prices. Views of hills and vines are consistently pleasing; the same can't always be said of the service.

13/20

Licensed
Open Thurs & Sun noon-4pm; Fri-Sat noon-9.30pm
Seats 62; outdoor seating
Owners Lindsay & Margaret McCall
Chef Mark Pearce
Cards AE BC MC V Eftpos
Prices entrees $14; mains $24; desserts $7.50
Map page 267 **Melway** 191 D9

Poffs'

INTERNATIONAL

164 Arthurs Seat Road,
Red Hill **5989 2566**

FEW chefs' resumes boast a stint at a private hospital, or claim to be born of refugees from the Bolshevik revolution. Then again, there are few places left like Poffs'. Surrounded by cottage gardens overlooking Red Hill vineyards, this peninsula stalwart is all olde-worlde charm. Butter curls and pottery wine coolers grace linen-clad tables, and uniformed young staff offer a cornucopia of house-baked bread. While the food doesn't set out to challenge boundaries, most ingredients are locally sourced and well cooked. Embrace chef Sasha Esipoff's heritage and order 'A True Russian Beginning' (herring, potato salad, caviar) with a shot of vodka, then follow with crayfish tail poached in chardonnay and cream. To its credit, Poffs' is one of the few remaining BYOs in the area and also sports an extensive list of regional wines and old-school Australian classics.

13/20

Licensed & BYO wine
Corkage $8 a bottle
Open Sat-Sun noon-3pm; Fri-Sun 6.30pm-late (Easter-Dec); Thurs-Sun 12.30pm-late (summer); Wed 6.30pm-late (Jan)
Seats 45; outdoor seating
Owners Lorraine & Sasha Esipoff
Chef Sasha Esipoff
Cards AE BC DC MC V
Prices entrees $12-$16; mains $25-$29; desserts $10-$12
Map page 267 **Melway** 190 J4

The Rocks

MODERN AUSTRALIAN

Mornington Yacht Club, 1 Schnapper Point Drive,
Mornington **5973 5599**

THERE aren't many restaurants that can brag about a waterfront setting as absolute as this one. The Rocks is as much a part of the harbour as the jaunty craft that dot the priceless bay views out yonder. Inside, the pitch is tasteful, relaxed dining for the masses. Service is swift, albeit a little over-enthusiastic, and the standard Mediterranean-inspired menu is augmented by a daily seafood list. Smaller dishes can be patchy: saganaki is overly chewy but Flinders black mussels in a spicy tomato and red wine sauce, and vine-ripened tomatoes stuffed with tabbouleh on a bed of smoky baba ghanoush both hit the spot. Main dishes sometimes lack polish, as in a slab of blue-eye on an oily fennel salad. The freshness and simplicity of the seafood mixed grill plays more to the restaurant's strengths. A grazing menu is available on the deck.

13/20

Licensed
Open Mon-Tues 9am-3pm; Wed-Sun 8am-3pm; daily 6pm-late
Seats 75; outdoor seating; private room
Owners Robert De Santis & Rocco Cirillo
Chef Michael Hoare
Cards AE BC DC MC V Eftpos
Prices breakfasts $6.50-$15; entrees $11.50-$21; mains $16.80-$60; desserts $11.50-$14.50
Map page 267 **Melway** 104 D9

Salix at Willow Creek

MODERN AUSTRALIAN

166 Balnarring Road,
Merricks North **5989 7640**

ONE of the peninsula's finest vineyard restaurants, Salix has floor-to-ceiling views over vines and pines. The food hovers between country heartiness and culinary flamboyance – you'll know when it's the latter because heads will turn as the dish is paraded to the table. Most of Sean Duggan's meals take an interesting piece of meat (lamb rump, juicy chicken, farmed rabbit loin) and go to town. The lamb might be rolled in zaatar then barbecued; chicken could come with a Thai curry crust and green mango salad and the rabbit might rest on a pea puree with bonus bunny pie on the side. Game also features in grilled pheasant sausages and the venison steak with spaetzle noodles and sour cherry jus. Desserts are lovely: don't miss the passionfruit brûlée if it's available. Well-priced Willow Creek wines are matched to each dish.

15/20

Licensed
Open daily noon-3pm; Fri-Sat 7-11pm
Seats 60; outdoor seating
Owner Michael Cook
Chef Sean Duggan
Cards AE BC DC MC V Eftpos
Prices entrees $10.50-$17; mains $23-$28; desserts $10.50-$15; set lunch menus $37 or $45 (2 or 3 courses)
Map page 267 **Melway** 162 H8

Vines of Red Hill

MODERN AUSTRALIAN

150 Red Hill Road,
Red Hill **5989 2977**

THEY keep sight of the little things at Vines: you can see it in the meticulously landscaped Tuscan setting and the well-balanced yet adventurous food. The stylishly sparse dining room has views of giant gums – you can get tree-huggingly close to them by dining under the vine-covered pergola. The menu runs from the light and zesty (asparagus and blue swimmer crab gratin with calamari salad) to the hearty and earthy (slow-roasted duck leg in filo with braised beetroot). Occasionally a dish suffers from an excess of creativity – as in crisp-fried gnocchi with cucumber, roasted capsicum and a chillied lime pickle – but most of the surprises here are pleasant. Mains leave room for thoughts of dessert: the chocolate tart served with local morello cherries and vanilla mascarpone makes for a wonderfully rich finish.

14/20

Licensed
Open Fri-Sun noon-3pm; Fri-Sat 7pm-late (extended hours Nov-Mar)
Seats 70; outdoor seating
Owners Jessica, Geoff & Helen Graham
Chef Steve Davidson
Cards AE BC MC V Eftpos
Prices entrees $13.50-$15; mains $19.50-$26; desserts $9.50-$14
Map page 267 **Melway** 191 D4

Afghan Marco Polo

AFGHAN

9-11 Main Street,
Mornington **5975 5154**

THIS family-friendly restaurant is a cheap, reliable option for Central Asian spice and flavour. The menu never changes but that means there will always be aashak (pasta parcels filled with braised leek and topped with spicy tomato sauce) and borani bonjon (fried eggplant with garlic yoghurt).

$ V

Licensed & BYO wine
Open daily 6pm-late
Prices entrees $4-$8.50; mains $15.50-$19.50; desserts $3-$5
Map page 267 **Melway** 104 D10

Arthur's Restaurant

MODERN AUSTRALIAN

Arthurs Seat Scenic Road,
Arthurs Seat **5981 4444**

THE unimpeded view across Port Phillip Bay feeds the soul at this Art Deco institution. Pleasing, mostly mod-Oz plates take care of earthier appetites. Seafood features: there's creamy crustacean chowder, scallops baked with pesto and parmesan, and ocean trout with lotus root and lemongrass. The wine list showcases the peninsula.

Licensed
Open daily 10am-5pm; Fri-Sat 6.30-9.30pm
Prices entrees $12.50-$16.50; mains $25-$27.50
Map page 267 **Melway** 159 E11

The Boyz 4 Breakie

MODERN AUSTRALIAN

1a Main Street,
Mornington **5977 2888**

RAINBOW banners adorn this cheerful double-storey cafe, but Boyz is more than just a niche venue: it's the most happening place in Mornington. Competent meals attract many, but weekend coffees are the main attraction – the espresso machine has pride of place in a central island and the flirtatious waiters bustle around it.

$

Licensed
Open Mon-Tues 8am-5pm; Wed-Sun 8am-late
Prices breakfasts $5.50-$18; meals $9-$28; desserts $6-$7
Map page 267 **Melway** 104 D10

Coast 2827

MODERN AUSTRALIAN

2827 Point Nepean Road,
Blairgowrie **5988 0700**

LAID-BACK Coast is a hit with city runaways and sea-change locals seeking lazy breakfasts and relaxed, stylish meals. Lunchers enjoy seafood linguine, tempura-battered whiting and dips with pide. Come evening, the mood mellows and the menu expands to offer baby barramundi and duck confit on orange and coriander mash.

Licensed
Open Mon & Thurs-Fri 11am-late; Sat-Sun 8am-late (daily in hols)
Prices breakfasts $5-$15; mains $17-$26.50; desserts $6.50-$9
Map page 267 **Melway** 167 G2

Dromana Estate Cellar Door & Vineyard Cafe

REGIONAL

25 Harrisons Road,
Dromana **5987 3800**

LAZY grazing, good wine and a veranda overlooking a lake: the Crittendens know what we want in a country luncheon. Tuck into a ploughman's platter, including pork terrine and aged cheddar, or a cheese plate with a glass of the acclaimed pinot. Dishes for one include pies and panini, perhaps with smoked salmon, avocado and lime.

$

Licensed
Open daily noon-3.30pm
Prices lunches $9-$18; desserts $7-$9
Map page 267 **Melway** 160 J6

Jill's at Moorooduc Estate

MEDITERRANEAN

501 Derril Road,
Moorooduc **5971 8507**

THE vineyard restaurant experience is particularly rustic at Jill's, three dirt-road kilometres off the highway. The journey is rewarded by the reliable menu, and the restaurant's modern lines and pastoral views. Seasonal, often organic, dishes may include funghi risotto, roast free-range chicken and walnut frangipane tart with spicy apples.

Licensed
Open Sat-Sun 12.30-3pm; Fri-Sat 7-10.30pm
Prices entrees $12.50-$14.50; mains $22.50-$23.50
Map page 267 **Melway** 152 H1

The Long Table

MODERN AUSTRALIAN

Centrepoint Shopping Centre, 159 Shoreham Road,
Red Hill **5989 2326**

REMINISCENT of a Cape Dutch farmhouse (whitewashed walls, exposed beams, straw ceiling), this home-style restaurant serves up comfy fare to a mainly local crew. South African boerewors sausages, slow-roasted lamb and local pinot are all good bets, as is a Hoegaarden with chips and mayo at the bar in the early hours.

Licensed
Open Wed-Sun 6pm-late
Prices entrees $8.50-$14; mains $14.50-$25; desserts $8.50-$15
Map page 267 **Melway** 191 B7

Mantons Creek Vineyard

MEDITERRANEAN

240 Tucks Road,
Main Ridge **5989 6264**

A TREE-LINED drive leads to attractive winery buildings and a modern dining room with a deck overlooking the vines. The hearty tucker recalls an upmarket pub (nut-crusted barramundi, marinated lamb fillets with eggplant). Taste the estate wines with your food, then head home with a crate of the fruity gewurztraminer.

Licensed
Open Wed-Mon noon-3pm; Sat 7-10pm
Prices entrees $8.50-$18.50; mains $17.50-$28; desserts $9.50
Map page 267 **Melway** 255 F1

Max's at Red Hill Estate

MODERN AUSTRALIAN

53 Shoreham Road,
Red Hill South **5931 0177**

MAX'S views are among the peninsula's finest, with a sweeping outlook rolling toward Western Port. The food caters to multi-generational daytripping groups by running with an easy-eating modern menu (calamari with caper mayo, Thai crab salad) plus a few retro flourishes (rich roasted chicken with brie and creamy potato).

Licensed
Open daily noon-3.30pm; Fri-Sat 7pm-late
Prices entrees $6-$20; mains $27-$30; desserts $10-$15
Map page 267 **Melway** 190 K12

Megumi

JAPANESE

433 Nepean Highway,
Frankston **9783 8975**

IF Megumi was judged by its street-strip location and uninspired decor, it would be empty indeed. But locals know to focus on the food, lining up along the sushi bar to see what's fresh or leaving it to the maestro to fill cane boats with sushi and sashimi selections. Also good is succulent nasu dengaku and melting gyutataki.

Licensed & BYO
Open Tues-Fri noon-2.30pm; Tues-Sun 6-10pm
Prices entrees $5-$12; mains $20-$25; desserts $5
Map page 267 **Melway** 100A C6

Rubira's

SEAFOOD

1 The Esplanade,
Sorrento **5984 1888**

A CITY institution before heading for the peninsula, Rubira's is synonymous with quality seafood. The impressive sandstone complex encompasses a chippy, bar, bistro and formal restaurant. Meals are unfussy, relying on quality produce in dishes like mussels in cream and white wine and expertly battered whiting. Service can be patchy.

Licensed
Open daily noon-4pm, 6-9.30pm
Prices entrees $12-$32; mains $22-$45; desserts $13
Map page 267 **Melway** 157 B7

Safi Buluu

MODERN AUSTRALIAN

41 Cook Street,
Flinders **5989 1165**

THE minimalist interior, deck and mandatory big breakfast are very welcome in sleepy Flinders. So is the varied menu, featuring tofu laksa, wood-fired pizzas and seafood. Reliably good berry puddings and citrus tarts are available all day while evening options include glazed chicken on wok-tossed salad and drinks in the adjoining bar.

Licensed
Open Thurs-Fri 11.30am-late; Sat-Sun 9.30am-late
Prices breakfasts $4-$16.50; mains $17.50-$22.50; desserts $7
Map page 267 **Melway** 261 K8

Smokehouse Sorrento

PIZZERIA

182 Ocean Beach Road,
Sorrento **5984 1246**

THIS loud, friendly local favourite is at the back-beach end of the main drag. An eclectic range of delicious thin-crust wood-fired pizzas is the main attraction. The fresh seafood pizza topped with prawns, scallops, calamari and spicy salsa is a winner. Mussels, pastas, steak and grilled fish are also on offer.

$

Licensed
Open Wed-Mon 6pm-late
Prices pizzas $11-$19.50; mains $11-$24.50; desserts $10.50
Map page 257 **Melway** 157 A8

GOURMET GETAWAYS

Pack the bags and head for the hills

Fairways Guesthouse
55 Golfhouse Lane, Lancefield, 5429 1903
The four-course fixed-price menu at Fairways draws heavily on host Lynne Champion's kitchen garden. After a dinner that might include farro (spelt wheat) soup with wild mushrooms, and chicken breast with orange-ginger reduction, retire to one of six tastefully decorated bedrooms. A beautifully renovated 1860s cottage with three bedrooms is also available.

Goldsmith's in the Forest
Harrison's Track, Lakes Entrance, 5155 2518
Hidden in thick forest about 10 kilometres north of Lakes Entrance, Goldsmith's is run by trained chef and teacher Darilyn Goldsmith and her husband Les. Guests enjoy three-course mod-Oz menus and can take part in cooking classes. Non-cooking partners can work up an appetite fishing, playing golf or bushwalking. Each of the four comfortable bedrooms has an ensuite bathroom.

Howqua Dale Gourmet Retreat
Howqua River Road, via Mansfield, 5777 3503
Whether you come for a relaxed weekend of country pursuits (bushwalking, tennis, swimming, fishing) or to participate in cooking classes, the food, wine and hospitality offered by Marieke Brugman and Sarah Stegley will be spectacular. Weekends are built around a casual Friday night meal, formal dinner on Saturday and a grand Sunday brunch finale.

Liberty Guest House
20-22 Mineral Springs Crescent, Hepburn Springs, 5348 2809
Run by Mary Ellis and Geoff Gray, the couple behind Cliffy's in Daylesford (see page 214), Liberty is a place to unwind and enjoy regional country cuisine cooked on a sturdy 1948 Aga stove. Gray describes the bohemian guesthouse as being like nanna's beach house. 'If you get up from a couch, you don't have to worry about fluffing up the cushions.'

Purrumbete Homestead
3551 Princes Highway, Camperdown, 5594 7374
Grand old Purrumbete mansion has been unsparingly renovated, its eight rooms fitted out in luxurious, olde-worlde style. The food is modern Australian, and the wine list is stunning. Among the 300-strong list are some remarkable Australian and French wines, including premier cru burgundies, first-growth bordeaux and Chateau d'Yquem.

Quamby Homestead
Caramut Road, Woolsthorpe, 5569 2395
Albert Park refugees Jane and John Murphy have established themselves in secluded Woolsthorpe, about 40 kilometres north of Warrnambool. Jane is a passionate cook whose country-style fare includes things like rack of lamb on pea puree and orange panna cotta with baked quinces. Accommodation is scattered around Quamby's beautifully manicured 1.2-hectare garden.

Strathvea Guesthouse
755 Myers Creek Road, Healesville, 5962 4109
While you're enjoying dinner in Strathvea's beautiful dining room, you can watch possums and sugar gliders come foraging for theirs in the spotlit garden. Strathvea's seasonal menu reflects a commitment to Yarra Valley produce. Hosts Di Clarke and Jan and Bruce Cormack have extended the 1920s guest-house, set in the Toolangi state forest, giving Strathvea 11 bedrooms, six with ensuites.

Woodman Estate
136 Graydens Road, Moorooduc, 5978 8455
This luxuriously appointed 1890s manor house will hold special appeal for frustrated aristocrats. Set in a large formal garden, both chalets and manor house suites overlook a private, trout-stocked lake. Stuart McKeon, formerly of Stokehouse and the Point, serves polished mod-Oz food. Take your pick of eating venues: formal dining room, casual brasserie or enclosed veranda.

Lancers Restaurant & Bar
Fully Licensed Restaurant

154-164 Ocean Beach Road
Sorrento, Vic 3943
Phone: 03 5984 1057
www.lancersrestaurant.com.au

RESTAURANT & BAR

STA5441

THE BEST MODERN CUISINE
specialising is seasonal seafood delivered fresh daily

AHA WINNER OF
BEST COUNTRY HOTEL 2002
RESTAURANT **BAR** LIVE ENTERTAINMENT
BOTTLE SHOP FUNCTIONS
OPEN 7 DAYS
CNR CANADIAN BAY RD & RANELAGH DVE MT ELIZA
T 03) 9775 2331 **www.canadianbay.com**

Yaringa Boathouse

RESTAURANT

BALCONY SEATING | ABSOLUTE WATER FRONTAGE
LUNCH & DINNER | FULLY LICENSED BAR

1 LUMEAH ROAD, SOMERVILLE
(Melway Map 149 K7) Bookings recommended
PH: 5977 3735

climax media 9770 0338

GEELONG & BELLARINE PENINSULA

Athelstane House

INTERNATIONAL

4 Hobson Street,
Queenscliff **5258 1024**

ATHELSTANE is a charming old guesthouse, where both the mood and the food are beachy casual. The venue looks well lived in, the staff are professional and welcoming, and Michael McSween's menu is a global jaunt of bright, simple flavours. Highly recommended are the Portarlington mussels, shiny black shells swimming in a creamy curry sauce spiked with salty juices. House-made crusty bread does a fine job of mopping up any leftover puddles. Good, too, are pork and ginger dumplings poached in a kaffir lime broth and served with a mild chilli sauce, and tender braised cinnamon-spiced duck with cannellini bean mash. The kitchen runs all day: a diverse breakfast spread includes the go-getting kitchen sink omelette; simple lunch offerings range from ploughman's platter and gnocchi to tandoori chicken pizza.

13/20

Licensed
Open daily 9am-9.30pm
Seats 48
Owners Clare Neville & Jeremy Dyer
Chef Michael McSween
Cards AE BC DC MC V Eftpos
Prices breakfasts $5-$11; lunches $8-$16; entrees $8-$16; mains $18-$28; desserts $8-$11
Map page 268 **Melway** 486 K12

Empire Grill

MODERN AUSTRALIAN

66 McKillop Street,
Geelong **5223 2132**

THE unassuming ex-motel facade gives little hint that Empire Grill is among Geelong's grandest dining experiences. The large candlelit dining room still feels intimate, crammed as it is with paintings and exotic artefacts – it's a great canvas for the creative fodder emanating from the kitchen. You might start with an impressive seafood dish, featuring shucked oysters over a bed of cucumber and cress, doused in a delicate consommé or a more straightforward glazed duck risotto with tiny button mushrooms. Mains can overdo it. A prosciutto-wrapped chicken breast stuffed with goats' cheese and rocket and served with prawns in a creamy velouté sauce recalls show-offy dinner party dishes of yore. But this is a truly lush dining experience: the waitstaff attend to every detail, the tables are set with fresh flowers and rich fudge comes with your coffee.

13/20 

Licensed
Open Tues-Fri noon-3pm; Mon-Sat 5.30pm-late
Seats 100; private rooms; bar
Owner Richard Kelly
Chef Dean Matthews
Cards AE BC DC MC V Eftpos
Prices entrees $8.50-$15.90; mains $27.50-$29.50; desserts $9-$13.50
Map page 268 **Melway** 401 G7

Giuseppe's Cafe

ITALIAN

149 Pakington Street,
Geelong West **5223 2187**

THIS stylish shopfront cafe is immediately welcoming: it's high-ceilinged with an Art Deco-inspired interior and buttery poster-filled walls. The bustling timber bar is just right for a snacky weekday lunch while quality table settings and a sassy Italian-oriented wine list make it a great choice for a romantic night out. Dishes don't stray far from a standard pasta and meat repertoire, but Giuseppe Barbagallo sneaks some attention-grabbing twists on to his plates. Your generous antipasto platter might include a slab of fluffy frittata, roasted baby beetroot and basil-marinated eggplant, while sage-scented saltimbocca turns up on a bright green bed of rocket and potato mash. Pasta standards always please, as in a good quality linguine served with a lemony fresh tuna and rocket sauce. All in all, a spunky little package.

13/20 $

Licensed & BYO wine
Corkage $5 a bottle
Open Tues-Sun 11am-late
Seats 50; outdoor seating
Owner & chef Giuseppe Barbagallo
Cards AE BC DC MC V Eftpos
Prices entrees $7.50-$15.90; pastas $13.50-$16.90; mains $18.90-$21; desserts $7.50
Map page 268 **Melway** 451 J2

Growlers Torquay

MODERN AUSTRALIAN

23 The Esplanade,
Torquay **5264 8455**

LIKE any good beach house, Growlers is casual, comfortable and has an atmosphere that suggests a party could break out any moment. Sit on the veranda with a view over Zeally Bay, or inside where there's polished timber flooring and a well-appointed bar. Chef Kate Newton's focus is on fresh flavours presented without fuss and her small menu takes inspiration from all over. You might eat a Mediterranean vegetable tart; potato, cashew and ricotta koftas; or kangaroo with tabbouleh and hummus. Asian flavours feature in the crisp wonton stack with shredded chicken, wasabi mayonnaise and pickled ginger: it's a nice mix of crunch, piquancy and easy-to-eat protein. Growlers doesn't do haute cuisine, but it is a fun place for a light meal – especially on a sunny day with a cold beer on the side.

13/20 V

Licensed
Open Fri-Sun 9am-3pm; Tues-Sun 6-10pm
Seats 80; outdoor seating; bar
Owners Murray Bingham, Nikki Buckley, John Hamilton & Cathy George
Chef Kate Newton
Cards AE BC DC MC V Eftpos
Prices breakfasts $5-$16; entrees $10.50-$21; mains $17-$25; desserts $9.50
Map page 268 **Melway** 506 B7

Harry's

SEAFOOD

Princess Park,
Queenscliff **5258 3750**

REGULAR diners at Harry's only ever seem to notice the positives: the excellent food (arguably the best seafood on the Bellarine Peninsula); the wonderful views of ships steaming past; the casual, heady atmosphere; the intelligent service. They hardly ever seem aware of the negatives: their darling diner inhabits a former toilet block and it's strictly BYO only. But their indulgence is hardly surprising – you'll be swooning too once you've experienced Michael Barrett's unforgettable mussels, steamed with wine, cream and spring onions. Other attention-grabbers include silver dory, which might come filled with crab mousse, wrapped in lettuce and steamed. Other dishes – say, duck with tamarind and star-anise sauce, or lamb with roasted garlic and shallots – are good, too, but when seafood is handled this well, it seems a crime to spurn it.

13/20

BYO
Corkage $2 a head
Open Thurs-Sun 12.30-3pm, 7-9.30pm (daily Jan & public hols; closed Thurs in winter)
Seats 65
Owner & chef Michael Barrett
Cards AE BC DC MC V
Prices entrees $14.50-$16.50; mains $25; desserts $7.50
Map page 268 **Melway** 487 A12

Joseph's at the Mansion Hotel

MODERN MEDITERRANEAN

Werribee Park, K Road,
Werribee **9731 4130**

WERRIBEE PARK may be a scant half-hour from the city, but there are few Victorian restaurants that have its grand country mansion appeal, and none with driveways that offer glimpses of rhinoceros stomping through an adjoining wildlife park. The modern dining room, decked in demure brown and aubergine, contrasts with verdant sculpture-strewn lawns outside. It's an appropriately luxe setting for accomplished dishes like creamy white bean soup, moist chermoula spatchcock with sherry vinegar, and roast cod with panzanella salad. Set lunches, while good value, can have a whiff of the production line, as with a bland brandade and overly chilled raspberry cheesecake. Green young waiters are overseen by excellent senior staff, meaning that service is generally smooth. A deep, rich wine list highlights the estate's Shadowfax Wines before scooting further afield.

15/20

Licensed
Open Mon-Fri 7-10am; Sat-Sun 7-11am; daily noon-3pm, 6-9.30pm
Seats 85
Owner The Mansion Group
Chef Barry Vera
Cards AE BC DC MC V Eftpos
Prices entrees $14-$15; mains $24-$32; desserts $12.50; Mon-Fri set lunch menus $29.50 or $35 (2 or 3 courses)
Map page 268 **Melway** 201 B4

Katialo Restaurant

MODERN MEDITERRANEAN

98 Newcombe Street,
Portarlington **5259 3580**

PERCHED on the hill a short doddle from Portarlington's main strip, Katialo is a relaxed and welcoming place for imaginative Med-influenced eating and drinking. Pick your way through an antipasto platter to get a sense of the restaurant's bold, comforting flavours: there might be steamed local mussels, smoked New Zealand eel, garlicky pork sausage, roasted mushrooms and an array of dips. Specialities include simply grilled whiting served with lemon and greens, and roast lamb medallions arranged around a citrus-infused heap of crushed potato and leek. A Greek bias is pleasingly evident in the kakavia (seafood soup) and the pigeon with skordalia. Desserts are fab: there's the Greek-accented karidopita (walnut syrup cake) and a moist, feather-light apple and poppyseed cake served with stewed rhubarb and a scoop of jaffa icecream.

13/20

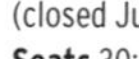

Licensed & BYO wine
Corkage $5 a bottle
Open Wed-Sat 9.30am-late; Sun 9.30am-5pm (daily 9.30am-late Boxing Day to Australia Day)
Seats 55; outdoor seating
Owners Steven & Alexandra Souflas
Chef Steven Souflas
Cards AE BC MC V Eftpos
Prices breakfasts $4.50-$14.50; entrees $9.50-$15; mains $21.50-$25.50; desserts $8.50-$9.50
Map page 268 **Melway** 444 H6

Kelp Cafe & Apartments

MODERN AUSTRALIAN

67-69 Lonsdale Road,
Point Lonsdale **5258 4797**

KELP opened at the end of 2002 and instantly raised the bar for Point Lonny dining a good few notches. The small dining room is sparse and modern, in keeping with the simple but classy food. A Jerusalem artichoke soup cleverly counterpoints the slight bitterness of the vegetable against a rich swirl of sour cream; gnocchi with sweet potato, prosciutto and parmesan is all elegant minimalism. Seafood dishes generally keep things simple: you may be offered pan-fried John Dory with boiled potato, roasted tomato and spinach or local mussels steamed with coconut and lime. More complex is a mild Sri Lankan chicken curry accompanied by sweet mango chutney and curried yoghurt. Cakes are baked in Melbourne and trucked in each day; cheeses come with quince paste. The wine list is petite but thoughtful, with local wineries well represented.

13/20

Licensed
Open daily 8am-9pm (closed July)
Seats 30; outdoor seating
Owners Kathy & Robert Hendrey
Chef Simon Thyer
Cards AE BC DC MC V Eftpos
Prices breakfasts $3.50-$9; entrees $8-$16; mains $9.50-$23; desserts $9-$12.50
Map page 268 **Melway** 499 J5

Kilgour Estate Winery

MODERN AUSTRALIAN

85 McAdams Lane,
Bellarine **5251 2223**

TUCKED into the top of a ridge, the barn-like dining room of Kilgour Estate offers stunning views across Port Phillip Bay's mussel farms. The all-day grazing menu includes crunchy duck spring rolls with hoisin, and warm chicken and bocconcini salad. But in such a setting, the 'seafood melange' seems an obvious lunch choice. Local mussels are crammed on the platter with crab, scallops, scampi and oysters; king prawns come in a coconut curry broth. Heartier meaty choices might include tender lamb shanks on pearl barley or eye fillet on warm potato salad – just right if there's a nip in the sea breeze. With brunch also an option (perhaps corn pancake with shaved ham or French toast with berries), Kilgour is a top Sunday drive destination. Wines are limited to those made and bottled on the estate.

13/20

Licensed
Open daily 10am-5pm; Fri-Sat 6pm-late
Seats 65; outdoor seating; bar
Owners Anne Timms & Rod Lilkemdey
Chef Leonie Eddy
Cards AE BC MC V Eftpos
Prices entrees $14-$16; mains $17-$26; seafood melange $80 (for 2 people); desserts $10-$13
Map page 268 **Melway** 457 D1

The Ol' Duke

MODERN AUSTRALIAN

40 Newcombe Street,
Portarlington **5259 1250**

ATTENTIVE service and quality food combine in this smart renovated hotel. Pick a spot on the deck for views across the foreshore reserve to the water or stay out of the breeze in the light, bright dining room. Uncomplicated yet skilfully prepared meals might include creamy roast pumpkin risotto or charred eggplant slices rolled with ricotta, spinach and pine nuts. The local catch dominates the specials board – perhaps a snapper fillet on laksa-style egg noodles. Other options include simple pastas (lemongrass-steamed Portarlington mussels tossed with noodles; gnocchi napoli) or easy-eating meat dishes like duck with hoisin and bok choy, chicken saltimbocca dressed up with Asian greens and chilli jam, or porterhouse with parmesan spuds. The wine list follows the same breezy formula, with a good selection by the glass.

13/20

Licensed
Open Mon-Fri 9am-late; Sat-Sun 8am-late
Seats 72; outdoor seating; private rooms; bar
Owners Melanie Pitman & Andrew Porter
Chef Emma Holbery
Cards AE BC MC V Eftpos
Prices breakfasts $5-$18; entrees $8.50-$14.50; mains $16.50-$26; desserts $8.50-$12.50
Map page 268 **Melway** 444 G6

Ozone Hotel

MODERN AUSTRALIAN

42 Gellibrand Street,
Queenscliff **5258 1011**

A NEW chef has given the food at the Ozone a real boost. Nothing much else has changed. The atmosphere isn't as formal as in Queenscliff's other grand old hotels: you'll still find yourself surrounded by seafaring images in the Boat Bar and, if you pick a good day, you can sit in the courtyard surrounded by flowering plants. Delicate vodka-cured salmon carpaccio makes a fine starter, served with attractive herb flowers and a dab of wasabi. Ocean trout fillet is indicative of the simple but well-cooked mains: it's crisply seared but gelatinous, with a balanced buttery citrus sauce and bok choy on the side. There's a great wine list and desserts are very good: the banana pizza is a nice spin on the traditional split, with slices of caramelised fruit, vanilla icecream and chocolate sauce on a spongy sweet pastry base.

13/20

Licensed
Open daily noon-2.30pm, 6-8.30pm
Seats 100; outdoor seating; bar
Owners David & Gillian Moffatt
Chef Cameron O'Mahoney
Cards AE BC DC MC V Eftpos
Prices entrees $7.50-$15; mains $22-$26; desserts $9.50
Map page 268 **Melway** 486 K12

Pettavel Winery & Restaurant

MODERN EUROPEAN

65 Pettavel Road,
Waurn Ponds **5266 1111**

FROM the moment you receive the clear tomato broth – ceremonially spooned over truffle-scented diced tomato – it's clear that Pettavel is the best restaurant on the Bellarine Peninsula by a country mile. It's quite a package: sleek timber and stone, with floor-to-ceiling views of the vines. The four-course set menu is encouraged in the formal dining area: three fixed entrees precede your choice of main, with dessert a $12 supplement. Most entrees work, as in the aforementioned soup, while some seem to be a compilation of what's left from the day before, perhaps sardines with avocado and ruby grapefruit. It's with the mains that chefs Dwayne Bourke and Richard Hooper (ex-Sunnybrae) weave their magic: Barossa pigeon with a shallot glaze; confit duck with white beans; pork with kipflers and cider. Desserts continue the theme and the wine list is admirable.

15/20

Licensed
Open daily 12.30-3pm
Seats 100; private rooms
Owners Mike & Sandi Fitzpatrick
Chefs Dwayne Bourke & Richard Hooper
Cards AE BC DC MC V Eftpos
Prices entrees $16; mains $26; desserts $12; lunch set menu $42 (4 courses)
Map page 268 **Melway** 463 G11

Poach

MODERN AUSTRALIAN

64b The Terrace,
Ocean Grove **5255 1521**

POACH is an oasis of modern cool in Ocean Grove's beach-burb strip. The feel is sophisticated: there's a funky dark-wood bar and a seductive lounge area with fireplace. Chef James White worked at Southbank's mecca – the influence shows in his loosely Middle Eastern-flavoured menu. Instant favourites include torpedo-shaped spicy lamb kofta with tabbouleh and mint yoghurt; wonderful mussels steamed in a tomatoey cumin-scented broth; and tender chilli salt calamari, lifted by the zing of a fresh coriander salad with palm sugar dressing. Desserts are good, too. Moist orange syrup cake comes with good jaffa icecream and the banana sundae has surprise honeycomb nuggets. A similar combo turns up in one of the all-day breakfasts: pancakes with banana and honeycomb butter. Otherwise, get fuelled with corn fritters or eggs – poached, of course.

13/20

Licensed
Open Mon & Thurs-Fri 9am-3pm, 6pm-late; Sat-Sun 8am-3pm, 6pm-late
Seats 40; outdoor seating; bar
Owners Melanie Pitman & Andrew Porter
Chef James White
Cards AE MC V
Prices breakfasts $5-$15; entrees $9-$14; mains $19.50-$24; desserts $10-$11
Map page 268 **Melway** 483 J12

The Queenscliff Hotel

MODERN AUSTRALIAN

16 Gellibrand Street,
Queenscliff **5258 1066**

BE seduced by this grand, romantic building and pretend that time stopped its march in the era of the Raj and the white linen suit. There's nowhere you'll feel more comfortable with a frosty gin and tonic in your hand. It's no surprise, then, that the dining room is firmly planted in traditional soil with the occasional nod to the exotic. Take, for example, the fine dukkah-spiced salmon served on a tomato, capsicum and basil peperonata with green olives, or sweet seared scallops paired with savoury prawns on slippery pappardelle in a rich saffron and tomato sauce. Creative twists lift desserts beyond the mainstream: chocolate mousse, for instance, is served with sambuca jelly. Chef John Schirmer has turned up the burners since last year and the restaurant seems set to find its way back to the glory days.

14/20

Licensed
Open Wed-Sat 7-9pm; bistro daily noon-2.30pm, 7-9pm
Seats 60; outdoor seating; bar
Owners Johann & Theresa Schuetz
Chef John Schirmer
Cards AE BC DC MC V
Prices breakfast buffet $27; entrees $10-$16; mains $27-$29; desserts $14; less in bistro
Map page 268 **Melway** 486 K12

Spray Farm

MODERN AUSTRALIAN

2275 Portarlington Road,
Bellarine **5251 3176**

THE homestead on this Scotchmans Hill property has been cleverly renovated to retain all its charm, and its awe-inspiring views across the bay toward the You Yangs. The bonus is that chef Paul Le Nourey is producing food that is easily interesting and sophisticated enough to tear your eyes from the panorama. Flavourful starters might include tender calamari fried with bok choy and ginger, or balsamic-drizzled goats' cheese with roasted capsicum and rocket. Main dishes start with basic protein, then dress it up to the nines: grilled lamb sits on smooth, musky hummus; parmesan-crumbed veal comes with artichokes and caramelised onions; chicken is served with a Moroccan-inflected melange of chickpeas, cous cous and sumac yoghurt. Wine service is good, but options are restricted to house labels. Call ahead – the Farm is a popular wedding venue.

14/20

Licensed
Open Wed-Sun noon-4pm (Sat-Sun only Jun-Sep)
Seats 120; outdoor seating; bar
Owners David & Vivienne Browne
Chef Paul Le Nourey
Cards AE BC DC MC V Eftpos
Prices entrees $13.50-$19.50; mains $23.90-$29.50; desserts $8.50-$15
Map page 268 **Melway** 443 F11

---

2 faces

MODERN AUSTRALIAN

8 Malop Street,
Geelong **5229 4546**

ENTER the world of Simon Yarham and Tim Mitchell. Mitchell runs front of house cheerfully and efficiently while chef Yarham gets busy with exotic ingredients and inventive flavour matches. Middle Eastern spices star in the bastilla, a Moroccan pigeon pastry, while beef carpaccio is tricked up with tempura vegetables. Sometimes Yarham's flavours seem to fight one another – as in a blue cheese miso sauce on a perfectly good eye fillet steak. More congruous dishes can be breathtaking, as in a zucchini soufflé with spinach and mascarpone cream. Desserts range from simple (crème brûlée) to complex (meringue roulade). It's great to see a Geelong restaurant with such passion for high-falutin' fodder but the 2 faces team might do better to pull a few of their wilder culinary punches.

14/20

Licensed
Open Tues-Sat 6pm-late
Seats 45; bar
Owners Simon Yarham & Tim Mitchell
Chef Simon Yarham
Cards AE BC DC MC V Eftpos
Prices entrees $14.50-$16; mains $24-$32.50; desserts $10.50-$16; tasting menu $74 (6 courses)
Map page 268 **Melway** 401 G4

Vue Grand Hotel

INTERNATIONAL

46 Hesse Street,
Queenscliff **5258 1544**

STEPHANE LE GRAND has clocked up 10 years in the majestic dining room of the Vue Grand and he's still producing some of the best food in the region. His passion for flavours and ethnic diversity is expressed in adventurous dishes that usually succeed. Take, for example, his sweet barramundi fillet: it's served with a crunchy coat of crushed sticky rice, on a corn galette adrift in a pond of mirin and sake. Excellent char siu-style duck breast is crisp-skinned, thinly sliced and served pink atop eggplant and ratatouille with a cherry and ginseng jus. Not all dishes fly – chutney and wasabi mayonnaise were not happy companions for heavily battered tiger prawns – but extravagant desserts, such as a crisp tower of almond tuile encasing a zingy passionfruit and citrus curd, are consistently good.

14/20

Licensed
Open daily noon-2.30pm, 6.30-9pm
Seats 100; bar
Owners Michael McNamara & Daryl Davidson
Chef Stephane Le Grand
Cards AE BC DC MC V
Prices entrees $15.50; mains $27; desserts $13.50
Map page 268 **Melway** 486 K12

Barwon Orange

MEDITERRANEAN/PIZZERIA

60 Hitchcock Avenue,
Barwon Heads **5254 1090**

BARWON ORANGE shines like a beacon: it's friendly, the service is great and there's terrific unfussy food like wood-fired tandoor-style chicken pizza with goats' cheese, and pumpkin and eggplant tagine with almond and potato roesti. Caramel panna cotta, banana biscotti and first-rate coffee make for a sterling finish.

$ V

Licensed & BYO wine
Open Mon-Fri 5.30-9.30pm; Fri 11am-2.30pm; Sat-Sun 8.30am-9.30pm
Prices pizzas & mains $10.80-$24
Map page 268 **Melway** 497 B3

Bazil's

MEDITERRANEAN

Corner Cunningham Street & Western Beach Road,
Geelong **5229 8965**

THIS Geelong stalwart is a fine bet for satisfying food. Sit on cane furniture amid the cosy clutter to eat impeccable gorgonzola risotto with fresh figs, hearty Greek-style lamb meatloaf, or sweet Moroccan chicken with apricots. While Bazil's food is well crafted, it no longer stands out in the much-improved local food scene.

Licensed
Open Tues-Wed 9.30am-4pm; Thurs-Sat 9.30am-late; Sun 9.30am-5pm
Prices mains $19-$23
Map page 268 **Melway** 401 H2

The Garage

GREEK

7 Bridge Road,
Barwon Heads **5254 1770**

THIS old petrol station is now a bright cafe serving good dips like fava (split pea) and feta whipped with capsicum, interesting mezze such as zucchini fritters and larger dishes like baby snapper and moussaka. The top tastes on Loretta Sartori's dessert list are crisp finikia pastries. Roll up to the takeaway window for fish and chips.

Licensed & BYO wine
Open Wed-Sun 11am-11pm (closed Wed Apr-Sep)
Prices entrees $8-$24; mains $17-$28; desserts $4-$8
Map page 268 **Melway** 497 B4

Koaki

JAPANESE

Rippleside Park, Bell Parade,
Drumcondra **5272 1925**

A JAPANESE restaurant in a boxy brick veneer on the banks of Corio Bay? Believe it. For 14 years Koaki has served well-presented sashimi, gyoza and simple rice and noodle dishes. The sashimi is good quality, the gyoza are handmade and hearty mains – like nabemono broth – brim with chicken, vegetables, bean thread noodles and chilli seasoning.

Licensed
Open Wed-Sun 6pm-late
Prices entrees $7-$11; mains $19-$24; desserts $9-$10
Map page 268 **Melway** 442 A10

Laurent's at Seaview House

EUROPEAN

86 Hesse Street,
Queenscliff **5258 1763**

LAURENT'S is a casual alternative to Queenscliff's grand hotels. It's a cosy, charming guesthouse dining room with traditional French-influenced food cooked by a chef from Alsace-Lorraine. The seafood is recommended, particularly the bouillabaisse-style soup with Moreton Bay bugs, and grilled catch of the day with saffron rice.

Licensed
Open Wed-Sun 6.30pm-late
Prices entrees $5.50-$14.50; mains $16.50-$22; desserts $7.50-$8.50
Map page 268 **Melway** 486 K12

Le Parisien

FRENCH

15 Eastern Beach Road,
Geelong **5229 3110**

WITH waterfront views of passing dolphins, it's not surprising that Le Parisien remains among Geelong's busiest – and most expensive – restaurants. Regulars come for the excellent pâté, the quail on roesti and the stand-out pepper steak. Try the seafood specials if you don't want old-fashioned French classics. Great wine list.

Licensed
Open daily noon-3pm, 6-10.30pm
Prices entrees $10-$15; mains $28.50-$30; desserts $10-$12
Map page 268 **Melway** 401 J2

The Pear Tree

MEDITERRANEAN

Shop 6, 7 Gilbert Street,
Torquay **5261 6339**

CHEF Italo Mostacci's friendly diner has brought big-city method and strong Mediterranean flavours to Torquay's shopping strip. Italophiles will kick off with pan-fried garlic olives, then be drawn by the chef's love of offal: grilled polenta with chicken liver ragu is one of four liver dishes on the list. Simple dishes work well; give desserts a miss.

Licensed & BYO wine
Open daily 8.30am-4pm, 6-10pm
Prices entrees $7-$16.50; mains $14.50-$26; desserts $8.50-$12.50
Map page 268 **Melway** 506 A6

Port Pier Cafe

SPANISH

Portarlington Foreshore Reserve (opposite pier),
Portarlington **5259 1080**

THE squat brick building down near the foreshore is no toilet block. It was the old fisherman's co-op; now it's a good little restaurant serving Catalan tapas and paella. You might share steamed mussels with garlicky aioli, marinated mushrooms and parsley-strewn sardines before tucking into paella studded with chicken, pork and fishy chunks.

Licensed & BYO wine
Open Thurs-Mon noon-3pm; Thurs-Sun 6-9pm
Prices tapas $3-$15; mains $12.50-$22.50; desserts $6.50-$7.50
Map page 268 **Melway** 444 H6

Sawyers Arms Tavern

MODERN AUSTRALIAN

2 Noble Street,
Newtown **5223 1244**

THE decor is classic country pub but the pub food at this family-run stalwart has more than a touch of class. Satisfying pan-fried kidneys come with prosciutto, and good, honest fillet steak is lifted by a side of mashed spuds dashed with truffle oil. Service is down to earth – airs and graces would be as popular as warm beer around these parts.

Licensed
Open Mon-Fri noon-2pm; Mon-Sat 6-9pm
Prices entrees $8.50-$13.50; mains $12.50-$25.50
Map page 268 **Melway** 401 C8

CELLAR DOORS

Somehow the wine always tastes better with a breath of country air

Balgownie Estate
Hermitage Road, Maiden Gully, 5449 6222

Balgownie's reputation rests largely on its shiraz and cabernet sauvignon, both made in a slightly restrained, savoury style, despite their impressive alcohol levels. Several other wines are on tasting, and pies, antipasto platters, coffee and cakes are served in the cafe. The wine museum is worth a look, and excellent accommodation is available on-site.

Brown Brothers
Bobinwarrah Road, Milawa, 5720 5500

Brown Brothers' cellar door combines the charm of a century-old family winery with the professionalism of a fully fledged tourist attraction. Well-versed staff guide you through a diverse tasting list that may run to 45 wines and always includes interesting back vintages available only at cellar door. After the tasting, call in at the neighbouring Epicurean Centre (see page 225) to see how the wines work with food.

Domaine Chandon
Green Point, Maroondah Highway, Coldstream, 9739 1110

Domaine Chandon is the epitome of the modern cellar door: a polished package of excellent wines and superb views. Wines are sold by the glass (five sparkling and three still wines), with a complimentary platter of bread and aged cheddar.

Phillip Island Wines
414 Berrys Beach Road, Phillip Island, 5956 8465

The entire Phillip Island vineyard, all two hectares of it, is draped in nets year-round to protect the vines from animals and the elements. This super-human effort is rewarded in the quality of the wines, particularly sauvignon blanc, chardonnay and pinot noir. Sit in the courtyard or on the veranda to savour splendid views of Bass Strait and the Gippsland countryside, along with simple cheese and dip platters.

Scotchmans Hill
190 Scotchmans Road, Drysdale, 5251 3176

There's not an espresso machine or an antipasto platter in sight at this traditional cellar door. Instead, you'll find a quaint 1920s stone cottage perched on a rise with views of Port Phillip stretching all the way back to Melbourne. The winery is famed for its chardonnay, pinot noir and sauvignon blanc, but small amounts of shiraz, cabernet sauvignon and riesling are available solely at cellar door.

Seppelt Great Western
Moyston Road, Great Western, 5361 2239

These days, the Great Western winery produces a vast range of sparkling and still wines for Southcorp. Its cellar door is set up in the 140-year-old Shaft House and offers about 15 wines for tasting, including Drumborg riesling, St Peters shiraz and Original sparkling shiraz. Picnic areas and barbecues are provided. Tours of the 1.6-kilometre maze of underground cellars are available for a fee.

Tahbilk Winery
Tabilk via Nagambie, 5794 2555

Tahbilk's cellar door is housed in the estate's National Trust-listed above-ground cellars and offers the full range of wines for tasting, including the revered 1860 Vines shiraz and the Reserve shiraz and cabernet sauvignon. A handful of varietal reds are sold at cellar door only, including Tahbilk's first release of sangiovese. The marsanne is one highlight among some very good whites.

Tuck's Ridge
37 Shoreham Road, Red Hill South, 5989 8660

Nestled in one of the peninsula's prettiest spots, Tuck's Ridge makes an increasingly acclaimed range of wines, the highlights of which are its pinot noir and chardonnay. Match them with a selection of simple, well-priced dishes such as barbecued calamari rings, bangers, lamb souvlakis, mussels and free-range egg frittata. BYO deckchair or use the outdoor settings and picnic rugs provided.

Bellbrae Harvest

MODERN AUSTRALIAN

45 Portreath Road,
Bellbrae **5266 2100**

THIS cottage cafe, tucked in the hills behind Torquay, is a smart blend of modern ideas and rustic flavours, using farm-grown produce where possible. Zaatar-spiked home-made pide with white bean dip and the peppery leek and cheddar soufflé are both entree staples. And the Locke family would have a hard time depriving regulars of the house-made beef and olive sausages served with chunky tomato relish and mash. Otherwise, there are pizzettas – perhaps with prosciutto, grilled mushrooms and feta – or focaccia with tandoori chicken and minted yoghurt. For dessert, it's hard to choose between fabulous berry flan, sour lime torte and house-churned icecreams (flavours might include white chocolate brûlée, orange blossom and lavender). If you roll up for afternoon tea, scones with Bellbrae Harvest jam and pure cream are a shoo-in.

Licensed
Open Thurs-Sun 9am-5pm (also Fri-Sat 9am-late in summer)
Seats 45; outdoor seating
Owners Barry & Verna Locke
Chef Sarah Locke
Cards AE BC DC MC V Eftpos
Prices entrees $10-$15; mains $18-$27; desserts $8-$12
Map page 268 **VicRoads** 93 E7

13/20

Dining Room One

ITALIAN

The Grand Hotel, Seventh Street,
Mildura **5023 0511**

MILDURA culinary mogul Stefano de Pieri has taken over the Grand Hotel's ground floor dining room and turned it into a smart pub restaurant serving very good food. A largely short-order menu keeps the grill busy: there are three cuts of aged Mallee beef, perhaps baby chook with ginger tomato jam and a clever mixed grill, which brings together petite lamb chop, expertly grilled minute steak, juicy chorizo and oney-marinated quail. A couple of excellent-value pastas, and a handful non-Italian dishes (Thai beef salad, chermoula-roasted lamb) round t the list. Service can be a little green, but manager Andy Williams ures things stay on the rails. Avoca Gondola, the 1877 paddleboat that is de Pieri's newest venture, is also an option for focaccias and ze (phone 5022 1444).

Licensed
Open Tues-Fri noon-2pm; daily 6-10pm
Seats 80; outdoor seating; bar
Owners Stefano de Pieri & Donata Carrazza
Chefs Jo Villeva & Tristan Allen
Cards AE BC DC MC V Eftpos
Prices entrees $12-$19; mains $19.50-$26; desserts $6.50-$8.50
Map page 268 **VicRoads** 203 P5

3/20

Dublin House Inn

INTERNATIONAL

57-59 Bank Street,
Port Fairy **5568 2022**

'WELCOME to our home' says the menu, and a warm welcome it is indeed. Cosy, quaint and filled with antiquey knick-knacks, Dublin House is a great place to sequester yourself on a cold coastal night. Enjoy a glass of sherry in front of the fire, then settle in for a pleasurable dinner. The prawn and camembert marriage may sound more 'shotgun' than 'made in heaven', but the crumbed and shallow-fried combination is worth a go. Rolled crepe stuffed with field mushrooms and topped with melted buffalo mozzarella, or kangaroo fillet served on a spinach omelette, are more representative of the vaguely mod-Oz menu. For dessert, steamed blackberry pudding, swimming in a dense jus, and with a crown of vanilla icecream and Persian fairyfloss, is a delight both to admire and devour.

Licensed & BYO wine
Corkage $5.50 a bottle
Open Mon-Sat 6pm-late
Seats 50; private room
Owners Glenn & Debbie Perkins
Chef Glenn Perkins
Cards AE BC DC MC V Eftpos
Prices entrees $9-$15; mains $22.50-$27; desserts $9.50
Map page 268 **VicRoads** 263 04

12/20 

Duffs Cafe

MODERN AUSTRALIAN

43 Gellibrand Street,
Colac **5232 2229**

DON'T zoom through Colac. Just one block from the Princes Highway is a cafe that's brought coffee culture and exciting flavours to the Western District's dairy capital. Situated in the restored 1891-vintage Oddfellows hall, Duffs does simple, attractive dishes with Mediterranean and Middle Eastern accents. Lunch fuel includes tangy dips, open sandwiches on Irrewarra sourdough, hefty salads (perhaps Greek-style marinated lamb with tzatziki or caesar salad with roasted chicken) and comforting hot dishes like roast pumpkin and pine nut cannelloni, or sparky chicken and cashew cakes with mint and coriander notes. Dinner dishes mine a similar vein, and also extend to family favourites like grilled fish or steak and chips. The coffee is sublime (all the staff have done coffee-making classes) and the cakes are worth a gander.

Licensed & BYO wine
Corkage $4 a bottle
Open Sun-Thurs 10am-4pm; Fri-Sat 10am-late
Seats 100; outdoor seating; private room
Owner Fiona Stewart
Chef David Allen
Cards AE BC DC MC V Eftpos
Prices lunches $6.50-$16; entrees $8-$13; mains $19-$23; desserts $5-$10
Map page 268 **VicRoads** 263 P4

13/20

Kosta's

GREEK/MEDITERRANEAN

48 Mountjoy Parade,
Lorne **5289 1883**

PEOPLE say they come to Lorne for the sea air – really, they're coming to feast at Kosta's. This Great Ocean Road icon, established in 1976, is still packing them in – so much so that there are two sittings at weekends and those who can't find a table cram at the horseshoe-shaped bar. There's a palpable sense of hospitality, a terrific Med/Greek-inspired menu dictated by the day's catch and, of course, Kosta holding fort at the door. It's a formula that never seems to fail. Start with wedges of grilled sheep's cheese and just-fried calamari. Then move on to char-grilled snapper fillets awash with a tangy sauce à la grecque, and a side of white beans, roasted parsnip and parsley or rabbit stifado, braised with red wine and thyme. Hipper – and better – than most Greek restaurants in the big smoke, Kosta's is further boosted by a decent wine list.

Licensed & BYO wine
Corkage $7 a bottle
Open daily 9am-1am (closed May-Jul; closed Tues-Wed Aug-Nov)
Seats 90; outdoor seating; bar
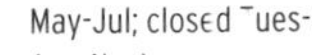
Owners Kosta & Pam Talimanidis
Chef Pam Talimanidis
Cards AE BC DC MC V Eftpos
Prices breakfasts $4.50-$12; entrees $13-$15; mains $22-$27; desserts $9.50
Map page 268 **VicRoads** 265 N5

14/20

La Bimba

MODERN AUSTRALIAN

125 Great Ocean Road,
Apollo Bay **5237 7411**

THE seasprayed dagginess of Apollo Bay's main street is loveable enough, but it's always a pleasure to escape up the stairs to La Bimba. Here, the bohemian mix includes a happy jumble of cushions and lanterns, with oak, mosaic and wicker fittings framing the blue bay below. Prices are a little high, but the best coffee in town, friendly service and the small luxuries of the room and the menu make the outlay seem worthwhile. Many of the best dishes – say, the unctuous duck on bok choy with cherry jus, the barramundi on lemony cous cous with harissa, and the Japanese spinach and noodle salad with orange and mirin – seem like direct copies of city restaurant favourites. But the eye fillet on garlic bread pudding, and the dark chocolate tart with candied orange are La Bimba originals.

14/20

Licensed & BYO wine
Corkage $5 a bottle
Open daily 8am-late (Dec-Apr); Wed-Sun 8am-late (May-Nov)
Seats 50
Owners Andrew Purves & Fiona Taplin
Chef Charles Boy
Cards AE BC MC V
Prices breakfasts $9.50-$13; lunches $9.50-$15.50; entrees $7.50-$12.50; mains $15-$25; desserts $12.50
Map page 268 **VicRoads** 264 D9

L'Orne

INTERNATIONAL

Erskine Falls Cottages, 5 Cora Lyn Court,
Lorne **5289 1622**

BILLED as the Great Ocean Road's 'newest restaurant', L'Orne (from the French 'orner', to adorn) is the brainchild of two go-getting Canadians – one a young, enterprising chef, the other the owner of the Erskine Falls Cottages, where this restaurant is located. In summer, deck dining with a coastal view beckons; otherwise, settle into a leather chair in the restaurant's 'cabin'. Start with, perhaps, asparagus and tarragon soup, mussels in a curry-spiked cream or a warm salad of duck breast, orange and sweet potato chips. Main courses travel the globe (coq au vin, bouillabaisse, jambalaya) and are mostly well cooked. An ambitious degustation menu defies the humble surrounds. The wine list is local, and while service is friendly, it's also amateurish. You may have to stumble through an ill-lit mini-golf course to get back to your car.

13/20

Licensed
Open daily 11am-4pm, 6pm-late (Sep-May); daily 9.30am-4pm (Jun-Aug)
Seats 50; outdoor seating
Owners Jamie Sellar & Corey MacLennan
Chef Jamie Sellar
Cards BC MC V Eftpos
Prices lunches $10-$20; entrees $10-$17; mains $28-$32; desserts $9-$10; degustation menu $100 (6 courses)
Map page 268 **VicRoads** 265 M6

@ A GLANCE

The need for caffeine doesn't stop at the city limits

FUEL STOPS

Cafe au Lait, 20 Mitchell Street, Bendigo, 5443 5126
This simple goldfields cafe does the important things well: good coffee and home-baked cakes.

The Coffee Room, 57 Piper Street, Kyneton, 5422 3555
In an old undertaker's chapel, this laidback temple to coffee draws folk from all over the district for their daily fix.

Flinders Bakehouse Cafe, 60 Cook Street, Flinders, 5989 0091
Break your excursion with coffee and a muffin at this homely cafe. And buy a loaf of fabulously dense fruit bread for the next leg.

Ripe, 376-378 Mount Dandenong Road, Sassafras, 9755 2100
The fireside sofa and back veranda are perfect spots for post-drive revival. Excellent espresso and a square of fudge will send you off with a happy buzz.

Marks

MODERN AUSTRALIAN

124 Mountjoy Parade,
Lorne **5289 2787**

WITH its blue and orange banquettes and breezily friendly staff, Marks is the epitome of a smart seaside restaurant. The specials list is always rife with creative seafood options: there might be baby octopus flavoured with lemon verbena and ginger, char-grilled whole baby snapper with oregano, and juicy fillets with a cumin and coriander crust. The neat, annotated wine list has many fruity white temptations to partner with your fish. Fortunately, chef Mark Purdie is a long-time Great Ocean Road restaurateur and he knows to balance the menu with hearty braised lamb shanks on mash, crisp duck with Chinese greens, hot apple and mulberry crumble and a long list of good reds. It's a smart move, because regulars know that Lorne can be one of the coldest beach resorts on earth, even in the middle of summer.

13/20 

Licensed & BYO wine
Corkage $6 a bottle
Open daily 6pm-late (closed Aug)
Seats 110; outdoor seating; bar
Owners Caroline & Mark Purdie
Chef Mark Purdie
Cards AE BC V
Prices entrees $7.70-$16; mains $17.50-$25; desserts $9.50-$12.50
Map page 268 **VicRoads** 265 N5

Pippies by the Bay

MODERN ITALIAN

Flagstaff Hill, Merri Street,
Warrnambool **5561 2188**

WHALES are Warrnambool's principal wildlife attraction but Pippies, tucked into the Flagstaff Hill redevelopment, is the pick of the town's restaurants. The chic dining room, in charcoal and olive tones, has blondwood tables, springy moulded chairs and great views across Lady Bay. Owners Peter and Jane McLauchlan (ex-Puds) have admirable credentials, and have recruited a chef with Florentino and Marchetti's experience. A passion for fine produce shines through in the Italian-accented food. Seasonal menus are augmented by outstanding specials like abalone polpette on salsa verdi or three-cheeses polenta perfumed with white truffle. Whether it's breakfast, lunch or dinner, Pippies wins with its sophisticated friendliness, discerning wine list, lovely outlook, reasonable prices and, of course, wonderful food.

15/20 

Licensed
Open daily 9am-late
Seats 80; outdoor seating
Owners Peter & Jane McLauchlan
Chef Chris Considine
Cards AE BC DC MC V Eftpos
Prices breakfasts $9-$15; lunches $7-$17; entrees $9-$14; mains $21-$26 desserts $8-$14
Map page 268 **VicRoads** 241 L10

Portofino on Bank

MODERN AUSTRALIAN

26 Bank Street,
Port Fairy **5568 2251**

PORTOFINO brings groovy city attitude to sleepy old Port Fairy. The menu and the mind-set mix modern and old world, but with none of the cloying cuteness that sometimes taints such combinations. Seafood is good: plump scallops, served in the half-shell, have a touch of sweet caramel where they've been seared; baked snapper is clean and fresh as the breeze. A particular treat is the duck, dusted with cumin and salt, then roasted. Crusty on the outside, juicy and perfectly tender inside, this dish comes with a mustard and pear pickle. Brains – crumbed, of course – make an appearance, as do slightly bitter bull's testicles, pan-fried with cannellini beans. A dish for the brave, it's more often ordered by men than women, according to management. Well-informed staff are able to guide you through the impressive, mostly mid-range, wine list.

14/20 

Licensed
Open daily 6pm-late
Seats 40
Owner Shane Clancy
Chef Allan Turner
Cards AE BC DC MC V Eftpos
Prices entrees $8-$12; mains $22-$27; desserts $10-$12
Map page 268 **VicRoads** 243 O4

reifs

MODERN AUSTRALIAN

84 Mountjoy Parade,
Lorne **5289 2366**

THIS food and drink zone on Lorne's main drag is doing plenty of things right. By day, the benches on its multi-tiered deck are filled with mums, dads, teens and tots sipping, supping and – often as not – soaking wet. They come for bumper breakfasts and the usual cafe crowd-pleasers like dips, bruschetta, risotto and fish 'n' chips. At night, the kitchen cranks up a notch, playing groovier tunes for a swankier crowd. Lunchtime's battered fish becomes dinner's tempura prawns; goats' cheese comes smeared on tapenade toast and the risotto is piled with truffled forest mushrooms. Sassy staff, Irrewarra sourdough and a well-priced and sourced wine list tick a few more boxes. Reifs is no virtuoso, but it knows who it's playing to and it gives them a damn good show every time.

13/20

Licensed & BYO wine
Corkage $6 a bottle
Open daily 9.30am-late (Sep-Apr); Fri & Mon 11am-late; Tues-Wed 5.30pm-late; Sat-Sun 9.30am-late (May-Aug)
Seats 90; outdoor seating
Owner Ross McCahon
Chef Alistair Hayes
Cards AE BC MC V Eftpos
Prices breakfasts $9-$15; entrees $3.50-$14.50; mains $16.50-$26.50; desserts $5-$8.50
Map page 268 **VicRoads** 265 N5

Royal Mail Hotel

MODERN AUSTRALIAN

Glenelg Highway (Parker Street),
Dunkeld **5577 2241**

A STRIKING monument to contemporary design and eco-friendly landscaping, the Royal Mail bears no resemblance to the Cobb & Co staging post it supplanted. The spacious restaurant is cleverly angled, separating it from the bustling bar, and ensuring terrific mountain views. Chef Jo Fraser prepares sophisticated, creative dishes that make use of quality regional produce, some of it from the Mail's own fields. A neatly composed tasting platter might include Warrnambool smoked trout, Shaw River buffalo mozzarella and Mount Zero olives. A house speciality is an eye fillet of Hopkins River beef. Juicy and tender (and expensive), the fillet rises from the plate like Mount Sturgeon, the southern sentinel of the Grampians looming behind the hotel. The extraordinary wine list offers 12,000 bottles for perusal.

15/20

Licensed
Open Mon-Fri 7-9am; Sat-Sun 8-10am; daily noon-2pm; Mon-Thurs 6-8pm; Fri-Sun 6-9pm
Seats 80; outdoor seating; private room; bar
Owner Dunkeld Pastoral Company
Chef Jo Fraser
Cards AE BC DC MC V Eftpos
Prices breakfasts $12.50-$17.50; entrees $9-$14.50; mains $22-$39.90; desserts $9.25-$10.80
Map page 268 **VicRoads** 229 R4

Stefano's

ITALIAN

The Grand Hotel, Seventh Street,
Mildura **5023 0511**

STEFANO DE PIERI'S flagship restaurant endures as one of Victoria's great dining experiences. The underground cantina has been serving its heartfelt food for a dozen years now, long enough for a love of food and wine to sing from every crevice. And sing it does: through the medium of salt-cured trout slices scattered with salmon roe; porcini risotto with blood-dark roast pigeon; wild barramundi doused in a creamy olive sauce; and coquettish panna cotta served with mango. There's no menu, so be prepared for a procession of dishes pushing the seasonal, regional line. The wine list is gem-studded as ever, with many offerings from de Pieri's homeland, and service is more consistent than it has been. Above all, Stefano's is a celebration of the simple – food, certainly, but also the basic, trusting ritual of sitting down and asking to be fed.

18/20

Licensed
Open Mon-Sat 7pm-late
Seats 60
Owners Stefano de Pieri & Donata Carrazza
Chefs Stefano de Pieri, Nathan Hoeksema & Ashleigh Allford
Cards AE BC DC MC V Eftpos
Prices set menu $75 (5-6 courses)
Map page 268 **VicRoads** 203 P5

The Victoria Hotel

MODERN AUSTRALIAN

42 Bank Street,
Port Fairy **5568 2891**

STILL the pinnacle of the Port Fairy food scene, the Victoria offers stunning contemporary cuisine. With an eye to taking advantage of whatever's ripest and freshest, chef Daniel Myers tweaks the five-course set menu every day, producing daring and lively interpretations of European favourites. A rich, verdant spinach and sand crab bisque is made even more fragrant and earthy with a generous splash of white truffle oil. Plump gnocchi in sage butter comes with crisped jamon. Char-grilled marlin steaks are served on a niçoise-style salad with quail egg. Subtle vanilla panna cotta comes with sweet and sour quandongs, making for an invigorating collision of the mild and the intensely tart. All dishes are beautifully and simply presented, without froth or excess. Augmented by smooth service, there's nothing to stand between you and culinary pleasure.

15/20

Licensed
Open Wed-Sat 6pm-late (daily 6pm-late school hols & folk festival); cafe daily 11am-late
Seats 55; bar
Owners Michael & Maureen Myers
Chef Daniel Myers
Cards AE BC DC MC V Eftpos
Prices set menu $55 (5 courses)
Map page 268 **VicRoads** 243 O4

The Vines Cafe & Bar

MODERN CAFE

74 Barkly Street,
Ararat **5352 1744**

CAFES as good as this are rare in country Victoria. Brightly attractive and refreshingly innovative, the Vines displays a dedication to the wines and produce of its region without lapsing into parochialism. It's a multi-purpose place: pause for coffee and house-baked cake in the covered courtyard, linger inside over a light lunch or weekend dinner, select the doings for a picnic from the little adjoining shop, and browse the boutique wine room. Eye-candy includes the work of local artists and Sandra O'Malley's daily-changing blackboard menu. She offers exquisite dishes like green prawns on lemon risotto with a tangy orange and fennel oil vinaigrette, or blue cheese frittata with pear and spinach salad. Magrets of duck with honeyed onion confit are a dinner favourite. Nearly 40 regional wines are available by the glass at quaffable prices.

14/20

Licensed & BYO wine
Corkage $1 a bottle
Open daily 9am-6pm; Fri-Sat 6.30pm-late
Seats 70; outdoor seating
Owners Ron & Sandra O'Malley
Chef Sandra O'Malley
Cards AE BC MC V Eftpos
Prices breakfasts $4-$16; lunches $9-$15; entrees $9; mains $23-$24; desserts $6-$7
Map page 268 **VicRoads** 226 E8

Waves

MODERN AUSTRALIAN

29 Lord Street,
Port Campbell **5598 6111**

PORT CAMPBELL used to be a seafarers' haven; these days it isn't even a fishing village. Still, it seems appropriate that seafood features on the menu at this thoroughly modern cafe-restaurant on the main street. The 10 or so fish dishes on the specials board spring from diverse traditions: there might be green Thai curry, sumac-seared marlin and citrus-baked ocean trout. But there's lots more besides: King Island scotch fillet, perhaps, or marinated pork fillet stuffed with orange marmalade. Most mains come with steamed potatoes and seasonal vegetables rather than individual garnishes. The day starts with leisurely breakfasts – on the sundeck if weather allows – followed by flexible lunches, as light or substantial as you like. There are no sea views, unfortunately, but there is a boutique hotel at the rear.

13/20

Licensed
Open daily 8am-late
Seats 65; outdoor seating
Owners Bill & Elizabeth Kordupel
Chef Rebecca Gorman
Cards AE BC DC MC V Eftpos
Prices breakfasts $3-$15; lunches $6.50-$19.50; entrees $5-$22; mains $17.50-$26; desserts $8.50-$12.50
Map page 268 **VicRoads** 264 G4

Chris's Sea-Grape Wine Bar & Grill

MEDITERRANEAN

141 Great Ocean Road,
Apollo Bay **5237 6610**

SEA-GRAPE can take much of the credit for the buzz around Apollo Bay these days. Grazers and latte sippers float in all day, flicking the sand out of their hair to order dips, pita, warm olives, fresh fish and pork souvlaki. While Chris's Beacon Point rebuilds after a devastating fire, this is the only place to try the man's Greek-inspired food.

V

Licensed & BYO wine
Open daily 9am-10pm
Prices breakfasts $4.50-$11; lunches $5.50-$16; entrees $7-$16; mains $22-$30
Map page 268 **VicRoads** 264 D9

Hamilton Strand Restaurant

MODERN AUSTRALIAN

100 Thompson Street,
Hamilton **5571 9144**

HAMILTON'S premier restaurant has moved to grander premises with a lovely outdoor dining area. Simple dishes with clean-cut flavours are based on quality regional produce such as Western District beef, lamb and cheeses, and fresh fish from down south. Conservative country tastes are judiciously livened with contemporary touches.

Licensed & BYO wine
Open Tues-Sat 10am-late
Prices breakfasts $6-$10; entrees $8-$16; mains $20-$26; desserts $6-8
Map page 268 **VicRoads** 230 G8

Kookaburra

REGIONAL

125-127 Grampians Road,
Hall's Gap **5356 4222**

MANY a competitor has fallen from its perch but Kookaburra has been a Hall's Gap constant for 24 years. Rick Heinrich's cooking isn't adventurous, but robust flavours shine through in heap-big favourites like venison pie and smoked pork. Venison fillet – from the Heinrichs' farm – comes with a splendid juniper-flavoured sauce.

Licensed
Open daily noon-3pm, 6-8.30pm
Prices entrees $8-$16.50; mains $19-$26; desserts $9
Map page 268 **VicRoads** 225 N4

Merrijig Inn

MODERN AUSTRALIAN

1 Campbell Street,
Port Fairy **5568 2324**

LOCAL seafood features at this cosy, slightly twee restaurant across the road from the Moyne River wharf. You might eat succulent Portland bay bugs with a piquant Vietnamese salad, pan-fried prawns on eggplant mousse, or marinated scallops. Warming options include duck breast in shiraz jus with a corn and pancetta risotto.

Licensed
Open daily 6.30pm-late
Prices entrees $10-$18; mains $25-$31; desserts $9-$9.50
Map page 268 **VicRoads** 243 05

---

moons espresso & juice bar

CAFE

108 Mountjoy Parade,
Lorne **5289 1149**

THIS surfside spot has more St Kilda dazzle – hip wait crew, funky stools, long tables – than coastal cruise. Lob in after a morning dip and chow on eggs with all the add-ons or kick back with an over-stuffed pide or baguette. Freshly squeezed juices and a handy selection of local wines take care of the various holidaymaker thirsts.

Licensed
Open Mon-Fri 8.30am-5pm; Sat-Sun 8am-6pm
Prices breakfasts $5-$14; lunches $9.50-$15; juices $5
Map page 268 **VicRoads** 265 N5

Puds Pantry & Deli

CAFE

60 Kepler Street,
Warrnambool **5562 5119**

THE proof of Puds is in the eating. Peter and Jane McLauchlan, now at Pippies, sold this popular bakery-cafe to their former pastry chef, Jason Bidmade, who is upholding its reputation for wonderful pies, quiches and daily hot dishes. The coffee is good, and the olde-worlde Chelsea buns are as delicious as they are nostalgic.

$ V

BYO
Open Mon-Fri 7.30am-5pm; Sat 8am-1.30pm
Prices pastries $2.60-$4.80; hot meals $6.50-$12.50
Map page 268 **VicRoads** 240 K9

The Stag Inn

MODERN AUSTRALIAN

22 Sackville Street,
Port Fairy **5568 3058**

NO longer frequented by rollicking sailors, the quaint old Stag now grooves to the sound of cracking shells as diners extract the last of the meat from juicy local lobster, served mornay-style, and accompanied by a free glass of bubbly. Other charmers include oysters with lemongrass and local eye fillet wrapped in prosciutto.

Licensed & BYO wine
Open Mon-Sat 6pm-late
Prices entrees $12-$18; mains $23.50-$28.50; desserts $10.50-$11.50
Map page 268 **VicRoads** 243 P4

Trentham Estate

MODERN AUSTRALIAN

Sturt Highway,
Trentham Cliffs **5024 8888**

THIS winery-eatery has beautiful views of emerald lawns sloping down to the Murray River. Take advantage of them by booking a table on the terrace, rather than in the dated dining room. Eat mod-Oz crowd-pleasers like risotto balls and crumbed prawns with lime and mint salsa, or buy some sausages for a DIY barbecue by the water.

Licensed
Open Tues-Sun 11.30am-2.30pm; Sat 6-8.30pm
Prices entrees $12-$18; mains $19-$26; desserts $10
Map page 268 **VicRoads** 3 E5

---

27 Deakin

CAFE/MEDITERRANEAN

27 Deakin Avenue,
Mildura **5021 3627**

DONATA CARRAZZA'S relaxed cafe, food store and Stefano merchandise stand attract Mildura's meet-and-greeters, city foodies and the odd backpacker. They're there for great coffee, big breakfasts – maybe roesti cakes with lush smoked salmon – and lovely, simple lunches like pasta carbonara or excellent baked-here baguettes.

$ 

Licensed
Open Mon-Sat 8am-3pm; Sun 9am-3pm
Prices breakfasts $3.70-$14.50; lunches $6.50-$16; cakes $6.50
Map page 268 **VicRoads** 203 07

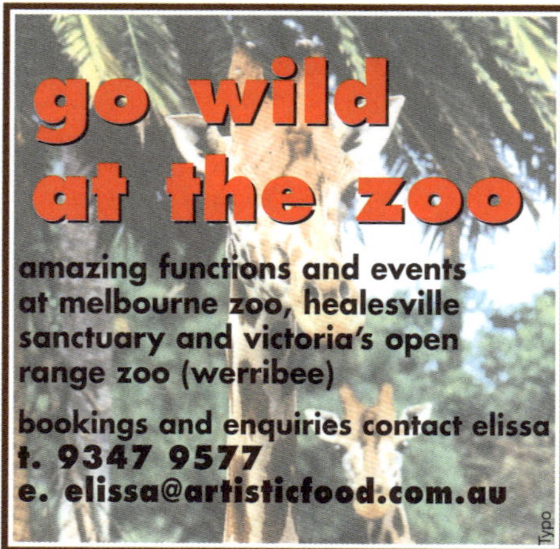

Shop for your certified organic food 7 days a week, 9am to 7pm.

PASSIONFOODS

219 Ferrars Street South Melbourne, Telephone 9690 9339.

Certified Biodynamic and Organic fruit and vegetables, groceries, eggs, dairy, meat, poultry, soy products, beer and wine. Enjoy our fresh cooked organic take-home meals.

For the passionate cheesemakers of King Island, cheese isn't just to be eaten; it's to be savoured, shared and enjoyed. They can explain why Brie should look creamy and plump with no chalky core. How much more enjoyable the eating experience becomes when you take time to let cheese warm, instead of serving it straight from the refrigerator.

Why it is, that when you let a small piece sit in your mouth, the flavour and aroma melt into one brilliant taste sensation. And why ripe, fresh cheese has a flavour that just can't be preserved. It's not information that will change the world, but it will give you a whole new perspective on the quiet joy of sharing fine cheese.

KING ISLAND DAIRY
PREMIUM QUALITY DAIRY PRODUCE
FARM HOUSE STYLE

Bad Habits Cafe @ The Convent

Be tempted by the Altar Bar/Lounge, take in the views of Daylesford as you sit in the conservatory enjoying a leisurely lunch, decadent dessert or just coffee

Mediterranean style cuisine

Great selection of local wines

Private functions available

Open daily 10am-5pm

Cnr Hill & Daly Streets, Daylesford

Ph: 5348 3211 for reservations

Typo

Waves

Waves is an oasis of intimate boutique-style accommodation, with outstanding dining facilities.

The Waves Cafe Bar and Restaurant offers an extensive seafood menu, often with delicious Asian influences.

Outside decking provides seating for up to 30 people.

29 Lord St, Port Campbell
Phone: (03) 5598 6111
www.wavesportcampbell.com.au

Superb contemporary B&B for couples in the *Heart* of town.
Sumptuous breakfast, licensed lounge with huge open fire. 4.5 star
www.captains.net.au
Ph (03) 5237 6771 Email: captains@vicnet.net.au

Typo

CENTRAL VICTORIA

Bazzani

MODERN AUSTRALIAN

2 Howard Place,
Bendigo **5441 3777**

OPPOSITE Rosalind Park, surrounded by mature plane trees, this 1860s building is Bendigo's place to celebrate milestones. The menu changes every six weeks and the food, while ambitious, is this majestic town's trump card. You might start with a warm salad of calamari and chorizo or sweet three-onion risotto, then follow up with fish and shellfish stew or maple-roasted pork on silken goats' feta mash. Desserts pivot around seasonal fruits, pastries and the house icecream. Bazzani has slipped on recent visits, a slide that coincides with the family spending more time at their Warrenmang property (see page 218). Culinary pairings are not always appealing (twice-roasted squab with bourbon-vanilla jus), some of the waiters seem inexperienced, and a deep and diverse wine list is let down by a limited selection by the glass.

14/20

Licensed
Open Tues-Sat noon-late
Seats 80; outdoor seating; private room; bar
Owners Luigi & Athalie Bazzani
Chef Brendan Tuddenham
Cards AE BC DC MC V Eftpos
Prices entrees $8.80-$16.50; mains $15.50-$28.50; desserts $8.50-$10.50
Map page 269 **VicRoads** 281 L13

Cliffy's

CAFE/FOODSTORE

28 Raglan Street,
Daylesford **5348 3279**

TAKE a pinch of Persian bazaar, a smidge of grandma's parlour, a touch of the Magic Faraway Tree and an eclectic collection of enticing produce and you've got Cliffy's. Its menu – handwritten on brown paper bags – offers the best that the Daylesford area produces. You might find a fragrant, sweet pumpkin curry, baguettes filled with whatever antipasto-type lovelies are in the larder, or an ocean of peppery gazpacho, with ice, cucumber and tomato 'bergs afloat. Fixtures include Tuki's grass-fed lamb pies and tart Musk Farm berry icecream, but the daily menu depends on what's fresh and who's cooking. The staff are enthusiastic and fresh, kids are smilingly welcomed and there's an interesting selection of local wines and beers: Cliffy's is a paragon of country cafes.

14/20 $ V

Licensed
Open Sun-Thurs 9.30am-6pm; Fri-Sat 9.30am-late
Seats 25; outdoor seating
Owners & chefs Mary Ellis & Geoffrey Gray
Cards BC MC V Eftpos
Prices breakfasts $4.50-$7.50; entrees $8.50-$10; mains $9.50-$20; desserts $4-$8.50
Map page 269 **VicRoads** 289 P9

Deco Restaurant at the Springs Retreat

MODERN AUSTRALIAN

124 Main Road,
Hepburn Springs **5348 2202**

THIS newcomer to the Spa Country scene has the goods to challenge the area's big players. For a start, it's in gorgeous surrounds, an iconic Art Deco hotel with more than a dash of Gatsby glamour. Chef Clinton Camilleri has a good pedigree, too, having worked at Blakes and Lake House. His food shows confidence and flair, backed by strong European techniques. Every dish has a little kick: the grilled swordfish salad is lifted with pomegranate molasses, quail strudel comes with fig compote and roasted chestnuts, marinated lamb loin anchors herbed gnocchi, a ratatouille timbale and a tomato stuffed with goats' cheese. Desserts are firmly continental, sticking to the soufflé, brûlée, tart triumvirate, usually matched with fruity sorbets and gelati. The ambitions of the food are not quite matched by the accessible, mid-priced wine list.

Licensed
Open daily 7pm-late
Seats 80; bar
Owner Malcross Ltd
Chef Clinton Camilleri
Cards AE BC DC MC V Eftpos
Prices entrees $13.50; mains $26.50; desserts $12.50
Map page 269 **VicRoads** 289 O3

14/20 

Emeu Inn

INTERNATIONAL

187 High Street,
Heathcote **5433 2668**

ONCE it was gold that brought the hordes to Heathcote. Now it's wine, and bottles of the region's best reds fill the cellar of this old butcher's shop and pub. Chef Fred Thies brings a range of influences to the Emeu's menu: there's his German training, a stint at the Southern Cross Hotel in the internationalist 1960s, and a fascination with native produce. You might try earthy yabby salad, robust kangaroo snags with house beetroot relish and a signature emu casserole cooked with native pepper leaf. European influences rule in the vigneron's platter – with sausage, pickle and rye bread – and the massive pork chop stuffed with sage and apple. Otherwise, go subcontinental with fragrant, skilfully made curries. Whether you're dining outside or in the cosy colonial dining room, Frank's wife Leslye always provides personable service.

Licensed
Open Thurs-Mon 11am-5pm, 6.30pm-late
Seats 30; outdoor seating
Owners Fred & Leslye Thies
Chef Fred Thies
Cards AE BC DC MC V Eftpos
Prices entrees $9.50-$16.50; mains $22.50-$27.50; desserts $7-$15.50
Map page 269 **VicRoads** 276 B3

14/20 

Farmers Arms Hotel

MODERN AUSTRALIAN

1 East Street,
Daylesford **5348 2091**

IT would be easy to drive past this unassuming pub and beeline for Daylesford's main drag. Not so fast. The Farmers' front bar is the real deal – all singleted blokes and frosty pots – but the dining room's white linen and antique clobber hint that there's more than pub nosh to the picture. True enough. There's been good food here for a few years, and with ex-Cicciolina chef Abbie Kitchin at the helm, meals are even better. Finely balanced entrees might include blue cheese soufflé in tomato coulis, and trout terrine over a bitey blood orange reduction. Mains are confident and invariably successful: salmon comes with a vermouth-dressed watercress salad; Italo-Asian roast chicken roosts on lime and spinach risotto; the ubiquitous vegetarian stack is reinvented with layers of polenta, roast beetroot and goats' cheese. The wine list has plenty of local interest.

Licensed
Open daily 6-9pm; Sun noon-3pm
Seats 60; bar
Owners Melissa Macfarlane & Frank Moylan
Chef Abbie Kitchin
Cards BC MC V Eftpos
Prices entrees $8-$16; mains $19.50-$24.50; desserts $7.50-$9
Map page 269 **VicRoads** 289 R10

14/20 

Frangos & Frangos

MEDITERRANEAN

82 Vincent Street,
Daylesford **5348 2363**

IT'S business as usual at the Frangos flagship (the family also owns the homewares shop next door and pizza cafe Koukla, page 220). In what is essentially a sparse room of grand dimensions, an atmosphere is created in broad, simple strokes: there's jaunty jazz, bistro furnishings and a striking wrap-around pew-style banquette. The regular presence of Jim Frangos, either at his corner table or a fireside perch, contributes to the ambience. The food is homely, honest – and somewhat expensive. There might be barley and kaiserfleisch soup, gnocchi with gorgonzola, or a bowl of tender calamari with chorizo and risoni. Local beef and pork 'bullboar' sausages are always around, perhaps on grilled polenta or creamy mash. Desserts are good, especially the luxurious lemon meringue pie; the fairly priced wine list is one of Daylesford's best.

14/20

Licensed
Open Fri-Sat 11am-late; Sun 11am-5pm; Mon-Tues 4pm-late
Seats 70
Owner Frangos family
Chef Andrew Bates
Cards AE BC DC MC V Eftpos
Prices entrees $10.50-$16.90; mains $18.90-$28.90; desserts $10.90
Map page 269 **VicRoads** 289 P10

Holyrood House

MALAYSIAN

51 Stanbridge Street (corner Duke Street),
Daylesford **5348 4818**

ARRIVING at Holyrood House without a reservation would be like crashing a friend's dinner party. Simply not done. But book ahead and your urbane host, Andrew Brownell, will welcome you to his elegant restaurant and guesthouse all smiles and cocktails. Meanwhile, in the kitchen, Brownell's partner Yong Teck Khee will continue painstaking preparations for the evening's feast. The Nonya-style set menu may begin with a clear chicken broth accompanied by spring rolls and steamed pork dumplings for dunking. It might be followed by firm chunks of fish in a tamarind sauce, fried pork with pineapple and a vegetable dish such as sauteed broccolini. The genteel culinary whirlwind always culminates with a great dessert, perhaps sticky shredded coconut baked in honey.

14/20 V

Licensed
Open Fri-Sat 7-10.30pm
Seats 20; outdoor seating
Owners Andrew Brownell & Yong Teck Khee
Chef Yong Teck Khee
Cards BC MC V Eftpos
Prices set menu $50 (3 courses)
Map page 269 **VicRoads** 289 P10

Lake House

MODERN REGIONAL
Country Restaurant of the Year

King Street,
Daylesford **5348 3329**

THERE are myriad ways to be pampered in Spa Country, but if you want to feel really special, come to Lake House. After 20 years of hospitality, this country dame is better than ever, overseen with passion by Alla Wolf-Tasker (winner of *The Age* Award for Professional Excellence). The gorgeous dining room has lake views, cushion-strewn banquettes and a large fireplace. Well-trained staff ensure a glitch-free experience. The food is pitched at diners celebrating special occasions – it's showy but careful not to sacrifice honest flavours. More than in the past, this is food to be enjoyed. The ardently seasonal menu may feature ruby-roasted kangaroo with chestnut mousse, subtle squid-ink linguine on smoked trout sausage, and exceptionally bright, pure apple sorbet. An excellent wine list further boosts what is one of Victoria's essential dining experiences.

17/20 V

Licensed
Open daily 8-11am, noon-5pm, 7pm-late
Seats 110; outdoor seating; private room
Owners Alla & Allan Wolf-Tasker
Chefs Alla Wolf-Tasker & Mathew Macartney
Cards AE BC DC MC V Eftpos
Prices entrees $10.50-$19.50; mains $28-$35; desserts $10.50-$15.50; Sat night set menus $92 or $102 (6 courses)
Map page 269 **VicRoads** 289 P11

La Trattoria

CAFE/ITALIAN

Lavandula Swiss Italian Farm, Main Road,
Shepherds Flat **5476 4347**

THIS pretty lavender farm is at once historical site, produce store, commercial farm and the home of La Trattoria, a tavern-like cafe. The whole shebang relies on the lavender growing in the fields surrounding the 140-year-old stone and timber barns: it's in the facial creams and soaps for sale, and it's in the scones and the glowing pink home-made lemonade. Thankfully, chef Annie Smithers offers dishes without lavender, too. Under grapevines on the veranda or in the ash grove out front, diners can share a meat platter – with salami, prosciutto and pickled vegetables – then move on to uncomplicated pastas, perhaps spaghettini with olive oil, parsley, chilli and garlic, or a niçoise-style salad with warm salmon over beans, eggs and juicy tomato. Finish with cakes, spectacular pavlovas or, of course, the scones.

14/20 $

Licensed & BYO wine
Corkage $3 a bottle
Open daily 10.30am-5pm (Sep-May, public & school hols); Sat-Sun 10.30am-5pm (Jun-Aug)
Seats 50, outdoor seating
Owner Carol White
Chef Annie Smithers
Cards AE BC DC MC V Eftpos
Prices scones $6; entrees $8.50-$14.50; mains $8.50-$16.50; dolci & biscotti $2-$8.50 (entrance to farm $3)
Map page 269 **VicRoads** 59 C6

Thai Issan

THAI

42 High Street,
Trentham **5424 1811**

THINK Trentham. Now think Thai. You may be forgiven for not linking this dozy one-street town with the uplifting scents of lemongrass, galangal and ginger, but Thai Issan is an accomplished Spa Country fixture. The shopfront dining room is intimate, warmly decorated with silks and looms sourced on the owners' numerous trips to Thailand. The menu reflects the chef's heritage (the Issan province in Thailand's north-east) in punchy salads and a choice of jasmine or glutinous rice (steamed and served in a traditional bamboo basket). But most offerings are fairly Main Street. There's an incendiary green pawpaw salad, a smoky, mellow yam neua of beef, and curries made from scratch and finished with fresh herbs. Desserts veer away from Thai offerings – instead, there's Rickett's Point lemon delicious and toasted coconut icecream.

13/20 $ V

Licensed
Open Fri-Sun & public hols 6.30pm-late
Seats 42
Owners Chaloem Chaiseeha & Bryan Derrick
Chef Chaloem Chaiseeha
Cards AE BC DC MC V Eftpos
Prices entrees $9.50-$13; mains $13.50-$28.50; desserts $8
Map page 269 **VicRoads** 290 B2

Tiggies

MODERN AUSTRALIAN

315 Learmonth Street,
Buninyong **5341 2999**

SOME would call it charming. Others, no doubt, would find Tiggies' exposed bricks and homely feel a little hokey. Either way, in an age of clone cafes, this welcoming restaurant in an old butcher's shop is to be admired for doing things its own way. The kitchen picks up on some trends (like bread with olive oil and dukkah) while steadfastly serving up its signature plum pudding for dessert, last recognised as a fashionable dish around 1843. John Hayes works his way through a range of cuisines: tomato and coconut milk soup has Thai influences; chicken with polenta has rustic Mediterranean appeal, served with attractively grilled slices of casalinga. The food's rarely flashy, but with good ingredients and hearty serves it doesn't have to be. The idiosyncratic wine list features Ballarat-area bottles and boutique cider.

13/20

Licensed
Open Thurs-Sat 6pm-late; Sun 11am-4pm
Seats 50
Owners John & Amanda Hayes
Chef John Hayes
Cards AE BC DC MC V Eftpos
Prices set menus $28-$48.50 (1-3 courses)
Map page 269 **VicRoads** 260 B8

Warrenmang Vineyard Resort

MODERN AUSTRALIAN

Mountain Creek Road,
Moonambel **5467 2233**

THAT'S a row of scarecrows you've just passed, not a line of people waiting to get in, although, with views this good, and such excellent food, who wouldn't queue? Antipasto might include velvety asparagus panna cotta, a cool gazpacho shot and rich venison rillettes – enjoy these accomplished morsels with a flight of Warrenmang wines. Wild hare braised in merlot and raspberries is fragrant and hearty, the sweet meat complemented by vanilla risotto and seared bok choy. Lighter vegetarian options might include a delicate tian with goats' cheese mousseline. And dessert? Scones and cheese vie with the cake of the day for your favours. Otherwise, sit back in the '80s chalet-style restaurant 'cabin' and let the well-informed staff recommend a bottle from the comprehensive list of Pyrenees wines. *Also Bazzani, page 214.*

Licensed
Open daily 8.30-9.30am, 10am-6pm, 6.30-8.30pm
Seats 100; outdoor seating
Owners Luigi & Athalie Bazzani
Chef Marreck Cleve Loren
Cards AE BC MC V Eftpos
Prices entrees $20; mains $30; desserts $15; all-day menu $12-$19
Map page 269 **VicRoads** 42 G9

14/20

Whirrakee

INTERNATIONAL

17 View Point,
Bendigo **5441 5557**

BUILT in 1908, this three-storey former bank overlooks Bendigo's historic Pall Mall. Past and present meet in the brightly lit, ornate dining room, where good modern food is prepared using traditional start-from-scratch techniques and served in generous, old-fashioned portions. International flavours might include fresh pasta triangles tossed with a simple breadcrumb, mascarpone and parmesan sauce; a seafood platter with tempura oysters and spicy prawns, and fat, juicy quail on rocket leaves. Hearty European dishes include grilled lamb with tomato tarte tatin and roast chicken on garlic mash. Chef Nikki Halleday's desserts are deliberately fun as well as being seriously good: passionfruit curd tart with a spiral cone of meringue perches atop the house icecream. Serious drinkers should explore the cellar wine list for well-aged local wines.

Licensed
Open Wed-Fri noon-2.30pm; Tues-Sat 6-9pm
Seats 60; outdoor seating; private room
Owner & chef Nikki Halleday
Cards AE BC DC MC V Eftpos
Prices lunches $13-$17; entrees $10-$16; mains $18-$27; desserts $10-$14
Map page 269 **VicRoads** 283 L14

14/20 

Wildings at the Cosmopolitan

INTERNATIONAL

Corner High & Cosmo Roads,
Trentham **5424 1755**

WILDINGS, in the weatherboard Cosmopolitan Hotel, is the rustic bistro from central casting: it's got the barn-like dining room and creaky floorboards, wood-and-wicker furniture, fireplace and rambling garden. But the fogeyish charm stops at the menu: Wildings' dishes are shot through with Chinese, Japanese, Middle Eastern and Mediterranean influences. For entrees, that may mean a layered Peking duck stack with hoisin sauce and deep-fried wonton skins, or calamari with Moorish spicing. Mains range from country comfortable (yearling rib-eye with mash) to highly finished, as in a refined duck gyoza. Simpler dishes tend to have a higher strike rate. Desserts are dreamy, and there's a compact but well-considered wine list. On Thursdays, the kitchen picks a cuisine – Greek, Indian or French, say – and crafts a menu accordingly.

Licensed
Open Sat-Sun noon-4pm; Thurs-Sun 6pm-late
Seats 45
Owners & chefs Anna & Chris Wilding
Cards BC MC V Eftpos
Prices entrees $8-$14; mains $19-$26; desserts $9; Sun night roast $18 (2 courses)
Map page 269 **VicRoads** 290 B2

13/20 

Ansonia Boutique Hotel

MODERN AUSTRALIAN

32 Lydiard Street South,
Ballarat **5332 4678**

THE Ansonia has been freshened up a treat – the dining room has a sleek new look with luxe carpet and stylish Jacobsen chairs. New owners took over as the *Guide* went to press; incoming restaurant manager Stephen Roddy (ex-Pettavel and Lake House) plans to focus on high-quality local produce and international flavours.

Licensed
Open Mon-Fri noon-3pm; Wed-Sun 6pm-late
Prices entrees $8.90-$15; mains $20-$25; desserts $7-$16
Map page 269 **VicRoads** 255 M12

Bath Lane Cafe

MODERN AUSTRALIAN

13 Bath Lane,
Bendigo **5441 5400**

OFF Bendigo's main drag, this bright cafe serves its food fast without forgoing freshness and flavour. Big portions compensate for any lack of finesse. The egg breakfasts are excellent (especially with hotcakes and hazelnut butter), the minestrone is reviving and the towering steak sandwich is serious enough to require a steak knife.

$ V

Licensed
Open Mon-Fri 7am-5pm; Sat 7am-4pm
Prices breakfasts $3.50-$13.50; lunches $5.50-$15.90
Map page 269 **VicRoads** 255 M12

Blue Pyrenees Estate

CAFE

Vinoca Road,
Avoca **5465 3202**

THIS homestead winery serves reliable nibbles at veranda tables with hazy mountain views. Partner a glass of sparkling wine with the antipasto or creative salads like eye fillet with semi-dried tomatoes and seafood with avocado. Settle in with the Reserve Red and decadent roast duck risotto with wild mushrooms and mascarpone.

Licensed
Open Mon-Fri 10am-4.30pm; Sat-Sun 10am-5pm
Prices antipasto $18.60; mains $13-$24; desserts $6
Map page 269 **VicRoads** 246 A3

Campaspe House

REGIONAL

Goldies Lane,
Woodend **5427 2273**

ONCE Richard Pratt's country retreat, Campaspe House is now a hotel and conference centre plus formal restaurant. Chef Brad Lobb (ex-Warrenmang, Frangos & Frangos) focuses on local foods, so you may eat Tuki trout draped over creamed spinach, or roasted saddle of Macedon hare with a Cope-Williams wine sauce.

Licensed
Open Fri-Sat 6pm-late
Prices entrees $15; mains $27; desserts $12
Map page 269 **VicRoads** 290 B12

Cope-Williams Winery

MODERN AUSTRALIAN

Glenfern Road,
Romsey **5429 5428**

MORE like a village than a winery, Cope-Williams offers cricket and royal tennis to whet the appetite. Afterwards, retire to the Hare and Spaniel Wine Bar for lunch – perhaps wild mushroom tart or lamb, spinach and pine nut sausages. Saturday evenings in the formal dining room might feature confit duck on a coriander noodle cake.

Licensed
Open Sat-Sun & public hols 11.30am-3pm; Sat 6.30pm-late
Prices entrees $9.50-$11.50; mains $18-$22.50
Map page 269 **VicRoads** 291 N8

The Grange Restaurant

MODERN AUSTRALIAN

Glen Erin Vineyard Retreat, Rochford Road,
Lancefield **5429 1041**

THE barn-like restaurant won't appeal to all, but there's no denying the appeal of the Grange's huge rib-eye steak, smothered in a tangy mustard dressing. The peripatetic menu covers Mediterranean tiger prawns, Chinese duck breast and char-grilled kangaroo. Leave room for the zesty lemon tart.

Licensed
Open Sat-Sun noon-3pm; Fri-Sat 6.30pm-late
Prices entrees $7.50-$16; mains $20-$29.50
Map page 269 **VicRoads** 291 M4

Koukla

MEDITERRANEAN

82 Vincent Street,
Daylesford **5348 2363**

DAYLESFORD'S hippest cafe is the diffusion-label Frangos & Frangos (see page 216). The crisp pizzas (say, gorgonzola and rocket) are terrific; the pastas and meat dishes show off regional produce (Tuki trout tossed with fettuccine, capers and lemon; 'bullboar' sausages with mash). Brilliant coffee and lemon tart top it all off.

$ V

Licensed
Open Mon-Tues 7.45am-4pm; Wed-Sun 7.45am-late
Prices breakfasts $4.50-$11; mains $12.90-$22.50
Map page 269 **VicRoads** 289 P10

L'espresso

MODERN ITALIAN

417 Sturt Street,
Ballarat **5333 1789**

THERE'S no better endorsement for a restaurant than bums on seats, and this worn-in cafe has some of Ballarat's warmest chairs. Enjoy bruschetta with mascarpone and figs or substantial options like salmon fillet with lemon aioli. Warm rhubarb and sour cream cake is indicative of the cafe's dedicated approach to indulgent endings.

$

Licensed
Open daily 7am-6pm
Prices breakfasts $4-$11; lunches $6.50-$16.50; cakes $5.50
Map page 269 **VicRoads** 255 L12

Ruby's

MODERN AUSTRALIAN

423 Sturt Street,
Ballarat **5333 3386**

WITH its strikingly minimalist dining room and wide-roaming menu, Ruby's is Ballarat's best option for after-dark eating. The food goes the extra distance, ranging from poppyseed pancakes and smoked ham and brie bagels to noodle dishes such as rabbit pappardelle or rice vermicelli with beef and black bean sauce.

V

Licensed
Open Tues-Fri 11am-late; Sat 9am-late; Sun 9am-4pm
Prices breakfasts $4-$11; mains $12.90-$23.90
Map page 269 **VicRoads** 255 L12

Saff's Cafe

CAFE

64 Mostyn Street,
Castlemaine **5470 6722**

SAFF'S juggles caffeine and a handy wine list to keep things buzzing day and night. Popular with locals and blow-ins, the cafe's regular menu bowls up simple fare like grilled saganaki, gargantuan burgers and fried chicken livers soaked in a rich, peppery jus. The reliably good specials board usually includes chicken, fish and vegetarian options.

V

Licensed
Open daily 8am-late
Prices breakfasts $4-$15.50; mains $10-$22.50; cakes $6.50
Map page 269 **VicRoads** 286 P6

Templeton Cafe & Accommodation

MODERN AUSTRALIAN

31 Templeton Street,
Castlemaine **5472 5311**

TEMPLETON is a stylish, simply furnished cafe offering modern but homely meals such as cumin-dusted black rice patties, Thai polenta sausages and a succulent shoulder of lamb cooked in red wine. In a quiet part of town, you can choose to dine on the front veranda or – better still – in a delightful courtyard shaded by a golden robinia tree.

Licensed
Open Thurs-Sun 10am-5pm; Fri-Sat 7-11pm
Prices entrees $8-$10.50; mains $16-$22; desserts $7-$9
Map page 269 **VicRoads** 287 P5

Tog's Cafe & Gallery

CAFE

58 Lyttleton Street,
Castlemaine **5470 5090**

DINING in Elissa and Jason Wilsher's lovely cafe might mean a hearty soup, curry or pasta by the double-sided fireplace, or a colourful deli tasting plate to share on the upstairs deck. Preserves and cakes are made next door, at Mulberry's Fine Foods, and passed through a hatch in the party wall.

$

Licensed & BYO wine
Open Sun-Thurs 9am-5pm; Fri-Sat 9am-late
Prices entrees $6-$11.50; mains $14.50-$18.50
Map page 269 **VicRoads** 287 P6

Tuki

REGIONAL

Stoney Rises, Newstead-Castlemaine Road,
Smeaton **5345 6233**

ROBERT and Jan Jones are on a winner – it's not everywhere that diners are encouraged to catch their own tucker. Once you've hooked your trout (or not, if fishing isn't for you), they barbecue it with lemon and butter, then serve it up with tremendous roasted potatoes. Tender roast lamb (no catching required) is also available.

Licensed
Open daily 11am-6pm
Prices entrees $9.80-$14.80; mains $22.50; desserts $5-$12.50; rods, tuition & main meal $22.50
Map page 269 **VicRoads** 58 H7

COUNTRY MARKETS

This little foodie went to market...

Central Geelong Farmers' and Produce Market
Market Square, Little Malop Street, Geelong, 5227 0841. Will run second Sat of month (Oct-Apr).
This monthly market is expected to draw more than 40 stallholders to the city centre when it cranks up in October 2003. Growers and makers from Geelong, the Bellarine Peninsula and the surrounding area will sell local wine, olives and oil, organic herbs, vegetables and fruit, and baked goods.

Hume-Murray Food Bowl Farmers' Market
Gateway Village, Lincoln Causeway (between Albury & Wodonga), 0438 582 996 or (02) 6058 2996. Runs alternate Sats, 8am-noon (summer), 9am-1pm (winter).
The Hume-Murray farmers' market continues to expand. Produce includes organic kiwifruit, persimmons, beetroot, zucchini flowers, melons and kaffir limes. There's also smoked trout pâté, organic lamb, German strudels and tiny orange cakes decorated with bergamot flowers.

Lancefield and District Farmers' Market
Mechanics Hall, High Street, Lancefield, 5429 2115. Runs fourth Sat of month (except Dec), 9am-1pm.
In winter, this market shelters in the Lancefield Mechanics Hall, but in warmer weather it sprawls across the main street's median strip. Combing Central Victoria's paddocks, groves, barns and kitchens for supplies, the market offers wines, preserves, lavender products, olive oil, fudges and cakes, plus Donnybrook farmhouse cheeses.

Phillip Island Farmers' Market on Churchill Island
Churchill Island (via Phillip Island road bridge), 5664 0096. Runs fourth Sat of month, 8am-12.30pm.
The tiny outpost of Churchill Island hosts a picturesque farmers' market overlooking Western Port. About 40 stallholders turn out each month, some of whom do the rounds of the Gippsland markets. Other supplies, such as asparagus, sprouts, spuds and native plants, are unique to the island market.

Red Hill Community Market
Red Hill Recreation Reserve, Arthurs Seat Road, Red Hill, 5974 4710. Runs first Sat of month, 8am-1pm (Sep-May).
Growers are strongly represented at this vibrant 29-year-old market. Look for Red Hill Cheese (made with cow's and goats' milk), smoked meats, fresh berries and seasonal vegies, and Red Hill Roast's coffee blends and takeaway coffee.

South Gippsland Farmers' Market
Memorial Park, Koonwarra, 5664 0096. Runs first Sat of month, 8am-12.30pm.
A monthly showcase for the bounty of fertile South Gippsland, this friendly market sells mushrooms, bushfoods, locally baked bread and cakes, smoked eel pâté, Fauder goats' cheese, Jindivick smoked meats and Terrané tapenade and olives. After selecting your haul, drop into the Koonwarra Fine Food & Wine Store (see page 240) next door for coffee.

Warrnambool Growers' Market
Civic Green, Liebig Street, Warrnambool, 5562 7030. Runs first Sat of month, 8am-noon.
At this relatively new market, set on palm-shaded lawns in the heart of town, you'll find creamy spuds freshly dug at nearby Koroit, carrots, honey, organic eggs, strawberries, blueberries, chutneys, cakes, smoked eel and local wine.

Yarra Valley Farmers' Market
Yering Station barn, 38 Melba Highway, Yering, 9730 0100. Runs third Sun of month, 10am-3pm.
At this monthly market, long-time participants Alloway Gourmet (buffalo bangers), Cunliffe & Waters (preserves) and Yarra Valley Icecream ply their trade alongside newcomers selling locally farmed Murray cod, rabbit, mushroom and chicken pâtés, and fresh pasta, sauces and antipasti, such as pickled beans and capsicums.

The Bank

MODERN AUSTRALIAN

86 Ford Street,
Beechworth **5728 2223**

THIS grand old bank has long been Beechworth's destination for showy food in a formal setting. A succession of recent chefs has stripped back some of the restaurant's more outlandish dishes – the emphasis is still on fusionist pairings but the strike rate is definitely higher. Dinner might be as straightforward as well-cooked lamb rump with wild rocket and leeks or local venison with roasted pears and creamy zucchini. Even complex dishes like coconut butter prawns with mango salsa, crisped rice paper, lime and kecap manis are cohesive and tasty. Desserts drift into prima donna territory, with swirling decorations and cockades of pulled sugar tarting up down-to-earth offerings like banana and macadamia semifreddo or hazelnut meringue. The wine list has local offerings at both ends of the price spectrum. Service is as crisp as the tablecloths.

Licensed
Open daily 6.30pm-late
Seats 48; outdoor seating
Owners Wayne & Denise McLaughlin
Chef Kristi Gladstone
Cards AE BC DC MC V Eftpos
Prices entrees $9.50-$18.90; mains $20.50-$28.90; desserts $12.50-$19.50
Map page 269 **VicRoads** 325 N9

13/20

Breathtaker Signature Restaurant

MODERN AUSTRALIAN

8 Breathtaker Road,
Mount Buller **5777 6377**

MULTI-LAYERED and set into the mountainside, this former ski lodge has morphed into Australia's first European-style alpine spa and all-suite hotel. It's also grabbed the baton to become Mount Buller's only all-year fine diner. The chic restaurant has a black glass ceiling, premium views and elegantly crafted dishes from Malaysian-born chef Tommy Chang. In summer, he balances exotic dishes (chicken with cous cous and a macadamia, chilli and coriander pesto) with the familiar (high country beef with mustard jus and red capsicum jam). Desserts – such as poached peach with lemon cream and a hazelnut crisp – are imaginative and delicious. In winter, when the mountain really springs to life, expect more robust dishes for hearty appetites. There might be smoked chicken risotto and Wannon River rack of lamb with roasted tomato and minty mushroom sauce.

Licensed
Open daily 7.30-10am, 6-9.30pm; brasserie daily 11am-3pm (also 6-8pm in winter)
Seats 70; bar
Owner John McDonald
Chef Tommy Chang
Cards AE BC MC V Eftpos
Prices entrees $17-$19; mains $28-$38; desserts $15-$18 (à la carte in winter only); set menus $25-$55 (1-3 courses); brasserie menu $6-$23.50
Map page 269 **VicRoads** 63 H4

13/20 

Cock 'n' Bull Wine Bar & Restaurant

MODERN AUSTRALIAN

17 Warren Street,
Echuca **5480 6988**

BUILT in 1876 on the banks of the Campaspe River, Cock 'n' Bull (formerly the Saleyards Hotel) seduces diners with a relaxed but intimate ambience and wonderful unpretentious food. Newcomers are greeted in the bar before being invited to the dining area, a series of small, interconnected rooms that are minimally decorated to highlight the original brickwork. Quality, rather than quantity, appears an overriding principle in refined starters like the moist Moreton Bay bugs and delicate crabmeat tortellini. Mains might include quail stuffed with bocconcini and sage, or baby snapper in garlic butter sauce. Desserts are sure to see you slouch ever more comfortably in your seat, whether it's poached cinnamon pears or spongy tiramisu ringed by chocolate sauce. A selection of six cheeses plattered with quince puree and muscatel grapes is excellent value.

14/20 

Licensed
Open Mon-Sat 5pm-late
Seats 65; outdoor seating; bar
Owners Stewart & Rand Coombes
Chef David Bowman
Cards AE BC DC MC V Eftpos
Prices entrees $14.80-$18.50; mains $22.20-$28.50; desserts $8.50-$14; cheeses $7-$17
Map page 269 **VicRoads** 266 E2

The Epicurean Centre

MODERN REGIONAL

Brown Brothers Vineyard, Bobinawarrah Road,
Milawa **5720 5540**

CHEF Chris Lee has an unusual brief. Instead of creating a dish, then coming up with a complementary wine suggestion, he begins with the wine, then crafts a dish to suit it. He tweaks his light, modern menus with the seasons and whenever the Brothers release a new wine. Sumac-rubbed salmon with goats' curd and shaved fennel is the foil for the limited-release riesling; quail with walnut pesto partners the Patricia merlot. Dessert marriages are particularly impressive: the moscato is heavenly with baked ricotta and honey-drizzled figs, and toffee pudding is a lovely match for the sticky wine. Meals would be even more enjoyable if the name-tagged waiters were as professional as they are friendly. Still, the restaurant, with its barrels, stone floors and glass walls giving on to shady trees, is an easy place to relax.

13/20 

Licensed
Open daily 11am-3pm
Seats 110; outdoor seating
Owner Brown Brothers Pty Ltd
Chef Chris Lee
Cards AE BC DC MC V Eftpos
Prices set menus $18-$40 (1-3 courses)
Map page 269 **VicRoads** 34 H9

Gigi's of Beechworth

ITALIAN

69 Ford Street,
Beechworth **5728 2575**

EVERY year Gigi's gets a little bit better. Home-made cakes and caffeinated aromas give it the feel of a gourmet cafe, but Alan Dale Robertson's bright interpretations of Italian regional dishes elevate this simple shopfront into headier realms. His dishes manage to be traditional without ploughing too many cliched furrows. There may be baby veal chops with beetroot chutney and spinach, orange and almond salad; fat, smoky eggplant polpette (fritters); and vibrant panzanella salad with dried ricotta and tiny capers. Even standards like the popular marinara and the featherweight tiramisu are above average. The culinary wallop is further boosted by the irrepressible Gigi working the floor, an outstanding wine list with an archive of Giacondas, and an ineffable glow that makes this the sort of place that delivers memorable nights out.

15/20 

Licensed & BYO wine
Corkage $7 a bottle
Open Mon-Tues & Thurs-Sat 9am-late; Sun 9am-5pm
Seats 45; outdoor seating
Owner Luigi Cipolato
Chef Alan Dale Robertson
Cards AE BC DC MC V Eftpos
Prices breakfasts $6.50-$9.50; entrees $9.50-$14.50; mains $17-$26; desserts $7.50
Map page 269 **VicRoads** 325 N9

the green shed bistro

MODERN EUROPEAN

37 Camp Street,
Beechworth **5728 2360**

A SMALL restaurant of considerable charm, green shed serves food with plenty of heart. The postage-stamp-sized front room with crackling fire works as a bar, as well as coping with any spill from the larger, convivial back area. Then there's the food – if it were any more rustic, it would be chewing on a straw. A chunky and robust tomato soup is crammed with basil and flavourful tomatoes, skins and all. Risotto is excellent, too, perhaps with a pungent pumpkin, walnut and blue cheese combo. There's always a pizza: the day's topping may be potato, onion and gruyère. More exotic dishes are less reliable: 'Moroccan' stew features good braised lamb neck but a herbed tomato sauce with preserved lemon overpowers the North African spices. Service is friendly but sometimes bumbles rather than hums.

13/20

Licensed
Open Fri-Sun noon-late; Wed-Thurs 6.30pm-late
Seats 60; outdoor seating; bar
Owner James Loveridge
Chefs James Loveridge & Richard Verrocchio
Cards BC MC V Eftpos
Prices lunches $9-$18; entrees $9-$13; pizzas $12.50; mains $22.80; desserts $8.50
Map page 269 **VicRoads** 325 N8

Harvest Home

REGIONAL

1-9 Bank Street,
Avenel **5796 2339**

SUZI McKAY has lovingly transformed a charming 1860s pub into an oasis with rambling gardens and buckets of atmosphere. And she's always making improvements: return visitors will notice the gazebo and a renovated rustic outdoor dining area. Some things don't change – meals still begin with a wonderful antipasto platter piled with home-made goodies like duck liver parfait with onion jam, smoked eel pâté and pickled cucumber. To follow, perhaps duck breast and confit leg with red cabbage, baked beets and, somewhat curiously, pork crackling. Desserts make the most of local fruits: there may be grilled figs or rich chocolate slice with berry icecream. But there are signs the expanded Home is taking its toll: the food is less consistent and the presentation less careful than in the past. There's a good wine list and cellared wines on request.

14/20 

Licensed
Open Thurs 12.30-4.30pm; Fri-Sat 11am-4pm, 6pm-late; Sun 10am-late
Seats 30; outdoor seating
Owner & chef Suzi McKay
Cards AE BC DC MC V
Prices entrees $14.50; mains $28.50; desserts $12.50
Map page 269 **VicRoads** 292 G1

Kirwan's Bridge Restaurant

MODERN AUSTRALIAN

Lobb's Lane,
Nagambie **5794 1996**

THERE aren't many modern restaurants serving innovative food in the middle of a paddock. But Kirwan's Bridge is exactly that. Originally a vineyard/restaurant, the winery side of the enterprise has faltered. This hasn't stopped chef Matt Milsome and skilled host Daina Winch from plugging away in their restaurant. French and Asian influences are evident in Milsome's food. His extraordinary signature dish comprises scallops and suckling pig, slow-cooked and slightly gelatinous, served with tofu salad. You might also find duck three ways, as gyoza, terrine and delicate smoked duck salad. Desserts also show team spirit, as in a chocolate plate with brownie, white chocolate mousse and chocolate wontons. The uninspiring wine list doesn't do the food justice, nor do the bedraggled grounds. Inside, it's all spacious comfort, with linen-clothed tables and comfortable chairs.

14/20

Licensed
Open Thurs-Sun noon-3pm; Fri-Sat 7pm-late
Seats 120; outdoor seating; private room
Owners Matt Milsome & Daina Winch
Chef Matt Milsome
Cards AE BC DC MC V Eftpos
Prices entrees $14; mains $24.50; desserts $13.50; degustation menu $55 (5 courses)
Map page 269 **VicRoads** 276 H1

Magnolia Gourmet Country House

MODERN EUROPEAN

190 Mount Buller Road,
Mansfield **5779 1444**

TO dine alfresco under the 115-year-old magnolia tree, especially when it is in full flower and wreathed in fairy lights, is magically romantic. The tree, brought from England as a sapling, is older than its namesake 1907 American-style guesthouse and restaurant. Austrian-born chef Christian Bergmoser (formerly at Mount Buller's celebrated Pension Grimus) and his wife Kim are the latest owners, but the Austrian influence is evident mainly in the desserts. The Salzburger nockerln (meringue soufflé with pour-it-yourself chocolate sauce) or Kaiserschmarren (caramelised pancake slices) are irresistible. Before that, Bergmoser presents artistically composed dishes like local tea-smoked lamb cutlets, stuffed duck breast on broccoli noodles and high country beef with peppery beetroot chutney. A small drinks list includes Mansfield and King Valley wines, some by the glass.

13/20

Licensed
Open Thurs-Sat 6.30pm-late
Seats 40; outdoor seating; private room
Owners Christian & Kim Bergmoser
Chef Christian Bergmoser
Cards AE BC DC MC V Eftpos
Prices entrees $11.90-$14.90; mains $21.50-$24.90; desserts $8.90-$12.90
Map page 269 **VicRoads** 330 E5

Milawa Factory Bakery & Restaurant

MODERN REGIONAL

Milawa Cheese Company, Factory Road,
Milawa **5727 3589**

THE food is very good, but if you come on a busy weekend, the setting lets it down: it's as though a hungry footy crowd has been plonked into Farmer Jack's shed. Cheese fans crowd around the tasting counter, smacking their lips over washed rinds and aged cheddar. Lunchers line up to order at the cash register, then pick a spot under the corrugated ceiling or on the shambling terrace. At dinner there's table service and much less palaver, all the better to enjoy Michael Ryan's terrifically accomplished meals. Warm up with a green bean and jamon stew, served with a garlicky doorstop of bruschetta; gnocchi baked with mushrooms, spinach and the home team's luscious blue cheese; or duck confit with cabbage and apple chutney. Cheese is an appropriate finish, plattered with fig salami and house-made sourdough.

14/20

Licensed & BYO wine
Corkage $5 a bottle
Open daily noon-3pm; Thurs-Sat 6.30pm-late
Seats 60; outdoor seating; private room
Owners David & Anne Brown, Adam Rivett & Will Flamsteed
Chef Michael Ryan
Cards AE BC DC MC V Eftpos
Prices entrees $12-$15; pizzas $12; mains $20-$24; desserts $9-$11
Map page 269 **VicRoads** 34 H9

Mitchelton Restaurant

MODERN AUSTRALIAN

Mitchelstown Road, off Goulburn Valley Highway,
Nagambie **5794 2388**

THIS striking winery is on the banks of the Goulburn River, with splendid views of gums and bush. It's a sprawling place with a freewheeling atmosphere. Pick up a grazing plate to eat on the lawns, or take your cheese, pork terrine and bean salad along on one of the regular riverboat cruises. Eating in means you can enjoy a glass of wine by the fire before moving to the classy dining room. The food stands on its merits – lightly crumbed then fried lambs' brains with salsa verde; tender eye fillet with horseradish mash and beetroot cooked in red wine – but is even better when enjoyed with the recommended house wines. Desserts are generous, as in the flourless chocolate cake that comes with chocolate sorbet and vanilla icecream. Excellent coffee tops off a stellar experience.

14/20

Licensed
Open daily 10.30am-4pm
Seats 120; outdoor seating; private room
Owner Lion Nathan
Chefs Brett Dobson & Matt Aitken
Cards AE BC DC MC V Eftpos
Prices entrees $13.50; mains $24; desserts $10
Map page 269 **VicRoads** 46 D6

Oscar W's Wharfside

MODERN AUSTRALIAN

101 Murray Esplanade, Echuca Wharf,
Echuca **5482 5133**

FRESH, uncluttered cookery, perceptive service, serene views of the Murray River's eucalypts and watercraft, and smart surrounds that could double as a showroom for the Timber Promotion Council: there's no mystery about Oscar W's popularity. In the heart of Echuca's historic port district, you can make the best of the view by coming for lunch, a judicious amalgam of light meals (club sandwiches, antipasto plates) and more elaborate offerings (zucchini flowers stuffed with goats' curd, pukka mushroom tarts with caramelised beetroot). Dinners continue the heartily formal theme: there's rabbit terrine, pork and fennel sausages, and grilled lamb shanks. Alcohol was once prohibited in these parts but there's nothing sly about the grog on Oscar W's stupendous list. There are about 20 wines by the glass, and the option of comparative tastings.

15/20

Licensed
Open daily 11am-late
Seats 90; outdoor seating; private room; bar
Owner Dean Oberin
Chef Scott Pitts
Cards AE BC DC MC V Eftpos
Prices tapas $6.50; entrees $9-$16.50; mains $23.50-$29.50; desserts $9.50-$14.50
Map page 269 **VicRoads** 266 F3

The Pickled Sisters Cafe

MODERN REGIONAL

Cofield Wines, Distillery Road,
Wahgunyah **(02) 6033 2377**

MOST tomatoes don't taste like they used to, but Pickled Sisters' semi-dried tomatoes are bursting with so much flavour that it's hard to believe tomatoes ever tasted this good. They're just one example of the exquisite flavours you'll encounter at this rough and ready cafe. Situated in a converted shed with winery machinery humming out the back, this is a friendly place with an emphasis on fresh local produce. A heartening attention to detail and an innovative spirit are evident in dishes like the luscious zucchini, bacon and chestnut soup, while the smoked chicken and sumac fattoush is the apogee of a warm salad. Superlative desserts include a creamy semifreddo strewn with honeycomb fragments and boysenberry sauce. The Sisters are child-friendly, so expect to encounter wayward toddlers wielding icecream sprinkle cones.

14/20

Licensed
Open Wed-Mon 10am-4pm; Fri-Sat (during daylight saving only) 7pm-late
Seats 80; outdoor seating
Owner & chef Alison McKillop
Cards AE BC MC V Eftpos
Prices entrees $9-$15; mains $18.50-$25; desserts $8
Map page 269 **VicRoads** 307 S8

Restaurant Merlot

MODERN AUSTRALIAN

Lindenwarrah Country House Hotel, Bobinawarrah Road,
Milawa **5720 5777**

LINDENWARRAH'S conference centre atmosphere has mellowed over time – it's now a pleasant place to eat. Whether you're in the flower-lined courtyard within earshot of the fountain, or in the austere dining room, you'll have the same appetising outlook on to vines and distant hills. Service is keen and there's a frisson of excitement about the menu, courtesy of consultant chef Andrew Blake. The on-site team does a better job with his simpler dishes, things like figs with prosciutto, lamb rump with tapenade and well-cooked beef rib-eye. But some dishes falter when the menu becomes more ambitious. Baby capers might overpower ricotta-stuffed zucchini flowers; the harissa could be innocuous. The $25 set lunch is decent value, especially considering that it comes with a glass of Lindenwarrah wine, which costs à la carte diners $12.50.

13/20

Licensed
Open daily 7.30-11am, noon-3pm; Thurs-Sun 6-9pm
Seats 120; outdoor seating; bar
Owner Lancemore Group
Chef Matthew Lello
Cards AE BC DC MC V
Prices entrees $14-$18; mains $24-$28; desserts $9-$14; lunch set menu $25 (2 courses)
Map page 269 **VicRoads** 34 H9

Roi's Diner

MODERN ITALIAN

177 Kiewa Valley Highway,
Tawonga **5754 4495**

TAWONGA is a Kiewa Valley whistlestop en route to the snowfields and this warm, eclectic restaurant is its heart. It's an inviting place, with a log fire, a clutter of local artwork and celebrity endorsements – Cathy Freeman, Judy Davis and the local Rotarians have all left their signatures. Dinner might start with a mango salad, steamed asparagus with a poached egg or smoked venison with caramelised onions. Mains could include a hearty risotto with quail and sage, roast pickled pork, and duckling with apples cooked in amaretto. More conventional dishes like veal shanks and stuffed chicken breast tend to make an appearance, too. Simple but thoughtful desserts include vanilla and raspberry icecream with a coconut crust. There's a well-priced wine list of mostly regional wines.

14/20

Licensed
Open Thurs-Sun 6.30pm-late
Seats 60
Owners Roi Rigoni & Sue White
Chef Roi Rigoni
Cards BC MC V Eftpos
Prices entrees $8-$10; mains $18-$19; desserts $8
Map page 269 **VicRoads** 327 S10

Sasha's of Bright

EUROPEAN

2d Anderson Street,
Bright **5750 1711**

THE name should ring a bell with Falls Creek and Kiewa Valley communities – this jovial Czech-born culinary veteran has conjured many a memorable meal over 20 years in the area. Now Sasha Cinatl has bobbed up in Bright, and infused the former Caffe Bacco with his inimitable middle European cooking and hospitality. His fortes are aged high country steak and roast duckling, perhaps preceded by a fiery goulash soup and followed by berry-filled crepes. His chateaubriand with bordelaise sauce is a dish of justified renown, and he is so proud of his duck that each one is commemorated with a number marked on a whiteboard. The glazed bird is sure to be crisp-skinned, minimally fatty and moistly flavoursome. It's not cutting-edge cuisine, but the regulars love it. There's an impressive choice of regional wines.

14/20 

Licensed & BYO wine
Corkage $7 a bottle
Open daily 6pm-late
Seats 45; outdoor seating
Owner & chef Sasha Cinatl
Cards AE BC DC MC V Eftpos
Prices entrees $6.50-$16; mains $16.50-$27; desserts $7.50-$8.50
Map page 269 **VicRoads** 327 P3

Simone's of Bright

ITALIAN

Ovens Valley Motor Inn, Corner Great Alpine Road & Ashwood Avenue,
Bright **5755 2022**

PATRIZIA SIMONE takes great local produce and transforms it with the sure touch of an artist. She might fill her handmade ravioli with wild nettles, then toss them with burnt butter, apples and walnuts; rich duck terrine could be pepped up with pickled cherries; and Flintstones-sized veal cutlet may be crusted with sage and parmesan and accompanied by an earthy whiff of truffles. Even the simplest dishes are lovingly reworked, as in the rocket and parmesan salad with preserved pears. Desserts – perhaps a chocolate plate with panna cotta, mousse and baci icecream – are demurely sweet rather than aggressively sugary. The wine list pays homage to the high country's best. Get in quick to farewell the 1970s motel dining room with shag carpet and copper fireplace. Simone's is planning to relocate to heritage-listed Victorian premises on nearby Gavan Street.

15/20 

Licensed & BYO wine
Corkage $5.50 a bottle
Open daily 6.30pm-late
Seats 60
Owners George & Patrizia Simone
Chef Patrizia Simone
Cards AE BC DC MC V
Prices entrees $14.90-$19.95; mains $19.90-$29.95; desserts $9.90-$10.90
Map page 269 **VicRoads** 327 M2

Stonelea Country Estate

REGIONAL

Connelly's Creek Road,
Acheron **5772 2222**

THIS tranquil resort has its own golf course, trout ponds, tennis courts and even a climbing wall. Taking advantage of the facilities will ensure an appetite for the sedentary pleasures of the restaurant, where cuisine and service are well above par. New chef Dianne Bradley upholds Stonelea's emphasis on quality local produce and subtly arresting flavours. Fish is handled deftly: baked Buxton trout comes on lemony dill risotto; grilled Yarra Valley salmon paddles in a carrot and champagne sauce. Creative thinking and careful hands elevate meat and veg dishes, as in roasted kangaroo with sweet potato puree and pickled beetroot. The delicate lavender-infused crème brûlée will send you to your lakeside cottage in a swoon. A wholly Victorian wine list mixes the state's hero labels with lesser-known players such as Peerick and Celtic Farm.

15/20

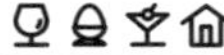

Licensed
Open daily 8-10am, noon-2pm, 6.30pm-late
Seats 80; outdoor seating; private room; bar
Owners George & Cathie Watkins
Chef Dianne Bradley
Cards AE BC DC MC V Eftpos
Prices breakfasts $25; lunches $7.50-$15.50; entrees $10.50-$18; mains $21-$32; desserts $12.50-$14.50
Map page 269 **VicRoads** 62 D6

The Terrace Restaurant

MODERN AUSTRALIAN

All Saints Estate, All Saints Road,
Wahgunyah **(02) 6035 2209**

THE TERRACE at All Saints Estate is well known for its grand elm-lined avenue leading to a heritage-listed mock castle. The food is a worthy match for the restaurant's imposing setting and for the estate's excellent wines. Local produce turns up in many dishes: smoked kangaroo salad has a Milawa blue cheese dressing; local greens are tossed with a raspberry and shallot vinaigrette; the coq au vin employs free-range Milawa chicken. Expect traditional dishes to be cooked and presented just so, as in the duck confit with crisp skin, a melting layer of fat and rich dark meat. The menu makes apposite wine-matching suggestions. Dessert – perhaps creamy mascarpone and honey parfait – is a must, if only so you can pair it with the excellent All Saints tokay. A new chef, Peter Quinn, started as the *Guide* went to press.

14/20

Licensed
Open daily 10am-5pm; Sat 6.30pm-late
Seats 110; outdoor seating
Owner Peter Brown
Chef Peter Quinn
Cards AE BC DC MC V Eftpos
Prices entrees $12.50-$19; mains $22-$27; desserts $9.50
Map page 269 **VicRoads** 307 U5

Tuileries

MODERN AUSTRALIAN

Jolimont Cellars, Drummond Street,
Rutherglen **(02) 6032 9033**

TUILERIES feels like a well-appointed but slightly bland hotel dining room; routine service and background muzak give the impression that it mainly caters to a wine tour bus crowd. The food is similarly democratic, with numerous Asian-style dishes on the entree menu (miso soup with chicken dumplings, five-spiced quail on crisp noodles) giving way to a Eurocentric list of mains. Most dishes work well: twice-cooked duck is accompanied by bright, refreshing rhubarb chutney; marinated lamb is perfectly char-grilled. But some dishes don't match their descriptions, as in 'game meat sausage' that turns out to be more of a crocodile terrine. Overall, the kitchen seems only mildly inspired by the stellar produce on offer in the region. The wine list, however, provides a good sample of outstanding local wines. A dedicated vegetarian menu is a bonus.

13/20

Licensed & BYO wine
Corkage $2.50 a head
Open daily 6.30pm-late; cafe Wed-Sun 8am-2pm
Seats 90; outdoor seating; private room
Owner Tony Lamb
Chef Leanne Oberin
Cards AE BC DC MC V Eftpos
Prices entrees $8.50-$15; mains $16.50-$26; desserts $11
Map page 269 **VicRoads** 306 F4

Beaumont's Cafe

MODERN AUSTRALIAN

84 Main Street,
Rutherglen **(02) 6032 7428**

PETER WEIR has cooked in many of Rutherglen's better restaurants. Now he and wife Birgit have opened their own place. It's quirky and casual with a fairy-lit courtyard. The food already shows impressive touches that only an experienced chef can achieve, like impeccable ravioli and the perfect onion tart.

Licensed & BYO wine
Open Tues 3-11pm; Wed-Sat 11am-11pm; Sun 9am-5pm
Prices entrees $8.50-$14.50; mains $23-$25; desserts $7-$9.50
Map page 269 **VicRoads** 306 F4

The Black Pudding Delicatessen

CAFE

525a High Street,
Echuca **5482 2244**

THIS small venue does great breakfasts and modest, tasty snacks throughout the day. The repertoire includes frittatas with chorizo, haloumi and mint, and soft panini rolls layered with herb-flecked crepes and crisp bacon. The deli stocks city-slick gourmet produce alongside country favourites like spicy rhubarb chutney from Ruffy.

$ V

Licensed
Open Tues-Fri 7.30am-5pm; Sat-Sun 9.30am-3pm
Prices breakfasts $4-$15; lunches $6-$15
Map page 269 **VicRoads** 266 F5

Bohjass Wine Bar

MODERN AUSTRALIAN

276b Wyndham Street (upstairs),
Shepparton **5822 0237**

BOHJASS is the latest venture for Min Innes-Irons, who, along with his brother Mat, previously ran Shepparton's Hotel Australia. The best dishes make good use of few ingredients, as in a green curry soup with firm-fleshed prawns, and duckling on buttery polenta. A new balcony and tapas menu add to the appeal.

Licensed
Open Fri noon-3pm; Tues-Sat 5pm-late
Prices entrees $8.50-$16; mains $16-$24; desserts $9-$9.50
Map page 269 **VicRoads** 273 L10

Cellar 47 Restaurant

ITALIAN

166-170 High Street,
Shepparton **5831 1882**

THE claret interior and formal ambience set the scene for plush Italian cuisine. Seafood figures prominently, perhaps green mussels or juicy tiger prawns to start, while mains include chicken escalopes with honeyed pine nuts. In such surrounds, you should end with a flourish: try luscious lemon pudding with a white chocolate swizzle stick.

Licensed
Open Mon-Fri noon-2.30pm; Mon-Sat 6pm-late
Prices entrees $8-$22; mains $18-$31; desserts $8.50-$9
Map page 269 **VicRoads** 273 M9

The Friar's Cafe

CAFE

127 Fryers Street,
Shepparton **5822 2181**

THIS one-time Baptist Church now has a red gum bar and a pleasing roster of light meals. A comprehensive breakfast menu, risottos and lamb souvlakis keep the brethren happy while the sun shines. In the evening, mod-Oz offerings might include kangaroo fillets and curry laksa. The hummingbird and carrot cakes are good, too.

Licensed
Open Mon-Sat 8am-late; Sun 8am-5pm
Prices breakfasts $3-$9.80; mains $15.50-$22.50
Map page 269 **VicRoads** 273 L9

King River Cafe

MODERN AUSTRALIAN

Snow Road,
Oxley **5727 3461**

OXLEY'S old general store now houses a cafe serving one of the best lemon tarts in Victoria. It's sharp and luscious with a nicely brûléed top. Savoury favourites include fried fingers of grated potato and honey-drizzled feta fritters; more ambitious dishes can be rather home-style in execution. Service is country-friendly.

$

Licensed & BYO wine
Open Mon 10am-3pm; Wed-Sun 10am-10pm
Prices entrees $9-$11; mains $13-$21; desserts $6.50-$8.50
Map page 269 **VicRoads** 34 H9

Lanterns at Willowbank

MODERN AUSTRALIAN

29 Coomb Street,
Taggerty **5774 7503**

INTIMATE, with a touch of class, this restaurant, gallery and B&B is countrified and friendly. A thoughtful selection of little-known local wines is a good match for the no-frills food. Barbecued steak and lamb are menu mainstays but delightful alternatives include chicken livers on rice and grilled salmon on crushed potatoes.

$ 

Licensed
Open Thurs-Sun 11am-4pm, 7-11pm
Prices entrees $14-$18; mains $14.50-$30; desserts $8.50
Map page 269 **VicRoads** 62 D7

Marmalades Cafe & Produce Store

CAFE

20 High Street,
Yea **5797 2999**

IF you ignore the espresso machine and refrigerated cabinet, this could be an 1887 country grocery store. Until you sit down for refreshments, that is. The coffee and cakes are good and there are plenty of freshly prepared mod-Oz meal options for the hungry traveller. New owners took over as the *Guide* went to press.

$ V

Licensed
Open Thurs-Fri 9.30am-9pm; Sat-Sun 9.30am-9.30pm
Prices entrees $8.50-$9.50; mains $14.50-$20; desserts $5.50
Map page 269 **VicRoads** 329 M2

Marylands Country House

INTERNATIONAL

22 Falls Road,
Marysville **5963 3204**

DON'T be put off by the guesthouse-cum-conference centre location. There are nooks to tete-a-tete, the wine list is a delight and the food is well-executed. Substantial Euro-based meals might begin with veal shank risotto then move on to oven-baked trout or kangaroo on braised cabbage. Chocolate soufflé is a de rigueur finish.

Licensed
Open daily 6.30-9pm
Prices entrees $14; mains $27; desserts $12
Map page 269 **VicRoads** 332 C10

The Mountainview Hotel

MODERN ITALIAN

Corner Mansfield & Cheshunt Roads,
Whitfield **5729 8270**

THIS place has everything you might want in a country pub: welcoming host, cheery dining room with fireplace, pub grub turned up a notch (like chicken parmigiana made with Milawa free-range chicken breast) and smashing desserts, like chocolate pavlova with berries. The wine list – long as your arm – features local Italian-style wineries.

Licensed
Open Tues-Sun noon-2.30pm, 6-8pm
Prices entrees $8-$14; mains $16-$22; desserts $8
Map page 269 **VicRoads** 48 H6

Raffety's Gallery Cafe

CAFE

Benalla Art Gallery, Bridge Street,
Benalla **5762 3777**

THE position's the thing here: eat on the big deck overlooking Lake Benalla, then have a squizz at the gallery after lunch. Decent food, coffee and wine make this more than just a pit stop. Choose from towering open sandwiches, reasonable curries and pita pizzas – perhaps with thick slices of smoked salmon, crème fraîche and caramelised onion.

$ V

Licensed
Open daily 10am-4pm
Prices lunches $5.50-$15; cakes $3-$6
Map page 269 **VicRoads** 309 Q6

Ruffy Produce Store

CAFE/FOODSTORE

Nolans Road,
Ruffy **5790 4387**

THIS revitalised country store is hidden behind oak trees in the middle of nowhere. The tiny menu includes a great-value platter, crammed with smoked ham and chicken from Euroa, herb frittata, excellent pickled fennel and Yea cheeses. Fill a hamper and head for the nearby swimming hole or drink local wine and elderflower cordial in the garden.

$

Licensed
Open Sat-Sun & public hols 8am-6pm
Prices lunches $6.50-$9.50; desserts $5
Map page 269 **VicRoads** 47 A9

Spirited Chef Foodstore & Pantry

CAFE/FOODSTORE

9 Bridge Road,
Beechworth **5728 1969**

JAYNE THATCHER'S Beechworth Preserves became so popular that it made sense to open a store to sell them, along with other local goodies. The bonus is that when you come to this rustic pantry to buy Thatcher's raspberry-shiraz jam or muscat butter you can sit down for Thai noodle salad, home-made terrine and real lemonade.

V

Unlicensed
Open Wed-Sun 9am-5pm (daily in school hols)
Prices rolls $7.50; mains $8; platters $9-$12
Map page 269 **VicRoads** 325 M11

Traawool Shed

MODERN REGIONAL

Goulburn Valley Highway,
Trawool **5799 1595**

WITH a new chef and a rejigged menu, the region's most stylish corrugated iron shed now serves up pizzas, fish and chips, lasagne and Thai beef salad. They're standards, sure, but done here with flair. Specials might include Moroccan lamb curry, baked flathead tails on a lime and chilli-dressed salad, and marinated chicken breast on basil mash.

Licensed
Open Thurs-Mon 9am-6pm; Fri-Sat 9am-late
Prices meals $8-$24.50; desserts $7.50
Map page 269 **VicRoads** 61 E3

Inspired Catering and Fresh Ideas

Quintessence Foods offers a dynamic approach to corporate, private and event catering in your home, for your business, or at one of our exclusive venues.

Romantically stylish, Mariana Hardwick has the ideal ambience for any special occasion, be it lavish weddings or intimate banquets. Modern and sleek is the image of Quella at Lamborghini, the perfect venue for extravagant cocktail parties and events. Your event is set to impress.

roma tomato olive and fetta tart

san choi bow presented on beetle leaf

vodka and frangelico breeze

Phone: 9509 0939
Mobile: 0419 899 919
www.quintessencefoods.com.au

looking for a venue?

browse hundreds of venues + services + products
tel 03 9354 2333 **email** sales@venues.com.au

venues.com.au

for your next fantastic occasion, come to events warehouse,
enjoy the view, the vibrancy, the venue

EVENTS WAREHOUSE

Events Warehouse

Shed 9 Southwharf Rd Southbank Victoria 3006
telephone 03 9699 4300 facsimile 03 9686 3640
web www.eventswarehouse.com.au
email info@eventswarehouse.com.au

ORLANDO
TRILOGY
Semillon
Sauvignon Blanc
Viognier
TRILOGY
Brut
ORLANDO
TRILOGY
Pinot Noir
Chardonnay · Pinot Meunier
ORLANDO
TRILOGY
Cabernet Sauvignon
Cabernet Franc
Merlot

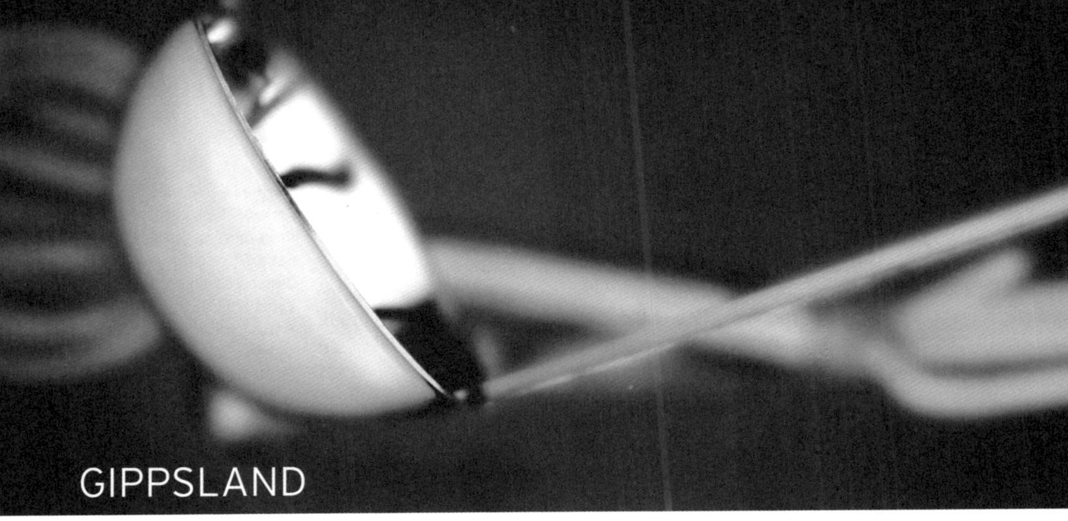

GIPPSLAND

The Berry Good Cafe

REGIONAL

315 Fisher Road,
Drouin West **5628 7627**

THIS idyllic Gippsland gourmet trailblazer is a veritable eco-tourism retreat of organic orchards, cottages and a rustic cafe. It's at its best from November to April, when more than 180 varieties of berries, stone fruits, apples, pears and nuts – many unavailable in shops – become progressively ready for do-it-yourself picking. But the homely cafe welcomes visitors all year for simple refreshments, made with Gippsland produce wherever possible. Expect platters of smoked trout, Jindivick cured meats and fat toasted sandwiches filled with Tarago River brie and farm-made plum paste. You've got the home paddocks to thank for fresh fruits, relishes and chutneys, and Joanne Butterworth-Gray's home-made pies and casseroles in the cooler months. To drink? Raspberry wine is just the ticket with blackberry pie, raspberry shortcake or apple flan.

Licensed
Open daily 10am-5pm
Seats 50; outdoor seating
Owner & chef Joanne Butterworth-Gray
Cards BC MC V Eftpos
Prices soups $5.50; mains $10.45; desserts $2.50-$6.45
Map page 269 **VicRoads** 96 F3

13/20 $ V ⌂

Bistro Blue

MODERN AUSTRALIAN

Shop 1, 23 A'Beckett Street,
Inverloch **5674 3339**

LAND prices in Inverloch may have soared but the local restaurant scene hasn't hit the same heady heights, making Bistro Blue something of a find. Blink and you'll miss it: the restaurant's austere grey facade and blue awning are identical to the adjoining solicitor's office and veterinary clinic on this busy seaside strip. Service can be patchy but an OK wine list and generous Asian- and Mediterranean-influenced dishes deliver good value for money. Filling starters include crisp Thai-style squid with sweet chilli sauce and scallops sauteed in lime and chilli with lemon-scented basmati rice. Equally ample mains include garlic-marinated rack of lamb and chicken roulade filled with feta, olives, capsicum and tomato. So generous are the savoury courses, in fact, that they leave you little chance of polishing off the bumper sticky date pudding.

Licensed
Open Wed-Sun 6pm-late
Seats 40; outdoor seating
Owners Greg Howson & Jenni Lovatt
Chef Adrian McGowan
Cards BC MC V Eftpos
Prices entrees $8.50-$17.50; mains $18-$29; desserts $9.50
Map page 269 **VicRoads** 358 F3

12/20

Bistro 115

EUROPEAN

115 Thompson Avenue,
Cowes **5952 6226**

OWNER-CHEF Harry Schmidt (formerly of Harry's Bistro & Cafe in Mornington) has moved to Phillip Island for a change of pace. His new operation's fine European-style food, tuned-in service, quaint cottage atmosphere and seaside location have ensured it a warm welcome. Service is relaxed but sophisticated enough to please weekenders who want something special; outdoor seating is pleasant and the wine list is varied. The food lifts it all a notch or two: crayfish bisque – served with a fish-shaped fleuron – might contain a few surprise scallops, but that only adds to its oceanic aroma. Roasted rack of lamb is cooked to rich, pink sweetness with a delicate herb crust and a dark, flavoursome rosemary jus. Desserts are old-fashioned and generous: indulge in profiteroles with chocolate sauce or bread and butter pud with rum 'n' raisin icecream.

12/20

Licensed & BYO wine
Corkage $5 a bottle
Open Tues-Sun 11am-late
Seats 70; outdoor seating
Owner & chef Harry Schmidt
Cards AE BC DC MC V Eftpos
Prices lunches $7.80-$15.50; entrees $7.80-$15.80; mains $17.60-$26.90; desserts $8.90-$14.60
Map page 267 **VicRoads** 302 H4

Boyle's at the Castle

INTERNATIONAL

7-9 Steele Street, Cowes,
Phillip Island **5952 1228**

THE moment you enter these intimate, tasteful surroundings your stress levels will plunge dramatically. The soothing decor reflects Jenni Boyle's calm, hospitable demeanour and showcases her striking paintings. By the time you study the beguiling menu, you're sure to be suffused with a happy glow. The same loving attention to detail that has furnished this oasis has gone into the food. An entree dish of sauteed scallops, champagne and cream topped with a pastry cap is light and luscious, while a hotpot of tender prime beef in a rich infusion of red wine and vintage port is fortifying and full-bodied. Take time between courses to linger on the outside deck and gaze over the tranquil garden. You'll return with enough vigour to tackle a petite piece of moist orange cake. Pure comfort food.

14/20

Licensed
Open Fri-Sat 6.30pm-late
Seats 30; outdoor seating
Owners Harley & Jenni Boyle
Chef Michael Ward
Cards AE BC DC MC V
Prices set menus $47.50 or $60 (2 or 3 courses)
Map page 267 **VicRoads** 302 J2

Bukhara

INDIAN

Shop 3, 12 Napier Street,
Warragul **5622 0025**

THIS is one of the best Indian restaurants in Victoria. Murphy Singh Aneja scorns the shortcuts taken by many urban restaurants, procuring the best ingredients and meticulously preparing his spices and curries in the traditional manner. The proof is in the subtle flavours of his tandoori delicacies and north-western frontier specialities. Dishes based on ancient recipes from the kingdom of Marwar (part of Rajasthan) are a recent addition to the extensive menu. There's nowhere else in Australia you're likely to find murgh jodhpuri (chicken in a cinnamon, clove and cardamom-flavoured yoghurt sauce) and shekhawti gosht (a dryish lamb curry made with individually roasted and pounded fennel, mustard and caraway seeds). Suggested menus come with all the trimmings, including a decorative chutney tray and tandoor-cooked breads.

14/20 $ V

Licensed
Open Fri noon-2pm; Tues-Sun 5.30pm-late
Seats 50
Owner & chef Murphy Aneja
Cards AE BC DC MC V Eftpos
Prices entrees $5.90-$9.50; mains $9.90-$23.90; desserts $6.50-$6.90; set menus $28-$38.90 (3-5 courses)
Map page 269 **VicRoads** 337 P9

Cafe Espas

MODERN AUSTRALIAN/SEAFOOD

Raymond Island Foreshore,
Paynesville **5156 7275**

DAWDLING boats, pelicans perched on the shoreline, yachts roped to timber jetties and tiny waves lapping the beach: to say that Cafe Espas had an idyllic setting would be a gross understatement. Step inside and you'll see the coastal landscape reinterpreted in co-owner Brendan Sims-Jeuken's paintings. His unique eye is also apparent in the nautical-themed accommodation. The dining action is all on the waterside balcony. A seafood-oriented menu starts with beer-battered fish 'n' chips, continues with a Thai seafood salad with chilli and lime notes, and ends up at salmon with dill and horseradish sauce. Popular desserts include cheesecake and a double chocolate mud cake. Don't expect culinary fireworks, but Espas is miles ahead of the local competition, and the whole family will love catching the ferry to get there.

Licensed
Open Fri-Sat 10am-late; Sun 10am-5pm (extended hours in hols)
Seats 50; outdoor seating
Owners Brendon & Maria Sims-Jeuken
Chef Maria Sims-Jeuken
Cards BC MC V
Prices entrees $7.50-$12; mains $15-$21; desserts $6.50-$8
Map page 269 **VicRoads** 350 J10

13/20 

Century Inn Terrace Cafe

MODERN AUSTRALIAN

Corner Princes Highway & Airfield Road,
Traralgon **5173 9400**

THE Terrace Cafe sounds dodgy: it occupies an unassuming annexe at a sprawling conference centre at the very edge of town. But as soon as you pass through the grand front doors, and are seated by crisply attired staff in the serene dining room, you know this isn't your average country motel. Cane furniture, antique sideboards and culinary-themed paintings by a local artist set the tone. The menu keeps things familiar; the flair is in the execution. An antipasto plate features house-made and local produce such as semi-dried tomatoes, crumbly feta and earthy eggplant. The calamari entree is a batterless mound accompanied by a green chilli sauce, while tender, tandoor-spiced chicken breast with coriander yoghurt shows a delicate touch. The wine list, while brief, contains some interesting local options from Bass Phillip and Narkoojee; coffees are excellent.

Licensed & BYO wine
Corkage $5 a bottle
Open Mon-Fri noon-3pm; Mon-Sat 6pm-late
Seats 50; private room
Owners Jodie & Mark Vogt
Chefs Mark Vogt & Kevin Campbell
Cards AE BC DC MC V
Prices lunches $3.80-$24; entrees $4.50-$18.50; mains $24.50-$28; desserts $9.50-$18.50
Map page 269 **VicRoads** 343 N7

13/20 

Gipsy Point Lodge

MODERN AUSTRALIAN

Off Macdonald Road,
Gipsy Point, near Mallacoota **5158 8205**

GUM TREES, swooping parakeets, the setting sun blushing the river: it's easy to feel that all's right with the world as you pick at your pre-dinner cheese platter in the slightly chintzy split-level dining room. When Ian Mitchell tells you what you'll be having 'for tea', expect to hear about things like grilled prawns with lime dressing, Cajun smoked trevally and lamb shanks with leek and saffron risotto. If you're lucky, he'll announce duck breast with an orange and cherry sauce that may well have you licking the plate. Desserts like crème de menthe semifreddo and raspberry meringue roll recall dinner parties of yesteryear. This is no high falutin' gourmet retreat, but the overall experience is no worse for the food being rather retro. The wine list is limited but reasonable. Booking is essential.

Licensed
Open daily 6.30-10pm (Jul-Aug by arrangement)
Seats 30
Owners Libby & Ian Mitchell
Chef Matthew Allen
Cards BC MC V Eftpos
Prices set menu $50 (3 courses)
Map page 269 **VicRoads** 70 C5

13/20 

The Koonwarra Fine Food & Wine Store

MODERN REGIONAL

South Gippsland Highway,
Koonwarra **5664 2285**

SUSTAINABLE, regional and seasonal are the bywords at this charming cafe, wine bar, produce store, post office, newsagent, live music spot and all-round hangout. Free-range eggs 'anyway you like' come with doorstops of organic toast. Avocado rice-paper rolls, chicken mango salad and beef burgers with Maffra cheddar and beetroot relish hit the plates around noon. Evenings are rustic and romantic, especially in the pretty garden, when you might dine on twice-baked goats' cheese soufflé, zucchini and haloumi fritters or venison sausages with Warrigal greens and gravy. All these fruits of Gippsland farmers can be partnered with beer from nearby Grand Ridge Brewery and wines from anywhere between Phillip Island and Ensay. Cakes are excellent and the barista understands what roadstop coffee should be all about.

13/20 $ V

Licensed & BYO wine
Corkage $2 a head
Open daily 8am-5pm; Thurs-Sat 6.30pm-late
Seats 50; outdoor seating; bar
Owners Maria Stuart, Melissa Burge & Thomas Burge
Chef Maria Stuart
Cards BC MC V Eftpos
Prices breakfasts $4.50-$16.50; entrees $8.50-$19.50; mains $18.50-$32; desserts $8.50-$12.50
Map page 269 **VicRoads** 102 J2

Nautilus Floating Dockside Restaurant

SEAFOOD

Western Boat Harbour,
Lakes Entrance **5155 1400**

WITH a name like Nautilus and an anchorage within cooee of the Lakes' fishing fleet, it's no surprise that this is a seafood restaurant. It's also among the slickest restaurants in eastern Victoria, with well-drilled floor staff. Plump for the fail-safe fish and chips or clever modern dishes like fat flathead chunks fried in crisp wonton wrappers, tiny, pan-fried scallops with an Asian dipping sauce, and perfectly cooked Eden mussels in a steaming light lemon thyme broth. Some fish dishes come with sadly old-fashioned touches like turrets of piped potato. The wine list is short and solely local (be warned you can't BYO anything that appears on it). This is a special place to land at sunset, when the last rays bounce off the water and on to the ceiling – they'll even deliver your martini in white gloves.

14/20

Licensed & BYO wine
Corkage $8 a bottle
Open daily 6pm-late (closed Sun-Mon Jun-Oct)
Seats 45
Owner McKenzie family
Chefs Ellen & Scott McKenzie
Cards AE BC DC MC V Eftpos
Prices entrees $8-$14; mains $22-$28; desserts $9.50
Map page 269 **VicRoads** 352 K6

Neilsons

MODERN AUSTRALIAN

13 Seymour Street,
Traralgon **5175 0100**

NEILSONS is forging ahead as one of Gippsland's culinary highlights. Situated in a gorgeously renovated home, the ruby walls, candles, polished boards and friendly staff all make a fine impression. Then there's the food: the kitchen is perennially hardworking and creative, as demonstrated in entrees like the dill pancake tower layered with smoked salmon and roasted capsicum salsa, and the beef carpaccio with horseradish mousse. Mains tend toward the meaty. Charred kangaroo fillets may come folded over parmesan-crusted potatoes; duck breast puddles in a biting mandarin jus. Simpler options include well-made pumpkin risotto and oxtail pappardelle. Desserts are refined: the warm chocolate tart with fresh fig and vanilla mascarpone is a standout. The wine list has plenty of interest at budget prices, though Gippsland wineries are scarcely represented.

14/20

Licensed
Open Tues-Fri 11.30am-2.30pm, 6pm-late; Sat 6pm-late
Seats 50; outdoor seating
Owner Brad Neilson
Chef Lewis Prince
Cards AE BC DC MC V Eftpos
Prices lunches $15-$19; entrees $13.50-$16.50; mains $14.50-$26; desserts $10-$14.50
Map page 269 **VicRoads** 342 G8

Post

MODERN AUSTRALIAN

Corner Princes Highway & Raymond Street,
Sale **5144 3388**

POST is a comfortable blend of urban savvy and country warmth, morphing as required from cafe to bar to restaurant. The food is imaginative, drawing together flavours in unexpected, but usually pleasing, ways. The gyoza are a case in point: Japanese in inspiration, the mushroom and herb dumplings sit on a Middle Eastern-style carrot and date salad with a drizzling of pomegranate molasses. Also playing mind games are the crab bisque served with smoked trout salad and baccala, and seared tuna on eggplant fondant with a lime dressing. Locals have had time to get used to – and love – menu stalwarts like the pear and gorgonzola risotto. Engaging chef and co-owner Jess Lazzaro often works the floor and her savoir faire is reflected in one of Gippsland's better wine lists. Post was looking for a new location as the *Guide* went to press.

14/20

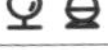

Licensed
Open Tues-Sat 9am-late; Sun 9am-6pm
Seats 45; outdoor seating; private room
Owners Jess & Sam Lazzaro
Chefs Jess Lazzaro & Shane Carter
Cards AE BC DC MC V Eftpos
Prices breakfasts $8-$14.50; lunches $8-$14.50; entrees $14.50-$16; mains $21.50-$26; desserts $7.50-$11
Map page 269 **VicRoads** 345 N7

The Riversleigh

MODERN AUSTRALIAN

1 Nicholson Street,
Bairnsdale **5152 6966**

SHARDS of chocolate poised on Tia Maria mousse signal that Riversleigh is a restaurant with serious ambitions. Chef Justin Moore's efforts with the food have been backed by some solid work on the wine list and a renewed emphasis on formal eating in the stately dining room. But don't stuff your shirt just yet: the relaxed atmosphere of the garden courtyard, the lounge with open fireplace, and the affable proprietors are still very much a part of the scene. A plain-language menu caters mostly to provincial tastes. Starters might include deep-fried camembert, Lakes Entrance garlic prawns in a wine and butter sauce and marinated chicken salad. Lamb souvlaki, char-grilled Gippsland sirloin and lightly fried veal escalopes are representative of the generous mains. Desserts do not sacrifice flavour as they strive for structural thrills.

13/20

Licensed
Open Wed-Fri noon-2.30pm; Mon-Sat 6.30-9pm
Seats 40; outdoor seating; private room; bar
Owners Jennie & Russell Field
Chef Justin Moore
Cards AE BC DC MC V Eftpos
Prices entrees $8.50-$20.90; mains $20.90-$26; desserts $9.90
Map page 269 **VicRoads** 348 G8

Tide Restaurant

MODERN AUSTRALIAN

70 Maurice Avenue,
Mallacoota **5158 0100**

KEITH ALLAN used to run Mallacoota cafe Strange Fruit. Now he's brought his casual and kid-friendly ethos to this modern restaurant of glass and wood, with soaring ceilings and open decking. Along with requisite camper fodder (Mallacoota has 1000 campsites) like fish 'n' chips and seafood pastas, you'll find more challenging dishes like wonderful little Eden oysters served with a Japanese dipping sauce and big blue mussels done provençale-style. During the summer holidays, Deb runs the juice and slushie bar and it's worth stopping in especially to try her fabulously fresh combos. Watermelon, blackcurrant and mint juice is great, but the 'ginger bang' is best of all. This inspired drink combines fresh ginger and pineapple juice with a scoop of home-made lemon and lime sorbet – it's hot from the root and cool from the slush.

12/20

Licensed & BYO wine
Corkage $3 a bottle
Open Wed-Sun 4pm-late; Sat-Sun 9am-3pm (daily 7am-late Dec-Feb)
Seats 85; outdoor seating
Owner & chef Keith Allan
Cards BC MC V Eftpos
Prices entrees $6.50-$13.90; mains $15.50-$26.90; desserts $6-$9
Map page 269 **VicRoads** 355 Q6

Archibald's Commercial Hotel

MODERN AUSTRALIAN

124 Main Street,
Bairnsdale **5152 3031**

TYPICAL country pub on the outside, foodie destination on the inside, thanks to Bairnsdale culinary identity David 'Archie' Archibald and partner-chef Jenny Boyle. Grilled lamb with Greek trimmings, pork kassler with orange and chilli glaze and herb-crumbed veal in tarragon hollandaise might appear on the flexible chalkboard menu.

Licensed
Open Mon-Sat noon-2.30pm, 6-9pm
Prices entrees $5.50-$12.50; mains $13.50-$25.50
Map page 269 **VicRoads** 348 C10

Boathouse Licensed Cafe

MODERN AUSTRALIAN

213 The Esplanade,
Lakes Entrance **5155 3055**

RECENTLY renovated and under new ownership, this simple cafe does good all-day breakfasts and excellent fish 'n' chips and fat sandwiches. Flathead tails often turn up on the specials board; the home-made cakes will make you forget all about those bathers you've got to squeeze into tomorrow.

Licensed
Open daily 7am-late
Prices breakfasts $4.50-$14.50; mains $8.50-$15.50; cakes $3.50-$5.50
Map page 269 **VicRoads** 352 K7

Breakfast at Allambie

BREAKFAST

169-181 Metung Road,
Metung **5156 2202**

YOU can't eat a great view, but it sure makes breakfast taste better at Allambie, one of charming Metung's original homestead properties. There's a good, served-at-the-table omelette, acceptable egg dishes and fruit platters, all served with an eyeful of Bancroft Bay. Coffee is superb and the service is friendly.

BYO
Open Sat-Sun 8am-noon (daily 8am-noon during hols)
Prices breakfasts $3.50-$18.50; cooked platter for two $35
Map page 269 **VicRoads** 352 D5

Carmichaels Restaurant

MODERN AUSTRALIAN

17 The Esplanade, Cowes,
Phillip Island **5952 1300**

THIS showpiece restaurant has captured its intended market so perfectly that it's entitled to pride of place overlooking Western Port. The menu dabbles in the new and the interesting (smoked quail, bush-spiced kangaroo) but mostly stays true to old faves like oysters kilpatrick and creamy spag marinara. Balcony seating is a bonus.

Licensed
Open daily 9am-11pm
Prices entrees $8-$18; mains $25-$32; desserts $10
Map page 267 **VicRoads** 302 H1

Croajingolong Cafe

CAFE

Shop 3, 14 Allen Drive,
Mallacoota **5158 0098**

THIS simple little spot is just the place to recharge the caffeine levels or grab a spot of lunch. Traditional breakfasts lead into worthy hot lunches like burgers with fresh salad. Daily specials often feature local seafood: you might luck upon impeccably fresh baked bream, pulled from the lake just hours earlier.

Unlicensed
Open daily 8am-4pm (closed Mon in winter)
Prices breakfasts $7-$12; lunches $6-$10
Map page 269 **VicRoads** 355 S5

Fisherman's Wharf Pavilion

MODERN AUSTRALIAN

70 The Esplanade,
Paynesville **5156 0366**

BRIGHT, friendly and seafood-oriented, the waterfront Pavilion serves the ubiquitous Lakes Entrance flathead tails, along with local prawns, scallops and tempura-style calamari. Less coastal and more ambitious is the kangaroo fillet encrusted with bunya nuts and served with native greens. Don't set sail before trying the verjuice sorbet.

$ 

Licensed
Open daily 9am-late
Prices breakfasts $6-$14; entrees $12-$14; mains $18-$30
Map page 269 **VicRoads** 351 H10

Iimis Cafe

MEDITERRANEAN

28 Seymour Street,
Traralgon **5174 4577**

EVERYTHING about Iimis is big: the space, the food selection, even the hearty welcome you receive from owners Peter or Costa Demetrios. The kitchen works all day, serving breakfast with the works, lunchtime salads – perhaps seared chicken with mango – and Turkish bread pizzas. Greek-inspired dinner options include marinated lamb skewers.

$

Licensed
Open Mon-Thurs 7.30am-9pm; Fri 7.30am-11.30pm; Sat 8am-11.30pm; Sun 9am-4pm
Prices mains $12-$18
Map page 269 **VicRoads** 342 G8

The Kiosk Cafe

MODERN AUSTRALIAN

Corner Ramsay Boulevard & Abbott Street,
Inverloch **5674 3611**

IN the 1940s it was Brown's Kiosk, a dinky-di camper's provedore. Architecturally, little has changed but this shack is now a trendy dawn-till-dark beachfront eatery. Breakfast tempters include a Cajun chicken toasted sandwich. Lunch means burgers or salads, while evening winners include smoked fish salads and vegetable curries.

$

Licensed & BYO wine
Open Sun-Wed 8.30am-6pm; Thurs-Sat 8.30am-11pm
Prices breakfasts $2.80-$14.50; mains $18.50-$23
Map page 269 **VicRoads** 358 E4

Larrikins Cafe

MODERN AUSTRALIAN

2 Wood Street,
Bairnsdale **5153 1421**

POPULAR with local artists, Larrikins is a casual cafe, exhibition space and home to the East Gippsland Wine Centre. The menu is dominated by focaccias and bagels but chalkboard specials might include roasted sweet potato and red capsicum terrine or cheese and silverbeet pie. New owners took over as the *Guide* went to press.

$ V 

Licensed
Open Mon-Fri 9am-4.30pm
Prices breakfasts $4.90-$14; lunches $4.75-$13.85
Map page 269 **VicRoads** 348 K8

Little Mariners Cafe

MEDITERRANEAN

Shop 3, 57 Metung Road,
Metung **5156 2077**

LITTLE MARINERS is better than ever, serving coffee all day and mod-Med meals in a modest space. The kitchen is trying harder with dishes like crumbed sardines with salsa, straightforward pastas and the inevitable Gippsland Lakes signature ingredient – flathead tails – done a variety of ways. Good, affordable seaside eating.

BYO
Open Tues 6-10.30pm; Wed-Thurs noon-10.30pm; Fri-Sun 8.30am-10pm
Prices mains $10-$27.50
Map page 269 **VicRoads** 352 D5

Orange Roughy

MODERN AUSTRALIAN

2 Old Waratah Road,
Fish Creek **5683 2207**

THIS cafe's easygoing vibe, unflappable staff and veranda-cum-beer garden are its best features. The food is decent without packing a brilliant wallop. You might try local calamari, coated with chilli salt and flash-grilled, lamb rack on cous cous or vegie noodles, best washed down with a Natural Blonde wheat beer from nearby Grand Ridge Brewery.

Licensed
Open Wed-Sun 10am-late (also Mon-Tues in summer school hols)
Prices entrees $9-$20; mains $15-$23; desserts $7
Map page 269 **VicRoads** 103 B5

Relish @ the Gallery

MODERN AUSTRALIAN

68-70 Foster Street,
Sale **5144 5044**

TRAPEZE lights, purple walls and other trappings give this busy gallery cafe a funky feel. Lunch is the go: nosh on wraps, open sandwiches or the chalkboard selection of pasta, salads and kebabs. Weekend dinners are more substantial. There might be roasted duck risotto, Thai-style baby octopus or Moroccan-spiced prawns with olives.

$

Licensed
Open Sun-Thurs 9am-5pm; Fri-Sat 9am-late; Sun 10am-5pm
Prices entrees $7.50-$18; mains $15-$25; desserts $6-$8.50
Map page 269 **VicRoads** 345 M7

Sticcádo Cafe

CAFE

Shop 6, The Village Walk,
Yarragon **5634 2101**

IF Sticcádo's menu has a beefy, cheesy bias, it's because the owners are farmers who believe in value-adding for survival. The excellent steaks, curries and pies are made with beef from their own farm; the cheeses (served individually or on a platter with toasted sourdough and grape jelly) are among Gippsland's finest.

$

Licensed & BYO wine
Open Wed-Thurs & Sat-Mon 10am-5.30pm; Friday 10am-11pm
Prices small meals $8.50-$10.50; mains $13-$25.50
Map page 269 **VicRoads** 335 S9

Waterwheel Beach Tavern

MODERN AUSTRALIAN

577 Lake Tyers Beach Road,
Lake Tyers **5156 5855**

THIS casual, quintessentially coastal newcomer features paintings of seahorses and snapper, and sweeping views across Lake Tyers to Ninety Mile Beach. Forgo the usual pub fare, find a spot on the deck and tackle the 'big-arsed seafood platter for two'. Grilled and fried fish sit alongside prawns, scallops, calamari and oysters. It's a feast.

Licensed
Open daily noon-2pm, 6-8pm
Prices entrees $5-$19; mains $15-$25; desserts $6
Map page 269 **VicRoads** 85 C7

The Wild Lime Cafe

MODERN AUSTRALIAN

18 George Street,
Morwell **5133 6381**

NONDESCRIPT George Street is an unlikely location for this cosy culinary oasis. Owner-chef Rohan Skee's deft touch is evident in tasteful dishes like crumbed eggplant parmigiana, pea samosas, herbed gnocchi and Vietnamese spring rolls. Those needing a steak fix can go the grilled rib-eye with baked potatoes and hollandaise sauce.

$ V

Licensed & BYO wine
Open Tues-Fri noon-2pm; Tues-Sat 6pm-late
Prices entrees $6-$11.50; mains $18-$23; desserts $5-$9.50
Map page 269 **VicRoads** 340 D6

INTERSTATE

Est

PURE SYDNEY
252 George Street, Sydney
(02) 9240 3010
Prices entrees $22-$26; mains $28-$38

PETER DOYLE'S move from Celsius to the Establishment Hotel has taken the food here to new heights, even for this seasoned Sydney chef. One minute it's steamed whiting in a gorgeous white wine nage, the next it's snapper with jacqueline sauce. Doyle's desserts are never disappointing; try the ruby grapefruit sorbet or anything with berries.

Sean's Panaroma

PURE SYDNEY
270 Campbell Parade, Bondi Beach
(02) 9365 4924
Prices entrees $15-$21; mains $19-$35

YEAH, yeah, so it's a cross between a cafe and a restaurant, where the waiters don't fuss and the decor is retro-funky rather than achingly cool. But the Bondi vista is pretty good, the attitude beachy keen and the flavours – from the duck-liver parfait to the white chocolate and rosemary nougat – simply lustworthy. Note: lazy lunches are the ticket.

Claude's

GASTRO TEMPLE
10 Oxford Street, Woollahra
(02) 9331 2325
Prices set price $125; degustation menu $150

LESS French and more individual than ever, the breathtaking culinary journey of owner-chef Tim Pak Poy has foodies entranced, even after nine years in this intimate Oxford Street bolthole. Caramelised wild oyster with a fine dice of tomato perhaps? A bitter almond soufflé? Say yes to something that's so light it's in danger of floating away.

Tetsuya's

GASTRO TEMPLE
529 Kent Street, Sydney
(02) 9267 2900
Prices set price $170

DON'T be scared off by the expensive and extensive set menu – a meal here is a lesson in harmony and perfection. Konbu seaweed graces satiny slow-cooked ocean trout; Murray cod may arrive with black bean and olive. And helping you on your journey to gastronomic nirvana are views of an exquisite bonsai garden and an encyclopedic wine list.

Icebergs Dining Room and Bar

HOT SPOT
1 Notts Avenue, Bondi Beach
(02) 9365 9000
Prices entrees $15-$25; mains $29-$46

PERCHED like a sea eagle hovering over Bondi Beach is Icebergs, the latest gastro-chic offering from Maurice Terzini (Melbourne Wine Room). Karen Martini's mod-Italian fare is beguilingly restrained and as fresh as the aquamarine fit out. The bug salad with snowpea leaf is awesome but beware – Martini's bistecca fiorentina has crossed the border.

Jimmy Liks

HOT SPOT
188 Victoria Street, Potts Point
(02) 8354 1400
Prices entrees & mains $15-$28

IT'S a very patient diner who'll wait up to two hours for space at a communal table in a dark, loud place. But the shiny people do because they hanker for Will Meyrick's take on Asian street food, from the stir-fried scallops with asparagus to a comforting, home-style beef and wintermelon soup. And the too-cool-for-school Asian-inspired cocktails.

MG Garage

FINE DINER
490 Crown Street, Surry Hills
(02) 9360 7007
Prices entrees $16-$29.50; mains $37-$43

GOODBYE Janni Kyritsis, hello Jeremy Strode, former Langton's chef. The suave dining room still boasts a real MG, but the raciness is left to this high-octane Melbourne import. No-one can cook a pig's trotter with sweetbreads and chicken mince quite like Strode or equal his stunning smoked eel on cauliflower panna cotta.

Rockpool

FINE DINER

107 George Street, The Rocks

(02) 9252 1888

Prices entrees $36-$39; mains $54-$70

WITH a smart million dollar-plus makeover last year, the now teenaged Rockpool has come of age. A surge of new dishes and a return to the bold spicing of old has kept Neil Perry's flagship a mod-Oz leader in a town of wannabes. Seafood is the star, with stratospheric prices to match, but when scallops come daubed with foie gras sauce, who cares?

Otto

FOOD WITH A VIEW

6 Cowper Wharf Road, Woolloomooloo

(02) 9368 7488

Prices entrees $18-$26; mains $24-$37

A CHANGE in owner and chef hasn't dented the popularity of this modern Italian casa for the bold and the beautiful. The Campari-lined bar and moody interior may remind you of Melbourne, but the attitude and views from this converted wharf are pure Sydney. Nab an outside perch and sample the prawn strozzapreti while checking out your

Quay

FOOD WITH A VIEW

Overseas Passenger Terminal, The Rocks

(02) 9251 5600

Prices entrees $26-$28; mains $34-$42

PETER GILMORE has really found his groove at Quay, home to one of the best views in town. There's the Bridge and the Opera House. There's an amazing salad combining quail poached in master stock with prosciutto and abalone. And as Gilmore was once a sweets cook, the desserts are as delectable as the vista before you.

Sailors Thai Canteen

FOREIGN AFFAIR

106 George Street, The Rocks

(02) 9251 2466

Prices mains $20; desserts $10

PUNTERS come throughout the afternoon to sit at the shiny communal table and select from a document as different from most Thai menus as Sydney is from Bangkok. Lone diners will do no better than the pad Thai, while the chilli-laden green papaya salad and murky, gently sour Chiang Mai chicken curry are perfect for sharing.

Yoshii

FOREIGN AFFAIR

115 Harrington Street, The Rocks

(02) 9247 2566

Prices set prices $80 or $110; less for sushi banquets

THERE are few Japanese restaurants in Sydney that can compete with Yoshii on decor, and fewer that come close to the food. Sublime morsels are delivered kaiseki-style – fish, gently smoking in a shroud of lit cedar as it's carried to the table, is glorious, so too the tofu and foie gras agedashidofu – or dine solo at the sushi bar.

Bathers' Pavilion Cafe

CAFE LIFE

4 The Esplanade, Balmoral

(02) 9969 5050

Prices entrees $13.50-$23.50; mains $19-$29.50

THE prettiest shell on Balmoral beach is still this delightful former 1930s bathers' shed turned restaurant-cafe. It's worth the weekend wait for a table so you can eventually ogle the view out to Middle Harbour. Go for oven-baked beans at breakfast, wood-fired pizzas at lunch or carrot soup with Jerusalem artichoke in the twilight hours. Bewitching.

Danks Street Depot

CAFE LIFE

2 Danks Street, Waterloo

(02) 9698 2201

Prices entrees & mains $10-$18

IT wasn't that long ago that taxi drivers wouldn't pick up in Waterloo. Now one of the best cafes you could imagine has popped up and the cabbies are filling fares like the Depot fills espresso cups. The food's as good as the crema, so chow down, in this swish converted warehouse space, on white polenta with asparagus or macho pasta with ham hock.

Aubergine

JAMES MUSSILLON'S cosmopolitan bistro oozes style, and it's not all down to the tiered space and caramel suede wall. Dishes like White Rocks veal on warm potato salad are nearly as ravishing as the seafood offerings. Aubergine's mixed fish, a stack of seafood with provençale vegetables, is so good it should be on display in the National Museum.

PURE CANBERRA
18 Barker Street, Griffith
(02) 6260 8666
Prices entrees $17.50; mains $27.50

Ottoman Cuisine

SERIF KAYA'S opulent modern Turkish cuisine continues to bedazzle. Syrian Aleppo pepper may grace the simplest of grilled tuna; a whiff of clove could accompany a dolma of salmon, while king prawns might arrive sticky with pomegranate sauce. Since the Ottoman empire upped camp from Manuka, Kaya's reign is unstoppable in his sumptuous new home.

GASTRO TEMPLE
Corner Broughton & Blackall Streets, Barton
(02) 6273 6111
Prices entrees $15-$21; mains $21-$27

Atlantic Restaurant

DESPITE a change of chef as Atlantic was scaling local heights, there's hardly been a hiccup. In fact, the place feels reinvigorated with the new-fashioned Euro-style menu (duck pot-au-feu with pork belly and savoy cabbage) on par with the swank, timber-clad dining space. The intelligent, wide-reaching wine list is also priced in the diner's favour.

FINE DINER
20 Palmerston Lane, Manuka
(02) 6232 7888
Prices entrees $16.50-$18.50; mains $27.50-$30

Water's Edge

BRIT-TRAINED Darren Vaughan cooks like an angel in this lakeside space between the High Court and the National Library with views to the War Memorial. Anything he does with game is superb, but the triumph is the darkly caramelised apple tart. Nothing escapes Vaughan's pursuit of excellence – even the bread and butter are made in-house.

FOOD WITH A VIEW
40 Parkes Place (North), Parkes
(02) 6273 5066
Prices entrees $14-$20; mains $22-$32

Silo Bakery

LEANNE GRAY'S bakery-cafe continues to be the hottest address in town, as cluey locals and visitors flock here for just-baked sourdough, the prettiest fruit tarts and the best breakfast around. More substantial offerings such as Toulouse sausages, or duck with cavolo nero, make the functional space feel that much warmer.

CAFE LIFE
36 Giles Street, Kingston
(02) 6260 6060
Prices entrees $4-$11.50; mains $13-$17

Hanuman

SOME say Darwin is the only place in Australia to eat Asian food, which might make Hanuman the country's best Asian restaurant. But that debate aside, this Darwin darling continues to deliver Indian and Thai Nonya treats to a loyal fan club. Don't go past the signature wok-tossed prawns. Also at Crown Plaza, Alice Springs.

PURE DARWIN
28 Mitchell Street, Darwin
(08) 8941 3500
Prices entrees $9.50-$13.50; mains $14-$27

Christo's

DARWIN legend Christo and his 70-plus mother Katie transform Top End seafood into Greek-style meals you only dream about down south. Choose from barra, bugs, octopus or prawns or sample them all on one gigantic platter. Also check out his latest Darwin venture, a huge taverna-like complex called Ducks Nuts Bar & Grill.

FOREIGN AFFAIR
28 Mitchell Street, Darwin
(08) 8941 1444
Prices entrees $10-$28; mains $19.50-$55

Lebrina

PURE TASMANIA

155 New Town Road, New Town
(03) 6228 7775
Prices entrees $16.50; mains $28.50-$32

IF it's found in Tasmania and it's good, Scott Minervini serves it up. Thorpe Farm goats' cheese joins Highland venison and the Island State's glorious seafood on a menu that finds its roots in Europe. Even the bread is made in-house, while the wine list is not only bargain-priced, but also locally biased. The 1840s colonial setting is enchanting.

Fee & Me

GASTRO TEMPLE

190 Charles Street, Launceston
(03) 6331 3195
Prices set menus $53.80-$69.75

CONSISTENTLY at the top of the culinary tree, chef Fiona Hoskin (Fee) continues to delight in this historic early 1800s house. Meals arrive as entree-sized offerings – three to five courses – ranging from light to rich. Fee always sources great produce, such as Flinders Island lamb, and the mammoth wine list is a worthy match for the stunning food.

Jackman & McRoss

HOT SPOT

59 Hampden Road, Battery Point
(03) 6223 3186
Prices entrees & mains $3.80-$9.90

YES, we know. We're still calling it hot, four years on. But this bakery-cafe continues to draw crowds, everyone from midweek mums to weekend market-goers stopping by for the great bread, chunky sandwiches, quiche and more. The coffee is in the French style (hot and milky or short and bitter), and the feeling warm and fuzzy.

Franklin Manor

FINE DINER

The Esplanade, Strahan
(03) 6471 7311
Prices set menu $65; degustation menu $85-$105

THE dining at stately Franklin Manor is worthy of nobility. Chef Meyjitte Boughenout's food is all crafted with care, from the serious (say, roasted lamb rump with green pea puree), to the frivolous, like the spiced beetroot lollipop. Come in summer, when the wind is less bone-chilling, or warm up by indulging in Tassie's best wine list.

Stillwater

FOOD WITH A VIEW

2 Bridge Road, Launceston
(03) 6331 4153
Prices entrees $14-$21; mains $24-$32

WHILE the best river views from this former mill are during daylight, the time to visit is at night, when talented Don Cameron rattles the pans. His brave and usually Asian-accented combinations are always well constructed and invariably delicious. Roasted squab may be matched with a delicate anise-scented sabayon and a Tamar Ridge pinot noir.

Orizuru

FOREIGN AFFAIR

Victoria Dock, Hobart
(03) 6231 1790
Prices entrees & mains $13.50-$18.50

IT'S rather splendid to find such a good Japanese eatery in such a fine location down at the docks. There are great views of sandstone factories and fishing boats bringing in their bounty. Bento boxes include a braised dish or tempura and are great for bargain-hunters, but it's Orizuru's spanking fresh sushi and sashimi that has diners hooked.

Sugo

CAFE LIFE

Shop 9, Salamanca Square, Hobart
(03) 6224 5690
Prices entrees & mains $5-14; desserts $7.50

WITH a name like Sugo and walls painted the colour of ripe tomatoes, what else would the menu offer but Italian-inspired cafe crowd-pleasers such as pizza, pasta and risotto? The coffee is Grinders, there's outdoor seating for when Hobart thaws out, and a co-owner has a hand in lovable long-stayer Kafe Kara in the city.

Urban Bistro

PURE ADELAIDE
160 Fullarton Road, Rose Park
(08) 8331 2400
Prices entrees $6.50-$21.90; mains $16.50-$23.90

WITH its lovely timber floors, choc-coloured chairs and intelligent table and wine service, Urban offers a slice of the good life just south of the city. Breakfast (from eggs, through strawberries with vanilla syrup, to Bircher muesli and beyond) is nearly the equal of their more substantial offerings such as peppered duck breast with porcini risotto.

The Grange

GASTRO TEMPLE
Hilton Adelaide, Victoria Square, Adelaide
(08) 8217 2000
Prices set menus $70-$110

WHILE the hotel venue has lost some of its sparkle, the food, from culinary wizard Cheong Liew, continues to entrance. From soused snook to black-bone chicken, the remarkable set-priced menus are full of mystery, flavour and intrigue. Vegetarians will be thrilled by many dishes, particularly those using tofu or smoked soybeans.

The Apothecary 1878

HOT SPOT
118 Hindley Street, Adelaide
(08) 8212 9099
Prices bar food $3.50-$9.90

IT'S all upstairs-downstairs at this fabulous red-hot wine bar in fast-changing Hindley Street. Great bar snacks taken in the salon-like ground-floor area might include fried olives, hummus and tzatziki. You can also enjoy your prosciutto and Maggie Beer pâté downstairs in the labyrinthine cellar, all the while supping great wines by the glass.

Bridgewater Mill

FINE DINER
Mount Barker Road, Bridgewater
(08) 8339 3422
Prices entrees $22; mains $31; desserts $15

LE TU THAI, arguably SA's best chef, is still ensconced at Petaluma's classy Bridgewater Mill, only 20 minutes from the city. The roasted Kangaroo Island chicken with scampi and Armagnac sauce is the stuff of legends. Don't leave without ordering dessert, and a six-pack of wine from cellar door to take home.

Star of Greece

FOOD WITH A VIEW
The Esplanade, Port Willunga
(08) 8557 7420
Prices entrees $7.50-$16.50; mains$19.50-$30

PERCHED like a fisherman gazing out over the Gulf of St Vincent, this smartened-up tin shed offers one of Australia's great dining experiences. The food, such as squid (fresh from that same gulf) with aioli, or goats' cheese soufflé, doesn't reach dazzling heights, but, given the magical setting, you'll fondly remember your meal here long afterwards.

T Chow

FOREIGN AFFAIR
68 Moonta Street, Adelaide
(08) 8410 1413
Prices entrees $2.80-$7.80; mains $8.60-$15.80

NOT so much a restaurant as a pulsating slice of humanity, T Chow is hot, noisy and full of locals who know the sun-dried scallops with bean curd are heavenly and the salt-and-pepper spare ribs lipsmacking. Regulars argue over whether the slow-simmered duck is better than taro-coated fried duck. Order both and decide for yourself.

Cibo

CAFE LIFE
10 O'Connell Street, North Adelaide
(08) 8267 2444
Prices entrees $16.50-$19.50; mains $20.50-$28

SOME come for the espresso, others for the familar service but most for the home-brand cornetti and gelati, and other honest Italian fare. Like any savvy Roman trattoria, Cibo still packs them in morning and night. The only difference? You might like a Barossa shiraz from the hefty wine list with your bistecca fiorentina.

Subiaco Hotel

NOT just a great watering hole, but a great hangout for flavour-chasers too. Regulars and in-the-know visitors flock here for mouth-watering dishes, such as a cauliflower and taleggio panna cotta or snappy duck fritters on rich Sichuan-style eggplant. The wine list is WA-centric, but that's just another reason to drop in.

PURE PERTH
465 Hay Street, Subiaco
(08) 9381 3069
Prices entrees $7.50-$18; mains $14.50-$25

Jackson's

NO wonder Neal Jackson is considered one of the best by his peers. His incomparable European technique, enriched with an Asian kick, makes this fine-diner a Perth institution. Count yourself lucky if the tea-smoked chicken with yabbies and crisp-skinned pork is on the menu, and don't leave without tasting one of WA's finest vintage reds.

GASTRO TEMPLE
483 Beaufort Street, Highgate
(08) 9328 1177
Prices entrees $17-$19; mains $28-$33

Must Winebar

NOT only does Russell Blaikie need his menu to be great in its own right, but also to match the stunning selection of wines (500-plus) at this Highgate hangout. Luckily, there's no compromise on quality, as the chicken liver parfait with grenache jelly is just as luscious as the rotisserie-cooked quail wrapped in prosciutto with radicchio salad.

HOT SPOT
519 Beaufort Street, Highgate
(08) 9328 8255
Prices entrees $9-$18; mains $22.50-$29.50

Star Anise

WHAT David Coomer can't do with ingredients isn't worth doing. This slave to mod-Oz food has the lightest touch, his smart minimalist bistro serving some of Perth's finest in the genre. Coomer's wok-tossed octopus with sweet pork and black noodles is lifted with tamarind, and don't miss anything he does with duck. Grab a courtyard seat in summer.

FINE DINER
225 Onslow Road, Shenton Park
(08) 9381 9811
Prices entrees $17-$22; mains $31.50-$36.50

Indiana Tea House

THE view over Cottesloe Beach is nothing short of breathtaking. The scene here is all shiny folk and happy families, and the menu, as you'd expect, is seafood-biased. But alongside beer-battered fish and chips or half-shell scallops with chilli salsa you might find pumpkin agnolotti. Kids are well catered for with their own special menu.

FOOD WITH A VIEW
99 Marine Parade, Cottesloe Beach
(08) 9385 5005
Prices entrees $14.85-$19.90; mains $22-$48.40

Altos

AFTER a minor refit, Altos remains a sexy thing. Antique posters still grace the walls, there's plenty of timber, and fans swirl lazily overhead. Many visitors come for the pappardelle with porcini ragu, the always-awesome risotto dishes and the devilishly good cassata. Others come for a wine list that drips with style and substance, listing over 400 top drops.

FOREIGN AFFAIR
424 Hay Street, Subiaco
(08) 9382 3292
Prices entrees $15-$22.50; mains $24-$30

44 King Street

PART of the city's fabric and seemingly always open, 44 King Street just keeps on keeping on. They still bake their own pastries and serve honest fare that would look good in any upmarket bistro, such as Andalucian baked chicken with patatas bravas. The coffee is top notch and the by-the-glass wine list (50-plus) will make your eyes water.

CAFE LIFE
44 King Street, Perth
(08) 9321 4476
Prices entrees $10.50-$18; mains $12.50-$29

Cru Bar & Cellar

WITH input from wine consultant Tony Harper (of the now-defunct Anise) and chef Paul Hoffman (formerly of the Grape) manning the stoves, this newcomer offers weekend breakfasts and all-day dining. There are about 40 wines by the glass, so tasting plates featuring chorizo with olive pâté, and rare tuna with artichokes and apple balsamic, are a sure thing.

PURE BRISBANE
James Street Markets, Fortitude Valley
(07) 3252 2400
Prices entrees $8-$12; mains $20-$24

Circa

OWEN LACEY is one of those indispensable Brisbane chefs who keeps getting better. Stunning green pea and ricotta ravioli may come graced by cepe cream, and seared Queensland scallops could come perched on a blini with bacon. Adding to the experience is an incredible wine list and glimpses of Story Bridge.

GASTRO TEMPLE
483 Adelaide Street, Brisbane
(07) 3832 4722
Prices entrees $17-$19; mains $28-$32

Telegraph Restaurant

ANYONE who liked PJ McMillan's food when he was at Arc will be overjoyed to find him creating equally fresh, interesting dishes down on Ann Street. His scallop tart with Jerusalem artichokes is heady with nutty roasted garlic. A nearly-niçoise salad finds rare tuna with beans, quail egg, tomato, sesame and basil, and the lemon tart is sublime.

HOT SPOT
GPO Hotel, Fortitude Valley
(07) 3252 1322
Prices entrees $9.50-$19; mains $27-$29

Gianni

GIANNI GREGHINI'S smart eatery continues to roll on, with a great take on mod-Med cuisine. Blue cheese and beetroot risotto may come topped with smoked tomato vinaigrette, lamb loin could accompany a polenta cake with madeira jus, and the desserts are amazing. The cellar, which boasts close to 5000 bottles, is worth the visit alone.

FINE DINER
12 Edward Street, Brisbane
(07) 3221 7655
Prices entrees $21-$22; mains $32-$33

Lat 27

YOU can see the river, the bridge and, even better, you can see Brad Jolly's roasted salmon with silky cauliflower puree and bisque. Jolly has worked with the UK's Marco Pierre White, but his menu here is more suited to sunny Brizzie days. Anytime is a good time to try the chicken sausage, redolent of roasted garlic and earthy truffled mushrooms.

FOOD WITH A VIEW
27 Macrossan Street, Brisbane
(07) 3839 2727
Prices entrees $14.50-$17.50; mains $27-$30

Bruno's Table

QUEENSLANDERS have been over the moon since esteemed Frenchman Bruno Loubet left his digs in London to set up in Brisbane – the difference is that here, mains cost less than $30. Dishes range from a classic boudin blanc of sweetbreads with braised beans to a quivery celeriac and cauliflower custard with crab velouté.

FOREIGN AFFAIR
85 Mesken Street, Toowong
(07) 3371 4558
Prices entrees $12.50-$17; mains $26-$28

Tomoko

TOMOKO'S great location and views of the rejuvenated parklands mean it doesn't have to try too hard with the food to impress. The good news is that it does anyway. From the coconut bread with cinnamon butter for breakfast, to hoisin chicken spring rolls or glazed Muscovy duck, it can be all things to all people, all day.

CAFE LIFE
1 Parkland Boulevard, Brisbane
(07) 3229 7777
Prices entrees $7.90-$10.90; mains $15-$21.90

Sassi Cucina

PURE QUEENSLAND

PORT DOUGLAS' brassy best, Sassi Cucina satisfies Top End resortees as well as those whose bathers and sarongs don't match. Modern Italian up front, with a strong emphasis on seafood – parmesan gelati and fish carpaccio are standouts – while out back there's a stylish sushi bar and cocktails all day. Bang on your best dress shorts.

4 Macrossan Street, Port Douglas
(07) 4099 6100
Prices entrees $16.50-$25; mains $25-$37

Ricky Ricardo's

GASTRO TEMPLE

RICKY'S is a study of how a resort restaurant should be. Generous hosts (Leonie Palmer and Steve Fisher), a captivating view, a laid-back bar for post-prandial digestifs and a Med-accented menu that's forward-thinking but not fussy. Start with a table laden with tapas and end with a 'Ricky's fizz' cocktail, and the setting sun. Perfect.

Quamby Place, Noosa Heads
(07) 5447 2455
Prices entrees $8-$20; mains $26-$33

Gusto

HOT SPOT

WHEN this riverfront restaurant is not packed with locals, it's brimming with the interstate jetsetters fleeing from overcrowded, overpriced Hastings Street. The roasted beetroot salad and Atlantic salmon on asparagus mash refuse to budge and so will you if the sun's shining and Gusto's glorious lemon tart appears.

257 Gympie Terrace, Noosaville
(07) 5449 7144
Prices entrees $9.50-$15.50; mains $17.50-$29

Fellini

FINE DINER

SPECTACULAR Broadwater views and equally mesmerising Italian cuisine from the Percuoco family have made Fellini a Gold Coast fixture. Matched by relaxed, yet always attentive service, and a smart and extensive wine list, there is no better way to enjoy the Coast. Don't miss the magnificent 'fungi and figs' dish.

74 Seaworld Drive, Main Beach
(07) 5531 0300
Prices entrees $16.50-$21.50; mains $25-$31

Season

FOOD WITH A VIEW

THERE are few places where thongs and sarongs are welcome. But by day they're almost mandatory at this perennial beach-front fave. Go fancy at night, however, and you'll be rewarded with Gary Skelton's hot-mod food. Wood-fired pizzas may be dressed up with rocket, and local seafood comes wearing olive oil and char from the grill.

25 Hastings Street, Noosa Heads
(07) 5447 3747
Prices entrees $15.50-$18; mains $23-$28.50

L'Unico Trattoria

FOREIGN AFFAIR

IN a tourist town that, incredibly, caters so poorly for the long luncher, L'Unico is a revelation. Thankfully, this Italian trat also takes full advantage of its setting, dishing up flappingly fresh fish with the postcard palm tree and sea views. The owners will be your best friends in minutes and hours later you'll be calling for the dinner menu.

75 Vasey Esplanade, Trinity Beach
(07) 4057 7137
Prices entrees $13.50-$17; mains $18.50-$38.50

Berardo's on the Beach

CAFE LIFE

MELBOURNE chef Matt McConnell has fled north and, along with his bathers, has packed his cous cous, sherry vinegar and strands of saffron. Perched right on the beach, this mod-Med diner is as good at breakfast as it is after the sun goes down. Also try their fine diner, Berardo's, 50 Hastings Street, Noosa Heads.

Hastings Street, Noosa Heads
(07) 5448 0888
Prices entrees $14.90; mains $24.90

Flower Drum

Cantonese Cuisine

Flower Drum Restaurant
17 Market Lane, Melbourne, Vic. 3000
Telephone (03) 9662 3655 Fax (03) 9663 5199

Dumpling King

Chinese Restaurant

Licensed and BYO

Now extended and tastefully renovated to seat 100. Famous Peking, Shanghai and Szechu Cuisine. New dishes including Peking Duck and live seafood.

570-572 Station Street Box Hill, Victoria 3128
Tel: (03) 9890 3719

RED EMPEROR

CHINESE RESTAURANT

Dining with sumptuous Chinese cuisine, surrounded by the wonderful panoramic view of the City & Yarra.

Multiple Award Winning Restaurant Fully Licensed
Upper Level, 3 Southgate Ave Southbank
Telephone: 9699 4170 Website: www.redemperor.com.au

Fully Licensed
B.Y.O. Wine Only

Experience exotic high standard Chinese cuisine prepared by Top-class Chef rarely found in Suburban area.

Cnr High Street & Kooyong Road Armadale
Phone: 9824 7710 or 9822 2217
Website: www.silkyapple.com.au

阿母
ah mu
www.ahmu.com
51 Bourke Street Melbourne
Telephone 9654 6800

东方楼
EASTERN BELL
CHINESE RESTAURANT – BYO
MSG FREE
Sunday Lunch
Dine-in 10% OFF
BELMORE PLAZA, 1ST FLOOR,
399 BELMORE ROAD, BALWYN
9857 4372 or 9857 4175

Bread

The Authentic Village Bakery 517 Malvern Road, Toorak, 9826 1955
Babka 358 Brunswick Street, Fitzroy, 9416 0091
Baker D. Chirico shop 3-4, 149 Fitzroy Street, St Kilda, 9534 3777
Firebrand Sourdough Bakery 69 Glen Eira Road, Ripponlea, 9523 0061
Gertrude Street Organic Bakery 226-228 Gertrude Street, Fitzroy, 9417 5998
Il Fornaio 2 Acland Street, St Kilda, 9534 2922
Kingfisher Bakery 371a High Street, Northcote, 9486 6648
Loafer Bread 146 Scotchmer Street, Fitzroy North, 9489 0766
Natural Tucker Bakery 809 Nicholson Street, Carlton North, 9380 4293
Phillippa's Bakery & Provisions Store 1030 High Street, Armadale, 9576 2020
Pure Bread Bakery 114 Union Road, Surrey Hills, 9836 3789

Caterers

The Big Group 38-40 Cubitt Street, Richmond, 9429 0910
Blake's Feast 1412 Malvern Road, Glen Iris, 9821 0669
Damm Fine Foods 31-37 Russell Street, Abbotsford, 9419 4922
Peter Rowland Catering 8 River Street, South Yarra, 9825 0000
Tim Hollands Catering 234 Gertrude Street, Fitzroy, 9417 7504

Cheese

Bill's Farm shop 17-18, Queen Victoria Market deli hall, City, 9328 2003
Cleo's Deli shop 816, Prahran Market, 9827 3074
Curds & Whey shop 12-13, Queen Victoria Market deli hall, City, 9326 9009
Dainties 549 Malvern Road, Hawksburn, 9826 3333
Fred Young of Kew 204 High Street, Kew, 9853 8306
The French Shop shop 1-2, Queen Victoria Market deli hall, City, mobile 0419 347 631
Nick and Sue's Gourmet Deli shop 17-19, Camberwell Market, 9882 8795
Pete 'n' Rosie's shop 713, Prahran Market, 9826 1260
Richmond Hill Cafe & Larder 48-50 Bridge Road, Richmond, 9421 2808

Coffee roasters and retailers

Beraldo Coffee 22 High Street, Northcote, 9482 2899
The Coffee Company 260 Carlisle Street, Balaclava, 9534 6604
Genovese Coffee 2 Nicholson Street, Coburg East, 9383 3300
Grinders Retail Coffee Shop 277 Lygon Street, Carlton, 9347 7520
Jasper Coffee Caffeine Dealers 267 Brunswick Street, Fitzroy, 9416 0921
Quist's Danish Coffee Shop 166 Little Collins Street, City, 9650 1530

Fruit and vegetables

Albert Park Fruit Palace 91 Dundas Place, Albert Park, 9690 4383
Cameron Russell stall 83, I Shed, Queen Victoria Market, City, 9329 3909
Colonial Fruit Company shop M5, Forest Hill Chase, 270 Canterbury Road, Forest Hill, 9878 5955
Mario's Quality Fruit 547 Malvern Road, Toorak, 9827 3714
Mecca Brothers Fruit City 346 Queens Parade, Fitzroy North, 9489 8650
Toscano's of Kew 213-219 High Street, Kew, 9853 7762. Also Victoria Gardens, Richmond, 9429 6064
The Wild Mushroom Specialist shop 116, Prahran Market, 9824 0805

Grocers and providores

David Jones Food Hall 310 Bourke Street, City, 9643 2222. Also 1341 Dandenong Road, Chadstone, 8531 4444
The Essential Ingredient Prahran Market, Elizabeth Street, South Yarra, 9827 9047
Leo's Fine Food & Wine 26 Princess Street, Kew, 9853 8314. Also 131 Burgundy Street, Heidelberg, 9458 4866
Simon Johnson Purveyor of Quality Food 12-14 St David Street, Fitzroy, 9486 9456. Also 471 Toorak Road, Toorak, 9826 2588

Markets

Camberwell Fresh Food Market 521 Riversdale Road, Camberwell, 9539 1361
CERES Saturday Morning Organic Market 8 Lee Street, Brunswick East, 9387 2609
Collingwood Children's Farm Farmers' Market, St Heliers Street, Abbotsford, mobile 0429 146 627
Footscray Market corner Hopkins & Leeds Streets, Footscray, 9687 1205
Prahran Market 163-185 Commercial Road, Prahran, 8290 8220
Preston Market between Murray Road & Cramer Street, Preston, 9478 3130
Queen Victoria Market corner Victoria & Elizabeth Streets, City, 9320 5822
Richmond Saturday Morning Market Gleadell Street, Richmond, 9205 5555 (Yarra City Council)
South Melbourne Market corner Cecil & Coventry Streets, South Melbourne, 9209 6295

Meat and poultry

Andrew's Choice 24 Anderson Street, Yarraville, 9687 2419
Belmore Meats 340 Belmore Road, Balwyn, 9857 9379
Brenta Meats 103 Station Street, Fairfield, 9489 0820
The Chicken Pantry shop 85-86, Queen Victoria Market deli hall, City, 9329 6417
Clarendon Street Meats 294 Clarendon Street, South Melbourne, 9690 2337
Donati's Fine Meats 402 Lygon Street, Carlton, 9347 4948
Excell Meat Company 307 Lygon Street, Carlton, 9347 5516
Geo Tennent & Sons Poulterers 6 Gold Street, Collingwood, 9417 4893
Hagen's Certified Biodynamic Meats shop 509, Prahran Market, 9827 1899. Also shop 16, Queen Victoria Market meat hall, 9329 5534
John Cester Poultry & Game shop 506, Prahran Market, 9827 6111
Jonathan's of Collingwood 122 Smith Street, Collingwood, 9419 4339
Peter Bouchier Butchers 551 Malvern Road, Toorak, 9827 3629. Also David Jones food halls City & Chadstone
Polkinghorne's shop 210, Bay Street, Port Melbourne, 9646 9304. Also Albert Park, 9686 3351, & Richmond, 9427 9136

Organics

Fresh at Elwood 130-132 Ormond Road, Elwood, 9531 4130
The Green Grocer 217 St Georges Road, Fitzroy North, 9489 1747
The Organic Grocery 318 Bridge Road, Richmond, 9429 9219
Organically Grown 190 Glenferrie Road, Malvern, 9500 9796
The Organic Union 137 Union Road, Surrey Hills, 9890 1292
Organic Wholefoods 452 Lygon Street, Brunswick East, 9384 0288. Also 277 Smith Street, Fitzroy, 9419 5347
Passionfoods 219 Ferrars Street, South Melbourne, 9690 9339
Plump Organic Grocery 24 Ballarat Street, Yarraville, 9687 6422
Rhubarb, Rhubarb Organics stall 138, Preston Market, 9478 7344
Superfruit 228 Waterdale Road, Ivanhoe, 9497 1055
Vic Market Organics stall 55-61, I Shed, Queen Victoria Market, City, 9328 1425

Pasta

Donnini's Pasta 398 Lygon Street, Carlton, 9347 1655. Also Canterbury, 9888 5722, & Toorak, 9826 9199
Farinacci Fresh Pasta 662 Glen Huntly Road, Caulfield, 9528 6076
Pasta Fresca 171 Centre Road, Bentleigh, 9557 5269
Traditional Pasta Shop shop 3-4, Queen Victoria Market deli hall, mobile 0419 322 785
Ubaldi Foods 307 Edwardes Street, Reservoir, 9462 3222

Seafood

Camberwell Market Seafoods shop 4, Camberwell Market, 9882 5019
Canals Seafood 703 Nicholson Street, Carlton North, 9380 4537
Clamms Fast Fish 141 Acland Street, St Kilda, 9534 1917
Claringbold's Seafood shop 510, Prahran Market, 9826 8381
Kingfisher Seafoods & Sushi shop 11, Camberwell Market, 9882 4467
Planet Seafood shop 4, Extra Fresh Centre, 284 Centre Road, Bentleigh, 9563 9211

Wine stores

Armadale Cellars 813-817 High Street, Armadale, 9509 3055
Boccaccio Cellars 1030 Burke Road, Balwyn, 9817 2257
Botanical Wine Store 169 Domain Road, South Yarra, 9820 7888
Dan Murphy's 789 Heidelberg Road, Alphington, 9497 3388. Other stores throughout Melbourne.
Prince Wine Store 2a Acland Street, St Kilda, 9536 1155
Randall The Wine Merchant 186 Bridport Street, Albert Park, 9686 4122. Also 324-26 Pakington Street, Newtown, Geelong, 5223 1141
Rathdowne Cellars 348 Rathdowne Street, Carlton North, 349 3366

World food

A1 Bakery (Middle Eastern) 643 Sydney Road, Brunswick, 9386 0440
Aegean Food (Greek) 32 Centre Way, Preston Market, 9478 5243
Casa Iberica (Spanish/Portuguese) 25 Johnston Street, Fitzroy, 9419 4420
Enoteca Sileno (Italian) 21 Amess Street, Carlton North, 9347 5044
Great Eastern Grocery (Asian) 185 Russell Street, City, 9663 3716
Minh Phat (Asian) 178-180 Victoria Street, Richmond North, 9429 4028
Oriental Food & Grocery (Korean) 117 Koornang Road, Carnegie, 9572 2341
Suzuran Japan Foods Trading (Japanese) 1025-1027 Burke Road, Hawthorn, 9882 2349
Thuan Hung Grocery (Asian) 55b Carrington Road, Box Hill, 9898 1612
Viva Spain (Spanish) 315 Victoria Street, West Melbourne, 9329 0485

Visit Williamstown – join Sam's Crew for a unique dining experience in their Heritage listed **Boat Shed Restaurant**.

Prepared by 5 star chefs, choose from an extensive a-la-carte, seafood or modern Australian menu or enjoy one of their gourmet wood fired pizzas.

Complement your meal with their fine selection of wines and international beers.

Relax and enjoy a unique experience.

Typo

3 Syme Street, Williamstown
Ph 9399 9959 Fax 9399 9294
Email: aatlanta@bigpond.net.au

BHOJ INDIAN RESTAURANTS

Docklands and Templestowe

Winner of Age Good Food Guide prestigious Chef's Hat four years in a row (2000-1-2-3)

We pride ourselves on showcasing the great diversity that is Indian regional cuisine and, in particular, the wonderful flavours of the tandoor and handi.

Bhoj Docklands Indian Restaurant
54 Promenade, Newquay, Docklands
(03) 9600 0884

Bhoj Indian Restaurant
Shop 14, 2nd level 114-116 James St Templestowe
(03) 9846 7799

Sirens invites you to come in, sit down and relax in the creatively restored Williamstown Bathing Pavilion. The original art deco building with its spectacular circular tower, wide deck and seaside location is a Williamstown landmark and the ideal setting for lunch, dinner, afternoon tea or that special function. There are two menus and dining areas to choose from, both with a Mediterranean/International flavour.

The restaurant section is more formally furnished, and has a menu to match, with polished timber floorboards, clean white linen and upholstery set to the theme of the beachside. The stylishly elegant restaurant provides a truly sophisticated dining experience. The exceptionally fine cuisine and extensive selection of local and imported wines has earned the restaurant an outstanding reputation amongst discerning diners.

The bistro could be mistaken for the interior of an ocean liner, with its wooden deck, freshly painted white walls and sea views. Dine alfresco on balmy summer nights or enjoy the warmth of the informal interior in winter. Indulge in a light meal from the modern eclectic menu, coffee and cake while taking in the bay views or a leisurely drink while watching the sunset.

Beach Pavilion, Esplanade, Williamstown
Phone: 9397 7811
7 days a week from 10am till close
www.sirensrestaurant.com.au

Typo

Roti Boti

513 Hampton Street, Hampton
Phone: (03) 9598 5511

A fully licensed family restaurant, Roti Boti has recently been renovated – the third facelift in its seven years of operation, demonstrating a commitment to keeping up to date with the constantly evolving world of cuisine.

BUKHARA

AMERICAN EXPRESS BEST RESTAURANT IN GIPPSLAND

Fully licensed multi award winning restaurant specialising in north-west frontier cuisine. Rendezvous for quality diners and food critics. Prior bookings are advisable.

3/12 Napier Street Warragul, Vic 3820
Telephone: 5622 0025

Curry Curry Indian Restaurant

Flavours as varied as the climate of India, and as exotic as the people. Each dish has its own distinctive flavour, which comes from selected herbs and spices that have to be separately prepared for each individual dish.

Curry Curry Indian Restaurant
Licensed & BYO (Wine Only)
931 Burke Road Camberwell Victoria
Telephone: (03) 9813 2753 **Fax:** (03) 9882 1689
www.currycurry.websyte.com.au

Gaylord

INDIAN TANDOORI RESTAURANT & COCKTAIL BAR

Open lunch Sunday to Friday, Dinner 7 nights. Seats 100. Private function rooms available. Fully licensed and BYO. Live Indian classical music Friday and Saturday.

4 Tattersalls Lane (off Lt Bourke St) Tel: 9663 3980

MELBOURNE CITY

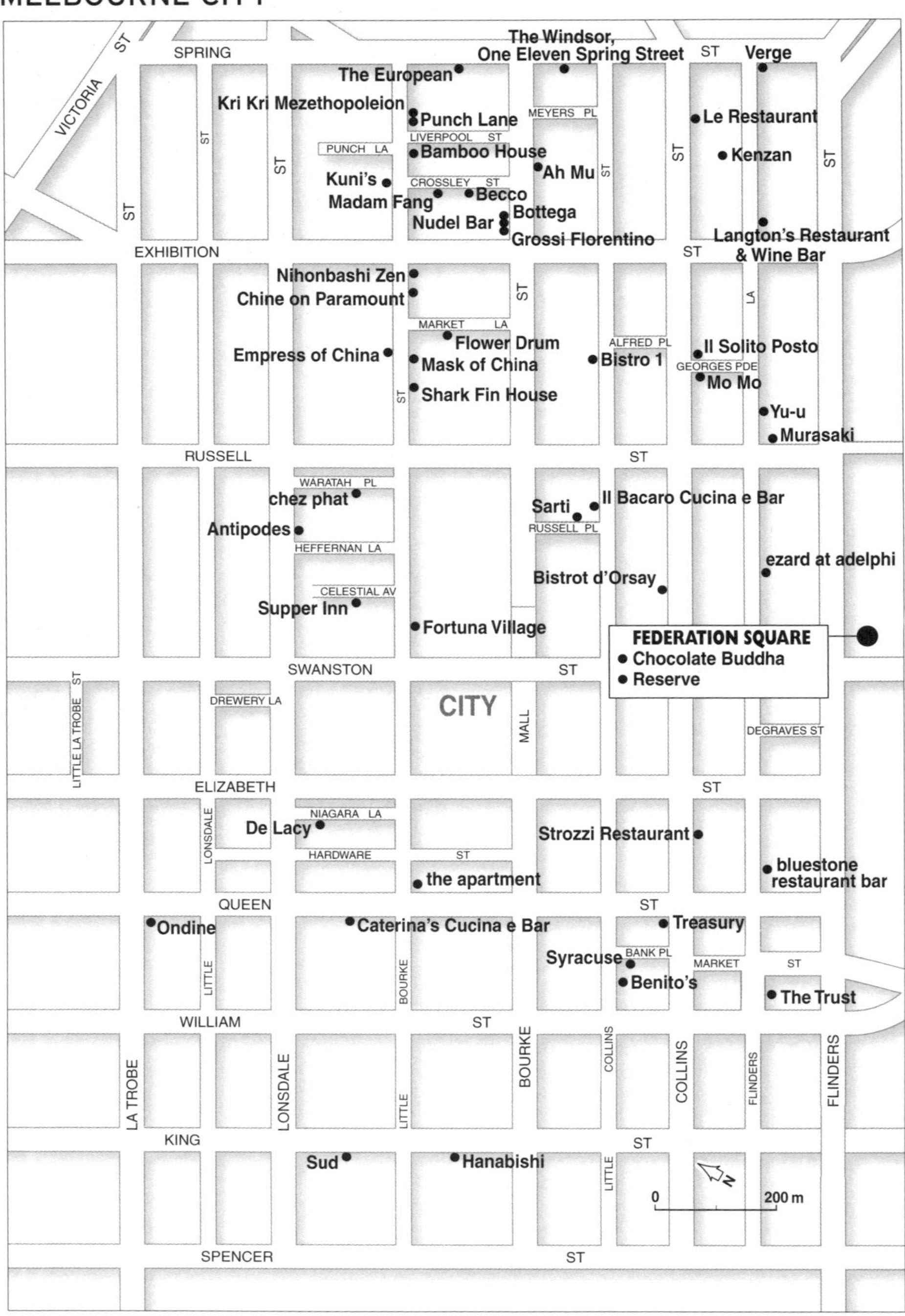

Roti Boti

513 Hampton Street, Hampton
Phone: (03) 9598 5511

A fully licensed family restaurant, Roti Boti has recently been renovated – the third facelift in its seven years of operation, demonstrating a commitment to keeping up to date with the constantly evolving world of cuisine.

BUKHARA

AMERICAN EXPRESS BEST RESTAURANT IN GIPPSLAND

Fully licensed multi award winning restaurant specialising in north-west frontier cuisine. Rendezvous for quality diners and food critics. Prior bookings are advisable.

3/12 Napier Street Warragul, Vic 3820
Telephone: 5622 0025

Curry Curry
Indian Restaurant

Flavours as varied as the climate of India, and as exotic as the people. Each dish has its own distinctive flavour, which comes from selected herbs and spices that have to be separately prepared for each individual dish.

Curry Curry Indian Restaurant
Licensed & BYO (Wine Only)
931 Burke Road Camberwell Victoria
Telephone: (03) 9813 2753 **Fax:** (03) 9882 1689
www.currycurry.websyte.com.au

MELBOURNE CITY

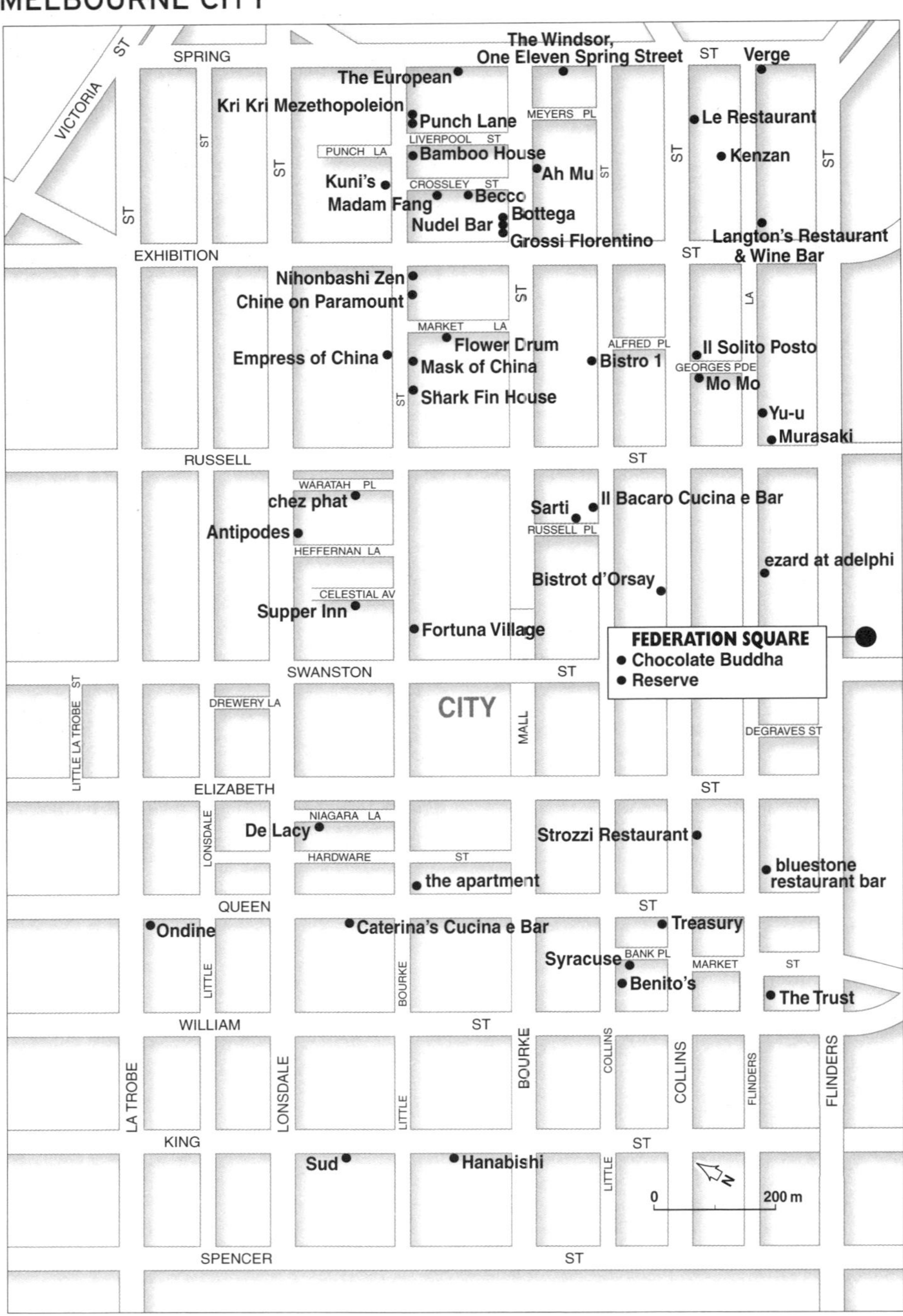

ST KILDA TO ELWOOD

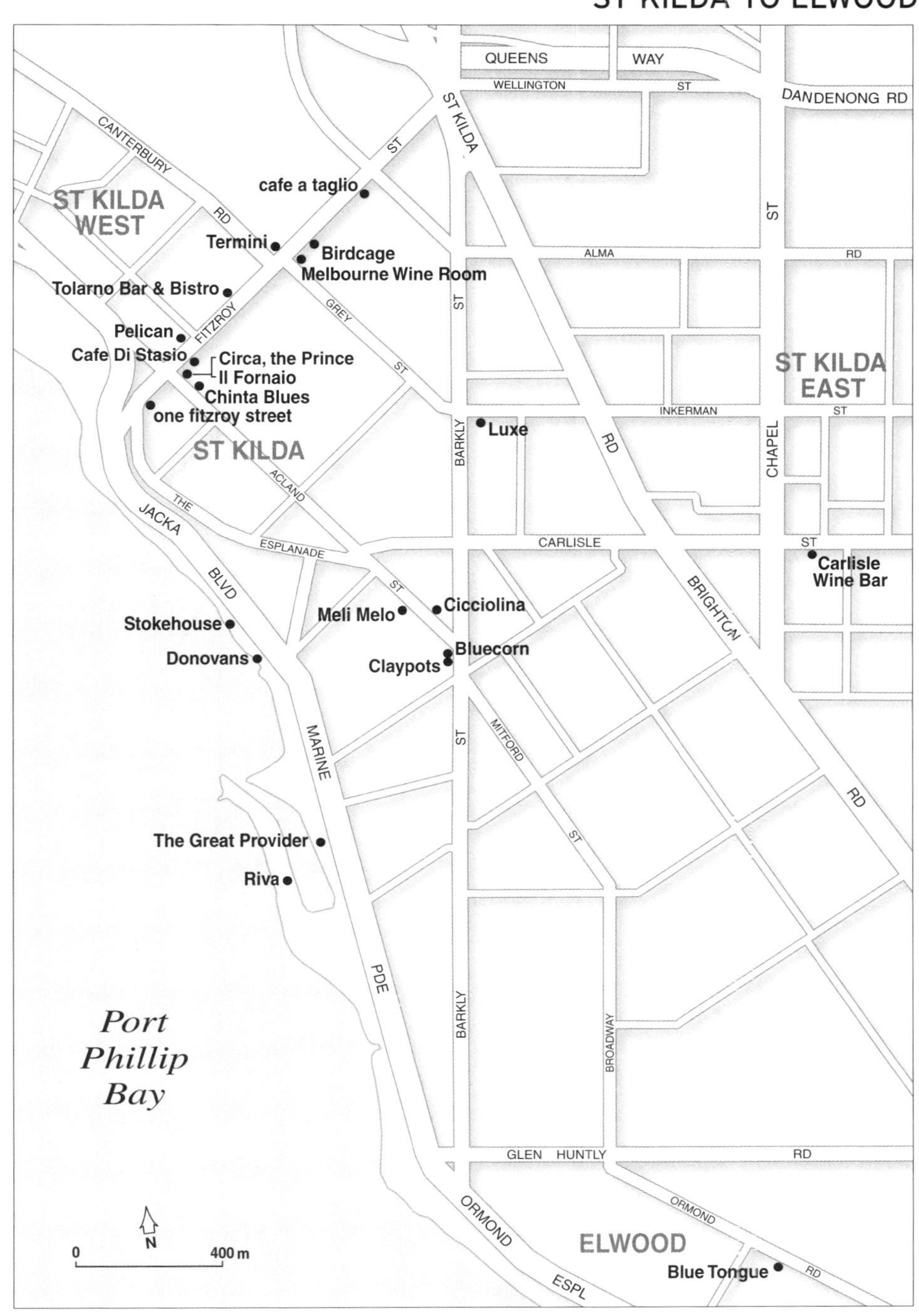

WEST MELBOURNE TO CARLTON NORTH

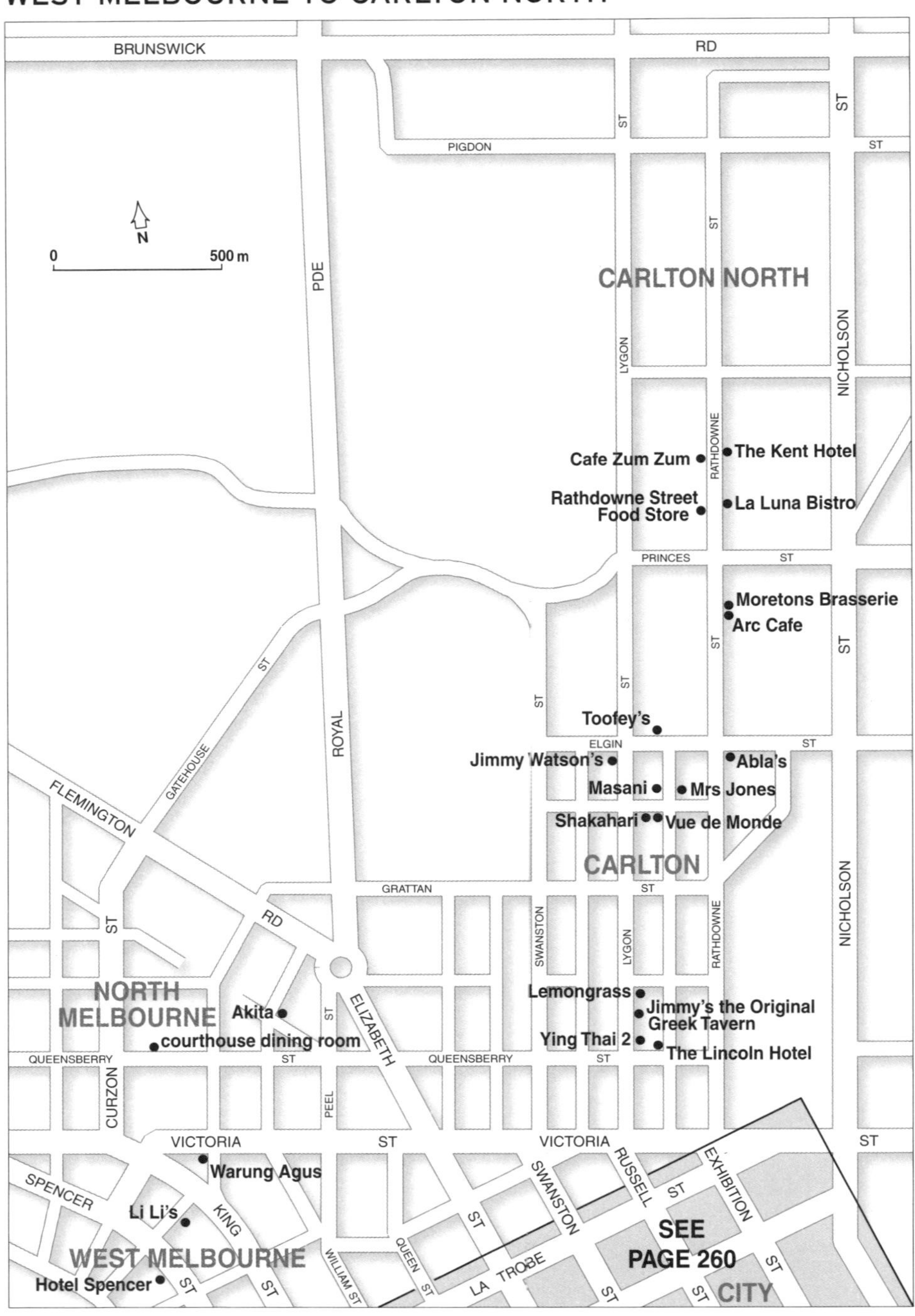

Hibiscus Restaurant & Bar
CLIFTON HILL
FITZROY NORTH
Matteo's
North Fitzroy Star
NICHOLSON ST
ST GEORGES RD
QUEENS PDE
HEIDELBERG RD
PRINCES ST
ALEXANDRA PDE
SEE INSET
JOHNSTON ST
Jim's Greek Tavern
FITZROY
Diningroom 211
Kazen
Red Rice
Blue Chillies
Old Kingdom
SMITH ST
NAPIER ST
BRUNSWICK ST
COLLINGWOOD
0
500 m
N
ABBOTSFORD
The Carringbush Dining Room
LANGRIDGE ST
GERTRUDE ST
VICTORIA PDE
Zio's Ristorante
Le Gourmet
ALBERT ST
radii
CLARENDON ST
SPRING ST
SEE PAGE 260
EAST MELBOURNE
Prodigy
Toey's
WELLINGTON PDE
JOLIMONT
CITY
HODDLE ST
SEE PAGE 265
RICHMOND NORTH
BRIDGE RD
LENNOX ST
idibidi
0
200 m
A & V Lazar Charcoal Grill & Seafood Restaurant
Pireaus Blues
Mao's

NORTHERN & WESTERN SUBURBS

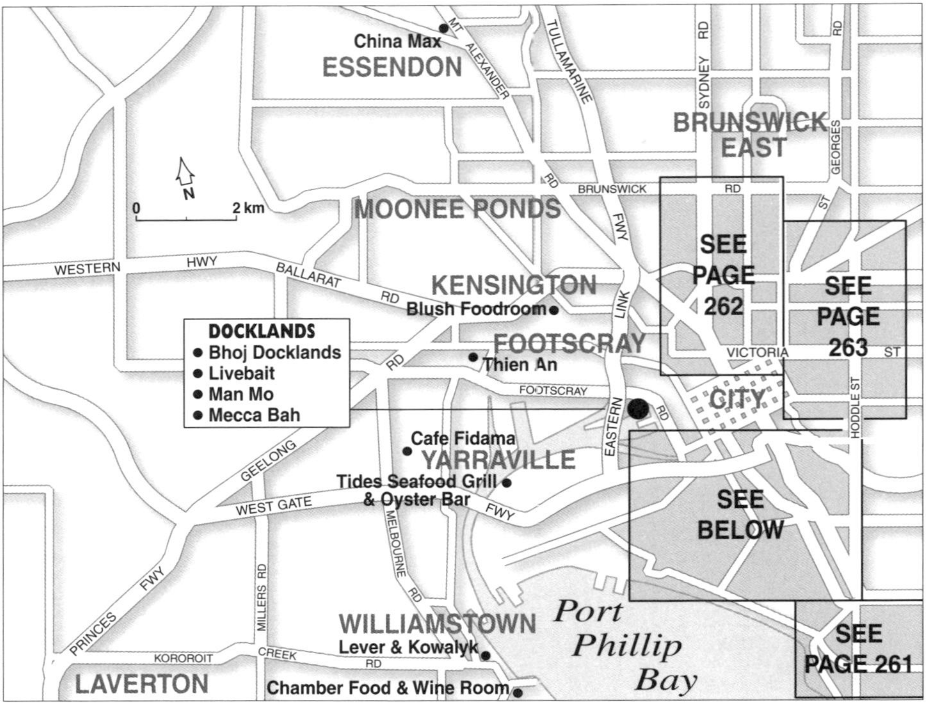

China Max
ESSENDON
MT ALEXANDER
TULLAMARINE
SYDNEY RD
RD
BRUNSWICK EAST
GEORGES
ST
N
0 2 km
RD
BRUNSWICK
RD
FWY
MOONEE PONDS
SEE PAGE 262
SEE PAGE 263
WESTERN HWY
BALLARAT RD
KENSINGTON
Blush Foodroom
LINK
DOCKLANDS
• Bhoj Docklands
• Livebait
• Man Mo
• Mecca Bah
RD
FOOTSCRAY
Thien An
VICTORIA ST
FOOTSCRAY RD
CITY
HODDLE ST
EASTERN
RD
Cafe Fidama
YARRAVILLE
GEELONG
Tides Seafood Grill & Oyster Bar
WEST GATE FWY
SEE BELOW
MELBOURNE RD
MILLERS RD
PRINCES FWY
WILLIAMSTOWN
Port Phillip Bay
Lever & Kowalyk
SEE PAGE 261
KOROROIT CREEK RD
LAVERTON
Chamber Food & Wine Room

INNER SOUTHERN SUBURBS

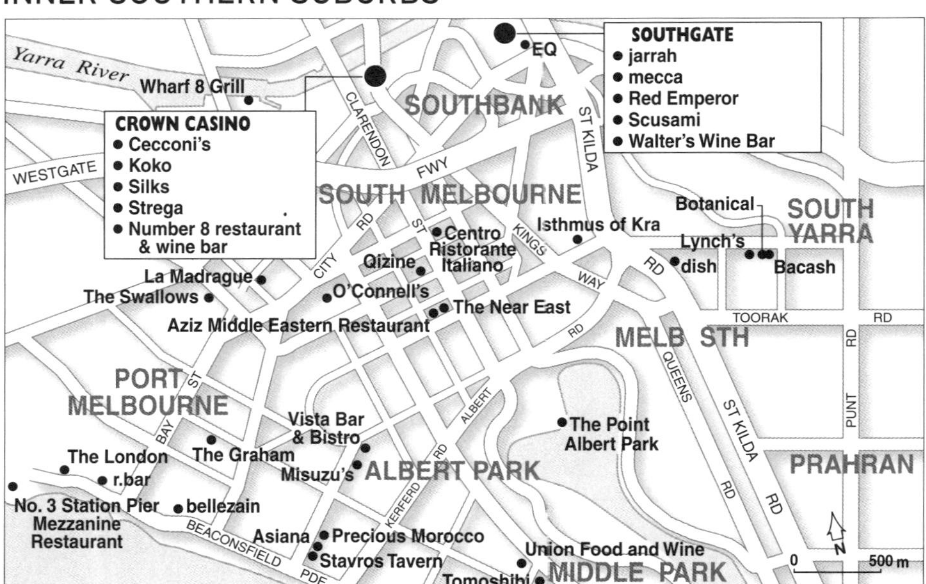

INNER SOUTH-EASTERN SUBURBS

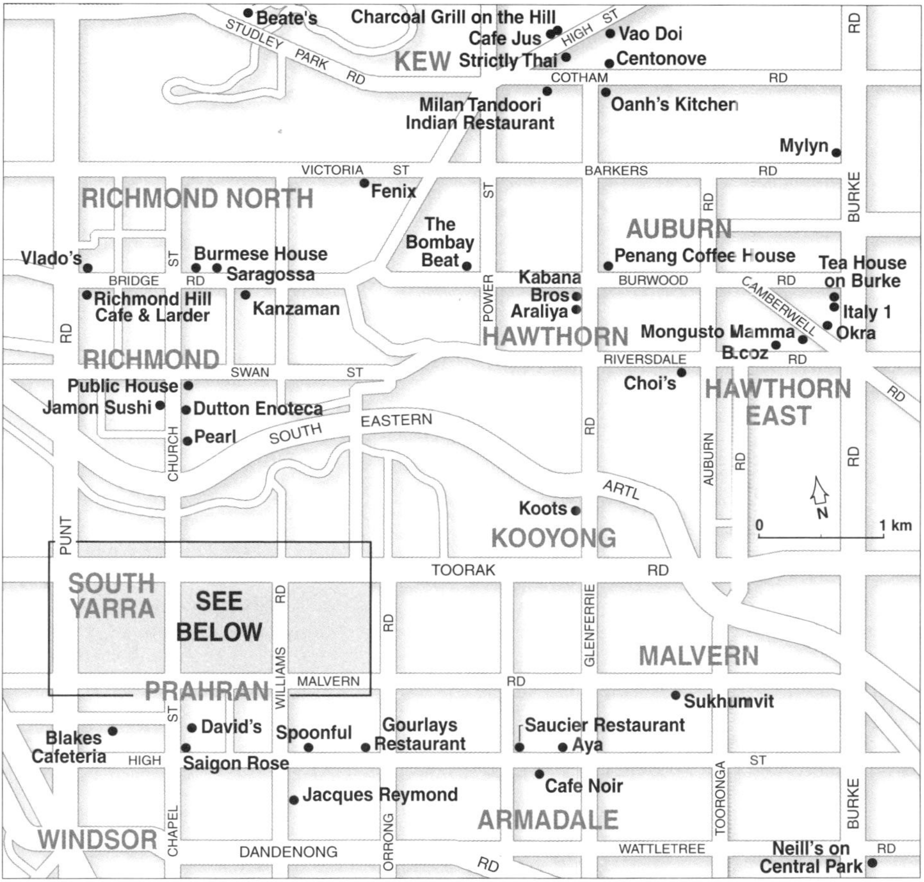

Beate's
Charcoal Grill on the Hill
Cafe Jus
Vao Doi
Strictly Thai
Centonove
KEW
STUDLEY PARK RD
HIGH ST
COTHAM RD
Milan Tandoori Indian Restaurant
Oanh's Kitchen
Mylyn
VICTORIA ST
BARKERS RD
RICHMOND NORTH
Fenix
The Bombay Beat
AUBURN
Penang Coffee House
Vlado's
Burmese House
Saragossa
BRIDGE RD
Richmond Hill Cafe & Larder
Kanzaman
Kabana Bros
Araliya
BURWOOD RD
CAMBERWELL RD
Tea House on Burke
Italy 1
Okra
Mongusto
Mamma
B.coz
RICHMOND
HAWTHORN
SWAN ST
RIVERSDALE RD
Public House
Jamon Sushi
Dutton Enoteca
Pearl
Choi's
HAWTHORN EAST
SOUTH EASTERN ARTL
CHURCH ST
POWER ST
AUBURN RD
BURKE RD
Koots
KOOYONG
PUNT RD
N
0
1 km
TOORAK RD
SOUTH YARRA
SEE BELOW
WILLIAMS RD
GLENFERRIE RD
MALVERN
PRAHRAN
MALVERN RD
Sukhumvit
Blakes Cafeteria
David's
Spoonful
Gourlays Restaurant
Saucier Restaurant
Aya
HIGH ST
Saigon Rose
Cafe Noir
Jacques Reymond
ARMADALE
TOORONGA RD
WINDSOR
CHAPEL ST
ORRONG RD
DANDENONG RD
WATTLETREE RD
Neill's on Central Park

TOORAK & SOUTH YARRA

Ciccia Bomba
France-Soir
Harveys
Da Noi
TOORAK RD
Orita's
Tribeca Restaurant Bar
GRANGE RD
Haggers
Pacific Seafood BBQ House
Viet's Quan
SOUTH YARRA
Caffe e Cucina
TOORAK
PUNT RD
CHAPEL ST
CROMWELL ST
WILLIAMS RD
MATHOURA RD
PRAHRAN
N
0
300 m
Bistro Thierry
Hibari
Cafe Latte
Mizu
Sweet Basil
Cafe Four Seasons
COMMERCIAL RD
MALVERN RD

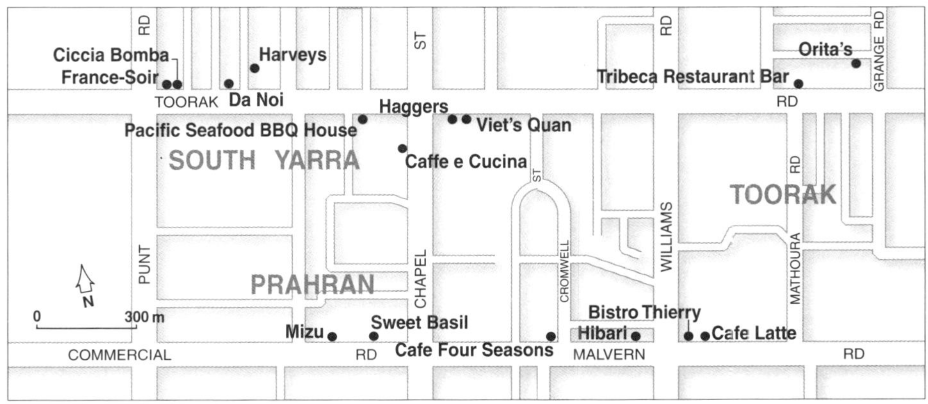

EASTERN & SOUTHERN SUBURBS

HILLS, YARRA VALLEY & MORNINGTON PENINSULA

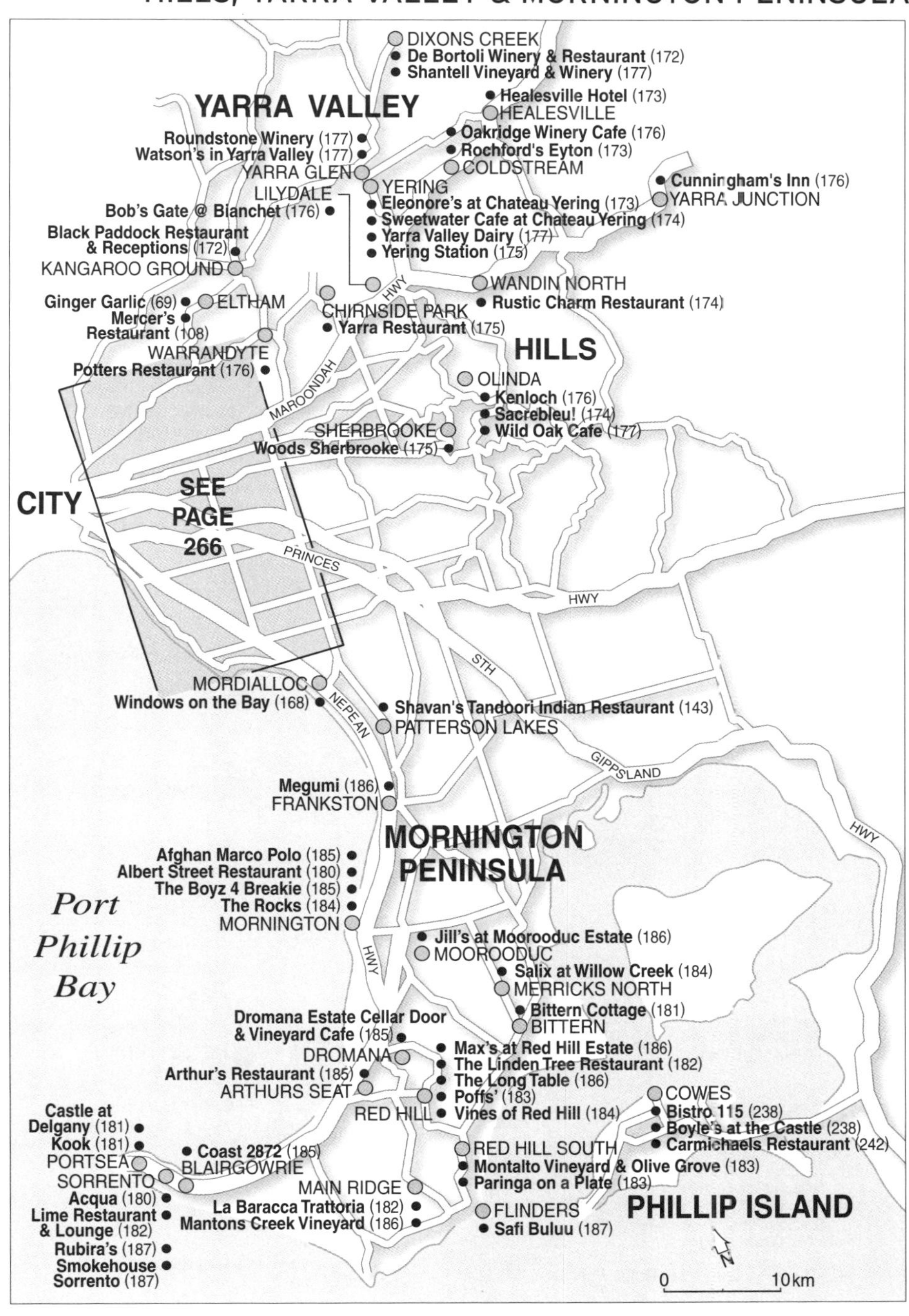

VICTORIAN COUNTRY

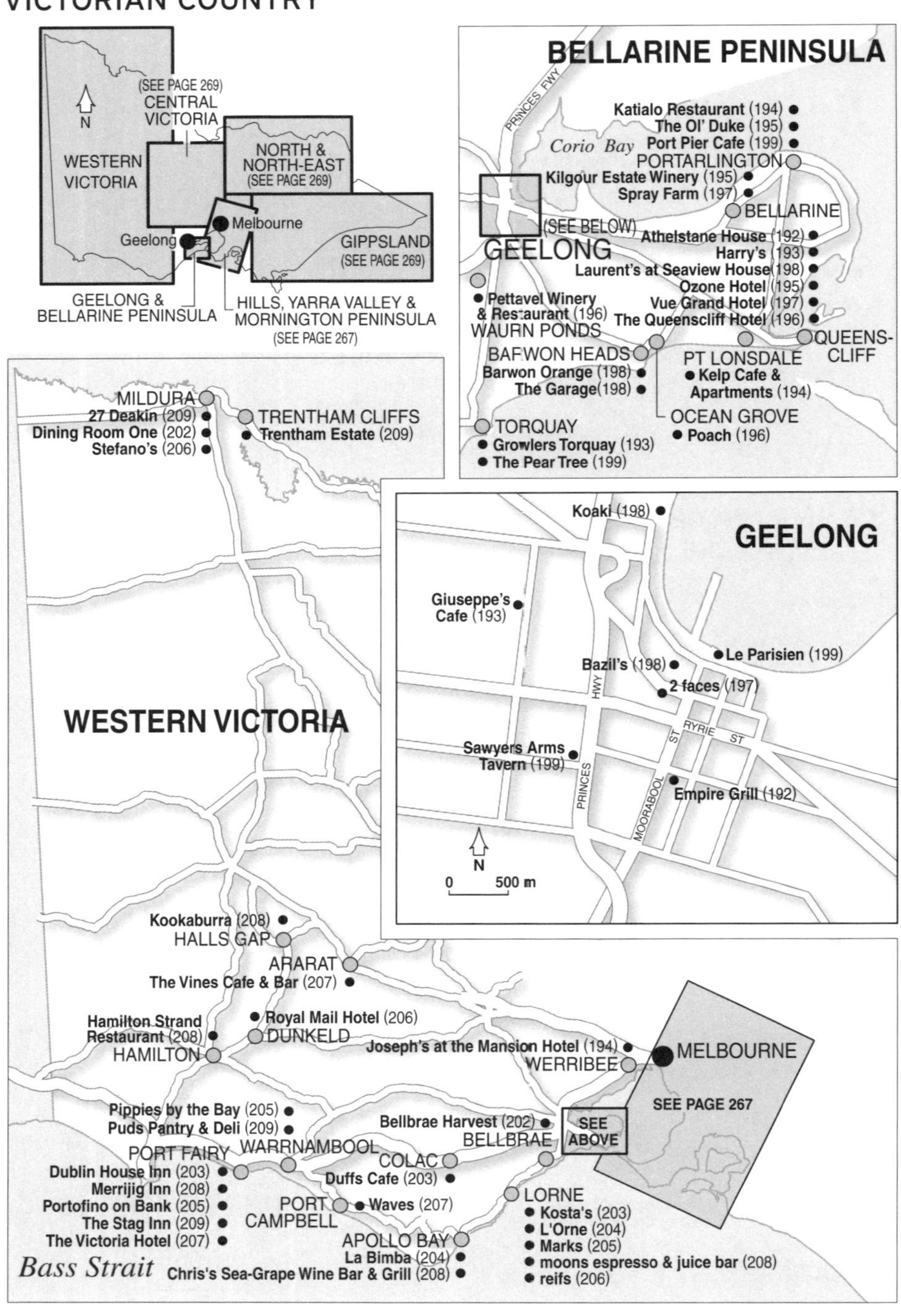

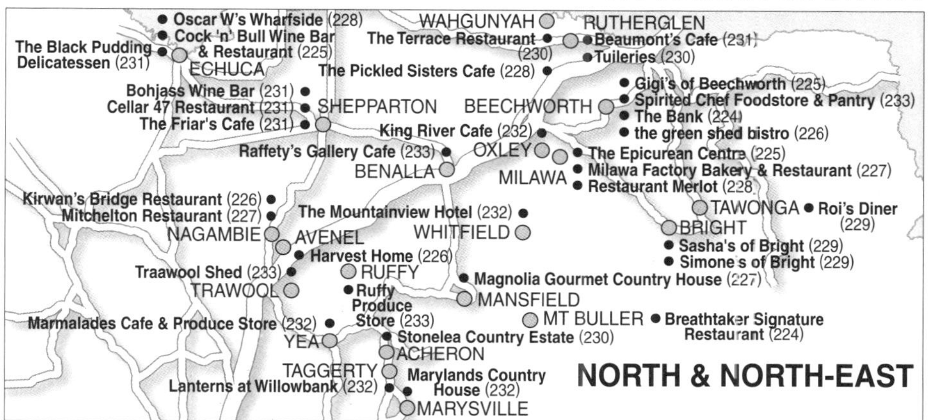

NORTH & NORTH-EAST
Oscar W's Wharfside (228)
Cock 'n' Bull Wine Bar & Restaurant (225)
The Black Pudding Delicatessen (231)
ECHUCA
WAHGUNYAH
RUTHERGLEN
The Terrace Restaurant (230)
Beaumont's Cafe (231)
Tuileries (230)
The Pickled Sisters Cafe (228)
Bohjass Wine Bar (231)
Cellar 47 Restaurant (231)
The Friar's Cafe (231)
SHEPPARTON
BEECHWORTH
Gigi's of Beechworth (225)
Spirited Chef Foodstore & Pantry (233)
The Bank (224)
the green shed bistro (226)
King River Cafe (232)
Raffety's Gallery Cafe (233)
OXLEY
The Epicurean Centre (225)
BENALLA
MILAWA
Milawa Factory Bakery & Restaurant (227)
Restaurant Merlot (228)
Kirwan's Bridge Restaurant (226)
Mitchelton Restaurant (227)
The Mountainview Hotel (232)
TAWONGA
Roi's Diner (229)
NAGAMBIE
AVENEL
WHITFIELD
BRIGHT
Harvest Home (226)
Sasha's of Bright (229)
Simone's of Bright (229)
Traawool Shed (233)
RUFFY
TRAWOOL
Ruffy Produce Store (233)
Magnolia Gourmet Country House (227)
MANSFIELD
Marmalades Cafe & Produce Store (232)
MT BULLER
Breathtaker Signature Restaurant (224)
YEA
Stonelea Country Estate (230)
ACHERON
TAGGERTY
Lanterns at Willowbank (232)
Marylands Country House (232)
MARYSVILLE

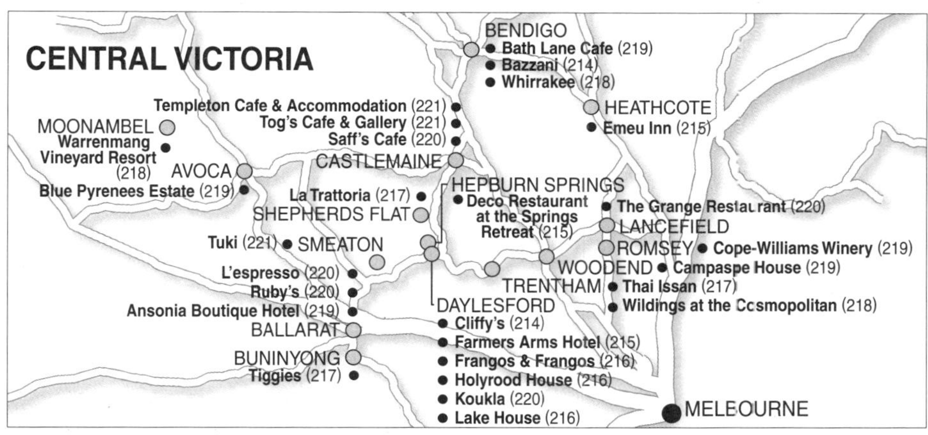

CENTRAL VICTORIA
BENDIGO
Bath Lane Cafe (219)
Bazzani (214)
Whirrakee (218)
Templeton Cafe & Accommodation (221)
Tog's Cafe & Gallery (221)
Saff's Cafe (220)
HEATHCOTE
Emeu Inn (215)
MOONAMBEL
Warrenmang Vineyard Resort (218)
AVOCA
CASTLEMAINE
Blue Pyrenees Estate (219)
HEPBURN SPRINGS
La Trattoria (217)
Deco Restaurant at the Springs Retreat (215)
SHEPHERDS FLAT
The Grange Restaurant (220)
LANCEFIELD
Tuki (221)
SMEATON
ROMSEY
Cope-Williams Winery (219)
L'espresso (220)
WOODEND
Campaspe House (219)
Ruby's (220)
TRENTHAM
Thai Issan (217)
Ansonia Boutique Hotel (219)
DAYLESFORD
Wildings at the Cosmopolitan (218)
BALLARAT
Cliffy's (214)
Farmers Arms Hotel (215)
BUNINYONG
Frangos & Frangos (216)
Tiggies (217)
Holyrood House (216)
Koukla (220)
Lake House (216)
MELBOURNE

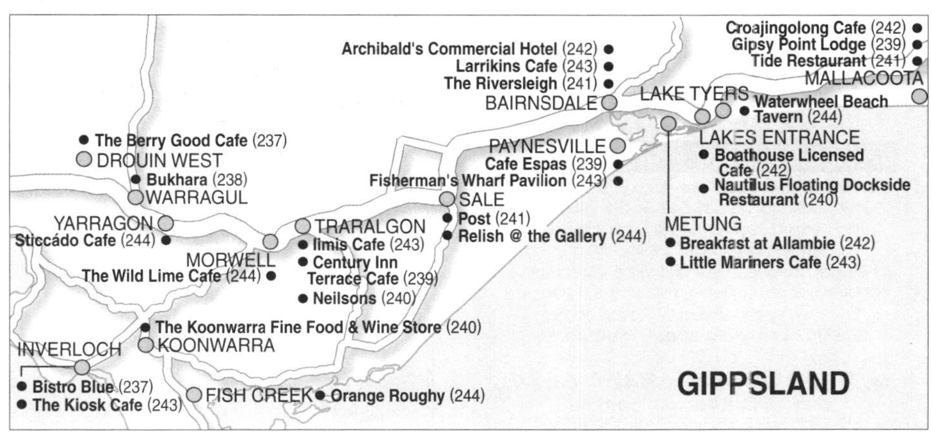

GIPPSLAND
Croajingolong Cafe (242)
Gipsy Point Lodge (239)
Tide Restaurant (241)
MALLACOOTA
Archibald's Commercial Hotel (242)
Larrikins Cafe (243)
The Riversleigh (241)
BAIRNSDALE
LAKE TYERS
Waterwheel Beach Tavern (244)
The Berry Good Cafe (237)
DROUIN WEST
PAYNESVILLE
LAKES ENTRANCE
Cafe Espas (239)
Boathouse Licensed Cafe (242)
Bukhara (238)
Fisherman's Wharf Pavilion (243)
Nautilus Floating Dockside Restaurant (240)
WARRAGUL
SALE
YARRAGON
TRARALGON
Post (241)
METUNG
Sticcádo Cafe (244)
Ilmis Cafe (243)
Relish @ the Gallery (244)
Breakfast at Allambie (242)
MORWELL
Century Inn Terrace Cafe (239)
Little Mariners Cafe (243)
The Wild Lime Cafe (244)
Neilsons (240)
The Koonwarra Fine Food & Wine Store (240)
INVERLOCH
KOONWARRA
Bistro Blue (237)
The Kiosk Cafe (243)
FISH CREEK
Orange Roughy (244)

Gurkhas

The Place for Nepalese food

Licensed & BYO wine

Experience the taste of Himalayan Kingdom at

Gurkha's Brasserie: 190 Chapel Street, Prahran. Tel: 9510 3325

Gurkha's Cafe: 360 Bridge Road, Richmond. Tel: 9425 9007

Gurkhas: 258 Lygon Street, Carlton. Tel: 9663 3119

Web: www.gurkhas.com.au

A refreshing cafe/restaurant/bar rich in urban cultures, with a menu that encompasses an array of light snacks through to more indulgent fare.

Innovative, yet simple.

330 Cardigan St, Carlton

Ph: 9347 0891

Open 10am til late

Breakfast Sat and Sun

Typo

AWARD WINNING

Greek Restaurant – Bar – Taverna

Dion is the fashionable new face of Melbourne's Greek precinct on Lonsdale St. (By the Age). Fully licensed, imported and local wines and spirits (limited BYO wine only).

Extensive seafood, meat and vegetarian menu.

Banquets for private functions up to 100 people.

DJ music upon request. Al Fresco dining.

205-207 Lonsdale Street, Melbourne

(next to MEDALLION CAFE – Cakes)

Tel: **9650 4050** Fax: **9484 6474**

www.dionrestaurant.com.au

Typo

Situated in North Balwyn and highly recommended by The Age Epicure.

Dunyazad offers banquets for groups and business functions – seating 180.

Belly Dancing every Friday and Saturday nights

OPEN 7 DAYS

9857 8778

329 Doncaster Road, NORTH BALWYN

BAMBOO TERRACE

Chinese Restaurant

Fully Licensed & BYO Wine

201 Bulleen Rd, Bulleen. Phone: 9852 0541

Only Ten minutes from C.B.D.

One can have

THE FINEST DINING EXPERIENCE IN PICTURESQUE GARDEN SURROUNDING WITH AMPLE PARKING

LUNCH & DINNER SEVEN DAYS

YUM CHA LUNCH DAILY

IT DOESN'T NEED TO BE A SPECIAL OCCASION TO PULL OUT THE

SILVER

SILVER SERIES

We've taken some old favourites and given them a polish to create our exciting new Silver Series. The range is made up of French Cask Chardonnay, Cabernet Merlot, Riesling, Shiraz, Verdelho and Sparkling Chardonnay Pinot Noir.

CLEMENGER 2532 WOR

INDEXES

Numbers in italics are minor references.

ALPHABETICAL INDEX

INDEX BY SUBURB OR TOWN

INDEX BY CUISINE/STYLE

BYO INDEX

GOOD BARS INDEX

GOOD BREAKFAST INDEX

GOOD VALUE INDEX

GOOD WINE LIST INDEX

GOOD VEGETARIAN INDEX

WINERIES AND WINE STORES INDEX

ACCOMMODATION INDEX

PRIVATE ROOMS INDEX

For People of Strength, Soul, and Spirit

Revised September 2012
First printing July 1996

ISBN: 1-4792-3701-9
ISBN-13: 9781479237012

For People of Strength, Soul, and Spirit

Seven Guidelines for Life & Career Success

Deborah L. Parker

Jackie,
All the best as you
use the power of
your strength, soul
+ spirit
Deborah
November 2012

Dedication

To the ancestors…

Family, blood, tribal, loved, community and beyond

From their memories, my soul responds

On their strength, I continue to climb

In their spirit, learning remains

"You are young, gifted, and Black. We must begin to tell our young, There's a world waiting for you, Yours is the quest that's just begun."
James Weldon Johnson

Books by Deborah L. Parker

- *Navigating Life's Roadways: Stories of Insight from My Odyssey and Inspiration for Your Journey* (Print and eBook Kindle) July 2011

- *Life is a Review! Observations and Collections of My Passages through The Times* (eBook Kindle only) June 2012

- Contributor, *Sister Strength A Collection of Devotionals for and From African-American Women,* compiled by Rev. Dr. Suzan Johnson Cook, October 1998

All books are available on Amazon.

Websites: www.navigatinglifesroadways.com
www.deborahlynnparker.com

"Reviews of Navigating Life's Roadways"

Warm, engaging and affirming
It amazes me that we think we are all different, yet our journeys have a lot in common. I enjoyed seeing the world through the lens Deborah uses in her book. The affirmation I felt while reading the book came from a deep resonance that in the end, we are all travelers to the same takes her road with grace, fortitude and her hands firmly on the wheel.

Fellow traveler
As a pancreatic cancer survivor, I felt like a fellow traveler with Deborah along life's roadways. Her descriptions are very

personal and extremely full of wisdom. I am a Japanese American woman whose life crossed paths with Deborah's briefly but deeply. I am so glad she wrote this book that continues to inspire me whenever I need to be challenged and uplifted!

Beautiful

What a wonderful book! Each section starts with a quotation that shows its relevance to Deborah's life … to all of our lives. I don't think there will be anyone who will not identify in some way with the challenges and triumphs that Deborah experiences.

On the Cover Image:

1. The view of a fishing village on the Gambia River near Banjul, The Gambia West Africa
2. A baobab tree in Senegal West Africa
3. Goree Island Slave Castle, Senegal West Africa
4. Family keepsakes: A family bible stories book that belonged to my great grandfather (circa 1908) beside a scroll of the 23rd Psalm (a gift I gave my mother for her last Christmas 2009)
5. My late mother doing what she enjoyed, working in the soil
6. The road I grew up on in Waverly Virginia
7. Family keepsakes: A stool my grandfather built (circa 1960), my mother's coffee pot and grandmother's baking pan (circa 1960)

Image Design by: Miss Sydne Brown (the author's niece)

All photos were either taken by or belong to the author, from travels to West Africa (1996) and of family keepsakes.

Table of Contents

Prologue–People of the Mighty

Our stories are timeless and tested. They are about us, a people of tremendous strength—from ancestral times to present day—who have survived the indignities of forced outsider status and deliberate degradation for far too long. Driven nonetheless, we have reconstructed and succeeded. Inscribed in our minds and in the books of the ages, this history both fuels us and angers us at times.

Even so, our songs are full of love and life—and the ups and downs of both. They are soulful with the rhythms of a heart that is in sync with nature and wonderment.

Our struggles are real and rugged. They beckon our memory to the highest callings of the spirit, to help us rejoice and to overcome. Led by a way to the truth of who we were created to be, in spite of the slights, we honor those who entered the all-consuming fight for freedom.

We need those stories, songs, and struggles. They are our trifecta! The world has bet against us, and yet we remain triumphant through it all. Circling the African diaspora, no matter where the forced ancestral boats stopped, these narratives ring true. They are—we are—resilient!

This skin hue binds us together. Our art, music, phrasings, and sassy personas root us in this journey from the huts, slave quarters, plantations, and shotgun houses of yesteryear to the varied residences in which we live in today. Our suffering has yielded progress. The fruits of a multitude's labor are seen in the extensive display of our talents and creativity as people of strength, soul, and spirit.

Now this is not meant to glorify our past, but yet, having survived the harshness of our journey to here, we have reason to shout "Hallelujah!"

Because we are: A mighty people!

And we are not done yet.

Why?

First it's time to recognize: our history and progress. As of this writing, 2013 stands to be a pivotal year in the African American story. On January 1, 1863—150 years ago—the Emancipation Proclamation ended slavery. On August 28, 1963—50 years ago—thousands rallied for the historic March on Washington, culminating with Martin Luther King Jr.'s "I Have a Dream" speech. April 4, 2013, marks the 45th anniversary of Dr. King's assassination in 1968, following his "I've Been to the Mountaintop" speech the previous evening. These are celebratory events and chronicles to sear deeply into our risings and goings.

Then, there's plenty of work still to be done. As the 1970's R&B group Harold Melvin & the Blue Notes sung in the words to *Wake Up Everybody,* "The world has changed so very much from what it used to be, There is so much hatred war an' poverty."

Yes, today's society, home, and workplace are challenging—on many scales, local and global. Much is expected of our resolve in this complex and fluid environment. Economic and job market woes lend no favor to us. The line between our traditional 'nine-to-five' and having any kind of life outside of work tends to blur. Unresolved pain from the past eats at our core and community. Personal habits lurk, ready to tear us apart from stress, technology or addictions. Around every corner a new and perplexing issue looms, summoning and quite possibly ready to ensnare our strength, soul, and spirit. Whether it is making career choices, enduring weariness on our journey, attending to family grounding, or confronting global dilemmas—these realities present threats to our wellbeing. And yes, race still very much matters, as a card played or stereotype portrayed. Other–isms are present and block as well, be they based on class, age, or gender.

There are also times when we can't identify the solutions to some very complicated problems. However there are points at which the answers are simplistic, based on fundamental guidelines that have weathered the years, tears, and fears of eras past.

Emancipated and thrust forward from groundswell movements, such as the one for civil rights, what can we now proclaim to guide us through?

"The elders of a community are the voice of God."
~ Nigerian proverb

In this shifting landscape, we may tend to forget "what the old folks say." Most of us probably now realize that our ancestors did indeed have it right! Their common-sense ways allowed them to get through the worst of conditions throughout history and still we thrive from their bold undertakings. We've packaged up our sorrows and created rhythm and blues in our "sweet soul music". Our strength, inner and physical, has helped us to carry our crosses; it has calmed our fears. These are our chronicles. And our amazing spirit rebounds. As the words of a popular gospel song, *Spiritual,* by artist Donald Lawrence & Co. reminds us, "You're not a natural being having a spiritual experience, but you're a spiritual being living this natural experience." We walk strong in this energy.

A conquering force sustained the old folks and now centers us. Forming a collective of comeback saints, let us rally behind them and move forward. We're called to a new awakening and application of what we've learned from those who've "looked over Jordan." We must now use those common-sense ways as our guidelines. Seven of them, symbolic of a rise to completion and for success in our appointed places are:

I. **Know Yourself–The Deep Sources of Your Strength**

II. **Know What You Want–Source Your Soul**

III. **Know Where It's Going On–Update Your Chronicles**

IV. **Know Your Resources–The Strong Do Survive**

V. **Know How to Take Care of Yourself–Ignite and Nourish Life's Fire**

VI. **Know Your History–From the Rising of the Sun**

VII. **Know The Creator–Invite Spirit**

Following these guidelines can firmly root us as we navigate through the challenges of our careers and lives, teaching us how to anchor our perseverance, gratitude, and faith.

Why This Book?

Because the season dictates it, reflected in the crises status of the current times noted earlier. These seven strategy-building techniques provide how-to's in addressing an imminent career or life situation. The guidance they hold could come in handy at any point, whether you are graduating, making a shift in your personal journey, dealing with life's inevitable setbacks, or changing course in your career. In these pages you'll find a message for action. If this isn't where you are, then perhaps you have a family member, community group, or friend who can benefit; use this information to advise them, or give them this book to assist as part of their "personal stimulus package." The goal is to get going wherever you are and supply whatever you need!

Within each of these seven guidelines I provide snapshots of a particular technique or tool to consider, based on your career or life dilemma. Your next step? Do your due diligence for any additional resources in areas where you identify as key strategies for following your declared path. This book is not a one-stop, get-it-all stocked way station of information, but it will encourage you to take the wheel and steer toward your success! Make it your very personal journey to get the results you choose.

Checklist-type exercises and thought-provoking questions are scattered throughout this book. They will be indicated with a **For You** and the symbol ⌖. Opportunities for reflection can yield personal riveting truths. My goal is to set a point, like a compass, with enough information for you to customize to your circumstances. These assessments are designed to help you discover your personal trifecta, the talents you uniquely possess, accompanied by ways of how you might deploy them wisely.

Although the majority of the first four guidelines address career related matters, it really is all related to everyday life. The two blend even more in today's hectic and super-connected world. Our life and career screen shots remain on and in tune with one another, and we constantly switch between the two, a version of multi-tasking.

So what can we further build on? Cultural traditions such as resourcefulness and involvement can support our endeavors for work and in the community. Yet, because of our particular inherited dose of soul, strength, and spirit, we may be inclined to try and go it alone. This independent, do-it-yourself thinking is not a part of our cultural mapping. We come from villages that support the essence of community. So here, within these pages, are a variety of guidelines—picture them as your narrative village.

The style in which this information is presented alternates between poetical and instructional. Statistics are included when necessary and you'll occasionally be given a good old-fashioned "talking to". I am glad to share relevant pieces of my personal anecdotes as examples.

The topics here are serious but I do weave in some levity, for humor is a quality that has sustained our community for centuries. Quotes from some of the foundational authors of our twentieth century writings are used for their guiding words still evoke much respect; they built the historical structure on which we stand. Organizing as they came out of slavery, these determined souls reconstructed and bonded to create a sustainable future. The wisdom of African proverbs is also dispersed in a few places to cement this winding legacy of knowing. Additionally, you'll recognize expressions or clips of songs from the music and musings of our community, lyrics from jazz, spirituals, or funk, which truly hone in on the messages of these guidelines. The rhythm is alive and hopeful and the message can be received.

Even when recording artist John Legend redid *Wake Up Everybody* in 2010, the powerful verses still prompt us to remember, "The world won't get no better We gotta change it, yeah." Just you and me." To create success.

That settles it!

Let the trifecta reign with strength, soul, and spirit.

Introduction

Seek, Know, Guide: Your Story as a Way Station

"He who learns, teaches."
~ Ethiopian Proverb

How does life speak to you? Tell you it's time to move or pause?

Usually an event happens to alert us; there are signs that evoke an awareness and call to take action. These signs are spiritual messages. Maya Angelou is quoted as saying, "Spirit is an invisible force made visible in all life." Clarity revealed.

Our ancestors relied on these spiritual signs as they walked through the bush of Africa, followed the drinking gourd of the Underground Railroad and marched the trails to freedom of the Civil Rights Movement. Having found purpose in Reconstruction, they trekked beyond their bondage and were led to way stations. There they had time to pause and gather energy, a way to return to their own strength. Passion for freedom continuously drove them forward. Migration up north in search of a promised land, ignited the prize of opportunity in their eyes. They steadfastly recognized these messages and felt the enormity of their power. Risks were taken. Weary, but confident, they forged on. So many stories, plenty of grit, goals achieved.

Do we have to reach that far back for these inspirational narratives? Today our current POTUS and FLOTUS possess significant melanin doses originating from the continent (they're black y'all). Gabrielle Douglas, gymnast extraordinaire, got Olympic gold. Bill Cosby moved from the Philly projects to stand-up comedian, actor, and PHD. Steve Harvey tells his listeners everyday that he "got a radio show." John H. Johnson came from his rural upbringing in Arkansas to starting an awesome reading staple of the Black community, Ebony magazine. Venus and Serena dominate tennis from L.A. to London. Ursula Burns went from a NY housing project to heading Xerox.

Your mama, granddaddy, aunt, cousin, YOU did…

Everybody has a story of their past to present, with the mess and miracles in between.

From peanuts to politics, the power of strength, soul, and spirit have covered and propelled our community.

We know these stories, don't we? Shared through media, family gatherings or books, these precious narratives are plain for us all to see. Can we be guided by this awesome energy of their potent accounts in our life and careers?

Are you attuned to the station to hear the message?

Seek Truths From Your Story

I'm open to hearing these telling tunes and sharing the lyrics.

They reveal my personal reasons for writing this book.

All too often I go into bookstores or search Internet sites and see shelves of books or eBooks on career and life success but only a handful actually cover the breadth of this topic, or so few are as targeted. In my sharing mode, there are times when I'm conducting a seminar, and someone of my hue approaches me for advice on a career challenge or difficult workplace situation they're facing. What I hear at times is often horrifying, in terms of discriminatory actions they're encountering. Or I sense from their explaining that they're possibly not aware of the array of career management options to consider. Also I receive phone calls or e-mails from friends and family, asking me to write or review their resume, along with suggesting ways to improve their job search. From our conversations, we discuss effective resources, (besides me), to assist them in these efforts, while the process still looms as a challenge. Or perhaps, the contact is regarding a personal life or relationship matter, and they need a listening ear. Insight is always welcome.

Reflecting on the crux of those situations—career or personal—I realize that many of us are missing that 'old folks' wisdom to guide us. Or we haven't always had the corporate savvy conversations around our dinner tables. Why? Our families are now more dispersed and the continuance of that 'mother wit' isn't as right up on us as it used to be and in previous decades our relatives weren't allowed to be employed in various types of organizations in significant numbers, not in white-collar positions anyway. Let me add that this does depend on your generation, pre or post Civil Rights era. Progress and social economic demographics have yielded better education and more exposure for those of us in our twenties versus sixties. Think about this. Did your early interpersonal environment include college educated family members versus "salt of the earth" folks? And all in between. This is not to say we didn't get the valuable common sense and hard work talk from our wise or blue-collar family experiences that can be applied to our current employment situations. The elders' sage advice for our personal challenges stands through the elements of time. Regardless of any of these factors, I maintain that we need to seek and to know.

So while books for the general demographics of the public on these subjects do offer some very good generic information, sometimes I have a need to read something that addresses my matters as an African American, a person in the trifecta of strength, soul, and spirit.

Let me expand on my background a bit more.

Through my work of over fifteen years in providing numerous workshops on career and life issues, a few other truths have become clear. Acknowledging the power of the array of backgrounds we come from plants us firmly to grow knowledgeable and bountiful. What does this mean? Simple: Each situation we go through—good or bad—teaches us something. From these experiences, we each bring a uniqueness, a bevy of our own personal thoughts that can enhance or hinder the steps on the route to achieve our goals.

Experience: Your Guide and Checkpoint

I feel it would be fitting to share more here about my story and stake in all this, for this book you are holding speaks to the energy of transforming dreams into reality. My vision to become an author first took shape in 1996, with an ad hoc published version of this book. As someone who's always loved to write, I started working on manuscripts and sending book proposals to agents after I'd finished a master's program in 1993. There were no immediate takers but I kept writing—and talking, to myself and others. Determined, the question was how could I go about this more creatively.

While preparing to speak at a Blacks in Government (BIG) Training Conference in Atlanta in 1996, a colleague in my writing support circle suggested that I bind one of my manuscripts to sell at the end of my presentation. I took that advice and sold several copies. Yeah! My first book sales! During that time, I'd also read Stephen Covey's *The 7 Habits of Highly Effective People* (1989) and had a desire to write a comparable book specifically geared at helping black folks. I stated as much to myself and a few others. Now, with today's technological advances streamlining processes in every industry, publishing included, the opportunity to make it more widely available has arrived. Checkpoint!

What I know now?

Sometimes we have to inspire and encourage ourselves through our personal narrative. To do that, we must start with what we've gleaned from life.

I view myself as someone who uses the wits and gifts God has given me, so I can be of service. The oldest child of a very determined single mother, I was raised in the home of my wise grandparents, and they all embedded in me the importance of a strong belief system. Watching them all persevere with hope for better times that would include more opportunities for our race is not something I will easily forget. Immersed in the segregated culture of our Civil Rights-era rural Virginia hometown, we were black, hardworking, proud and Baptist.

My mother, in particular, instilled a love of reading in me. Education mattered to her, as evidenced in a few ways. First, after I was born, she returned to high school to finish her senior year. That would be no easy feat for any young, new mother, especially one from a poor family in 1955. After my siblings came along and we became of school age, she invested in a set of *World Book Encyclopedias*, to help us do our homework—in spite of our poor economic condition. My mother read to us, with a wonderful focus in her eyes and voice. She also bought us a set of Bible storybooks to cement the study of our faith. I internalized her visible actions, was a good student and decided with my mother's encouragement, to go to college. This foundation for the importance of knowledge, faith and determination prepared me for a journey that would ultimately offer its variety of twists, trials, and triumphs—every one of which has been instructional.

After graduating college, I embarked off on my own, making a variety of career stops along the way. Social worker, Army reserve officer, and stints in the corporate sector with human resources, leadership, and operations positions. I discovered a way to combine those pursuits and start my own enterprise. In 1993, DPJ Associates was born. As a tribute to the spiritual wisdom of my late grandparents along with my own name, Deborah, Pearl, and Joseph, I felt strong in this business's foundation. (In 2007, I renamed to The DPJ Training Group).

Next, I went on a quest to gain more experience, find opportunities, and of course, support myself financially. First

I volunteered by providing seminars at my church and community organizations, along with writing résumés, which gave me momentum and validation in my choice of work. Part-time opportunities such as teaching courses through adult education programs at local schools strengthened my experience. Eventually, I hit pay dirt! My first major project was facilitating career transition training for hundreds of military service members preparing to enter the civilian workforce due to a force drawdown. Since I'd gone through that process myself when I left active duty, here was a chance for me to share what I knew, both conceptually and experientially. Later, as many corporations started downsizing, there was further need to support those affected with job search, résumé-writing, and interviewing techniques, so more work surfaced in this area. I also offered individual coaching. One key area included helping people through the emotional trauma and impact of unexpected job loss by listening and identifying the next best steps to take.

Continuing to find ways to use what I knew in my business, I expanded the type of training projects within my capabilities, adding leadership and diversity. From my experiences as the oldest child of a single parent and an Army reserve officer, there were lessons I could share. Leadership was in me! Growing up in the 1950s–70s and witnessing this country's move from segregation to integration and the reactions of those around me, I gleaned much about the impact of race, a key diversity concept. With the entwinement of opportunities for my education and career that came with Civil Rights policies, my path further solidified in understanding the societal dynamics of this topic. In other words, I could testify about a thing or two! Objectively of course.

I pressed on. Not alone.

Along the trails of my life and career, I've encountered numerous people who have helped me. Family, caring teachers, strangers, and friends have each added precious pieces to the puzzle of my life, helping me put it all together. Business connections have provided referrals that have led to wonderful client engagements. Fellow consultant friends have coached me when I have stumbled off course, professionally and personally.

Staying ever grateful and faithful has allowed me to maintain my resolve not only in victories, but also through the roadblocks that have come my way. Life ultimately just happens. Even as I pen these guidelines, neither mine nor your life is or will be perfect. I, like many of you, have had my burdens to carry, and I've had to discover when it was time to lighten the load. Of course there have been tough patches and challenges too: cancer, relationship difficulties, and business letdowns, to name a few. Tumultuous storms have zapped my strength, but it is a determined spirit that allows me to get back up when I fall. More details about other aspects of my setbacks and successes can be found in my motivational memoir, *Navigating Life's Roadways* (www.navigatinglifesroadways.com).

Reworking strategy, letting go, and repeating lessons are things that I've had to do at times. In the process, I developed some guidelines and perspectives to keep me operating.

On a personal front, I'm a committed aunt to a nephew and two nieces. I share what I can with them to help them avoid serious mistakes, mainly sound life and cultural principles that will hopefully guide them through their young adult journeys and beyond.

Travel, national and international, is one of my passions; the ability to take nice vacations is a success factor for me (in addition to a few other indulgences). I love exploring history, food and culture.

Involvement with my sorority, church, and other community groups keep me grounded in benevolent activities.

Through it all, my soul remains anchored in God, the ultimate 'way station'.

My family's background has served as constant guide. Wise, persevering, and resourceful describe them. Out of their missteps and my own, dignity remains.

I continue to seek all lanes as I explore my purpose and encourage you to do the same.

So...What's Your Story?

We all get to be experts when we harness our life experiences. I disclose these facets of my career and personal sojourns as an example of how we ALL can find our own individual truths and opportunities—big or small—from the maps of our strength, soul, and spirit. Don't model mine! There's no bragging here—just facts. What's mine is mine, and what's yours is yours—all struggles, successes, detours or triumphs. Pinpoint. Fold up for later. Ready for you to open. Are you committed to...?

Through what lens do you view your journey? Critical. Reflective. Thankful. Find your own way to capture the majestic elements of your story. Root yourself in the survival of coming out of any tragic pieces of your personal chronicles. How 'you got over', and found your way to where you are—in spite of—is your way station, a stop worth revisiting.

So get on board the right TRACK.

Tenacious. Resolute. Able. Caring. Kindred.

Claim the whole of your truths, 'good, bad, or ugly', as part of the guide to make the words I share in this book real... for YOU!

Then, as James Brown, the "Godfather of Soul," sang, "Say it loud! 'I'm black, and I'm proud!'" Get ready for greatness. Exclaim your strength, soul, and spirit narratives in a bold way, letting them be your guide to success.

Find them, file them, and do not forget them.

Section A

Recognize: Stay on the Main Track and Get–isms Out of the Way

"There is little hope for us until we become tough-minded enough to break loose from the shackles of prejudice, half-truths, and downright ignorance. The shape of the world today does not permit us the luxury of soft-mindedness. A nation or a civilization that continues to produce soft-minded men purchases its own spiritual death on an installment plan."
~ Martin Luther King, Jr., *A Testament of Hope*

Quota hires. Driving While Black. Incarcerated disproportionately.

Conflict, scape-goating, the weaker sex, human nature, stereotypes, tribal dynamics, the bottom of a dry well, politics, "old dogs and new tricks."

"N word" fever. Angry black women. Crack-carrying kids. Profiles.

Disparities. Chronic Unemployment.

A modern day Klan.

–isms of Race, Gender, Class, and Age.

Should we always drink the Kool-Aid?

Terms and conditions that can get us off track...if we let them.

A portion of an old, old story is here.

The election of President Barak Obama didn't end it.

Gaping holes exist in gender equality.

Silver hairs aren't always viewed as spikes of wisdom.

Serious News

But what statistics support this? Race, gender, and age discrimination or harassment account for anywhere from up to 35 percent of complaints filed with the Equal Employment Opportunity Commission. Found in employment, housing, or financial practices, institutional barriers still reside in this society, crushing the glow of "the American Dream" for many of our history and hue. According to the Bureau of Labor Statistics, over eleven million jobs have been lost in this country over the past five years, with employment in the black community hovering between 12 and 16 percent, up to double the national average of 8 percent. The imprisoned population consists of around 40 percent of our folks (the majority of them black males), despite our 13 percent makeup of the overall U.S. census numbers. Even Hollywood can be blamed for not always supporting diverse portrayals of the totality of our community. We can't ignore those other unflattering messages in media steams of television and radio programming. Are they operating full steam ahead to ghettoize our demographic? Then, there are the myriad of familiar anecdotes from our relatives, co-workers, neighbors, and friends, sharing what has happened to them in different situations because of... You got it, fill in the blank.

Troubles Anywhere?

Ascent into the middle class and beyond, for many African Americans, has been derailed in a few ways. Home foreclosures have impacted a once solid investment strategy for our communities. Our families, youth in particular, are under constant cultural attack, from forces both internal and external. Negative media, gaps in various lifestyle sectors, and our "own stuff" gain too much power in our psyches. Education rates, crime statistics, violence, and economic indicators don't always come back with the good numbers we'd like to hear or see concerning our condition. Slights and innuendos of a racial nature, while seemingly just annoying, do build up, affecting our 'souls as black folks'. The National Urban League's Annual State of Black America Report uses a variety of statistical and narrative measures to document these trends. Their goal, then, is to launch targeted initiatives and engage stakeholders in conversations about next steps regarding health, education, and job growth efforts for our community.

Clogs, Movements, and Causes

However, even in the midst of so much grim news, good news should not be forgotten. Tremendous gains have stationed a recognizable portion of us in those "dee-luxe apartments in the sky!" Mentionable "moving on up" has occurred.

I was raised in a home with no indoor plumbing. Now, I live in a home with more than one bathroom—a few, in fact—and that's big time on my scale! There's nothing like going from outhouse to in-house, on the main sewer line!

College education rates and other success indicators have certainly bumped upward since the Civil Rights Movement. Our collective comeback shimmers in the strength of our major victories won!

There's always that mixed bag though. When we look at the causes of some of the issues that clog our progress, impediments we face as a people, we see that most of them have their origins in institutional or localized racism. The residual effects of slavery and Jim Crow still temper the way for significant segments of our community. Driving, shopping, or just hanging out as a black person can still garner us a shamelessly discriminatory and harassing response from other human beings with whom we share the planet.

Are there steps we can take to deal with these situations? What about sanctioned resources? Yes and no, but whatever the process, it demands that we draw on our skills and outreach to develop effective strategies to deflect this dilemma of discrimination. I think we all know that racism and those other–isms aren't going away anytime soon. I've encountered my share, but I know there are plenty more still lurking around out there.

Sexism and ageism are forces to be reckoned with too, still rampant today. Just like racism, they drain and disappoint our inner constitution. For a little perspective here, a truth about the human dynamic is that it predisposes us to not like someone because of something. Think about it: Even within our families, some of these conflicts bear out. Birth order, pigmentation, abilities, education, material possessions, and other demographics create favorites, outcasts, or uppities. Got it? So, let's get back to the biggies. These three–isms of race, gender, and age tend to be prominent, since they are linked to the first things people notice in our human interactions. History books show us that this has been the case since the beginning of time; it has always gone unchecked and amok.

But where do these unwelcome forces show up? They permeate facets of our daily lives: hiring practices, financial lending, or the checkout line at a retail establishment. Entity or individual can be the perpetrator.

What else is there to think about? Class dynamics are real. The haves and new money are ensconced proudly on one end of our community, while the permanent poor, the have-nots, wait on the other for a new ship to come in. Is there a Willie Lynch among us? (In case you don't recognize the name, Lynch was a seventeenth-century slave owner who encouraged intergroup discord amongst slaves as a way to control them). Do we help or encourage the bootstrap approach? This is a question to consider in our families, as well as the larger reaches of African Americans.

Even so, it is imperative to put racism and those other–isms on lockdown at some point in our lives. I think most of us know when to call them, when we see these forces play out. Sometimes the behaviors are subtle, yet we're sure of the uncomfortable or angry feeling we're having. Our next step is to decide what to do about the situation. Here's where self-knowledge comes in. My stance has always been that we should examine what vehicles are available to assist us in the complaint process, decide how important the issue is to us, and determine if we are emotionally equipped to do the questioning and the waiting that is usually associated with filing a complaint or other procedure. Resources focus on the desired outcome, and patience is far more than a virtue: It is a required strength in these instances.

The Good Report: In Spite Of

Since my 1996 version of this book, we, as a people, have made huge strides in many venues from government, corporate, entrepreneurial, and sports to cultural fronts. We've gone from carrying greasy bags with biscuits to having major gravitas. We've traded in our tattered hand-me-downs for high fashion, from mud-walking to driving a Mercedes…and everything in between—low places to high places, starting with the biggie, an African American President and First Family, residing in the ultimate "big house." Many of us are "living large," as defined by common success indicators of education, lifestyle, career, and material achievements.

But how did they—and we—get to this place in time? Debates still abound on the role of government in creating success by "leveling" the playing field. Many Civil Rights-era baby-boomers, like me, willingly acknowledge that if it weren't for affirmative action and other such initiatives, we probably wouldn't be where we are. Now, before anyone gets upset, let me expound. As usual, our personal stories validate much.

I, like many, come from a proud family. My mother didn't want to receive welfare, in spite of the fact that she'd been abandoned by my stepfather to raise four children on her own. She worked as a domestic for seventeen dollars a week before a better job at a factory came along. I remember her stance and struggles, which are vividly etched in my mind. We lived with my grandparents in a rented shotgun-style house (no hallways or indoor plumbing). When the financial toll got too heavy, we did have to succumb to "government cheese," if only for a short period of time.

Free monies also helped me get an education, as I was poor, black, and smart. The Basic Education Opportunity

Grants of the 1970s funded a significant portion of my tuition. As a college student, I went on food stamps when I became self-supporting, releasing the burden on my mother, who had three more children to care for.

But promising days did come.

My mother eventually bought her own home, as did my grandparents. Federal lending programs for our demographic helped make it so.

Without those programs, I doubt I'd have such a story to tell. My career options, my own business, my writing a book, or many other possibilities would not be part of my biography without that help, a foundation that I could build on.

Many have gone through variations of this path before, with and without government assistance, and their stories continue to inspire. Barack's is among them, and most of us know about Michelle's as well—right along with Madam CJ Walker's, W.E. B. Dubois's, your parents', your grandparents', and your aunts' and uncles'. Then there's Miss So-and-So from the neighborhood, that teacher, that minister, a few truck drivers, Pullman Porter's, and The Help; they've all got their own narratives of "making it" in spite of...well, everything.

So, what's your life's *good* news report? Again, find it, file it, and do not forget it! Sometimes even the saddest of stories can end up in a more productive place.

A Reality Check: Why Now or Later?

For job situations, I refer back to the statistics mentioned at the beginning of this chapter, because looking for a job or staying and growing in a current career field in today's job market is a very challenging process for everyone, but especially for African Americans. In a preretirement workshop I conducted for a government agency a number of years ago, a participant stated, "I'm a forty-three-year-old black male. Who's going to want to hire me for anything the way things are now?" I understood what he was saying, but what a self-defeating statement! We can't let those thoughts block our actions.

Due to these current market variables, it's important to recognize at the outset that a lot of effort is required if we are going to get the opportunities we want. Not dwelling on negative things, while dealing with reality and recognizing certain potential barriers, yet not letting them control the outcome, is key. We need this grit.

Unfortunately, our encounters with ignorance and hatred will continue. Especially in the workplace, this is where racism rears its ugly head in many ways. We sometimes have to prove ourselves to others, conflicting our foundational beliefs of confidence. As W.E.B. DuBois wrote in his classic, *The Souls of Black Folks*, "One ever feels his twoness—an American, a Negro; two souls, two thoughts, two unreconciled strivings; two warring ideals in one dark body, whose dogged strength alone keeps it from being torn asunder." Where are we now, a century later?

There's still this pervasive thought that there's no way we can be as qualified as other demographic groups, especially white males. Whenever we're put into a position or extended an employment opportunity, there's still a sense, at times, that the offer doesn't come from our merits or abilities, but because it's a quota, a requirement, a diversity or affirmative action hire. In my career transition work, I've encountered whites who have feared being overlooked for a job they were qualified for because of a perceived mandate to fulfill quotas. Some even indicated that recruitment interviewers had stated a desire to bring them in for the position, but they couldn't because of the affirmative action mandates. How stupid on many counts!

Also, in this era of tweets, likes, linking, sharing, and pinning, the hateful and the weird have found a refuge to disperse their rants. Cyberbullying. Instances of Facebook harassment among colleagues has surfaced in the work environment through posting disrespectful comments or photos.

Is there a way to counter and add voice?

Workplace encounters offer their share of stupidity as well. In corporate positions, the pressures to show thyself extra competent are there. Maybe we will be eyeballed differently in retail jobs, scrutinized for any and all signs of potential stealing. Curiosity about our hair, dress, food, or music might display disdain, clouding what would otherwise be effective interactions. During my diversity seminars, I'm periodically approached by fellow African Americans who share their accounts of being denied well-deserved promotions or access to other developmental opportunities. Racial bias is the perceived and real cause in most of these cases. Based on the context, I take a moment to ask some questions and do some due diligence to pinpoint the rest of the story. Many of my diversity courses are mandated by the client organization, often in the aftermath of an incident or an increase in EEO complaints. I often face staredowns by whites in the audience, especially those who are not there voluntarily or feel their required presence is a punishment. Several discussions reveal outdated views on race and ethnicity. My job is to be objective and manage the opposing views, yet be instructional. It's not always easy, but I do enjoy the work.

For any of us, the situations noted above can eat at us and cause us to get sucked into that game. Especially now, as resources and opportunities get leaner, that scenario becomes more real.

I recently gave a presentation on change management to a dinner networking event for human resources professionals. As I reviewed the feedback, I happened upon a comment from an attendee, inquiring as to what made *me* qualified to talk about the topic. During the program, my bio was read, and I offered plenty of examples of my previous work in other organizations, handling similar issues. I didn't understand why my qualifications were being questioned, and it made me angry.

Then I realized, for me, the word "qualified" ranks as one of those super-hot buttons that can be easily pushed. Backing off, I remembered something: I know what I know, and that anger was not my reality. I know I have to maintain professionalism and integrity at all times, even in such charged situations.

Recognize when it's time to back away and inject another guideline to center your emotions around these slights, biases, and stupidity. You know what you know, and don't let anyone make you feel that it's not enough.

Home Training and Back-in-the-Day Rules

When we look at getting off track in the conditions of education, family, and economic challenges, I tend to go back to old-school thinking. I addressed a breakout session at the National Council of Negro Women at their National Convention in May of 2012. My topic was "Readying Youth for the Future Workforce." In that presentation, I reiterated the importance of home training as the baseline for success in whatever the endeavor. From unfortunate stories on the chaos of many school classrooms due to unruly behavior to generational residue on a sense of direction, signals abound on the work that needs to be done.

What is that work? The same as it's always been.

Adults establish rules, and make our youngsters aware of the need to do the right things. This is a continuous struggle and need. Shaping character counts! Embed gratitude. Hover over them to impart the meaning of being a good citizen and "handling your business". This is also where the village concept can help—in personal, narrative, or virtual forms. "Back in the day," children were exposed to various life rituals or events when they were old enough to understand and make use of such vital lessons. Boundaries and safety for young people was a priority. Aretha Franklin's "R-E-S-P-E-C-T" reigned, especially for our elders. Grown folks, even outside of the family, were entitled to give children a good, old-fashioned talking-to if they are seen misbehaving, and no one was concerned about a filing a lawsuit over it. Adults looked out for everybody's children. Teachers were woven into the fabric of the community; they were at church, in stores, or visiting around in the neighborhood on the weekends. Manners were emphasized.

We can each find a way to keep young people on track, whether we're parents ourselves, extended family members, or just Mr. or Miss So-and-So in the neighborhood.

Kinfolk, Neighbors, and Friends

The 'old folks' found ways to help each other out. In our ancestral land, the village operates much the same. This was particularly important in our segregated and poor communities. Counting on others was a way to keep on getting by. Going next door to borrow a cup of flour or sugar from a neighbor so a meal be could prepared—and returning the same when you could afford to buy your own—was a way of life.

Many of our families have similar experiences and beginnings, whether it was a county or city hometown. The core family name stayed in the town, and those members who never left became keepers of the homestead, providing some sense of continuance. Now, this is not so much the case. Here, too, progress is a mixed bag, particularly as it pertains to the status of our families and communities. Because of relocation in order to achieve the desires or demands of our careers, the nuclear family is often dispersed, living in various places. We're often far away from kinfolk and the others we grew up with.

When family members relocate for their work, the challenges of time and resources can restrict their ability to reconnect as often as they may like. But what can we do? Even military or diplomatic members, the traditional "away families," find themselves struggling for support and a way to connect with family and friends. From childhood to adulthood, family to faith, the longing for the ties that bind is present. It is an inborn human need, and we all seek ways to satisfy it.

So, we discover ways to create community. Finding playmates, soul mates, or officemates is essential to our humanness. As I like to say, "We're all just big children." We still need raising up, no matter how grown our driver's license says we are. Through book clubs, sports clubs, or hobby groups, we look to quench our desire to share space and conversation with like-minded others occasionally. Our places of worship, professional associations, and community groups continue to provide a cultural sanctuary and a forum to address those–isms that undeniably hover around us all.

Of course, not all of the good ol' days were really so good, but in them there did exist some fundamentals that are constant and consistent. My grandmother had a saying: "Right ain't changed in all these years." In spite of today's progress and perils, a few principles remain true. Children need guidance. Sharing is good for the soul. The importance of a sense of continuity reigns. And lineage matters!

Getting Ourselves Straight and Ready

Upon recognizing that many personal and fiscal resources are needed for this career and life strategizing, a solid, actionable process is a good posture. This is not a slow-moving world anymore, and we have to hustle. The work before us is not an easy feat. Our assets in this quest, beyond our willingness and determination, also include an open mind and positive outlook, along with good organizational and communications skills. Access to people, places, and things such as a strong network, libraries, organizations, and social media tools are essential.

So how do we deploy these seven guidelines for strength, soul, and spirit to be ready? Leadership is one route—first of ourselves.

Mainly, the goal for any leader is to succeed, to move past obstacles and problems, and to claim a triumph! We do this all the time in our lives. From this experience, a personal victory narrative can take shape, one that becomes solid and surefire. One critical thing that a leader must do is show him- or herself strong. We cannot allow fear to take us down! Remember those who firmly postured for freedom in the face of trackers, dogs, and horses.

Next, it's important to ensure that complex situations get the right amount of attention. Too often, we dust off serious issues, dismissing them as trivial. While they may seem simple and insignificant on the surface, these problems may have layers of stuff that needs to be waded through. This is the case for racial, gender, or age bias confrontations. Other issues with our youth, education, or healthcare require us to address root causes. Pay attention to the signs of trouble!

This era of microwave magic, solving a crime in sixty minutes of television, and hurry-up approaches to reconciling tough matters has led to impatience with the processes that are often necessary if we are to find enduring solutions. Instead, some of our most daunting challenges continue to surface. How do we put them under and out of the way? We must lead, be thorough, and use our strength, soul, and spirit.

Success: Define and Claim the Destination

What is and where is success? This can be defined differently for each of us, based on who and where we are. From employment in a job or career that provides fulfillment, to the ability to take care of a family, to economic stability, to being a good neighbor, to being respected in the community and place of worship, to being in good physical health or having solid, loving relationships—the range of how success is defined is personal.

Prosperity on these important fronts brings its own richness to life: degreed or not, the color of the collar in your work situation, the address of your residence, whether your cash flow is stuck or surging, bounty or barely holding on. Recognize your personal obligations that prevent or propel. Call your life as you see it. Are you in a sweet, enriching spot or rotting hole? Prosperity can be rooted in the emotional—peace of mind or strong faith. It should not be locked in worries. Are you passionate about your interests or hobbies? Satisfied or wanting a change? These are your choices, and it is your challenge to figure them out and define success as you see it.

Our ambitions, along with our own measure of strength, soul, and spirit, add to the meaning of success. To claim this status, let's start by discovering and working on eliminating any barriers to our personal progress.

Are you stationed and ready?

Making It with a Vision

"Every great dream begins with a dreamer. Always remember, you have within you the strength, the patience and the passion to reach for the stars to change the world."

~ Harriet Tubman, Conductor of the Underground Railroad

Imagine freedom. Done.

Vision: A plain message to prevent personal perish.

From Kunta Kinte to Harriet to Martin to you, we harbor plenty of iconic images of what it has taken and takes today to achieve the right to be. Shackles to shacks and now suburbs, this new life shape is unfolding. From you to me, can we model their grit and, yes, sacrifice? Whatever it looks like in time, energy, money, effort, or even loss, make the picture of your envisioned reality as plain as it needs to be. Imagine your career, your family, and your everything else.

The dream triggers this new thing that you want. Measureable and to the point is how to capture this goal. Ask yourself: How badly do I want this? What am I willing to go through to get it? Only you have the answer!

As Earth, Wind, and Fire sing, "Keep your head to the sky."

Dream, imagine, and take a risk!

Back on Track? The Way Forward

First, let's fortify for the opposing forces and be sure we know the truth about ourselves, our people, and our purpose. Read positive, recent, and industry-targeted information. Don't rely solely on the local newspaper or news broadcasts for accurate accounts of our life or situation in America. As is protocol for all things Internet, proceed with caution before completely trusting everything on the websites that scroll before your eyes. Be ready and resilient to pursue what's for you. Rightly know your personal constitution.

We now become the griots of our struggles and story. Having our own main track of information is a great place to start! Shoulder these pillars of the seven guidelines and go. Find your beacon. Help yourself and others continuously along the way. Pace yourself. Be gentle. Realize that sometimes along the route, we all need a little P-U-S-H: **p**urpose, **u**nderstanding, **s**upport, and **h**ealing!

Section B

The Seven Guidelines

"Never, never rest contented with any circle of ideas, but always be certain that a wider one is still possible."

~Pearl Bailey, Actress and Singer

Guideline I

Know Yourself—The Deep Sources of Your Strength

"I am what time, circumstance, and history have made of me, certainly, but I am also much more than that. So are we all."

~ James Baldwin, Writer and Activist

Assess and Respect Yourself!

Our ancestral beginnings. A plethora of persevering and enduring people.

The cramped and wretched Middle Passage. Taken to a wintering continent of despair. Auctioned and forcibly labored. Denied. Vilified.

Those that boldly came before wouldn't let anyone turn them around. Freedom seared as a goal of their souls. It kept them hardily keeping on, in spite of unfathomable toils. Every day they reached down deep to strengthen themselves to, at the very least, survive. And now these stalwart known and unknown figures serve as our personal pillars. They passed on some of what they were made of to us.

What we came from can be a source of hope and pride. Although it's an ugly and painful past, can we honor what it took, the role this historical turmoil plays to stage us where we are today. These tough circumstances yielded a cultural nucleus. Respect it!

We each possess some of the strengthening residue—mammy to modern-day woman, sharecropper to CEO. We've worked hard to re-create those unflattering images.

From the ancestors, generationally passed down to the 'old folks', and now to us, there's a treasure trove waiting to be discovered. Be not ashamed of the weight from their shoulders. Bring it! We certainly are somebody, aren't we?

Understand the Wealth of Your Skills, Abilities, Assets, Liabilities, and Limitations

Who are you at the core?

Each of us has an eternal spring that keeps us pressing on through adversities. Do you know how to draw from that well? It is that ancestral reserve of perseverance and endurance, the nature of your past applied to your current environment, the source to nurture your family circumstances and attend to the challenges and opportunities of the present day. What does this well of abundance look like for you?

Your journey to your current place in time is unique here, and you are accompanied and your story is enriched by the baggage you hoist.

Now, it is totally and measurably about you. So what makes you stand out? Do you also recognize your less-desirable personality quirks that could sabotage your success? Can you identify how to stay out of your own way?

Self-awareness and knowledge are critical in this shifting landscape. Knowing the 'good, the bad, and the ugly' of your personality will afford you the realism needed to fuel your drive down your individual path. This information about ourselves is a valuable tool for negotiating new territory and exploring unrealized opportunities, both professionally and personally. Referred to today as "emotional intelligence," this knowledge supports us as we navigate a variety of interpersonal situations. In addition to enhanced relationships, this information will help you to "Respect yourself," as crooned by the 1970s R&B group, The Staple Singers.

Why Not Know Our Core Selves?

Unreconciled shame? Afraid to be aware?

Sometimes we conceal ourselves from our true identities. We may not want to acknowledge the person we truly are, in all our special gifts, until we are forced to face the wealth of what life has taught us. A failure to know our true selves may be the result of a lack of engagement, being stuck in a rut, or simply feeling unfilled.

We may rely on such crutches until we grow into an ever-evolving bloom of life, eventually facing ways to find insight, after challenges have found us with no meaning in our life story. Then, circumstances lead us to start the quest to find value in our personal narratives. Have no shame! Rather, take pride in the pieces that have come together to create the place and meaning of your today.

I believe we are each bestowed with abilities of wonder, making us each a unique blend all our own. From arts, culinary, mechanical, scientific, or plain common sense perspectives, the range of what we bring to the world is vast. Some gifts we are born with, and others are inspired or grown within us as the results of how parents, caregivers, and teachers have instructed us. Eventually our own choices and pursuits add to this list of areas in which we can excel.

Our goal is to find these talents at the right time and with the right count. Do not delay. Do not let others keep you from this treasure. These attributes shelter us in the turmoil of today, becoming our fallback in challenging economic and career times.

Recognize it!

In order to gain such awareness, a few informal exercises to gauge and guide the journey to self-definition are included on the following pages. Recommendations for other formal methods are listed too. However, there are several points to acknowledge from the beginning.

- **Recognize that assessment is continuous (of self, skills, and situation).**

Why? Because things change. We grow as we have new experiences and acquire fresh knowledge. Making decisions prompts new insights. Otherwise, we stagnate when the status quo becomes too comfortable. Sometimes a situation changes and causes us to reassess our options. Life's interruptions can sway us, forcing us to shift in another direction. Family additions or losses challenge or comfort us. Societal issues impact our lives, be they global conflict, budget cuts, innovations in our industries, or any combination of these or various other factors. Windfalls in personal finances or new technology cause us to rethink our plans. Our strengths are zapped or recharged in these moments.

- **Don't underestimate or downplay yourself.**

Learning to package ourselves with all of our talents, skills, and abilities is Task One. What has brought you to where you are? Wherever you are now, stand proudly there. Too many times, I hear people say, "I'm *just* a..." when asked about what they do. Think about all you have to offer, and be able to put it out in the universe with power. All career fields and jobs have value in this world. Single or married, college educated or GED-earner, suburban, rural, or inner city—it's all good! Solidify your place to be and give.

- **Capitalize on your strengths.**

Who's the best person to...? The 'old folks', like we do now, asked this question to identify resources for everyday survival. Mostly, the sources were individual enterprises, built on strengths. From raising children, to doing or cutting hair, to project management to cooking to playing basketball, we each bring our unique talents to our professional and personal lives. Figure out what you do well and market that skill or talent to the max! Just do you...naturally. Proudly claim your abilities and use them smartly. Use those gifts that will allow you to circumvent and morph through daily and sustaining challenges. Bring them on with enthusiasm!

- **Acknowledge weaknesses (development areas), liabilities, and limitations.**

None of us are perfect, and we all have issues and likely baggage of some sort. Knowing our weaknesses helps us determine which of these we can correct and provides a degree of direction for improvement. With awareness of our liabilities in tow, this data helps us to avoid wrong careers or environments. Then there are some tasks or skills we just cannot do; these are limitations. Various aspects of our personalities help or hinder us. Patience, attention to detail, or being outgoing or shy can be among these, and we are all a very different combination of these attributes and hindrances. Own up to where you lack or need to make improvements...and get busy making them!

Teachings from Your Setbacks and Achievements thus Far

How do we find out what these strengths, assets, limitations, or liabilities are? Sometimes by trying and failing or succeeding. And learning from both. Or pulling from the past to affect future success.

Educator and author Booker T. Washington wrote, "I have learned that success is to be measured not so much by the position one has reached in life as by the obstacles which he has overcome while trying to succeed."

For You: Reflect on some of the highlights of your life, your setbacks as well as triumphs. A setback could be a financial downturn, an illness (yours or a loved one's), or a failure (education, relationship). Triumphs might include graduating, starting a family, a promotion, a longed-for and hard-earned vacation, or buying a home. These are a few examples. Pick your own and then flesh them out to discover more about your core.

- Do you feel that you have a delivered natural ability (DNA)? Either someone remarked that you were born with it, or it was noted at a point in your early years.
- What tasks bring you excitement and good energy?
- Think of an achievement that you accomplished. What made you go after that goal in the first place?
- Consider a trial you've experienced in life. Describe how it happened.
- What hurdles did you encounter?
- How did you get over them? What actions did you take?
- Were there any guiding perspectives that kept you focused (sayings, faith, perseverance, self-control)? If so, what were they?
- Who else was involved? Who supported or hindered you?
- What unique talents have shown up for you in your triumphs and setbacks?
- Describe those situations in which you feel most confident.

Answering these questions will inspire you to start the process of getting in touch with your resilience assets, giving you a push forward. Important assets of your core will come to light. Think about whether you inherited these skills or traits from family members, as part of the scientific or environmental DNA. I constantly reflect on my beginnings as the oldest child and product of a determined, proud single mother. In addition to that, I was raised in the home of resourceful and wise grandparents; these beneficial elements comprise my nexus. It isn't that I've been immune to baggage left over from some of my background, but that only makes me cognizant of those liabilities and limitations.

The message here is this: Know what sends you into the dry zone. Replenish it.

Find your center, the wellspring. Be proud of whatever that force is for you.

In terms of identifying more of your good, bad, or ugly, I recommend taking the Myers Briggs Type Indicator (MBTI), a personality assessment instrument. Through your responses to statements, the scored rankings point to why you may like to work alone, why you come alive around lots of people, why you rely on intuition, or why you prefer to engage in analytical thinking. More specifics will be detailed in your personal results. This helpful, effective tool also provides possible matching of personality type to careers. Check with local libraries, adult education programs, and community colleges for MBTI offerings or learn more at www.myersbriggs.org.

Other informal ways to find out what careers or environments for which you are best suited include skills assessments that will help you know what you're working with. The list below is by no means all inclusive, but it provides you with a good idea of the wide variety of skills that we tap into based on our experiences and exposure:

For You: Inventory your skills by reviewing the list (see instructions). Remember that many skills are transferrable across different environments, so mark the skill whether you use it at work (current or previous), home, in a community activity, or at your place of worship. These skills are also known as functional skills. Turn them into verbs (–ed) and they become

POWER words that are useful in writing a résumé, indicating action!

Seven Skills, Seven Successes, Seven Seeking

Put a check mark (☑) by the skills you have, a plus (+) by those skills you enjoy, an (x) by those skills you do well, a question mark (?) by those you want to learn, and a circle (o) by the skills you'd like to use on your next position, opportunity, or career.

SKILL ASSESSMENT LIST

administering programs
analyzing data
arranging functions
assembling apparatus
auditing financial reports
budgeting expenses
coaching individuals
compiling statistics
conference management
conflict management
coordinating events
designing systems/programs
displaying artistic ideas
driving vehicles
editing publications
estimating requirements
evaluating programs
exhibiting ideas/plans
fundraising causes
handling complaints
interviewing applicants
investigating incidents
managing projects
marketing products
motivating others
negotiating contracts
operating equipment
persuading others
planning social events
political advocacy
programming technology
promoting events
providing personal care
physical labor, fixing, lifting
repairing equipment
remembering data
researching options
reviewing programs
running meetings
selling products

inspecting results	supervising others
insuring compliance	teaching students
implementing ideas	writing papers

OTHER SKILLS:

Now, personalize your skill list by adding to the ones above. These skills can be put in categories such as communications, interpersonal/people skills, leadership, program/project management, financial, analytical, information management, transportation, manufacturing, health services, information technologies (IT), education, and telecommunications. Also, be aware of the current terminology, buzzwords and jargon that are being used in your industry today. List these other skills below:

____

____

Formal methods available to do skills assessment include the Campbell Interests and Skills Survey and the Holland Self-Directed Search. Contact a career coach or look for offerings at a local community college or university career services office to take advantage of these helpful tools. Whatever skills you determine are your strengths, think about how they can be assets in this current employment market.

What Makes My World Go 'Round?
Life and Work Style Attributes

On a daily basis, we deploy parts of ourselves to get by and through life's variances. The old folks relied on a set of tried-and-true attributes to do what they had to do to get by and to cement a future for us through extremes of these limited, but determined circumstances. How do we see them in hindsight? Sages of wisdom, focused souls, strong spirits who, with God by their side, made a way out of no way? That's my image.

Think about *your* current image. What personal qualities do you bring to your life and the workplace? How do others see you? If there's a match between these two views, this can be a confirmation of your special gifts.

In my seminars, I ask participants the following question to get them thinking about this: If I walked into your office and asked a few of your colleagues or friends to share three words to describe you, what would they say? Although this is an informal way to get feedback on the image people are projecting out there, the point is that perceptions are reality—of ourselves and of others. How do you want to be seen?

The list below also gets to that same view issue as well as the who-am-I-at-the-core question mentioned at the beginning of this guideline. This is another informal way to describe who we are in relation to work and the world. Some of these can be actual strengths in certain environments.

For You: Put a checkmark by those traits/qualities/characteristics that you would use to describe yourself.

adaptable
admit mistakes
adventurous
ambitious
analytical
appreciative
articulate
artistic
believing
listener
likeable
loyal
mannerly
mesmerizing
motivated
naysaying
organized
patient

bountiful
caring
cerebral
cooperative
creative
decisive
detail-oriented
dedicated
disciplined
energetic
fair
good-humored
innovative
intuitive
knowledgeable
positive
precise
quality-minded
responsible
resourceful
risk taker
sensitive
spontaneous
strategic
supportive
task-oriented
thorough
trustworthy
triumphant
truthful

Now, try this. Reflect on the top three attributes that you bring to work situations. Which three do you use in helping others in personal or other professional situations?

PULLING IT ALL TOGETHER

Time to wrap up and assess, but before that, there's one other piece to add here: Do you remember your first job? Whatever it was, whether it was delivering papers, serving fast food, or working retail, think about what that experience taught you.

Mine was working in the café in my hometown as a dishwasher—for a whopping fifty cents an hour! Talk about minimum wage! Of course, now that I'm self-employed, the long hours sometimes average out to the same amount of pay at times! Nevertheless, sustaining and inspiring, the remembrance keeps me focused, and I make sure to share the story with my nephew and nieces, as well as other young people I encounter. Why? Because no matter where we start, our launch into the world of labor is a core life ritual.

First jobs:

- Shape our character.
- Teach responsibility.
- Help define our career path.

Life is a series of building, carving, and rebooting efforts. Each step of the journey, there's an addition or subtraction that shapes our being.

Think about all the things you checked, circled, or exed in the previous assessments. How did your ancestral or other DNA recognition contribute to the list? Does that now give you a better picture of how important these types of inventories are in making career and life decisions? What's emerging for you? Remember, self-awareness is a journey; hopefully, this guideline has started you on a voyage to victory. But this begs the question: Are you willing to take the risks to get there?

For You: Write down or record your thoughts at this point—particularly any discoveries about your life purpose. How has your own strength, soul, or spirit been revealed?

Guideline II

Know What You Want— Source Your Soul

"Those that don't got it can't show it. Those that got it can't hide it."

~ Zora Neale Hurston, Writer

Bounty hunters went after those who sought freedom. Slaves had value, an identified price for their labor. Identify your bounty. What's of importance to you?

Do you want something so deeply?

"We all need it. Got to have it..." As James Brown wails the words to "Soul Power," he adds how attitude helps us get what's missing. There's usually a hankering for something in our lives that hits us in our souls.

Nurture whatever it is. Fuel that passion.

Is it...

A career-related quest? Go after that opportunity.

A community outreach effort? Define the scope.

Better relationships? Strive to touch.

To create, write, build, discover? Decide and act on your dreams.

There is no time for drying up! Encourage yourself when no one else will. Know what's for you and explore.

Have an attitude of "I deserve..."

March on!

Feeling good about where we are and where we're going is a powerful state. Alignment of our personal elements—mind, body, and soul—ignites an energy to be recognized, and we must burn it to get there.

How do we arrive in this space or place? Is there a way to find the "true north" to achieving our goals?

Explore Your Internal Routing:
Motivations, Goals, and Values

The reality is that in moving on down the roads of our journeys, we gain and lose ground. All is aligned with great momentum one moment, but in the next, we get misdirected and wonder how we'll find our way. Most of the time, we eventually do get there—somehow. This leads us to ponder: Is there some kind of GPS for life to keep us on course?

I've surmised that we all have an IPS (internal positioning system) to steer us. Just like an automobile navigation system—with its GPS, dashboard, and features—we, too, can punch in coordinates for where we want to go in life. We have attributes, strengths, and limitations to direct us. Our motivations, habits, and wits contribute to how we handle the inevitable bumpy roads. We set destinations for our career, family, health, quality of life, or relationship goals, and we can arrive at these places based on how we deploy the elements of our IPS dashboard.

I've found that this IPS, like the GPS technology, has worked for me sometimes and malfunctioned others. In my car, when the quirky voice of the dashboard is silent, I check to see if the GPS is on, particularly if I'm in unfamiliar territory. Likewise, in my life, if I'm not adhering to the right messages, I sense a system failure. The signal for me, then, is that maybe my IPS is not on. I feel lost, literally, on my life quest. "Is this a place I need to explore more?" I question. "Or, maybe I need to press the source and go to my dashboard!

So what are parts of your dashboard's on button for syncing that IPS?

- **Discover your unique routing.** Understanding how your life works in terms of its unique cycles and circumstances provides a map for focus. This is where the power of your story resides. How so? Knowing the design of our route helps us navigate and heed the messages in the hills and potholes of life.

I have come to realize that an off-road collision in a low place is part of my special path before I slowly make my way out to higher ground and another level that God has waiting for me.

We all get sidetracked, but the cargo we accumulate on that not-so-pleasant part of our journey can be helpful when we finally launch in another direction. Whether it's good or bad, we all carry this load. It can keep us on a realistic route as we move toward destination success.

- **What's the fervor that's with you?** This IPS is part of our drive, an engine that fuels us every day. It takes us through storms and other bad conditions. Our IPS is composed of gifts and wits, perspectives, willingness to admit and learn from mistakes, humor, gratitude, wisdom, faith, and the list goes on. These are the blocks of our being, in varying quantities—our confidence chest! A good deal of this force comes from our early life values and grounding.

For me, being raised poor, Baptist, in a rural town, and in a family who encouraged me to "git my lesson," equipped me to set out on my sojourns of accomplishments and failures. These grounding rays are securely locked in my soul, constantly instilling a hopeful motivation.

- **Recognize your hardwiring**. What's inbred in our biological, physiological and psychological circuits? There's that DNA (deliberate natural ability) mentioned earlier, which shapes us to withstand or withdraw based on the conditions we encounter. When our purpose is unclear, we stall. Sheer will and a strong work ethic can get us unstuck.

Know the operating hardware and software of your IPS (internal positioning system). Name what resides on your dashboard, especially the main engage button, which keeps you pressing on.

Our destiny and destinations are ours. Source them.

Inside and outside of us, there's a vitality field at work. It comes from a solid and sure place, our souls. Think about the slaves in search of freedom, navigating the Underground Railroad. Their IPS pointed toward the North Star. Walking, dodging, hiding, and hoping, they forged ahead.

Are You Synched and in Motion?

Before going to a deeper level on this topic, there are other commitments to be realized from the beginning. Thoughts come to mind about the best environments in which we operate as our best selves. Having some vision of where we perceive this place to be will help us put our IPS on course.

Getting in touch with what we want, then exploring the steps to get there isn't always easy. Again, these pursuits will tax our internal resources, but it's very much worth it!

"Soul power" is needed in the following areas:

TIME—BE A WIZ

Finding the desired career or life situation is not an overnight process. It will take loads of hours to organize, plan, research, network, and interview to find a niche in a work or community environment. From sunup to sundown, making a schedule is a good idea to track time expenditures and allotments. Know what period of the day is best for you to do tough work and be creative, when you operate on maximum cylinders.

MOTIVATION—YOUR BIG PAYBACK

What's the initial focus of your career or life strategy? Take the time to sort out what's really important and propels your energy to act—or, as the 'old folks' call it, your 'gumpshun.' Be willing to make hard decisions at every step. These decisions help ensure that the effort and time expenditure are being properly used. It will help us avoid those 'wild goose chases', running after situations that don't match up with our best selves. Once that process is done, you're ready! In the words of the R&B song "Ain't No Stoppin' Us Now," performed by McFadden & Whitehead, "But we won't let nothin' hold us back... We've got the groove!"

To get on with it, let's identify what I call the "major groove-makers," the factors that will keep us committed and on course. When we're working and going about our lives deeply immersed in these major groove-makers, there's a sense of being in stride. They can also reel us in when we lose focus. Life's strokes are easier when we're in alignment with our gifts, wits, talents, and purpose—when our IPS is engaged and functioning strong! The major groove-makers are listed below:

For You: Ponder and participate in this section by reflecting on what really motivates you to do the work you do, brings the most smiles to your soul, or gets you out of bed on your worst day. Consider ranking these items with a rating system of your own choosing (maybe 1, 2, 3 or some other system). The benefits become clear as you do.

MAJOR GROOVE-MAKERS

- **Salary—The Goods**

Are you looking for a position or career field that plays the tune "Mo' money, mo' money, mo' money"? Of course we all need dollar bills to pay living expenses and meet our financial obligations, but the question is: Is it all that you're after? If it is, that's okay, but consider the other major groove-makers to follow. What else is important?

- **Challenge—Go Forth and Charge!**

Is your ideal position one that allows you to stretch and grow? Does this opportunity incorporate your core skills? Do you feel you're being all you can truly be? The desire to be a part of the type of organization with a management culture that allows for employee intrapreneurship, where innovation is encouraged could be on your radar. Intrapreneurship is when an employee feels they operate as an enterprise within a larger organization. They are given the go-ahead with ideas for new services or processes that bring results. Support, not stifling, guides the way. This motivator could also show up in your volunteering choices.

- **Flexibility—Any Way**

Being able to have a measure of control in terms of how we spend our time and the results we achieve can be satisfying. A sense of destiny and influence follows. With other responsibilities on our plate, a work and lifestyle that allows for flexible schedule options can rank high as a major groove-maker. This is especially true with family care issues (elderly and children) that are quite prevalent in our society. Some companies offer work-at-home, telecommuting, or alternative worksites to allow their employees to meet other professional and personal obligations.

- **Intrinsic Reward—Get Some Satisfaction**

Many people choose careers that enable them to help others or make a contribution to the larger community. Experiencing that internal feel-good factor keeps them pumped! In some cases, their work really makes a significant impact on individual lives, such as in education, ministry, nonprofit organizations, and human services. Pro bono efforts bring this same sense of doing something for the greater good. The up-close aspect of seeing people grow or providing a necessity in their lives creates very rewarding scenarios.

- **Location, Location, Location!**

Some parts of the country or the world offer appealing qualities in terms of climate, cost of living, cultural events, or overall enjoyment of life. Big-city life versus small town, versus the in-between are worth considering on the choice meter. Also keep in mind that some parts of the country have lower or higher populations of black folks, which could impact cultural and social opportunities and requirements. Deciding what geographic area is most conducive to our lifestyle is a pondering point. East Coast, West Coast, Midwest, Down South, South East, New England, out of the country, in the boonies, or in the core of the city—it's all about location!

On a personal note, back in 1988, I realized how critical location is as a variable when it comes to evaluating potential opportunities. I interviewed for a position in a small town in a state I won't mention, as my object here is not to offend. I arrived in that little burg, which played host to only one motel and the biggest event was the grand opening of a local Hardees. Race relations were still of the plantation variety, and the nearest social hub was forty miles away, a drive on a two-lane back road. Thanks but no thanks! The salary and responsibilities were good, but I would've spent every weekend and most of my salary trying to get out of there. It was a lesson learned: That location would not have been good for my soul, no matter what kind of paycheck I was bringing home.

- **Security—Holding On**

To some, the potential for longevity within a company is enough to make their dent in the world of work. Be advised that job security is now rather elusive. Few industries or organizations can make that promise of the gold watch in twenty-five years in today's competitive and global economic market.

This has been a trend for a while. Back in 1997, I attended a seminar at my college homecoming. The keynote speaker was a business professor who declared, "The psychological contract between employer and employee is null and void." In the past, that contract meant that if I, the employee, did a good job for the employer, that employer would keep me around. Such contracts no longer hold water, and everyone is subject to being downsized. Even top corporate executives are not immune, and that's a tough reality that we have to face. No matter how long you'd be willing to stick it out, you might not have the chance to stick around.

I jokingly say to participants in my career workshops that the only possible job security exists in mortuary sciences and with the IRS: Death and taxes really are the only certainties. Thus, the key to any type of security is personal preparation for the next opportunity. Keep your skills current and marketable and your network alive!

- **Combo of Two or More**

Some have major groove-makers deep in two or more areas. Challenge, intrinsic reward, and flexibility are mine. Being able to use my DNA skills, help others professionally and personally, as well as manage my own schedule keeps me tracking. Spoiler alert! Being self-employed presents a variety of challenges, some unwelcome, but the point about discovering your motivators is what keeps me going in spite of those worst days.

What does it for you? What keeps you in your groove? Remember that major groove-makers might CHANGE later on, based on the milestones you reach. For instance, when we're first on our own after graduating, the motivator could lean toward money, in order to buy the new car. After stabilizing in a job, the focus is on getting the first apartment or house. Mid-career, the quest for a challenge could show up as the major groove-maker. Later, security for retirement reasons could be the motivator. Family status and responsibilities could alter what motivates us. Schedule flexibility might declare itself as what's most important. Later on, some people who have been geared toward making a lot of money change careers because they suddenly want to give more to the community. Again, the choice is yours. Now the question is: How do we make choices that satisfy our major groove-makers?

Building a Personal Reserve

As we march forward in reaching the wants of our core, there are other stakes to put in place. Stocking these attributes constantly will keep us built to last, whether we're operating in a paid or volunteer situation or managing our lives.

- **A Little But Good Attitude**

The rules and conditions will keep changing. There will be failures and setbacks It's easy to become bitter. Staying focused and positive is essential to present ourselves well and concentrate for the best decision-making. There may be times to fight the–isms noted earlier. Gratitude, for whatever the situation, is necessary as well.

- **Get It Together—Organizational Skills**

Rounding up all needed documentation, such as résumés (old and new), transcripts, evaluations, job descriptions, and letters of recommendation may be time consuming, but it has a huge return on investment (ROI). You don't want to go on a fishing expedition when something is needed right away. Next, put them in some type of logical order. A tracking process to catalog research data, log phone calls, résumés sent, and networking cards will also be needed. Use supporting technology in this effort, and don't forget to record those passwords for company websites when applying online! The same tactics work for tracking any financial expenditures, especially for tax purposes.

- **Who Knows You? References**

Have you 'done good'? Can anyone attest to that? Compile a list of people who've known you in a professional setting, such as supervisors or co- workers. Also include those who can speak to your character. Include personal friends with a solid background; teachers, professors, or family friends. Make sure position titles, addresses (e-mail and postal mail), and phone numbers are current. Contact your references to let them know of your career plans, especially if you haven't communicated with them in a while. The last thing you want is for a potential employer to call a reference who doesn't remember you or thinks you're no longer among the living.

This who-knows-you concept isn't just for job situations. Many community and professional associations may also require references. Due to the worst of human nature (molesters, scammers, and the like) background checks, of the financial and character type, are now the norm.

Ensure that your social media presence reflects an image that's aligned with who you are professionally, especially on LinkedIn. Recruiters and interviewers do use Google to check out prospective hiring candidates. Censor your tweets and Facebook posts based on the type of opportunities or community positions you seek.

I Like It Like That
Values/Preferences List

Another main thing to consider in our soul search are values. They guide the situations we choose, for they represent the set of variables that are the most important to us—the things we truly place value on. We develop preferences in our career and work lives around these values. True convictions aren't easily compromised. Values are part of our reserve and resolve. How do they play out? Well, in a variety of ways. They force us to answer this question: What kind of environments or situations do I like to work in? What groups do I choose to be a part of in the community? Are they in line with my personal responsibilities for my family situation? Being specific on these types of preferences helps us manage time more effectively and to be more on target with our desires. It will help you to know where you are and what falls within your realm of choice. Not to negate the fact that sometimes 'we have to do what we have to do'. Only you know your situation.

For You: Below is a list of values and preferences that people often seek in their career and life circumstances. Rate these on a scale of 1-5 (1 being of low importance, 5 of the highest importance) in terms of where they fit to your choices of a place to work or other environmental aspects. They may also blend in with other pieces of your life. Go ahead and dream, but be specific. This subtle focus can produce your ideal! And why not dream?

_____ achievement/awards offered
______aesthetic work environment (looks good)
______athletic programs/sports leagues available
______autonomy/independence

_______benefits program
_______childcare facilities on site
_______decision-making authority
_______educational opportunities
_______entrepreneurial spirit encouraged
_______exposure and visibility through special projects/ assignments
_______flexible schedule
_______government agency
_______help others in my work
_______high pressure
_______near downtown area office and/or residential location
_______near rural area office and/or residential location
_______nonprofit organization
_______prestige
_______private industry
_______promotional opportunities
_______public contact
_______public transportation availability
_______set routine
_______secured facility
_______travel opportunities
_______variety in work
_______work alone
_______work inside
_______work outside
_______work with team

Other values or preferences that are important to me in choice of career and community environment are:

____

____

Now identify your top three variables in determining the best fit for you.

1.
2.
3.

How do these value factors connect to your major groove-makers?

Make Up Your Mind—Decision Time

The mapping process of your career to life route continues.

For You: Take a close look at your skills and attributes (from the assessment in Guideline 1) in conjunction with these values. See how the information connects to data you've gathered from other opportunities or research.

Questions to ask yourself at this point:

- What have I found out about me?
- What have I discovered about me as it relates to my current career environment?
- What are my options? (Choose all that apply.)

1. Stay in current job field at same level.
2. Look for a position offering advancement in my current field.
3. Change my field.
4. Change environment (government, private sector, nonprofit, entrepreneurship).
5. Change industry (defense contracting, education, health services, technology).

- What do I specifically want to do in this area? (policymaker, manage projects, supervise people, office support, technical, analyst, customer service)

- Does this choice match my major groove-makers?
- How do these choices connect to my life outside of work?

It may take some time to merge these items, but this is an opportunity to look at the steps and start some preliminary thought. As things continue to change and you find out more about yourself, be prepared to revisit this again from a fresh perspective.

Remember, options is the key word here. Sometimes we feel stuck, and unfortunately, that's sometimes our own fault. Maybe we limit ourselves or listen to the wrong people or pay attention to any self-imposed limitations. Remember, you have some control. You have some choices.

Press Toward the Mark—Setting Goals

What's behind you that provides fuel for your soul? That gives action to your dreams.

Identify your future, considering the real work before you. Once you've developed a sense of where you want to be, the next step is to set some goals. Why? Taking things as they come may work for a while, but goals give our IPS a sense of direction and give definition to our purpose. Have a plan to keep them moving!

How do you expand your trifecta, the massiveness of your strength, soul, and spirit? By continually goal-setting and applying the process to all areas of our lives, not just for career issues. Goals can be set in the following areas: **Financial** (savings, investments, distributions), **Physical** (weight loss, fitness programs), **Recreational** (travel and fun), **Spiritual** (worship and/or meditation), **Relationship** (enhancement and quality or quantity).

Basic principles to understand and follow in goal-setting are:

- Set goals that are specific. Then claim them.
- Make sure they are realistic. Do they fit YOU?
- Establish a timeline for completion. Make check-points.
- Lay out the steps to make it happen. Mind the details.
- Prioritize and put in logical life order. What's your Number One?
- Review and revise goals as necessary. Assess yourself.
- Write them down to make them more real. Be diligent in doing.
- Share with a supportive person who will hold you accountable.

For You: List your goals in at least one of those areas mentioned above. Start to outline the steps that will enable you to accomplish them within your timeline.

Goal:

Timeline:

Steps:

As you consider the source for what you want, make sure it aligns with who you are. Make sure that you're not keeping up versus keeping on. Overlay these goals with spirit. Ground these desires in good faith and wellbeing.

Guideline III

Know Where It's Going On—Update Your Chronicles

"Knowledge is the prime need of the hour."
~ Mary McLeod Bethune, Educator and Activist

Messengers. Drum beats. Griots. Spinning tales.

Newspapers. Gossip. Nosy neighbors. Telephones. Party lines.

Information superhighway. Social media.

There's value in knowing and doing so 'by any means necessary'.

From the beginning of time, from chattel to colored to citizen, we've done that, realizing there are timeless messages from the annals of history that prepare us for the present and future.

So the list for learning grows. Events and residue of the worst and best of times ensue. It has to.

The New Three R's Plus Two: Re-careering, Reinventing, Resourcefulness

Knowledge of the outer world and its impact on us individually, as well as the various segments of our lives, is also a critical guideline to follow. There are new principles of education to acknowledge and proceed accordingly. The three R's used to be reading, 'riting, and 'rithmetic. At one time, we could depend on them to get us through our work lives. They were, and still are, the basic skills. However, the three R's list has changed and expanded. It sheds new light on the issues of today's job market and greatly affects the working lives of many African Americans. Our ancestors, and many others in the struggle, worked so hard to get the opportunity for us to have those first three R's. Now the rules and realities of what it takes to get ahead are changing due to the new three R's… plus two.

Restructuring and Reduction in Force (RIF)

Quite frequently, we hear news reports of some major company announcing that it is cutting hundreds or thousands of jobs. Back in the mid 1990s, when I first started doing career management work, the military, once a solid avenue of upward mobility for African Americans, reduced its force by approximately 25 percent. Technological innovations, along with other factors, impacted this decision. In turn, the Department of Defense, other federal agencies, and private companies, in direct support of the military, had no need for as many civilians to augment the force. Major government contractors were affected since the requirement for aircraft, equipment, services, or weapons shifted.

The federal government, also a secure career avenue for many African Americans, shut down for periods of time during that same time and offered early retirement programs. Plans were underway to reinvent the government and to reengineer organizational structures.

And then the trend started to hit everywhere.

IBM, AT&T, Xerox, GM, and even old reliable Sears have made major cutbacks, closing stores and trimming their organizations down to the "right size." Steel, rubber, textile industries, or factory jobs, also once a means of securing middle-class wages for African Americans, have all dried up or gone overseas. Mergers and acquisitions are commonplace. Economic woes have brought about several recessions and more organizational cutbacks. Technology has also enabled organizations to do more with less people. Reorganization is also a way that major companies are trimming the numbers and expanding employee responsibilities. Employers also offer work-at-home options and flexible work schedules as a result of smart technology. Impacts on construction, building management, and other industries can be observed with this trend.

Even though some of this data looks at what was happening back in the 1990s, this same cycle of change is still occurring in all types of organizations today. The prosperity years of the late 1990s gave way to the tragedy of 9/11. National security, fear, economic turmoil, and fear again impacted every level of our society. The airline industry is almost unrecognizable; it is not what it once was. It has been a slow slog back to recovery. Wall Street's woes with corporate greed and the housing crisis balanced against the wonderful technology of smart phones and apps have us in a paradox. Small business growth has also weathered its share of headwinds and tailwinds.

Yes, there's a whole lotta downsizing going on, and for a variety of reasons. Because of it, competition is stiff for the jobs and career opportunities that do remain. Add on welfare, education, and healthcare reform, and the complexities and issues expand. Our challenge definitely becomes how to stay in and not out of the market. There are other issues that we, as African Americans, must come to terms with in plotting our career strategies in this new era. **Establishing our own three R's is instrumental to survival in today's competitive society. Realism, Reaping, and the Right attitude are essential; plus Resourcefulness and Reinventing ourselves.**

Who Tells the Tale? Myths and Realities

The following skit reading delves into these Three R's plus two. With a link to other points noted so far around relooking our thought process and options, along with some comic relief. Enjoy!

Scene

Tony, a bright marketing assistant with a public relations firm, is somewhat dissatisfied with his career and life right now. He's been in his present position for five years and would like to see his career blossom. He feels capable of doing so much more with himself. Right now, he just goes to work and comes home. Work has ceased to challenge him; he can do it on automatic. Tony would like to become more involved in some activities or sports but just doesn't know what to do. He has a soulful godfather who used to help him with these issues, but he hasn't seen him in ages. *Where is he when I need him*? he wonders.

Opening

(Tony is pacing the floor in his living room.)

Tony: Oh, soulful Godfather, where are you? You haven't been to see me in years. My life is out of control. Maybe if I put on some R&B music and go to sleep, he will show up. Yeah, that's what I'll do. I'll try to dream about him real hard. He'll surely get the message that I need to see him.

(Tony stops pacing, puts on his favorite beat song, and drifts off to sleep).

Tony: I'm dreaming! I'm dreaming.

(Soulful godfather appears.)

Soulful Godfather: Hey, did someone dial my psychic hotline number? Who's been looking for me?

(Tony wakes up.)

Tony: Hey, soulful Godfather, you're here! I sent for you. Where have you been? It's been a while.

Soulful Godfather: Well, my work load has been reduced. I'm actually on the retired list. You know, that granting-wishes and making-dreams-come-true stuff kind of gets to you after a while. People work you to death, wanting this and wanting that.

Tony: But you can't be retired! I have some wishes. My career is at a dead-end, and my social life is down the tubes. I feel like life is quickly making me a bystander.

Soulful Godfather: Man, have I heard a lot of that in my day. But that was mainly during the sixties and seventies. People felt they didn't have a lot of choices back then. But this world has changed so much. People change careers more often now, and it's okay—more acceptable. There are alternative work styles to choose from that blend more with your unique life situation. Employers are doing so much more to make the workplace rewarding by offering skill enhancement training and career planning courses to employees. Along with community organizations, they're encouraging citizens to get involved in their local governments and volunteer activities. Professional, recreational, and social clubs exist as outlets for cultural and other interests. And everybody talks about this E word, empowerment. They tell me it means encouraging people to take charge of themselves, being responsible for what happens to them in their careers and lives. Empowerment is about making choices and taking the steps to make it happen. Well, I tell you, with all of that going on, it's a wonder we soulful godfathers weren't RIF'D right away. But the transition wasn't that swift, and there are people who needed a push to get started in taking control of their lives.

Tony: So, in other words, I have to get with the program? You're not going to grant me three wishes or anything like that?

Soulful Godfather: Tony, you're a smart brother. I have been observing you over the past few years. You have a lot of untapped potential. I will grant you what I call my charge.

Zap!

(Soulful Godfather touches Tony with a wand)

Soulful Godfather: The spark has now been plugged into your mind. From this visit and our conversation, you'll know what to do. You've been empowered. Good luck, Tony.

Tony: Thanks, soulful Godfather. I can feel the optimism and motivation already. Will you be back?

Soulful Godfather: I'll always have your back, but in a different role these days. Remember, you're in control. I'll keep reminding you. May the Zap be with you!

(Soulful godfather disappears.)

Tony: Time to get busy!!!

And for us too, it's time to get busy! No one is going to totally take care of our career needs. Only we can give ourselves permission to have a life. Gone are the days when people deserve a promotion because they've sat in a particular chair for x number of years. There is no soulful godfather who will automatically make things happen in our lives or communities. Our charge is to take the steps necessary in finding new opportunities or horizons to expand our level of living. Managing our work and lives, along with the many transitions they will go through, takes grit. Strive to incorporate the elements of **CHOICE, CONTROL, COMITTMENT and PLANNING. Our new three R's can also include taking Responsibility, Reinvigorating ourselves, and Releasing our potential** to get what we want professionally and personally.

Take a Look Around: The New Job Market

If you've been in the same job or career for over five years, chances are the employment market process is quite different from when you last sought a new opportunity. Rapid and complex might be the best words to describe it. Wrapped up in the day-to-day tasks of doing our work, it's easy to forget to look outside of our area to see what's happening around us—the shifts, subtle and seismic.

Some of this information is probably not new to many of you, but keeping up with these career evolutions can be overwhelming. It certainly ain't what it used to be! So much more is expected of us as citizens and employees. Employers are looking for employees who can contribute to an organization to keep it competitive, along with well-informed people who exhibit potential.

But just how do we follow these shifting chronicles in the job market?

As you read this book or others and listen to a variety of recommendations on career topics, be aware of a couple of things. Each decade has brought its progress and predicaments. First, if the person making recommendations is telling you to just go to the employment office and apply or look in the newspaper classifieds, chances are they're a bit out of touch. While such advice may be well intended, times have warped forward. Yes, there used to be a time when longevity in a position, qualifications, and hard work would earn you a promotion. Or maybe you could have tried pounding the pavement, visiting several companies and putting in an application or submitting a résumé, hoping for an interview and a subsequent job offer. These days, this is rare. Technology prevails. Now, an online presence is not only helpful, but also essential. CareerBuilder, Indeed, Monster, and log-ins to company websites are required and consume time in a job search. LinkedIn, Facebook, Twitter, and other social media outlets can provide job leads. Whether it's the old way or the new way, a well-planned strategy will land you interviews, jobs, positions, opportunities, and career promotions.

What's Going On? Some Things You Ought to Know

As society changes, organizations restructure, and people grasp new options; invariably, so does work and how we define it. Predictions have even come to visualize the end of the job as we know it. A serious look at the transformation of work was tackled based on the information contained in a report entitled "Workforce 2000," a 1987 study done by the

Hudson Institute for the Department of Labor. The purpose of that late-eighties study was to examine demographic, technological, and organizational shifts to assess their impact on the workforce toward the year 2000. Anyone working in America today ought to know a bit about this report and what it means in totality. It is the catalyst for a lot of the changes we see happening in every industry, agency, and workplace today, as well as in society, and what we will see in the tomorrows.

The major findings of the 1987 study were as follows:

1. By the year 2000, over 80 percent of the new entrants in the workforce will be white women and men and women from various cultural/ethnic groups. The causes are many. Let's break down the statistics and the causes a bit.

A. Over 45 percent of new workforce entrants will be women. An increase in the number of women in the workforce has occurred due to a variety of economic and social issues. Traditional family roles and structures are shifting. More women are unmarried and self-supporting. Due to the high cost of living in many areas, it takes two incomes to survive or have a desirable lifestyle. There is also an increase in the number of single-parent families (due to divorce and non-marriage); the majority of these have females as the head of the household.

B. Members of various European, Asian, African, East Indian, Hispanic, Caribbean, Latino, and Arab nationalities continue to come to the United States. Their reasons for coming to America are many. Among the most common are presumed opportunity and escape from oppressive governments. In turn, the workforce is becoming increasingly culturally diverse.

C. African Americans now make up about 12 percent of the U.S. population. The fastest-growing cultural group is under the Hispanic ethnic umbrella, which includes Latino, Puerto Rican, Cuban, South American, and Mexican.

D. These statistics also reflect the result of the two major social movements of the 1960s, Civil and Women's Rights. Although we're forty-plus years beyond these united efforts, further legislation has cemented the dynamics of these demographics.

2. The Department of Labor reports that over 90 percent of new jobs and opportunities will be created in the service-producing/industry sector. Transportation, communication, utilities, trade, real estate are service-producing areas. Business, education, health, information, retail trade, and public service are industries for job growth, and the majority of these jobs will be located in small businesses. Higher skill levels will be required for employees. More than 50 percent of these new jobs will require some type of formal education beyond high school, especially a firmer grasp of math, language, and reasoning abilities. Most will be in managerial, professional, and technical capacities, indicating the need for a solid combination of education and experience.

It is also important to note that most major job losses will occur in those occupations involving manufacturing, production, and agriculture.

3. Technology will continue to expand; innovation and creativity will be emphasized in organizations. The information superhighway will ride through our homes and offices. Also, due to personal computers, fax machines, voice, and e-mail, plus various software applications, employers will offer alternative work options such as flex time, satellite work stations, and work-at-home schedules.

4. Organizations will continue to grow globally, especially as U.S. relationships continue to develop with foreign countries and trade agreements are finalized.

5. Organizations will continue to look for ways to reorganize, downsize, or merge with other companies to keep competitive, diversify their product bases, streamline operations, and get more out of less employees.

6. As employers grapple with numbers, money, and personnel, many are opting to use temporary employees or contingency workers in professional and administrative areas to satisfy contractual or other short-term human resource requirements. Over 25 percent of today's workforce consists of temporary workers. Other terminology and alternatives for this trend includes outsourcing and staff-leasing. Job-sharing is another alternative being used to deal with changing work styles and commitments to home/leisure pursuits.

7. All of these realities bring up issues of job security, career change, and company loyalty. More than ever, people are willing to change positions, industries, and/or careers several times throughout their work lives, either by choice or necessity. People don't marry the company much anymore. It's a matter of what you can contribute while you're there, of learning what you need to move on to the next opportunity. Employer and employee are expected to not necessarily be loyal to each other, but mutual respect for the nature of the business and everyone's right to make career choices is a better perspective. Job-hopping, once a negative term, is now the norm.

Were these predictions on point? If you've been in the workforce for over fifteen years, how did you see these predictions become reality? If you've been in the workforce for less than fifteen years, how will these predictions impact your career choices?

FYI, "Workforce 2020" spins off of the 1987 study. It continued to look closely at what is happening globally, demographically, and technologically.

Again, I include the history of this report because sometimes we wonder how we got to now. Our current economic and workplace conditions, positively and negatively, emanate from these trends. Understanding these dynamics gives us a degree of healthy perspective. Never a bad thing to have.

Where the Jobs Are

Yes, it's a tight and tough job market, but opportunities do exist. As mentioned earlier, most new job growth in the next ten years will remain in service industries and in small businesses. According to the Bureau of Labor Statistics, the hottest industries and occupations with the most job growth in the next ten years are:

✓ Medical and Health Services (home health aides, occupational therapists, nurses)
✓ Software Engineers
✓ Market Research Analysts
✓ Financial Planners
✓ Human Resource Managers
✓ Veterinary Sciences
✓ Dental Hygienists
✓ Meeting and Event Planners
✓ Language Interpreters and Translators
✓ Mental Health Counselors and Family Therapists
✓ Registered Nurses
✓ Trades: Brick Masons, Iron Workers, Carpenters

These are just a few areas that are predicted to be career hits. Check them out as a means to stretch and grow. Thinking of only of traditional jobs is fine if that's what works well for you. Back in the mid 1990s, I was amazed at the number of folks who looked to the post office as a career option; this is not to denigrate postal work in any way. I only mean to say I didn't know the role this career choice held in our community because in my hometown, there weren't any black folks working at the post office, so it had never entered my mind. A friend of a friend of mine was leaving the military as a captain, with graduate degrees in hand. When I offered help in his job search, he said plans were already in place for him to take the Postal Selection Exam. When I inquired further about what seemed to be an odd pursuit, his answer to me was, "I figured it'll be a good job." I made some other suggestions, but his mind was made up.

Check out your script. Is it stereotypical? Consider other untapped career fields that may be geared to your strengths and abilities. It's worth it to do additional research on these occupations and industries, for many offer measureable growth opportunities. Other publications and reference books from the Department of Labor are good sources to consult as well.

Do Your Thing: Entrepreneurship

George Washington Carver and Madam CJ Walker. Barbers, beauticians, washerwomen, caterers, or toolmakers. Enterprising souls are a part of our history. They have used their DNA (delivered natural abilities) in their enterprises. Small business ownership can be a winner under the right conditions. In the midst of working on the revisions of this book, actor Sherman Hemsley, aka "George Jefferson" of *The Jeffersons* fame passed away. Various mediums commented on his portrayal as a wealthy black entrepreneur during the 1970s, an anomaly that provided lessons for current day. Hemsley's character was bold and proud. Time, commitment, and effort were his operative words: "Clean it up!" Tapping into our unused talents, assets, and abilities is worth considering to make our East Side. Resources to make it happen can be found at the Small Business Administration.

Holding the Future: Twenty-First-Century Challenges and Opportunities

As we root ourselves further into this century, there are new questions begging answers: What does this entire slate of information mean for me, as a member of the workforce, as a member of society, and as an African American? Do I have the skills, education, and experience for those types of opportunities? Do I have what it takes to be an entrepreneur? What do I have to offer my community?

Below is a list of what I consider some of the biggest challenges for African Americans, based on what's happening in this complex environment.

- ***ZAP*! EMPOWERMENT**

From ejected, enslaved, and emancipated to empowered. What a journey!

Remember our scene with Tony and his soulful godfather? Tony was reminded that he's in control of his life and his career. Empowerment means using your creativity and initiative to be responsible for you and self-start as well as self-govern; to deal in solutions with any presented problems; and to use our brain power to put on our A game, bringing the ultimate outcome for ourselves, our organizations, and our lives.

- **DIVERSITY—COLORS OF THE WORLD**

Our ancestral homeland consists of a wide array of tribal and ethnic groups. The ones on the boats mingled and mated; thus, contrary to what others may think, we are not all alike! As African Americans, most of us share a common struggle, history, and a vision for heightened equality. However, when we look into a crowd of us, there are plenty of different hues, ways of dress, ages, physical abilities, and gender. When we talk to or listen to other African Americans, we hear different beliefs, attitudes, religions, or experiences. We know there are socioeconomic and class differences among various lifestyles, education levels, and geographic regions as well. Generational segments around pre- and post-Civil Rights era, technology, and terrorism bring vivid variety. Those differences aren't just among us, but exist in other cultural groups as well.

What works to our great advantage is to try to understand others for who they are, within and outside of our community. The successful employee and citizen of today and the future knows this. Realize that "everybody likes chicken." Our success in today's society and workforce depends on it! Getting in touch with our prejudices, likes, and dislikes of others or their cultures is a task before us. Listening to each other and experiencing other ways of living can raise our awareness. For me, growing up in a rural Virginia town, I thought every black person was Baptist and mainly poor like my family. When I enrolled in college and encountered black classmates who were Catholic and had parents who were doctors or attorneys, I was amazed. I hadn't been exposed to black folk like that before—not to mention encounters with anyone who was Mexican, Korean, or German. My hometown demographic was black and white, period. Fortunately, the years ahead yielded much cultural education for me, mainly courtesy of Uncle Sam assigning me to travel in different countries, and also thanks to various vacations I took abroad. I parlayed these experiences into doing programs in the workplace diversity consulting arena. Experience truly is the best teacher!

So yes, our knowledge of the variety of the world can support our pursuits in other ways. Due to globalization, there is also an increased market for employees with multicultural, international, or global experience. The economic vibrancy in other countries can create new business experience. For instance, if Africa is a continent of interest to you, try volunteering for global organizations to broaden your expertise and knowledge. Then parlay that to your advantage in the job search. Find those companies that are expanding their business interests in Africa, but also be aware of Africa's diversity.

Show your content and character through the colors of the world.

- **PRODUCTIVITY—GIVE IT ALL YOU'VE GOT!**

More than ever, employers are looking for people who will work smart, not hard. What does this mean? It means you will be expected to use all of the human, fiscal, and physical resources available to help you get the job done in an effective and efficient manner. Tapping into the know-how and experiences of others is a must. Don't reinvent any wheels. Make friends with technology, and think of better ways of doing business. If it ain't broke, break it! Just because something is still in operating condition, that doesn't mean it's functioning as effectively and efficiently as it could. Why is this important to know? Because performance evaluation processes have undergone revisions with a focus on results and quality. This comes up at some of my client sites when staff members who look like me complain about this issue. Racism is thrown out as a cause, and that's exploration time for me, in coach mode. I hear their complaints and ask, "What have been your major accomplishments during the rating cycle? And does this information show up on your résumé?" I'm just saying, as a realist, I do take the time to fully examine their assertions and the proof.

- **BALANCE THE LOAD—WORK AND LIFE ISSUES**

Strive for career opportunities or jobs that match your life interests in some form. Employers now try to bring the two together by establishing recreational activities, daycare facilities, on-site fitness areas, transportation options, and a variety of other initiatives to address and enhance quality of life issues. A family-friendly workplace is the goal of many organizations that want to recognize the whole-person perspective. Many families are involved in elder care as their parents age, and some grandparents are raising their grandchildren. There is now a focus on health and wellness as obesity rates rise. Taking care of all aspects of mind, body, and spirit is essential. The reasoning? A happy employee is a productive employee. Morale is high, customer service is good, and profits are up. Everybody wins!

- **LEARNING NEW SKILLS—IT'S IN OUR HEAD**

As mentioned earlier, the three R's—reading, 'riting, and 'rithmetic—are still important; however, new skills are essential to keep relevant. Technological smarts are needed, but problem-solving abilities still reign as a way to make it happen when stuff breaks down. Written and verbal communications skills are crucial. Our speaking and writing abilities are still questioned, or amazement is shown when we are articulate. Clear enunciation with good grammar can cause a teasing frenzy with our youth, known as "talking white." Let's get this out of our head!

Classes on communications topics, as well as leadership, are not just for upper management. They're for all levels of employees. Don't wait for your employer to send you to these classes. Use your own fiscal resources to take classes at community colleges or other locations. Check for free offerings in your place of worship, through community organizations, and at the public libraries. Read books on the topics as a route of informal education.

- **CUSTOMER SERVICE AND BRANDING—GIVE IT TO THEM**

It's an old management theory made new again: Service to the customer with a smile and an understanding of his or her need. Various management gurus have introduced new programs that I think make good sense and are here to stay for a while. At the core, these methodologies are about consistency in results and giving your full attention to and working well with customers in and outside of the organization. Your customer can be the person sitting next to you at work or the vendor that brings paperclips. Each of us can find better ways of doing business, whether it's in a new filing system, new ideas for managing a department, devising a new form, or the way in which we answer the phone. Everyone from the top to the bottom gets involved to improve the processes of the organization. Also, reengineer your business processes as a way to develop your internal and external brand. Evaluate how you work and what your organizational systems are. These same principles apply to career strategies. We're a product, so we market our skills, knowledge, and abilities to an organization. Our individual quality and processes are what we're selling. And what about your online presence? Do you have one? If not, you should! Does your brand stand out? What's a consistent message on your Facebook profile or in your tweets?

- **CHANGE AGENT—ALL HAS A SEASON**

What's your change fear factor? To make one or implement one? Knowing when it's time to go with the flow, resist, or suggest an alternative plan of action requires a mindset of being open to change. Without this, stagnation and resignation take over. Recognize the benefits of change for our growth and development as well as that of the organization to put us on a path for success. Change does involve risk. Historically, this is another area where we'd be lost without the sacrifices for freedom exhibited by our ancestors. As Frederick Douglass stated, "If there is no struggle, there is no progress."

- **COMPETITION—OLYMPIC MOMENTS**

It's bound to happen, with many vying for the same jobs, careers, and opportunities. Ask yourself some questions: How competitive am I? What do I have that gives me an edge over the next employee, applicant, or interviewee? The answers can be very illuminating! Just saying, "I know my job," "I do a good job," or. "I'm a hard worker," won't cut it today. There are literally millions of other people out there saying the same thing. To bring this point into my workshops, I often refer to the Yogi Bear principle. Polling participants on their recollections of the cartoon character, I ask, "What did Yogi Bear say about himself?" The answer? "I'm smarter than the average bear." What makes you beyond average or unique? This is where the attributes list from **Guideline I** comes in—your core assets. Yeah, you've done well, but what you can do in the future is what employers want to know. What's your potential?

For You: Have you taken this information to heart? What would it take for you to make any changes you may have identified as necessary? Reflect on what you've gleaned from these first three guidelines. What will be helpful for you to develop your triple threat of strength, soul, and spirit?

Guideline IV

Know Your Resources—The Strong Do Survive

"This country can ill afford to continue to function using less than half of its human resources, brain power, and kinetic energy."

~ Barbara Jordan, Late Texas Congresswoman

The village collects.
A community shares.
The tribe protects.
Family takes care.
A congregation gathers.

What do these represent? Individuals coming together to support each other to survive: feeding the collective body, recognizing spirit, imparting values, developing norms and honoring boundaries.

We need other people. Belonging and sharing anchor us. We are each other's resources in many ways. Generations and cultures thrive on what has passed through and down, joining their gifts in the quest for survival. Communicating with the beat of the drum, voice of the knowledgeable, or the smoke of the fire, a message rallies. From the location of the best watering hole, dangerous places to avoid, or births and passings, our ancestors have relied on beacons of essential messages or coded music to relay information.

So what do we do now as we live in the age of warp-speed knowledge? Is there a continuance of these time-tested norms?

Today followers, likes, and fans show up on our social maps. How many we have determines our presence, both online and in the global sphere.

The right tools and the strongest support are needed to keep focused in the midst of these innovations. Our balance and perspective in a world of shifts depends on stocking our personal lists so they're on hand as tools to support our success.

Who You Know: Personal Connections as Supply

Tapping into the knowledge of those we encounter professionally or personally for our job search, advocacy work, or fellowship needs serves as a useful strategy for achieving our goals. Gleaned from casual conversations, meetings, or online exchanges, there's authoritative wealth in sharing resources. Social media sites such as Facebook, LinkedIn, or Twitter create technological connections, allowing us to virtually supply to and receive help from others. Having a solid and ready 'elevator speech', a 60 second pitch of your strengths, background,—or what you're looking for—can land results. Further dialogue follows once awareness of your need is put out in the atmosphere. These, along with other interpersonal methods, provide ways of gathering information from people in formal and informal settings. Truly, networking rules the way today!

Working the Net

Let's face it: In today's competitive society, it's all about contacts and finding the route through them to the people with power of the pen. Many career opportunities are not advertised and exist only in the hidden job market. Coveted in the minds of a very few people or on limited pieces of paper, these gem positions are uncovered through networking.

This concept of networking isn't just for the job search. Used in many parts of our lives to put us in touch, these actions help us take care of business (TCB) Looking for a new doctor? A handyman? A new place of worship? We usually ask someone, using a version of the elevator speech format. When moving to a new location, oftentimes we seek out people who can share referrals for shopping or community resources. Even inside organizations, hunting for the go-to person to get the inside scoop on goings-on and resources is a must.

Networking is an approach that is part of the action of the ages: reaching out to touch someone, as the old phone ads used to put it. Still seen by some as a complicated communications system or brown-nosing—that it is not. Our ancestors networked, and it contributed to their survival. The oral tradition of storytelling and sharing permeates the chronicles. From griots to gossip, we can spread some information. Now, more than ever, the goal is to get accurate accounts of goings-on that are connected to our objectives.

And keep in mind that networking is a giving and sharing process. In our encounters, we should also look to gather helpful data that could benefit friends, colleagues, or others we know who have current career or life needs.

Link the Six Degrees of Separation

To get in touch with the expanse of our network, initially it's a good idea to make a comprehensive list of all of the people you know and have known. The range of interactions from work, family members, friends, grocery store, bank, place of worship, organizations, or the gym can be included. Now is a good time to look at how to further expand that network to maximize your resource base. Remember, it's not just who you know, but who they know, and who they know, and so on. This is the concept of "six degrees of separation," which states that in this small world after all, we're probably only six people removed from anyone we need to meet in the world. More specificity in the elevator speech facilitates the possibility of getting to the right resource person. The goal is to eventually have the right persons know us or know of us, to assist us in our career and life endeavors.

Think about your current organizations as well. Increase your network there by volunteering for projects or getting in on special meetings to get more exposure. The goal is to be ready to make a move so you won't be caught without a fall-back plan.

⌖ **For You:** List at least seven people you know. Write their occupation, place of employment, and other information you are aware of about them such as family status, organizational memberships, hobbies, or interests.

Name	Type of Work	Interests/Activities
1.		
2.		
3.		
4.		
5.		
6.		
7.		

Develop a few questions you would ask network contacts to get the information you need on a potential career opportunity.

1.

2.

3.

Also practice your elevator speech. I am... I help others...I'm looking for...

TIP: Questions should address areas designed to expand your base of general information, possibly about professional organizations, or other places to make solid connections of resource people.

This is how your network base explodes! Now, think about how you can use it effectively to find out information on career opportunities or specific life interests such as hobbies, membership in a particular organization, or something else.

Next, follow through on these contacts with a phone call, e-mail, text, tweet, or face-to-face. Do something! Check in occasionally just to say hi. The timing could be on your side as people in your network become aware of new opportunities or information crosses their line of sight. Keep yourself on the radar. And, of course, do be sincere in your check-ins. Have conversation-starters in mind, based on commonalities or current events.

A networking resource list can also help you with our next personal contact process.

Chatting and Informational Interviewing

If you ask the right question, invariably, you'll get a useful answer. Such is what happens in informational interviewing. It is just what the title implies: an interview to gather information about career fields, organizations, or positions that may be of interest.

When I started my business, I used informational interviewing to speak with several consultants about the ins and outs of being a single shingle. I asked about how to find clients, the best places to get updates on the training industry, and other administrative matters. These exchanges were extremely important, and the contacts were very open to share. Another human dynamic is that we really do like to be asked questions and seen as experts in something.

For seeking information in an organization, asking staff who work in the human resources department. It is also good to get a feel for current recruitment occupational requirements. This process can take place informally, such as in networking encounters or telephonically and possibly lead to a formal style, where the interview takes place in the office of the information provider. It's important to remember not to ask for a job in the informational interview.

⌖ **For You**: List careers, jobs, or companies in which you think you may be interested (refer back to the hottest career list).

1.
2.
3.

List places or people you can contact to gather information on that career field or company.

1.
2.
3.

List questions you would ask.

1.
2.
3.

TIP: For career-related questions, center on qualifications for positions in terms of education and experience. Responsibilities, travel, licensing, or special requirements such as association memberships can be addressed in this process. In addition, projected trends in the industry, growth potential, or relevant buzzwords can be captured. A similar line of inquiry can be used for information regarding community or lifestyle matters.

Sample Informational Interview Questions:

1. Tell me about some of the responsibilities of your position.
2. Describe a typical workday in your office.
3. What skills, traits, and knowledge are necessary for success in your career field?

Life and Work Matter: Hook-Ups that Help

We can't know it all or do it all. The key is people, people, people! Others' assets, connections, and expertise are needed to help us on this journey. As you look at the concepts below, recognize that some may require you to get outside of your sphere of comfort.

Right approaches and interpersonal principles can pay off in engaging others for support. Gauge which of these concepts will stretch you to a more beneficial zone. These options also increase our networking territory. Be seen! Go forth! Learn anew!

- **MENTOR**

How do we best tap into the lessons learned of others? A mentor is someone who can help us by providing guidance and insight based on their career experiences. To find one, use formal or informal methods. Some organizations have matching programs to create these relationships. Informally, mentors are found through interactions and connections within the workplace, professional associations, or career resource meetings. A variety of mentoring structures exist: one-on-one, circles or quads (one mentor and several mentees meet at the same time), and virtual, just to name a few. Based on your aspirations, decide which structure best supports you.

There are a few things to consider. Do you want to find a mentor in your place of work because they have the savvy and know the inner politics, or do you prefer one outside of the organization due to their objective perspective? Your choice should be based on your direction. Also, it is possible and recommended to have more than one mentor, formally and informally.

- **VOLUNTEER WORK**

This is a low-cost way to gain experience in a new career field and give back to the community. Being a volunteer can rack up extra points on résumés and in the interview process. Giving your time and energy freely can be viewed as another character-shaping opportunity.

- **INTERNSHIPS**

As a means for recent graduates or career changers, this can be a strategy to gain entry into a new opportunity sphere. These programs are usually coordinated through schools or directly with the target organization.

- **PART-TIME WORK**

What a great way to check out a new career field! Before making a full-fledged commitment or leaping into something you're not prepared for, why not earn income while exploring your next new venture?

- **TRAINING CERTIFICATION PROGRAMS**

This is an educational investment that is useful in helping you with the transition of changing careers and to gain the new skills needed in an educational or worksite program.

- **PROFESSIONAL AND COMMUNITY ORGANIZATIONS**

A group exists for just about everything we have going on in our lives: career, advocacy, political, fellowship, alumni, worship, learning, and countless others. Join at least one.

- **HOBBIES AND INTERESTS**

Expanding into new activities (and possible entrepreneurial ventures) as well as contacts can emanate from doing those things we enjoy.

- **SUPPORT GROUPS**

We're so proud that seeking the help and input of others is sometimes viewed as a sign of weakness. It's not our fault. This is part of our mis-education process, where asking for help brought negative, stinging comments from the slave master. Rethink this! Our original culture is based on a tribe, a supportive entity. Sharing our concerns and strategies with others can be very releasing and therapeutic. This type of dialogue also helps to know that we are not alone in our challenges and feelings about our situation, whether career or life related. Many libraries and other community organizations offer these venues for voicing.

Communications, 411, and Traveling Buddies

Overlaying all of the information up to this juncture—whether you are in career search, personal assessment mode, better understanding the landscape around you, or further connecting with others—has been the importance of messaging. How we project ourselves to a potential employer, present to a community group, or give instruction to children all involve effective communication. Blended with Human Relations 101, these skills are life constants that shape the nature of these interactions.

- ✓ Engage in open communication so the people in whatever lane you're traveling in at the moment will be clearly aware of everything important to a situation.
- ✓ Honesty builds trust in relationships, and trust is necessary to get the optimum value from our interpersonal connections.
- ✓ Don't make assumptions. Be willing to seek the truth. Remember that when we assume we make a…well, you know…out of U and ME.

- ✓ An awareness of the effect we have on other people postures us to listen and be ready to resolve our part in disagreements.
- ✓ Stop thinking you can change others, especially not into miniature models of yourself! Understand their core and work within that when necessary. Build on their assets when working together. Ask questions to understand others' perspectives.
- ✓ Establish priorities, but understand when a shift is necessary from our daily doing routine. Flexibility is essential!
- ✓ Don't take everything personally. It's not always about us. Be willing to receive and give feedback. We all have blind spots; others can sometimes see behaviors and faults in us that we are completely unaware of. These could be challenging or complementary to whatever effort we're involved in.
- ✓ Get a handle on our expectations. Be open to the unexpected. Loosen that pressure on ourselves and others.

⌖ **For You**: As I mentioned in the introduction, the first four chapters would address the majority of career connected topics. So these skill assessments, values, attribute identification, networks, and other resources are critical elements to put somewhere. What will you do with this information? Come up with plans, to fill in the gaps and have something to fall back on.

How about creating your personal stimulus package? To aid in your recovery from or to... (a career change, job loss, a business start-up, move to a new location, community effort)

Then work long and prosper from it!

Guideline V

Know How to Take Care of Yourself—Ignite and Nourish Life's Fire

"Hurrying and worrying are not the same as strength."
~ Nigerian Proverb

Dance with fervent moves. Adornment in nature's jewels. Circles of sharing.

Talking to the Master. Feeding from the Earth. Gathering to join or mourn.

Ancestral cries ignite these rituals. Spirituals sung. Live!

Bathing at the river. Planting. Growing.

Let it all go now.

Find serenity!

Release through pouring the mental and physical residue of the moment becomes its own freedom. No stress and no worries. Our relatives of the ages knew these coping and relaxing actions were necessary, but do we? A hectic world of instant access, microwave-speed responses, or search engine optimization can wreak havoc on our sense of what's important. Long commutes, multitasking, and demands from our smart phones or people may all drag our physical and mental resources. Bad news, overexposure, and always having to be on and reachable are not good for our soul. Technology is wonderful, but it is also addictive. Kindle Fires may diminish our life fire if we let them. Our personal spark can be diminished in the midst of these factors.

Really...is it worth it?

Personal Perils and Burnout

Facing this new reality of today's 24/7-on society and workforce may cause some of us to relook our approach to what we dream of. Making changes to our mental outlook may be necessary in order to thrive. Constant stimulation can be disruptive to our strength, soul, and spirit.

Illness too can offset our trifecta. Obesity, diabetes, cancer, and heart disease threaten our community in unacceptable proportions. Mental health issues are still often tough to acknowledge within our demographic. As the economy sinks, so can our spirits.

Reports on disparities in healthcare for African Americans are real issues to contend with. Personal stories abound of doctors paying less attention to our medical symptoms and complaints surmount about the lackluster speed at which they are diagnosed. My mother, who had leukemia, told her doctor for months that she felt more tired than usual. He never ordered a common blood test that would've shown the decline in her critical red cell count. When she finally couldn't move another step, he admitted her to the hospital. Further testing revealed her fatal condition. I'm not saying an earlier diagnosis would've changed the final outcome, but that could be the story for many others. So what's my point? Being advocates for ours and loved one's health is critical. It's time to pay attention!

Our personal habits stand ready to rob us of our vigor. We fill the voids with shopping, drinking, eating, or whatever escape routes we choose to distract us from our best selves.

Taking on other peoples burdens is another condition that extracts our verve. Other people's problems have the potential to take us off course. For parents, caregivers, or those with a personality of caring and listening, shaping realistic boundaries in interactions with others can be difficult. We can become a dumping ground, expected to always be there to help and save everyone, often not being appreciated for those compassionate, selfless efforts. This results in resentment and other emotions that damage relationships, another factor that can produce personal burnout. This happens in families, friendships, and professional settings. For a little transparency, this tends to be one of my challenges as that oldest responsible child.

What else is perilous? Career threats loom. People are getting pink slips (or whatever color they are now) every day, being escorted off the premises of a workplace they've been a part of for years. Family and lifestyle situations are economically challenged when this happens. For corporate clients, I've conducted venting sessions for those employees who've just been downsized out of their jobs. The goal, to support the person in their initial release of their disappointment and fear in the immediacy of what has just occurred. I lent my ear, just letting them be angry or express other emotions. Common outcries included: "How did this happen?" "What will I do?" "I've got bills," plus a few expletives! Add on the fact that looking for a new job or changing to a new career is scary these days.

These reactions are normal. Any type of adjustment, modification, or change in one's life can bring about a certain amount of stress. What's important is that we acknowledge these feelings, along with the range of conditions they generate. If not dealt with, stress can affect our emotional wellbeing, causing illness or injury and interference with our goals.

I know of two individuals who were downsized out of the military, which came as a complete shock to both of them. They both remained in denial, blended with anger, for a couple of years. Further unable to take action, marital discord, along with family suffering and personal pain settled in. When approached with opportunities, they couldn't effectively sell themselves because of pessimism; they were unable to release the buildup of disappointment over this career interruption. Getting over stuff that happens is difficult to do, and many of us have probably been there.

Even under normal conditions, the tensions and pressures of life can be overwhelming. Success itself can bring a measure of downfall. Being catapulted into a new station in life can open up expectations for material or personal gains that sedate not nourish the soul.

What does this mean? Mainly, stress can be caused by good or bad events, and the body can respond in a number of ways. Working on your career and life matters can be pleasant or unpleasant, so be aware of how you perceive it.

Our perceptions of how we view work and living affect our attitudes. That, in turn, determines our response to stressful events. Our thought patterns influence our attitudes about our situation. Dump stuff in, and trash runs amok. What outlook do we have? As usual, the mind is a repository for the positive, a stress buster.

Sourcing Your Stress with Fuel

For You: Take a few moments and complete the following exercise. Put a checkmark by those words that represent your current perceptions of work and life in the corresponding column. Be honest!

I view work as	I view my lifestyle situation as
a challenge	adventuresome
opportunity	confining
pleasure	draining
a drag	exhilarating
tedious	buoyant
new experiences	neutral
repetitious	carefree
wearing	overextended
consuming	balanced
new contacts	harried

reports	worrisome
e-mail hell	successful
growth-oriented	pleasing
a hassle	growth-inducing
endless	oppressive
energizing	rapid-paced
professional	relaxed
turmoil	fulfilling
tantalizing	anxiety-laden
dull	joyful
stimulating	questionable
rewarding	superficial
stifling	casual
delightful	meaningless

Think about where you put those checkmarks. What's the message from both columns?

How does it affect your sense of purpose? Which ones don't settle well with you?

Reflect on how to ignite the energy in those areas.

Dance. Or...

As the R&B group *Earth, Wind & Fire* sings, "When you feel down and out

Sing a song, it'll make your day."

What There Is to Fear

Let's say you see some aspects of your life and career that you want to change. Any idea how? This can be scary, and stress is also caused by fear of the unknown—particularly when things don't go our way or we get overwhelmed. Our own monsters and demons may not cooperate in allowing us the energy needed to make any desired changes.

⊕ **For You**: Take a moment to think about your greatest fears in revamping aspects of your career or life.

Some possible fears are:
1. I won't find a new job if I'm downsized.
2. It's so hard to be happy in this awful world.
3. I don't know what I want to do.
4. The expectations of others are bearing down on me. I feel pressured to do something.
5. Things have changed a lot. I can't keep up.
6. I'm concerned about the future of my family.
7. This work isn't supposed to be fun. I have responsibilities.

Others:
1.
2.
3.

Our fears are valid, and everyone experiences them at various junctures. What's important is that we don't let them control us. Remember, having a planned process reduces the possibilities of those fears becoming realities. Acknowledge the scary moments and use the energy to bring about positive results. Dance if you need to!

Whatever perils we're experiencing, it's important to recognize the alerts. Stress becomes a problem when it's in overabundance; this is known as distress. There are usually signals that warn us of being in this state of too much angst.

Warning signs of distress may include:
1. Irritability
2. Inability to concentrate
3. Excessive sleeping or not sleeping well

4. Intake of more alcohol or food than normal
5. Forgetfulness

Other symptoms you experience:

1.
2.
3.

We can better manage the stress in our lives if we're aware of how it manifests in us individually. Other key things to remember about stress are:

- Stress is cumulative. Things pile up. Deal with it as it comes.
- Stress is in the 'eye of the beholder'. What may be stressful for me may not be stressful for you.
- Stress can be channeled for better productivity. It can be a trigger to take new actions to solve undesirable aspects of our situations.
-

How to Rekindle the Fire: Whole, Worthy, and Well

Remember that stress is a wellbeing issue, hitting us at all levels of our natural existence. How do we return to a more proportionate, manageable place in our strength, soul, and spirit? Take a moment and reflect on those days when your overall countenance exudes this balance. Describe your thoughts and feelings in that moment. I think many of us might categorize this state as being whole, worthy, and well. Individually, in trying to obtain this condition, we might answer these questions.

How do you define wholeness?
What are you worthy of?
Who are you when you are well?

For many of us, a basic sense of feeling in control of our lives, showing up authentic, taking care of our physical, mental, and spiritual being with a healthy sense of self-esteem would be filtered into the answers to those questions.

So why aren't we always there? What gets in the way; are there things that become deflators? Certainly, life's disappointments, our habits, motivations, and perspectives can flow out in each of those areas to send us spiraling downward, but we can rise up to feel we're getting the best of ourselves from life. Our wellbeing deserves a way and space to rebound from the onslaught of life's pressures. Through the techniques listed below, we can get whole, worthy, and well.

- **BALANCE—MIX IT UP**

Make time to do something for your emotional, physical, spiritual, intellectual, and vocational wellbeing every day. Prioritize your life quests. There is time to do everything that is important to us if we're clear on what those tasks are.

- **SPIRITUAL—GET RIGHT NOW**

Keep in touch with your faith and beliefs in a higher power. Pray for guidance. Rely on spirit power to calm your fears. Participate in your religious services. Remember the age-old wisdom of our ancestors. Speak life into your language.

- **EXERCISE—MOVE IT UP AND DOWN**

Research shows that exercise releases those natural high ingredients in our brains, those endorphins that make us feel good. Walking, biking, jogging, lifting weights, yoga, swimming, and aerobics are all good. Do whatever fits your time and inclinations.

- **NUTRITION—GOOD SUPPER TIME**

We've packed up leftover crumbs and made cuisine and called it 'soul food'. Even though most of these delicacies (as we see them) are scrumptious, they aren't always good for our body. Some do rate on the healthy scale, such as the yams and collard greens, when prepared with less salt and other fatty ingredients. Also, watch the Kool-Aid and soda consumption or anything with too much sugar. Eating right does have a correlation to how we feel.

There is also a comeback of a variety of home remedies, such as castor oil and iodine. Other alternative medicines and therapies can also keep us well.

- **SENSE OF HUMOR—HAVE A COMEDY HOUR**

Being able to laugh at ourselves and different situations can be stress-relieving. At many family gatherings, time is often spent looking back and reflecting on 'how we got over', with compelling stories that can be very healing. Individually thinking about our lives in totality, successes and trials can bring good perspective. Reading and watching sitcoms can bring laughter for the soul too. This is one of my outlets; I've seen more *Cosby Show* and *Sanford and Son* reruns than I'm willing to admit!

- **IT AIN'T ME! DEPERSONALIZE THE EVENT**

Some things are out of our control. The job loss may have nothing to do with you and your performance or who you are. Instead of saying, "I gave that company, person, or organization the best years of my life, and look what they did to me," tell your inner self, "I learned a lot from my work at XYZ or my relationship with ABC, and those skills and experiences will take me far in my next opportunity."

Other life realities hit us as well: relationship incidents, societal issues, personal accidents ... It seems like stuff is out there waiting to pounce. We can't deny these realities of living. Look forward, not back, for these events could be masked blessings.

But sometimes we do move toward the edge, with despair and loss of hope. Depression can creep up fast. Recognize the signs that come from low moments or a case of the blues, for these are normal feelings during challenging times. Mental health concerns should be addressed just like our physical health symptoms. There's often reluctance for many of us to admit to these conditions. We're supposed to have coping skills, but the courage is really in coming forward and getting the needed help.

- **SUPPORT GROUPS—NEEDED TO GET BY**

Life happens: frustration, illness, family disruptions, tragedies, and all sorts of other disappointments. Getting through or by these things isn't easy, especially alone. Hospitals, local libraries, places of worship, and other service organizations now offer everything from cancer to career support groups. If not, get your own group together, a gathering of people with a purpose, to strategize ways to overcome setbacks and seemingly insurmountable obstacles.

- **GET OTHERS INVOLVED—IT'S A FAMILY AND FRIEND AFFAIR**

Seek the input of those close to you in your career or life decisions. A wise sage's ear comes in handy here, especially if you're considering relocation, starting a business or going back to school. Ask yourself how this will affect those closest to you and your relationship. Keep the communication channels open and in good receiving condition.

- **RELAX—COOL RUNNINGS**

Find things to help you wind down. Seek hobbies that allow for tinkering, piddling, or sending your mind off on a journey. Are you a gardener or golfer? Do you fish or play cards? The picture of my mother on the introduction page for this guideline shows her poking around in the soil. After eight hours in a noisy, tedious factory, this was what she did to release and replenish. She found beauty in the dirt.

What's your centering activity? Occasionally schedule goof-off days. The break can be rejuvenating!

- **SET BOUNDARIES—BE A TERRITORY**

If you're one of those folks who has difficulty saying no, if you too often take on other people's burdens and can't seem to carve out a space just for you in your home, you've realized how draining this can be. The people in your life aren't going to point this fact out; instead, they'll stick with their comfortable way of dealing with you. A little rule setting, the way it's going to be, will help you regain your lanes. Based on your situation, some explanation to your tribe may be necessary too.

Also, think about where you are in the season of life. Are you in a burning or subsiding place, in respite or reinventing? We all have appointed times to be in either of those seasons, based on career or family or personal circumstances. Relish each of them for what they teach and contribute to our growth.

- **DOWN BY THE RIVER—SPA MOMENTS**

Our ancestors knew the value of the waters—of bathing and relaxing in the pond, stream or ocean. Take to them! At home, use your bathtub or old basin. Got discretionary funds? Find a local day spa or full-service one. Whatever you can or choose to do, the goal is to treat yourself to a little pampering. Nails did. Hair done. Feet rubbed.

- **LOVE—'NUFF SAID**

Love yourself enough to take care of yourself. Love others enough to encourage them to do the same.

Now...create alignment and balance in the life you want. Let this state be revealed in a big way. Make a shift when needed. Practice discipline to change any unwelcome habits.

This is hard work for these hurried times. We can get used to this always-on persona, and when that happens, it's easy to forget to take care of our mental and physical temple. We can start by putting at least one step on our schedule. Chunk it up.

We are worth it! Ignition of the senses, support of the soul, and renewal of strength can position us on a wellness track and feed our spirit with abundance. Ready what works for you. Then fire it up to blast away burnout. Simplify for less stress.

Encourage and engage...yourself!

Guideline VI

Know Your History—From the Rising of the Sun

"History is the landmark by which we are directed into the true course of life."
~ Marcus Garvey

Alex Haley dared to tell it.

Stories circulate. Truth sought.

Ancestral soil connected. The bush, brokenness, boat, and big house.

Kunta, kente, and kinfolk form our present kaleidoscope.

Middle passage, slavery, emancipation, marches, and legislation.

Freedom—a prize that focused a movement.

Over thirty-five years ago, a nation was mesmerized, sitting front and center of their television screens. The horrors and triumphs were vivid, and reality loud and large, as the *Roots* miniseries showed us what the history books wouldn't. Past, blood, victory, and Providence boldly portrayed.

The backward-looking African sankofa bird tells us, "Go back and fetch it."

No doubt where we came from.

Pivotal stakes in the new land.

Honor the firsts.

Continuing to make a way.

Inventors, instigators, and inroads.

But what do we do with this information?

Roots: Personal and People

Successful people are able to draw from the past and utilize it as a teaching tool; as a source of strength; a base for personal power; a device for direction. The truth—with its horrors and happiness—makes them free to embrace this totality. Many victories of African American leaders, heroes, role models, and groundbreakers stand as products of the pages and chronicles of the past.

On every front, our presence has made a difference. Hands and minds that are storehouses of creativity; inventions, agriculture, military, art, music—the list is enormous. We were there!

And, as with most things, it's about the "in the beginning." Carter G. Woodson, author of the classic, *The Mis-Education of the Negro*, wrote, "Those who have no record of what their forebears have accomplished lose the inspiration which comes from the teaching of biography and history."

Where to Dig

There are several ways to increase the knowledge of our history. Read and see about the past by visiting museums and meaningful cultural sites in your city and others. Dig for information, wherever you are. Convention and visitors' centers of some major cities have special directories or guides that list African American historical sites, events, attractions, and entertainment. From coast to coast and in between, a wide array of places to chart our history exists. Baltimore Maryland has the Great Blacks in Wax Museum, depicting several important eras of the history of African Americans, from the motherland to the Harlem Renaissance, to the fight for Civil Rights. Los Angeles is the location of the California African American Museum, with an emphasis on the Western frontier, the cowboys and cowgirls, and those pioneering spirits. Detroit Michigan hosts The Charles H. Wright Museum of African American History, with a focus on education through interactive and online resources. The Schomburg Center for Research in Black Culture in the New York Public

Library system is renowned for its vast collections, documenting the totality of experiences within the African Diaspora.

And then there's my home state of Virginia, ground that bears the first documented African footprints to step on American soil in Jamestown. Head north and Mount Vernon, the home of this nation's first president, houses on its acreage a slave burial ground. Partnering with other historical organizations, a local Fairfax County group, Black Women United for Action (BWUFA), spearheads an annual Slave Memorial Wreath-Laying Ceremony at Mount Vernon. I was very active with BWUFA back in the mid 1990s, thoroughly enjoying the solemn and spiritually moving nature of this event.

No matter what corner of the country, the contributions of our people are coming to life and being dug up—and beyond. From a chance networking encounter, BWUFA also joined forces with our Canadian sisters and brothers, many of whom are descendants of slaves that escaped through the Underground Railroad. There was an instant kindred connection, in purpose and personality, so mutual visits were made, BWUFA to Halifax, Nova Scotia in July 1995, and the Black Nova Scotians to Mount Vernon for the Slave Memorial Wreath-Laying Ceremony the following year. A special contingent came back for a Black History Month program at the Canadian Embassy in 1996 (a first-time event). Through these collective efforts between countries and continents, the goals of our dual existence are being realized and revitalized, to be viewed as an integral part of the development and destiny of the world.

For Our Victories: Venue Variety

The National Park Service maintains a listing of black historical sites in various states. For instance, Montgomery, Alabama has a Civil Rights Memorial, providing a timeline of the legislative hurdles and lives lost in the quest for equal status in this country. Fort Leavenworth Kansas is the home of the tribute to the Buffalo Soldiers, unsung African American soldiers, and heroes who fought and died in the defense of this nation. Much artwork is also now available depicting the military pursuits of African Americans in the Old West. For now, we appreciate the chronicles and pictorial representation of our people who have been 'proud to serve.'

And what a history there is!

There is a rich military legacy indeed, from the 555th, "Triple Nickel", the first black parachuters, to the Tuskegee Airmen, who gained fame during World War II as the first black fighter pilots. Associations honoring these stalwart defenders still continue to meet and share their history with the community. Other military service heroes and firsts have been honored legislatively and through books as well such as the Montford Point Marines and Golden Thirteen Naval Officers.

We also honor our role in commerce. Black Expo USA is an annual event that focuses on entrepreneurship and economic empowerment. Featuring workshops, cultural artifacts, and products that speak to our innovations, the program appears in several cities.

On every front, we've put a stake: Olympian medals and championship rings. There are many firsts here too. We run, jump, play tennis, flex muscles, and yes, black people do ski! And we've expanded the list and formed clubs around some of these activities.

How do we share the knowledge, for *perpetuity?*

Several mainstay books on the market by prominent authors and historians give a comprehensive timeline of the arrival, cultural contributions, and struggles of African Americans; such as the classic works of John Hope Franklin and Lerone Bennett, Jr. The earlier writings of Carter Woodson, W.E.B. DuBois, and others are good starting points. These phenomenal writings reconnect how far we've come and the progress the world is making to understand the fullness of the African American experience.

For an African worldview, read the research of Cheikh Anta Diop and supplement it with the works of Ivan van Sertima and Asa Hilliard. Discover more about the African Biblical perspective with Reverends Cain Hope Felder and Walter McCray. Don't know who they are? Google them. Research and dig. Many of these authors have set the bar; creating a tsunami-like interest as to how vital this anthropological knowledge is on all fronts.

Our organizations are also a source of history. The NAACP, NCNW, and National Urban League greatly mirror our successes and struggles. We should all pledge our support to at least one of these organizations, as was implored at events such as the epic 1995 Million-Man March.

The work continues. Our sociology, demography, and theology bring a truth. Sororities, fraternities, Masons, and Eastern Stars remind us of commitments to service, education, culture, and, yes, good times. We can't deny it! We like to party too. Just imagine the role these groups have played in each of our lives, and they still do because they are still needed. Many have even celebrated the momentous centennial recognition, 100 years of bringing the force of community organizing to create justice and a village of support. I am a proud member of Delta Sigma Theta Sorority Incorporated, and our plans are underway for our 100-year recognition in 2013.

Reflecting back on these organizers' boldness, courage, and foresight ranks high on my awesome meter! Their adversities of the time with limited resources and only decades removed from bondage present extraordinary lessons on strength, soul, and spirit for the ages.

Steady the Words and Pictures Trod

Reading and writing are guides to direct us to the roots of history. Since the 1980s, the surge in the popularity of the works of African American authors has been wonderful. Terry McMillan showed the publishing industry that we can 'get our groove back'. Tony Morrison's winning of a Nobel Prize for literature in 1993 was a victory long coming. Not to forget those creative forerunners who took to pen during The Harlem Renaissance, their words still very much anchor and inspire.

Whether they are fiction or nonfiction, these syllable extensions pierce the essence of the evolution of our culture: the joy and pain of African American men and women. They provide generational stories, knocking at our own individual memories door. Integrating historical tidbits, they entertain and educate the reader at the same time. Now many follow in the pen steps of Phillis Wheatley, a 17th century slave, who became the first African-American poet and first African-American woman to publish a book.

Subscribing to African American print or online focused magazines, newspapers, or other periodicals keep us up to date and in touch with what's happening nationally and locally with our communities. Ebony, Jet, Black Enterprise or Essence continue as cornerstones.

Art exhibits depict the rich value and traditions imbedded in the works of premier international, local, and regional creatives of the Diaspora. Around the holidays, marketing and promotional organizations sponsor ethnic art and gift shows in various locales. Art tells the stories of our natural existence in its own way. History has also been captured in photographs through the collections of James Van Der Zee and Gordon Parks.

Steady but sure, our people have kept at their creative crafts, plodding along until this power is now recognized. It's an explosion of talent!

Take It Home

Let us not underestimate the extraordinary effect of landmarks in our lives, whether cultural, family, or personal. They give us a base, a starting point, in our widespread destinations after our ancestors disembarked from the ships. Retracing our steps can rejuvenate, as we reminisce on fond moments after acknowledgement of the painful. Going back to our hometowns for reunions allows us to reconnect with people and our beginnings, the source of our strength, soul, and spirit. As the old folks remind us, "Don't forget where you came from!"

The relevance of knowledge of our past has hit other arenas. Black History Month continues to be honored through special activities in many organizations. Participate in those observances at work, your place of worship, and in the community. Attend African and Caribbean festivals, as well as other cultural events. Make it a yearlong celebration; let's not confine it to February. Volunteer to help with these activities, ask questions, read the literature, eat the native dishes, and appreciate the sights and smells of the multifaceted traditions. Enjoy the vibrancy of the African Diaspora.

Our food in itself narrates, sharing the palettes and cuisine pieces our ancestors brought with them. The slaves ate yams to sustain them on the Middle Passage. No major holiday table is complete without a dish of them present in many of our families. My grandmother used to bake sweet potatoes for my after school snack and I still have the pan she used! Even though I've had the privilege of traveling through a good deal of the world and sampled a mixture of delicacies, I still get excited over fried chicken, collard greens, cornbread, and chitterlings, to name a few of my favorite dishes. To me, those foods really are good for the soul. Historically, some even have medicinal purposes, such as the use of the juice from greens, pot licker, for colds and other ailments.

Share your heritage proudly. Talking to older members of the family can help us gain historical perspectives, a sense of accomplishment on how far we've come along with more depth of the family's roots. Attempts to trace our genealogy are becoming more frequent and yielding results. A visit to the archives section in the library or vital statistics office of our family's birthplace, along with online resource genealogy sites is a good start. Sharing and gathering this information can bring about self-understanding and mutual respect. Drawing strength and courage from those who have gone before can propel us forward. The past is a basis for being, so dig into it wherever you can!

Continent of the Sun

Why talk about Africa, some might ask? I say, why not Africa? The relevance of this continent to our future is waiting to be discovered. First, from all archaeological indications, God created our humanness of body and spirit in Africa. We are all children of that continent.

The realization that I am the descendant of a man and woman, who made an unwilling journey, under wretched conditions, on a cargo ship across the Atlantic, is a soul-stirring lesson in the power of survival. What strengthens me is that my family's generations made it to this shore. Through procreating, re-creating, and creating, I'm here...and so are you.

And that's our story throughout the African Diaspora. When I visit the Caribbean and note the similarities of the folks I encounter, I often think it's only a matter of where the boat stopped and who was forced off in various locations.

Years ago, I took my eleven-year-old nephew to a slave ship exhibit at the Blacks in Wax Museum in Baltimore. As we wandered down in the replica of the ship hold, the sounds of moaning and groaning, back dropped against the noise of ocean waves and winds, could be heard. He got scared and turned around. I comforted him and told him we had to see this. We slowly moved though the wax figure exhibits of scantily dressed slaves with neck irons and chains, sitting in close quarters. The exit area featured a tank of Atlantic Ocean water with cups for pouring libation, a solemn and healing ending. My nephew later told his mother, "It was awesome. We poured water in a fish tank for our dead relatives." *The symbolism will come later,* I thought. It did, for he's now twenty-eight and still remembers the power of that moment.

My interest in Africa really started while I was in college. I took an anthropology course entitled "People and Cultures of Africa," which provided a forum for me to learn important research on Africa, such as the remains of the earliest humans. I've also come to recognize the opportunities I had not fully utilized due to my lack of proper education on African culture. Several students from Nigeria were on campus, presenting a tremendous opportunity for an authentic cultural exchange. My classmates and I admittedly initially ostracized these students, because they seemed different. Eventually I came to know them better and did gather some insights into their tribe, the Yoruba of Lagos, Nigeria. I did a paper on their family and kinship structure for a sociology class and even earned an A.

How has the relevance of Africa played out for me since then? Read on!

To even further take it the root, how about using DNA to find your African ancestry? I've done this test and discovered my family is of Nigerian descent, specifically Yoruba-Fulani on the matriarchal side. One of my uncles did the patriarchal side, and the results also showed Nigerian-Ibo on the male side.

Wow! So I made sure to let my former classmates from Nigeria know!

We used the company African Ancestry in Washington DC for our testing. The fee is around $300, and the testing kit can be ordered online. Instructions for using the saliva method are explained well, and once sent in, the company returns DNA results in about six weeks. This technology has not always been available, so we claimed the whole continent for identity. Now, through this scientific process, we can know specifics. I found it affirming, an ultimate answer in my roots beyond my hometown of Waverly, Virginia.

Also, why not venture to the motherland if given the opportunity? The door of no return, where our ancestors transited from the various slave ports on the west coast of Africa, now swings open.

My thinking about this led me on a spiritual and biological quest. I knew that my existence in ancestry, soul, and blood reached out across the ocean, before the year of 1619. There is another home for me—not just the one I know and treasure, some 170 miles southeast on Interstate 95 in Virginia, but a planetary one on another continent. And not just for me, but for all my sisters and brothers that comprise the 12 percent of African American population of this country. I clearly began to recognize that in order for me to grow and strengthen my faith and purpose, the past, present, and future are vehicles linking many answers and holding much authority. I've taken two trips—to Senegal, the Gambia, Ghana, Togo, and Ivory Coast—and found these pilgrimages very spiritually sustaining. More sojourns to Africa are in my travel plans, especially Nigeria, now that I know it's the local of my ancestral beginning.

A place of beginning that has its challenges and residue, the continent remains wrought with this mixture, juxtaposed against an inspiring land mass and people of tremendous resources and downfalls. Nevertheless, many African countries are versions of role models for forging ahead from which lessons can be extracted. Nelson Mandela's story is epic: for South Africa. Ghana's history is notable. Technology, social media, and tourism have further linked the continent in the global economy, swaying some of the dark myths surrounding it. Africa is on the rise!

Now the question is: What are you doing to know, understand, and apply your history? Will you enter the space to a new awakening?

Guideline VII

Know the Creator—Invite Spirit

"Our creator is the same and never changes, despite the names given Him by people here and in all parts of the world. Even if we gave Him no name at all, He would still be there, within us, waiting to give us good on this Earth."
~ George Washington Carver

The healing of music. The fervor of prayer.
The awesome Provider. Foot stomping. Hand clapping.
A Whisper. A leaf moves. The Presence is there.
Grace and Mercy for the Journey. Call and Response.
Hope. Ancestral Sorrow Songs.
The Blues. Overcoming. From darkness to day. Victory.
Every time the spirit is felt at heart and soul level, do something.
Falling down and getting back up.
Acknowledge it. Trust it.
Send a revival!

Numerous conditions have tried to rob us of our fervor and out of the hold of spirit. Slaves were forbidden to openly worship, but they found a field or a shack to talk to the Master, and the Spirit was in the midst. Hallelujah!

For people of strength, soul, and spirit, God has been our rock in a weary land. Some of us have come up the jagged sides of hills and out of the lowest plains, yet God has snatched us back. The blessings have been bountiful, His purpose unfolded to us on a daily basis.

Let me acknowledge that we have a blend of religious as well as spiritual beliefs and practices in our community. Whether you are Christian, Muslim, Buddhist or any faith, our commonality resonates in the surrender to something greater than our natural selves. And it shows up greatly as another guide to help us operate in love and purpose.

This Spirit moves through us to take us to higher levels, if we let it. His will, 'making a way out of no way', leads us to excel.

Now is not the time to forget the guidance that God has provided for us as a people, particularly since our arrival in this land. Through the hardships there have been hope and understanding to keep our ancestors moving toward amazing and freer days, knowing that through it all, He is faithful, just, and purposeful. The joy of this Presence, its own source of spiritual muscle, is an awesome pillar on which we stand.

Welcome the Energy

In our current times of increasing negative messages, media attacks and disdaining accounts on the status of our community, particularly our youth, we need spiritual remembrance. Passing on to the next generations, our personal and community stories of how God has been on our side in the midst of being 'buked, scorned, and bet against, can be an effective mental counterattack.

Then use the goodness of spirit to shun evil, however it looks in the ugliness of behaviors that make us act in ways that are not good for ourselves and others. Be aware of false professing. As a realist in my faith and praise, I know that good things are not always present, even in our places of worship. My grandmother told me when I was leaving for college, "Be aware of some of those city churches you find. Some of the biggest devils you'll ever want to see are up in there." Noted... and she was probably right.

And we can't forget some of the not-so-pleasant residue of our history that contributes to crime, scams, and misuse of power—to name a few—some even invoking spirit as a front. Call it what it is in blocking the flow of our blessings.

Invite spirit, a voice of victory instead. Ask for sage wisdom in all things.

Spirit beckons us to forgive and forge onward, to put what is behind, behind. There are some in our community who still have shame around slavery, the aftermath of emancipation, and sharecropping. To answer that angst, Providence, destiny, or order come to mind. Somebody survived and thrived, and that's how we're here. The strength of that reality is compelling. Healing results. Without the past, we wouldn't stand firmly in where we are. No matter what your circumstances, take the appointed time to reconcile it!

Knowing when to let go, when to hold on, or when to turn it over to something bigger than we could ever imagine is part of a spiritual cycle. The ancestors knew this, that their plight was not forever. God's plan would reveal itself in order to change their condition. Referring to the victory 'over yonder', they held true to the power of faith as an expressed future condition—not of ready-made appearances, but of things to come, right on time...guaranteed! In the meantime, they held on, trusted, and did what they had to do. While still carving a unique rhythm in how they sung and moved, they brought out their soul. It was greatness acknowledged in an awesome way.

The majesty of miracles will show up.

Messages of sprit show up in the natural cycle of life. The sunrise and sunset of our transitioned loved ones, and ours to come, provide memories that can be catalysts for achieving our goals. Their sacrifices to get us to this day—somebody prayed for us—are all strongly ensconced in the collective. I remember my loved angels most vividly during quiet moments, particularly when I'm out for a walk by the woods or water. Nature, too, is a provider. Earth, wind, and fire—the elements—remind us of this power.

Anchoring in the Principles of This Force

How do we get to this place of spirit?
Stand fast.
Hold firm.
Cease action.
Listen.
The spirit then moves.

God wants us to be successful. He created us for it, in however we measure our achievements. Vivid memories of watching my family continue on in the face of adversity with no excuses inspire me, raising me and others, a mission of value accomplished.

So meditate. Ask Him. Then acknowledge this super force that hovers over us, waiting to be tapped to support our deepest yearnings.

Many of you may remember what it was like to go to church or your special place of worship with family or community elders. I know I do. My experience is based on my southern rural Baptist upbringing. The renditions of hymns, full of hope and praise, moved me. A recognized other presence was no doubt in the midst. Somebody testified. Holy! A roll of preaching energy, then someone got happy. Speaking their faith into the atmosphere, this person electrified the moment. Those paper fans (usually from the funeral home) were needed to calm them down.

Your own worship experiences may be similar or different, yet our commonality is that this faith expressed energy is what got our family and other loved ones over. They acted on spirit, which they placed in their hearts as another 'personal stimulus package'.

Bringing these principles of reality into our communities is so important now. Those adverse images and messages that threaten the minds of our succeeding generations stand to take over. A grounding and personal grassroots effort to invite this critical life piece of spirit at an even deeper level is part of the work to do. Each of us, whether parent or extended relative, or any way in which we impact a child, can do this. We can communicate faith. In many churches or other venues, young people are often recognized for making the honor roll, graduating, or other significant events. It's a good thing to acknowledge these youngsters, but the next step is to make sure *they* see it as a blessing. Instill in them a gratitude to the Creator.

How else does this spirit show up in the universe? It seeds our creativity. When invited in, this spirit envelops us, sending energy to nourish our souls. Music, food, and art abound from this state. I often listen to sixties or seventies R&B and find it deeply touching. The symbolism is so real, as an answer to societal and personal maladies, resounding so full of hope. These melodies bring joy; moving my overall spirit from lackluster to luminous. Faith and thanking the Lord so warmly sung in the messages.

Whatever the season of life, it is paramount to have a faith foundation. Think about your first steps in trust. Your walk matters. Stand on the promises of His will and way. Picture alignment of life.

Belief that something sure and steady sits at the helm of our lives is the way of spirit. The turns and twists of midlife have presented many challenges for me with huge losses on a personal, as well as professional scale. Having the right thing on hand, my faith, keeps me soldiering on. Listening to the gentle guidance of God's spirit and my loved ones who now reside with Him points the way!

How do find your place to invite spirit?

Anchor in your special spot. Seek an environment for focus—a no-enter zone from those we share space with. Walks along a quiet path or near water are good for me. I've even discovered a rock in the midst of a grassy area in my neighborhood; when I stand on it, a sense of spiritual energy illuminates any dilemma I may be facing, and on that rock, the answer is revealed.

Find your sanctuary. Claim this base as your return to home, a place to ponder, and then act.

Spirit calls us to invite others in too. Don't forget to treat others well, in fellowship, in love, and in support. As Mahalia Jackson so inspirationally and brilliantly sang, "If I can help somebody, as I pass along…if I can cheer somebody, with a word or song…then my living shall not be in vain." Be led to recognize the evidence presented when we need to reach out to others, even in our worst moments. There's purpose in these acts.

Then there's the personal realm of our belief. That we will get… (fill in what your desire is), in due time. Posture yourself in a realm of knowing that what is for you is for you and will surely come. Don't forget to hope for good reports…and for purposeful days to fulfill your divine assignment.

A magnificent force is standing by, to charge your traveling energy. Make sure it's a button on your IPS (internal positioning system) for your success and life in the spirit!

Section C

Epilogue: Get the Power and Steer Toward Success

"I have discovered in life that there are ways of getting almost anywhere you want to go, if you really want to go."
~ Langston Hughes, Poet and Activist

Freedom came. Movements worked.
And so now what's on our to-do?
Success, elusive or real—ours to claim in work and life.
All is within us to achieve.

Deploy every talent you have in order to get yours. Stop waiting for a soulful godfather to grant your wishes. Find a spiritual place for reflection. Discover those waves of strength that keep you forging ahead.

As the 'old folks' continue to remind us, in this life we will have some hard times. These tough patches are vehicles to mold and shape our character. Dark moments come, and I'm reminded of the words of one of my favorite songs, "*Better Days*," by the R&B artist Diane Reeves: "You can't get to no better days lest you make it through the night."

Calling on our resolve, let it truly anchor mind and body to move on down the road to our selected destinations. In spite of…

Therein resides the multitude of lessons that shape our personal guidelines. Supporting our trifecta of strength, soul, and spirit, these made for us teachings are grounding.

How to best summarize them?

Read on for tweaking these guidelines to your journey.

Thoughts to Keep You Moving Forward

- Be determined to move strong, in spite of uncertainty and storms (whatever they look like for you: slow economy, job market, relationship challenges).
- Rudder at the right signs. Stay anchored in your values, visions, and interests. (Revisit your lists.)
- Open all lanes for learning. Detours and potholes are there for a reason. (If you fall in or go the wrong way, so what? Find a way out or around.)
- Explore the right realms, your major motivators. What's the gas in your engine? (passion, giving back, your expertise, challenge, taking care of your family)
- Acknowledge fellow travelers. We don't journey alone (Get support from friends, mentors, and networks.)
- Plot a route to success that's realistic. Be confident in who you are and pace your journey to your style. Do you!
- Rejuvenate. Stop and rest. Take a break, vacation, or staycation (Have a special way to fuel you.)
- Boldly remain a believer in your own success. See it to the right, left, front, and rear as you check your mirrors. (Engage!)
- Claim victory at critical times. Segment your successes for each leg of your journey (Small wins are good).

Don't Be Afraid to Use the Power

- **Purpose and Passion**

There's a mission in recognizing your destiny and what gets you genuinely excited.

- **Overcoming and Opportunity**

Setbacks can often yield your next success point.

- **Winning and Wonder**

How we or I got over and through is still a subject for amazing stories.

- **Expectation and Elevation**

A believable and solid vision can take you to the next level.

- **Released and Recharged**

Let whatever it is that's holding you back go, go, go! Then mount up for the future.

So wrap all that is you in this powerful abundance for your days ahead and beyond. Hustle when you need to. Be attuned to the ribbons of grace and love. Stay grateful, even on muddy trails, forced marches, or when you need to go underground.

We will stumble along the way, but even the worst experiences of our lives can yield the discovery of that new path. Move from pitiful to prosperous. Find highlights in those most unwelcome of events. Reboot your IPS (internal positioning system) when you feel a bit sluggish. Tune up and in to the true direction dictated by your measure of strength, soul, and spirit. Whisper thank-yous to the world, and most importantly to Him, who makes us able, God.

Do gifted, witted, and purposeful you. Always! Then you will discover all you were created, niched, and fitted to be.

What Guideline Will You Leave Behind?

The 'old folks' left a mark. The ancestors were marked, literally. The slaves built landmarks. The freedom-seekers laid out a route. The marchers created movements.

And if you don't know what to do with this history?

Then leave a footprint, the legacy of your effective deployments of your triple threat. Engage in reflection about what you want that mark to be. In your children, your unique works, or your community presence, a clear remembrance of your journey should be clear.

What has been left to us?

As I've shared parts of my personal story, you may remember references to my mother's determination and my grandparents' wisdom, along with their strong sense of hope. What's yours? Reflect on those hand-me-downs from those you love, big or small—a favorite recipe, life lesson, humorous or sage saying, writing, craft, value imparted, or family business. These stand as left behinds of value. Cherish them. The character traits we inherit from our DNA (delivered natural ability), scientific or other ways enabled—embrace them. Tally these talents and attributes up. Decide how you will spread them to your circle, the lives you touch in some way through family, fans, friends, or followers.

How will you cement that powerful part of you, the part that will be remembered? Make it a pillar for the future, so that someone else will shoulder it firmly, as a foundation for achievement.

Time for Action

A while back, as I was boarding a flight home after being away on a business trip, I noticed the writing on the piece of paper with my baggage check: "Keep this receipt for the rest of your journey." Wow! As usual, I found all sorts of applications for this message—mainly that we carry a massive load of mess and miracles in our consciousness. They can either be a triple threat for failure or a launching pad for triumph.

Poke through your personal baggage, find those ancestral items, and combine them with your assets. Then make them a keepsake to open for perseverance through the best and worst of conditions. Maintain them to sustain you.

Here, at the end of this guidebook, is your time for setting an action plan to achieve that success that God, 'the old folks', family, friends, and ultimately YOU want to have. Start to reflect on all that you have read and capture it in a series of strategies to revive your trifecta: strength, soul, and spirit.

Your Personal Constitution

Emancipated and free!

What are you resolved to do?

Make a few demands on yourself. As this quote by Frederick Douglass still reminds us, "Power concedes nothing without a demand. It never did, and it never will."

Compose the principles you stand on freely. Let them be your "I, the person." Your preamble is waiting for a new start. Decide where you will declare and make your imprint. Concede not.

Take authority. Over what, you might ask? Choose from these seven places: your health/wellness, career, home, community effort, with people, a specific organization, or place of worship, the rally for success beckons.

Then execute! Call out the what, how, and when.

For You: Seven Actions I Will Employ to Achieve Life and Career Success:

I.

II.

III.

IV.

V.

VI.

VII.

Let these steps you take toward action be part of your 'personal stimulus package,' to soar in prosperity. Create your mighty! Engage the three R's. Recognize the cornerstones of your life. Opt in. Commit. Reconstruct. Deal! Get on track for greatness.

If you do these things, you are on the way to becoming your own triple threat. Position yourself for it—with unimaginable strength, deep-felt soul, and amazing spirit!

Now, go get your bounty and blessings for success!

Godspeed!

Deborah

About the Author

Deborah L. Parker is Chief Inspirer and Speaker of The DPJ Training Group, a leadership and personal development company based in the Metropolitan Washington DC area. For over fifteen years she has provided numerous workshops and coaching programs for federal, Department of Defense and private sector clients.

Viewing herself as someone who uses the wits and gifts God gave her to be of service, Deborah helps others grow professionally and personally into their next season. Building on a career life that has taken her to positions as a social worker, Army reserve officer, corporate manager, and now entrepreneur and author, Deborah understands what it means to make a change, sometimes the hard way. She holds a B.A. in Sociology from the College of William and Mary and an M.A. in Human Resources from George Mason University. Deborah has also completed the U.S. Army Command and General Staff College.

The author of two other books, a motivational memoir entitled *Navigating Life's Roadways: Stories of Insight from My Odyssey and Inspiration for Your Journey,* released in July 2011, Deborah shares poignant narratives about her setbacks and successes, to include honoring the lessons from her family and heroes that provide her solid identity. And in *Life Is a Review: Observations and Collections of My Passages Through the Times,* released in June of 2012, she invites readers to browse her twenty-five-year compilation of essays, blogs, speeches, and poems around family, career, history and relationships.

Staying connected in the community, Deborah is a member of Delta Sigma Theta Sorority, Inc., NAACP, Metro DC Chapter of the American Society for Training and Development, Military Officers Association of America, and Mount Pleasant Baptist Church in Herndon, Virginia.

When taking a break, Deborah enjoys travel, reading, and long walks.

15464437R00087

Made in the USA
Charleston, SC
04 November 2012

Purpose PUSHERS

The Journey of Discovering & Walking in Your Life's Purpose

Presented by
Dr. Trenace Richardson

Purposed Publishing
Company, LLC
Bowie, MD

Purpose Pushers: The Journey of Discovering & Walking in Your Life's Purpose.

ISBN: 978-0-578-60817-4 (paperback)
Library of Congress Control Number: 2019920151

Purposed Publishing Company, LLC
1019 Fallcrest Ct.
Bowie, MD 20721
www.purposedpublishingcompany.com
info@purposedpublishingcompany.com

Cover design and Formatting by Stephen Fortune at Skycon Media, LLC
Editing and Proofreading by Monica Settles

Printed in the United States of America

Contents

PHASE II

PHASE III

Contents

Introduction

Butterflies are such magnificent creatures. They come in so many different shapes and colors. Because of their seemingly effortless beauty, we often fail to appreciate the process they go through to get that way. We know it in our head perhaps, but rarely when we are looking at a butterfly do we think about what they used to look like, or what they might have gone through to get to this place of wonder and admiration today.

So it is with us as people, too. We often look at the sister to our right or left and sum her up based on what we currently see. We assume that since she looks great, smells good, works hard, and smiles bright that she must be living her best life. And social media does not help us with our perceptions. For if we allow them to, the pictures, videos, and posts that show someone WINNING can become that person's whole life in our minds, and not just the brief moment it actually was.

This is no ordinary self-help, how-to book. We wanted you to meet twenty amazing butterflies and allow you the opportunity to hear, see, feel, and understand their miraculous metamorphosis. And even though we are certain that these butterflies are twenty of the most beautiful you have ever seen, the change process they have each endured to be present with you in this book has not been pretty by any means. At times, it has been downright ugly, messy, and painful. Change is inevitable. None of us can avoid it, no matter how much we try. But these women teach us that if you confront and surrender to the metamorphosis, beauty can be found in the process and in the outcome.

You are about to get a sneak peek into the private lives of twenty remarkable women. They have dared to share with you their most intimate thoughts and feelings about significant moments in their lives that have pushed them toward their purpose in life. Some of them are still in the midst of figuring out their purpose. Some have discovered it but have not yet surrendered to their purpose. And some are fully walking in their purpose and desire to share some significant lessons learned. We are certain that no matter where you are in life right now, you will be able to connect with, relate to, or learn from these women at one or more of these stages. We invite you to see them at every phase of their process and to witness how their life experiences have pushed them toward their purpose, and to be encouraged, knowing that what's happening in your life is doing the same for you. Meet your Purpose Pushers. They are here to help you discover and walk in your life's purpose!

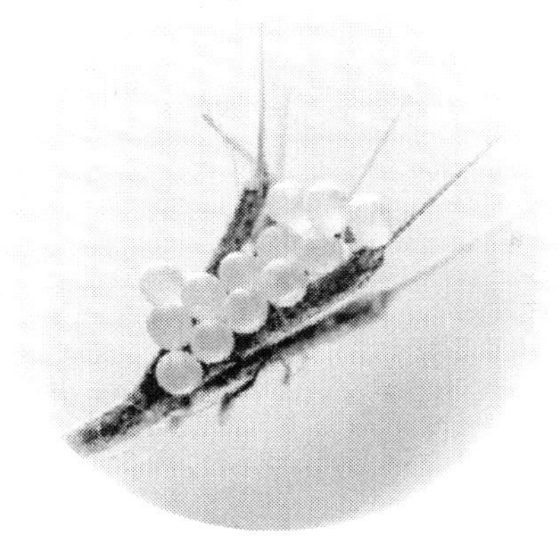

Phase I

"Happiness is a butterfly, which when pursued, is always just beyond your grasp, but which, if you will sit down quietly, may alight upon you."

Nathaniel Hawthorne

I'm Hoping: The Infancy Phase of Purpose

The Egg/Infancy Phase of the Butterfly's Growth

Butterflies at the egg/infancy phase of their lives look and act absolutely nothing as they will in their final phase of adulthood. No one looking at the small, almost unassuming egg would ever guess the wonder that lies within. The eggs laid by the Mama butterfly are so small, several of them could fit on the eraser head of a pencil. She typically lays them on the underside of leaves to give it the best chance of survival, because the harsh truth is that most butterflies don't make it past this initial phase of their lives.

You see, if they manage to remain undetected by any bugs or birds that might scoop them up while foraging for food, they spend several days growing inside of the egg unassisted by the Mama butterfly. Once they are too big for their eggshell, they begin the arduous task of breaking it open so they can get out. Both their rapid growth inside the egg and the work involved in getting out of the egg makes them so hungry that they eat the eggshell they were once housed inside before they begin to devour the actual leaf they were left on by their Mama. They emerge as caterpillars constantly in search of nourishment to grow, and constantly in danger of being devoured by a hungry bug or bird in search of the same nourishment. At this stage of their lives, it is simply survival of the fittest. They have no clue what their purpose is and WHY they were hatched.

At this infancy phase of their lives, it's all about hoping that they will survive the harsh realities of life without succumbing to the pressures of simply BEING who they were created to be. Meet our Purpose Pushers who are currently HOPING that their egg/infancy growth phase will lead to an amazing future for themselves and help ignite or revive the hope for your life's purpose.

A Journey of Purpose

by Carla Freeland

As a baby I was nurtured, fed, and clothed along with sufficient shelter. My purpose at that time was to learn the basics in becoming independent in life.

In elementary school, my only obligation was to attend school and get good grades. I had to use my manners, be kind to others, and respect my elders. I did what I was told and I got by in school. I didn't have a care in the world, other than my toys and my best friends. This was my life. This was all I was supposed to be as a little girl.

I went on to middle school and I changed a lot. My interests went from toys to boys, clothes, and hair. My main priority was to get into a good high school that had a decent trade to pursue a career; but, at this time of my life, my focus was a little off. I knew there were high expectations of me to be successful, but I wasn't willing to put in the effort. I was told that my priority was just to finish school, and even though this was not so important to me, I finished middle school anyway.

Finally, I make it to high school. I'm a little fuller and more mature. I still like boys, clothes, and hair, but I'm not as interested in it as I was before. At this point, I really had no dream to be anything other than a secretary. But now that I am in high school, I was told that my main objective was to graduate and go to college. High school was supposed to prepare me for adulthood. That's all I heard. Graduate. College. "Blah, blah, blah." I wanted to graduate but my intention was not to attend college. I certainly didn't want to do anything extra to get ahead, I just wanted to get by. I had no motivation at all and I cared less and less about education.

I didn't understand this mood and so I just went with the flow. This mentality continued throughout the rest of my time in school until I dropped out. The pressure of it all and my lack of concern about the consequences had won. I felt like, "Why do I have to graduate when I can just get a job?" or "What is the point of all of this?" A diploma served no purpose to me. I had no purpose in my life.

I'm an adult now. The time is close to a year since school has ended and I am doing nothing with myself. Hopeless. Unmotivated. No passion. Insignificant. From the time I was a little girl until my teenage years I was told that you have to graduate and go to college. You have to get a good job to support yourself. I shrugged my shoulders. Some people thought that getting married and having some kids was a woman's purpose. "HA!" So, accomplishing these things will give me the perfect life? That's my purpose? Well, this was portrayed on TV and in some books I read. I even heard it from some people around me. Is that the life I am supposed to be living? If so, I wasn't living it. I didn't graduate high school. I had no job. And now my life means nothing. I messed up. I'm a disappointment. I'm so hated now. "Who am I supposed to be?" and "Who is the person I want to be?" I asked myself these questions, but I didn't know the answers to any of them. "What is my purpose?"

I am older and wiser now. I understand how important education is and that a high school diploma is a requirement. I ended up getting my GED and after that, I went to a school and learned how to type. I took some college courses after that, but I didn't finish. I was content with working. Single with no kids, I would hang out with my friends and then come home. I was only responsible for myself. This was my life, my commitment to me alone.

A few years later, I began to feel different about my life. I wanted a relationship but was afraid of getting hurt. I was not a mother, but I wanted to be. I thought I couldn't have children because it had not happened yet. I was having baby fever so bad, but I believed it just was not in the cards for me. So I let it go, accepting that I am only here to work, be a friend, a daughter, retire from work, and then go off to my final resting place. I had adapted to this life. This was my purpose. Then one day, I found out that I was pregnant. Happy could not express how I felt on that day! Finally, I knew what my purpose was: to be called 'Mommy.' From there, I had a smooth pregnancy and a healthy son. My purpose was fulfilled as a mother.

But now, I'm feeling sad and alone. Guilty and shameful. I have resentment and I feel defeated. My son is a young adult now, and a lot has changed over the years. I have lost loved ones, and experienced a lot of challenges in life. When these challenges happened, my perspective on life changed. The relationship with my family was now different. I looked at them differently but how I felt about them remained the same. I wanted to do more for my mother at this point in her life. I felt somewhat responsible for my son's trials and tribulations. Now, I am taking a good look at myself. I feel like something is missing, but what? What am I looking for? Is it too late to find my purpose? I needed an outlet other than my friends. I needed to find like-minded people that I could talk to about my issues. I didn't want therapy because I didn't feel comfortable. I tried journaling, but that meant I had to write down how I felt, and that wasn't going to help me. So then I said, "Girl, if you don't find something you gon' lose yourself."

Right then I knew I wanted to be a better me. I found a gym, started working out, and I changed my eating habits. I was able to lose a significant amount of weight. I found this group called REAL Women on a social group app. The topic was "Things Mama Didn't Tell Us About". I said, "Ok, I'm in." I went expecting to be around women who would be talking about that specific topic. You know what I mean. "My mother didn't do this" or "My mother didn't teach me that". After listening to some of the stories and sharing my own, I realized that it was so much more than that. The topic was addressed but on a deeper level. At that moment, it was like I had gone back in time to when I was a little girl and I understood why certain situations were that way because of how my mother grew up. I had a different perspective for my mother, a better understanding of her without even asking her anything, and it made me judge her less. Some of my "Why?" questions were also answered in that women's group. That day my eyes were opened to something I knew I had to embrace and accept. At that first visit, I was ready for this journey of change. The REAL Women sister circle is actually a safe space for women to self-improve and be empowered. This dynamic was what I was looking for and I have been going ever since. Attending the circles has really changed my insight because self-awareness is an important key when you start walking the path to learn about yourself. You have to be open to new experiences and accept the changes that will come after new explorations. As a result, I have read about meditation and spirituality. I have gone to yoga classes. I attended a class that made me ask myself, "Who are you?" and "What do you want from yourself?" Powerful! I can look in the mirror and see beyond the surface. I now know that where I am right now is ok. I realize that at this point my purpose is to become a better me.

I encourage you to ask yourself, "Who am I" and "What do I want?" You'll find that the answers to these important questions will be revealed as you open yourself up to new experiences and new perspectives. Know that where you are right now is the perfect place to start toward a better you. Look in the mirror and begin to see beyond the surface. Your purpose today is YOU.

It's Darkest Before Dawn

by Lorrie A. Roberts

Time has stood still from the moment I was informed that my mother had passed. I have been groping around in the dark ever since I received the phone call confirming what I already knew. At 7:15 am on November 14, 2018, my mother had passed away. As if time stood still, I could feel her presence slipping away. The lights and sounds of life went out, and it has been eerily quiet and very dark in my world since then. Time no longer had constraints and I felt as though I existed in a jelly-like substance. No music, no background noise, none of the millions of voices that normally occupy my mind, and no song running through my head. Nothing!

There have been so many moments in this last year where I have just felt stuck. These moments have stretched into days, weeks, and months as if my heart is being crushed with the weight of missing my mother. For my entire life she had been my sounding board, listening to every farfetched, nonrealistic, out-of-this-world idea that I have ever had. She always encouraged me to reach for the stars, to keep a song in my heart, and a smile on my face. This advice has gotten me through every crazy time in my life from Desert Storm in 1990, to losing my job in 2014 due to a workplace injury, which led to me being diagnosed with Complex Regional Pain Syndrome - the most debilitating pain known to man without a cure.

Dealing with this condition, coupled with my mother's death, caused me to begin questioning my worth, my purpose, and my place in the world without her. I didn't know if I would be able to survive the overwhelming feeling of loss. I felt myself succumbing to the crushing weight of her being gone, while not knowing what I was supposed to be doing with myself. I was lost and broken. I began seeking out people who I thought would be able to get me through the darkness. I went to my siblings, close friends, and family members, but to no avail. The thread that bonded us together was the loss of a loved one, and we were all grieving differently. I began to understand that no one could "help" me through this process but me. I had been looking for a lifeline in all of the wrong places. I had come full circle, back to where I started on my knees in prayer. I wanted to believe that God's plan was a bit flawed. It had to be because at this point in my life, I had lost my job, gained a rare debilitating chronic pain syndrome, AND He took my mother. How could this be His plan? I was angry with God and felt myself slipping into the abyss of nothingness. I felt that I no longer had a purpose for continuing to be in this place at this time. I had begun to isolate myself from everything and everyone.

I realized that I had been stuck and in the dark with no noise because I did not get to say goodbye to my mother. During the REAL Women's Summer Intensive 2019, held in Ocean City MD (which was my mother's most favorite place to be), I was able to tell my mother goodbye while quietly looking out over the ocean. This singular act of letting go released a tremendous weight from my heart. As tears of joy, sorrow, and happiness streamed down my face, I began to hear the familiar sounds of music float back into my heart. I began to feel the energy of life as it started to flow through my body once again.

Long before my mother's death and even more since she died, I struggled with where I belonged and what I was supposed to be doing with my life. My entire adult life had revolved around my mother, making sure she had what she needed or wanted. I would help her, as best as I could, to find relief from her daily life of pain from complications with diabetes. As far back as I can remember, I have been researching or concocting some natural remedies in the hopes of enhancing my mother's quality of life. She battled diabetes for over forty years.

I sustained a knee injury at work in August 2013. Six years, two surgeries, and numerous procedures later, I also researched natural remedies for myself. After my second surgery, I ran into complications immediately, including intolerance to most narcotics, nonsteroidal anti-inflammatory drugs and nerve medications. I lost mobility in my knee and my pain management team was unable to control my pain. Finally, the doctors told me that my current chronic debilitating pain was the best it was ever going to get. With this news, I found myself having to learn to live and somehow thrive with a rare chronic pain disease. On most days, I wanted to jump off a bridge, but on the good days, I managed to just barely eke out a smile.

At this point, I asked God to show me how to live with this debilitating pain naturally and not have to rely solely on man-made medicine. Thus began the research into more natural ways to combat pain, and the first of many concoctions were born. During the research for a healthier alternative for pain, I was also looking for ways to wean my mother off of the forty-plus pills she was taking daily. In three years of researching and coming up with concoctions in the kitchen, I am pleased to say we were able to lower my mother's AC1 down by several points, and was able to wean her off of twenty-two of the forty pills she was taking. With this decrease in pills, she was more mobile, had more energy, and was more focused with a better quality of life.

At some point during the process in our lives, we have to stop looking for answers outside of ourselves. We've been taught to seek wiser counsel, too often forgetting that the ultimate counsel is God. This journey of finding, discovering, accepting, and stepping into my purpose started with God slowing me completely down, not by a step or in a stride, but with a solid brick wall. I believed that I would one day return to my passion, which was computers, but He gained my attention. Every path, every sign, and every detour was steering me away from computers.

On this journey, I lost my job, gained a chronic pain disease, AND He took my mother away from me. Again, how could this be His plan? I now realize that I needed to have these drastic changes and the pitfalls in life to prepare me to walk into my purpose without excuses. I could no longer blame the lack of time on "I'm just working so hard on the job." I could no longer fall back on the excuse of "My time will come later; I need to look after my mother." I now realize that "nothing is wasted." In our times of darkness, we are being prepared for the light. He was preparing me to step into my purpose with boldness, focus, and balance by being uninhibited by the normal constraints that we place upon ourselves. I was too small-minded and unequipped to handle the responsibility of educating people, specifically black women, to a more natural process of healing our bodies. I came to see that:

It is darkest before dawn.

But then the sun comes up and
the birds begin to sing

And the most beautiful melodic
melody assaults your ears

With a crescendo of the most beautiful
memory of you, Mom.

As you consider your own circumstances, remember this: Whatever the size of your challenge, whatever the scope of your problem, God is bigger. Much bigger. He will instruct you, protect you, energize you, and heal you if you let Him. Pray fervently, listen carefully, work diligently, and treat every single day as an opportunity for praise and worship.

From Crisis to Righteousness

by Kerneacia Nimmons

Growing up, I was the middle child with an older brother and a younger sister. My mom raised us by herself. My dad...let's just say in 1984 he was sentenced to life in prison. So, growing up as the oldest female in my house, I had a lot of responsibilities which included cooking and cleaning. My mom was either at school or at church. She stayed in church a lot. I would not understand why she stayed in the church so much until later in my life.

My middle and high school years were very difficult. I was searching for that love that I missed from my father in all the wrong places. I called myself following my cousin: I looked up to her because she was cool, beautiful, knew the latest slang, was cool to be around and wore the latest fashions and hairstyles. She taught me how to do my hair, and taught me how to use tampons and pads when my menstrual cycle came. I would envy her when we would go out. She was the pretty one, and it seemed like everyone would look past me to see her. It made me feel like I was invisible. I tried to dress like her and be like her, so when that time came for someone to like or notice me, I thought I was ready. I lost my virginity when I was about 16 to a young boy that I thought was in love with me. Little did I know that there was a "bet" placed between him and his friends that he would take my virginity. Losing my virginity was one of the worst experiences of my life because it left me feeling like I was nobody.

One night, many years later, I was in a hotel room with a verbal abuser, who manipulated me and made me feel unworthy, useless, and powerless with no voice. Once again I felt like I was nobody. I was trapped and didn't know who I could talk to or who could help me. When he left me in the room for a very long time, I stood at the window crying uncontrollably. I looked up at the sky and asked God *to please get me through this!* I was afraid and I felt abandoned, but I remembered that *GOD loves me, and God cares for me - Kerneacia*. That night I felt God's love covering me and from that point on I felt and knew I had been delivered and that my life had a purpose. The grip the enemy thought he had on me was NO longer. God saved me, wrapped His arms around me, and comforted me. After that experience, I left the abusive relationship and grew in my relationship with God. I also met my Prince Charming who is now my husband and we went on to have a family with five beautiful children.

Even though God had opened my eyes to see life clearer, the enemy still tried to find ways to discourage me; like the night I was sitting in my family room and all I could hear in my head was: *You are not worthy! You are not worthy of this! That is why you are sitting, slumping, tired and laying around because you are not worthy!* I kept hearing these words over and over in my mind. Everyone was smiling, and the kids were laughing and playing, except me. I just sat there and pretended that everything was okay, but it wasn't. While sitting there I came to realize that it was the enemy again, trying to attack my mind and get me back down that dark, lonely path called *depression.*

Why? It all makes sense now. Over the years, praying, meditating, and putting on the whole armor of God before I started my day, kept me going. It gave me the energy and strength that I needed to get through the day, and it also prepared me for the obstacles that I would face. However, I had gotten away from my daily routine, which left me feeling disconnected from God. I needed to stay close to Him to receive the strength I needed to keep moving forward.

To reestablish my connection with God and practice loving me the way that God does, I decided to write myself a "Dear Younger Me" letter. It said:

> *"Kerneacia, what do you want to be when you grow up? The first step is to get the information you need to become what you want to be and GET it. You are very smart, and the sky is the limit. You can be anything and everything you want to be. Start achieving good grades. If you don't understand something, raise your hand and ask for a tutor. Help is all around you, Kerneacia. Apply to the best colleges. Yes, people are going to tell you that you can't apply for one reason or another, but you must stand firm and stand your ground. Continue to ask God to lead you and guide you because along the journey, there WILL be distractions and setbacks. But know it's going to be okay; you will get through it. Once you stumble and fall, get right back up and keep dancing; no one will ever know unless you tell them. Some trials will make you stronger and wiser.*

But remember that you will be sharing this to help someone else along in the future. You are an encourager. You will speak joy and happiness to those who are hopeless. Keep that smile on your face because you are awesome, loving, kind, smart, beautiful and passionate. Do not let anyone tell you otherwise because they will. Let those words, negativity, and anger roll off of you like rain on a windshield. Do not let that negativity stick! You are doing an awesome job and that is why the enemy and people are trying to keep you down.

Kerneacia, you come from a strong family of women, but know this: You are a "chain breaker". You have broken the cycle and the generational curse. It may look like you went down the same path, but you didn't. Pray and ask God for direction. He will lead and guide you. He will not steer you in the wrong direction. Again, you may stumble and even fall, but you MUST get back up and dance. You don't have to change yourself for anyone.

Also, Kerneacia, love yourself. Sometimes things may seem very overwhelming or impossible to get through, but give it to God. How? By praying. Once you pray about it-let it go. Don't try to figure it out or work it out - give it to God and let it go. Read and stay in the Word of God. All of the answers you need is in the Bible. Spend quality time with GOD because He wants it and YOU need it!! Everything is going to be okay. Trust me!

Years and years from now, you will have five beautiful children and a supportive husband. You will have an amazing family that needs you in a special way. You've got this, Kerneacia. How do I know? Because I am looking at you. See how far God has brought you and remember that He has you in the palm of His hand. He loves you. Trust in Proverbs 3:5-6, your favorite scripture, and know that everything will be just fine."

Love, Kearneacia

Writing this letter to myself helped me to see who I am and how much I've grown. I'm no longer the little girl searching for her father's love because I have the love of God. I no longer feel like I'm nobody because I realize that I'm special. The enemy no longer has a grip on me because I know that I'm God's child. I recognize that who I am and what I've survived is all for a greater purpose. While that purpose is being revealed, I will continue loving myself in the process.

I encourage you to write a "Dear Younger Me" letter to yourself to get clear about who you are now and where this will take you in your next steps. Leave room for yourself to love, to grow, and to change. You deserve it.

Finding Hope in Burnt Rubble

by Yalonda Blizzard Smith

September 11, 2001 is a day I nor anyone else will ever forget. The day started out like any other day. I was a 25-year-old, naïve young woman, working as an auditor for the Department of Defense. That day, I remember waking up and feeling like playing hooky from work, but remembered I was scheduled for a training class at the Pentagon in Washington, D.C. I quickly changed my mind, got myself together, and headed to work. The training class I was in started out a little rocky. Our instructor was late and claimed we had the start time wrong, so we spent the first ten to fifteen minutes arguing about who was right. Eventually, class started. Then that's when it happened - a marine burst into our training room and told us to exit the building immediately, but he did not say why. My class was located in the Pentagon concourse where the banks and vendors were located. The classroom's wall leading into the concourse was glass and we could see people walking briskly or running to the exit. I just thought to myself, "This must be a drill." As I walked to the exit, I remember two ladies casually walking in front of me talking about regular day-to-day issues in their lives when a soldier approached them and said, "I said exit the building! Let's go!" I thought, "What's dude's problem?"

I didn't realize the extent of what was happening while we were being evacuated. It wasn't until I saw the grayish, black sky, and heard people talking, saying that "We were under attack," that I realized it was not a drill. In the chaos that ensued in the aftermath, I felt like I was walking through a dream. I checked in at my office, which was across the street from the Pentagon because everyone had to do a headcount of personnel. As we stood outside of our office building, we felt the earth move under our feet. We were told later there was a second explosion and the plane was settling into the Pentagon. I was in utter shock and disbelief. I was on the opposite side of the Pentagon when the plane struck.

September 11th caused me to re-evaluate my life and come to the realization that tomorrow truly is not promised to anyone. That night is when I accepted Christ as my Lord and Savior. When I got home I called out His name, repented for my sins, and thanked Him for my life. I remember watching the news that night and President Bush made a statement like "America would not turn and run like cowards," but that we would report to work in the morning as a sign of solidarity and courage." I remember thinking, "I'm going to work alright!" I went to work, filled out a leave slip for the remainder of the week, and went to North Carolina to see my parents. The following days, I watched the news still in disbelief and saddened by the loss of life, but at the same time grateful for mine. Shortly after my return to Northern Virginia, I decided to visit a church I'd previously visited. That's when I felt and knew God was real and would give me what I needed. Unlike my first visit, I understood everything the pastor was preaching about and I could see how it all applied to my life. I was open to receiving the Word of God. I became a "Bible junky" and was at church almost every time the doors opened. I went to midweek Bible study and I continued to attend Bible studies at work. I was hungry for the Word of God.

As I studied God's Word for myself, my life began to change. Initially, it was extremely difficult to change because I had the same friends that were doing the same things as before. But I really wanted a change. I prayed to God for some saved friends and He delivered them. He began introducing me to true women of God who were diligent about studying His Word and serious about living holy for Him. He introduced me to people who taught me how to study and encouraged me. God built a support system around me.

However, the enemy is never far behind with something that could either make or break us. At the beginning of 2002, I met a man at church and began dating him. He had all the lingo and appearances of a good Christian man. I was still new in my faith, but I just knew God was blessing me with a husband. It's hilarious as I reflect on it now, but this relationship at that time had the power to pull me out of my faith in God. As the relationship progressed, I reverted to old patterns and became pregnant. When I told him, my Prince Charming turned into a nightmare. He accused me of trying to trap him and refused to come see me or take my calls. This stressed me out. I was heartbroken. I remember during that time reading and praying Psalm 23 and asking that God's will be done. I thought that His will was for me to have the baby; it was not. I started bleeding shortly after my doctor confirmed the pregnancy, and I miscarried. I know there is a God because in a situation that could have easily pushed a new Christian away from Him, this drew me closer to Him. I grieved and worked through my anger while maintaining my relationship with God. During this time, I learned about spiritual disciplines such as prayer, fasting, meditation, and submission. I immersed myself in the Word of God.

This is just one small fraction of my journey. During these experiences I felt as though my life was blowing up or burning down. These experiences were powerful and changed the trajectory of my entire life and the lens through which I view it. My journey has been one of trauma, significant loss, and challenges, but it has also been one of discovering an enduring and indestructible love - God's love. In moments where I felt like my life had burned to the ground, or that God was trying to kill me, when the smoke cleared, I found hope, victory, strength, and purpose. God used everything I experienced and built something beautiful. A life of purpose. He is more than willing and able to do the same for anyone willing to trust and obey Him. He gives us hope in the midst of our burnt rubble, whether is in in broken relationships, loss of life, or adversity.

As you grow to love yourself and your purpose DO NOT, and I repeat, DO NOT fall into the trap of comparison. Our culture is consumed with comparisons and works overtime to make us feel as though we are inferior and therefore must compete with each other. Not so! As I grew in my personal relationship with Christ, there were many times I mimicked others trying to find my voice. This mimicking was always unnatural and inauthentic. But when I embraced myself, flaws and all, I started to take notice of the gifts God gave me. Comparison had me questioning the validity of my call and purpose to preach the gospel. Comparison also caused me to become dissatisfied with my life as a single woman. I desired companionship and a partner to build a life with and I wanted a family. I remember being so caught up in comparing my life to others that I became very judgmental. Instead of working on yourself, comparisons can cause you to think more highly of yourself than you ought, and destroy your relationships. Comparison is a waste of time and is a serious tool employed by the enemy to keep us distracted. Don't fall for it. Whatever God has purposed you to do, the Kingdom needs it!

As a takeaway, I wish that you and all women and girls will know that they are enough and that they are worthy of love. Stop trying to mold yourself into what other people believe you ought to be. God did not create a world of duplicates or imitations. God created diversity! He created variety! We all have different experiences that will shape and influence who we become. Each of us is designed for love, with a specific purpose to fulfill. And that purpose is NOT to be like anyone else. Learn to love those things that set you apart, the freckles on your face, your wide nose, your wide hips, your flat or fat butt! Embrace and love it all. Love yourself first!

And always pray! As I have grown as a woman, I understand that any maturity, wisdom or strength was not attained on my own. It was a gift from God. The gift came and was recognized because of prayer. Prayer is always in order!

From Pain to Passion

by Kimberly Cleveland

Have you ever asked yourself, "What is the purpose of life?" I believe at some point in our lives we have all asked ourselves that question. You may have been like me, in a place where you were not satisfied with life. A place where there is a void and you don't know why. From the outside, everything appears to be great. You have a great job, family and friends, a decent car, nice clothes and a decent place to live in. But you still feel discouraged and frustrated! So, you ask yourself, "Why do I have this void?" And something in you knows that there must be more to life than this.

This is exactly how I felt when I set out on the discovery of my purpose. I felt guilty, honestly. From the outside looking in, my life was pretty good. I was blessed, but I could not shake these feelings. I knew I was just going through the motions of everyday life, and it wasn't fulfilling. I was doing what I had been told to do by my parents. I was surviving but not thriving, and I was lost. I couldn't really articulate it then, but now I know I was wanting to live a life of passion and purpose. I wanted to feel alive!

I kept asking myself, "What is the purpose of life? What is my purpose on this earth? Why am I so unfulfilled?" Over time, that inner voice inside of me began to answer back. It said, "What do you truly want out of life? What will make you happy? What dreams do you have that you have not accomplished?" When I began to reflect on these specific questions and really take the time to answer them, I received revelation, enlightenment, and clarity.

I didn't receive the answers to the questions overnight. It truly was years of circling around those questions and years of deep introspection in learning who I am and what I truly wanted. It was such a process for me because I had to throw away what my parents wanted for me and who they wanted me to be. I had to stop being such a people pleaser. I had to make myself sit alone, away from all of the distractions, and answer each of those questions. However, I had no idea the answers would come from my pain.

My divorces almost choked the life out of me, but they propelled me into my passion and purpose. They were very traumatic because being a wife and a mother were my deepest desires. From a little girl, I knew beyond the shadow of a doubt that I wanted to be a wife and mother. I idolized my grandmother, who raised me for the first six years of my life. She was a stay at home mom of seven kids, and she and my grandfather were married for over sixty years.

You can imagine how devastated I felt after failing twice at my lifelong dream. I cried every day and fell into a deep depression. I had tried twice and failed. I just kept asking myself why was my greatest desire being dangled in front of me like a carrot and then snatched from me like a cruel joke? I dwelled on the lies that said that the future I desired and longed for were out of my reach. I would no longer have a happy family, nor love someone and be loved. My son would not have a two-parent household. I thought, "Who is going to want to marry a woman who has been married twice and has a son?" I felt like used goods. The loneliness was debilitating.

On top of feeling unlovable, depressed, hopeless, and abandoned, I wrestled daily with shame and guilt. I had failed not once, but twice. The guilt and shame were there because I couldn't figure out how to make my marriages work. I had shame because I wasn't valuable enough for my husband to want to stay or even try and work it out. As a Christian woman, these feelings were like a scarlet letter worn on my chest. Everyone knew I had been divorced twice. I felt like a disgrace and an outcast, and I no longer wanted to live. The pain was too great, and I didn't think I could carry it anymore, along with the child I was carrying in my womb.

But through the pain of my divorces, my passion and purpose were birthed. I knew I had to heal and come out of the deep depression because my unborn child needed me. I didn't want the pain and depression I was feeling to affect my unborn child. He became my will to live and the drive to find my purpose. I chose not to become a bitter woman and I chose to forgive my ex-husband. I still believed in and felt very passionate about the institution of marriage. I knew there was nothing wrong with God's divine institution. Therefore, there must be something we as humans were doing wrong. I wanted desperately to learn why marriages everywhere were failing. I asked God to reveal to me through His Word what the divine design for marriage is and what His purpose is for a husband and a wife. He revealed that we need to invest more time in preparing for marriage. This is where I found my focus, passion, and purpose, and I am now helping women be their best selves to have a happy and fulfilling life and marriage.

Every woman experiences challenges, setbacks or trauma in their life. But the question becomes, "What are you going to do about what you experienced?" Are you going to let those experiences stifle, debilitate, and choke the life out of you? Or will you push through to the other side and use those experiences to shape and model you into the woman God called you to be. He has a purpose for your life. Those experiences are all part of the plan. You have to overcome those experiences so you can now go on to do something great!

I have come to learn that the things you go through in life are not just about you. You have a responsibility to take those obstacles and the pain you endured and use them to help someone else, so they can be encouraged by your testimony and learn from your trials. The pains, challenges, and obstacles in our lives often lead us to our purpose in life. If you want to live a life full of passion and purpose then identify your gifts and talents, use them in the areas you are most passionate about, and start doing what brings you joy and happiness.

Steps to take to help you figure out your purpose

You must get clear on what you want and begin working towards your purpose. Begin with these 7 steps:

1. Get clear on what you want out of life. Write it down.

2. Determine what brings you joy and happiness. What are the things you like to do that bring you joy and happiness?
3. What are your gifts and abilities?
4. Write down your dreams.
5. Write down those things you are passionate about. These are the things that you light up about, that excite you, and that makes you feel alive.
6. Create a passion card[1] on a three-by-five-inch index card (see the example below). Whenever you are faced with a choice, a decision, or an opportunity, choose in favor of your passions.
7. Once you determine what you want out of life, what you are passionate about, and what you enjoy, then start setting goals and a timeline for living a life of purpose and passion.

1. From the book *The Passion Test* by Janet Bray Attwood and Chris Attwood.

LIVING MY LIFE OF PASSION

My life is ideal when:

I am ______________________________

I am ______________________________

I am ______________________________

I am ______________________________

I am ______________________________

Date ____________

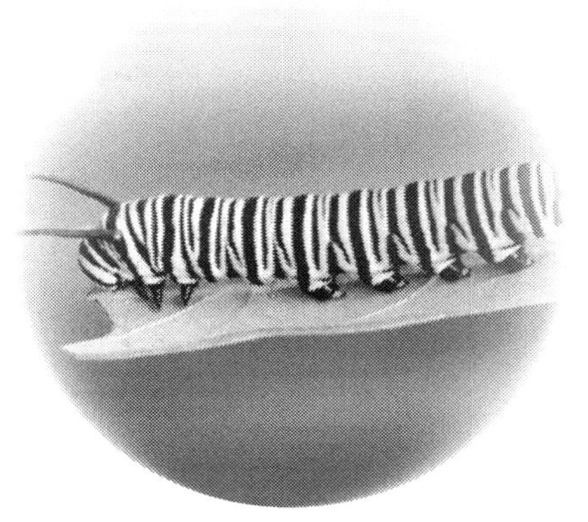

Phase II

*"We delight in the beauty of the butterfly,
but rarely admit the changes it has gone
through to achieve that beauty."*

Maya Angelou

I'm Learning: The Discovery Phase of Purpose

The Larva/Caterpillar Phase of the Butterfly's Growth

Once a caterpillar has successfully made its way out of its egg, its primary focus is to eat. At this larva phase, taking in as much food as possible to continue growing is the caterpillar's sole purpose in life. In order to do that, the caterpillar is constantly traveling from leaf to leaf or plant to plant simply to take in new nourishment. This travel results in a tremendous amount of learning, growing and changing. The more the caterpillar eats, the bigger it grows. And the more it grows, the more it changes. The skin on a caterpillar sheds about four or five times during this discovery phase. It is literally growing out of its own skin, and it is constantly taking in food. Some of the food will be stored and used at later phases of growth, but much of it will be used in this current phase to ensure necessary growth takes place. The caterpillar is instinctively taking in what it needs to grow about 100 times its size when it first comes out of the egg!

At this discovery phase of their lives, it's about absorbing and digesting all they can to ensure they have everything needed to grow in future phases, while at the same time, nourishing themselves right here, right now, in the present moment. Meet our Purpose Pushers who are currently LEARNING and discovering new things about themselves in their Larva/Caterpillar phase of growth and will help you figure out how your life's pieces fit into the bigger picture of purpose.

The Mirror of Me

by Angela Richardson

As I stand on the crest of turning fifty years old, I find myself nestled in the discovery level of purpose. How is this? How is that, at almost fifty, I remain in the perpetual state of discovery? There are feelings of shame, of being forgotten, and of guilt. It seems that no matter how many times I travel life's journey, all paths lead me back to the crossroads and dead ends of why and what. Why am I here and what do I want? Why do I continue to find myself looking at the same wall of emptiness? What do I need to do to move from this level to the next? What do I need to get there? With each day the weight of these unanswered questions becomes too hard to carry or comprehend. It created the cloud and darkness that hid my purpose; but, there was a light.

As I sat in my first REAL Women Intensive meeting, the answer presented itself to me as a beacon of light to a weary traveler. I do not know who I am. As I sat there God brought a memory back to me. When I was a young girl, I would ask the same question, "Who am I?" I remember staring in the mirror and I would ask, "Who am I? What am I?" and then it would change to say, "Who are you?" As I stared at this little girl staring back at me, I drifted further away to the point where I did not recognize the person staring back at me. I wanted to see inside her, beyond the outward and into the innermost part of me. There had to be more. I would do this several times a month. It seemed like everyone around me knew who they were and knew their purpose. I felt like the only person in the world who did not possess this precious knowledge was me. Through life's circumstances, I went further and further away from any meaning and understanding of that person staring back at me.

I'm not sure when it happened, but one day I came to the startling awareness that I could no longer look at that little girl in the mirror. I only used the mirror now to serve a practical purpose, like applying makeup and getting dressed, no longer for discovery. Through many tears and disappointments, it became too painful to look at the shell of the little girl who used to be able to seek who she was in the mirror. The image became blurred and I felt that my life was a haze. How painful is it to look at the one person you should know, but don't? How is it that I don't know who I am when I spend every waking day and sleeping night with myself? Shouldn't I know myself better than anyone else? This is my purpose in this season of discovery. To embrace and discover the woman who has eyes like mine. In this stage, I must sift through my life and sort out the definition of me from who God has made me to be.

Throughout my life people have defined me as "Angie with the pretty hair," or "light skin Angie," or "Angie from NW," and sometimes even "pretty Angie". Interestingly enough, I did not like my hair, I did not feel pretty, I wished I had any complexion other than my light hue, and I wanted to be transported to someplace else. I became an assemblage of descriptors, all being external and not internal. I allowed others to define me both by the negative and positive descriptors. I would hear people say, "She thinks she cute," so I would work hard not to think I was too cute. First, I heard teachers say, "I was smart," so I believed I was smart. Then it transitioned to, "She's not very smart, she can't write," so I believed that "I'm not smart and I can't write." I embraced what others said I was and was not. I was so lost, I accepted any form of direction.

Where do we get our definition of who we are? Is it from our parents, life, friends, or family? I think initially it's from our parents, but if our parents are struggling with who they are, how are they able to create the space for you to discover your own identity? Shouldn't home be the first safe space for self-discovery? If so, this space was not fully realized in my life. I was sixteen when my mom passed unexpectedly, and I felt my identity die with her. From there I became angry, out of control, and lost. On one sunny spring afternoon, my life spiraled out of control. I believe on that day I lost the will to know who I was in my own identity. I gave up. I no longer wanted to know who that girl was looking back at me in the mirror. All I knew was that she was lost, crushed, betrayed by death, empty, and in need of a rescuer. So which do I choose? Am I pretty or not, smart or not, a good person or not?

My rescuer came when I least expected it. I finally allowed God to enter into my life. The relationship with Him became a series of transitions, transformations, and healings. I realize now that God had to heal the broken places, peel away the layers of darkness, and love the little girl in the mirror. Throughout my life, I always wanted things to be different. I wanted to be like everyone else. I walked into rooms and tried to assimilate to others. I wanted to eradicate all the trauma and sadness I had experienced in my life. However, as I was sitting in the REAL Women Intensive meeting, I began to understand that it is a culmination of these events, actions, and experiences that make me who I am. I began to open my heart to see the little girl in the mirror. This time it was different. I did not look in the natural mirror hanging on the wall; I began to look at God's mirror, the Bible. This is when I realized that although my earthly father and mother, who love me very much, was unable to create the space for self-discovery, my heavenly father can.

As I spend time with God and His Word, He shows me what I am and what I am not. I am not a culmination of the hurt and pain hurdled at me from hurting people. I am not a lost little girl. I am not reduced down to my external features. I am a child of the most high God! I can be a little extroverted as well as introverted, and that's okay. I am kind, I am loving, I am a trauma defeater, I am a hurt overcomer. I love nature and adventure; I am giving, I am compassionate, I am Angela, an Angel-like messenger. I am love, and I am me. As I stand in this place of discovery, I stand learning to believe who I am. As God teaches and reveals to me this wonderful creation He's made, I'm learning to see what He sees. Although I have not completely discovered who I am, I am marching, and sometimes crawling, toward the light of discovery. There are days when I can shout from the mountain tops, "I am me and I can tell you who that is!" Then there are days when I shy away from the mirror of me and feel more comfortable to assimilate. Whether I'm shouting or hiding, I know she is in there, and whoever or whatever she is, she is uniquely designed just for me. As I discover me, I will discover my purpose. The more I embrace the parts of me, even on the cloudy days, the clearer my life becomes. This will lead me to my purpose. Learning who I am is not a one and done event but a walk of life, a walk with God, and a walk with me. Through each time of prayer, worship, tears, and doubts, God says, "Baby girl, I love who you are, and so will you."

As you walk through your life of self-discovery, be open, be brave, be accepting, and be willing to be introduced to the many parts that make up YOU. Our purpose is intertwined into our discovery of who we are as individuals. If you are in this stage, I encourage you to trust the process and never stop looking in the mirror. God is there, and so are you.

The Perfectionist

by Moanne Joseph

I cannot remember the exact moment when I developed "the plan," but from a young age it existed, and I was prepared to execute it. "The plan" was the master timeline and expectations that I developed for my life. However, I did not know there were going to be detours, missed exits, and eventually a period where I would have to abandon the path altogether.

I lost my father when I was ten months old, before I could comprehend how that loss would shape my life. My parents were Haitian immigrants living in America when my father died. My father was the provider for his family in America and Haiti. It is common for immigrants living in America to send money to Haiti to help their families; however, when my father passed away, his family lost a big source of income. In my young mind, I decided that my plan would revolve around a profession that would be highly respected in my Haitian community and adequately provide for my family in Haiti. I would carry on my father's legacy and also fulfill our tradition of providing for our family. The masterplan included going to college, law school, and getting a lucrative job as an attorney.

The plan brought me comfort. It was my security blanket. In a world where uncertainty was my birthright, the plan became my assurance. In a world where I could not choose whether my father lived or died, the plan became my choice. Since I did not have control of his life, I decided that I would control mine.

I took pride in making to-do lists and completing them. I rejoiced at the thought of completing a project exactly as planned. This helped me to thrive in school. I could control how much I needed to study to get the desired grade. Eventually, the perfectionist in me took center stage. Her role was to make sure that I followed the plan. If I pursued the path as planned, I would reap the benefits such as receiving praises for following cultural norms and pleasing the people in my life. While I traveled on the path, when things were going as planned, I rejoiced in my achievements. However, when things were not going as planned, I would crumble. The perfectionist in me wanted everything to be perfect, and deviating from the planned path and risking an unfavorable outcome was out of the question. However, God had other plans for me, and his plan looked nothing like mine.

The first detour and roadblock came when I did not complete law school. I was devastated. I had been a great student in college and the perfectionist in me thought that I could achieve the same outcome in law school. During my first semester of law school, I encountered challenges that kept me from performing to the best of my ability. These difficulties included illness and severe emotional strain. I suffered from digestive system problems which left me drained from the pain and nausea. My two-hour commute to school each way left me extremely exhausted. I was also an emotional wreck after losing two cousins to sickle cell anemia. The perfectionist who was used to getting everything done was no longer able to function. The day I received my final grades for my first semester in law school, I crawled up into a ball on the floor. I remembered thinking that I will never be able to get off of the floor, literally and figuratively. I felt like a failure. I was ashamed. I placed all my value into becoming an attorney, and the devastation of not completing the task left me questioning my self-worth.

During this difficult time, I met the man who would become my husband, and he loved me through my struggles. Eventually, with his help and with my confidence somewhat restored, I decided to start over. I went back to school and received a Master's degree in Paralegal Studies with a 4.0 grade point average. I found a job in a law firm where I worked for three years, earning a good salary, and I sent money home to my father's family in Haiti. The plan was progressing, but my life took another turn.

I left my job at the law firm to become a stay-at-home mom. Even though we made the best decision for our children, I felt like the plan had failed again. The remittances to Haiti had to stop. I began to isolate myself to avoid questions about the original plan. Later, I decided that I would start a personal training business, and not pursue a career in the legal field. The business was successful, but again I lost my confidence because personal training was not one of the prestigious professions in my community, which furthered my isolation.

I did not count the cost of perfectionism and isolation. It created bitterness, resentment, and insecurities which took root in my heart. I was afraid that others would look at me as a failure and that I would not be respected in my community. I became a shell of the person that I felt I was truly meant to be. While I presented to others that all was well by taking care of my family and friends, I pushed myself further down the to-do list. I neglected my needs, my desires, and tragically, any form of dreaming. There was no sparkle left in me. Thankfully, the story did not end there. I did not wake up one day and abandon my need for perfection and approval, but change slowly came, and it taught me some valuable lessons.

First, I had to take the limits off the master plan, change my perception, and let go of the expectations that I placed on my life. If I continued to let the perfectionist take center stage, I would not be able to settle into the beauty that is my life. My life did not end because law school failed. My value is not based on a particular profession. I had the freedom to choose to take another path that accommodated my family and provided me with flexibility. I learned that my purpose can be multifaceted. I can choose to fill the purposes in the seasons that God has for me right now, even if it was not in my original plan. I am now open to live my own life and to find all the purposes God may have for me.

I am learning that I have to be patient by making time to discover myself. I have to invest in myself with the same time and effort that I freely give to others. The original plan had everything to do with others and nothing to do with me. I formed a plan based on continuing my father's legacy, but I never took the time to determine the kind of legacy that I want to leave for me and my family. Now, I am committed to the time and work it will take to create the life and legacy that I want for myself.

I am learning that it is crucial to be courageous and take risks. As a perfectionist, this can be a true stumbling block. I usually need a guarantee that whatever move I make next will not only be the right move but the perfect move. Instead, I am learning purpose can be found outside of my comfort zone. Brene Brown, a best-selling author and research professor, said it best in her book, *Daring Greatly*, "You can choose courage or you can choose comfort. You cannot have both." Therefore, I am choosing courage. I understand now that it took courage to pick myself up and apply for a new program. It was also courageous to enter the world of marriage, motherhood, and leaving a job as a paralegal to pursue personal training, none of which was in my original plan.

Courage is embracing each purpose in my life, especially in marriage and motherhood by loving my husband and children well. Courage is releasing the pressure to fulfill my father's legacy. Courage is freeing myself of cultural norms that do not fit in my life. Courage is emerging from isolation to share my story of loss and pain. Courage comes with resilience. Courage will look different for everyone, but courage is a must in finding your purpose.

The perfectionist in me would have never told you this story before now. However, purpose can also be found in the one place you would never allow people to enter. That is where someone can learn from your story. I am calling all my fellow perfectionists, planners, and cautious people on this journey in finding your purpose to take the limits off of your master plan, invest in yourself and, most importantly, be courageous and take risks. You can take them cautiously if you must, but I urge you- take them!

A Leap and Some Pieces

by Christian Belton

"What am I doing?" "What if I'm making a mistake?" "What was I thinking?" "I don't even have a plan, really." "Girl, who do you think you are?" "What if I fail?" "Ugh! You know you hate failing!" "This is the craziest, stupidest thing I've ever done." Just keep smiling.

It's September 1, 2006, and these are the thoughts that flood my mind as I stare out the passenger window of my father's black Nissan Maxima. The trunk and back seat were jam-packed with my suitcases, my laptop, and a few boxes. My mother was driving and with every passing minute, we were going further down the highway. With every mile marker that we passed, I soon realized that I was getting farther from home and closer to what would become my new home. "Is this really a good idea?" is all I kept thinking as my mom drove confidently down the highway. It was as if her presence was trying to assure me that everything would be okay.

Earlier that year, I had briefly mentioned that I thought about moving from Philadelphia, Pennsylvania to Maryland. I didn't really have a plan. By the summer I had a fresh Bachelor's degree and no job leads. Did I mention I didn't have a plan? I just kept feeling like I needed to branch out and discover life outside of the state that I knew as home for most of my life. I took a step back, prayed about it, and felt the release to make the move. Make the move. I was definitely moving alright. I moved from certainty to confusion, from familiar to unfamiliar, and from comfort to discomfort. I did not realize at first how much change was about to take place on the other side of this move. I just knew that there was more to me than I had experienced. I knew that it was time to discover who I needed to become in order to find and then fulfill my purpose. That isn't to say that I could not have done that in Philly. But sometimes there is an unexplainable call within that requires you to do something you have never done before, like relocate without a good idea of what you're going to do when you get there.

I'm a planner and I am analytical, but when it came to THIS decision a lot of that went out of the window. It was as if my soul was pulling me to this place with such great force that my mind had to cater to the directives of my soul. It did not make sense to some people and rarely did it make sense to myself, but I was in a place in my life's journey where I knew I had to try something. Perhaps this something would be the very thing that would push me into my purpose. I had already played it safe in the past; it was time to try something different. Some would say that moving from your parents' home to your aunt and uncle's home in Maryland is still pretty safe, but for me, it was the leap that I needed to uncover and discover me. And that's what finding your purpose really is: it is just one leap, big or small, after another. It is making the decision to choose more. It is journeying from existing to evolving so that you can become the greatest version of yourself and be able to handle the responsibility of your purpose. For me, the physical move helped facilitate the evolution that would take place. This one relocation was the beginning of the events and experiences that began to prepare me for my purpose. It was this season in my life that taught me about who I am and who I could become. As I stepped out and did one new thing after another, I learned things that would bring me closer to my purpose. Through different jobs, my knowledge and capacity increased. This season taught me to recognize the opportunity for growth and to not underestimate the daily moments of purpose.

When pushing towards your purpose, don't forget to pause from the grind and the stress of survival. Pause and pick up the pieces of purpose along the way. These pieces of purpose were all around me and they continued to show up in different ways at different jobs until I learned the lesson or skill necessary. One piece of purpose along the way connects to another piece and then another until all the pieces tie into the greater puzzle called purpose. Even if I could not see it at the time, it would work towards my purpose later. Substituting years ago helps me in planning my paint parties today. The things I learned as an Administrative Assistant helps me run my business today. Being an assistant and watching someone run their business gave me the courage and inspiration to run my own business years later. What are the pieces of purpose that you might be ignoring? Is there a common thread between the jobs that you have had? Or maybe there is a common thread in the volunteer tasks that you seem to gravitate towards. In this phase of life, get access and then assess. Get access to knowledge, people, and places that will teach you what you need to know for your future. And once you have been given access then assess the information and discover the impact or influence that it may have on your purpose. It all has a purpose.

But let's be real, this getting to our purpose thing can be all kinds of frustrating. I remember a couple of years into my move to Maryland when I began to pursue ordination in the African Methodist Episcopal church. I started seminary in Washington, D.C., and I will never forget the day I drove to my first class. I had my directions in hand, a tank full of gas, and I was making my way through rush hour traffic. I couldn't wait to get there to start this new chapter of my life. I remember getting into the city and I was about fifteen minutes from the school. Washington, D.C. has a lot of roundabouts and I clearly did not know how to navigate them well. You have to be in the right lane at the right time to make sure you can exit the circle in time. Well, again it is rush hour, I'm not exactly familiar with this circle situation, and I keep exiting the circle at the wrong time. Over and over again, people aren't letting me over and I keep having to go all over the place just to get back to this circle and try again. All I wanted to do was exit the circle at the third exit so that I would end up on Massachusetts Avenue, Northwest. I was so frustrated that I started crying. So now, I'm driving in rush hour traffic in D.C., tears clouding my eyes, and I yelled, "I just want to get THERE!" After a good ten minutes I finally got off at the right exit and arrived at the school. All was well. I was a little late but because it was the first day of school, I didn't really miss anything at all.

As you journey through this thing called life, you might feel like you are going around in circles and you aren't making any progress. Tears of frustration and anxiety might cloud your vision because the more you go around, the more time you feel is being wasted and there is still a great distance between you and your destination. But rest assured your "there" is waiting for you. Every time you go around the circle you are learning a new trick to get into the right lane at just the right time to make it to your destination. All of our destinations and purpose in life is different, but your purpose is not going anywhere. Release the anxiety. Wipe your eyes. You will not miss a thing. Your purpose is waiting on you and you are getting closer to it every single day.

If you are in this phase, here are some things to do:

- Celebrate your progress and leaps of faith. When we are focused on a destination we sometimes forget to enjoy the journey. Take yourself to lunch, buy that book, or light a candle to commemorate the leaps you courageously took.
- Pause and pick up the pieces of purpose along the way. Learn and receive as much as you can.
- Breathe and remind yourself that you will not miss your purpose. Seriously, take a breath right now and say out loud, "I am not going to miss it!"

Purposefully Me

by Kimberly Cabbagestalk

As a second-generation female preacher, finding my purpose should have come easily. Just follow in the footsteps of those who preceded me and voila...purpose! At least that's what I thought. The journey of discovery has been one that I would not have chosen for myself, yet it has shaped me, most times, into the fearless leader that I am becoming. The experience of learning to find my own voice and my unique ministry style has been coupled with joy and pain (and ok, and maybe a little drama here and there) but nevertheless, I found it.

In my early years as a minister, I fell right into the cookie-cutter model of ministry designed by my church. I was often the youngest minister at every church I joined from age twenty-seven to forty. I don't know how I managed to do this, but it frustrated me each time they would put me over the youth ministry by default. Being the humble and submitted servant I was trained to be, I would serve as the youth minister without much passion. I actually served in a lot of positions in church just to fill the emptiness, while the yearning to fulfill my purpose remained void. When the yearning became so great I could no longer ignore it, I started making changes. Changes that caused me to be misunderstood, rejected, denied and criticized on one end, while simultaneously bringing me a sense of purpose, alignment with destiny, and authenticity on the other end. My purpose has always been to help other women break free of the superficial molds placed on them, which causes them to be who others want them to be at the expense of never being who God created them to be. My process is my purpose. I have come over a few hurdles and while I am still learning and discovering greater dimensions of what it means to be a Purpose Pusher, I don't hesitate to share my journey with others.

It's hard to feel purposeful when you feel you have been discarded. The lingering feelings of the last time my dad left home were of pain, rejection, abandonment, and anger. The insecurities and feelings of vulnerability were like those programs running in the background which drain the battery on your cellphone. These negative emotions were running in the background of my life's story, becoming the grid through which I saw my life and the influence of my self-perception. I was functionally dysfunctional as the years went by, masking the pain with overachieving aspirations and high performance. Being a people pleaser, dumbing myself down to be accepted, and seeking validation and approval from people was a norm for me. There was a hole in my soul the size of my dad that I was trying to fill with things that could never really quench that thirst. Then, one day I got desperate for the pain to stop and the cycle to be broken. I was desperate to shut down all those negative emotions running in the background and to refresh the browser of my life. I was ready to live out loud the life that I knew God had dreamed for me. When I allowed God to fill the hole in my soul with peace, joy, and abundance, I began to flourish. Sometimes we are not able to discover who we really are and what we are purposed to do because it is hidden beneath the layers of our pain. Pain can be so profound that we feel hopeless about our future. Whether there has been a divorce, loss of a loved one, abuse, or abandonment, these things must be dealt with before you can flow in your purpose. If not properly dealt with, these thing will sabotage every effort to live a life of fulfillment. The first step to discovering my purpose was to get healed and become whole. I have met a lot of broken leaders in my day and I watched them singlehandedly destroy everything they built because they would not identify, acknowledge and be healed from the trauma of their past. I have watched as the cycle of pain was passed on to those they were called to train and develop. I have seen ministries and businesses fold because this one critical part of the process was avoided.

Soon after, I began to exist from a healed place and I became confident in my identity. It became clear to me that I'd been functioning under a false identity in many ways. I was the person that people wanted me to be instead of the person I was purposed to be. I was like a chameleon, transforming into a version of myself that would fit in with every new environment. The need to be accepted was suffocating my desire to just be myself. If I went to a church that was a teaching ministry, I would try not to elevate my voice while preaching. If I went to a church where they would proclaim the Word with force and an elevated voice, I would follow suit even if I lost my voice while doing it. One day with a hoarse and raspy voice, I began to pray and ask God to show me what He had in mind when He created me. What was the sound in the earth that was designed to come from me? What is the ministry He purposed me for in the earth?

I began to ask God some very specific questions and I got very direct answers. Once I was a little clearer about my purpose, I no longer needed the validation of man because I was now living under the approval of God. I decided that I would not spend the entirety of my life being a cheap knock off of my authentic self. The affirmation that I longed for from my natural father was quenched by my heavenly father.

Confronting my childhood trauma was not easy, but nothing was as hard as leaving the cocoon of familiarity and spreading my wings. One of the hardest things I ever had to do was leave my mother's side in ministry. My mother raised me, my sister, and brother as a single parent. I owe so much of my development as a wife, mother, and minister to her. She has been an example of what it looks like to overcome insurmountable odds and pursue purpose with dignity and grace. I served with her in her early ministry assignments and it was under her ministry that I gave my life to Christ and became an ordained minister. When God told me it was time to leave her ministry, I was challenged with doing so, but I knew if I was going to spread my wings and learn to fly I had to bust out of the cocoon. While the cocoon is a safe place to develop, it is not designed to be a permanent place. On the journey of discovery, you will find yourself in places for a time of development. These places of growth are so easy to become attached to but they are temporary spaces which must be vacated at the appropriate time. I previously made the mistake of staying in places for too long. The cocoon that is designed to protect you as you mature can become the place that handicaps you if you stay there too long.

While I believe that my journey of discovery will be life long, here are a few things that I've learned so far that I hope will encourage you:

1. To be anything other than who God designed you to be dishonors Him and it dishonors you—the authentic you.
2. Serve with purpose from a place of healing and wholeness. Pray, meditate, get counseling if necessary.
3. Don't make temporary places permanent. Staying in a place past its time can only turn out to be detrimental. I'm not saying it will be easy, but I am saying it will be necessary.
4. Relationships with people that are very close to you will change as you begin to walk in your purpose. The new you will not be palatable to everyone but it will be God's sweet delight.
5. For everything God has purposed you to do, there is a place, there are people, and there is provision.

Be fearless and intentional about discovering and fulfilling your purpose. Until you do, the world is void of your genius, your creativity, your wit, and your sensibility....don't keep us waiting too much longer! Press into your purpose!

My Mask was Fierce

by Rhonda Ragsdale

Death is a life changer. I know this is a morbid way to start our discussion, but it is so true. I was so clear and focused on my calling, purpose, and passion in life until death paid a visit to my family. I was destined to be active in a Christian education program at my local church as either a teacher, supporter, or director. I had received my license to preach the gospel and I was getting ready to start my second year in seminary. My path was set and I was sure that my life goal was to teach faith in Jesus Christ to help believers figure out the answers to their questions, to give them tools for their struggles, praise for their victories, and to understand the traditions of the church with biblical truths. Once I retired from my "day" job, the plan was to work for my local church in their Christian education program. As I saw it, my steps were ordered by God and I was on my right path, until that faithful day in September 2012.

On Saturday morning, September 8, 2012, I received a call from mama, who was in the emergency room with major pain. The doctors had found something that concerned them. Test after test revealed that she had stage four pancreatic cancer that had spread throughout her body. The prognosis was that the cancer was terminal, and the doctor's goal was to give her the best quality of life the hospital could provide. On April 17, 2013, nine short months from diagnosis, she was gone and my world changed forever. For the next three years, I was a pillar of strength while internally I was dying and so was my passion for teaching in all forms, especially in the church. I continued to teach but there was no longer the excitement, fervor, and zest for it, and I was just going through the motions. The sad thing about this season was that people never realized that I had lost my passion because I had the "everything-is-good" mask on. During my time of mourning and grief I was lost. I learned that I could hold back my emotions and press forward in a manner that no one would know that I was dying inside. While wearing my mask, I was an effective teacher, but my love for teaching had diminished. My passion for teaching had decreased so much that I dreaded having to prepare lessons and avoided it as much as I could. I was lost trying to figure out if this was because I was grieving or if this was a transition for me. Now as I sit back and consider my emotional state during this season, I pray that I didn't do anyone harm. My mask game was just that fierce!

I walked into the REAL Women's December 2016 Intensive meeting, where I had been asked to participate on a panel discussing life lessons from women in their forties. In this space full of strangers, I was given permission to remove my mask and feel the emotions I had been hiding for years. These sisters discerned my mask game and gave me a safe place to slowly remove it. I decided during that weekend that I would become active in REAL Women; it was a gift to myself and I began to start healing from the loss of my biggest cheerleader, my mama.

My first official sister circle was in January 2017, and I've been engaged from that moment on. My personality won't allow me to just be a part of an organization and not be fully engaged and active. Even though I told myself, "I'm only attending to get through my grief and get some balance in my life," my mask slowly came down and I began really learning who I am at my foundational core. I was learning to love myself and all of who I am, which was critical for me at my age. At forty-eight, I did not fully know myself. I had my mask game on and I was living to get people to love and accept me instead of loving and accepting myself. Being among these women helped me to learn that it is never too late to get to know, accept, and love myself.

I got involved in the operations and building of REAL Women. The first time I facilitated at a REAL Women's event I was so excited and could hardly contain myself. Oh my goodness, the passion I was feeling was intense, and it was just as exciting as it was when I was teaching – and maybe even more so. Here was a room full of women, and I wasn't telling them what to do or how to do it, but I was facilitating a discussion that helped us all work through the issues that kept us from being the best version of ourselves. Unlike teaching, as a facilitator, I wasn't responsible for knowing the answers or solving their problems. I was giving the ladies tools to figure out the answers or solutions for themselves. I was confused by this unexpected feeling of exhilaration so much that I immediately discounted my feelings. But aren't these the feelings that I wanted standing in this new improved version of me?

Until death came to visit me, I loved teaching and it gave me the excitement I was now feeling while facilitating at REAL Women events. Teaching gave me fervor when there is dialogue and exchange between myself and the students and I took every opportunity given to me to stand before people to teach something. I was pumped and hyped for every opportunity to teach, but now I was getting that same feeling from something other than teaching. I was learning that the skills I developed as a teacher were transferrable and could be used to help build a safe space for women to do personal development work on themselves. And in the process, I get healed.

It's been three years since I joined the REAL Women family. Each day I strive to be my authentic self and I'm learning that my gift to break down information and convey it in a manner that helps people understand it is both useful teaching in the church and facilitating for REAL Women. Both situations allow me to pour into others and challenge them to live their best life. Just recently, I was told by a dear friend that I have the ability to sow into people and that, in this season, I'm learning how to be comfortable in this part of my purpose. In essence, she was telling me that I needed to learn how to be the powerful vessel that I am. So, this internal struggle to choose whether I should be teaching Christian education or facilitating REAL Women events is more about me being comfortable with the impact of my voice in the world, and not what type of teaching I engage in. So the moral of my story is that no matter what I call it, teaching or facilitating, I have to be comfortable with the impact of my voice in the world. Sometimes the pivot in life isn't about what you do but more about who you are and how you see yourself. With this as the backdrop of discovering my purpose, I offer you the following tips to survive your discovery season:

1. When loss occurs, allow yourself to grieve. As hard as grief is, it is a necessary part of life and it comes to do a work in us that no other experience can do. Seek help from a professional or trusted friend to help you if you can't handle it on your own.
2. Allow yourself space to process your emotions – the good ones, the bad ones, the scary ones, and the indifferent ones. Processing your emotions is freeing and opens you up to make space internally for what life brings your way.
3. Age is nothing but a number. Age doesn't keep us from learning and working to know thy own self. This gives you permission to walk into any room as your true, authentic self. Your authentic self is not only good for yourself but for those you encounter because someone needs to see you living your truth so that they will have the courage to live theirs.
4. Embrace your gifts, talents, and skills, and do not put limits on when and where you can use them. When you open yourself up and try different things, you will be surprised where you land. No experience will be wasted; it will all help you discover your purpose.

Phase III

"Adding wings to caterpillars does not create butterflies, it creates awkward and dysfunctional caterpillars. Butterflies are created through transformation."

Stephanie Marshall

I'm Changing: The Transition Phase of Purpose

The Pupa/Chrysalis Phase of the Butterfly's Growth

In order to get to the butterfly stage where flying is possible, a caterpillar must first completely shed its current form, create its own protective shell to isolate itself from everyone and everything around it, and then allow its muscles to dissolve and liquefy in order to be reshaped and reformed into the butterfly we all love and admire.

This is the pupa/chrysalis phase where massive transition and transformation take place for the caterpillar. Once the caterpillar is full grown, it stops eating. At this point, the caterpillar instinctively knows it is time to affix itself to the underside of a branch. It is here, while suspended in the air that the caterpillar begins to produce and release a hormone called *ecdysone*. This hormone causes it to cast off its outer coating, similar to that of a snake shedding its outer skin. But underneath the shed skin is a hard shell, similar to the exoskeleton of a beetle. The caterpillar allows itself to be taken over by this hard shell and is now considered a pupa or a chrysalis. The chrysalis that embodies the pupa, formerly known as a caterpillar, is not a cocoon or shell around the pupa, it IS the pupa's actual body! Talk about major change! But it doesn't stop there.

The pupa then undergoes a much more gruesome change while encapsulated in its own body. It releases enzymes that rip apart and dissolve cells in its muscles, digestive system, and other organs. This total deconstruction only leaves parts like breathing tubes that keep the pupa alive during the change. It is during this unbelievable process that specialized cells called imaginal discs begin to reproduce and take over. These discs have everything the pupa needs genetically to form into the butterfly we will soon see.

At this transition phase of their lives, it's all about surrendering to the changes that inevitably come in life, no matter how tragic or difficult. Meet our Purpose Pushers who are currently CHANGING during their pupa/chrysalis growth phase knowing that on the other side of this transition awaits a higher purpose and calling not just for them, but for you too!

Travailing in Transition

by Monica Leak

The word travail doesn't exactly suggest joy, happiness, or pleasure. The mere mention of the word can trigger thoughts of pain and suffering, especially for women. Travail is defined by Merriam-Webster as "work especially of a painful or laborious nature; labor, childbirth." To travail is no easy task; yet, it is a process that once it begins, you must see it through to completion. Like me, you may have hit a point of great travail in your life, where you're on the brink of fulfillment of God's promise to you and on the edge of God's great manifestation in you. We undergo transition which signals the first stage of labor where the contractions are most intense. There can be great pain when changing from one state to the next. Maybe you've been praying and fasting, or doing things to help yourself and others like: ministering, teaching, exercising, eating healthy, writing, seeking therapy, finding your tribe, or journaling to find the things that give the needed support during this process. For me, I was putting forth my best effort reading books, listening to CDs, and attending conferences to receive this great manifestation. I'm travailing on the brink of birthing something; however, I am stuck in transition because it did not come with ease, nor did it align to my timeline or plans.

I was stuck in a place where my self-esteem was shot to hell. I was good enough to invite to gift-giving events because people knew I was a giver. I was good enough to be that listening ear or presence in the room, but I was not worthy enough of time and real connection with others. Emotional, verbal, and physical abuse in relationships and fear of not measuring up or fear of launching into new territory had me stuck. What is that something that is causing pressure and hindering you from birthing your purpose? What is it that is causing you pain, blocking your revelation and understanding? What is it that is causing confusion and intercepting your receipt of wise counsel and support? You are right there. You can feel it, you can sense it, and you're ready to bring it forth, but you continue to find yourself stuck in transition.

Take the story of Jacob and Rachel found in Genesis 35:16-19 in the Holy Bible. Rachel was the daughter of Laban and the favored wife of Jacob. Rachel was found to be barren which during that time was looked upon as a reproach. She not only grieved about her condition, but she was angry, too. Two major mistakes Rachel made were casting blame on others and following her own plan. Rachel started out by blaming her husband, Jacob, going as far as to tell Jacob to give her children or else she would die. We, too, can blame our friends, the job, coworkers, spouses, the environment and other factors for things not manifesting in our lives; however, we have to see our responsibility and our role in what is happening around us. We must acknowledge our blind spots and our need to be right all of the time. I was like

Rachel and made the same errors she made. However, I had to stop the madness of blaming everything and everybody and like the therapist I am, do my own evaluation. If you did a self-check, you may discover your similarities with Rachel as well.

Rachel then continued in her plan by stealing the household gods and images from her father, which represented the legal deed to all that her father owned. Then, when she was not able to give birth, she gave Jacob her maidservant so that she could claim the child as hers. Today, we don't commonly use idols or other women to make up for physical deficiencies, but in our hearts, we have the same motive – manifesting what we want. After blaming everybody from the spouse to the dog, we figure we're going to help God out a little because things are just taking too long and our patience is wearing thin. We expected that miracle check in the mail today. We expected the house and tangible blessings to be within our grasp and when God's way did not appear to be working in our favor, we came up with our own alternative. So, I took an extra job whose hours kept me from being fully engaged in worship, fellowship opportunities, and personal time of devotion and reflection. I took money once earmarked for our tithes and offerings to pay the debt I shouldn't have gotten into in the first place. I took what was supposed to be invested for self-care to fully invest time and energy on projects, programs, and events that drained and depleted me but pleased everybody else. I did everything to improve my physical condition, not realizing that I was hindering the very thing God wanted for my life.

If we are going to travail in this transition, we need to change our position. It's time for some spiritual alignment, moving from our agenda to the will of God. I am a planner and I love my planner! I have my layout and everything is written with meetings, projects, programs, and proposals in the works. I had this five-year plan for myself that included my completion of graduate school, being gainfully employed, and if not married by thirty-five, then I would pursue my doctoral degree with plans to start my own private practice. That was the plan, but in all my planning I didn't change my position. I was in my Chaka Khan mode, singing, "I'm Every Woman…it's all in me!"

Nothing could have prepared me for the transitions that hit me in life: the loss of my best friend, a series of abusive relationships, and the loss of a child. None of this was anywhere on that plan. I found myself in so much turmoil and pain to the point of just wanting to end it all and make everything stop. Here I am trying to make moves and push forward in life, and all of these changes were interrupting my flow and running interception with my dreams. What helped me through this part of the process was having a series of birthing coaches, my sister-friends three states away who will call me, pray with me, and make sure I'm breathing. My next coach was team 'get out of the house' and 'no, you will not fall into the abyss of pints of ice cream, potato chips, and Lifetime movies.' Each in their own way helped me to change position, which allowed me to broaden my point of view, see life through a different lens, and check myself to acknowledge how out of order I was. Making the change in position may not be comfortable but it sets you up to push into your manifestation. You must walk it out, according to 2 Corinthians 5:7 (NRSV), "for we walk by faith, not by sight." What you see physically is based on your vantage point. The earth looks really different from a satellite versus the view from a plane or a car. We are pushing through to see that promise come to fruition.

It's your unwavering faith that keeps you pushing forward even when you're wondering about resources, what else can be done, who I am supposed to connect to, and all of those questions that have you up early in the morning. You need to gird up your inner strength and put one foot in front of the other and keep walking. Walking helps the labor to progress; take the next step.

Focus on your breathing. In a season of constant movement, this need can be forgotten with all the to-do lists and days of our lives. It took a long time for me to realize that I wasn't breathing. I was doing everything for everyone else, and I still lost. Exercise in the Word of God: inhale the strength, power, and identity of who God called you to be, and exhale the shame and the past and just breathe. How can you expect to live and move without being mindful of your breathing? Every breath is a gift from God. Allow each breath in to receive what is necessary from the Spirit, and each breath out to release the toxins. Try voicing a mantra or daily declaration from scripture. Wash and allow the cascade of water to release the tension or pressure that you've been holding inside. Let the water not only cleanse but also refresh you inside and out. My final recommendation is that of healing through touch whether that is a massage or another form.

These recommendations will bring you through the travail, transition, and final delivery. If we fail within the travailing stage through which transition enters, we suffer the possibility of not reaching our destination and we will labor harder than normal, have a preterm birth, or a miscarriage. Destiny awaits you so continue to push through your transition to deliver what God has purposed for your life.

Stop Fighting the Pain

by Nephateria McBride

On April 7, 2018, I watched my grandmother take her last breath. The English language lacks the words necessary to describe the pain I felt that night. My mother called earlier that day and told me that my grandmother had been rushed to the hospital. She had been ill and in and out of the hospital since January, but there was something different about this call. I was leaving a women's event when I got the call. When I heard my mother's voice, I somehow knew. I knew it was time. I immediately jumped in my car, drove home, grabbed my clothes and got on the road headed to Pennsylvania. I thank God for traveling mercy that day. A trip that is normally five hours from Maryland, took only four hours. When I arrived at the hospital around 8 pm, no other family members were there. It was as if God had ordained these precious moments alone with my grandmother. As I stood beside her bed watching her go in and out of consciousness, the doctor came in to talk to me. He told me that they could not raise her blood pressure and the medication he had given her was the only thing keeping her alive. The only thing he could do at this point was keep her comfortable. It was time to call the family in.

We all gathered in her hospital room around 11 pm. We decided to take her off of the medication to ease her suffering. Within seconds of stopping the medication, her blood pressure and heart rate began to drop. As my family stood around the hospital bed watching the numbers drop, we sang praise and worship songs. We watched in agony as the number went to zero and a flat line ran across the monitor. As the alarm sounded, my older cousin said, "That's it. She's gone." The nurses came into the room to pronounce her time of death and started removing the tubes from her body. There was an eerie silence in the room as we watched them. Reality was slowly settling in. Then like firecrackers, the heartbreaking, soul-wrenching cries of my mother, aunt, uncles, siblings, daughter, and cousins began to sound off in the room. Our matriarch had transitioned.

I stood silently and looked around the room. I immediately started doing what I do best, take care of everyone else. I went to console my Mother. I then noticed an older cousin breaking down, so I went to wrap my arms around him. While consoling him, I saw my daughter crying in a heap on the floor in the corner so I immediately ran to her rescue. Then it hit me like a ton of bricks. I stopped moving and stood staring at my grandmother's now lifeless body lying in the hospital bed. Ma was dead. My fiercest supporter and biggest cheerleader. My heart. The number I dial when I want to ask a question about anything. She was gone. In that moment, it felt like I stopped breathing. I only recall my daughter shaking me and asking if I had my inhaler. I fell backward into a nearby chair and released a cry from the depths of my soul. My heart shattered into a million unrecognizable pieces that night. Life would never be the same, but the pain I felt that night would not be wasted.

The seconds, minutes, hours, days, weeks, and months after my grandmother transitioned were a roller coaster ride. Some days were a blur and some seemed to stretch on forever. It felt as if I were suspended in time. It felt like a never-ending loop of pain. But God did something incredible during this season of my life. It was in the waves of grief that I discovered my most authentic self. It was during this season that my purpose started becoming clearer. Grief came, snatched, and encased me as a cocoon of silk encases a caterpillar ready to become a butterfly. Unbeknownst to me, grief had come to transform me. I became so familiar with grief that I started referring to it as "She." She wouldn't allow me to pretend that I was okay. So, she stripped me of the ability to project a façade and left me too exhausted to engage in people pleasing. When I tried to fight her, she tightened her grip and pushed me deeper into relationship with God. She stripped away religion and taught me how to experience true intimacy with God. When I tried to return to the hectic pace of life that I lived before my grandmother's death, she shut me down physically or emotionally and taught me how to practice self-care. Grief is a bad girl! She even taught me the beautiful art of saying no, how to set boundaries, and how to honor my commitment to self.

Why am I sharing this? I want you to understand that sometimes the pain and trauma of what you are experiencing is necessary to push you into purpose. It hurts and you may be ready to throw in the towel, but trust me when I say that nothing will be wasted! When grief first came to visit me, I did not understand her purpose. When she started spinning her cocoon around me, I felt like she was trying to hurt me and keep me isolated. She wasn't. She had come to transform me from the inside out. While in the cocoon, I began reflecting on how tired my grandmother was in her last days. I recalled how she had one consistent message for me: Live your life. As I thought about what that meant, I declared that I was only going to do things that made me come alive. As a result, I began assessing the things on my plate. I started asking myself hard questions like, "Why are you doing that?" "Is this something you really want to do?" "Do you feel obligated to do this?" "Are you trying to please others by doing this?" Essentially, I got clear on my "why" for the things I was doing. If it did not align with who I was becoming, I began to make changes. I stepped down from ministries. I declined activities and developed healthy boundaries. From a space of grief, I found me…a vessel of healing.

I had been doing some healing work through REAL Women, a wonderful organization that exists to create safe spaces for women to do personal development work on themselves. Therefore, I was present to the fact that I am one of God's vessels of healing. My plan - notice that I said MY plan - was to leave my federal government job in the near future to work full-time for REAL Women. However, on May 8, 2019, all that changed. Who I was destined to be became clearer that day. My granddaughter was having surgery in Pittsburgh. While sitting in the surgical waiting room with my divorced parents, I facilitated a beautiful conversation between them where they discussed their divorce and topics never discussed before. God used me to facilitate healing between my parents that day. Everything within me came alive! Later that day, I told my father I wanted to be a counselor, yet, the thought of going back to school discouraged me from processing the thought any further - until a week later. I had an intense meeting at work that left me discouraged, frustrated, and on the brink of tears. While sitting in my car, I declared I was done with my current job! By the end of the next day, I enrolled in the Master of Arts in Clinical Mental Health Counseling Program.

I am in the process of transitioning from an auditor to a counselor…the vessel of healing I was created to be! This season of my life is exciting and filled with many unknowns, but I am exactly where I am supposed to be. Every tear I have cried and every sleepless night is worth being in this beautiful, transformative space. This is what I want you to know. I stepped into my purpose when I stopped trying to be who others or who I thought I was supposed to be. The metamorphosis occurred when I began to allow God to breathe life into the woman I was becoming. Trauma and loss knocked me to my knees. Grief transformed and healed me. But it was learning to surrender to the process that unlocked the key to my life's purpose. So, the question is, what are you going to do? Remain stuck in your pain and trauma or allow it to transform you into a new being and move you toward purpose? The choice is yours.

Here are a few nuggets of wisdom that I hope will encourage you:

- Trust that nothing will be wasted. Everything, even pain, has a purpose.
- Don't be afraid to go against the current. Be the fish that swims upstream when others are swimming downstream.
- Figure out who YOU are and be authentically YOU!

Strength through Adversity

by Tajala Lockhart

Growing up, I never realized what things truly meant. For example, my mother was a single mom and a hair stylist. I spent my entire childhood in her hair salon, *Thee Rose Hair Studio*. Over the years, I listened to so many women and young girls share their stories. My mother loved roses so everything she did ensured that she had roses everywhere, naming her business after the flower as well. I did not know why she loved them so much, but I found out why after losing her on September 3, 2012. It was Labor Day that year and I learned that there was a biblical meaning behind the rose. She loved God and loved to share His Word with others, and the rose in the Bible symbolizes love, strength, fire, and luxury. That was definitely who she was and the example she set for others.

Through life's obstacles and challenges you have to find what gives you strength through adversity. The roses that my mother used to decorate the house and salon with, and even the salon name, was a constant reminder to her of what her God-given gifts were. Growing up in a town where we did not have much, we had love from family and our community. The love and support taught me so much despite any circumstances. I learned a lot from my mother's example and from my hometown community, and knowing that there was more in this life, I had to go and find out just what was waiting for me.

Since my mother was a single mom, I knew college would be too much of a burden on her, so I decided to take a different route. After my high school graduation, I started working different jobs at quite a few different companies that would eventually land me an opportunity to work with Marriott International. During my tenure, I found the opportunity to attend college through Marriott's college tuition reimbursement for employees. I jumped at the opportunity and later earned my Associates in Applied Science degree in Hotel & Restaurant Management. I built a successful career in the hospitality industry for more than twenty years.

However, a shift started to happen within the industry and in me. I felt like I had learned all that I could in hotel operations. In addition, I continued to carry with me the loss of my grandmother, two uncles, and my brother. Other major events also occurred in my life. I became a mother, found out that my biological father was indeed not my father, and then finally, in 2012, I suffered the ultimate loss of my mother. It took a lot of strength, but I had to find my way through this first shift. I did the only thing I knew to do which was pray and ask God to give me the strength and guidance to move forward. The answer to my prayers came in the form of a teaching opportunity to do what I loved by teaching about the hospitality industry to at-risk youth.

I taught for a couple of years, but I didn't really want to commit to it because of talks about a federal government shutdown. I needed a stable income so I continued to ask God for guidance and soon after an opportunity arose to become an Assistant General Manager at a local hotel fifteen minutes from home. Girl, I was so excited not to be in traffic every day! Things were going so well at the hotel that it led to the dream opportunity for me to become the General Manager. It was a blessing from God! I was so excited, but very emotional because my mother knew how much this industry meant to me and she was not here to celebrate this achievement.

I continued to work in that role for a few years only to find my spirit shifting like nothing I have ever experienced before. I started missing the students I taught, but I didn't think going back would be the best choice for me financially. Then things at the hotel started going downhill due to ownership choices, which led to me to leaving that job. About a month later, I received a call from one of the companies where I previously taught, inviting me to return since the federal government shutdown was over. An awesome sense of peace came over me and I accepted the offer to return. I taught there for about six years until I felt that shift in my spirit again, prompting me to stretch myself in a way I never had before. The teaching was a test of trusting God with the guidance I had prayed for in the previous years. This shift lead to me becoming the founder of a nonprofit organization and a published author.

Through my work and writing, I was sharing my mother with the world which was great for me. I continued to teach during this new shift which I started to call my "discomfort zone". It was something about achieving these two things, starting a business and being a published author, that made me feel different on the inside and about myself as a woman. I started to feel like I really had something to offer. I did not know what it was or what to call it, but it made me scared in a good way. In this newfound space within myself, God led me to have a conversation with my husband about branching out even more to start another business. Yes sis, in addition to my nonprofit business! After talking things through with my husband, I resigned from my teaching job and successfully launched a second business, while continuing my nonprofit. Things have been challenging; however, I continue to feel that I am doing the right thing.

Now, are you ready for this? If that wasn't enough, I started feeling that there was more to my journey that I needed to do. This was super uncomfortable, but I couldn't shake the feeling. I wanted to run for office to have a seat on my county's board of education. So, I did it! I ran for the board member seat for the Charles County Board of Education in Maryland. Naysayers told me I was not qualified. They said, "You do not have a master's degree to be a board member." What they didn't know was that their comments only fueled this young project girl who grew up on welfare. That fuel awarded me an opportunity to defeat two incumbents and two Apple Ballot candidates for a seat as a Governing Board Member of the Charles County Board of Education. In addition, I was able to host my first Cherish Her Brunch event that had over four hundred attendees and one hundred women walked away with my book!

What does this have to do with being a Purpose Pusher? Everything! God had a different plan for me than what I thought and continued to open doors of opportunity to utilize my gifts and talents. As I started praying through the pain, emotions, loss, and fear of walking this earth by myself without my mother, I learned to tap into the spirit of my mother and to lean on God's guidance. The young women that I serve, the students and second chance adults I teach, and the school system that I support provide me an opportunity to push others into their purpose despite the adversity.

Through my journey, I realized I could endure more than what I thought I could handle in life, and succeed. What I thought was an uncomfortable zone became my comfort! God wanted me to realize that teaching was just a part of the bigger picture of beginning to live and walk in my purpose. I just needed those people and God to remind me that I mattered.

God gave you a purpose too. Don't allow the noise of others to keep you from finding or realizing that you may already be walking in it. If you feel stuck in your current position but not ready to take that leap of faith, use your skills and talents to create opportunities for additional streams of revenue. Remember that your purpose is not just for you - it's the answer to someone else's pain. Don't let fear keep you in bondage. Be courageous enough to allow the fear to lead you to your purpose. You, too, can be a Purpose Pusher!

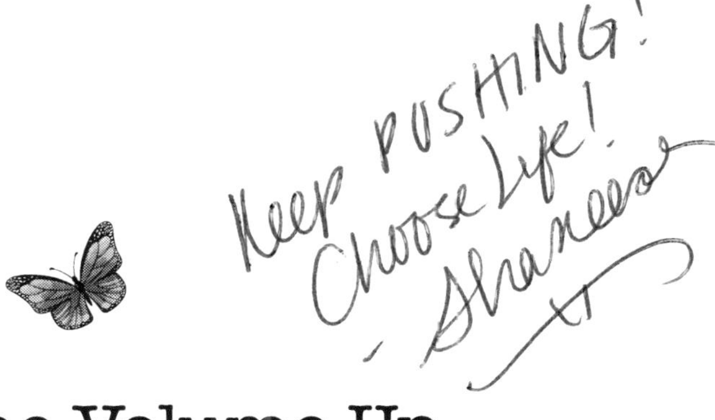

Turn the Volume Up

by Shareese Strong

You are a product of your past, but
not a prisoner of your past.

Rick Warren

I've heard it said that we are as sick as our secrets. My secrets made me ill. My mind was sick, my body ached in pain, and my soul was dehydrated from years of emptiness, deprivation, and thirst for a greater and more purposeful life. Secrets kept me isolated and afraid of getting too close to people for fear of them seeing who I really was as a person. More importantly, secrets kept me from seeing who I really am.

During my childhood years, I faced many years of sexual abuse. I lost my voice early on in life. My identity was robbed by trauma, dysfunction & fear. Shame became my interpreter. Oftentimes, scared of my own shadow, I would hide into my shell, which became my safe place. I was very timid, shy and afraid of people. I didn't trust anyone and thought everyone wanted something from me. I was scared of the world that I lived in and lost my voice during those years.

My parents' divorced when I was a pre-teen. My dad was my best friend. I have such fond memories of us laughing and joking together. He became addicted to drugs which ultimately landed him in prison, breaking my already fragile heart once again. My mom tried her best to take care of my brother and me while dealing with mountains of debt, heartache, and her own inner demons. Life can be tough.

As a teenager, I continued the rhythm of dysfunction and trauma and entered into an abusive relationship. I remember the times I wanted to leave the relationship. Like the time he drove his fast Z-28 close to one hundred miles per hour on a dark country road, threatening to kill me if I were to leave. Or the time I was beaten and punched repeatedly because I looked outside of the window to get a glimpse of "light". A dark place became a common place. Sometimes, I would fight back but more often than not, I would numb the feeling of pain as if nothing had happened. During my tenth grade year, at the age of 16, I gave birth to my baby boy. My son was five months old when I received a telephone call from my mom asking me to take a look at the local newspaper. To my surprise, my boyfriend's picture was there on the front page. He had been on trial that week and was sentenced to prison for twenty-five years for a crime he had committed before we had even met. A part of me felt relief that I wouldn't be his punching bag any longer, but another part of me was still scared for my life.

After that relationship, I tried to change the trajectory of my life and my son's life. I graduated high school with a 3.8 GPA and enrolled in a trade school for computers. I landed my first job on a contract with a company that supported the White House and the Executive Office Buildings, and with that income

I purchased my first home at the age of twenty-four. Shortly after purchasing my home, I met a gentleman at the church I attended. Within nine months of knowing each other we were married. We divorced fourteen years later.

I have struggled with feelings of emptiness and sadness most of my life. I was taking a couple of anti-depressant medications and attending therapy sessions regularly. During my divorce, I hit another all-time low. I was asked to leave my five-bedroom, three-car garage that sat on a three-acre plot of land I had helped to build from the ground up. I lost nearly everything. I felt numb, lonely and broken. I had been around people with mental illness my whole life. Sadly, there are millions of people who are living in a "secret" hell, trying to live a productive life while having a mental illness. I was one of those people. Eventually, I was diagnosed with Clinical Depression, Post-traumatic Stress Disorder, and Adjustment Anxiety Disorder.

In one of my many therapy sessions, I learned about the flight and fight response. Basically, it's a physiological reaction that occurs in response to a perceived harmful event, attack, or threat to survival. I spent the first half of my life in survival mode. I needed to protect myself in order to feel safe. My guards were up all of the time. I stayed in defensive mode feeling sheltered and alone. The years of abuse taught me that fear is strategic. It's planned. It serves the purpose of keeping people out, including yourself. Fear paralyzes you, numbs you, keeps you in bondage, and feeds shame and fear. It wasn't until later in my adult years that I actually started looking people directly in the eye because I couldn't at first. I was afraid that if we meet eye to eye that they will "SEE" me. The paradox is that I've always wanted people to "SEE" me. The real me. However, shame created a buffer for that not to happen. Shame gave excuses for me to continue to hide. Shame validated my insecurities. You can't live in shame and vulnerability at the same time. They are one another's competition. Fear is shame's companion.

Beloved, even with all that we have experienced, it's not the end of our stories. I spent a lot of years trying to find my voice. There was always something inside that told me I was unique, powerful and strong, but I couldn't find the voice or the courage to express it. It took me nearly forty years to realize that the voice never left me, it had just been muted.

I love the passage in Isaiah 43:18 of the Holy Bible, which encourages us to think on the new and not to dwell on the past. That's hard to do, but the truth is that life is lived forward and understood backwards. It was now time for me to live forward. The enemy had stolen enough of my past and I was not letting the same thing happen with my future. I started to develop strategies that only focused on where I wanted to be in my life. My vision was forward focus. My purpose was becoming clearer. I no longer spent energy in blame and regret. I started moving my thoughts and my heart in a forward posture. I began to visualize what success and victory looks like in my life. Slowly but surely, the past was becoming a launching pad for my PURPOSE.

After many continual years of counseling, therapy, and research, I'm a living witness to how we can turn something so very painful into something very purposeful. In 2019, I formed a non-profit organization called LifeTeam, Inc. My company provides service, advocacy, support and awareness for individuals and families who have experienced sexual abuse and mental illness, or for those who have a mental illness. I've transitioned from a victim and someone "stuck" with the stigma to someone who is thriving, successful, healthy, happy, and living beyond "crazy". My PURPOSE is to get the "secret" out! I want to stop the mental health stigma. I'm no longer hiding in Shame! Abuse is an old chapter and not welcomed in the new.

It's a tragedy to go through life and never know who we really are and what our purpose is in life. Beloved, there is nothing you've ever experienced that will be wasted. Every single step you have taken, no matter which direction or turn you took, has gotten you to this very point. You matter and your experiences, all of them, have shaped you.

Dear Heart,

I invite you to come out of hiding. I invite you to use your experiences, the good, the bad, and all the ugly stuff in between as a launching pad to your purpose. Let nothing be wasted. Use everything. No shame. No fear. No guilt. No filters. Just your story, your vulnerability, and your courage. It's now time to see what GRACE, REDEMPTION, RESTORATION, and WHOLENESS looks like. It's time to turn your mistakes into messages, pain into purpose, and suffering into service. Let's make some noise together....I got the coffee!

—Shareese

Beyond Bankruptcy to Blessings

by LaDonna Mixon

I will never forget the day I had to file for Chapter 13 Bankruptcy. I was being sued by the Homeowners Association (HOA) of the community I lived in, and the only option I had at the time to prevent my home from being sold was to file. I sat in my Attorney's office feeling defeated. Ironically, the money I spent to retain an attorney was more than the actual debt that was due to the association. In addition to feeling ashamed and embarrassed, I felt like a fraud. I mean, here I was, in the cusp of fantastic growth of my salon business, having resigned from Corporate America three years prior to focus on my entrepreneurial goals full time. I had big dreams and big plans but didn't have one single idea of how this process would shift my life's course. I remember feeling like I didn't want to continue on with the ideas that were birthed on the inside of me. It felt like my spirit and my mind had fallen into quicksand and I was sinking deeper and deeper into despair. The fire in my belly to thrive became a slow simmer of fear and disillusionment. Have you ever felt like you messed up so bad in life that you weren't sure how you were going to recover? I questioned my abilities and my confidence in my purpose waned. Why had I chosen this experience for myself? Where was the lesson in this experience?

In the days that followed the filing and appearing at the federal courthouse, I became numb to positivity. My credit cards and any type of capital I had access to was frozen. My credit plummeted. I had to dig deep to find the resources to not only pay the attorney's fees, but the past due amount of the HOA fees, the court costs, budgeting classes, as well as sustain my lifestyle. I was angry at myself for not staying on top of everything. One of my close friends tried to encourage me with words of wisdom that this too, however dismal I saw it, would also pass. Her attitude was upbeat as she encouraged me with a vision of my life being restored with this experience ultimately becoming a story of triumph. At the time, I was too heartbroken and mentally defeated to accept this prophetic consolation as a possibility of truth.

Up until this point, I had worn my achievements like a badge of honor. Everything God entrusted me with, I wanted it to prosper. There was no room for failure in my success equation. I placed high value in these components: being a woman who didn't finish college but was still able to become a thriving multi-business owner who balanced motherhood, marriage, career, and service in ministry. None of this had any merit when I was faced with the possibility of homelessness. It was here, in these times of isolation and struggle, that I was stripped bare. Without any of my souls' decorative attire, I was able to own my stuff. I had to claim and clear the feelings of smallness and the multitude of times I allowed insecurity to be my pivot foot out of fear. I was getting to the root of the deliberate self-sabotage and poor decisions made from a mindset of lack. Within the still small space of my mind, the divine revelations needed for my transformation began to unfold and reveal the gift of mastery working in tandem with my life's purpose.

Growing up in poverty and in drug infested and crime riddled areas, sometimes I did not know where my next meal would come from or if the clothes on my back would be sold for drugs. I know that much of my sense of security is rooted in those earlier experiences of not having enough. I made a personal vow to not return to those experiences ever again. To fulfil this vow meant that I had to adapt to making excellent grades, working hard, and staying busy earning accolades and achievements. They were badges of honor stacked against the hardship of all I endured as a child. An important part of my growth in transcending this part of my self was to walk courageously on a path I had never seen. It was clear that I needed to adjust my focus toward reframing my self-worth. You see, who I am as a child of God, ordained and equipped to usher others to the inner work of their soul, is not diminished because of financial mistakes, or any mistakes for that matter. The sum of my value as a human being in this lifetime is to be recognized as a priceless commodity- far exceeding anything I could have dreamed or imagined. Why do we believe our sole reason for existing is wrapped up in the things we do or accomplish, but it not be a part of our divine make up? I believe the essence of our divine selves is realized most in the darkest nights where we are forced to search in the deepest part of our heart to remember just how powerful we are.

During the three-year period of the bankruptcy plan, I got a glimpse of God's grace in my life as unfailing and steadfast.

I started speaking with authority and confidence regarding the promises over my life, and I reminded myself of this daily with affirmations of being an overcomer. The beauty of seeing yourself victorious at your lowest point is that you also come to renew your mind to the idea that God always provides the capacity for you to walk in your purpose regardless of how dire the situation may seem. In the face of losing my home, the quintessential symbol of the American dream, I was still fully equipped with every resource I needed to not only fulfil my destiny but to help others along the way. I gained a perfect opportunity to help them call their greatest selves forward by pointing them to the light within them, all because I was able to do it for myself. I became a change agent for my own life! I was on an incredible, earth shifting assignment to transform my own heart. I shifted my focus from seeing myself as small, limited, and stuck, to a God-infused powerhouse with unlimited potential and endless capacity to manifest anything my heart desired. I became bolstered with coming up with creative ways to finance my business and personal endeavors. I found avenues of capital that was available to me, which allowed me to live freely and abundantly while doing all that I loved. Each year in bankruptcy, I experienced miracles that only God could have orchestrated with the expansion of my business operations and partnerships. I became energized with coming up with ways to pay down the balance of the debt and finally, it was complete. The trustee discharged me from the chapter 13 with a refund check. My credit was on the mend. I sold my home and moved on to a new property lovelier than I could have imagined.

A mentor once told me that the answer is in the room with the question, which means that nothing will be hidden from the heart that diligently seeks. I chose to release the burden of shame surrounding this experience, starting with giving voice to this story, in hopes that you will be encouraged to face any hard times with a renewed sense of peace and encouragement for better days ahead.

Surrendering in obedience to your own purpose creates avenues to experience a beautifully orchestrated life. We have the power to release ourselves from the holding patterns of self-destruction and shed the toxic stories we tell ourselves. Get comfortable with the discomfort that comes with taking giant leaps of faith. By taking a seat of power to your own healing, you are intimately aware of divine goodness flooding your life. Your soul's purpose in this life is not tied up in the mistakes you make, but sustained in the inherent nature of who God created you to be. Hold yourself accountable to become the conduit of change in your thinking and feeling- choosing to live fully in both the shadows and in the light. Uncover the parts of you that you keep locked away and bring that into the light of God's plan and promises. Take a deliberate stand to sever anything - people, places, environment, mindsets, or belief systems - that no longer serve you. And ultimately, choose to not grow weary in the well doing. Even in my mess, the purpose of my life is being fulfilled in this moment to bring a message of hope and encouragement in your journey. Allow the treasure found in life's transformations to provide peace through seasons of unfortunate circumstances. Graciously and confidently accept your personal assignment to call yourself to life's mastery while on the road to redeeming grace.

Phase IV

"Beautiful and graceful, varied and enchanting, small but approachable, butterflies lead you to the sunny side of life. And everyone deserves a little sunshine."

Jeffrey Glassberg

I'm Sharing: The Re/Productive Phase of Purpose

The Adult Phase of a Butterfly's Growth

Once the imaginal discs have fully produced and formed a butterfly, the chrysalis begins to soften and allows a full-grown butterfly to emerge. The wings of the butterfly initially come out a bit withdrawn and closed in. But as blood and fluid is pumped through the veins of the wings, they begin to spread to their full length. This butterfly looks totally different from what it looked like as a caterpillar. It is now admired for its growth and beauty and all that it has been through to get to this point is lost on most of the people who appreciate it at its present state.

But looking good is not the butterfly's only duty in this adult phase of existence. The female butterfly now spends her brief days on earth: feeding on her favorite flower plants, carrying pollen from plant to plant to help fruits, vegetables, and flowers produce new seeds, mating, and laying eggs to start the life cycle all over again. The main purpose for the adult butterfly is to feed herself so she has the strength to reproduce more of her own kind.

At this sharing phase of their lives, it's all about using what she's been through in the other phases of her life to get her to this place of helping others grow. Meet our Purpose Pushers who are currently SHARING during their adult growth phase since they are now clear about their life's purpose. They have learned lessons along their journey and want to share them in hopes that you will be inspired to reproduce too.

From a Daughter's Heart

by Shelia Bullock

As a southern, quiet country girl growing up in a home with both parents, an older brother, and a German shepherd dog, there were lessons to learn regarding my purpose here on earth that my mother was not able to teach me. My mother, the dominant personality of the house, ruled the family. I struggled with low self-esteem and my mother became the giant I tried to please without any confrontation. I faced fear because I had no sense of direction to help shape my goals nor did I have someone to guide me through life. As the years passed, I noticed my mother's memory began to change. She was getting confused and had difficulty completing normal tasks. The signs were there and I had to take action because I was concerned for her safety. I faced the fear that something drastic was going to happen if I did not take charge and become her caregiver. Her energetic spirit and affectionate disposition towards things that interested her had changed. The fear of being her advocate put a heavy burden on me. I asked myself the question, "Will I be able to make the best decision for mom?" I had juggled with continued doctor appointments, changing medications, emergency room visits, interviewing of clients, different agencies, and time missed from work, lack of extra curriculum activities, and the lack of sleep! I knew the time had begun for me to move past my struggles and accomplish the higher achievement award of seeing my mother get the care she so deservedly needed.

Today my dad, my brother, and even my German shepherd are gone, and mom's Alzheimer's disease has advanced. The struggle of having to take the lead over mom's welfare without any previous experience triggered past hurts and failures. I was scared of failure! After all, leading from within was not something I was familiar with doing. I had to figure out some action plan that took my mind off of self-pity. Why Lord, why did you take my daddy and brother away from me and leave me here to take care of mom? How was this little girl going to be all grown up and make grown-up decisions? I was of legal age but I did not feel like I was old enough to handle mom's affairs all by myself, nor did I want to. The roles had switched and I had to take care of mom. I had become mom's advocate! The caregiver journey has taught me and reminded me of my favorite scripture in Jeremiah 29:11 (NKJV): "For I know the plans I have for you, declares the Lord, plans to prosper you, and not to harm you, plans to give you hope and a future." Those years of Sunday school, church services, and revival have rooted a love deep down inside of me to be pleasing to my Lord and Savior, Jesus Christ. He has continually placed the right gifts inside of me to help me deal with the hardships that still come. But I am an overcomer!

No longer walking in fear, I know I can make a difference for my mother and myself. I am no longer silent when I need to speak up on behalf of my mother or myself. I am an overcomer of that fear and I am now a voice that was once silent! I no longer walk in fear of the unknown because I dig deep to find answers for my unanswered questions. I have walked through the valley of shadow of death with my heavenly father guiding me. My mother does not remember that many of our family and friends are deceased and having to share this with my mother repeatedly is like walking through the valley of the shadow of death. However, I know my heavenly father is with me every step of the way. She has memory loss where she can recall things that have happened years back, and yet does not remember yesterday's events. Daily she continues to ask about her loved ones and wants to know why no one told her they had died. Jesus said He would never leave me nor for sake me, and as I sit and share these truths with my mother, I feel the Holy Spirit protecting and leading me. In a sweet voice, I let mom know each time she asks about the deceased, "Mom they are in heaven now. They died a long time ago." God comforts my heart making it easier to share these truths with my mom. Many situations in life can leave deep wounds, but when healing takes place you become ready to spread your wings and fly.

I was a caterpillar that became a butterfly! While maturing into adulthood, I realized why my mother was so strong-willed and controlling when I was a child. She wanted me to experience more out of life than what she had experienced. It was her way of pushing me out of my shell. Just as the butterfly has to take that first flight, my mom pushed me forward allowing me to spread my wings and fly for such a time as this! I learned to figure out life's situations on my own and realized I may not have the answers for everything, but I could ask questions, research, and find the answer. The fear factors that haunted me – those 'what ifs' in choosing jobs, relationships, and more – can no longer haunt me, as I have learned to not allow them to determine my destiny. My defining moment that made me aware of my new growth was when I actually enrolled my mother into the long-term care facility. Years ago, mom said, "Shelia, if I ever get to the point where I can't take care of myself you can put me in a nursing home." Well, I struggled and tried to work around that decision but nothing else was attainable. Today, I am free of the guilt and shame knowing I made a sound decision that I am able to rest with peaceably.

As I continued overcoming my fears of using my voice and making life changing decisions, I connected with anointed women of God in Monday night and Saturday prayer meetings. I began to peel back the levels of hurt and disappointment I experienced in my life. After years of praying and seeking God, I was able to allow the hurt and pain of rejection to heal from the inside out. Because this assignment was mine, I had to go through the unbearable in order to get to the bearable! The dry season was over. This caterpillar began to come out of her shell and earn her butterfly wings. I was walking on new turf and the challenges became easier each day! I was no longer at the stage where I just took whatever was dished out to me concerning mom's care; I prepared the menu myself with God stirring my hands and leading me through this valley. I have come too far to think about quitting on my voice and authority now. I am able to help someone else walk through their valley experience. Believe me the day will come! I have gone through the stage where I ate from everyone else's plate trying to find comfort out of junk food and unfamiliar journeys. I have had dry seasons where I sat under several anointed leaders in revivals, women's conferences, and Sunday morning services trying to find the right medicine to enter into my sick, wounded soul. Nevertheless, I found healing in my heart and mind, and comfort in overcoming my fears.

I encourage all of you to get with a prayer ministry with sisters in Christ that have different spiritual gifts, and a church that has a Bible-based agenda. Anointed women of God pour into your spirit and have an assignment to help you overcome your challenges. God has plans for each one of us to prosper and be in good health. Take Him at His word! I did and as a result, my life has been filled with promise and purpose!

Navigating and Normalizing the Journey

by Myranda Harper

I never lost nor let go of my purpose, but having an unexpected pregnancy and birth, followed with post-partum depression, all while managing and maintaining my full-time accounting firm, my fiancé's restaurant business, and some legal woes left me exasperated and depleted. October 31, 2017, the day I discovered I was pregnant, through August 2019, was a complete whirlwind. I felt I was losing me and I grieved my past life. Yet, through it all, I still pushed and led a purposed-driven, but not fulfilling life. You can have purpose and still be unfulfilled. How? Because you're not in tune with the present, which is a gift. You are doing things just for the sake of feeling and being busy, but not being consciously or actively engaged in what you are truly doing. That was me.

Yet and still, the journey to get back to being consciously and actively engaged has not been easy by far, but it has been a necessary, enlightening, and meaningful journey. How'd I get back to this place? March 16, 2019, 7:58 am, I randomly found my "Dream" journal and began reading previous entries and random notes. It was the "shake-up," the "wake-up" call, and the reminder I was desperately seeking, but could not seem to previously locate. I began to move with different authority or, as some may call it, "swag." And the morning of September 5, 2019, after spending my first day alone and in quiet in almost two years, I wrote in the "Dream" journal how I was going to continue moving purposefully and fulfilled through my new life as a woman, a soon-to-be wife, new mother, CEO of my firm, and contributor to society: I had to focus on my self-care. I had to not feel bad for taking time to pour into myself, and to do things in my time – using my power in saying no, but creating balance with the power of my yes. I had to remind myself that a "setback" is nothing but a reset for a step up! Now, I can continue normalizing and navigating the journey, while educating and encouraging others to do the same.

So, what does this mean for you? The first thing about navigating and operating in your purpose is remembering your "why." What is your reason for that purpose? Having the purpose is not enough. You must have vision and with vision there is a constant need for clarity and a keen grasp of why it all matters in the first place. You must keep your "why" in the forefront of your mind. It will be the push you need when the trials and tribulations of life rain on you. My "why" in life and in my firm is to be an educator so the knowledge serves as a catalyst in a chain reaction for people, not just to know better, but to do better for themselves and others. Becoming pregnant and later giving birth shifted my "why" a bit. It became more intimate because my "why" now had two eyes staring back at me, needing me to educate her just as much as everyone else I pour into. I now have a responsibility to pour into her first so she can develop into a loving, selfless individual who will make a positive impact in everyone's life she enters. At first, this bothered me because I did not know how to split myself and my time for the "why" in my purpose. Being the CEO of a company already comes with great requirements, but motherhood required even more of me, giving more of myself than I was ready to do. Long story short, I cracked and postpartum depression set in hard.

Of course, everyone around me called it my "hormones," or stated some insensitive, unsupportive, inappropriate societal witticism that ended with me "just needing to get over myself" or "suck it up, welcome to motherhood." None of that was helpful and it did the exact opposite of what they may have been intending for their words to do. It muddied my waters. It made my "why" harder to see. The vision was not clear and the purpose-filled life I was living seemed stolen or at least forgotten. It all made me yearn even more for the life I had, which included the firm. But the lesson gained while navigating through this part of my life has been to get in tune with myself and practice self-care first. I must be the best for me FIRST before I can be anything, yet alone the best, for anyone else. Think about it! How are you supposed to give to others mentally, physically, spiritually or in any other manner, if you are tired, exasperated, and running on empty yourself? An empty carafe cannot help to top off or fill a glass. Thus, taking care of yourself cannot be a second thought. When I made that decision on September 5th to re-live my life purpose-filled, I chose me! For once, it was not the fiancé, the baby, the firm, the clients, the friends, the family, or anything else. It was me! I decided not to feel bad for taking the time to pour into myself, and that's what you must do first when practicing self-care.

Of course, everyone may not be pleased with your stance on your self-care mechanism or choosing you first. It may be frustrating because you are in a battle trying to get others to understand how self-care is necessary for you to be anything else. The battle itself can impact your self-care and revert you back to some old habits of putting off your "me time" to accommodate others. Stay focused! Choose you! Give yourself grace and understand that everyone was not charged with your purpose. Therefore, you must do what you need to do to preserve yourself while on this journey. It is imperative!

Doing what I need for me does not just embody self-care, it requires doing things in my own time. Being an accountant and owning a firm, deadlines are always around. The various IRS deadlines, an organization's internal deadlines, fiscal year deadlines, state deadlines, and more. There is something needed for and from each organization and each individual every day. The demands seem never-ending and sometimes they can be quite taxing. Yes, I want the firm to be of service and to help as many as we can, but I found myself hating my own company. I had created a "job" that I did not like, which was crazy! I work for myself, so why was I growing dim and disgusted? It was because my time was being dictated by everyone else. They were telling me what to do, when to do it, how to do it, and why I needed to do it. Let's not forget, I also had the demands of motherhood and family. All of it was going against the grain of my why and my purpose. The dictating had to stop and it had to start coming from no one other than me! Your time is the most valuable item on your purpose-filled journey. Thus, you must respect and manage it with care. You must discover or rediscover the power in saying "no" while creating balance with the power in saying "yes." I hope that by doing this, you, as I have, will gain more brain capacity and ability to exercise clearer thinking while operating in purpose.

You will need that clear thought process along the purpose journey because setbacks will occur. I cannot count the many setbacks I have experienced, especially as of late. Motherhood, the loss of the restaurant, and legal woes didn't just rock my life, it rocked my firm. I could no longer operate in the same ways as I did before when it was just me. Despite my efforts to transition some clients, some could not deal with my shifting priorities. I lost so much. So many tears shed as I watched things within my life disintegrate. It seemed like everything I touched during this time turned into dust. I felt my purpose was pointless. I was just going through the motions and did things for the sake of feeling "busy." What I came to realize was that a setback is nothing but a reset for a step up!

Life moves so fast that often times we do not take the time to truly be present and enjoy the moments. Thus, when rough patches happen we are in shock and dismay. The reality is that the signs were probably there during these times, but we simply ignored them out of "being busy." When the setback hits, express and process your feelings, but don't stay there. Shift your mindset, become present and engaged again, and start preparing for the step up. Be grateful for that setback because it will help you to go back and remember your "why," practice self-care, and manage your time so you can continue pressing on with purpose!

Preparation, Power, and Perseverance

by Dr. Karla Kornegay

The year was 1984 in Albany, Georgia, and at twelve years old, I can say that my life as a preteen was sheltered. My parents ensured that my sister and I were well taken care of during our lives. My father built our home from the ground up and after about five years, it was completed. My father was a hard worker and everyone knew it. Needless to say, many of his friends and family members had become very envious of his accomplishments. My father, who was a very prideful man, did not believe in asking anyone for help, and this characteristic eventually became his downfall.

Once my father completed the construction of our home, many marveled at the sight of it. It seemed that they could not believe that one man could build such a home with minimal assistance. Of course my father's ego seemed to go through the roof, and it began to show in the most negative ways over time. My father worked for the federal government while serving his country in the Army Reserves, and my mother was a homemaker. Periodically my mother had odd jobs to keep from being bored and to have money of her own. Relying on my father for an allowance seemed to bother her often. With my father being the man that he was, he forbade my mother to work, so she became the after-school caregiver for many of the children in our community. My mom loved looking after children, but as time went on, I noticed that her zeal for this thankless task was beginning to dwindle. She did not seem as fulfilled as she once was, and her joy seemingly faded away.

While my father was a great provider, he could also be quite a scrooge. My mother had to always ensure that my sister and I had everything we needed and most of the things that we wanted. She did this by using the stipend she received from my father along with the monies she earned from being a babysitter. With my father being the breadwinner, this seemed quite hard for my mother, but she always ensured that my sister and I never went without anything even if she had to rely on her parents for financial support at times.

My father, a very strict man, did not allow my sister and me to go to many places, and he gave my mother a hard time about leaving the house unless she was going to visit my grandparents, who lived fifteen minutes away from us. Even at such a young age, I had a hard time understanding this because he was rarely available to us as his family. My father seemed to find solace in partying with his friends until dusk on most weekends. When he was not with his friends he found comfort in visiting his mother, who eventually succumbed to cirrhosis of the liver from alcoholism. My grandmother's demise did not surprise me in the least because even at the age of twelve, I understood that her death by alcoholism was inevitable. My grandmother was always drunk when we visited her, and my mother often said that many of my grandmother's siblings were alcoholics, too. I later came to understand this sick cycle to be a generational curse.

I often saw my mom praying and sometimes when she was unaware, I listened to her pray. She always asked God to keep my sister and I safe from the spirit of alcoholism. I never understood that prayer nor did I understand what she meant by the spirit of alcoholism, but I knew that it was serious. I did not realize that there was something called a spirit of alcoholism, so this was puzzling to me. As time went on, my father's behavior began to take a toll on us. It was bad enough that my father's family lived in close proximity to us and was always meddling in my parent's affairs. My father also began to consistently come home drunk every weekend and would verbally and physically abuse my mother. Things had begun to spiral out of control, and my sister and I found ourselves nervous and scared more often.

Over the course of a few months, my father's bad behavior towards my mother worsened, and it really took a toll on everyone. My mother began to drink alcohol heavily, which only made the fighting worse. Shortly afterward, my father traded in his verbal and physical abuse towards my mother and began to use a gun to intimidate her instead. He used the gun as a scare tactic because my mother, over time, had grown tired of the abuse and began to retaliate in ways that took my father by surprise. He was not used to my mother defending herself. My sister and I dreaded the weekends because we knew that they were going to fight, and we never knew when our father would decide to actually fire the gun that he so often pulled out to frighten my mother. I always wondered why my mother kept us in that horrible situation. She would leave, only to return to the chaos that never changed for the better. I later learned that she only stayed for financial reasons.

One weekend my father came home drunk and began to argue, incessantly, with my mother for no apparent reason, as this had become the norm. While I stood in the kitchen, my sister in her room, I saw my father go for his gun. He pointed the gun at my mother. I yelled out to my mother, "Mom, he has a gun pointed at you!" My mother looked at my father and ducked right before he fired a shot at her. Horrified, I yelled obscenities at my father. Then I turned to my mother and stated, "If you do not leave, I am leaving! If we stay in this house, someone is going to get killed!" I saw my sister crying in shock at what just took place. She remained in her room, barely peeping around the corner of her doorway. My mother was crying, I was crying, and my father stood in a corner of the house, dumbfounded. I pulled myself together and ran next door to my grandfather's house to get help and tell him what had occurred. My grandfather came to the rescue. He didn't alert the authorities, but he made my father leave the house on that dreadful evening. The next day, my mother packed us up and her parents took us to live with my aunt in Atlanta, Georgia, where I finished school and went on to attend college in California. I did not realize how the series of events during my childhood, which consisted of rejection, control, witnessing low self-esteem in my mother, violence, substance abuse and a slew of other issues, would impact my adult life and set off a chain of events. Was the pain meant for a bigger purpose? At the time, I could only wonder.

I understand now that it was my faith that brought me through the hard times in my life. Being introduced to the church and to spirituality at a very young age led to me having a relationship with the Lord.

As a youngster, I experienced some unexplainable spiritual encounters. I did not understand the encounters at the time, but for some reason I felt that I was special in a sort of weird way. I now understand that the spiritual encounters I had as a child were preparing me to share the love of Christ with others as an adult. Helping people understand the spiritual world through scripture has helped them in their Christian journey. Although I am still a work in progress, I know that the Lord is guiding me, healing me from past trauma, and placing people in my path to help. For this, I credit the Lord, my mother, my willingness to be obedient, and Minister Kevin LA Ewing of the Bahamas for helping me to grow spiritually on a daily basis. People that I have helped have told me that they never wanted to read the Bible until they met me, and now they are excited about learning about the Lord and all that He has to offer them as His children. My purpose, in this regard, is still being fulfilled.

Other ways that I am walking in my purpose is through the many gifts and talents that God has given me to include singing, the arts, and modeling. I also served my country in the U.S. Air Force and accomplished several goals over the years, including owning multiple properties, starting my own company, becoming a community and political activist, working on my first book, running for political office as a Board of Education Candidate, earning twelve degrees before the age of forty-seven, and most of all, being a mother to two successful college students. With the Lord's help, the support of life coaches, relationship coaches, and Minister Kevin LA Ewing, I am well on my way to doing bigger and better things in this life. I can say that I am not afraid to go and conquer the world because my father told me that I could and most of all, he showed me. There was, indeed, a purpose for the pain that I endured, and I am not done yet!

Despite my childhood, which consisted of enduring the most difficult of times while also thriving in my gifts, and talents, I still made it. I took those things that were good and developed them into a path for my life that has brought much success and fulfillment. My hope is that you, too, will deal with and heal from the negative experiences in your life, and embrace those things that help you accomplish your purpose and so much more. You can persevere and become a Purpose Pusher too!

The Tale of Two Moms

by Victoria

When I was 18, I learned of my actual identity. Before October 1972, I believed that my mom and dad were my real parents. Then my stepsister, desiring to be the only child in their lives, decided to reveal my birth mother. She felt a need to point out that neither my mom nor our dad was my parent, and therefore devised a successful plan to have a relative drive me to her house to ask me a series of questions that would lead to the breaking news. My stepsister wanted to be known as the only daughter so that she would inherit everything as my father's only child. She succeeded in that endeavor and after she passed away, it was confirmed that money and jealousy were the factors that drove her behavior.

My stepsister's malicious acts did not pay off at that time. She told me not to tell anyone the big news, so for three days I was in a daze, wondering what to do and who to talk to. My world had been turned upside down. Although I knew who God was, I did not have God's Word stored in me as I do now. Before finding out the truth, I thought I had a near picture perfect family. We lived in a three-bedroom, two-bathroom home with a two-car garage as a middle-class family. However, that picture was shattered when I found out my birth mother was my mom's younger sister.

On the third day after receiving the news, I found the courage and opportunity to confront my mom. I asked her, "Are you my real mama?" At the time, she was washing dishes with her back facing me, so I wasn't sure what she was thinking when she heard my question. Although I couldn't see her face, I did witness her shoulders droop with a whimpering sound. It was the very first time I noticed my mother crying. She asked, "Who told you?" At this point, I knew it was true. She asked if a particular aunt shared the news because that aunt had always felt that I should know the truth. My mother then proceeded to tell me about my birth mother and the decision to change my name and my identity. As a result of this revelation, many relationships in our family suffered.

After this I realized that my mother had a remarkable way of being indifferent toward me. Rather than love and nurture me, she felt it was her duty to instruct me and make me feel as if I owed her for the part she played in my life. However, I had to learn not to take responsibility for a decision I had no control over. There were times when I really felt alone; but I wasn't lonely. I praise God for perseverance which allowed me to move to a place where I could love others and myself. I learned that love will always find a way to make things right!

As I began the journey to love myself, I sometimes found love in the wrong places. I was letting the world know that I had lacked real love in my life. However, it is an amazing epiphany when you learn to truly love yourself and you know the difference between real love and inauthentic love. People will treat you as well as you treat yourself, so loving yourself first is key.

You will be able to see things ahead of time and better prepare for any situations you may face. It took costly therapy sessions, reading positive books, and surrounding myself with positive people to figure out how to start loving myself.

When I got older and had my child, my birth mom said to me, "Let me raise him. It is the least I can do." I could tell she was carrying the guilt of not rearing me. However, I encouraged her to forgive herself for what she had done to me and receive God's forgiveness. After that conversation, I knew I needed to be intentional about taking care of me and my son so that I wouldn't have those same regrets. Although I had experienced feelings of rejection, I shifted my focus to loving myself and others. I started my mornings by speaking love to myself and continued with these affirmations throughout the day. This practice helped me to change the trajectory of my mind, body, and spirit.

Loving yourself is not being selfish. It is just a reminder to be true to yourself so that you can be true to others. Setting boundaries is one way that allows you to be true to yourself. For example, when you have a cold, you keep yourself warm, take the medicine, and drink hot beverages. You wrap up in a warm blanket for comfort and make sure to stay out of the environment that will keep you from getting well. The same is true for loving yourself. Take all the necessary precautions to keep yourself well-nourished and hydrated so that you can heal and grow. Sometimes that means removing yourself from places or people that keep you sick. Doing so helps you to be the best for yourself and to give of your best to others.

Because I made the choice to love myself, I am the loving, supportive, caring and giving mother that I always wanted. I can now bring love to the table in my marriage, too. And where

I couldn't love those who hurt or rejected me, I now can love them, even if they don't love me. I don't have to allow their actions to affect me anymore, and it won't stop the love that I can still show to them. I can even love and take care of my ninety-five year old mother with joy and loving kindness.

My beginning is definitely not my end! Love has redefined me and allowed me to re-imagine my true self. Make true love a part of your fiber. Let love redefine you so you can re-imagine your true self! To do this, find what makes you happy and take the small steps until you are able to take the big steps. Reward yourself every step of the way. As you journey, write down your pain, learn your triggers, and then learn how to avoid or manage your triggers. Let others take ownership for their actions, and do not allow them to project their pain onto you. If necessary, you may need to end or redefine any hurtful relationships that keep you from truly loving yourself or others. You have the power to make that choice. Lastly, praise God for all He has done in your life! It may have been tough, but you will survive so you can LIVE!

This, Too, Shall Pass

by Dr. Melissa Scotch

I am not a cold-weather person. The sun and the sand had always been home, regardless to living near or far from the warmth. Living in northeast Pennsylvania, I struggled with the cold winters. Snow! Sleet! Freezing Rain! Wind chills that can cut right through you! It was numbing at times. I had two young children with 'special' abilities. Staying out of this cold was simply not an option. I was running to various therapies and activities for two young children, minimally five days a week. There was not an option to avoid the cold. There was not an option to 'not show up.' Their therapies were so critically important. Add to the setting additional life and financial stressors, and I found myself fading. I was not tired - I was exhausted to my core. The exhaustion was mental, physical, spiritual, and beyond.

Finding that I was not feeling well, and struggling to keep up with my needed schedules, I sought medical support. I wanted to feel better. I wanted to not be exhausted. I desired on the deepest level to be 'my old self,' the one that was full of energy. I liked that person. And not only was I dealing with the many challenges to my life, but I also did not even like who I was seeing in the mirror. I no longer recognized that woman.

As per the usual, one doctor's appointment led to yet another. Instead of feeling better, I was more stressed than ever, trying to take two young children to therapies, doctor appointments, and more. Then it happened. I was called into the actual office of one of my doctors. He asked me to sit down and he began talking. After repeated appointments, he recognized a decline in my health, particularly in my physical appearance. Asking some personal questions, hoping for further understanding and confirming his thoughts, he walked around his desk and leaned against it; he appeared somewhere between a standing position and a sitting position and crossed his arms. The desk was a solid wood with a red tint and a shiny glass-like top. Behind the desk were floor to ceiling bookshelves filled with endless medical books. Then I glanced to my right at a small window, perhaps 24 inches x 18 inches. The vertical blinds were open, but not quite all the way; however, they were opened far enough to be reminded that it was January. It was cold, there was snow outside, and the sky was dark and dreary. As I turned back around to the doctor, I noticed he kneeled down in front of me, put his hand on my knee, and in the calmest, caring, yet strong voice he said, "Your stress levels have been a major contributor, and you have to change everything if you want to be here for those beautiful children sitting right outside of my office. You have cancer, and you will need to be strong, and do better." I did not cry, yet the tears were falling. He handed me some tissues. I pulled it together and as I got up and started walking out of his office, he says, "I think you should sit down. I will have the nurses tend to the kids." I told him, "No, thank you," and with tissues in hand, I walked out to see my soon-to-be five and four-year-old 'babies' sitting there playing their educational games. The chairs were green. Not a Crayola green, but more of a sea foam green. And as they stood up to put on their winter coats, I sat down next to them. I was numb, but not from the cold Pennsylvania weather! I did not know what to do, where to go, what to feel, and yet these beautiful children stood there, just staring at me, trying to figure out what was happening.

I am not entirely sure how long I sat there in silence. Both children leaned on each shoulder, kind of hugging me, with concerned curiosity. Why was mom not moving, speaking, or responding? It could have been ten minutes, perhaps twenty. I took one of the deepest breaths I can ever remember, took the tissues in hand and blotted my eyes as to not wipe or use a large motion to alert my children. I hugged them both and we left. As cold as it gets in northeast Pennsylvania in January, as much as I cannot stand the bitter cold, and as much as it would make me numb for months at a time; I had just slid down some horrible continuum that the winters of Pennsylvania could no longer compete with. I was not cold on the outside. I was literally numb, only this time it was from the inside. I felt nothing and it was as if I was watching the next few hours from outside of my body.

Right around the corner in town, only about a mile away, both children had their occupational therapy appointments. We went! As one went to therapy, I played with the other. Then they switched. It was my daughter that went second that day, and then I played with my son in the waiting room. We drove home. I made dinner. And the next day we simply resumed a normal schedule. I told no one. It was not until another cold day in January, but now a year later, that I returned to my doctor. A complete year of habituating, not living. I was not well. I was weak. I spent a lot of time in bed. My son at the age of five would make our dinners. I cannot even count the number of times he fed me and his little sister. It was always a plate with five crackers, a piece of cheese, and some green grapes, yet to date, some of the best dinners I ever shared.

When I returned to my doctor, I spent the next year under constant watch and care. With few options on the table, and another year gone we were again back at the doctor's office on a cold, dark, and dreary January day. After weighing my options and having a long discussion with my doctor, it was almost exactly two years to the date that I decided surgery was the best option. I was scheduled almost immediately.

There are not enough adjectives in the human language to describe the range of emotions I was feeling going into surgery. When waking up from my surgery, I can clearly remember opening my eyes, and realizing that life would never be the same. Although I went through indescribable stress during these years, even though I carried the burden by myself for a year, and even though I had just woken up in a hospital bed with excruciating pain, I was grateful. The numbness was gone. I was feeling pain, and I was grateful!

At that moment life changed. I no longer desired to be that younger version of myself. She may have had endless energy, but she did not have this knowledge. I was empowered with a sense of purpose. A knowledge and understanding of the world that could never be taken away.

Now, I am no longer habituating. I work, live, and love each day with and from a place of gratitude. I went back to school and earned both my master's degree and my Ph.D. for the sole purpose of being able to live in-service of others, to support my children in developing into wonderful community members, and to be able to not only positively impact my family, friends, and students, but their children, and perhaps even generations to come.

As I have found my purpose, I share with you that it is vital to understand, we need people! Be willing to reach out for support, or support others in need. Be gracious. There is always something to be grateful for, so write them down, hang them on your refrigerator, or share them with a friend. Be willing to be vulnerable. You do not always have to be the 'strong one.' Be flexible. We cannot always change what's around us, but we can always choose how we respond. And most importantly… be the 'captain of your ship!' Just as a physical ship would have difficulty finding its way out of a port without its captain, you ARE the captain of your metaphorical ship. You will need to develop goals to have a path. What do you want written on your epitaph? How do you want to be remembered? If you are reading this, being remembered in a positive light is important. If you can recognize what the end of your journey will be, you have a path. A positive path to start now, your point A. Your point B is how you want to be remembered. The rest is simply your journey, your path, your ability to live with purpose. And always with gratitude!

Your Next Steps

Wow!!!! You have heard the stories of 20 amazing women who have overcome challenging and even traumatic life events that led to HOPING, LEARNING, CHANGING, and SHARING their purpose. They have shared their trials and triumphs; and victim to victory situations, for the purpose of encouraging and inspiring you to become a Purpose Pusher! Even if your story didn't mirror theirs, I hope you were able to glean some nuggets to apply to your life. Speaking of your life…now that you've read these women's stories, think about the stage of purpose you're in and write a few words to describe that stage below.

I'm HOPING ______________________________

____

I'm LEARNING ______________________________

____

I'm CHANGING ______________________________

____

I'm SHARING ______________________________

____

Now that you have identified your current stage of purpose, what's next for you? What do you want to see happen in your life? What do you want to create? What inner promptings or shifts do you notice? As you begin this new year, I encourage you to set intentions for how you desire to live. If you're unsure of where to begin, go back through this book and review the nuggets shared by these Purpose Pushers. No matter what stage of life you find yourself in, you too can be a Purpose Pusher! Start today by taking that next step!

—Dr. Trenace Richardson

Purpose PUSHERS

The Journey of Discovering & Walking in Your Life's Purpose

Presented by Dr. Trenace Richardson
Contributing Authors

Angela Richardson
Carla Freeland
Christian Belton
Dr. Karla Kornegay
Dr. Melissa Scotch
Kerneacia Davis-Nimmons
Nephateria McBride
Kimberly Cabbagestalk
Kimberly Cleveland
LaDonna Mixon
Lorrie Roberts
Moanne Joseph
Monica Leak
Myranda Harper
Rhonda Ragsdale
Shareese Strong
Shelia Bullock
Tajala Lockhart
Victoria
Yalonda Blizzard Smith

For more information about these authors,
visit www.purposedpublishingcompany.com

Made in the USA
Middletown, DE
22 December 2019